America's Story in Events and Personalities

The First People Through The 1870's

By

Ronald E. Rhodes

Table of Contents

Dedication

I dedicate this book to my sons, Kevin, Jamie and Jonathan, and my adopted son, Saverio Occhipinti, with the hope that one of them might, one day, pick it up and realize how deep was my love for the America in which I grew up, and how deep was my love for them.

I dedicate the book also to my wonderful Dad and Mom, John and Dorothy Rhodes, hoping they'll look down from Heaven and say "Look! Ron finally did something productive!", and to my Grandma Leola "Dee" Russler, who taught me early in life that learning stuff can really be fun.

Most importantly, I dedicate this book to my wife, Kathy, who is an extraordinary lady, and who did all the chores for years while I claimed I was "working on the book".

I would be deeply remiss if I did not express my deep and sincere gratitude to the people who encouraged me, assisted me with advice and constructive criticism and motivated me to keep plugging along. I want to thank my friends Carter Shelton, Tom Jaggard, Ernie Cash, Mike Loving, Vickey Setters and Bill Freund. My memory isn't what it used to be, and I'm sure I've left some deserving people off of this list, and, to them, I sincerely apologize.

I also want to express my gratitude to Anna, my connection to the publishing house, who was patient with, and always responsive to, my "rookie ignorance" throughout the process of preparing the manuscript for publication.

Finally, I have to mention my little brother, Kerry Dane, and his kids, Joshua Rhodes and Abby Rhodes Fansler, along with my beloved nephew, Mike Fansler. They did nothing to assist with the book, and may have even scoffed at the audacity of my project, but I want them to see their names in such a prestigious publication. I also must mention my little sister, Jana Jo, and her two daughters, Paige and Amber, who have been relentlessly supportive.

Thank you all!

Prologue

I've attempted to be careful to verify the information I share with credible, responsible sources. I've tried to keep it in a rational and more or less chronologically correct linear sequence. I have tried to keep any form of political bias entirely clear of these writings. It is written in an informal format, intended for no particular age group. I am trying to write the American history book that I wish I'd have been able to read when I was young.

It is perfectly acceptable to use it as a resource to acquaint yourself with specific episodes in our history, rather than reading from beginning to end. Much of the "history" is shared by seeing it through the lens of individual biographies of interesting or significant persons.

Each segment is written with the intent to include "the good, the bad and the ugly" aspects of historical events and personages. The issues of slavery in America, our Native American history and the history of the Women's Rights Movement are threaded throughout the fabric of the text. Hopefully, this will offer parents a source from which they can resist the "revisions", "re-writings" and "poetic imaginings" of our history, which are so popular in our "dumbed down" era.

What I have written I am confident you can trust to be a true and accurate presentation. Time and space don't permit writing comprehensive accounts of every interesting event in our history, so I've tried to select the events and the biographies that will best give one a meaningful understanding of the times. So, friends, let's begin at the beginning.

How Did We Get Here?

Examinations of long-lost human settlements and of fossils recovered from times long past, tell us that human beings most likely "evolved" from primates, as there is evidence that humans share a common ancestor with the apes. There will always be debate between different schools of thought, with some believing the process of evolution was managed by "God" and some believing the process was independent of any universal being and purely determined by natural science.

Some important differences between the apes and modern human beings are that apes walked primarily on all fours, while men walk upright on two legs; and that the biggest brains in primates are much smaller than the smallest brains in humans.

Most archaeologists believe human beings (Homo sapiens) originated in Africa, around 350,000 years ago and slowly migrated to all the other parts of our planet. Early migrations settled and lived in all different climates. As the centuries passed, newer migrations arrived and over-ran or chased away or even destroyed the prior settlements, which had been established in earlier times.

The history of men on earth is a constant story of one group being overcome and replaced by other groups. In general, the more modern, better equipped, more evolved populations ultimately, inevitably, over-run, replace and supplant those who came before them. It's a process that appears to be part of the destiny of mankind and a natural part of the development of civilization, though those who have been overrun and supplanted undoubtedly feel differently.

Hundreds of thousands of years were passing by, creating our history along the way. Groups of humans whom, scientists seem to agree, all started out being of one "racial description" eventually settled in widely divergent climate types. Some in the dark coldness of the far northern and far southern parts of the planet, while others settled in equatorial areas of the bright, hot sun. Some learned to thrive in the deserts and others in the mountains. Eventually, each group began to develop characteristics that made them more successful and more likely to survive, within the environments they had chosen. Skin colors changed. Physical characteristics formed. Humans began to diverge in their appearances and behavioral characteristics, based on the needs presented by their own environments. Still, all of today's humans originated in the same "family" of ancestors, back in Northern Africa.

There is, over time, evidence of a long series of "versions" of upright humans. Around 100,000 years ago, man had developed to what we now call "**Neanderthal**" status. Neanderthal man walked upright, made some kinds of primitive tools and was using fire for warming their caves and for cooking the animals they hunted.

Thirteen thousand years is a long, long time for us. It amounts to about 170 human lifetimes strung end to end or about 464 generations of families. Scientists tell us that the first "**indigenous**" people to come to North America arrived around thirteen thousand years ago. For a long time, it was believed that all of those first "**Native Americans**" walked across a long land bridge. The bridge, called the **Bering Land Bridge**, connected Russia's Siberia to America's Alaska, though, of course, they did not yet have those names. Some anthropologists believe the earliest migrations into North America may have begun as far back as 50,000 years ago.

We don't know exactly how many early humans came across in this way or from which places they originally came. Going back to the very beginning, all of us originally came from Northern Africa. Today, though, scientists believe that many, by the time of the first migrations into Northern America, may have made their way from parts of Asia, having previously made their way from Africa.

Modern scientists believe that, while the Bering Land Bridge was an important path, some humans also came to North America by making boats and floating down the western coast of what is now the United States. We know that, according to anthropologists and archeologists, there were at least three major migrations of groups of humans. The very earliest migrations arrived, as we said, between about fifty thousand years ago and up until about thirteen thousand years ago.

Scientists break periods of time down into stages or eras. These very   first Americans are called "**Paleoamericans**", and they lived during the "**Paleoindian**" or the "**Lithic**" era. The **Paleoindian** era lasted for approximately eight thousand years, until around 5,000 years B.C., about 7,000 years ago. The **Paleoindian** era overlapped with the more recent "Archaic" era, which lasted from about 8,000 B.C. to 1,000 years B.C. The "**Woodland**" era lasted from about 1,000 years B.C. to about 1,000 years A.D. The "**Mississippian**" era lasted from about 1,000 years A.D. to 1,600 years A.D., which was approaching the more modern, "**Age of Enlightenment.**"

The humans from those three early major migrations into North America soon diversified into hundreds of distinct subcultures. Anthropologists today believe that there may have been many smaller migrations of people from different parts of the world. Each of the migrations brought different languages and different cultural characteristics.

Climate scientists tell us that the general climate conditions during those very early times were very similar to conditions we experience today. The earliest arrivals in North America would have lived during the most recent Ice Age, which reached its furthest drift southward around 20,000 years ago. The ice-covered areas were as far south as present-day Missouri and Illinois.

Life in Very Early American Cultures

How did people in those earliest American cultures live? The three big migrations led to three large cultural groups. One, for example, is called the **Clovis culture**, which spread over much of North America and even down into South America. The Clovis people are identified by artifacts such as highly unique spear points, now found as evidence of their existence in various locations.

The Clovis culture was primarily a hunting culture. These early Americans are known to have used some kinds of primitive tools. Some were nomadic, meaning they traveled throughout their lives, following food and water sources. They built a variety of types of homes. Some of those people became the ancestors of today's Navajo and Apache Native American tribes. They had villages and they constructed multi-family dwellings, which served as winter homes. In good weather, they traveled to track bison and other animals for food and to seek good fishing locations and edible plants. In winter, they returned to their villages and dwellings. Other tribal people lived in sod huts, adobe cliff dwellings, "wigwams", "tipis" (tee-pees), "wickiups" or, as pictured, "long houses".

Native American Longhouse

The Clovis culture was very widespread in North America. It was well established in time around 25,000 years ago, which was also the time when Earth's most recent ice age was at its greatest extent. The people of Clovis lived for many thousands of years in the forbidding atmosphere of that ice age.

As centuries passed, the many different cultural groups developed clear, unique characteristics. Some were primarily still hunters. Others became "gatherers" who first sought out edible foods in nature and, later, learned to plant and grow crops. Some groups were nomadic, while others tried to retain specific land boundaries.

Over time, they developed mastery of more skills and learned to make more kinds of tools and more kinds of weapons. Some of the tribes were generally peaceful, while some

3

were dangerously hostile and aggressive. Some, like the **Iroquois** nation, were known for violently driving other cultures out of their tribal homelands and stealing their properties. It was common for tribes to attack other tribes. Captives from war parties were sometimes tortured in hideous ways.

Some captives, especially women, were turned into slaves and were sometimes very badly abused. Slaves were sometimes traded to other tribes for valued objects. On the other hand, **indigenous** people soon learned the benefits of friendly cooperation among nations. There is much evidence of co-management of resources, sharing water sources and hunting grounds and establishment of "trade routes".

Indigenous people sometimes agreed on the use of certain locations, often around the merging points of two or more waterways, to meet and trade goods and services. In some cases, many tribes were known to meet at regular times each year, to trade and market their goods. Some groups traveled for days or weeks to reach those trade gatherings.

Let's take a big jump now, to approximately 1300 B.C., after many groups have lived and developed their cultures for 8000 years or so, all in various North American areas. There were now several major "language-based" cultures. Those groupings, based on common languages, were the **Iroquoian** (American Northeast), the **Algonquian** (American Northeast), the **Mississippian** (American Southeast), the **Archaic** (American Plains), the Puebloan (American Southwest), the Thule (Far North) and the **Late Marine** (American Northwest).

These language-based cultural groupings pretty much persisted, sometimes thriving, sometimes struggling for their survival, all the way through 1700 A.D. and even further into modern times. **Vikings** visited Canadian Newfoundland as early as 1000 A.D. The Vikings established a "colony" there named **Vineland**. This was probably the first instance of "**colonization**" in North America.

Colonization is a nice way of saying that some powerful nation has moved into some other nation and, usually by force, has taken control. Colonization has been an integral and probably inevitable, part of the world's history going as far back as there are records or archeological evidence. Colonization was a good thing, in terms of modernizing cultures and sharing knowledge and goods. The "colonizing nation" was sometimes benevolent to the resident and indigenous population, bringing needed resources and educational benefits. Colonization was too frequently, though, a bad thing in terms of stripping original residents of rights, power and ownership of their resources. In its worst forms, colonization included violent abuse, theft, barbaric behaviors and enslavement of original residents. Perhaps the worst consequence of the practice of colonization was its vital part in the spread, all around the globe, of the horrible institution of slavery.

The True History of Slavery in the World

It would be an unforgivable omission to fail to address the history of slavery in North America. We can't do that without learning HOW slavery came to be and HOW it arrived in America. The archeological evidence tells us that slavery was part of mankind's earliest known history, going back to pre-historic man. The very earliest civilizations (Mesopotamia, Egypt, Africa, India and China) ALL incorporated slavery as an institutionalized factor in their economies.

In many cases, male slaves were not as common as females, because males were killed rather than captured. Women were generally enslaved for use as field laborers or as "**concubines**". History's earliest known formal system of law, known as "**The Hammurabi Code**", recognized and regulated slavery as a legal entity. The first well-organized, true "slave society" emerged in ancient Greece, around the years 400 to 600 A.D., when, almost unbelievably, almost one-half of the population consisted of slaves. In these early times, because of the locations, most slaves were white people.

Over the centuries, times changed and more dark-skinned people began to be enslaved. In many parts of the world, the awful institution of slavery persisted for many thousands of years. Arabs were the most prolific purveyors of slavery, taking huge numbers of African slaves as early as the 1100s A.D. Arabs sold slaves in the Middle East and in Asia for many centuries. As early as the 1300s, Europeans were using slaves from Russia and Africa to provide labor on Italian sugar plantations. Slavery was commonly practiced in Arabian lands, Africa and Asia long before Europeans joined the shameful activity. By the 1500s, African slaves were being captured, not only by Europeans, but also by their own African brothers and sold into slavery. Soon, dark-skinned people from the West Indies were being sold into slavery.

It should be noted that, in earlier times, slavery sometimes looked differently than it has appeared more recently. In Greece, for instance, slaves were not considered the lowest level in society. Some slaves were teachers, poets, scholars and physicians . . . but they were still slaves. In those times, slaves often served as farmers, household servants or concubines and ownership of slaves was a measure of wealth and prestige. In the New World, though, slavery was much more a function of a "slave economy" in which slaves were primarily a source of free labor. Not all slaves were treated brutally, but brutality was way too common and included all kinds of physical abuse, sexual assaults and, even murders. Sadly and shamefully, various forms of slavery are still practiced in some parts of the world, including Africa and Asia.

How did slavery come to America? Africans were captured, often by other Africans and cruelly marched, sometimes hundreds of miles, to locations where they were sold to the slave trade. "**Slavers**" packed the Africans into the miserable cargo holds of "**slave**

ships" for "**The Middle Passage**". The Middle Passage was the label given to the cruel shipment of new slaves across the ocean, to be re-sold in various parts of the world. As many as 40%, 40 out of every 100 slaves, died during the forced marches to get to the ships or during the passage of the slave ship across the ocean.

We know now that approximately 300,000 Africans were subjected to The Middle Passage and sold into slavery somewhere in North America. The 300,000 who were sold in North America amounted to 2.5% of the total of all the slaves that made the Middle Passage. The best information available tells us that a total of about 12.5 million Africans were victims of The Middle Passage, the overwhelming majority being sold into slavery in the Caribbean, the West Indies and South America.

The True History of Slavery in America

The Portuguese were very active, for many centuries, in the slave trade business. In the year **1619**, the "**Sao Joao Bautista**", a Portuguese slave ship, was sailing for Mexico. The slave ship was captured by two pirate ships, both under the British flag. By that time, nearly half of the slaves aboard had already died, due to the horrific conditions on the ship. It is on record that many of the slaves on the ship had been captured, by black African slavers, in Angola. Angola is a state located in Southwestern Africa. The black captives are believed to have been, in their native African homes, members of the African tribes or kingdoms, known as **Ndongo** and **Kongo**. They would be, inadvertently, bringing elements of their African culture, history and language with them to the new world.

This is the true story of how slavery first came to America's shores:

After being seized by the English, the slave ship, the "Sao Joao Bautista", was re-directed to an English colony at Point Comfort, near the tiny village of **Jamestown**, in what is now Virginia. Jamestown, at that time, was twelve years old and had been suffering many hard times. One prominent colonist, **John Rolfe**, wrote that "a Dutch Man'O'War ship" had come to anchor near Jamestown. The ship's officers sold or more accurately "traded", more than twenty black slaves in return for "victuals" (food and supplies).

An interesting note here is that John Rolfe is the same guy who married Pocahontas in 1614. **Pocahontas** was the daughter of a **Powhatan** chief and had been baptized as a Christian. She gave birth to a son after marrying Rolfe. We'll have much more to say about Pocahontas later.

Powhatan Indians

Diaries, journals and records of a 1621 census indicate that there were 23 black slaves living somewhere in the English colonies at that time. Most of the slaves lived in the homes of their "owners" and they shared in the immense workload of all of the colonists. They worked inside the homes and in the fields. Slaves were considered valuable assets. As American tobacco became a product in huge demand in Europe, most slaves of those times eventually worked in the tobacco fields. (A couple of hundred years later, as the tobacco market slackened, many slaves were sold to cotton plantations, further south and life became even far more difficult for them).

Life was, unquestionably, very hard for all the colonists and, undoubtedly, even much harder for slaves. By 1619, many of the colonists had already died, succumbing to illnesses, the cold winters, starvation and even to some attacks by the indigenous natives. These colonists, of course, were not Americans, they were English. America, as an independent nation, would not exist for another 160 years. We'll be discussing the institution of slavery a bit more when we come to Columbus's story and to the birth of America as a new nation.

When America's **Founding Fathers** began researching all the governments of history, working to create a new government which they hoped would keep the best elements and eliminate the flaws, of those former institutions, the subject of slavery was a constant part of their planning. Many of America's founders wrote of the evils and unsustainability, of the institution of slavery, even though they owned slaves.

Remember, less than 25% of Americans ever participated in the shameful institution of slavery on any level and most Americans were very much opposed. Many of the earliest

American settlers came to America in reaction to religious persecution in Europe. The new Americans were generally Protestants or Quakers and, for many, slavery was considered an "abomination", which, indeed, it was.

While the Founding Fathers recognized that slavery was immoral and unsustainable in the long term, their more immediate problem was the hard fact that some of the colonies were extremely dependent on free slave labor. America's plan to fight for independence from England was sketchy, at best and the odds against their success were tremendous. The support of EVERY colony was essential.

The nation's founders were painfully aware that, if Southern colonies refused to cooperate, there would be no possibility of successfully revolting against the British. There would be no way to win American independence without the full support of the Southerners. The founders knew that the Southern colonies, if they refused to join the other colonies in the Revolution, would afford the English safe ports of entry, through our Southern seaports. The Southern colonies would provide access to the British, in return for British resources and funding. The British would be able to bring armies and war materials into the battle. The Southern colonies would provide for England a "Southern front", which would effectively entrap American colonists, putting the British in control of areas both to the North and to the South. Under those conditions, the Revolution had no chance of success.

If the Founding Fathers forced the abolition of slavery into their plans, the Southern colonies would side with the English and America would not ever exist. Slavery might STILL be thriving in the Western hemisphere. The war for independence could not possibly be fought without the full support of the Southern colonies. In order to create a nation free from England's domination and exploitation, America had to table the slavery issue, to be dealt with after the nation was actually established.

Slavery was a part of some cultures for thousands of years. In some parts of the world, it still exists. In the new America, it persisted for only three generations. The Republican Party was founded in 1854, with the primary goal of putting an end to the institution of slavery in America. The **Emancipation Proclamation**, fathered by **Abraham Lincoln**, was signed on January 1st, 1863. It read "All persons held as slaves are and henceforward shall be, free". Over the next six years, **Amendments** to the **United States Constitution** would be passed to forbid discrimination based on race and to guarantee American Black people the right to vote.

The Amendments were essential because the Emancipation Proclamation did not actually "free" any black people. The slaves in the South were still owned by people who did not recognize Lincoln's government, and their owners disregarded the Proclamation. Slaves held in the North were not freed because they lived in states governed by our Constitution, which meant they could only be freed by Constitutional Amendment. The

13th, 14th and 15th Amendments were the foundation for freeing the slaves and for guaranteeing certain civil rights for all Americans. Unfortunately, women were still denied the right to vote.

Abraham Lincoln and **General U.S. Grant** made plans to ensure that Southerners would abide by the new laws, but Lincoln was quickly assassinated. Grant continued to work to protect black people, many of whom had fought courageously under his command during the war. Even so, real freedom, in many Southern states, was still far away.

Southern Democrats, after the Civil War ended, reacted to reforms demanded by Northerners by establishing new restrictions on black people living in the South. Laws were established, formal and informal, creating rules which forced black people to live in an unjust, unfair, cruelly enforced life of subjugation to Southern white people. "**Reconstruction**" or "**Presidential Reconstruction**" was a period in which Northerners attempted to prevent the exploitation and continued abuse of black people.

President Andrew Johnson became president following the assassination of Abraham Lincoln. Johnson was no advocate for the abolition of slavery, though his opinions changed dramatically as he grew older. He became a strong supporter of rights and resources for African-Americans. Southerners, during the period of Reconstruction, began to implement **"Black Codes"**, local laws that restricted and oppressed black citizens." Later, after Reconstruction, Southerners enacted **"Jim Crow"** rules, which restricted all forms of activity for black Americans.

The Republican party, in response to those "black codes", became more radical in its demands for real freedoms for black people. They passed, in spite of great opposition from Democrats, **"The Reconstruction Act of 1867"**, which provided the first constitutional guarantee that black people could participate in and have a voice in, government. It is the passage of the Reconstruction Act that most believe was the trigger that initiated the resistance, in the South, that led to the creation of the **Ku Klux Klan** terrorist organization.

In the early years following the war, Southern Republicans were mostly made up of recently freed black citizens. Southern Democrats continued to resist black freedoms all the way through several more decades, until their last, filibuster-driven, fight to try and prevent the passage of the **Civil Rights Act of 1964**. It was nearly a century after the **Emancipation Proclamation** before terrible practices, such as school segregation and separate dining and restroom facilities for blacks and whites, were finally purged from America's South. Racism and discrimination still exist, though in less visible forms and may never be totally eliminated . . . until we all have blended and merged to the point that our differences can no longer be recognized.

Early Explorations of North America

By the mid-1600s Spanish explorers and **Conquistadors** were exploring vast areas of the American Southwest. The Spanish contributed to the development of Native American cultures, in a huge way, when they introduced horses to America. The lifestyles of some indigenous tribes changed drastically as they learned to raise and utilize horses. The ability to own and ride horses changed the way food was obtained, the way travel was accomplished and, sadly, the way war was made.

In the meantime, in Europe, the "**Middle Ages**" were being replaced by "**the Renaissance**". The "**Protestant Reformation**" was banging up against the Catholic Church's "**Counter-Reformation**". The concept of "individual rights" was growing in importance. Technological advances were being made in the areas of navigation, shipbuilding and trade systems. Soon, European nations began to hunger for exploration of "**The New World**" . . . North and South America.

History labels the years approximately 1400 through 1550 as being "**The Age of Discovery**" or "**The Age of Exploration**". The established world, the nations in Europe, Africa and Asia, which were thriving and ambitious, all began seeking sources of new lands to acquire and occupy. They were hungrily seeking gold, silver, precious stones, silk, spices and, shamefully, slaves.

Portugal as early as 1480 was the early home of European explorations, but mostly focused on Africa in their searches. Then, an Italian named **Christopher Columbus**, in 1492, talked Spanish rulers Ferdinand and Isabella, into funding an exploratory voyage. Columbus convinced the Spanish royalty that he could find a new path to China, Japan, India and the "Spice Islands" (Maluku Islands near New Guinea). Columbus sailed to the West with his three ships, the **Pinta,** the **Nina and** the **Santa Maria**. Columbus found the Bahamas and then Cuba, though he mistakenly thought he was sailing the Indian Ocean. He did not, on this trip, actually arrive in North America. Columbus took back with him, to Spain, coconuts, tobacco, sweet corn . . . and tales of dark-skinned natives, whom he labeled, because he thought they were in the Indian Ocean, "Indians".

Columbus never did, though he made several additional voyages, actually set foot on North America. The continent was ultimately named, by a German geographer, in honor of an early explorer whose name was "**Amerigo Vespucci**". Amerigo Vespucci actually did reach the Americas, in 1502, but he walked onto the southern tip of South America, not North America. So, neither Columbus nor Vespucci ever saw North America!

Note: Slavery existed around the globe during the times Columbus sailed. There is little doubt that, on some of his voyages, he was involved in the slave trade in some way. This author did his best to research claims of bad behaviors attributed to Columbus. Little of it seems based on any actual evidence. He did make many notes describing practices of slavery which he observed in some of the locations he visited. It's very likely he was involved in some ways. Many of the crimes attributed to Columbus were based on extensive writings by Bartolome de La Casas, shared by "The Zinn Education Project". Bartolome was never in the New World at the time Columbus was there and the bulk of the Zinn claims against Columbus seem to refer to crimes committed by other New World governors at times later than Columbus's visits. With little hard evidence to go on, it is difficult to justify the acrimonious attacks on Columbus. Columbus did not, as is often claimed, introduce slavery to the New World. It had existed for at least hundreds of years prior to his explorations. For instance, the Aztec culture, in South America, had employed a highly structured system of slavery for centuries. North American tribes of indigenous peoples also practiced forms of slavery. Remember, Columbus never actually set foot on the North American continent, so it would have been impossible for him to be a factor in slavery in North America.

The First Settlements in America

Ponce de Leon, a Spanish nobleman, explorer and "conquistador", sailed with Columbus (second voyage) in 1493. He returned in 1513 and explored parts of Florida and undoubtedly claimed the land for Spain. Decades later, in 1565, the Spanish returned to establish a base that has become the oldest city in North America . . . **St. Augustine, Florida**.

During the mid-1600s several nations had established some sort of presence in North America. The Spanish were already well established in the Southwest, Mexico and Florida; the French occupied a part of Eastern Canada and the area that would become the American Northeast; and the English were developing colonies all along the eastern coast of what would become America. The **Jamestown Colony** was founded in **1607** and the **Pilgrims** came to **Plymouth Rock** in **1620**. Many early colonists, especially the English, fled to **"The New World"** to escape religious persecution in Europe. Many of the colonists, especially in the Virginia and Massachusetts areas, received substantial help from indigenous tribes. They learned to use native sources of food, such as corn (maize) and tobacco soon became a big cash crop in the Virginia area.

Over time, conflicts over land and resources led to hostile interactions between indigenous tribes and Europeans. The inevitable spread of new immigrants across the New World had begun, though still in its infancy and the result would be catastrophic for Native Americans. Indigenous people suffered great losses due to infection with diseases carried by Europeans and some Europeans suffered from illnesses to which they had no immunity. Severe winters, crop failures and illnesses led to many deaths among the settlers. There were times when indigenous natives assisted settlers and times when natives were hostile and laid siege to some settlements.

The mid-to late-1600s saw the population of Native tribes decimated as they were infected and succumbed to, European diseases for which they had no immunity. Europeans were steadily gaining control of more and more land. Natives did not understand the concept of "owning property", as many believed only Mother Earth, God or the Universe could own land. They saw themselves as stewards or caretakers, of the lands, but not as "owners", though they did see certain areas as being the rightful province of their own tribal nations. Tensions increased between colonists and Natives. In 1675 a **Wampanoag** tribal chief named **"King Philip"** also known as **"Metacomet"**, led a coalition of his people, the **Pocumtuc** people and the **Narragansett** people in an attack on a colonial settlement known as **Swansea**. The tribes of the coalition were all part of the Algonquian nation of indigenous peoples. Some indigenous tribes, including the **Mohawk** people, joined with the colonists in the fight, known as **"King Philip's War"**, which lasted about two years. Every colony was impacted by the conflict. By the time it was over, around 3000 natives were killed and more than 600 colonists were killed. About a dozen colonies were completely burned to the ground by King Philip's warriors. Sadly, many atrocities were committed during King Philip's war, both by colonists and Natives. It is significant that all of the colonies joined together, all providing troops and resources to the cause, in a unified defense in the conflict. A "union" was developing. King Philip's War ended in August of 1676.

Another notable event happened during this same time period. In the colony known as Virginia, a man named **Nathaniel Bacon** gained the support of hundreds of Virginia planters to lead what became **"Bacon's Rebellion"**. The dispute is now viewed as the first armed insurrection, in the colonies, against British rule. There had been ongoing conflicts between Virginia planters and several native tribes. The English governor refused to support the desire of the colonists to bring in English troops to drive off the indigenous tribes. It is most likely the planters hoped to gain control of much more land, taking it from the natives during the conflict. Bacon's group objected to their treatment by the English Governor who ruled over the colonists. They believed they were taxed unfairly, the Governor was appointing his friends to high positions and the Governor was failing to protect the colonists from attacks by native tribes. The conflict quickly became a form of civil war, with Virginia planters, native tribes and large numbers of "**Loyalists**" all fighting one another. "Loyalists" were colonists who were loyal to the English King. Bacon's rebels ultimately chased the English Governor from the colony's capital, Jamestown and Jamestown was burned down. Bacon himself died before the conflict ended. Ultimately, by May 1677, Bacon's rebels had been defeated and the rebellion ended. Some historians believe this "insurrection" was the first chapter in the eventual **Revolutionary War.**

The Colonies in the Early to Mid-1700's

Times were volatile in Europe. Wars were being fought. Religious conflicts were dividing groups and nations. The voyage to "The New World" was arduous and dangerous. Still, given the harsh conditions in Europe, many were willing to risk the trip. Many wanted to go to America to escape religious persecution or because they felt their governments did not represent them fairly. The population of colonists in North America basically tripled between the years 1700 and 1750, by which time one million, one hundred thousand settlers were in place somewhere in the colonies. Some, by then, had already been in America for several generations and knew nothing of their European homelands.

America, in the 1700's, was known as "The 13 Colonies" or "Colonial America". Life was hard. Most colonists lived in simple one or two-room houses, with large families. Many infants did not survive their first few months of life. Disease was a constant threat. Even though most homes were small, residents often took in lodgers, who helped with money and chores. Few owned slaves, but, for those who did, the slaves often lived in the homes with their owners. Travel from the colonies could take several weeks, often enduring very bad conditions. Travel within the colonies was often by walking, though some had horses or mules. A trip that might take an hour today could easily take several days. In many areas, only dirt (often mud) trails existed or no trails at all. Along the coast or along the rivers, some traveled by canoe or boat. Sailing on a ship from South Carolina to Massachusetts sometimes took more than a month.

There was no telephone or telegraph and news traveled only as fast as the travelers. There were no power tools . . . and no power! Settlers had to clear their lands of trees and rocks using only their hands and some hand tools. Horses, mules and oxen were precious possessions. They had to build their own homes, using simple tools and available resources. Most colonists, including women and children, spent almost all of their time working. Nourishing food supplies were a constant concern. Settlers had to plant and maintain their own crops, which were sometimes raided by natives and they hunted local wildlife and fished the streams and lakes. Many poor people, and there were many poor people, lived mostly on bread and potatoes. In many homes, meat was a rare luxury. Beer was popular, as it had been in Europe.

There were no post offices in the colonies until after the American Revolution. **Benjamin Franklin** was made Postmaster General of the "United Colonies" and, later, the **Second Continental Congress** formally established the **American Postal Service**. Franklin was the best guy for the job. As early as 1753 he was already creating elements of what would eventually become our postal system. Franklin, before America was America, created efficient routes, cut the times for deliveries between major settlements in half, established a system for payment (based on weight and size of packages) and even set up a weekly mail wagon delivery system. Of course, in rural areas, mail was still carried by whoever was traveling in the right direction and was often left in taverns or inns where addressees could pick it up.

In the mid-1700s, colonists had been building villages, clearing land for homes and farms, exploring the New World and establishing a culture for nearly 150 years. Several generations had already been born and lived out their lives in America. The English controlled most of the Eastern seaboard. The Spanish were still living in the Southeast. The French controlled a large area that began in Canada and included, going south, the Mississippi River basin all the way down to Louisiana. Borders were only vaguely defined.

The French and Indian or "Seven Years' War"

Conflicts sprung up frequently between the French and the English. Ultimately, in 1754, the great war known as the **"French and Indian War"** or the **"Seven Years' War"** began. In America, it was the French and Indian War, but globally it was known as the Seven Years' War. One side of the fight was represented by French colonists and France, the nation, along with their many indigenous allies. The other side was represented by English settlers and England, the nation, along with the very large **Iroquois Nation** of Native Americans. The incident that lit the fire of the French and Indian War was probably when a young Lieutenant Colonel of the British colonial infantry, **George Washington**, led an attack that hoped to drive the French from the Upper Ohio Valley. The French resisted and succeeded in repelling Washington's attack. The war followed, with many significant encounters between forces.

The conflict eventually involved France, colonial America, England, Spain and even India. Early on, the French were mostly successful, but, as time went by, the English gained more and more ground. The French were defeated in Canada by English forces in 1759 and the British gained control of Canadian provinces.

In 1762, Spanish **King George III** offered to step in and deliver assistance to his French cousin **King Louis XV** and they signed what was known as **"The Family Compact"**. It promised that should the Seven Years' War not come to a rapid close, the Spanish military would join with the French to defeat the English in America. In response, the British declared war on the Spanish. As it turned out, the Spanish weren't much help to France and both were finally defeated. Along the way, the British took advantage of the wars with Spain and France to secure control of numerous new holdings. They took the French Caribbean islands, Spanish Cuba and the Philippine Islands. The French and Indian War ended in 1763 with the **Treaty of Paris.** As a consequence of their win, the British kept possession of all of the French territory east of the Mississippi River, large new sections of America between the Atlantic and the Mississippi and Spanish Florida, though they did allow the Spanish to keep Cuba.

The British "won" the French and Indian War, but not without paying a huge price. The war cost a lot of money and the British compensated by extracting large increases in taxes from the shallow pockets of the colonists. The British also began to try to control and restrict the expansion of the boundaries of the colonies as they grew westward. Colonists blamed the British for inflaming the hostility of indigenous tribes during the war. Colonists were also angry that, following the war, King George III issued a royal decree known as **"The Proclamation of 1763"**. The new edict prohibited settlement, by colonists, in any area west of the Appalachian mountains. The King believed his declaration would mollify the anger, resulting from the war, among Native Americans.

Unfortunately, many colonists were already living on property that they had acquired and developed, but which was located in the King's now forbidden territory. Resentment for the Crown, among many colonists, was growing.

American Government Before the Revolution

The 13 American colonies were not a homogeneous group. For instance, New York had a heavy Dutch influence, while Florida had a Spanish foundation. Many settlers in the New World came from Germany, France, Switzerland and other origins where English was not spoken. An "American" version of the English language began to emerge, influenced by many other linguistic bases. Overall, though, the colonists were dominated by the influence of old England and the forms of government that developed were heavily colored by English laws.

The earliest settlements, such as Jamestown, Massachusetts Bay and Plymouth were founded by private company charters. They were not ruled by the British crown, except as the companies, who paid the bills, were ruled by British law. They had no Royal affiliation. Other provinces, such as Maryland and South Carolina, were **"Proprietary Charters"**, meaning they did have a Royal Charter, but the charters gave control or **"sovereignty"**, to the local proprietors in the New World. The specifics of government varied widely from province to province and there was no central oversight.

By the mid-1700s, the colonies had mostly settled into a system of general loyalty and submission, to the English crown. Still, there were clear differences, from colony to colony, in how the government worked. "Town Meetings" were the basis for governing in the colonies of New England, which were deeply impacted by their "Puritan" backgrounds. Other colonies had more diverse populations and more diverse systems of government. Some were based on counties, while others were based on parishes or other structural foundations.

Law enforcement provisions were beginning to appear in various forms. In many of the colonies, formats similar to old English law were starting to emerge. In the colonies dominated by Puritans, mostly in New England, "crime" was often equated with "sin", combining religion and secular law. In those rigid systems, conviction rates exceeded 90%. In other parts of the New World, convictions for the accused were often lower than 25%. The concept of "law" was already subject, in America, to widely divergent interpretations. It's still true in today's America.

While we acknowledge the diversity in government, from province to province in early America, we also acknowledge a generally common basic system. In most cases, there would be a "Governor", who represented the interests of either the Crown or the chartered proprietor. The Governor frequently controlled all of the three essential branches now seen in our modern American government: **Judicial**, **Executive** and **Legislative**. In support of the Governor, there would often be a "Council", which would be made up of individuals appointed by the Governor or by the Crown. Finally, in one form or another, there would likely be an **"Assembly"**. The Assembly was most similar to the English House of Commons, the lower house of their Parliament. Assemblymen were often elected to their positions. They were able to have some control over expenditures and new legislation. As time went by and tension between the Crown and the New World began to intensify, it was often the Assembly of the various colonies that stood up to represent the interests of their people. The population of "natural born" citizens, born in the colonies, steadily increased throughout the 1700s. This meant the influence of the original settlers, all born in Europe, was steadily degrading, as their percentage of the total population rapidly decreased. By the mid-1700s, there were many Americans whose fathers, grandfathers, great-grandfathers and great-great-grandfathers had ALL been born in the New World. Still, for the most part, they still viewed themselves as being "English" and most were still quite loyal to the Crown.

The Causes of the American Revolution

In simplest terms, the **American Revolution** came about because the people in the 13 original colonies were beginning to resist efforts by the English Crown to increase British control over colony business. **King George III** also wanted to charge taxes on colonists to repay the Crown for the costs to England of fighting the **Seven Years' War**. Colonists, by that time, had lived in America for 150 years. Many were loyal to the King and happy to remain in the status of English colonists. Many other colonists had begun to resent English controls, English Governors and expenses related to English taxation and tariffs. **"Tariffs"** are a kind of tax imposed on products imported and exported out of the country. Colonists believed the English were enforcing tax and tariff conditions that punished the colonists to the benefit of the English.

The earliest spark to initiate the fire that became the American Revolution probably was struck at the end of the French and Indian, Seven Years' War. At the conclusion of the war, England wanted colonists to pay England's expenses related to the war. Colonists were already angry because they believed the English intervention in the war created a more hostile relationship with some indigenous tribes. They were also angry because, as a condition of the treaty that ended the war, **"The Proclamation of 1763"**, American colonists were forbidden to settle in areas where many were already living.

The method George III chose to gain reparations from colonists was to implement **"The Stamp Act"** in March 1765. The Stamp Act was designed to tax a variety of colonial products and services, with the money going to the Crown. One part of The Stamp Act taxed colonists for every piece of paper they used. Prior to this, colonists had been able to determine their own tax systems. Colonists believed that England was trying to squeeze money from their shallow pockets to pay the costs of England's war with France. Colonists did not react well at all to the Stamp Act. Riots occurred all over the colonies. Benjamin Franklin, already well-known in America, convinced the British to rescind the Stamp Act. One consequence of the whole episode was that colonists learned that, if they were motivated to do so, they could successfully resist British interventions. This change in mindset clearly did have some impact on growing thoughts of independence.

The concept of **"Taxation Without Representation"** was beginning to gain awareness in the colonies. The phrase 'Taxation without Representation" was probably coined by a secret group of powerful American businessmen known as **"The Sons of Liberty"**. This was a reaction to the fact that England was able to make rules and regulations, create laws and establish tax mandates which negatively impacted colonists in America. Colonists came to believe this was an egregiously unfair arrangement because they had no part in the government that was controlling their lives. Colonists were governed by a system in which they had no representation. By "no representation", they meant that the colonies were given no seats, no presence, no vote and literally no participation in the creation and enforcement of punitive laws that had a great impact on their daily lives and their financial welfare. Some began to feel that they were not treated as equals to their English brothers in London, but rather as servants.

The British Parliament, in 1766, passed the inflammatory **"Declaratory Act"**, permitting England to tax colonists in the same manner in which they taxed British citizens in England. This aggravated the already bad feelings colonists had about being taxed while having no representation in the taxing body, the English Parliament.

In England, in June 1767, Parliament, the assembly in the English government responsible for making laws, created **"The Townshend Acts"**. The Townshend Acts, coming on the heels of the bitterly resented Declaratory Act, was a system of taxes or tariffs on English goods shipped to America. Products such as paper, lead, china, glass and tea all had "duties" or taxes, imposed upon them. The result would be to increase prices and increase the amount of American money going to England. Colonists were not happy and saw the new taxes as another effort by the English King to exploit their work. In response to the Declaratory Act and the Townshend Acts, American colonists began a year-long boycott of English goods. Ships bearing English products were blocked from discharging their loads. British officials were harassed. Consequently, the British sent troops to American cities. Seeing British troops in their streets inflamed the anger of many Americans.

The Townshend duties were meant to specifically tax products that the British believed would be difficult for Americans to make on their own. One result was that Americans devoted their efforts to begin producing those products at home. Again, "independence" was beginning to gain more and more support. More colonists began to understand that it would be important for them to become independent of other nations to meet basic needs. Even so, many colonists remained devotedly loyal to the Crown.

The one-year American boycott of British goods began in January 1768. At the time, Boston had a population of about 16,000 Americans. The British, in response to American boycotts and harassment of British officials, had shipped 2000 troops to Boston by 1769. The stage for conflict was being set. Tensions were increasing between three basic categories of people: the American colonists, "patriots", who were beginning to thirst for independence, the American colonists who were still loyal to the Crown, known as **"Tories"** or "Loyalists" and, finally, the recently arrived English troops.

Fights began to break out between patriot colonists and British loyalists and British troops were sometimes involved. On February 22, 1770, a group of patriots gathered to attack, throwing rocks at a store run by a loyalist. A British customs official, **Ebenezer Richardson**, fired his gun out of his window, killing, probably accidentally, an eleven-year-old boy named **Christopher Seider**. This further angered the patriots. More bloody confrontations regularly occurred.

The Boston Massacre

On March 5th, 1770, a bitterly cold winter night, British Private Hugh White was on guard. His post was assigned the protection of the King's money, which was stored in a Customs House, located on King Street in Boston, Massachusetts. A group of hostile patriots accosted White with insults and physical threats. At some point, White struck a colonist with the bayonet on his rifle. The patriots then responded with snowballs, ice and stones. Bells started ringing, usually warning citizens of a fire, but, this time, resulting in a rush of male colonists onto the streets. Private White was knocked to the ground. His reinforcement appeared in the person of British Captain Thomas Preston. Capt. Preston brought a few supportive troops and formed a defensive position opposing the colonists. The patriots continued their assault on the soldiers, using sticks and make-shift clubs. Things quickly escalated. There are inconclusive reports as to how it happened, but, somehow, a soldier fired his rifle. The shot triggered the other soldiers to fire their weapons, too. Ultimately, five of the colonists died in the skirmish. Among those who died was Samuel Gray, a maker of ropes. Records say he suffered a "fist-sized" hole in his head. James Caldwell, a sailor, shot twice, also was killed. Perhaps the most well-known casualty of the conflict was **Crispus Attucks**. Attucks was a worker on the docks of Boston Harbor and was a person of mixed racial heritage. Crispus Attucks may have been a person of color who was a mortal casualty of the early events leading to the American Revolution. You have probably guessed that this dark episode became known, the world over, as **"The Boston Massacre"**.

The British soldiers involved in The Boston Massacre were arrested and jailed, even though most records show the colonists actually initiated and pushed the confrontation. Months later, the soldiers went to trial. They were represented by a lawyer who would later become an essential player in the revolution. **John Adams**, a colonist lawyer who would one day be an American President, defended the British troops. Adams was no fan of the British occupation, but he was dedicated to fair applications of the law. Capt. Preston and most of the British soldiers were found not guilty, due to Adams' effective defense. Two of the soldiers were found guilty of manslaughter and their punishment, as was the rule in England, was to be "branded" on their thumbs.

Captain Preston later wrote, of the Boston Massacre: "None of them was a hero. The victims were troublemakers who got more than they deserved. The soldiers were professionals who should not have panicked. The whole thing shouldn't have happened".

The news about the Boston Massacre was probably manipulated to the advantage of the colonists and to the detriment of the British soldiers. Regardless, as it passed through the colonies, the story further inflamed the anger of many patriots toward Britain and the Crown.

The Boston Tea Party

Boston Tea Party

Under King George III, because England was suffering economic distress following the French and Indian/Seven Years' War, which was very costly to them, the British Parliament imposed a series of taxation laws. The laws were applied to the colonies and caused a wave of resistance among the colonists. The Stamp Act, passed in 1765, required colonists to pay new taxes on paper products such as legal documents, wills, playing cards, business documents and newspapers. Colonists responded by boycotting British goods shipped to America. The Stamp Act was eventually rescinded. Only two years later, the Parliament passed The Townshend Acts, which colonists felt were even more unfair than the Stamp Act had been. The Townshend Acts put taxes on products essential to the colonists: paper (again), lead, glass, paint and . . . tea.

The refrain of "No Taxation without Representation" was gaining currency among the colonists. Some of the Townshend taxes were rescinded, but some, including the tax on tea, were maintained. Colonists began boycotting all tea coming into the colonies from the British East India Tea Company, which was soon brought to the edge of bankruptcy. Colonists smuggled tea in from the Dutch to serve their vast appetite for tea. In 1773, Parliament passed **The Tea Act**, which established the British East India Tea Company as the only supplier of tea to the colonies. Colonists were angered by this move, which they rejected, as they believed it not only taxed them unfairly but created an illegal monopoly to their economic detriment.

Colonists continued to refuse entry to ships carrying British tea and continued to refuse the discharge of any British tea in their ports. Thomas Hutchinson, however, the Royal Governor in Boston, chose to permit entry to Boston harbor of three ships bearing loads of British tea. The ships were Dartmouth, Eleanor and Beaver.

On the night of December 16, 1773, 60 patriots boarded the three ships. They were disguised as Mohawk Indians. They dumped 342 chests of tea over the rails of the ship and into the cold water of the harbor. This act of protest became known as **"The Boston Tea Party"**. The patriots were members of a group of colonists known as The Sons of Liberty and one of their leaders was **Samuel Adams**, who would become known as one of the key figures of the coming Revolution.

British Parliament was enraged and inflamed by what they saw as the wanton destruction of expensive British property. They quickly passed, in response, the **"Coercion Acts"** or **"Intolerable Acts"**. The Intolerable Acts were a big stimulant to the move toward a desire for independence in the colonies. The Intolerable Acts did several things that the colonists would respond to with great anger. They required colonists to board British troops in their homes. They closed down the Boston harbor and instituted British military rule in all of Massachusetts. The Intolerable Acts also made British governors and troops immune to prosecution for any crimes committed in America. The spark had been created to light the fire of revolution. The colonists responded to the Intolerable Acts by calling into session the first **"Continental Congress"**.

Key British Players in the American Revolutionary War

King George III

King George III

King George III was King of England and Ireland from 1738 to 1820, after which he became King of the new United Kingdom of Great Britain and Ireland. George ruled during turbulent times. He lived during a period in which Catholics had been persecuted and laws were in place intended to restrict all forms of Catholicism. George reigned over changes that eliminated anti-Catholic laws, allowed Catholics to lease land in England and allowed Catholics to vote in Irish elections. He continued, though, to block any allowance for Catholics to sit in Parliament. While George III was King, England was fighting a war with Napoleon's France and, simultaneously, a war to retain control of the American colonies. He was on the English throne while the Stamp Act, the Townshend Acts and the Intolerable Acts were imposed on the American colonists. They led to the American Revolution, during which George III ruled in England.

General Thomas Gage

In the very early days of the revolution, **General Thomas Gage** was Commander-in-Chief of all British forces in America. In June of 1775, Gage distributed a proclamation that granted pardon to all "traitors" who would reverse their course and pledge loyalty to the crown. The proclamation specifically excluded patriots **Samuel Adams** and **John Hancock**, meaning if they were apprehended, they would be imprisoned or hanged.

Colonists were engaged in a reasonably successful siege of the British-occupied city of Boston. General Gage and other recently arrived British Generals, planned efforts to break the siege. They planned an amphibious assault, land and sea, to occupy the high grounds at Dorchester Heights and then to attack colonists who had established a position at Roxbury. Dorchester Heights and Roxbury are neighborhoods in today's city of Boston. From these positions, their plan was to continue on to capture the headquarters of the local colonists in Cambridge. The battle was to be known as the **Battle of Bunker's Hill**, though most of it actually took place at nearby **Breed's Hill**.

The patriots had received intelligence informing them of the plans of the Redcoats and had heavily fortified the Breed's Hill location, stopping the progress of the British. The British lost one-third of their fighting force while attacking the colonists at Breed's Hill. The Redcoats did, ultimately, take possession of Boston's Charleston Peninsula, including Bunker Hill, but the battle was generally considered a defeat for the British. Within days after receiving the news, George III recalled General Thomas Gage. The King replaced Gage with General William Howe.

General Thomas Gage, several years later, would return to America to continue the fight.

General William Howe

General William Howe was sent to America in early 1775. The American Revolution began while he was making the ocean crossing from England. Howe replaced General Gage and was made Commander-in-Chief of all English forces. General Howe led British troops in the **Battle of Bunker Hill**, which was actually fought on **Breed's Hill**. **Colonel William Prescott** led about 1000 patriots. General Howe led three assaults on the city of Boston and was finally successful in occupying the city. Prescott was credited with telling his troops, in an effort to conserve ammunition, "Don't fire until you see the whites of their eyes". The cost of the victory, for General Howe, was great, as around 1000 British soldiers were killed. Following the British occupation of Boston, resistance was constant from the residents of the city and Howe eventually pulled out of Boston.

General Howe led British troops in the long campaign to capture New York City. He commanded troops through the **Battle of Long Island**, at Throg's Neck, Pell's Point, White Plains and at Fort Washington. At that point, British troops took full control of New York. George Washington and his troops retreated across New Jersey. It was late in 1776, weather was terrible and Howe settled his troops down for the winter, around New York. Historians have criticized Howe for not aggressively pursuing Washington and achieving a decisive victory, which might have ended the war and the revolution for independence.

In 1977, Howe attacked and occupied the city of Philadelphia. It took several battles and several months and was not considered a well-planned campaign. Washington, leading the Continental Army, attacked at Germantown. Howe's troops were forced to withdraw to go back closer to Philadelphia. Howe's poor leadership was blamed for the weak performance at Germantown and for the failure of British **General Burgoyne's** failed Saratoga campaign.

British weaknesses highlighted at Germantown and Saratoga encouraged the French to enter the war on the side of the colonists. This became an essential factor in the ultimate success of the revolution.

Howe resigned and returned to England, never to return to America.

Admiral Richard Howe

Richard Howe was brother to William Howe and the two brothers coordinated activities between troops on the ground and ships at sea. The British Navy, under Admiral Howe, conducted blockades to prevent supplies from going in and out of the colonies. They also provided cannon fire support to British troops fighting battles near the sea and the harbors. Admiral Howe ferried General Howe's troops to a landing point from which they were able to attack and eventually occupy, Philadelphia. General Howe assigned his brother, Admiral Howe, to meet with representatives of the Continental Army, to attempt a reconciliation following the **Battle for Long Island**. It was unsuccessful.

General Henry Clinton

General Clinton, like General Howe, came to America in 1775, with the Revolution beginning while his ship was still en route. He participated in the costly Battle of Bunker Hill, about which he later wrote: "A dear bought victory, another such would have ruined us". General Clinton, in 1776, commanded a fleet that landed near Sullivan's Islands, off the Carolinas, where he managed a naval bombardment. It did not succeed and he returned north to support General Howe's assault on New York City. Once the British had occupied New York City, in 1777, Admiral Clinton was left there in charge of operations.

When General Howe returned to England, General Clinton was appointed Commander-in-Chief. In 1779, while George Washington was focused on fighting the war along the American frontier, General Clinton successfully raided an important crossing of the Hudson River, located at Stony Point, New York. Americans soon drove them out and regained control of the crossing.

General Clinton, on June 30, 1779, declared what is now recognized as **"The Philipsburg Proclamation"**. The proclamation formalized a British Army offer to set free fugitive slaves who enlisted in their forces. The Continental Army, at that same time, was also recruiting African Americans. The Philipsburg Proclamation, though, served to complicate the issue of slave repatriation as the war was ending. After the war, slave owners whose slaves had run away during the conflict sought to have what they considered their rightful "property" returned to them. It would be another eighty years before Abraham Lincoln delivered the Emancipation Proclamation.

In 1780, General Clinton laid siege to the city of Charleston, South Carolina and eventually captured and occupied it. In 1782, after British General Cornwallis surrendered to the Continental Army at Yorktown, General Clinton was replaced and returned to England.

General Charles Cornwallis

Cornwallis, as a Lt. General, began his military career in the colonies under General Henry Clinton. Cornwallis was in charge of the first siege of the city of Charleston, South Carolina, which failed to dislodge the Americans. Both Clinton and Cornwallis then participated, under General William Howe, in the campaign to occupy New York City. Cornwallis's division of troops carried out the Battle of Long Island and then chased George Washington, as Washington led the retreat of patriot troops through New Jersey, after the fall of New York City to the British.

General Cornwallis, who had been promoted to second in command under General Howe, took a large force south in 1779. Cornwallis, along with General Clinton, then coordinated the siege of the city of Charleston, which ultimately succeeded. Continental forces in Charleston, led by Benjamin Lincoln, were forced to surrender. Cornwallis retained control in South Carolina, driving out all Continental forces. He then began moving his troops north into North Carolina.

General Cornwallis eventually took part in the siege of Yorktown, near the end of which he had to surrender to George Washington. Ashamed and embarrassed, Cornwallis claimed illness and sent another General, in his place, to formally surrender his sword. Washington, hearing of Cornwallis' plan, sent his own second-in-command, General Benjamin Lincoln, to accept Cornwallis' sword. Cornwallis, along with the also disgraced Benedict Arnold, returned to England in 1782.

Lieutenant General John Burgoyne

General Burgoyne arrived in the colonies in May of 1775, not long after the first shots of the Revolution were fired. He participated in the Siege of Boston, but, being an ambitious man and not seeing growth opportunities for himself in America, soon returned to England.

Burgoyne returned to North America in 1776 and led British reinforcements sailing up the Saint Lawrence River. His troops provided respite to the British, who were under siege in Quebec City, by the Continental Army. General Burgoyne, under British **General Carleton**, successfully drove the Continental Army out of Quebec province. Carleton and Burgoyne, later, failed an important attempt to capture **Fort Ticonderoga**, located in Vermont near the border to New Hampshire.

General Burgoyne, in 1777, was put in command of a large contingency of British troops who were charged with taking possession of Lake Champlain and the Hudson River Valley. The British plan was to divide New England from all the colonies to the south, which they hoped would put an end to the Revolution or what they called the **Rebellion**. Burgoyne was told he would gain substantial support, which did not materialize, from Native Americans and from colonists who were loyal to the Crown. Burgoyne had early success in the campaign and regained control of Fort Ticonderoga. In recognition of this accomplishment, Burgoyne was promoted to Lieutenant General.

When Burgoyne pushed his force beyond the range of communications with British leadership out of Quebec, he found himself soon surrounded by the Continental Army, which was led by American **General Horatio Gates**, at Saratoga. Burgoyne attempted several times to drive his forces through the American lines, but found no success and ultimately was left with no alternative but to surrender his entire army.

General Burgoyne's defeat at Saratoga is believed to have been a major turning point in the war for independence. Confidence and optimism bloomed strongly in the colonists. The British Parliament blamed Burgoyne for the losses and he was returned to England in disgrace. The reversal of fortunes in the war, favoring the colonists, gave France confidence to join in the conflict, taking the side of the new Americans against old England.

Key American Players in the American Revolutionary War

George Washington

Revolutionary General and America's First President

Geoorge Washington was the son of **Augustine Washington** and **Mary Ball Washington**, Augustine's second wife. He was born February 22, 1732, at the family's home, a plantation in Virginia, which was, at that time, a British colony. The family was wealthy and young George was probably educated in private institutions and had private tutors. Affluent families of those times often had extensive personal libraries and Washington was no exception.

George's father died when he was eleven years old and George, the oldest son, would have soon begun helping to manage the farms. His formal education was complete by the age of sixteen. He spent a great deal of his time at Ferry Farm, a family plantation near Fredericksburg, Virginia. The family owned numerous slaves who served both in the homes and in the fields. (By the time of Washington's death, it is believed the family, on their several farms, owned around 300 slaves. Washington's will provided that all of the slaves would be given their freedom on the death of his wife, Martha).

George Washington, in his studies, showed a good aptitude for mathematics and learned to be a land surveyor. He undertook numerous surveying expeditions on wilderness lands to the West, which gained him enough income to begin acquiring more land of his own. His surveying activities also offered an opportunity to explore unsettled lands, seeking optimal conditions for future purchases.

George's younger brother, Lawrence, was the victim of tuberculosis and passed away in 1752. Lawrence had been privately educated in the fine schools of England and, though younger than George, became one of George's teachers and a mentor to his older brother. George inherited Lawrence's estate, known as **Mount Vernon**, located on the Potomac River not far from Alexandria, Virginia.

Probably due to his family's status, young George Washington was made a commander of the Virginia militia, though he had no military experience. He demonstrated courageous leadership during the **French and Indian War** and was soon in command of all of the colony's militia. After that conflict ended, Washington returned to Mount Vernon and served in the Virginia House of Burgesses for about fifteen years.

Washington married a wealthy widow, **Martha Dandridge Custis**, in 1759. Martha had two children, for whom George became a loving step-father. As an adult gentleman farmer, George grew the family's properties, five farms or plantations, substantially. He was skilled in agriculture and experimented with the current knowledge of ways to conserve the land and to optimize crop production. He was a breeder of mules, which were the tractors of the times and he established a fishery. He successfully grew fruit orchards, wheat, corn and more.

As the 1760s arrived, colonists were beginning to chafe at British taxation and other restrictions on their growth and production. Washington began to contemplate the advantages, to the colonists, of independence from England. George Washington was a delegate when the **First Continental Congress** convened in Philadelphia in 1774. Only a year later, the **Second Continental Congress** was convened and the **American Revolution** had already begun. Washington was declared Commander-in-Chief of the new **Continental Army**.

As the war ended, Washington had become a legendary American hero. He rode a wave of the nation's affection into the first Presidential election. At that time, the first President was to be chosen by a count of the votes of 69 "electors". Electors came from each state. Washington was elected unanimously. Electors voted for two people. The person who had the most total votes would be President. The person with the second-highest total would become Vice President. **John Adams** became our first Vice President. Washington would go on to win the second Presidential election, once again voted in unanimously.

George Washington never lived in the White House, which had not yet been constructed. The seat of the government was, in a sense, mobile, following the location of the President. Washington, at times, served from New York and, later, from Philadelphia.

Congress passed the **Residence Act** in July 1790. The act provided for the establishment of a permanent capital. It was to be located in what would become Washington, D.C. and was to lie along the banks of the beautiful Potomac River. Washington personally supervised the building of the new capitol building. He also determined the locations of the President's mansion (the White House) and the actual Capitol building.

Our Constitution vaguely described the need to create some executive positions to assist the President in his duties. Washington filled out the concept and established our first **President's Cabinet**. As he developed it, there were, initially, only four Cabinet positions. They were not to be elected officials but were to be chosen by the Executive or President.

Washington's first Cabinet included a **Secretary of State**, who was Thomas Jefferson, a **Secretary of Treasury**, who was Alexander Hamilton, a **Secretary of War**, who was Henry Knox and an **Attorney General**, who was Edmund Randolph.

Washington intentionally selected people with a diversity of viewpoints, rather than "packing" the Cabinet with people who would all support his own positions.

President Washington, in 1789, created the first **national holiday**, designating November 26 as a **"National Day of Thanksgiving"**. His intention was to bring citizens together to express gratitude "to the Almighty" for caring for Americans during the revolution and thereafter. Washington personally celebrated the date by attending church at St. Paul's Chapel in New York City and by donating food and beer to imprisoned debtors. (In those days, those who could not pay their debts could be imprisoned).

The Whiskey Rebellion arose in 1794 and is covered in a different section of this history. The rebellion was the first internal threat to the health of the new nation. Washington, while meeting his other essential responsibilities, also recognized his duty as Commander in Chief of America's armed forces. He personally collected a militia force to quell the rebellion, which he did effectively. Washington's firm and prompt response to the insurrection added stability to the strength and ultimate authority of the federal government.

Washington visited Newport, Rhode Island in August of 1790, where he was welcomed warmly to the Touro Synagogue. He seized the opportunity to speak on the importance of religious freedom in America. In his letter directed to the synagogue, Washington declared that they should be received with more than just "tolerance". He carefully clarified his position, saying "It is now no more that toleration is spoken of as if it were the indulgence of one class of people that another enjoyed the exercise of their inherent rights". He meant that their freedom to exercise their own religious beliefs should never be dependent on the approval of others. Washington added "The Government of the United States, which gives to bigotry no sanction, to persecution no assistance, requires that they who live under its protection should demean themselves as good citizens in giving it on all occasions their effectual support". His words of that day put in place a precedent for the protection of religious freedom which is still relevant in today's American society.

These states were all welcomed into the union during Washington's administration: North Carolina, 1789; Rhode Island, 1790; Vermont, 1791; Kentucky, 1792; and Tennessee, 1796.

As Washington's two terms neared an end, he completed his **Farewell Address** to the nation. He was 64 years old and suffering from the pains of serious dental problems and rheumatism. The document had been drafted much earlier, at Washington's request, by **James Madison**. When the time came to leave office, the initial draft was edited by **Alexander Hamilton** and Washington. The address was printed as a letter to the citizens of the country and first was revealed by a Philadelphia newspaper on September 19, 1796.

It has become one of our country's most revered documents. In the farewell address, Washington explained his refusal to run for a third term. He cautioned citizens against allowing their regional differences to divide them as a nation. He emphasized the importance of remaining firmly unified. He expressed his concerns about the development of opposition political parties because he feared the effects of adhering to political party loyalty rather than loyalty to the nation. He warned against "a spirit of revenge" and the appearance of "cunning, ambitious and unprincipled men" who might "usurp for themselves the reins of government". It almost sounds like he could foresee some of the problems pervasive in our modern-day government. Finally, his farewell address also expressed his advice to future leaders about **"isolationism"**. He believed that America should attempt to stay free of obligations to foreign nations and neutral regarding conflicts between foreign nations. He recommended that America "Steer clear of permanent alliances with any portion of the foreign world." He reasoned that should we bond with one nation, we will likely be antagonizing other nations. He believed neutrality would help the United States avoid foreign wars and would protect our trade routes with all concerned.

George Washington and Slavery

Washington grew up in the community of Virginia plantation farms. Slaves provided the free labor that made the plantations profitable and virtually all plantations used slave labor. It was unconscionable, but deeply established after centuries of global practice.

George inherited slaves at the age of eleven when his father died. George's home, Mt. Vernon, was located in Fairfax County, Virginia. In 1754 a full 40% of the total population was made up of enslaved people. The "slave labor culture" was an integral part of life for everyone young George knew.

We know that, as a young adult, George, who had inherited ten slaves, purchased several additional slaves. When George married Martha Dandridge Custin, in 1759, he acquired another large number of slaves and more properties. Over the next couple of decades, he added about 40 more slaves. Most of the additional growth of his "slave census" came as a result of births among his existing group. At the time of his death, the properties held approximately 300 enslaved African Americans.

A visitor from Europe, traveling around America, wrote that Washington "dealt with his slaves far more humanely than do his fellow citizens of Virginia". The same writer shared the opinion that most Virginians typically treated their slaves harshly, providing only bread, water and blows". This opinion appears to have been shared by Washington, himself, as he is known to have offered criticism of his fellow plantation owners, saying owners "who are not always as kind and as attentive to their slaves' wants and usage as they ought to be".

Nearing the end of his remarkable life, Washington wrote, of his slaves: "The unfortunate condition of the persons, whose labor in part I employed, has been the only unavoidable subject of regret (in his life). To make the adults among them as easy and as comfortable in their circumstances as their actual state of ignorance and improvidence would admit; and to lay a foundation to prepare the rising generation for a destiny different from that in which they were born; afforded some satisfaction to my mind and could not I hoped be displeasing to the justice of the Creator". Washington was saying he recognized the injustices in which he participated and he hoped he had treated his slaves well and he hoped God would take mercy on him. His comments about the state of the Negro reflect the ignorance of the times.

It seems that, as Washington matured and as he experienced the American Revolution and fought on the basis of equality for all, he gradually became, in his philosophy, an abolitionist. He witnessed, in his war travels, the successful approach to agriculture undertaken in other parts of the country, in which slave labor was rejected. Seven months into the revolution, Washington approved permitting free black soldiers to join the Continental Army. He witnessed the brave performance of those black soldiers during horrific battles. Washington also had a cherished relationship with the **Marquis de Lafayette**, a Frenchman who passionately opposed slavery. At some point, he evolved to the point that he made a firm commitment to never again buy or sell a human being. He could not, however, bring himself to free the slaves who made his financial survival possible.

George Washington wrote to his friend, Robert Morris, regarding the abolition of slavery: "I can only say that there is not a man living who wishes more sincerely than I do, to see a plan adopted for the abolition of it; but there is only one proper and effectual mode by which it can be accomplished and that is by legislative authority; and this, as far as my suffrage will go, shall never be wanting".

At age 46, Washington, after being a slave owner for 35 years, wrote to a cousin: "I long, every day, more and more, to get clear of ownership of slaves". When he became President, he consistently supported legislated moves to abolish slavery, but he would not live to see real progress toward that objective. Emancipation would have to wait for the appearance of another great leader, three generations down the road of American history.

Terms of Washington's will:

George Washington was never involved in public movements favoring abolition. He believed emancipation would have to happen in gradual measures. Washington died in December 1799. In his will, he left clear instructions to emancipate or free, after his wife Martha's death, all the slaves owned by himself. At the time, there were 317 slaves at Mount Vernon, but less than half were owned by George, himself, and the remainder were part of Martha's family's properties. Mount Vernon was still home to 153 slaves after Martha died and all the property was reverted to the Custis family estate.

Washington's will stipulated that elderly slaves or those too sick to work, were to be supported throughout their lives by the Washington estate. Furthermore, slave children without parents or slave families too poor or indifferent to the education of their children, were to be assigned to masters who would teach them reading, writing and useful trade. All the slave children were to be emancipated at age 25. Martha Washington, in 1800, signed a **"Deed of Manumission"** which freed all of George's slaves, which transaction is still found in Fairfax County Court Records. George Washington's slaves were finally freed on January 1, 1801

John Adams

America's Second President

John Adams was born a British subject in the British colony of Massachusetts. John's father was a leather craftsman and an educated farmer. John was an avid reader as a child and his father, a Deacon in their church, encouraged him to pursue a career in the ministry. John, after graduating from Harvard University, became a grammar school teacher for three years. He studied the law on his own and soon began practicing law in Boston.

John married **Abigail Smith**, daughter of a minister, who was well-educated and who served as a balance, throughout their lives, to John's irascibility and volatility. Letters between John and Abigail, over the decades of their lives, reveal two people deeply in love, who both display unusual intellectual capacities. The letters are famous for their passion and their emotional "love letters". The two of them had four children (and one who did not survive) and their son **John Quincy Adams** would become an American President.

John Adams never owned a slave, nor did his wife, Abigail and they were deeply opposed to slavery. He was not, however, a proponent of **"abolition"**, as he believed an abrupt, forced end of slavery would create enormous problems. In the late 1700's there were approximately 900,000 slaves in the U.S., most of whom were born in America.

Adams' political career began to develop as his law practice grew. Tension was growing in the colonies between the British rulers and the Americans. Adams became a known representative of the resistance of the colonists to Parliament's passing of the **Stamp Act** and then the **Townshend Act**. He argued, with others, that the British could not tax Americans under conditions in which the Americans had no representation in the government in England.

When the **"Boston Massacre"** happened, Adams stepped in to provide legal representation to the British Soldiers. He was excoriated by many for defending the Redcoats, but he insisted that everyone, regardless of guilt or innocence, has a right to a fair trial. His insistence on upholding the rights of the soldiers gained him some anger on the part of some colonists but also became part of his growing reputation for being highly principled.

John Adams was elected, by Massachusetts colonists, to participate in the **First Continental Congress** of 1774. Along with his cousin, **Samuel Adams**, the two of them became leaders of the rebel cause. They argued that England had no right to tax or legislate, on behalf of Americans. In 1775, the **Second Continental Congress** convened, by which time Adams was acknowledged to be a leader of the "rebels", known to be promoting the idea of gaining American independence from England.

The Americans were beginning to develop a new organized militia. John Adams successfully nominated George Washington, who was then appointed Commander of the new **Continental Army**. Adams then selected Virginian **Thomas Jefferson** to be the primary writer of the American **Declaration of Independence**. Adams emerged as the most dominant speaker during the debates about the Declaration and about whether or not to proceed in the pursuit of independence.

In 1776, Adams wrote the **"Plan of Treaties"**, which choreographed a peace with France, critical as the Revolutionary War progressed and which included concepts that would impact America's foreign policy guidelines for the next hundred years. Congress made Adams the Director of the "Board of War and Ordnance" and he was essential in raising funds, garnering support and equipping the new Continental Army. He was responsible for the creation of the **American Navy**. Congress had previously sent Benjamin Franklin to Paris, France, to solicit French assistance for the war. Adams was sent to join Franklin when progress seemed to be coming slowly in furthering relationships with the French government. He sailed for England, along with his 10-year-old boy and future President, John Quincy. It was an unusually rough voyage across the Atlantic. Adams, surviving the crossing, was then instrumental, along with Franklin, in coordinating the execution of the critically necessary alliance with France against the English.

John Adams returned to America in 1779, arriving in time to participate, that summer, in the Constitutional Convention for the state of Massachusetts, his home. His extraordinary knowledge of governments around the world and their constitutions, made him the obvious choice to write the constitution for Massachusetts. The document he drafted officially became the state's constitution in 1780 and it became the primary source for the creation of the nation's new constitution. Adams created a government that included clear **separation of powers**, **checks and balances** and a **bicameral** (two separate sections) legislature . . . which became our **House** and **Senate**. Jefferson was the primary writer of our Declaration of Independence and Adams was the father of our Constitution. The two of them would be friendly adversaries on many issues moving far into the country's future. They both served as Presidents of the United States. They lived long lives and, amazingly, died on the same day, July 4th, Independence Day, 1826, fifty years after 1776.

Congress soon sent Adams back to Paris, with instructions to assist Franklin in negotiating an end to the war with the British. Franklin was a social butterfly, engaged in many personal relationships and was very popular with French society. Adams was not so likable and was more of a blunt, direct negotiator. The two shared a strained relationship. Together, though, the combination of their attributes yielded a successful outcome. The **Paris Peace Treaty** was signed in 1783, finally ending the long Revolutionary War. Thomas Jefferson was sent to Paris in 1784 to replace Ben Franklin. Adams and Jefferson, while frequently in disagreement, became fast friends and remained so for the duration of their lives

Following the negotiations for peace, Adams was sent, by Congress, to represent America as an ambassador in London, England. He was not treated with great affection in the old country, as much bitterness persisted about the rebellion of the colonists. Thomas Jefferson joined Adams in England in 1785. The two of them were able, while in London, to negotiate critical loans from the Dutch. The new nation was in dire financial straits after the war and the loans helped them survive.

Adams returned to America, where he served as the nation's first **Vice President**, under unanimously selected **President George Washington**. Washington had served two terms as the nation's first President and was asked to run for a third term. Washington refused, explaining that the American President should not be given unlimited time in office. Washington was very concerned that the American President NOT become a "King".

The new nation's first true, contested election took place in 1796, after Washington's second term. Adams was elected President, with **Thomas Jefferson** gaining the position of Vice President. Jefferson would become the nation's third President, following his friend Adams into the position. John Adams was the first President to reside in the mansion that would become known as **"The White House"**.

Thomas Jefferson

America's Third President

Thomas Jefferson's father, **Peter Jefferson**, a cartographer and a planter, owned a plantation known as Shadwell, near Charlottesville, Virginia. His mother, **Jane Randolph Jefferson**, was a member of a wealthy and prominent Virginia family. Thomas was the third of their seven children.

Jefferson attended the College of William and Mary, from which he graduated in 1762. He was known for studying many long hours each day and then spending hours more practicing violin. Thomas went on to study the law under the same Virginia attorney, George Wythe, who tutored **Chief Justice John Marshall** and highly respected American statesman **Henry Clay**.

Jefferson worked as a lawyer and was soon elected to Virginia's House of Burgesses. He was building a reputation for his knowledge and his quiet nature. His reputation spread when he wrote, in 1774, a pamphlet known as **"A Summary View of the Rights of British America"**. British America was, of course, the American colonies. The pamphlet built a rationale explaining that the British Parliament had no rightful authority to legislate over the Americans.

When Jefferson's father died, while Thomas was a teenager, he began pursuing plans to build a brick home, on their property, on top of a mountain he was clearing. The home would become the national landmark **Monticello** mansion. Jefferson was deeply interested in botany, livestock breeding and architecture. Monticello would eventually be the base for many experiments and much research. Jefferson built an immense library over the years, which eventually was sold to the government to begin rebuilding the **Library of Congress**, which had been burned by the British during the War of 1812.

Thomas Jefferson kept voluminous and detailed written histories of all aspects of life on his plantation. He kept records related to gardening, breeding animals, management of slaves, daily weather reports and various experiments. He corresponded regularly with European experts on many subjects.

In 1772, Thomas married a young, attractive widow, **Martha Wayles Skelton**. They eventually gave birth to six children. Only two survived to adulthood, Martha and Mary. Sadly, Jefferson's wife, Martha, died at the young age of 33. Thomas was devastated and deeply depressed long after. He never again married.

Sally Hemings was sent to England and then to France when she was around 16 years old, with the purpose of accompanying Jefferson's daughter on a trip to join her father. While in London, she was entertained by John and Abigail Adams, who were serving in

England at the time. In France, slavery was not permitted and Sally functioned as a free citizen but continued to serve, with pay, the Jeffersons. It is believed that it was during this episode, while serving in France, that Jefferson initiated intimate relations with the young Sally. It is thought that Sally could have remained in France as a free citizen, but desired to return to Monticello, where she had family. One of her sons, **Madison Hemings**, revealed that it was known in their family that Sally had negotiated with Thomas Jefferson to get him to agree that, if she returned to Monticello, he would promise to emancipate all of her children on his death. Some believe that Jefferson and Hemings produced six children, though only four survived to grow into adults.

As the **American Revolution** developed and tensions between the British and the colonists heated up, Jefferson was selected to represent Virginia as a delegate to the **Second Continental Congress**. Known to be a gifted writer, he was soon assigned the task of writing a **Declaration of Independence**, meant to express the desire of the colonists to gain freedom and the reasons behind that desire. **John Adams** and **Benjamin Franklin** were sources of information and ideas to support Jefferson's efforts.

Jefferson returned to the Virginia House of Delegates in 1776 (previously known as the House of Burgesses). In the course of his service, Jefferson wrote the **"Virginia Statute for Religious Freedom"**, which most consider the foundation for the **First Amendment** in our **Bill of Rights**. It provides legal protection guaranteeing that all people can worship as they choose.

Thomas Jefferson was elected Governor of Virginia, a post in which he served from 1779 to 1781, after which he once again served in the **Congress of the Confederation**, which became today's **Congress**. Benjamin Franklin was returning from his years of service in France in 1785 and Jefferson was assigned to replace Franklin in Paris. His occupation in Paris prevented his participation in the **Constitutional Convention of 1787**. Jefferson did, however, make known his suggestions and support for term limits for Presidents and for the introduction of a **Bill of Rights**.

On his return, in late 1789, from Paris, France, President Washington appointed him the position of the young country's first **Secretary of State**. While holding this important office, Jefferson and **Alexander Hamilton**, who was **Secretary of the Treasury** at the time, began a long history of opposition to one another's policies. Jefferson resisted the formation of a strong central (Federal) government and wanted power retained by the states and local governments. He was afraid of the voice of the people being lost in a big government. Jefferson was one of the founders of the **"Democratic-Republican"** party, which was meant to form a foundation for opposing Hamilton's "Federalist" party. The **Federalists** wanted a strong central government, with much power over the states. Many years later, the Democratic-Republican party split and the majority of its adherents went on to form today's **Democrat** political party. The remainder created the **"Whig"** party, which eventually morphed into today's **Republican** political party.

John Adams and Thomas Jefferson both ran for President in 1796. Adams got the most votes, with Jefferson having the second highest number. According to the laws at that time, Jefferson became Vice President. In 1800, Jefferson and Adams again opposed one another in a very bitterly fought campaign. Jefferson won, due to a flaw in the electoral system which was later remediated by the Twelfth Amendment.

Jefferson's inauguration, March 4th, 1801, was the first held in Washington, D.C. and he eschewed the traditional carriage ride, instead walking to and from the formal ceremony. During Jefferson's first administration, he accomplished, in 1803, the **"Louisiana Purchase"**, at a cost of $15 million. It brought, under American ownership, more than 800,000 square miles of new territory, ranging from the Gulf of Mexico to the Rocky Mountains and back to the Mississippi River, an immense new acquisition. Jefferson sent American explorers **William Clark** and **Meriwether Lewis** to survey and map the new territory. The Louisiana Purchase virtually doubled the size of the United States. Aside from mapping new territories, Lewis and Clark returned with vast new records detailing plant and animal life, indigenous tribes and the geography of America between the two oceans.

Jefferson won re-election in 1804, defeating Federalist candidate **Charles Pinckney**. His second term was marked by a conflict between France and the English, in the course of which both combatants began harassing American merchant ships. In response to the aggressions, Jefferson employed the **"Embargo Act of 1807"**, which blocked American ports to foreign shipping. The act was not popular, due to the harm it caused to the American economy and was eventually repealed. America was very reluctantly drawn into the **War of 1812**.

After serving his two terms as the third President, Jefferson eagerly returned to Monticello. He spent his remaining years pursuing his intellectual and agricultural interests. He was a founder of the University of Virginia, where he designed some of the buildings and helped develop academic curriculum. He built one of America's most expansive libraries. He insisted that the school have no religious connections or affiliations, hoping that people of all religions would feel welcome.

Thomas Jefferson and his old friend and foe, John Adams, remarkably both passed away on the same day, July 4th, 1826, exactly 50 years after the adoption of the Declaration of Independence. Jefferson is buried at Monticello, but, at the time of his death, he carried substantial debt, so the plantation had to be sold. "The mansion, the contents of the mansion and most of the slaves were sold, though Sally Hemings and few "special cases" were set free."

Thomas Jefferson and Slavery

Historians believe Thomas Jefferson had a life-long relationship, following Martha's death, with a "house slave" named Sally Hemings. Sally was Martha's half-sister, a result of previous owner-slave relationships. Records suggest Thomas was deeply devoted to Sally and they produced children together. Descendants of Sally Hemings are now considered part of the Jefferson family.

Slavery was a terrible, shameful institution. Our Founding Fathers, Jefferson included, believed it to be morally indefensible. Free slave labor was essential to the successful management of plantations growing tobacco and, later, cotton. In spite of his acknowledgment that slavery had to one day be ended, Jefferson owned slaves throughout his life. At one time, he wrote of a plan for the gradual emancipation of slaves, but it never was seriously considered. While Jefferson wrote, passionately, in the Declaration of Independence, that "all men are created equal", his personal writings reveal that he believed there were biological differences between the races which would mean they could never peacefully coexist in society.

His father bequeathed approximately 175 slaves to Thomas and Thomas is believed to have owned, during his lifetime, in the neighborhood of 600 slaves. When Thomas died, most of the slaves on the plantation were sold. A few "special cases", including Hemings, were set free.

Alexander Hamilton

Alexander Hamilton's childhood was difficult, to say the least. His family lived on the Caribbean island, Nevis, in the British West Indies. His mother, **Rachel**, had been married to a man who had her imprisoned, charging her with adultery and who spent most of her fortune. Rachel later had a relationship with Scottish trader, **James Hamilton**, though they were never married. Rachel and James had a son together, Alexander Hamilton. When Alexander was born, his mother was still married to her first husband.

Alexander's family was abandoned by James Hamilton in 1766. Historians believe it is likely, since Rachel was still married to another man, that James left to protect Rachel from being imprisoned for bigotry. Rachel passed away only two years later, leaving Alexander an orphan. Alexander, only eleven years old, went to work for a trading company located on the island of St. Croix. Alexander became an avid reader and was largely self-educated. A terrible hurricane struck the island in 1772. Alexander penned a remarkably eloquent letter illuminating the results of the hurricane. He gained a reputation as a scholar, stirring local supporters to gather funds that they used to transport Alexander to America, where he could continue his studies.

In 1772, American colonists were beginning to prepare for their war for independence. Alexander Hamilton arrived just in time to become an early supporter of their objective. He soon became known as an ardent **"Federalist"** or supporter of a strong central government and was instrumental in creating the Constitution and in getting the Constitution ratified.

Hamilton, still just a teenager as the war for independence heated up, quickly became well-known for the pamphlets and articles he wrote, supporting the desire for freedom from England. He was ambitious and sought ways to contribute to the actual combat in the fields. Hamilton brought together an artillery company. He served at the **Battles of White Plains**, **Trenton** and **Princeton**, and soon was in demand, with several high-ranking officers hoping to add him to their staffs. When George Washington requested Hamilton become Washington's **Aide-de-Camp**, Hamilton quickly acquiesced. Their relationship rapidly deepened and they became very close. Washington became something of a father figure to Alexander and treated the young man as a son.

Hamilton was rewarded for his major part in creating the new government by being appointed America's first **Secretary of the U.S. Treasury**. He proceeded to structure a financial system and economic foundation for the new nation. His chief opponent in politics was the brilliant Thomas Jefferson, who favored a limited central government and wanted the powers of government centered in the individual states. Hamilton created the **"First Bank of the United States"**.

The well-known differences between the preferred policies of Hamilton and those of Jefferson became the triggers for the creation of the nation's first two political parties. They became the **"Federalists"**, supporting Hamilton's philosophy and the **"Democratic-Republicans"**, supporting Jefferson's philosophy.

In 1780, Alexander married **Elizabeth Schuyler**, often called Eliza or Betsey. Eliza was born to a wealthy and influential American family. Alexander was born in poverty and became an orphaned immigrant to the colonies. Their romance was celebrated in the high society of the times. (It is the basis for much of the award-winning Broadway play, 'Hamilton'. Alexander and Elizabeth had eight children together. Hamilton was especially fond of his eldest son, Philip. Philip was killed in a duel with one of his father's political opponents after that man insulted Philip's father during a speech. The Hamilton marriage was devastated by the loss of young Philip. The marriage was further assaulted when the **"Reynolds Scandal"** erupted, revealing an adulterous relationship between Alexander and another man's wife. Eliza, though, persisted through the difficulties and remained true and loyal to her husband. Elizabeth was the co-founder of the first private orphanage in New York City.

In 1793, war again broke out between France and the British. The feud between Jefferson and Hamilton continued. Jefferson favored joining in the battle to support France, returning the enormous favor France delivered to the colonists in their own war for independence. Hamilton, more of an **"isolationist"**, wanted America to retain its neutrality in the French-English war.

While Hamilton returned to his law practice in 1795, leaving his post as Secretary of the Treasury, George Washington was refusing a third term as President. Alexander Hamilton, along with **James Madison**, wrote much of Washington's **"Farewell Address to the Nation"**. Hamilton continued, from behind the curtains, to impact political events. John Adams became the second President and the Adams-Hamilton rifts had the effect of diminishing the strength of the Federalists, leading to the election of Thomas Jefferson to be our third President.

Alexander Hamilton was well-known and well-liked, especially by the Federalists. He would most likely have eventually been a powerful Presidential candidate. Unfortunately for him, in 1797, the notorious **"Reynolds Pamphlet"** revealed Hamilton's acknowledgment of a sexual affair with the wife of James Reynolds. It created a scandal from which Hamilton's political career could not recover.

Hamilton had an ambitious, aggressive personality. He became engaged in frequent passionate debates. In those times, when a "polite society" man felt he'd been insulted, it wasn't unusual for the offended party to challenge his offender to a duel, armed combat. Weapons might be fists, swords or guns. Historians write that Hamilton was engaged in no fewer than ten duels or "affairs of honor". Sadly, in 1804, on July 11th, just such an affair was played out between Hamilton and **Aaron Burr**. The two had been long-time political rivals and each had many complaints about the other. Burr, on this occasion, had heard that Hamilton had disparaged Burr at a dinner party. Challenges ensued. They faced one another with pistols. Hamilton's shot went wide, easily missing Burr. Friends at the time believed Hamilton never really meant to hit Burr. Burr's shot, however, mortally wounded Hamilton, who died the next day.

In our modern world, we see Alexander Hamilton's face on our ten-dollar bills.

Alexander Hamilton and Slavery

Notes on Alexander Hamilton and slavery: Historians seem to agree that, philosophically, at least, Hamilton was deeply opposed to the shameful institution of slavery. In real life, though, evidence has accrued which suggests he did engage in some elements of enslavement. As a lawyer, he sometimes represented slave owners in legal arbitration. His father-in-law, Philip Schuyler, Eliza's father, "owned" as many as thirty enslaved African Americans. Hamilton was a member of the **New York Manumission Society**, which was an abolitionist organization. Recent research appears to indicate that Alexander Hamilton did, indeed, own a small number of slaves, called, in his family, "servants".

Benjamin Franklin

Josiah Franklin, who had come to Boston from England and his second wife, **Abiah Folger**, from Nantucket, became parents to **Benjamin Josiah Franklin** on January 17, 1706. Theirs was a family of modest means. Josiah had been born into a modest farming family and, as an adult, made candles and soap. Benjamin was the eighth of ten children born to Josiah and Abiah. Benjamin's father also had nine children with his first wife, Anne Child, who passed away.

Benjamin Franklin benefited from very little formal education, which had ended by the age of ten, as was common for the times for children of families of modest means. He was a prodigious reader, though and became well-educated by his own work. Ben soon became a proficient writer, as well. He was "apprenticed" at age 12, by his father, to an older brother, James, who was a printer in Boston. Working for James, Ben learned the art of printing and became strong carrying the extremely heavy boxes of lead type, which was used to produce the printed content.

Ben's good writing skills soon found him publishing essays in their newspaper. He used the pseudonym **"Silence Dogood"**, hiding his own identity and protecting himself from hostile reactions to his writings. Ben bridled under the thumb of his older brother, resenting harsh treatment and what Ben felt to be unfair conditions. He ran away from his apprenticeship, illegally at the time and escaped back to Philadelphia, essentially as a fugitive from the law. If James pursued him, the pursuit was unsuccessful.

In Philadelphia, Benjamin became a printer under his own authority. In 1724, he decided to travel to London, England, where he again worked as a printer. The American Revolution was still fifty years into the future. By 1726, he had returned to his hometown, Philadelphia, where he opened his own print shop. He printed and published a wide range of content, including documents for the government, government currency and all types of pamphlets. His business became quite successful.

Benjamin acquired his own colonial newspaper in 1729, which was known as **"The Philadelphia Gazette"** and which grew very popular. He published **"Poor Richard's Almanac"**, which drew a vast readership and was known for his common sense and humorous statements. The almanac was published regularly for twenty-five years.

Franklin pursued a long relationship with **Deborah Read**, who was generally acknowledged as his "common-law wife". They could not legally marry because Deborah was, technically, still married to a man who had abandoned her. Ben and Deborah produced a son, who died at age 4 of smallpox; a daughter, Sarah; and a second son, William, whom one day served as the final colonial governor, under the British, of New

Jersey. William refused to support the revolution, when it occurred and eventually died in England.

While living in Philadelphia during the 1730s, Ben Franklin created the nation's first **"lending library"**, which became the country's largest library for the next hundred and twenty years. Franklin, after devastating fires, established the first **"fire company"**, using local volunteers to manage fire fighting equipment. He initiated a **"police patrol"** for the protection of citizens. Ben created the **"American Philosophical Society"**, which was a sort of brain trust, bringing together skilled and educated persons to discuss the issues of the day. He built a solid reputation as an asset to the community and became a well-known personality of the times.

Franklin organized the original Pennsylvania militia, necessary because Pennsylvania was still an English colony and the English didn't offer much local protection. He was active in local civil matters and raised money to pay to have the city's streets paved and lighted. He was a key player in the creation of the **"Academy of Philadelphia"**, which eventually became today's University of Pennsylvania.

Benjamin was the founder of America's postal system. In 1737, the British governor made Franklin the postmaster of Philadelphia and he ultimately became the **postmaster general** for the colonies as a whole. He was fired from the job in 1774 when the British decided he was too friendly to pro-colonial interests, in opposition to British rule.

By 1750, Ben was in his early 40s and had become quite successful through his printing business and his popular writings. He turned over the daily works of his print shop to others and became engaged full-time in other pursuits, including colonial civic interests. During this period, he engaged in experimentation related to the understanding of the potential of electricity, including his famous "kite" experiment, which proved lightning consisted of an electrical charge. One result was his invention of the **lightning rod**, which protected buildings, including homes, from fires caused by lightning.

Franklin was one of the nation's first great inventors. He studied and wrote about, a wide range of scientific subjects, including the causes of the common cold, the potential benefits of refrigeration, the impact of oceanic currents and meteorology. He invented a stove that generated much more warmth but required much less fuel and the stove, named, of course, **"the Franklin Stove"**, is still in use in some places. Ben invented **"bifocal"** eyeglasses, which could be worn to improve both long-distance viewing and up-close reading. Mozart and Beethoven wrote music specifically to be played by an instrument invented by Franklin, which was known as the **"glass armonica"**.

The Continental Congress was convened, in Philadelphia, in 1775. Congress made Benjamin Franklin the **"First Postmaster General of the United States"**. His son-in-law would one day succeed him in that position and the first U.S. postage stamps were illustrated with images of Benjamin Franklin and George Washington.

Friction between the colonists and their British rulers was growing strong and fast. A group of representatives from the various colonies came together in 1754. The meeting was held in Albany, New York. Ben wrote a plan that described a method of uniting all of the colonies under the leadership of a single national Congress. It was known as **"The Albany Plan"** and, though it was never adopted, it is recognized to be the foundation for the **Articles of Confederation**, which led to the construction of the first **Constitution of the United States**, which was ratified in 1781.

Benjamin Franklin was a member of the Pennsylvania Assembly and went to London in 1757. There, he worked on numerous issues related to the activities of the British as they impacted the colonists. He was, initially, a supporter of the Royal monarchy. He stayed in London for several years and was there as the British began to institute the series of actions that eventually led to the American Revolution. He testified, in the British Parliament, in opposition to the imposition, on the colonists, of the notorious Stamp Act.

Soon after the revolution had begun, Franklin returned to his home in Philadelphia. He was a delegate to the **Second Continental Congress** and he was one of the five men on the committee that drafted the American **Declaration of Independence**. Franklin was shipped back across the Atlantic in 1776, where he was engaged, for years, in efforts to gain financial and military support from France in America's fight for independence. Ben became an extremely popular figure in the "high society" of the King's court in Paris and was generally believed to have enjoyed the company of many of France's "ladies of court society". John Adams eventually was sent to join Franklin in building America's relationship with France. In 1778, while Franklin was America's Minister to France, a formal military alliance between the American patriots and the French government was signed. Most historians believe that had Franklin and Adams failed, the colonists would very possibly have failed in their fight for freedom from British rule. In 1783, Franklin was instrumental in drafting the **Treaty of Paris**, which ended the Revolutionary War.

Back home in Philadelphia again, in 1787, Franklin was a delegate to the Constitutional Convention. At age 81 years, he was the nation's oldest participant in the convention. The Constitution was ratified in 1788 and General George Washington was then inaugurated as the new nation's first President in 1789. Benjamin Franklin was the only American whose signature decorated all four of America's critical documents: the Declaration of Independence, the Treaty of Alliance with France, the Treaty of Paris and the United States Constitution.

Benjamin Franklin died only one year after Washington assumed the Presidency, at the age of 84. He left funds, in his will, which were to be used to create a trade school, a science museum, a foundation for scholarships and funds for various civic projects. We see Franklin's face on today's one-hundred-dollar bills and his name graces many towns, streets and schools.

Franklin was famous, in his own times, for his witticisms and wisdom, reflected in quotes taken from his writings. Here is a short list of some of the favorites, which have aged well through the many decades since his death:

- Never leave that till tomorrow which you can do today.

- Guests, like fish, begin to smell after three days.

- They who can give up essential liberty to obtain a little temporary safety deserve neither liberty nor safety.

- Three can keep a secret if two of them are dead.

- We must, indeed, all hang together or, most assuredly, we shall all hang separately.

- An investment in knowledge pays the best interest.

- By failing to prepare, you are preparing to fail.

- It takes many good deeds to build a good reputation and only one bad one to lose it.

- Well done is better than well said.

- Tell me and I forget. Teach me and I remember. Involve me and I learn.

Notes on Benjamin Franklin and Slavery

Benjamin Franklin, as a young adult, did own slaves. Records show he owned two slaves, who worked as household servants. He also carried advertisements for the sale of slaves and the recovery of fugitive slaves, in his newspaper, the Pennsylvania Gazette. During that same period, he also published pamphlets and essays decrying and condemning slavery. His personal writings consistently displayed his recognition that the institution was cruel, immoral and unsustainable. As he grew older, he became an avid and vocal, abolitionist. He took the office of President of the Pennsylvania Society for Promoting Abolition of Slavery in 1787. The organization provided assistance to help integrate freed slaves into society. Franklin's final public act, in 1789, was a petition to Congress that requested the abolition of slavery and the termination of all slave trading.

Samuel Adams

Samuel Adams

Samuel Adams was born into a well-to-do Puritan family in Boston, on September 27, 1722. His father, **Samuel Adams, Sr.**, was a respected merchant, a deacon in the church and an active player in local politics. Samuel's mother, **Mary**, was also from a successful and respected family.

"Puritans" were members of English Protestant church denominations. They were very influential in politics in England and in the colonies in New England. Puritans were known for very strict religious doctrine, especially as it relates to recreation, pleasurable activities and sexual behaviors.

Samuel was a student at Boston Latin School and later attended Harvard College, where he was enamored of the writings of philosopher **John Locke**. Locke was influential in the **"Age of Enlightenment"** and was a supporter of the growing belief that people have certain inalienable birthrights, which could not be taken away and that governments should only exist through the will of the people. Samuel produced a master's degree thesis, in 1743, more than 30 years prior to the beginning of the American Revolution, which illuminated the legalities of resisting the authority of English rule in the colonies. He may have already been considering independence from the mother country.

Samuel's father, Samuel, Sr., passed away in 1748 and Samuel inherited the family business, which was the production of ingredients necessary for the brewing of ales and beers. A newspaper, in 1751, carried an advertisement that read that he was offering for sale: "Strong beer or malt, for those inclined to brew it themselves, to be sold by Samuel Adams, at a reasonable rate". There is still today, in America, a very popular brand of beer named "**Sam Adams**".

Samuel soon learned he was not a great businessman and his father's business went bankrupt. Sam was appointed as a city tax collector, but his skills were lacking or his motivation and his records were off by very large amounts. He lost that job. It became clear his strengths were not in the areas of finance or business management, but, fortunately, he was revealed to be a very good writer.

"The Public Advertiser", a newspaper started and managed by Adams and some of his friends was used to publish Adams' editorial opinion pieces. He used that pulpit to preach the importance and precious nature of individual personal rights and freedoms. Sam Adams, unlike most prominent people of his day, left little in the way of journals, letters or diaries to illuminate the details of his personal life. He did, though, write prodigiously, often under various pseudonyms, letters and articles that were published in colonial newspapers. He wrote to incite opposition to British rule, usually regarding rules, regulations and taxation which he believed to be attacks on the freedoms of colonists. As time passed, his writings grew more and more antagonistic to England and more and more openly supportive of American resistance. He sometimes "embellished" his stories, occasionally to the point of dishonesty, to make British rulers appear as overbearing and unfair as possible. Sam was very effective in building anger and outrage against the English governors, military and tax collectors. His contributions were so important, in the decades prior to the Revolution, that some historians believe that the Revolution may never have happened without the "cauldron stirring" of Samuel Adams.

His words became more significant during the 1760s, during which the English were imposing the **"Intolerable Acts"** (the Stamp Act and the Townshend Acts).

Articles written by Samuel appeared widely in print, claiming the British had no right to "tax the colonists without representation" in Parliament and claiming the Intolerable Acts were designed "to destroy the liberties of America".

In 1765, the year of the Stamp Act, Adams won election to the House of Representatives in Massachusetts, where he would retain the office for nine critical years. He became a member of political activists known as **"The Loyal Nine"**, a clandestine group that encouraged independence. The Loyal Nine eventually morphed into the **"Sons of Liberty"**, which, at the time, was considered to be a radical organization. It was still a decade before the American Revolution began.

Boston was occupied by British troops in 1768, as the Crown attempted to stifle the infancy of the rebellion. Adams wrote prolifically, under various pen names, to stimulate support for independence for the colonists. Boston merchants, in Adams' writings, were encouraged to boycott all British goods.

The Tea Act was passed by Parliament in 1773. It forced the colonists to purchase their tea, which was an enormous market product at the time, from the British East India Company. Rebellious colonists, probably including Samuel Adams, made plans for ways to interfere with the British tea shipments. He is generally believed to have assisted in planning and carrying out the **Boston Tea Party**, which took place in Boston Harbor on December 16, 1773. Protesters, many dressed up to look like Indian warriors, ditched 342 large chests of tea, taken from several British merchant ships, into Boston harbor. Samuel Adams wrote, after the Tea Party, that the protesters "have acted upon pure and upright principle".

British authorities responded with outrage after the **Boston Tea Party**. They considered themselves to be the rightful authority in their colonies. They believed themselves to be the "protectors and defenders" of the colonists. The Crown sent **General Thomas Gage**, in 1775, to lead soldiers to Lexington from Boston, with the objective of arresting both Samuel Adams and his fellow rebel, **John Hancock**. When American spies discovered the British plan, they organized rebel militiamen (**"Minute Men"**) to repel the British in Lexington. The **Battles of Lexington** and **Concord** soon followed, meaning the actual **American Revolution** had finally begun.

Sam Adams was appointed delegate to the Continental Congress and was a signer of the Declaration of Independence. Throughout the long years of the war, Adams continued to deliver passionate rhetoric through the printed press. He attacked colonists who were "Tories" or "Loyalists" and who remained true to the Crown. He wrote, about them: "If ye love wealth better than liberty, the tranquility of servitude than the animating contest of freedom—go from us in peace. We ask not your counsel or arms. Crouch down and lick the hands which feed you."

Samuel Adams, in his role as a delegate to the Continental Congress, was active in the drafting of the **Articles of Confederation**, which were the foundation for the United States Constitution. After the war, Sam continued to participate in American politics. He became President of the Massachusetts Senate and Lieutenant Governor and, when his friend John Hancock died, he took over as Governor. Sam was re-elected Governor three times.

Samuel Adams died in 1893, when he was 81 years old, after finally retiring. Many of his written quotes are still remembered today. This is a favorite:

"Among the natural rights of the Colonists are these: First, a right to life; Secondly, to liberty; Thirdly, to property; together with the right to support and defend them in the best manner they can. These are evident branches of, rather than deductions from, the duty of self-preservation, commonly called the first law of nature."

Samuel Adams and Slavery

Samuel Adams wrote often about the unsustainability of the institution of slavery. He opposed slavery and supported efforts to find relief for its victims. Adams always, though, was more concerned about preserving the unity of the colonies and, eventually, states, than he was concerned about slavery. One of his biographers, Ira Stoll, wrote that "Of all our founding fathers, he is the one perhaps most likely to have dreamed of a black President". He was a member of Boston's Town Meeting assembly, which sent directions to the General Court proposing a law that would prohibit all "buying and selling of slaves in the state of Massachusetts". The legislature did not pass that law but did pass a law banning any new importation of slaves into Massachusetts. No slaves were owned by Sam Adams, but his second wife, Elizabeth was given a slave named **Surry**. When Adams learned of the acquisition of Surry, he is reported to have declared that "No slave can live in my house; if she comes here she must be free". Records are not clear as to whether Surry was ever actually emancipated. Adams' personal letters seem to indicate, in many reports, that Surry was well-received in the family and treated as a family member.

Thomas Paine

Thomas Paine, born January 29, 1737, in England, was the son of a Quaker, **Joseph Paine** and his wife, **Frances**. Thomas benefited from minimal formal education, learning only basic reading and arithmetic skills. He went to work at age 13 for his father, who was a tenant farmer who made corsets. Thomas worked making corsets and soon tried a series of other occupations, being mostly unsuccessful. He became an "officer of the excise", which meant he pursued smugglers and collected taxes. Thomas used his earnings to purchase basic scientific equipment and to buy books.

When he was sixteen, Thomas attempted to sign on to work on a ship named "The Terrible", the captain of which was named "Captain Death". His father put a stop to Thomas's efforts and he never served aboard The Terrible. Paine did, three years later, serve one year on the crew of "The King of Prussia", during the **Seven Years' War**.

Thomas experienced two failed marriages, while still living in England and found little occupational success. His situation was tenuous, at best, when he was introduced to Benjamin Franklin, who was representing the colonies in England. The American Revolution was still a few years into the future. Franklin suggested he try his fortune in America and provided some "letters of introduction" to ease Paine's entry into the world of the colonies.

Thomas Paine arrived in America and the city of Philadelphia, in November of 1774. Ben Franklin's brother-in-law connected Thomas with Robert Aitkin. Paine and Aitkin founded and edited the **Pennsylvania Magazine**, which offered Paine the opportunity to publish numerous articles and some poems. He often used pseudonyms or published anonymously. One of his well-known pieces was an article entitled **"African Slavery in America"**, which was a blistering attack on slavery, as it existed in the colonies. He signed the article **"Justice and Humanity"**.

Tensions in the colonies, between loyalists and American patriots, were rapidly intensifying at the time when Thomas arrived in Philadelphia. Philadelphia was the home of much of the rebel resistance. Paine was an "early adopter" of the drive for American independence. He wrote a fifty-page pamphlet entitled **"Common Sense"**, in January 1776 and it became a primary driver on the road to the Declaration of Independence.

Thomas Paine served with the Continental Army as an aide-de-camp to **General Nathaniel Greene**. Between 1776 and 1783, Paine published sixteen papers, the **"Crisis Papers"**, each of which he signed **"Common Sense"**. The very first of the sixteen, "The American Crisis. Number 1", reached George Washington at a most critical moment during the Revolution. Washington's army was encamped at Valley Forge, suffering bitter cold, starvation, sickness and few resources and was falling apart. Washington was so moved by Paine's article that he instructed his officers to read it to all of the troops. The opening of the piece became one of the most inspirational passages in American literature. This is the opening that Washington's troops heard:

"These are the times that try men's souls. The summer soldier and the sunshine patriot will, in this crisis, shrink from the service of his country; but he that stands it now deserves the love and thanks of man and woman. Tyranny, like hell, is not easily conquered; yet we have this consolation with us—that the harder the conflict, the more glorious the triumph. What we obtain too cheap, we esteem too lightly: It is dearness only that gives everything its value. Heaven knows how to put a proper price upon its goods and it would be strange indeed if so celestial an article as freedom should not be highly rated. Britain, with an army to enforce her tyranny, has declared that she has a right not only to tax but "to bind us in all cases whatsoever," and if being bound in that manner is not slavery, then is there not such a thing as slavery upon earth. Even the expression is impious, for so unlimited a power can belong only to God."

"Common Sense" had such an impact on the minds of colonists that John Adams wrote: "Without the pen of the author of 'Common Sense', the sword of Washington would have been raised in vain".

In 1780, the General Assembly of Pennsylvania passed abolition legislation that delivered freedom to 6,000 slaves. Thomas Paine wrote the preamble to that legislation.

In 1791 and 1792 Paine published his famous **"Rights of Man"**, which was relevant, at the time, to what was happening in the French Revolution. Paine went to France to supervise a French translation of his work. "Rights of Man" was a series of 31 articles, which supported his belief that a popular revolution is acceptable, if and when the government refuses to safeguard the natural human rights of its citizens". Paine was eventually charged with treason in France. The charge was based on his writings in opposition to the mass use of the death penalty, especially with the use of the guillotine and his objection to the execution of Louis XVI. He was jailed, but James Monroe, the American ambassador to France, secured his release.

In the years from 1794 through 1802, Paine published his two-volume manifesto entitled **"The Age of Reason"**. The books offered unpopular criticisms of some aspects of Christian theology and were widely misunderstood to represent atheism, which they did not do. Among the content was a consideration of the divinity of Jesus Christ, which was not well received. Just prior to this time period, Paine had engaged in a disagreement with George Washington. His break with Washington, and the interpretations of his writings in The Age of Reason, combined to terminate much of his popularity.

Paine was broke, again, at the end of the revolution. His patriotic articles and pamphlets were purchased by hundreds of thousands of colonists, but Paine refused to accept any profit, preferring that his writings reach those who could not pay. In the years after the war, Paine was given, by the government, a sum of money and a farm. He spent much of his time writing and working on scientific inventions. He worked on the development of a smokeless candle, which would be a great benefit in homes of the day, in which numerous candles were often used for lighting. He also worked on the creation of an iron bridge requiring no piers.

Time passed and enmity toward Paine was dimmed. He was able to sail to Baltimore, where he was welcomed by President Thomas Jefferson, with whom he had become acquainted during his time in France. Subsequently, Paine became a frequent visitor to the new White House.

Thomas Paine was in New York City, near his farm in New Rochelle, when he died on June 8, 1809. His doctor, as Paine died, asked Thomas if he "wished to accept Jesus Christ" before passing away. Paine responded, literally with his dying breath, "I have no wish to believe on that subject".

In 1809, a British journalist, William Cobbett, came to America and stole Paine's remains, which he spirited back to England. They have been lost.

Nathan Hale

Nathan Hale was born in 1755, in Connecticut, in the American colonies. His parents were **Richard Hale**, a Deacon in the church and **Elizabeth Strong**. Nathan's great-grandfather was a key player in the **Salem Witch Trials** of 1692. One of Nathan's descendants was **Edward Everett Hale**, a well-known activist in the fight to abolish slavery. One of Nathan's classmates at Yale was **Benjamin Tallmadge**, who would become a spy for the Continental Army. Nathan graduated from Yale with honors and would go on to become a teacher.

Once the revolution began, Hale served as a Captain in the 19th Regiment of the Continental Army. At a critical time in the conflict, Washington was desperate for information about the activities of the British military. He asked for a volunteer for an especially dangerous mission. Captain Nathan Hale stood forward to request the assignment. Thusly, he became one of the first spies for the American army.

Hale took on the disguise of a Dutch schoolmaster and, eluding British watch guards, slipped behind the Redcoat lines. He was able, for many weeks, to maintain his disguise and to gather critical information, which was spirited through the lines and back to Washington. The British invaded Manhattan, New York, on September 20, 1776 and proceeded to burn the town down. Redcoats were warned to watch carefully for potential spies. The night after the fire, Nathan Hale attempted to sail across Long Island Sound, in an effort to return to American forces. British sailors captured him and he was taken to redcoat **General William Howe**, who interrogated him. Hale was found to be in possession of documents that clearly identified him as an American spy.

General Howe, the next day, commanded the execution of Nathan Hale, by hanging, for the crime of spying against the Crown. Nathan Hale was marched to the gallows for his hanging. Hale stood, with the noose around his neck and was asked if he had any "last words". He is reported to have famously responded **"I only regret that I have but one life to lose for my country"**.

Aaron Burr

Aaron Burr was born, in February 1756, into a wealthy and well-known American family. His parents were **Aaron Burr, Sr.** and **Esther** and both died when Aaron, Jr., was still a young child. He and his sister, Sarah, were cared for by an uncle and one of their grandparents was the famous theologian, **Jonathan Edwards**.

Burr completed his education at Princeton University, known at that time as the 'College of New Jersey', where his father had served as the school's second President. Aaron graduated from college at the tender age of 16, during the time that the American Revolution was being born. He soon became an aide-de-camp for a colonel in the Continental Army. He also served under **Benedict Arnold**, before Arnold defected to the British. At one point, he was assigned to General George Washington's staff, but their relationship was not warm and Burr was reassigned to serve as an aide to **General Israel Putnam**. Burr was awarded a Congressional commendation for serving bravely in battle. Poor health caused Burr to resign from the army in 1779.

Following the revolution, Burr became one of many of the nation's founders in their efforts to build a new republic. Burr was a staunch defender of free speech and he was an early promoter of abolitionist (anti-slavery) movements. He continued his study of the law and opened a practice in New York City. He was married to a widow, **Theodosia Bartow Prevost** and the marriage lasted until her death in 1794. Burr was elected to the state assembly and then appointed Attorney General of the state of New York in 1789.

Aaron Burr became the nation's third Vice President in 1801. He did not enjoy a good relationship with President Jefferson. He was engaged in a long-standing hostile rivalry with the Secretary of the Treasury, Alexander Hamilton. Hamilton was often involved in a series of unpleasant political interactions which impacted Burr. The two exchanged unpleasantries and disagreements on numerous issues. Burr blamed Hamilton for his political difficulties. Hamilton wrote papers speaking unkindly of Burr. Historians believe Burr thought that Hamilton had made offensive comments about Burr in public. Burr challenged Hamilton to a duel, with pistols being the weapons of choice. The duel took place early on the morning of July 11, 1804. Hamilton's "seconds" or supporters at the event, have suggested that Hamilton sent his shot "wide", having no intention of actually killing Burr. No one can know whether or not that is accurate. In any case, Burr's shot was true and fatal, leading to Hamilton's death the following day.

Following the duel, in the face of accusations that he had "murdered Hamilton", Burr fled out of state. It is believed that he was involved in attempts to create an opposition government involving Mexico and lands to the west of the Mississippi. He was tried for treason, but acquitted. No longer trusted in America, Burr departed for Europe, where he tried to sell Napoleon on the idea of invading America. Eventually, he returned to New

York, broke and without prospects. He practiced law and he re-married, to a very affluent widow, **Elizabeth Brown Jumel,** and promptly blew through most of her fortune. Elizabeth sued Burr, based on charges of adultery, for divorce. The divorce decree was granted on the very day Aaron Burr died, September 14, 1836.

Benedict Arnold

General for BOTH the Americans AND the British

Prior to the war, **Benedict Arnold** was a merchant who traded via ships on the Atlantic Ocean. As war tensions built, he joined the Continental Army. Arnold had leadership abilities and ultimately advanced to the rank of Major General.

Arnold gained a reputation as a capable strategist and a man of courage. He was placed in command of a force which, joined by **"The Green Mountain Boys"**, in May of 1775, successfully captured **Fort Ticonderoga**. Ticonderoga was an important gateway to other targets for the rebels. Cannon and other armaments from Ft. Ticonderoga were dragged to Boston, where they assisted in breaking the British siege of Boston.

Benedict Arnold, late in 1775, led a force that attempted the first ever American military **"amphibious assault"**. His troops used birch-bark canoes to invade Canada in an attempt to capture Quebec. Americans expected Canadians to happily join in their efforts to dislodge the established French forces in the area. Canadians did not cooperate and the plan failed miserably. Most American troops were either wounded, killed or captured. Arnold was shot in the leg but escaped. The Americans did not try again to approach Canada during the war.

Benedict Arnold successfully led rebel troops in several more battles, until he was badly wounded at Saratoga. A bullet ripped into his thigh and he was pinned beneath his fallen horse. His leg was damaged so severely that he was unable to join in combat for some years afterward. During those times, Arnold believed he had been unjustly passed over for promotions and that other officers were taking credit for his accomplishments. Arnold had invested much of his own money in funding his forces and felt the colonial government was failing to properly reimburse his expenditures. He became plagued with bitterness and resentment. He was involved in numerous conflicts with the Continental Congress. Arnold secretly decided to switch sides.

While Arnold began to clandestinely negotiate with the British, the Americans, believing him to still be loyal to the revolution, put him in command of the fort at **West Point**. Arnold made arrangements to surrender the fort to the British. American troops captured **British Major John Andre**, who was in possession of written plans which exposed Arnold's treachery. Arnold's plan to turn the fort over to the British was foiled.

George Washington's forces had been informed of Arnold's nefarious plans and were looking for him everywhere. Arnold, knowing he was targeted, fled down the Hudson River, where he narrowly escaped Washington and was able to board the British warship Vulcan.

Benedict Arnold was subsequently made a Brigadier General in the British army. He led several raids on American forces before the war ended. He died in London, England in 1801.

Prussian Baron Friedrich Wilhelm von Steuben

Wilhelm Von Steuben grew up in Russia and the Prussian area in Germany. He was made an officer in the Prussian army at the tender age of 17. He pursued a military career in the infantry and was impressive enough in his service to be promoted to a position in the headquarters of **Frederick the Great**. Captain Von Steuben was a superior military expert of his time but was discharged from the army under a cloud of clandestine rumors about his lifestyle. In today's world, it is considered most likely that von Steuben was openly gay. Records of the time seem to offer ample evidence to support the assumption.

After his discharge from the army, von Steuben was involved in government positions in Germany. He was deeply in debt and seeking pathways to better his position. After serving in armies in Austria, Baden and France, von Steuben learned that Benjamin Franklin, serving the colonists in France, might be able to refer him to a position with Washington's army. Franklin, on advice from the French Minister of War, who was acquainted with von Steuben's history, enthusiastically recommended von Steuben to General Washington.

Washington's army was suffering through the extreme winter at Valley Forge. Von Steuben, after being celebrated by Congress in York, Pennsylvania, reported to Washington on February 23rd, 1778. Von Steuben did not speak English, but he was fluent in French. Washington's aide-de-camp, Alexander Hamilton and General Nathaniel Greene were both able to serve as effective interpreters. Von Steuben had agreed to serve without pay and Washington soon had him working to train the troops.

Baron von Steuben created a systematic format for training that is still, in some ways, followed in today's world. He also implemented a system of sanitary strategies that undoubtedly quelled some portion of the illnesses that were rampant through the camps. He performed with distinction in many battles until the war's end. Von Steuben was in command of a division at the **Battle of Yorktown** as the war drew to its finish.

After the revolution, Baron von Steuben elected to remain in America. He became an American citizen and was prominent in local affairs. The American Congress was negligent in payment of funds due to the Baron until long after the war and financial problems plagued him. Friends, including Alexander Hamilton, helped him to obtain an estate in New York State, where he lived his life. His estate was left, on his death, to his two aides, William North and Benjamin Walker.

The Green Mountain Boys

The Green Mountain Boys" were a rebel militia group made up of men from the Vermont-New Hampshire area. They were known for their loyalty to their leader, **Ethan Allen**. They were instrumental in, along with militia forces under Benedict Arnold, taking Fort Ticonderoga.

The original Green Mountain Boys were re-formed as the Green Mountain Continental Rangers, to fight as part of the Continental Army. The Rangers fought several battles in the Revolutionary War, under the leadership of Seth Warner, while Ethan Allen went on to fight with the Northern Army segment of the Continental Army.

The Green Mountain Boys regiment has persisted throughout American History. They formed up to fight in the War of 1812, the Civil War, the Spanish-American War, the Viet Nam War and wars in the Middle East. Today, the Green Mountain Boys are known as the modern Vermont National Guard.

The Marquis de Lafayette

The **Marquis de Lafayette** was an affluent French aristocrat. His full name was Marie-Joseph-Paul-Yves-Roch-Gilbert du Motier, Marquis de Lafayette. Lafayette was one of the most powerful people in France, where he championed the cause of a 'constitutional monarchy". He was instrumental in the French Revolution, which began about the time of the end of the American Revolution and in France's "July Revolution" of 1830.

Lafayette was orphaned at a young age but inherited a substantial fortune. He was a respected member of the court of France's King Henry XVI. He traveled to America, paying his own expenses, about two years after the Declaration of Independence. The Revolution was in full progress. Lafayette was only 19 years old when he arrived in America. Lafayette came to America with very strong references, and was introduced to General Washington when the Marquis arrived in Philadelphia in 1877. He had no combat experience, but he had significant resources and was recognized as a valuable liaison with the King of France. Washington appointed him Major General in the Continental Army, recognizing Lafayette as an important asset, despite his lack of experience in battle.

All records indicate that George Washington quickly developed a sincere affection for the Frenchman. Historians read into it the possible significance of the relationship of the childless General Washington and the young orphaned, Lafayette. Their relationship took on the characteristics of a father-son bond. Lafayette took on any task he was assigned with enthusiasm and professionalism and quickly proved his value.

Lafayette led a command in the **Battle of Brandywine**, near Philadelphia, in September of 1777 and served there with distinction. He was soon after given command of his own division of the Continental Army. He led troops in a series of confrontations for the next two years and returned to France in 1779, where he worked with Benjamin Franklin and John Adams to encourage Louis XVI to provide supplies, troops and funds to support the American rebels.

Lafayette, after successfully lobbying Louis XVI for more resources for the colonists, returned to America in April of 1780. Following him were 6000 French troops and six fully equipped "ships of the line". Ships of the line were large sailing ships, of a kind built up until the mid-1850s, which were outfitted for combat. Lafayette then was assigned command of a division located in Virginia, with which he harassed a British force commanded by Benedict Arnold, the American traitor who was now serving the crown. Lafayette's army then pursued the army of British commander **Cornwallis**, which he chased across Virginia and eventually pinned down at **Yorktown**. Yorktown became the final stop for the English army. Cornwallis surrendered on October 19th, 1781. The revolution was over and Lafayette was one of the greatest of its heroes. He was acclaimed as a **"Hero of Two Worlds"** and returned to France, where he was promoted to become Brigadier General. Lafayette returned to the United States in 1784, where he visited friends in several states and was celebrated as a great hero.

Patrick Henry

John and Sarah Henry came to America from Scotland, where John was college educated. John was a planter and had a farm in Virginia, where young Patrick, born in 1736, grew up. Patrick was home-schooled by his father. As a young adult, Patrick found little success in business, failing repeatedly at running a store and at being a planter, like his father. He studied, on his own, the law, and opened a law practice while simultaneously working as a tavern manager.

Patrick Henry, in the course of running his law practice, became well-known for his emotional oratory. His speeches were compelling, combining effective persuasiveness with passionate intensity.

Patrick's first big legal case became known as **"The Parson's Cause"** and was later considered one of many early events leading to the American Revolution. In the Parson's Cause case, a legal challenge was raised to question the authority of the crown to regulate affairs in the colonies. The case had to do with issues around the payment of salaries to British Ministers in the states. The ministers were paid not in coin, but in tobacco, which was quite valuable. The case argued the right of the Crown to interfere in the valuation of tobacco in the colonies. As he prosecuted the case, Patrick Henry made an emotional speech that became well-known and established him as a thought leader among the growing numbers of rebels.

When parliament passed the notorious **"Stamp Act"**, Henry wrote an eloquent missive that included a number of **"resolves"** which came to define the position of the colonists regarding taxation. Henry's resolves were distributed throughout the colonies. They explained the rationale behind the colonist's objections to being taxed by England while having no representation in the English government. The resolves declared that the Americans should only have to pay taxes imposed by their own representatives. Henry risked charges of treason when, as part of the speech in which he introduced his resolves, he insinuated that King George III might suffer the same ending as Julius Caesar if England's oppressive policies continued.

The Second Virginia Convention met in Virginia, in 1775, to develop a strategy in opposition to the British. It was at this convention that Patrick Henry gave his famous **"Give Me Liberty or Give Me Death"** speech. Here is the relevant section of text from that speech:

"Gentlemen may cry, 'Peace, Peace,' but there is no peace. The war is actually begun! The next gale that sweeps from the north will bring to our ears the clash of resounding arms! Our brethren are already in the field! Why stand we here idle? ... Is life so dear or peace so sweet, as to be purchased at the price of chains and slavery? Forbid it, Almighty

God! I know not what course others may take; but as for me, give me liberty or give me death!"

The speech inflamed the passions of colonists, swayed the opinions of some dissenters and was credited with stimulating efforts to begin preparing troops for war. In response, the British Royal Governor of Virginia, **Lord Dunmore**, stripped all gunpowder stores from local magazines, hoping to disarm rebels. Not long after, Dunmore would issue the famous **"Dunmore's Proclamation"**, which declared martial law in Virginia and promised to free any slaves who would escape and come over the line to fight with the Redcoats. The proclamation infuriated Southern colonists and further impassioned anger toward the Crown.

Following the Declaration of Independence, Patrick Henry became the new state of Virginia's first governor and he repeated, later, as the sixth governor. He was an "anti-Federalist", meaning he feared a powerful central government and was an advocate of "state's rights". Henry refused to sign the Constitution, as he believed it granted too much power to the federal government. He was the writer of some of the (anti-) **Federalist Papers**, which argued for human rights and against a large central government. The Federalist Papers later became powerful sources in the development of the **Bill of Rights**.

Most plantations, given enough size and enough work to do, involved ownership of slaves and Patrick Henry was no exception. He owned 67 slaves by the time of his death. As did many slave owners, Henry recognized the evil of the awful institution and opposed it. His writings confirm that he supported abolition of slavery and supported efforts in that direction, in spite of his own family's dependence on free slave labor. He wrote, "I am the master of slaves of my own purchase. I am drawn along by the general inconvenience of living here without them. I will not, I cannot justify it". Henry labored in an effort to terminate the importation of any slaves into Virginia and was successful in doing so in 1778.

Patrick Henry never held national office and died in June 1799, at his Southern Virginia plantation, now known as **"The Red Hill Patrick Henry National Memorial"**.

Francis Marion

(The Swamp Fox)

Francis Marion grew up on a family plantation in South Carolina. At age 15, Francis was aboard a ship bound for the West Indies, which sank at sea. He survived a few days on a lifeboat, was rescued, and was able to return home to help run the plantation.

Francis Marion became known as the legendary **"Swamp Fox"**. He emerged as a military officer in the Carolinas, serving with the Continental Army. He was never in command at any major battles but was a powerful force in disrupting Redcoat activities. He was, by the end of the war, a Brigadier General leading South Carolina troops. Marion became known for his "hit and run", ambush tactics of harassment and is considered a father of modern guerrilla warfare. He is considered an ancestor of today's **Army Rangers** and of the **75th Ranger Regiment**.

Prior to the war, Marion's family "owned" slaves who performed field and house duties on the family's plantations. During the war, some slaves fled to serve in the Redcoat infantry. The family's Pond Bluff plantation was confiscated by the British and several slaves left or joined the British. Following the war, Francis Marion borrowed money to purchase additional slaves, to continue working the fields and running the houses. Some, according to records, moved from Pond Bluff to Belle Isle, another of the Marion plantations. Some slaves, as was not uncommon, were designated by the family and assigned in family wills, to "special" treatment conditions. Among those slaves were "Buddy", Francis Marion's "manservant"; field overseer "June" and his wife "Phoebe", who was Buddy's sister; and daughter of June and Phoebe, "Peggy". Those, plus at least ten others, returned to Pond Bluff following the Treaty of Paris.

Francis Marion, in the years following the war, served in the South Carolina Senate and was made commander of Fort Johnson, for which he was paid $500 annually.

Casimir Pulaski

Casimir Pulaski

Kazimierz Michał Władysław Wiktor Pułaski of Ślepowron, or **Casimir Pulaski**, came to America to fight with the colonists in the revolution. He was a Polish nobleman, a soldier and a proponent of the use of horses in cavalry as an effective tool of war. He convinced Washington, General Gates and Congress to support the development of a command of forces on horseback. Pulaski is generally known as the **"Father of the American Cavalry"**.

Pulaski was introduced to Washington in August 1777, near Philadelphia. Pulaski demonstrated his horsemanship, displaying expertise in an array of riding stunts and sealed his future with the Continental Army. It took several months for Congress to approve a military rank for him, but he ultimately was made Brigadier General and led forces in several battles. Pulaski was given the title "Commander of the Horse". He organized a corps of horse-mounted troops to be known as the **"Pulaski Cavalry Legion"**, which was based in Baltimore.

Pulaski served through mid-1779 but was mortally wounded during the siege of Savannah, Georgia.

Andrew Pickens

In South Carolina, rebel colonists were engaged in a series of conflicts with British loyalists (Tories) and the Cherokee people, who were supporting the British. One of the colonists who developed, during this period, into an effective military leader for the patriots was **Andrew Pickens**. He became a Colonel in the Continental Army.

In February 1779, Pickens led a small group of rebels in a surprise attack on a much larger British force in Georgia, gaining a victory that dampened enthusiasm among loyalists. Pickens later was forced to surrender a fort and about 300 troops. The British "paroled" Pickens, with the agreement he not participate in the remainder of the war. After loyalist raiders destroyed his property and terrified his family, Pickens rejoined the war effort with renewed vigor. He fought in several more battles.

Late in the war, Pickens led a small contingency of 25 militia in a battle, known as the **"Ring Fight"**, against 150 Cherokee warriors. His defeats of the Native Americans ended with the **"Long Swamp Treaty"**, which caused the natives to give up large sections of land. Pickens, though, earned the respect of the Natives, who gave him the name **The Wizard Owl"**, after a highly respected King from their own tribe.

When the wars were over andrew Pickens served in the South Carolina House of Representatives until 1794.

Native American Tribes in the American Revolution

Indigenous tribes, for the most part, would have preferred to stay clear of the revolution. Some, however, due to location and economic relationships, were pressured to participate. Some supported the British and some supported the Americans. Some tribes were parts of larger **"Indian Nations"** and were split, with some serving one side of the conflict and others supporting the other side. Some groups were, based on changing conditions, in support of the British at times and the Americans at other times.

Both the British officers and American George Washington had fought in the French and Indian War. They had gained a firm understanding, from personal experience, of the effectiveness of tribal warriors.

The **Cherokee Nation** and the **Iroquois Confederacy**, which included six indigenous tribes, were very large and covered huge territories. Each of the two large contingencies was split, with some parts supporting the British and some supporting the Americans.

King George III's Proclamation of 1763 proclaimed all lands west of the Appalachian mountains to be preserved for Native Americans. Many colonists already had settled out West and were isolated. Americans weren't supposed to venture out there, but trading routes were established all along the rivers. The English, the French and the Americans all were in the area. The British had a series of military forts strung through the territories where they traded. Many native tribes felt that the English and French, who still dominated the trading routes, were the safest alliance for them. As the war proceeded, some changed sides.

The **Oneida** and **Tuscarora** nations sided with the colonists, while the **Mohawk** nation and the **Cherokee** sided with the British.

British officers encouraged and supported vicious raids on American settlements by tribal warriors. American colonists were enraged and demanded protection from the raids. General Washington, in response, in 1779 ordered an expedition to respond to the carnage. **General John Sullivan** commanded the expedition, which became one of the major exercises of the Continental Army. The objective of the mission was to destroy Native crops and villages and it did a lot of damage. The expedition earned General Washington the name, among the Iroquois, of **"Town Destroyer"**.

The end of the Revolutionary War, in 1781, sadly, did not end the hard times for tribal peoples. There was residual resentment, among the colonists, because of tribal affiliations with the British and because of atrocities, real and imagined, committed by the tribes during the war. **1782** became known as the **"Bloody Year"** for the indigenous tribes. As America's troops became free of involvement in the revolution, many became involved in aggressive moves against the tribes.

The treaty that ended the American Revolution, The Treaty of Paris, 1783, included an agreement that all lands East of the Mississippi and South of the Canadian border would thereafter be a possession of the new United States. An enormous tract of land, then, became a part of America. The masses of Native Americans who lived throughout that land had no say in the matter. Their homelands became, with a stroke of the treaty pen, the property of the American government. Colonists moving to the West, to the American frontier, were often resentful of natives, believing all of the natives supported the British and were complicit in wartime atrocities. The settlers were sometimes brutish in their efforts to drive away natives residing in highly desirable locations.

The end of the Revolutionary War, in some ways, marked the beginning of a long, shameful era of abuse and exploitation of native tribes. In too many ways, that condition persists today. Native American tribes, in modern America, are far too frequently isolated on dismal reservations. Rates of education are very low, numbers living in extreme poverty are too high, healthcare is poor and acts of violence and suicides are much too frequent. Much needs to be done to correct many decades of deprivation and negligence. The U.S. government eventually identified **574 different tribes** of Native American peoples within America's borders.

The Continental Congress of 1774

Twelve of the thirteen colonies sent representatives to the **First Continental Congress**, which took place in Philadelphia on September 5th, 1774. Only Georgia, which was involved in a conflict with indigenous tribes and was dependent on British military support, did not send a representative. George Washington, John Adams (future American President) and John Jay (future Supreme Court Justice) were among the participants. The first Continental Congress had been convened primarily in response to the **Intolerable Acts** imposed upon the colonies by Britain.

The First Continental Congress was carefully formed with the basic intentions of creating a foundation for free speech, open debate and the presumption of equality for all participants. The Congress completed several significant tasks. The **Articles of Association** were passed, which declared that colonists would no longer accept shipments of British products unless the British rescinded their **Coercive Acts**. It also passed a **Declaration of Rights**, which stated that the colonies were still loyal to the Crown, but that the Crown had no right to tax them without representation, in Parliament, for the colonies. The Congress also passed a declaration that should Britain NOT rescind their Coercive Acts, the colonists would cease all shipments of American goods to Britain. It also planned a Second Congressional meeting to be held in May of 1775, if the conflict continued by that time.

The **Second Continental Congress** did, indeed, meet in May of 1775. The revolution had begun. On June 14th, Congress established a fighting force made up of militia from each of the colonies, a united force to be known as the **Continental Army**. The following day, George Washington was designated Commander-in-Chief of the new army of the colonies.

In July, the Second Continental Congress issued what was titled "**Declaration of the Causes and Necessity of Taking Up Arms**", written in part by Thomas Jefferson, another future American President. The declaration constituted a lengthy, carefully crafted, detailed explanation of the reasons for and justifications for, the threatened rebellion by the colonists. It was followed by what was titled the "**Olive Branch Petition**". The petition was basically an appeal, a "last ditch effort" by the colonists, addressing **King George III** personally, asking him to work with them to resolve the various conflicts between the Americans and the English government. The King, in a move that proved ill-advised, dismissed the petition without consideration.

The ensuing year saw the Continental Congress managing the beginning of the war over the rights of the colonists. Entering 1776, there was still a great divide among colonists as to whether they did, or did not, support the move to separation from England. Support for the British waned as resentment built over military engagements.

Thomas Paine, an immigrant from England, published a pamphlet titled **"Common Sense"**. It made clear the reasons colonists would benefit from, and deserve, independence and self-government. The pamphlet quickly made its way through the colonies and stimulated more enthusiasm for independence.

The colonies, through early 1776, began to direct their Congressional representatives to begin to seriously consider separation from England. **Richard Henry Lee**, a Congressional delegate from Virginia, formally presented a proposal for independence. A committee was appointed to create an initial draft of a provisional **Declaration of Independence**, to be used should an actual declaration be approved and passed. The committee was composed of five delegates, including **Benjamin Franklin** and **John Adams**, but most of the actual writing was done by **Thomas Jefferson**. Jefferson wrote eloquently, composing a document to be known and revered by free people the world around. His declaration included a beautiful expression of the **natural rights** of all people.

The Continental Congress made several revisions to Jefferson's work. Sadly, one element that was removed was Jefferson's attack on the morality of the awful institution of slavery. His original intention was that ALL men would be free in the new nation. Unfortunately, at the time, the thirteen colonies were considered big underdogs in the upcoming battle with the far better-funded, staffed and armed British military. Every colony had to be fully committed for the Americans to have any chance of success in gaining their independence. Jefferson was, himself, a plantation owner and slave owner, but his writing indicates that he was fully aware that slavery was wrong as wrong could be and was unsustainable over time. Most of those involved in producing our early plans for the government were opposed to slavery and knew it couldn't last. They also knew they had to have full support from the Southern colonies to fight England. It became clear that those Southern colonies, where free slave labor supported their agriculturally based economy, would never join a united force that, if successful, would end slavery. Our **"Founders"**, as a group, realized that the issue of slavery would have to be tabled until some future time when Americans had established a functional new government.

On July 4th, 1776, the **Continental Congress** voted for approval of the new nation's **Declaration of Independence**.

America's Declaration of Independence

(The Complete Text)

When, in the course of human events, it becomes necessary for one people to dissolve the political bands which have connected them with another and to assume, among the powers of the earth, the separate and equal station to which the laws of nature and of nature's God entitle them, a decent respect to the opinions of mankind requires that they should declare the causes which impel them to the separation.

We hold these truths to be self-evident, that all men are created equal, that they are endowed by their Creator with certain unalienable rights that among these are life, liberty and the pursuit of happiness. That to secure these rights, governments are instituted among men, deriving their just powers from the consent of the governed. That, whenever any form of government becomes destructive of these ends, it is the right of the people to alter or to abolish it and to institute new government, laying its foundation on such principles and organizing its powers in such form, as to them shall seem most likely to effect their safety and happiness.

Prudence, indeed, will dictate that governments long established should not be changed for light and transient causes; and, accordingly, all experience has shown, that mankind is more disposed to suffer, while evils are sufferable than to right themselves by abolishing the forms to which they are accustomed.

But, when a long train of abuses and usurpations, pursuing invariably the same object, evinces a design to reduce them under absolute despotism, it is their right, it is their duty, to throw off such government and to provide new guards for their future security. Such has been the patient sufferance of these colonies and such is now the necessity that constrains them to alter their former systems of government. The history of the present King of Great Britain is a history of repeated injuries and usurpations, all having in direct object the establishment of an absolute tyranny over these states. To prove this, let facts be submitted to a candid world.

He has refused his assent to laws the most wholesome and necessary for the public good.

He has forbidden his governors to pass laws of immediate and pressing importance unless suspended in their operation till his assent should be obtained; and when so suspended, he has utterly neglected to attend to them.

He has refused to pass other laws for the accommodation of large districts of people unless those people would relinquish the right of representation in the legislature; a right inestimable to them and formidable to tyrants only.

He has called together legislative bodies at places unusual, uncomfortable and distant from the depository of their public records, for the sole purpose of fatiguing them into compliance with his measures.

He has dissolved representative houses repeatedly, for opposing, with manly firmness, his invasions on the rights of the people.

He has refused for a long time, after such dissolutions, to cause others to be elected; whereby the legislative powers, incapable of annihilation, have returned to the people at large for their exercise; the state remaining in the meantime exposed to all the dangers of invasion from without and convulsions within.

He has endeavored to prevent the population of these states; for that purpose obstructing the laws for the naturalization of foreigners; refusing to pass others to encourage their migrations hither and raising the conditions of new appropriations of lands.

He has obstructed the administration of justice, by refusing his assent to laws for establishing judiciary powers.

He has made judges dependent on his will alone, for the tenure of their offices and the amount and payment of their salaries.

He has erected a multitude of new offices and sent hither swarms of officers to harass our people and eat out their substance.

He has kept among us, in times of peace, standing armies, without the consent of our legislatures.

He has affected to render the military independent of and superior to the civil power.

He has combined with others to subject us to a jurisdiction foreign to our constitution and unacknowledged by our laws; giving his assent to their acts of pretended legislation:

For quartering large bodies of armed troops among us;

For protecting them, by a mock trial, from punishment for any murders which they should commit on the inhabitants of these states;

For cutting off our trade with all parts of the world;

For imposing taxes on us without our consent;

For depriving us, in many cases, of the benefits of trial by jury;

For transporting us beyond seas to be tried for pretended offenses;

For abolishing the free system of English laws in a neighboring province, establishing therein an arbitrary government and enlarging its boundaries, so as to render it at once an example and fit instrument for introducing the same absolute rule into these colonies;

For taking away our charters, abolishing our most valuable laws and altering fundamentally the forms of our governments;

For suspending our own legislatures and declaring themselves invested with power to legislate for us in all cases whatsoever.

He has abdicated government here, by declaring us out of his protection and waging war against us.

He has plundered our seas, ravaged our Coasts, burnt our towns and destroyed the lives of our people.

He is at this time transporting large armies of foreign mercenaries to complete the works of death, desolation and tyranny, already begun with circumstances of cruelty and perfidy scarcely paralleled in the most barbarous ages and totally unworthy of the head of a civilized nation.

He has constrained our fellow citizens, taken captive on the high seas, to bear arms against their country, to become the executioners of their friends and brethren or to fall themselves by their hands.

He has excited domestic insurrections amongst us and has endeavored to bring on the inhabitants of our frontiers, the merciless Indian savages, whose known rule of warfare is an undistinguished destruction of all ages, sexes and conditions.

In every stage of these oppressions, we have petitioned for redress, in the most humble terms. Our repeated petitions have been answered only by repeated injury. A prince, whose character is thus marked by every act which may define a tyrant, is unfit to be the ruler of a free people.

Nor have we been wanting in attentions to our British brethren. We have warned them from time to time of attempts by their legislature to extend an unwarrantable jurisdiction over us. We have reminded them of the circumstances of our emigration and settlement here. We have appealed to their native justice and magnanimity and we have conjured them by the ties of our common kindred, to disavow these usurpations, which would inevitably interrupt our connections and correspondence. They too have been deaf to the voice of justice and of consanguinity. We must, therefore, acquiesce in the necessity, which denounces our separation and hold them, as we hold the rest of mankind, enemies in war, in peace friends.

We, therefore, the representatives of the United States of America, in General Congress assembled, appealing to the Supreme Judge of the world for the rectitude of our intentions, do, in the name and by authority of the good people of these colonies, solemnly publish and declare, that these United Colonies are and of right ought to be free and independent states; that they are absolved from all allegiance to the British Crown and that all political connection between them and the state of Great Britain is and ought to be totally dissolved; and that, as free and independent states, they have full power to levy war, conclude peace, contract alliances, establish commerce and to do all other acts and things which independent states may of right do. And for the support of this declaration, with a firm reliance on the protection of Divine Providence, we mutually pledge to each other our lives, our fortunes and our sacred honor.

The Articles of Confederation

Following the publication of the Declaration of Independence, arguments were strong concerning just how the new nation should be configured. Many colonists were very reluctant to establish a "central government" which would rule the lives of residents in all of the different colonies. Americans were determined to preserve their rights to freedom of speech and freedom of religion and to retain their ability to govern themselves. In response, several efforts were made to "codify" a system that would protect citizens while providing effective government.

Benjamin Franklin, in mid-1775, presented the first attempt to write up rules for a system everyone could support. Other efforts soon followed. A Philadelphian named **John Dickinson** presented the draft that, after many revisions, was finally approved for presentation to the states. The final revision, approved in 1777, provided that each state remain "sovereign" and an independent entity. The Continental Congress, the "central government", was to provide a way to resolve disputes between the individual states and was to be responsible for treaties and international relations, maintaining a military force to defend the union and coining money. Individual states were, otherwise, to be responsible for their own governments. The emphasis was to keep control in the hands of the citizens, rather than in a central government. The central government was NOT to be allowed to levy taxes on citizens and was NOT to be allowed to regulate commerce in the free economy.

The **Articles of Confederation** named the new union **"The United States of America"**. Pointedly, it was not named "The Federation of States of America". Our Founders were determined that the new government be a government of the people, a **"Republic"**. In a "Democracy", the government is based on a simple "majority rules" structure. Whoever has the most votes, wins. The most powerful groups have the only meaningful voices. Minority voices are disregarded and irrelevant. In a "Republic", the government provides protections that guarantee that the minority voice will always be heard and can have an impact on decisions. The men who wrote our Declaration of Independence and our Constitution were well-educated in history. They studied all past forms of government and were determined to create the first government in which the voice of the people truly was the foundation for all operations.

Issues arising from the Articles of Confederation soon led to the formation of the **Constitutional Convention of 1787**, intended to create a system of laws, under the Constitution, for the new "Republic". Life was changing rapidly in the new union, the economy was growing, people were moving west to the frontier, disagreements were cropping up and pressures led to the need for a more comprehensive constitution. The Articles of Confederation, while they served a temporary need, were inadequate to meet the complex needs of a new nation. Ten years after the Articles of Confederation were approved, growing tensions led to the Constitutional Convention of 1787.

The Constitutional Convention of 1787

The **Articles of Confederation** served as the first framework for governing the colonies as a new union. They left the states largely in a condition of self-government or sovereignty. It had become clear that, in order for the diverse groups to work together for their mutual benefit and defense, a stronger central government was necessary. The big concern was how to provide this stronger government without infringing on the rights of the people, as represented in their individual states. The delegates, in 1787, created a system that required three separate branches of government, the **Executive**, the **Judicial** and the **Legislative**, meant to ensure a system of **"checks and balances"**, which would limit the powers of any one branch.

As it became clear that the Articles of Confederation would be inadequate to address all the needs of the new republic, a young attorney from New York named Alexander Hamilton called for a new constitutional convention. The Confederation Congress invited representatives from all 13 states.

The State House in Philadelphia, now known as **Independence Hall**, was the home of the **Constitutional Convention of 1787**. The Declaration of Independence had been signed there, eleven long years earlier. 12 states sent representatives, 55 delegates in all, with only Rhode Island refusing. Rhode Island did not want a central government interfering in its business.

The delegates elected, by unanimous vote, national hero George Washington as President of the convention. The Revolutionary War being over, George Washington had been back at Mount Vernon, his home in Virginia, trying to rebuild his estate. He had to be talked into attending the Constitutional Convention. Benjamin Franklin was the oldest delegate, at age 81. American patriot Patrick Henry refused to participate, due to his own concerns about giving too much power to a central government.

One issue that was debated hotly was the question of how states would be represented in the new Legislative branch. Bigger, more populous states, wanted population counts to determine the number of representatives from each state. Smaller states, of course, wanted equal numbers of representatives, regardless of state populations. After much debate, the **"Connecticut Compromise"** was approved. The Connecticut Compromise provided for a **"Bicameral"** legislature. It created the **Senate**, wherein each state would have an equal number of representatives and the **House**, wherein representatives would be determined proportionally by population count.

Another controversial topic was slavery. Although some Northern states had already started to outlaw the practice, they went along with the Southern states' insistence that slavery was an issue for individual states to decide and should be kept out of the

Constitution. It had become clear that including any restrictions on slavery would mean the Southern states would refuse to join the union. Without the full participation of all of the thirteen states, there was no chance for the new nation to survive. For the purposes of taxation and determining how many representatives a state could send to Congress, it was decided that enslaved people would be counted as three-fifths of a person. Additionally, it was agreed that Congress wouldn't be allowed to prohibit the slave trade before 1808 and states were to be required to return fugitive enslaved people to their owners. The moral and economic issue of slavery had to be tabled, to be dealt with after the new nation was established.

It was September 17, 1787, when the Constitution, having been debated and revised for several months, was finally signed. It replaced the Articles of Confederation and created a stronger central government. It provided for the three branches, executive, legislative and judicial, with a framework of checks and balances intended to guarantee a government controlled by the people and to ensure that no one branch has too much power.

The first delegate to sign the new constitution was George Washington. 39 of the 55 delegates signed their approval. Some had left Philadelphia and weren't present to sign. Three delegates refused to sign. It then became necessary to gain **"ratification"** of the document. Ratification required the passage of approvals from nine of the thirteen new states. Some states resisted ratification based on concerns that the new document provided too little protection for certain basic human rights.

There were still many Americans who opposed a centralized government and did not initially support the new constitution. Founding fathers **Alexander Hamilton** and **James Madison**, with some input from **John Jay**, wrote a series of 85 essays in support of ratification. The essays were published in newspapers and pamphlets under the pseudonym "**Publius**", which is Latin for "public". The 85 essays, collectively, were to be known as the "**Federalist Papers**".

Negotiations among delegates continued and, finally, on June 28th, 1788, New Hampshire became the ninth state to ratify. An agreement had been reached which assured some of the resistant delegates that prioritization would be given to the passage of new "amendments" to address the need for protections for basic human rights. The first of those amendments would be known as the **"Bill of Rights"**. The new constitution was scheduled to take effect on March 4th, 1789. Events came in quick succession, then, as George Washington was inaugurated on April 30th, 1789, having been unanimously selected during the Constitutional Convention of 1789. The U. S. Supreme Court was in session for the first time ever on February 2nd, 1790, which event signaled the first date on which the new government was fully operational. Rhode Island, always independent, became the final state to agree to ratification of the constitution, on May 29th, 1790.

The **Preamble to the Constitution** explained the purpose and fundamental principles of the document. This is the full text of the Preamble to our Constitution:

"We the People of the United States, in Order to form a more perfect Union, establish Justice, insure domestic Tranquility, provide for the common defense, promote the general Welfare and secure the Blessings of Liberty to ourselves and our Posterity, do ordain and establish this Constitution for the United States of America."

Benjamin Franklin, the oldest participant, was quoted, once the Constitution was signed, as saying: "I agree to this Constitution with all its faults, if they are such, because I think a central government is necessary for us... I doubt too whether any other Convention we can obtain may be able to make a better Constitution."

You can see the original Constitution document today at the National Archives in Washington, D.C. We recognize the historical document on September 17 each year on "Constitution Day"

The Bill of Rights

The new constitution was being ratified by all of the states, with Rhode Island, persisting in its independent mindset, becoming the last state to sign, on May 29th, 1790. The new government was already being formed and institutionalized. The House of Representatives, the most direct connection to the voice of the people, was already working. **James Madison** had already followed up on agreements, made during the creation of the Constitution, to add a series of amendments to the basic document. The intention was to provide guarantees, to all citizens, for certain fundamental human rights. The issue of slavery was always a dark shadow behind all of the discussions of personal rights and was a living contradiction to some of the commitments being made.

Madison, a member of the new House of Representatives, introduced a total of 19 new proposed amendments to the Constitution. Only twelve of the proposed amendments were actually adopted and those twelve were forwarded out to the states for ratification. Ultimately, ten of the amendments were passed, ratified and appended to the Constitution. Those ten became known collectively as **"The Bill of Rights"**. Final ratification took place on December 10th, 1791. **James Madison** was integral in the writing of the amendments and in the process of getting them ratified. He in known now as the **"Father of the Constitution"**, just as **Thomas Jefferson** is generally credited with the writing of the **Declaration of Independence**.

The Bill of Rights was meant to guarantee to all citizens certain basic protections. Those included freedom of speech, religion and the press; the right to bear and keep arms; the right to assemble peaceably in public; protection against unreasonable search and seizure; and the right to a speedy and public trial by an impartial jury of peers.

The process of adding amendments to the Constitution is laborious and time-consuming. It must be approved by the House and the Senate and then ratified by three-fourths of all states. Since 1790, only seventeen more amendments have been added. Most recently, in 1992, Article XXVII was ratified. It addresses protocol for Congressional pay raises.

The Bill of Rights

(The Complete text)

Amendment I

Congress shall make no law respecting an establishment of religion or prohibiting the free exercise thereof; or abridging the freedom of speech or of the press; or the right of the people peaceably to assemble and to petition the government for a redress of grievances.

Amendment II

A well-regulated militia being necessary to the security of a free State, the right of the people to keep and bear arms shall not be infringed.

Amendment III

No soldier shall, in time of peace, be quartered in any house without the consent of the owner, nor in time of war, but in a manner to be prescribed by law.

Amendment IV

The right of the people to be secure in their persons, houses, papers and effects, against unreasonable searches and seizures, shall not be violated and no warrants shall issue but upon probable cause, supported by oath or affirmation and particularly describing the place to be searched and the persons or things to be seized.

Amendment V

No person shall be held to answer for a capital or otherwise infamous crime, unless on a presentment or indictment of a grand jury, except in cases arising in the land or naval forces or in the militia, when in actual service in time of war or public danger; nor shall any person be subject for the same offense to be twice put in jeopardy of life or limb; nor shall be compelled in any criminal case to be a witness against himself, nor be deprived of life, liberty or property, without due process of law; nor shall private property be taken for public use without just compensation.

Amendment VI

In all criminal prosecutions, the accused shall enjoy the right to a speedy and public trial, by an impartial jury of the State and district wherein the crime shall have been committed, which district shall have been previously ascertained by law and to be informed of the nature and cause of the accusation; to be confronted with the witnesses against him; to have compulsory process for obtaining witnesses in his favor and to have the assistance of counsel for his defense.

Amendment VII

In suits at common law, where the value in controversy shall exceed twenty dollars, the right of trial by jury shall be preserved and no fact tried by a jury shall be otherwise reexamined in any court of the United States, than according to the rules of the common law.

Amendment VIII

Excessive bail shall not be required, nor excessive fines imposed, nor cruel and unusual punishments inflicted.

Amendment IX

The enumeration in the Constitution, of certain rights, shall not be construed to deny or disparage others retained by the people.

Amendment X

The powers not delegated to the United States by the Constitution, nor prohibited by it to the States, are reserved to the States respectively or to the people.

The American Revolution Begins

Aseries of events, over a twenty-year period, brought North American English colonies to the brink of revolution. Those events included the French and Indian War, the Boston Massacre, the Boston Tea Party, the Stamp Act, the Declaratory Act and the Townshend Acts. Together, the series of acts were known, by the colonists, as "**The Intolerable Acts**" or "the Coercive Acts". In spite of these conflicts and perceived harassment, many colonists remained loyal to King George III and to the monarchy in England. They were known as **"Loyalists"** or **"Tories"**.

Historians consider the battles at **Concord** and **Lexington**, on April 18th, 1775, to be the beginning of the actual military conflict that became the **Revolutionary War**. The war constituted an "**insurrection**" by the 13 colonies, with the objective of gaining freedom and independent **"sovereignty"**, escaping British rule. The colonists were rejecting the right of England to rule over them. England, of course, under **King George III**, refused to accept the right of the colonies to revolt. The future potential, in terms of riches and resources, of the **New World** was extraordinary and England intended to keep control of all of it.

Hundreds of British troops, on April 18th, 1775, marched to Concord from Boston. Their objective was to capture a cache of weapons, ammunition and gunpowder which the colonists were collecting and storing. **Paul Revere**, a patriot, rode to deliver a warning to the colonists of the approaching British.

A True History of the Legendary Ride of Paul Revere

While Paul Revere is the best-known of the patriotic riders, others also participated. Legend has it that Revere, a respected silversmith, flew through the colonies shouting "The British Are Coming . . . The British Are Coming!" In reality, Revere and the other riders went about their intended business very quietly. Colonial loyalists and British citizens and troops were scattered through the area and Revere would not have wanted their attention, as they would likely have terminated his mission.

Joseph Warren, a colonial physician and patriot, gained information that British troops, known as **"Redcoats"**, were marching that very night on Concord, Massachusetts. Warren was a member of the **Sons of Liberty**. He quickly directed two couriers, the silversmith **Paul Revere** and a tanner named **William Dawes**, to ride fast as possible through the small towns to warn civilians and militiamen that the British Redcoats were on their way.

Dawes and Revere took different paths on their rides through the countryside to Boston. Revere had to cross the Charles River, with his horse, on a boat, so he could reach Charlestown. In Charlestown, patriots were awaiting information about the British troops and had been told to watch the steeple of the **Old North Church**, which still stands today in Boston. The steeple was the highest and most visible, point in the area. Once informed, the patriots had been instructed to hang one bright lantern on the steeple if the British were coming by way of the land. Two lanterns hung in the steeple were to mean the British were coming by sea, into the harbor.

Revere accomplished part of his mission in Charleston and Dawes his in Boston and the two continued their rides, to meet up in Lexington, just East of Concord. Patriots **Samuel Adams** and **John Hancock** were in hiding. Adams and Hancock convinced Revere and Dawes to flee the area, to avoid being captured. As the actual "fighting" part of the war was beginning, the British considered the American colonists who supported the revolution to be traitors. Traitors were likely, if captured, to be hung.

As Revere and Dawes took flight, they were joined, along the way, by **Samuel Prescott**. While history has given Revere much of the credit for the ride to warn colonists, it was actually only Samuel Prescott who actually made it all the way to Concord. Paul Revere was captured by a British patrol. William Dawes had to walk back to Lexington after being thrown from his horse.

Famous American poet **Henry Wadsworth Longfellow** wrote a well-known short poem, commemorating the famous ride. The poem was entitled **"Paul Revere's Ride"** and it went like this:

"One if by land and two, if by sea;

And I on the opposite shore will be,

Ready to ride and spread the alarm

Through every Middlesex village and farm

For the country folk to up and to arm".

The Revolutionary War, for the colonies, was fought by a rag-tag force of largely inexperienced, poorly paid, inadequately supplied militiamen. There was a national force, the Continental Army, led by Washington and there were individual "state militia" groups in each colony. Militia were often called to duty for periods of only three months at a time. Discipline was notoriously poor. Leaders in the various colonies brought men together and assigned their duties. Officers were generally elected and often came from influential families. Many of the troops were farmers, who sometimes left their military companies to return to take care of fields in the spring, to plant and in the fall, to harvest. Some never returned to the army. It was a huge challenge for George Washington and other leaders to keep a strong Continental Army in the field. There were rarely as many as 30,000 colonial troops in the field at any one time.

Colonists, without the advantages of numbers and resources, quickly became a "hit and run", guerilla-type fighting force.

British troops, on the other hand, were very well trained in the military arts and worked within a framework of very strict discipline. They were well-outfitted and had access to better weapons and other resources. British troops were trained in the traditional tactics of presenting an organized front line in battle, with additional lines of troops and cavalry behind, ready to move forward. The British began the war with approximately 42,000 regular army troops. They believed they had the greatest Navy in the world. They added "mercenaries" from Germany, mostly Hessians, who were paid by the English to fight on their behalf in America.

Hessian troops gained a reputation for fierceness and effectiveness in battle. Their officers were well-trained and experienced. The Hessian soldiers were "rented out" to the British by their homeland Princes. Thousands of Hessians were killed in the war and more than half of the remaining troops chose to stay in America after the war ended. Hessians fought in every battle during the revolution, from 1776 to the end.

Colonists were outnumbered and out-gunned, but they had one big advantage. The British military detachments were, for England, a very expensive force. They were fighting thousands of miles from home, depending on supplies shipped on slow ships from Europe and they were simultaneously tied up with other international conflicts. The British knew they were limited as to how long they could stay and fight and how much they could invest in the battle. The colonists were at home in a vast new world. They could fight in selected positions and then run and hide, waiting for a new opportunity. They had all the time in the world to wait out what they now considered a British invasion. The land was on their side and time was on their side. Washington surely knew that, if he could inspire the colonists to persist, if they could just hold on, eventually the English would have to give up and go back home.

The Battles at Lexington and Concord

In the wake of the Intolerable Acts of 1774, **General William Gage** was commander of all British forces in America. He commanded fewer than 5,000 troops, from his headquarters in Boston and the British Parliament believed that would be sufficient to intimidate the colonists into submission. General Gage began, as early as 1774, to "seize" stores of weapons, ammunition and gunpowder from the colonies. This frightened patriots and because of this and other concerns about British rule, they began to organize. Groups such as the Sons of Liberty began to gather recruits and resources.

Colonists learned that the British planned to seize a large cache of weapons and powder held at Fort William and Mary. On December 13, 1774, Paul Revere, who would become more famous for a later ride, was dispatched to warn the colonies that the British were coming. Several hundred patriots beat the British to the fort where they took down the British flag, removed the cannons and took weapons and large supplies of gunpowder.

On April 14th, 1775, General Gage was informed that Massachusetts was in a "state of revolt" and he was ordered to go there to arrest all "Actors and Abettors". Colonists quickly learned of his plans. Paul Revere was, once again, directed to ride to warn colonists. Revere, William Dawes and Samuel Prescott completed the ride, though only Prescott went all the way to Concord. The famous "two lanterns" were confirmed, by the Sons of Liberty, to be hanging in the steeple of the Old North Church in Boston. The stage was set for confrontation.

Gage's 700 troops were staged on the Boston Common on April 18th, 1775. Their orders were to march to seize the colonial armory located in Concord, Massachusetts. On the map, the march doesn't look very long, but, in real life, at that time, it was very difficult. British troops, Redcoats, had to be transported across the Charles River, then had to march through a bog or marsh of brackish water which was waist-high in places. They were cold and soaked by the time they reached Lexington, at around five o'clock in the morning.

The Redcoats were met by 77 colonial militiamen, who had been expecting them. The two forces lined up in a traditional manner, two lines, parallel, facing one another. Officers on both sides had ordered their troops to stand ready but not to fire their weapons. No one today knows who fired the infamous **"Shot heard round the world"**, which is credited with formally beginning the American Revolution, but someone did. Troops on both sides began to shoot. Seven patriots were killed and the colonists retreated. The battle at Lexington, the first in the war, was over.

The British moved on to Concord, their mission destination, where they were met by a much larger force. Colonists had several hundred troops in place. The British had marched far, under bad conditions, fought a skirmish in Lexington and were tired and running out of ammunition and supplies. The colonists retained control of their armory, much of which had been stolen from British caches. The Redcoats left the field and began their return to Boston. American snipers picked off many British troops along their way. Fortunately for the British, 1100 reinforcement troops arrived in time to prevent a total defeat for the Redcoats.

Including the skirmish at Lexington, the short confrontation at Concord and the march in retreat back to Boston, British forces suffered 273 dead. The Americans lost 95 militiamen.

The war had begun.

The American Revolution

An Overview

Colonists were triggered by the skirmishes at Lexington and Concord and by the battle at Bunker Hill and began to gather a fighting force. Colonists who supported the revolution were known by the British as rebels or traitors to the Crown. In the colonies, though, Americans supporting the revolution considered themselves to be patriots, seeking to gain their own rightful independence. Colonists who continued to support the Crown and there were many, were known as Loyalists.

King George III and the British Parliament had in place their Generals Sir William Howe, Sir Henry Clinton, John Burgoyne and, soon after, General Charles Cornwallis. The Generals who carried the "Sir" tag were those who had been "knighted" by their King. Each General arrived at the colonies with a band of reinforcements.

As rebels began to gain in numbers and gather forces, the Second Continental Congress was convened in Philadelphia, where George Washington was appointed to lead the Continental Army. Rebel militia was gathering and taking up arms throughout the colonies.

In Virginia, the British Governor, Lord Dunmore, in Dunmore's Proclamation, offered freedom to colonial slaves who would agree to fight for the British. Approximately 1500 black men, many fugitive slaves, did join Dunmore. Months later, a patriot force defeated Dunmore at Great Bridge, Virginia.

Washington, as a military leader, faced great obstacles. The colonies, not yet being a nation, had no established military force and no surplus of funds. The troops were often poor colonists, with a mix of weapons, no resources, poor supplies of ammunition, no training and little readiness for the extreme deprivations they were about to experience. Uniforms were sparse and some troops traveled and fought without shoes. He faced an opponent, England, which had the world's greatest navy and a long-established military community. Washington soon proved to be a truly great leader, though he was no genius in terms of military strategy. He always led his troops personally and went among them to keep their spirits high. He turned out to be a brilliant motivator for men. His troops wintered at Valley Forge, Northwest of Philadelphia in Pennsylvania and were the victims of a brutally severe, bitterly cold season. Conditions for the troops were devastating, but Washington's inspirational leadership kept them together and motivated them to serve the cause of independence.

Washington led the Continental Army through eight miserable years of war. The patriots lost many battles, but survived, often due to Washington's "hit and run" tactics.

In October of 1781, Washington, with the assistance of the French, defeated British forces at the **Battle of Yorktown**. This defeat suffocated any remaining British desire to continue to war. Washington was elevated to the status of a great national hero.

The **Treaty of Paris** was signed in 1783, formally ending the war. Washington was eager to leave the military and to avoid politics. He returned to Mount Vernon and resumed his role as a gentleman farmer, in which he would have happily persisted. He was asked, though, in 1787, to attend the Constitutional Convention in Philadelphia and to be the chair of a committee charged with writing the new constitution. Delegates recognized Washington's great leadership and some wanted him to assume the role of "King" in the new nation. Washington believed it was essential that the new government be led by an elected official, a "President" who would hold a limited term in the position. He rejected proposals that would have added layers of pageantry and luxurious trappings to the position, in the style of European Kings and Monarchs. Washington was elected President in the new nation's first election, after the successful fight for independence, in January 1789.

American Revolution Chronology of Events

During the fall and winter of 1775-1776, British Redcoats were in occupation of the American city of Boston. General Washington's forces were attempting to contain the Redcoats in the Boston area. The capture, by Washington's rebels, of artillery taken from Fort Ticonderoga added substantial military leverage. The British, under General William Howe, evacuated Boston in the spring of 1776 and retreated to Canada. Howe was planning a major attack on New York City.

Most colonists had, by the spring of 1776, been converted to support the American rebels in their battle for independence. The patriots adopted their Declaration of Independence, on July 4th, 1776. The British government, George III and Parliament were determined to crush the American rebellion. They launched a fleet carrying nearly 35,000 armed troops to the New York area. General Howe's force of Redcoats routed Washington's Continental Army off of Long Island.

In September 1776, Washington was driven out of New York City and had to evacuate all of his troops back across the Delaware River, forced south to Valley Forge, Pennsylvania. Washington struggled to keep his army together during the bitterly cold winter months. Resources were scarce and many of the troops were poorly clothed and poorly fed. Some abandoned the Continental Army and returned to their homes. Morale was poor following several defeats in the field. The British seemed to be winning. Washington's inspirational motivation is credited with retaining a force strong enough to do battle. Washington decided to risk everything in a surprise attack on British forces. The freezing Delaware River separated him and his troops from his proposed target. He planned a bold and dangerous surprise Christmas Eve attack.

Crossing the Delaware

On Christmas day in 1776, Washington executed the famous crossing of the Delaware, a historic military exercise. In the icy cold, on a miserably wet, freezing night, Washington collected a fleet of all manner of boats from up and down the Delaware River. **Hessian troops**, in Trenton on the New Jersey side of the river, fighting for the British, were busy celebrating Christmas late into the night. Washington loaded 2,400 of his 5,400 troops onto the floating "armada" and they all quietly made their way, throughout the night, across the wide, mostly frozen river.

Washington had approximately 3000 additional troops, whom he divided into two other attacking forces, so, in his plans, he was sending a three-pronged ambush. Unfortunately, the two divisions not led personally by Washington did not successfully make it to the meeting points across the river. Those divisions were to bring critical artillery. Washington, though, split his remaining troops into two columns. They attacked the Hessians, who numbered about 1500 troops, from two sides, early in the morning on the day after Christmas. The patriots surrounded Trenton. The Hessians were completely surprised. Groggy and disoriented after a long night of celebration, they were ineffective and were routed. Approximately one thousand Hessians were captured. Americans lost only four lives. Americans won the battle, but Washington had to withdraw because most of his force, including much of his artillery, had failed to make the crossing.

The successful American attack at Trenton was a great and much-needed, boost to morale for American forces. Washington followed it up quickly with a second successful attack on British forces at Princeton, New Jersey.

The War in 1777

Entering 1777, the war was going in favor of the British. Washington's success at Trenton against the Hessians was a big morale booster for the colonists and for his Continental Army, but Americans were still to suffer a series of painful defeats.

The British attempted to split American forces into two parts, dividing New England from the other colonies. Redcoat **General John Burgoyne** moved his forces south from Canada, to join Redcoat General Howe's forces near the Hudson River. In July 1777, the Americans holding **Fort Ticonderoga** were overcome by Burgoyne's troops, suffering a damaging loss.

Meanwhile, General Howe brought his Redcoats south from New York to confront Washington's Continental Army. In September 1777, the British, under Howe, dealt the Americans another defeat at **Brandywine Creek** in Pennsylvania. The British were then able to occupy Philadelphia.

The Continental Army followed up with a successful attack, harassing the British at Germantown, now a part of Philadelphia. As winter approached, Washington withdrew and collected his army back at **Valley Forge**.

Redcoat General Howe's decision to move his troops south inadvertently left General Burgoyne's army, gathered near Saratoga, New York, open to attack. A division of the Continental Army, commanded by American **General Horatio Gates**, soundly defeated the Redcoats at **Freeman's Farm** on September 19th, 1777. The conflict is known now as the **First Battle of Saratoga**.

The British quickly suffered another defeat at Saratoga, on Bemis Heights, on October 7th, the **Second Battle of Saratoga**. On October 19th, General Burgoyne was forced to surrender all of his forces to American General Gates.

Events at Saratoga are now recognized as being a critical turning point in the war. The British people were losing interest in supporting war, as they were simultaneously involved in other international conflicts. The American successes at Saratoga gave the French new confidence in the likelihood of ultimate American success. The French had quietly been supporting the colonists but were now committed to openly taking the side of the Americans. The French formerly declared war on the British themselves, in 1778.

Things were looking up for the Americans, but they were destined to endure many more hardships. Washington's army was about to suffer through a terrible winter in the field.

Valley Forge

Washington at Valley Forge

Historians believe nearly 12,000 troops had gathered around the Valley Forge headquarters for General Washington. By December 1777, conditions were horrible. Horses and oxen were hard to find and men were harnessing themselves to carts to move materials. A couple of thousand crude huts had been cobbled together, using whatever materials could be found. Weapons and ammunition were in short supply. Many of the troops were without shoes, coats and blankets. The winter was unusually severe. Nourishment was minimal, with solid food supplies being scarce and practically no meat was available. Nearly one-fourth of his troops were listed as "unfit for duty", being ill and/or starving. Washington recognized the importance of finding a way to offer hope to the troops and to the country. He was regularly beseeching Congress, with little success, to provide more funds and resources for the new army. Some officials were questioning his competence, after suffering a series of defeats.

There were, however, a few positive things happening within the Continental Army. The colonists were not, from the outset, a "finely tuned military instrument". They were ragtag, poorly armed, poorly dressed, poorly disciplined and largely unskilled farmers and tradesmen. The Prussian officer, **Baron Friedrich von Steuben**, had been delegated to the Continental Army by the French, who were now American allies. Von Steuben was an experienced, well-trained, very professional career soldier. Washington put him in charge of training and instilling discipline in, the troops. He was very effective and his impact was clearly observed during the coming campaigns.

A second good thing coming out of the hard winter at Valley Forge was the participation of the **Marquis de Lafayette**, who had come from France to join

Washington's army. Lafayette would prove to be a superior officer and a close friend to Washington and the Americans. He would also serve to help promote financial support from France for the colonists. The French were in conflict with England, as was America, so being allies made each of them stronger.

The American Revolution Draws to a Close

By June of 1778, British General Howe had been replaced as supreme commander by **General Sir Henry Clinton**. The British were in occupation of Philadelphia but were attempting a move to New York. The Continental Army, under General Washington, attacked the British near Monmouth, New Jersey, a battle that ended in no victory for either side. Clinton's army and supply train were able to gain entry to New York.

The Continental Army, with an assist from a newly-arrived French fleet, attacked the British forces at Newport, Rhode Island. When that attack failed to dislodge the British, the war in the Northern colonies fell into a stalemate.

In the years from 1778 through 1781, the American colonists were beginning to question the war, some wondering if they wouldn't have been better off staying under British rule. The Continental Army experienced its first "mutinies" and Washington had difficulty motivating troops to stay the course. **Benedict Arnold** fled to the British side of the conflict and became a leader among their forces. Americans experienced a series of losses in battle.

The British occupied Georgia, in 1778 and South Carolina, in 1779. **General Cornwallis**, in August 1780, led British forces in defeating Americans, under General Horatio Gates, at Camden, South Carolina. It was a shameful defeat for Gates, who had far superior numbers of troops. Gates had also suffered a humiliating defeat three years earlier, at Saratoga. Following his embarrassment at Camden, he never led a major force again. He was replaced by **General Nathaniel Greene**.

American troops under the command of General Greene, led by **General Daniel Morgan**, defeated British troops in January 1781, at Cowpens, South Carolina.

General Cornwallis and his Redcoats, under steady pressure from General Green's Americans, were driven, in retreat, to the Yorktown peninsula in Virginia, near the Chesapeake Bay. It was the autumn of 1781. **The Battle of Yorktown** ensued. George Washington led his troops, supported by a division of the French army, together numbering 14,000 soldiers, against the British. An armada of 36 French warships floated offshore, preventing any escape in that direction by the British. Another American force, led by Major General Lafayette, blocked any flight by land. General Cornwallis was surrounded and out-gunned. He had no alternative but to surrender his entire army on October 19th, 1781.

Humiliated, Cornwallis refused to indulge the traditional courtesy of "surrendering his sword" to Washington. He sent, in his own place, a deputy to perform the formalities. Washington, knowing Cornwallis wasn't showing up, sent his own deputy, **Benjamin Lincoln,** who took possession of Cornwallis' sword.

While the Battle of Yorktown did not officially terminate the revolutionary war, it did put an end to any major conflicts. The British continued to occupy some parts of the colonies, including around the Charleston area and in New York City. In the latter part of 1782, the British, acknowledging defeat, began withdrawing their remaining forces.

Negotiators representing the new United States of America and Britain met in Paris, France, in September 1783. The **"Treaty of Paris"** was written and signed, meaning Britain formally recognized the United States as an independent sovereign government. At that same conference, Britain signed peace treaties with both France and Spain, both of whom had had their own conflicts with the British, while also supporting the American colonists.

The Northwest Ordinance of 1787

The year 1800 saw half a million American settlers living on America's western frontier, west of the Appalachian Mountains. The **"Northwest Ordinance"**, in 1789, provided a plan for absorbing western lands into the United States.

"The Northwest Ordinance" followed the **Ordinance of 1784**, written by Thomas Jefferson, which laid out protocols to govern the way new lands, described as being north of the Ohio River, could be assimilated into the United States. Jefferson, a slaveholder, included terms that prohibited slavery in any new lands added under the Ordinance.

"The Northwest Ordinance" passed in July of 1787, detailed a process by which territories located north of the Ohio River could achieve statehood. The area designated included territory that would eventually become the states of Illinois, Indiana, Michigan, Wisconsin and Ohio, as well as parts of Minnesota. "The Northwest Ordinance" provided that all Native American land treaties with the U.S. must be honored. Inevitably, many American settlers had little respect for the treaties and were concerned only with obtaining land for themselves. As Americans moved further and further west, encounters with Indian nations sometimes resulted in violence. Understandably, the Indians resisted the loss of their native lands to the new settlers.

A **Miami Indian** Chief, **Chief Little Turtle**, formed a confederacy of several Indian tribes and tried to fight off the constant encroachment of white settlers. Congress, in the early 1790s, formed the first **U.S. Army** to exist during a time of international peace. The new army was sent to take control of Chief Little Turtle's forces and end the Indian resistance. Chief Little Turtle was able to successfully fight off the Americans for a couple of years, but was finally defeated in 1794. This pattern of engagements would be repeated many times over the coming decades.

The Residence Act

As the new nation grew and began to establish a national identity, "The Residence Act" was passed in 1790. Philadelphia was designated the temporary capital and held that position until 1800, when the federal government and the capital, were moved to the District of Columbia. President Washington chose architect Pierre-Charles L'Enfant to design the new capital city of Washington. L'Enfant's design for the city, formed in spokes reaching out from a core consisting of the two houses of Congress and the home of the President, still stands today.

America in the 1790's

The 1790s were rich with "firsts" for the new nation. Our first **State of the Union Address** was delivered on January 8, 1790, by American hero, President George Washington, who was almost universally popular. Weeks later, America's **Supreme Court of the United States** was convened, in New York City, for its first session. Our nation's first official **Census** was commissioned by Congress in March, 1790. It revealed that 3,929,214 citizens lived in America, with the highest population being in the state of Virginia, home of George Washington and Thomas Jefferson.

The first census reported that there were approximately seven hundred thousand slaves living in the thirteen new states. The number would expand dramatically in the coming decades, as the cultivation of tobacco and cotton crops required vast amounts of manual field labor. By the time of the Civil War, there would be more than four million slaves. The shameful institution, over time, gradually shifted more and more to the Southern states, as the tobacco crops on the East Coast lost market value and the cotton crops were grown further South.

Eli Whitney and the Cotton Gin

Eli **Whitney** was born in Massachusetts in 1765. As a youth, Eli showed early signs of his skills as an inventor. He built, for instance, a violin and a forge for making nails. He graduated from Yale College, (now Yale University) and moved to the South.

The institution of slavery was boosted, in 1794, with the introduction of the **"cotton gin"**, which Eli Whitney invented. The cotton gin mechanically removed unwanted seeds from the cotton "bolls". Whitney, at the time, was staying on a plantation owned by the widow of **General Nathaniel Greene**, **Catherine Greene**. Some historians believe it may have been Catherine who originally gave Whitney the idea for the cotton gin. The availability of the cotton gin soon made cotton America's number one export.

One human laborer could clean seeds from about a pound of cotton each day. Whitney's cotton gin could clean up fifty pounds of cotton each day. Unfortunately, the machine served to make slave labor even more important, as more slaves meant more cotton for the machine to clean and more money for the plantation owner.

Eli Whitney, a rather prolific inventor, was later able to secure a contract to build muskets for the government. His work on this project reflected his novel idea of using standardized, identical parts for each item, which made the assembly, repair and replacement of parts far easier and less expensive. Whitney's successful use of mass production techniques was revolutionary and contributed significantly to America's growth. As the **Industrial Revolution** approached, toward the end of the 1800's, **Henry Ford** and other manufacturers would "fine-tune" and capitalize on Whitney's methods of **mass production**.

Eli Whitney married Henrietta Edwards in 1817, at which time he was more than fifty years old. They produced four children in their eight years together and Eli died in 1825, at the age of 59.

America in the 1790's . . . Continued

Americans in the 1790s had a new nation, a new government and a new constitution. The list of critical "things to do" was very long. Plans had to be made and actions taken, to establish a protective military, create a judicial system, develop a fair system of taxation to pay for government services, expand a postal system, etc.

Lacking a judicial system, laws could not be enforced. The military was worn down following the revolution. The navy was essentially non-existent.

George Washington, a man who had always listened carefully to the counsel of others before making decisions, quickly created a **"cabinet"** of advisers.

Departments of State and Treasury were soon created by **Congress. Alexander Hamilton** became the first **Secretary of Treasury** and **Thomas Jefferson** became the first **Secretary of State**. In the same sequence, Congress created the federal judiciary, the **Supreme Court. John Jay**, who had already declined Washington's offer to be Secretary of State, accepted an appointment as the nation's first **Chief Justice of the Supreme Court**. The federal judiciary initially was composed of the Chief Justice, five associate justices, three circuit courts and 13 district courts.

Washington's administration reigned over the adoption, on December 15, 1791, of the **Bill of Rights**. The Bill of Rights was written to protect the fundamental human rights of American citizens. It soon became part of the debate about how the shameful institution of slavery would be handled in the United States. The obvious contradiction between parts of the Bill of Rights and the treatment of slaves, would fester for decades before finally boiling over into the civil war.

Throughout the 1790s, the number of migrants, from Europe, into the new country, grew rapidly. Colonists continued to stretch the boundaries of America's western frontier, moving to Ohio, Kentucky and Tennessee Territories. Production of critical necessities, such as grain, cotton and tobacco was steadily increasing. Rich farmlands were being cleared and developed.

The Industrial Revolution, which had been born in Europe, was emerging dramatically in the United States. The American shipping industry had quickly grown to become the second-largest in the world, behind only England. American producers were exchanging goods with China, selling furs to the Chinese and bringing back to the states precious commodities such as silk, tea and various spices. Essential textile-producing companies were opening up in New England. Glass, iron and paper were being produced in Pennsylvania, New York and New Jersey.

Terms ending the American Revolution resulted in America taking possession of territories previously held by Spain, Britain and France. Washington developed policies that stabilized the rush to move into those territories and take possession of properties in those areas. He oversaw the admission of new states Vermont, Kentucky and Tennessee. As he left the office of the Presidency, in his Farewell Address, Washington warned Americans of the dangers of international politics, advising the nation to "steer clear of permanent alliances with any portion of the foreign world". He believed America would be safer, more secure and more stable if it stayed away from foreign politics and conflicts. It was a policy of **"Isolationism"**, which persisted in American foreign policy for many decades.

Washington oversaw the creation of the **First Bank of the United States** in 1791. In associated moves, a federal mint was created, to expedite the creation of a stable currency and policies related to federal excise taxes were put in place.

In 1791, a man named **John Fitch** obtained a patent for the **steamboat**. Steamboats would become essential components of passenger travel and cargo distribution, as the rivers of America were opened up for safe travel.

The Whiskey Rebellion

Taxes were always, and still are, a very sensitive issue in government. They are essential for funding government services, supporting the military, running the postal system, etc. Arguments have always been rampant around the right and authority of the government to tax citizens and in what conditions taxation is appropriate.

The first big conflict over taxes in the new nation came up with **"The Whiskey Rebellion"** in the spring of 1791. The new government imposed an excise tax on all "distilled spirits". An excise tax is a tax imposed by the government on sales of certain commodities or services.

There was great opposition to the "whiskey tax", especially in Pennsylvania. There were still many experienced soldiers in the population, now home after the revolution. Several groups of armed protesters were formed. The protests soon grew violent and federal tax collectors were attacked. President Washington quickly responded by calling up militias from several states. He personally led a force of approximately 13,000 armed men, which marched into Pennsylvania in the fall of 1794. Faced with the approach of the famous and very popular General Washington and his troops, the rebellion quickly fell apart. Washington took around 200 captives and two or three people died in the fighting. More people, about a dozen, died from illness or accidents than from shootings. The protesting groups were disbanded and the whiskey rebellion was over.

In his response to the Whiskey Rebellion, President Washington established an important precedent. His actions demonstrated that citizens, in America, under our constitution and Bill of Rights, are free to protest. They are not, however, free to introduce violence into their protests and, if they do so, the government has a right to respond to that violence.

In 1792, **The French Revolution** broke out. France entered a military conflict with Great Britain and other European powers. Americans were still in clear remembrance of the essential assistance, financially and militarily, that the desperate colonists received from France during their own revolution. Many Americans believed their country should take the side of France and return those favors. President Washington took a realistic look at the condition of the infant nation's financial and military resources and took the position that America must stay out of the European conflict. His point of view was consistent with his philosophy of isolationism, as well as in response to his evaluation of America's resources and capabilities. Washington delivered the **"Proclamation of Neutrality"** in April 1793, which soon became the **"Neutrality Act of 1794"**. This declaration of policy, codifying isolationism, became an American staple of foreign policy for the next one hundred years.

Pinckney's Treaty

The Treaty of San Lorenzo

In the years following the revolution, many disputes about territory borders and trading conditions, continued to flare up. Spain and the United States had conflicts that had to be resolved because they impacted western settlements and American-Spanish trading policies. In 1795, America's **Thomas Pinckney** met with Spanish representatives to complete the "**Treaty of San Lorenzo**". The treaty finalized the determination, for that time, of America's southern border, below which Spain continued to hold control. The treaty guaranteed American's free navigation of the Mississippi River, all the way south to New Orleans, which was then a part of Spanish Louisiana. Among other provisions, the treaty required both sides to control the aggressive actions of Indians residing within their borders.

The Treaty of Greenville

As they saw the colonists absorbing more and more property, from the times before the revolution up until 1785, Native Americans became more and more concerned about the loss of lands that had been their homelands for centuries. In 1785, several large Indian nations joined forces, in an effort to stop the flood of immigrants and to resist the new nation's growth.

American settlers along the western frontier were angry that their government wasn't offering protection against Indian aggression. Indians, of course, believed that they had every right to protect their homelands. Washington recognized the danger of allowing the conflicts to continue. He first sent his **Brigadier General Josiah Harmer** to put down what he considered a rebellion. The Indians defeated Harmer.

Washington responded, one year later, in 1791, by sending a new force commanded by **Major General Arthur St. Clair** to suppress the Indian nations. St. Clair, too, was badly beaten by the Native Americans, at the **Battle of Wabash River**. More than 600 American soldiers were killed in the battle. The Indian concept of war was based on "guerrilla tactics", fighting from cover in the wilderness, ambushing troops and then vanishing into the forests and "hitting and running". American forces, accustomed to fighting in organized, disciplined formations, were confounded by the strategy.

Washington, after seeing two of his Generals fail, now turned to **General "Mad" Anthony Wayne**. Wayne took the time necessary to thoroughly train his troops. He taught them the combat methods of the Indians. On August 29, 1794, General Wayne led his troops to a decisive victory against the Indians at **The Battle of Fallen Timbers**. The battle signaled the end of The **"The Northwest Indian War"**.

"The Treaty of Greenville" was signed by all combatants in 1795. It cleared the way for Americans to begin legally settling in the territories then known as Ohio, Michigan, Wisconsin, Indiana and Illinois. America continued its steady expansion from the Atlantic coast toward the Pacific.

Federalists and Republicans (Democratic-Republicans)

Alexander Hamilton and Thomas Jefferson were at the core of the development of political parties in the American government. George Washington opposed the idea of having opposing parties. Hamilton, the first Secretary of the Treasury, was a strong advocate of a strong central government and the party known as "Federalists" grew up around him and his ideas. Jefferson, the nation's first Secretary of State, believed our constitution supported a concept more focused on the rights of individual states and the voice of the people. He opposed the development of a large, centralized federal government. Those who supported him and his political philosophy became known as **Republicans**, also known as **Democratic-Republicans**.

The conflict between Jefferson and Hamilton brought about the formation of the first "two-party" or **"bicameral"**, government in the Western world. Federalists primarily promoted the interests of tradesmen and manufacturers. They were skeptical of the abilities of the common man being up to the task of governing. Federalists leaned toward strong support for England and the English form of government.

Hamilton, the de facto leader of the Federalists, was never a candidate for political growth, due to issues in his personal life. He was, however, recognized for his ability to organize an efficient Treasury and to introduce a national central bank, stable currency and other necessary elements of governmental infrastructure. Hamilton was afraid that a weak central government would have to result in chaos and anarchy. He believed in a solid structure and a well-ordered government.

Republicans leaned more toward a focus on agricultural interests and political values. They were not big supporters of bankers and had little interest in manufacturing. Republicans opposed a strong central government. They would likely not approve of the massive American government we see in today's world. They feared that a central government that grew too strong would soon be a source of oppression. Republicans enthusiastically supported state's rights and the rights of the individual citizen. Thomas Jefferson declared "I am not a friend to a very energetic government".

Going forward, the two parties, the Federalists and the Democratic-Republicans would grow more organized and more clearly defined. They would be key factors in America's government through future decades. In today's world, the Republican party still exists and the Federalists eventually became today's Democrats. The philosophies of the two parties have been modified continuously and bear little resemblance to their original charters.

Other parties have gained various levels of support over the years, but none have challenged the two primary parties in terms of numbers of supporters or political influence. Modern politics include "Independents" (who claim to support no major party), "Green" groups (who support environmental priorities), "Libertarians" (who represent the rights of the individual and oppose big government) and others.

America in the 1790's . . . Continued

October 13, 1775, is the date claimed by our Navy as the time of its original establishment. At that time, the Second Continental Congress, preparing for war with England, created the **"Continental Navy"**. Following the end of the revolution, the American Navy was essentially dismantled. As time went by, after the war, it became clear that American merchant ships needed protection. **"Barbary Pirates"**, from several North African Muslim States, were routinely attacking the merchant's cargo ships, costing huge losses in products and ships, which were sometimes captured and held by the pirates. Under our second President, **John Adams**, Congress passed legislation known as **The Naval Act of 1794**, which mandated the creation of a permanent standing **United States Navy**.

During the late 1700s and early 1800s, America fought to become a viable member of the international community. The states were largely driven by a farming economy, with small, family-owned farms dominating the New England and Mid-Atlantic states. Farming was even more prevalent in the southern states. A few large cities, such as New York and Philadelphia were rapidly growing into commercial trade centers. There was a steady traffic of merchant sailing ships back and forth between the United States and Europe and Asia.

The institution of slavery continued to be a constant source of friction in the states. The Northern states were slowly trending toward the elimination of slavery entirely. The Southern states were "digging in", defending the necessity of slave labor for planting and harvesting tobacco, rice and cotton crops. While the Constitution stipulated that "the slave trade" be terminated in 1808, that date came and went with little impact on behavior. There were so many slaves living on the plantations of the South that they produced large numbers of children, who themselves became working slaves. The overseas trade for slaves was no longer necessary. Slavery was integral to the southern economy, even though most southerners owned no slaves.

America's Economy in the 1790's

Before the American Revolution, the colonists benefited by having stable trade conditions with their English rulers. The British Navy protected American shipping. Favorable tariffs were observed, which, while sometimes criticized, encouraged American trade. Following the revolution, America's merchants and tradesmen had to cope with the loss of much of the business that had previously been nurtured by the Crown. The American government, still very much de-centralized, had no authority to manage conditions. States were more concerned with their own financial stability than they were with the new nation. The economy was in trouble.

The English were hoping to "starve" the new America with restrictive trade practices, hoping to see the new nation fail. American leaders met in 1785, at the home of George Washington, to seek solutions to their economic problems. They decided that the new government would have to become more powerful and more centralized if it were to survive. Two years later, in 1787, a convention of delegates from the new states met to create the Constitution which would give the government power over economic issues. Those issues included powers of taxation, trade regulation, contract negotiations, coining money and printing paper currency. It was a big step toward stabilizing the new country's economy.

In 1776, the year America claimed its independence, **Adam Smith** wrote his **"Inquiry into the Nature and Causes of the Wealth of Nations"**. Smith was opposed, as was Thomas Jefferson, to a strong central government. He believed in a free market, with minimum interference and few tariffs imposed by the government. Gold had, historically, been the singular measure of wealth throughout the world. Nations had collected colonies, all around the world, in their attempts to seek gold. Adam Smith believed that gold may have been a measure of wealth, but that it was not the true source of wealth. He believed that agriculture and trade goods were the real foundations for growing wealth. Thomas Jefferson and James Madison believed that America's economy should be based on a small government and on agriculture. Alexander Hamilton believed that the economy would have to be based on a strong central government, on the creation of a healthy, central national bank and on the development of manufacturing capacity.

Trading with Native Americans

In the many decades prior to the American Revolution, several European nations were engaged in very lucrative trade practices between themselves and American Indians. England controlled much of the Ohio River Valley. In Canada, the French had established an empire and they aggressively defended their relationships with the natives. The fur trade was immensely profitable for them. American merchants from Philadelphia maintained a trading relationship with Indians located on the far side of the Alleghenies. They sent manufactured goods, such as cloth, cooking utensils, alcohol and weapons to the West, where they traded for furs supplied by the Indians.

Most trading done by the Indians was conducted by their women. It was beneficial for both the natives and the Europeans to maintain the trade routes. The appreciation the Indians had for the white man's manufactured goods undoubtedly curbed many impulses to resist the white settlers.

Alexander McGillivray's parents were a Scottish trader and a **Creek Indian** woman. It's likely his father had married his mother to cement profitable trade relations with the natives. Alexander became a leader of the Creek tribe during the 1780s. in Florida. The slow process of assimilation had begun, as the white invaders slipped into more and more sections of Indian land and personal relationships developed between the races.

The Europeans, primarily the French and the Spanish, had good reason to assist the Indians in resisting further incursions, by white settlers, into Indian properties. They wanted to keep the colonists out of the West, so they could protect the vast trading of furs. They wanted the land free of settlers and farmers, so the deer and beaver, essential to the fur trade, could flourish. The Indians collected the fur from the animals and the Europeans collected the fur from the Indians.

Congress, in 1796, enacted legislation that created **"Indian Agents"**. At the same time, Congress made it illegal for private individuals to engage in trade with the Indians. Government agents were to be the only people allowed to trade with the natives. Europeans and colonists regularly manipulated trade agreements to take advantage of the Indians, which left many of the natives deeply in debt. This indebtedness made it much easier for colonists to buy up Indian lands, which they did very aggressively.

Native Americans were inclined to view Earth as, in a sense, their "Mother", rather than being a commodity that could be purchased and "owned" by an individual. Their philosophical beliefs made them easy prey to colonists, who believed that they could survey the land, stake out farms or residential properties and then forbid anyone else from using that property. The whole concept was foreign to many natives.

By 1801, during Thomas Jefferson's administration, the government had quietly begun a program of systematic removal of Native Americans from their ancestral homes. Programs intended to encourage white colonists to settle on Indian lands began to take effect and would continue for decades. Systematic destruction, by white settlers and soldiers, of the immense herds of buffalo quickly eliminated a primary resource for the survival of the tribes. Some believe the killing of the bison was done intentionally to make the Native Americans weak and dependent.

Thomas Jefferson believed that the "**Louisiana Purchase**", an act that vastly increased the boundaries and doubled the size, of the United States, would offer an area to which the Indians could be sent to "re-settle". He seems to have intended to forcibly displace all Indians living east of the Mississippi to make them live within the confines of the Louisiana Purchase. A later President, **Andrew Jackson**, much more aggressively pursued a policy of relocating all Native Americans to the far west or to reservations.

The Fugitive Slave Act of 1793

The tension between those who did and those who did not support slavery was always an undercurrent to daily American life. One point of contention was around how a "runaway slave" should be managed if apprehended in a "free state". Some of the new states completely prohibited slavery, some "tolerated" slavery and others were very dependent on the cheap labor provided by their slaves. Slave owners would pursue runaway slaves, who often attempted, in their flight, to gain entrance to slave-free areas. **"Bounty hunters"** would stalk runaways, in hopes of collecting reward money for the return of the slaves to their owners. In 1793, **The Fugitive Slave Act** was passed. It mandated that escaped slaves be returned to their owners. It essentially made" bounty hunting" for runaway slaves permissible, even in free states. It is recognized, in today's world, to be a remnant of a barbaric practice and not an action for which the Washington administration could take pride.

America in the 1790's . . . continued

Throughout the 1790s, colonists continued to move westward, settling in the Ohio, Kentucky and Tennessee territories. The land was relatively cheap to acquire. Parts of Pennsylvania and Virginia began to produce large harvests of wheat. Farmers began to focus more on producing extra products, not for their own needs, but to sell to the domestic or overseas markets.

While the **Industrial Revolution**, already well underway in Europe, was only beginning to be a factor in the American economy, it was visible in advancements in manufacturing techniques and the use of water power to drive operations. Americans were marketing textiles, grains, iron, tobacco, paper and glass products. American merchant ships were sailing back and forth to the Orient and to Europe.

The Barbary Pirates and Thomas Jefferson

In the early 1800s, pirates from the "Barbary States" of North Africa were routinely stopping American merchant ships. **The Barbary Pirates** stopped and boarded American vessels. They stole products and held ships and sailors for ransom. (Somalian pirates still operate very effectively in our modern world, holding huge cargo ships for ransom.)

President Thomas Jefferson refused to acquiesce to the demands of the pirates. When Jefferson refused to pay "tribute" to the pirates, Tripoli declared war on America. Jefferson didn't like the idea of committing American military resources to a foreign operation, but the cost of allowing the pirates to dominate was too great to ignore. Without going through Congress to formally declare war, Jefferson directed the new American Navy to engage the pirates.

American marines attacked Derna, a city in Tripoli, in April of 1805 and conflicts would continue until peace was negotiated. The naval battles, fought primarily off the shores of Tripoli in Libya, persisted throughout 1805. While the pirates were never completely eliminated, Jefferson was able to keep the trade routes open for American merchants, which was his objective. Somalian pirates continue to operate in modern times.

The **American Marine Corps** anthem is the oldest of the armed forces anthems. The opening lines are "From the halls of Montezuma to the Shores of Tripoli", honoring the marines who stopped the Barbary Pirates under President Thomas Jefferson.

The actual battle referenced as the **"Halls of Montezuma"** in the anthem took place long after the conflict with the Barbary Pirates, but the song worked better citing the later battle first. The **Battle of Chapultepec** happened on Sept. 13, 1847, near Mexico City, when U.S. Marines stormed Chapultepec Castle. The Halls of Montezuma were within the castle.

America Moves into the 1800's

America, in the early 1800s, grew explosively. New states were joining the union. Americans were moving and settling farther and farther into the West. American Indians were being displaced and relocated for the convenience of the new arrivals. Millions of European immigrants came to join the "New World". The issue of slavery continued to grow more and more contentious. The developing Industrial Revolution was changing the world of manufacturing and, with the invention of the cotton gin, agriculture. The Louisiana Purchase doubled the size of the new nation, offered a location for the temporary placement of Native Americans and gave the United States an invaluable new shipping port at the mouth of the great Mississippi River.

As the American population rapidly expanded, growing to more than 10 million citizens by 1820, more and more citizens moved west of the Appalachian mountains. Subcultures typical of various regions had begun to develop so that social and political opinions characteristic of certain regions were being transferred into the new territories. The issue of slavery began to be the predominant differentiator between the Northern parts of the country and the Southern parts of the country. Resistance to slavery was characteristic of New England, home of the Quakers and Puritans, the Middle Atlantic, Chesapeake and the Carolinas. The abolitionist sentiments of that area were carried into the Northwest territories which became Ohio, Indiana, Illinois, Michigan and Wisconsin. The sentiments in favor of slave labor, on which their agrarian economy vitally depended, were carried into the areas that were, or would become, Arkansas, Kentucky, Missouri, Tennessee, Mississippi and Texas. The tension over the institution of slavery would persist and grow, infecting the nation for several more decades and would culminate in the Civil War.

Around the House in the Early 1800's

Prairie Sod House

Today's Americans would likely find living in the year 1800 very tough. Consider that most of the population was far from wealthy. Most homes had one or two rooms. A two-room house generally had one room to sleep in and another room for every other need. There was no electricity, so no furnace, no air conditioning and no lights. Windows had no glass. Homes were constructed of wood, for the most part or of sod. Houses were drafty and cold and it wasn't unusual for snow and frost to be on household items and beds.

On the frontier, the land had to be cleared. There were no power tools, so wood was cut with hand saws and axes. Trees had to be cut down and then cut into planks or used as logs for construction. Water had to be carried back each day from streams or lakes and then boiled. Wood had to be gathered for fires.

Clothing was mostly homemade, meaning people had to grow hemp for use in making linen. Most adults had, at most, two outfits. One for church. One for work. Women used spinning wheels to make the thread they used to weave clothing. Women assisted with crops, with home defense, when necessary and did the cooking and cleaning.

Infant mortality was very high. Diseases would sometimes kill large numbers of settlers. Families often had several children, knowing the odds against survival were sometimes poor. Clothing would be handed down from child to child.

Horses, oxen and mules were luxuries many families did not possess. Those who had them enjoyed easier and more efficient methods of planting and harvesting crops, traveling into town and socializing with neighbors in their communities.

Grocery stores or "General Stores" or "Mercantile", often had little to offer outside of, hopefully, some sugar, some coffee or tea, some flour and maybe some sewing supplies. Some citizens could not afford to shop at all.

Modern medicines, such as vaccines, antibiotics, analgesics, etc., did not exist. Physicians were not available in many places. Half of all children born did not survive to the age of six years, victims of smallpox, dysentery, measles, typhoid or scarlet fever. Native Americans exposed to the diseases of the white man inevitably died, sometimes losing whole villages. Homesteaders learned to sew up their own open wounds.

Settlers had no herbicides or plant nutrients, other than fertilizers provided by livestock and crop failures were not uncommon. A bad year for crops made a bad year for food for the family. Homesteaders had to learn to do their own carpenter work, horseshoeing, blacksmithing and well-digging.

It was common for people of that time to spend their entire Sundays at church. Every other day was spent, sun-up to sundown, in one way or another working.

Families living in larger cities had access to luxuries such as glass windows, whale oil or kerosene for lamps.

Cleanliness was a constant concern. Water had to be carried to the house from a hand-dug well or a stream. A simple pan was often the only source to hold water for cleaning. A single tub of heated (hopefully) water served as the weekly bath for the entire family. It wasn't unusual for people to go for weeks, especially during winter, without bathing at all. Infants either wore no diapers or wore cloth diapers, often no more than rags.

Many people wore no shoes for most of the year. Before the mid-1800s, shoes were not made for "left and right" feet.

The Early 1800's in America . . . Continued

President John Adams was America's second President. He was the first, on November 1, 1800, to live in the new White House. His stay was short as he was soon to be replaced, in February 1801, by our third President, Thomas Jefferson.

When the votes were counted for the 1800 Presidential election, Thomas Jefferson and Aaron Burr were locked in a tie. The tie had to be broken by a vote of the House of Representatives and Jefferson won that contest.

The very first Chief Justice of the Supreme Court was **John Jay**, appointed in 1789 by the first President, George Washington. Jay was followed by John Rutledge, Oliver Ellsworth and then **John Marshall**, who took the position on February 4, 1801. Marshall served as Chief Justice for the next 34 years and had a great impact on the ways our Constitution is interpreted.

The Supreme Court, in February 1803, for the first time overturned a case previously decided by a lower court. This action was the foundation for the concept of **"Judicial Review"**, leading to a pathway for future appeals. It was significant because it validated the Supreme Court as being equal to the other two branches of the government. There was now an avenue for the court to modify legislation created by Congress.

The Louisiana Purchase

Spain owned Louisiana Territory in 1800 and they were not well established. America's leaders did not believe Spain would inhibit further American expansion. The Americans were dismayed when the French, ruled at the time by **Napoleon Bonaparte**, purchased the Louisiana Territory from Spain. Thomas Jefferson was much more concerned about the French than he had been about the Spaniards. Napoleon was ambitious and aggressive. Napoleon was making plans to send troops to New Orleans. Jefferson believed New Orleans to be extremely important, both for defensive purposes and for mercantile purposes. He sent **Robert Livingston** and **James Monroe** to New Orleans to try and purchase the area around the port of New Orleans and parts of western Florida. They were authorized to spend ten million dollars on the purchase. In the meantime, Napoleon had given up on his militaristic plans for Louisiana. To their amazement, Napoleon offered to sell the United States all of the Louisiana Territory for only fifteen million dollars. The amount exceeded what Jefferson had approved, but the pair, Livingston and Monroe, quickly approved the purchase. This single action opened the door to America's growth westward from the Missouri River to the Pacific Ocean. The Louisiana Purchase was concluded with Jefferson's approval on April 30, 1803. It added 828,000 square miles, including all or parts of fifteen of today's states. It can generally be described as all of the lands between the Mississippi River and the Rocky Mountains, including the port area around New Orleans. The actual per acre cost of the purchase worked out to about three cents.

The Lewis and Clark Expedition

The Corps of Discovery

Thomas Jefferson had always been interested in science and exploration. Following the purchase of the Louisiana Territory, he was very curious about what riches and resources the United States might have acquired. Trappers and explorers had wandered the area for decades, but little surveying or mapping had been accomplished. Native Indians of various tribes were inhabitants of various locations and were not likely to recognize the authority of Americans to "own" the land. Jefferson was most anxious to learn what opportunities and challenges might lie beyond the great Mississippi.

Captain Meriwether Lewis was a close friend and a former secretary to Jefferson. Jefferson approached him about leading an expedition to explore the new territories, create maps and evaluate the possibility of finding a **"Northwest Passage"** that would allow easy movement from America's East all the way across the Rocky Mountains. Congress approved $2500.00 to fund the operation. The adventure was to be known as **"The Corps of Discovery"**.

The expedition actually began in May of 1804. Supplies were gathered, support staff was added and the journey began. A total of $669.50 was spent to accumulate gifts for use in negotiating with natives. Meriwether Lewis had been named Commander. He arranged for materials to be gathered from a government armory at Harper's Ferry and from government stores at Philadelphia. Everything was brought together at St. Louis.

The expedition, led at that point by **Second Lieutenant William Clark**, left St. Louis and proceeded up the Mississippi River to Camp Dubois, which was near today's Wood River, Illinois, on the east side of the Mississippi. Clark was the son of America's **General George Rogers Clark**. Lewis, who had been making plans and gathering resources, met the group at Camp Dubois, from where they began their travels. They began, on May 14th, 1804, to sail up the Missouri River to the west. The Corps of Discovery was formalized as a function of the U.S. Army. It was made up of more than 30 volunteers and would be supplemented by a few 'attached parties' and new additions.

The Corps was joined by a French-Canadian trader named **Toussaint Charbonneau**. He was hired to join the expedition because Lewis learned that his wife, **Sacagawea**, could speak Shoshone fluently. Charbonneau was not much admired by Lewis and Clark. A member of the expedition wrote that Charbonneau had been stabbed by an older native woman, using a canoe awl, while in the act of raping a native girl. His wound caused him some difficulty in walking. Charbonneau was accompanied by the native woman named Sacagawea, whom he had either purchased or won while gambling. He also "owned" another native woman, who was named Otter Woman.

Sacagawea was the daughter of a **Lemhi Shoshone** tribal Chief. She was born in what is today's Idaho, near what is now the Montana border. **Hidatsa Indians** raided the Shoshone village in 1800 when Sacagawea was about 12 years old. Many were killed. She was then a captive of the Hidatsa, in the area we now know as North Dakota. The Hidatsa tribe sold Sacagawea to the **Mandan Indians** as a slave. Approximately a year later, at age 13, Sacagawea was sold into a forced "marriage" to Charbonneau.

Sacagawea became a valued asset to the Corps of Discovery, smoothing over relations with different cultures that were encountered and providing information about the geography and history of the lands they explored. At one point, she rescued the precious journals of Lewis when a canoe capsized in rough waters. In 1805 she gave birth to a son whom she named John Baptiste. In one of the diaries, a member of the Corps wrote that "powdered rattlesnake rattles" were administered to ease the birth. Lewis and Clark wrote warmly about their gratitude for her valuable services. After the expedition, Charbonneau and Sacagawea joined Clark in St. Louis, where he adopted and provided for the education of John Baptiste.

The Corps of Discovery, with much assistance from Sacagawea, navigated across Montana and the Continental Divide. They encountered the Shoshone there and Sacagawea was reunited with her brother, whom she had not seen since they were both kidnapped. Sacagawea's familiarity with the tribe was a blessing to the explorers, who, with her help, were able to purchase horses to facilitate their continuing travels.

The story of the expedition is a fascinating history and some great books are available to learn more about the many chapters of the great adventure. The journey ended back in Washington, D.C., in 1806. The explorers then shared the story of all of their adventures with Thomas Jefferson, who was very eager to learn all he could from them. Lewis and Clark failed in their primary mission, which was to find an efficient route to traverse the nation, from east to west, through what all had hoped would be found to be "The Northwest Passage". They did, however, succeed in surveying the land between the Mississippi and the Pacific Ocean. They generated a massive amount of new information, including volumes of maps and journals full of information about the botanical and biological riches of their new world. They gained valuable trading information and essential knowledge of the native tribes. They completed a two-year journey that was fraught with dangers from the harsh geography, the rough waters and shallows of the rivers and some of the Native Americans they encountered. All of this they accomplished while losing only one member to death and while avoiding almost all violence with natives.

The journals and diaries of the Corps of Discovery documented the maps they created, the information they gained about the land, the identification of more than 120 different specimens of animals and descriptions of natives and their lifestyles. Also preserved were more than 200 samples of plants with which they were previously unfamiliar.

All in all, the Lewis and Clark expedition gained, at a cost of only $2500, an immense amount of priceless new information. It would contribute vastly to the coming mass migration of Americans all across the land.

Lewis and Clark were rewarded by Jefferson with 1,600 acres of land for each of them, as well as doubling their salaries for the trip.

Lewis became Louisiana Territory's Governor. He became a problem drinker of alcohol and wasn't a very good Governor. Lewis was never married and he had no known children. He died in 1809, sadly, of two gunshot wounds, believed to have possibly been self-inflicted.

Clark was much more successful in his post-expedition life. He became a Brigadier General of Militia in Louisiana and would also be an Indian Agent for the federal government.

The Early 1800's . . . Continued

While the Corps of Discovery was getting a first look at America's new Western frontier, life was going on back in the States. New Jersey, on February 15, 1804, became the final "Northern" state to formally abolish slavery. The line of distinction between Southern "slave states" and Northern "abolishment" states was growing more clear and more divisive.

Thomas Jefferson, in the election of 1804, easily defeated challenger Charles Pinckney. Our third President would serve two full terms.

America's first long-distance, trans-state highway was approved for funding ($30,000), by Congress, in 1806. It would be a **"National Road"**, called the **"Great National Pike"** or the **"Cumberland Road"**. It was a highway that would extend from Cumberland, Maryland, through Pennsylvania and Ohio. The road was completed in 1837, during which time it became the second road surfaced using the new **"macadam"** process, which had been developed by a Scotsman named **John Loudon McAdam**. The Cumberland Road ran 620 miles and became a primary resource for the western movement of thousands of settlers.

The Treason Trial of Aaron Burr

In February of 1807, the former Vice President, Aaron Burr, best known for killing Alexander Hamilton in a duel, was arrested for treason. He was indicted for conspiring to unite Mexico and portions of Louisiana to create an independent republic. His reputation had been stained due to various political intrigues and his killing of Hamilton. Jefferson had dropped him as Vice President. Burr's treason trial was held in Richmond, Virginia.

It was revealed that Burr had organized a small army on America's Western frontier. Some historians believe he planned to create an independent republic made up of parts of Texas, Louisiana and Mexico and to make himself Emperor thereof. Burr had been in communications with the English Crown, hoping to gain their support, knowing the British had hopes of regaining possession of all or parts of the states.

Burr's best-known co-conspirator was the highest-ranked officer in the American army, **General James Wilkinson**, who was known to be, on occasion, devious. Wilkinson, as was learned much later, was also an undercover agent, collecting pay from Spain to work on their behalf. By the time Burr had brought his forces together and was ready to launch his campaign, Wilkinson had guessed the enterprise had no hope of success and had informed Jefferson of Burr's nefarious plans. Jefferson ordered Burr's arrest.

In the meantime, believing he was as prepared as he could be, Burr began to work on his plan. He was disappointed when he found that only about 100 men would support his efforts, but loaded them onto flatboats to float downriver on the mighty Mississippi River. Burr was informed of Wilkinson's double-cross as his boats approached New Orleans and found out that Jefferson had ordered his arrest. He attempted to run, hoping to evade capture, but was arrested in February 1807, in the vicinity of today's Mobile, Alabama. He was taken to Richmond to stand trial.

Jefferson insisted that Burr be charged specifically with treason, as it carried with it the death penalty. Supreme Court **Chief Justice John Marshall** presided over the trial, which lasted for several months. Testimony during the trial was inconsistent and contradictory. Burr's lawyers engineered a strong defense, mostly by questioning the reliability of the testimony against him. They proved Wilkinson had tampered with documents used against Burr. With little hard evidence and confusing testimony, the jury ultimately found Burr "Not Guilty" of treason.

Many Americans were unhappy with the outcome of the trial. Burr was judged guilty in the court of public opinion and was "hanged in effigy" in many locations. He left America to live in Europe for a while but returned to America in 1812, where he once again practiced law. Aaron Burr died in 1836.

New Developments Related to Slavery

Southern states had forced passage of legislation, **Article 1, Section 9**, that would ban any prohibition of importing slaves until the year 1808. It took effect with the approval of the Constitution, Later, in 1794, Congress passed legislation banning the construction of any ships built to serve the slave trade. As the 1808 date approached, abolitionists dreamed of finally being able to put an end to the shameful institution. Thomas Jefferson led a movement to end the importation of slaves, in harmony with his failed attempt to get the ban included in our Constitution. Jefferson voiced his condemnation of the slave trade in his State of the Union address in December of 1806. He continued, though, to use slave labor on his farms.

Long before the revolution, various attempts to end slavery in the colonies had been made. The slave trade, though, providing a source of free labor, was responsible for the low prices by which Europeans could obtain American exports. The British, before the revolution, wanting to protect this beneficial economy, overturned and obstructed any early efforts to ban slavery.

Five Northern states had already banned slavery or set firm dates when it would be banned. (Connecticut, Rhode Island, Pennsylvania, New Hampshire and Massachusetts).

Anticipating the end of the legislation protecting the slave trade, to occur in 1808, Congress passed an Act, on March 2, 1807, that would end the importation of slaves through any and all American ports of entry. The Act was written to take effect on the first of January, 1808. Many hoped that the Act would actually end the practice of slavery, but it definitely did not do so. It didn't even succeed in stopping the importation of new slaves, as approximately 50,000 additional souls were brought in over the ensuing fifty years, prior to the civil war.

John Jacob Astor

John Jacob Astor was born Johann Jakob Astor in what is now Heidelberg, Germany. Johann worked, as a child, in his father's butcher shop and also became a dairy salesman. At the age of 16, Johann moved to London, England, where he worked for an uncle, who manufactured pianos and flutes. There, in London, he learned the English language and he anglicized his name to become John Jacob Astor.

Astor married **Sarah Cox Todd**, whom he declared had a sound mind for business, in 1785. He gave her credit for assisting him in many of the details of his businesses. She managed the businesses when John was traveling. Together, they produced eight children. Sarah brought a three- hundred-dollar dowry to their union, which provided the funds by which they opened their first business, selling musical instruments, which provided the ignition for Astor's eventual vast business successes. Sarah became the expert on evaluating and processing furs and was an important factor in John Jacob's ultimate success.

When the American Revolution was over, in the early 1789s, John moved to the United States. He arrived, first, in the port of Baltimore, bringing with him a shipload of his family's flutes. Astor soon recognized the potential of the fur market and began to operate a fur trading business. He was very successful in the fur business and formed the **American Fur Company** in 1808, becoming the company's sole shareholder. Astor bought or traded for, furs from Native Americans. He prepared the furs himself and sold them domestically and internationally. As the American Fur Company grew, Astor became a wealthy and influential citizen, befriending the most important business and political leaders, including such luminaries as Thomas Jefferson.

Astor gained control of much of the very profitable fur trade in America's Northeast, lower Canada and America's Northwest. After the Louisiana Purchase, he gained control of much of the fur business in that vast new marketplace. His trading post, established in 1811 on the Columbia River, called Astoria, was the nation's first community on the Pacific Coast. Astor funded an exploration, known as the **Astor Expedition**, taking place from 1810 to 1812, which discovered the **South Pass** through the Rocky Mountains. The South Pass became the doorway to the West through which hundreds of thousands of settlers would pass. The Oregon, the Mormon and the California trails all used the South Pass.

Astor soon expanded his business interests. He became a land and property owner, purchasing precious real estate along New York's waterfront and in the business centers of the rapidly growing city. He was known as a patron of American arts and culture, supporting groups like the Audubon Society and he founded the Astor Library.

Astor's fur business suffered during the War of 1812 when the British captured some of his trading posts. Perhaps this was the stimulus that pushed Astor into the illegal opium trade. He had been trading for Chinese tea and silk and so already had a route through which he could move the opium. Astor obtained massive supplies of opium from the Ottoman Empire in Europe and transported it on his ship, the Macedonian, to the shores of China. The opium was loaded off the Macedonian and moved to smaller vessels, which then moved the opium ashore. Astor received tea, silk, fabric and pottery in return for the opium, which products he sold, at a great profit, in American and London. Astor was in the opium trade business for about ten years and undoubtedly contributed to what became a flood of addicted souls in China and, to a lesser degree, in America. Astor wasn't alone among famous Americans who participated in the opium trade. Warren Delano, the grandfather of future President Franklin Delano Roosevelt, also made a fortune in the business.

John Jacob Astor's fur business expanded westward until the American Fur Company became the world's largest fur supplier. His real estate interests remained focused on his East Coast properties, which were extremely valuable. By the time of his death in 1848, he was the wealthiest man in America, valued in excess of twenty million dollars. His wealth would equal about $780 million dollars in present-day money.

America in the Early 1800's . . . Continued

The Supreme Court of the United States, in February of 1809, delivered a decision that clearly defined the status of the federal Supreme Court as it relates to the courts of the individual states. The case of the **U.S. vs. Peters** yielded a SCOTUS decision that would have the impact of cementing the superiority and authority of the federal courts over the decisions of the state courts. The Chief Justice was, at the time, **John Marshall**, and his written words were "If the legislatures of the several states may, at will, annul the judgments of the courts of the United States and destroy the rights acquired under those judgments, the constitution itself becomes a solemn mockery; and the nation is deprived of the means of enforcing its laws by the instrumentality of its own tribunals". The decision guaranteed citizens of America that rights given them by federal SCOTUS decisions could not be taken away by state courts.

James Madison

America's Fourth President

James Madison was born on March 16, 1751, in Orange County, Virginia. He was the oldest of twelve children born to **James Madison, Sr.** and **Nellie Conway Madison**. The family-owned a plantation named **Montpelier**, on which James grew up. Montpelier included 2600 acres of land and was worked by as many as 100 slaves. He left that plantation at the age of eighteen and attended the College of New Jersey, which we know today as Princeton University.

James Madison was around twenty-four years old when the American Revolution was initiated. He was appointed to be a colonel in the Orange County militia but was not suited for military life. Small in stature and sickly in health, James soon abandoned the military and focused on politics. The Virginia Constitution Convention was convened, in 1776, to organize a new state government, as British rule was terminated.

Madison met and became a lifelong close friend of Thomas Jefferson. Madison became a strong advocate for religious freedom in America, declaring it an individual's birthright. When the Continental Congress met in Philadelphia in 1780, Madison was there as a delegate from Virginia.

James Madison was a key player in the creation of the new nation's constitution. He had completed an extensive study of world governments throughout history. He became, along with Alexander Hamilton, an advocate for a strong central government, putting him sometimes at odds with his dear friend Jefferson. Madison also fought to promote the concept of a "system of checks and balances", which he believed essential to ensure that no one element of government gain too much power.

America's **Constitutional Convention** was convened, in Philadelphia, in May of 1787. Madison presented his **"Virginia Plan"**, which defined three branches of the new government: the **Executive**, the **Judicial** and the **Legislative** components. The Virginia Plan became the foundation of the United States Constitution. While Madison stated that the creation of the constitution was "not, like the fabled goddess of wisdom, the off-spring of a single brain", but rather was "the work of many heads and many hands". In spite of his attempt to share the credit, Madison became known as the **"Father of the Constitution"**. His work continued as, while serving in Virginia's House of Representatives, Madison was one of those who structured and wrote the federal **Bill of Rights**.

As the new constitution took effect, Madison began leaning away from the idea of a powerful central government, which was promoted primarily by Alexander Hamilton. The **"Federalist"** political party emerged, which supported Hamilton. Madison became an ally to Thomas Jefferson, who was an avid supporter of the rights of individual states to govern themselves. Madison and Jefferson were the founders, in 1792, of the **"Democratic-Republican Party"**, creating thereby the first "opposition party".

In 1794, James Madison, then 43 years old, married the love of his life, **Dolley Madison**, a 26-year-old widow. Dolley had one son and was a Quaker. Madison, quiet and reserved, was not known for socializing, but Dolley was much more outgoing. She became well-known for her love of entertaining guests at receptions and dinner parties. In today's world, she would be a "networking" success and her events offered many opportunities for James to engage with influential people in society. Dolley and James were married for 41 years and were rarely separated during all that time.

Thomas Jefferson became the nation's third President in the election of 1800. He quickly appointed Madison his Secretary of State. Madison worked, along with Jefferson, on the monumental purchase of the Louisiana Territory from the French. The Louisiana Purchase essentially doubled the geographical area of the United States.

Britain and France were at war with one another in the early 1800s. Both warring nations were angered that America insisted on remaining neutral in their conflict. Ships of Britain and France began attacking U.S. ships at sea and forcing American sailors into their service. Pay was very low, the work was very hard, the job was dangerous, the voyages were very long and unpredictable and it wasn't easy to entice men to serve on the ships. The British, for many years, used the practice of "Impressment" to obtain sailors. Impressment, or "crimping" was their habit of capturing or kidnapping unwilling men to force them to serve. Madison, supported by Jefferson, employed an "embargo" against all British and French trade goods, blocking their tradings in and out of the U.S. ports. Unfortunately, the trade embargo ultimately was a greater punishment for Americans than for the Europeans and Jefferson terminated it when he left office in 1809.

James Madison became America's fourth President in the election of 1808. The war between France and Britain continued to be a thorn in the Madison administration. The British **"Impressed"** or forced into their fleet service, approximately 15,000 American sailors between the years 1793 to 1812. Britain also continued to support American Indians in their continuing conflicts with American settlers. The United States declared war on Great Britain on June 18th, 1812. A review of that conflict will follow our account of Madison's life.

The War of 1812 was unpopular among many of America's citizens and the Federalist party opposed many of Madison's efforts. American forces lost most encounters during the war, but the American Navy developed into a formidable fleet. Its ships were superior and became the foundation for today's navy.

Madison once again won in the election of 1812. Times were hard during the War of 1812 and many citizens blamed Madison for their hardships. The British were aggressively pursuing the war. New England threatened to exit the union. The Federalist party blocked Madison's political agenda. British troops invaded Washington, D.C., in August of 1814. They burned much of the capital, including the capitol building itself, the new White House and the Library of Congress. Exhausted by the war, the United States and Great Britain negotiated a settlement to end the war. The **Treaty of Ghent** was signed in December of 1814. News of the treaty did not reach everyone quickly. The United States, in December of 1814, with a force commanded by **Andrew Jackson**, engaged with the British in the **"Battle of New Orleans"**. The conflict ended with a clear American victory, which meant little, as the war had ended, but which left a sweeter taste in the mouths of Americans regarding the execution of the war. There were other key American victories during the war and Madison was credited for the outcome.

Madison served two terms as our fourth President. History praises him as a great communicator, writer, statesman and possessor of a gifted mind. He exited Washington, D.C., as his term expired and returned to the plantation Montpelier. He was accompanied by his beloved wife, Dolley. They remained active, after their return to Virginia, in civic affairs. James died in June of 1836, a victim of heart failure, at the age of 85.

President James Madison and Slavery

President Madison, like many Americans of his time, engaged in a paradoxical mindset regarding the institution of slavery. His writings reveal clearly that he was painfully aware of the evil of the institution of slavery. He supported the banning of the international trade of black people. He supported a gradual approach to achieving the emancipation of all slaves. A French visitor wrote that Madison was a young man who "has had the humanity and courage to propose a general emancipation of the slaves". Madison's letters home, while he was abroad, clearly refer to some slaves as family members. Still, he continued to use slaves as cheap labor on his property.

One favored slave, named Billey, was given to James when James was a child, to be a companion. At some point, Billey became **William Gardner**. Billey was with Madison at the Continental Congress. He became a problem, of sorts, as he gained knowledge about the writings of the Declaration of Independence and the Constitution. Billey was "contaminated" with new opinions about freedom for negroes. He attempted to run away more than once and Madison considered selling him to gain funds to buy books. Madison did, indeed, sell Billey, or William Gardner, into **"indentured servitude"** for a term of seven years. Following his release from that period of forced servitude, Garner became a free merchant's agent. As such, he worked again for Madison and for other colonists, including Thomas Jefferson. Billey married a lady named Henrietta, who worked as a launderer and they started a family.

As the constitution was being written, Madison recognized the hard fact that, if slavery were to be banned in the document, Southern states would never ratify it and the United States would never be formed. He agreed to a "twenty-year compromise" which was written to project 1808 as the year when the slave trade would be ended. Sadly, 1808 came and went and some importation of new slaves continued.

The War of 1812

America's involvement in the War of 1812 actually was initiated in the early 1800s. By 1803, England and Napoleon's France had fallen back into all-out war with one another. The American government tried to remain neutral and to continue to trade with both of the warring nations. Both Britain and France attempted to "blockade" the movement of trade products into the ports of their enemy. American ships which tried to "run the blockades" to transport their product loads were often intercepted.

The British Navy was a harsh employer and many British sailors tried to desert their ships, leaving the British ships short of experienced seamen. Consequently, British ships would frequently stop American merchant ships and would "impress", meaning kidnap, American sailors to work on their warships. Several thousand American sailors were impressed with the English navy during these years. The American government had to find a way to respond to the aggression.

The U.S. ship Chesapeake was stopped by the British ship H.M.S. Leopard. The two vessels were within American territorial waters. The British attempted to impress a number of American sailors. They also took custody of four Americans, whom they believed had committed crimes against Britain and whom they eventually executed. The Americans resisted. The Leopard then fired cannons at the Chesapeake. Following this incident, President Jefferson continued to abstain from military action, continuing his favored policy of neutrality and focusing on marketing tactics to deter the warring nations from aggression against Americans.

The British continued their practices of impressment and restrictive trade policies. Jefferson continued to rely on a series of legislative acts creating embargoes, tariffs, etc. In 1807 he banned all exports and imports from both Britain and France. This had the unfortunate side effect of creating a serious recession in the American economy. Still, Jefferson resisted any movement toward a serious military response.

The American economy continued to pay a heavy price, due to trade restrictions brought about by the war between France and Britain. Conditions deteriorated to the point that Americans began to favor an American military response.

War was finally declared on June 18th, 1812. Congress was deeply divided on the issue. James Madison had been elected America's fourth President. Madison listed impressment as one of the justifications for America's declaration of war. Americans demanded freedom from interference with American merchant ships. Congress resisted efforts to raise large sums of money to finance the war. Americans enjoyed few meaningful successes in the conflict. The British burned the new American capitol building, located by then in Washington D.C., in 1814.

Not many good things happened as a result of the war, but American production of goods and services did begin to thrive. The Industrial Revolution was continuing to impact the nation's growth and development. Unfortunately, increasing market demands also increased the need, in Southern states, for cheap slave labor. Industrialization also illuminated the growing problems associated with urban poverty, which still plague our country today.

The English had, at that time, substantial holdings along the eastern coast of today's Canada. As that was the area most convenient for American naval forces to attack, much of the war was fought along that coastline. The English had developed a very profitable timber trade in Canada and it is likely Americans considered the possibility of invading and acquiring that land. Later in the war, more of the naval conflict was carried out farther into the mid-Atlantic ocean and also focused on American territories in the area of the Gulf of Mexico.

The War of 1812, for the Americans, began with an American attempt, with several forces, to invade British territories at Detroit, Montreal and Niagara. The invasion was not well planned, American troops weren't well trained and the operation was not successful. British troops were supported by American Indians led by the great Indian leader **Tecumseh**, including warriors from the **Shawnee**, the **Delaware** and other native American volunteers. Indian aggression toward the Americans was undoubtedly founded in their resentment of American expansion into their homelands.

The forces under British **General Sir Isaac Brock**, aided by several Indian forces, captured America's Detroit in August of 1812. American invasions of other Canadian locations either failed or were simply canceled. A late attempt, by American **General James Winchester**, to regain control of Detroit, ended badly, with Winchester surrendering his army to the English and Indian forces.

America's victories during the early part of the War of 1812 were mostly victories by the new Navy, on the open Atlantic. The **USS Constitution** sank the HMS (British) vessel Guerriere. **Captain Stephen Decatur's USS United States** captured the HMS Macedonian. Then, the Constitution defeated HMS Java. A group of British ships, on Lake Erie, was defeated soundly by American ships led by **Commodore Oliver Hazard Perry**. Perry's victory ended British naval dominance in the area.

Late in 1812, American forces under **Major General William Henry Harrison**, (a future American President), began to establish some American victories. Harrison's army troops, joined by troops from Kentucky, took back Detroit. British troops, losing naval support after their defeat by Perry, had little hope of holding onto Detroit. Soon after, Harrison took his forces to the **Battle of the Thames**, at which time he eradicated the alliance between the Indians and the British.

The Battle of Thames took place on October 5ᵗʰ, 1813, along the Thames river, located in Southwestern Ontario. The Americans brought 3,500 soldiers. The British brought 800 English troops who were joined by five hundred Indians, led by the great Indian leader and warrior, **Tecumseh**. The Americans had already captured, the day before, a large store of English armaments and food supplies. The English were living on only a fraction of normal food rations and morale was very poor among their troops. English cannoneers got off only one shot before fleeing. The British were totally defeated and many of their troops fled the battlefield. The Indians fought with courage and determination but had no chance of victory. The great warrior, Tecumseh, sadly, died on the field.

A British force, in August of 1814, led by **General Robert Ross**, campaigned through Maryland. Ross defeated the Maryland militia at the **Battle of Bladensburg**. Ross's troops went on to capture and burn government buildings in Washington, D.C., including the new White House. General Ross was later killed in a failed attempt, with British naval support, to occupy the city of Baltimore. During that same battle, Americans at Fort McHenry fought off a fleet of British ships. It was a battle that was furious in intensity and lasted 25 hours. It was this battle, **Fort McHenry**, near Baltimore, that inspired the writing of our American national anthem, by **Francis Scott Key**.

After the failure at Baltimore, the British re-focused their attention on America's Gulf Coast. America's **Andrew Jackson**, another future President, won a stunning victory against the British in the **Battle of New Orleans**. It was January 8ᵗʰ, 1815. Unknown to Andrew Jackson, the war had actually, formally, ended on December 24ᵗʰ, 1814, with the signing of the **Treaty of Ghent**. President Madison ratified the treaty in February and the **War of 1812** was officially over.

The war took the lives of 15,000 Americans. The treaty assured the Americans that the British would stop impeding American merchant ships and the British would stop supporting Indian aggression.

The Indians probably took the worst beating in the War of 1812. They lost their alliances with the French and the British. Tecumseh was killed. They had dreamed of a British victory, which might have improved their standing in America. Their hope was that the British would win and would formally recognize the Indian nations, protecting their sovereignty. The loss of British support, British money and British weapons eliminated the resources Indians needed to defend their homelands and attack American forces. American expansionism was inevitable.

Tecumseh

Shawnee Tribal Chief

Leader of Indian Nations

Chief Tecumseh

A Poem by Chief Tecumseh

Live Your Life

So live your life that the fear of death can never enter your heart.

Trouble no one about their religion.

Respect others in the view, and demand that they respect yours.

Love your life, perfect your life, beautify all things in your life.

Seek to make your life long and its purpose in the service of your people.

Prepare a noble death song for the day when you go over the great divide.

Always give a word or a sign of salute when meeting or passing a friend, even a stranger, when in a lonely place.

Show respect to all people, and grovel to none.

When you arise in the morning, give thanks for the food and the joy of living. If you see no reason for giving thanks, the fault lies only in yourself.

Abuse no one and no thing, for abuse turns the wise ones to fools and robs the spirit of its vision.

When it comes your time to die, be not like those whose hearts are filled with the fear of death, so that when their time comes, they weep and pray for a little more time to live their lives over again in a different way.

Sing your death song and die like a hero going home.

Shawnee Tribal Chieftain Tecumseh

1768 - 1813

Shawnee Chief Puckeshinwa and his wife **Methoataske** were blessed with a son in 1768. They named him **Tecumseh**, which name means "shooting star" or "blazing comet". They lived in the Ohio Valley. Chief Puckeshinwa was killed, in 1774, in the **Battle of Point Pleasant**, part of **Lord Dunsmore's War**. **Lord Dunsmore's War** was a conflict between the Virginia colony and the Mingo and Shawnee American Indian nations. Tecumseh's mother, Methoataske, on the death of Puckeshinwa, left for the Missouri territory, following much of the tribe. She left Tecumseh and his siblings to be raised by Tecumapease, an older sister.

Tecumseh learned the history and structure of his Shawnee tribal culture from Tecumapease and an older brother, Cheeseekau. Cheeseekau also groomed Tecumseh to be a Shawnee warrior. As he matured, Tecumseh came to hate the white Americans, whom he had seen occupying his homelands and whom he knew to have committed awful atrocities against the Indians. Historians note that he also was appalled by the brutal activities some Native Americans visited on their enemies. Tecumseh, after seeing a white man burn out the stake, warned his allies against such brutal practices. He was clearly opposed to barbaric behaviors, whether practiced by the white man or by his own people.

Tecumseh, joined by his older brother Cheeseekau, along with a small gathering of Shawnee warriors, carried out many raids on white settlers. They went to the Tennessee territory, where they joined with **Cherokee Chickamauga** warriors to continue their raids. Cheeseekau died in a skirmish, leaving Tecumseh to lead the Shawnee warriors. They followed him to Ohio, where they assisted **Chief Bluejacket**, another Shawnee war Chieftain. They pursued resistance to the U.S. Army. Tecumseh, in 1791, under Bluejacket's leadership, led a war party against the Americans. The U.S. army, under **General Arthur St. Clair**, was overwhelmed and completely defeated. It was a bloody battle and 925 of 1000 American troops were killed in the action. The gory conflict became known as the **Battle of Wabash**. The luck of the Native Americans was soon to wear out, though and the joined forces of Indians were defeated, in 1791, by **General Anthony Wayne's** forces at the **Battle of Fallen Timbers**. The defeat was played out on the Maumee River in Ohio.

Following their defeat at the Maumee River, the Indian nations signed, having little choice, the **Treaty of Greenville**. The treaty mandated that the natives forfeit most of their land in the new Northwest Territory. Tecumseh, however, refused to sign. He believed in the Native American philosophy that all of the land was owned, in joint, by all of the Indian Nations. He didn't believe it was possible to simply sign it away. As it turned out, the Indians pretty much abided by the Treaty of Greenville, but the white settlers and the American government did not.

Tecumseh then settled in the Ohio territory, where he became, during the early 1800s, a well-known and highly respected leader and war chief. He was recognized as an effective orator and a good ambassador for his people. Tecumseh's younger brother, Lalawethika, in 1805, deeply under the influence of alcohol, experienced a "vision". It stimulated Lalawethika to believe he was destined to lead the Indians in a consolidated effort to regain their property and protect their culture. He became, under the new name Tenskwatawa, known as **"The Prophet"**.

"The Prophet" accurately, in 1806, somehow predicted a solar eclipse. He gained many new followers from several Indian tribes. Two years later, The Prophet and Tecumseh re-located their burgeoning tribal confederation to the Indiana territory, in close proximity to the Wabash and the Tippecanoe rivers. The settlement was to be known as "Prophetstown".

Tecumseh traveled incessantly, mostly on foot, all around the Western and Northern territories, attempting to bring the major tribal nations together. He believed the only possible way to stop the invasion of white settlers and to protect their homelands, was for all of the Indian nations to join together to consolidate their forces. His speeches were powerful in his quest to unite all of his people. He began to successfully consolidate a confederation of tribes.

Tecumseh, in 1811, made his feelings clear about the importance of bringing all Indians together to resist the onslaught of white settlers. He said "Where today are the **Pequot**? Where are the **Narragansett**, the **Mahican** and the **Pokanoket**? Will we let ourselves be destroyed in our turn without a struggle? Give up our homes? Our country bequeathed to us by the Great Spirit? The graves of our dead and everything that is dear and sacred to us? I know you will cry with me "Never! Never!"

The Indiana Governor, a future American President, **William Henry Harrison**, led American forces to march against Prophetstown. It was 1811. His objective was, reportedly, to destroy the Indian village. Tecumseh, at the time, was far away, pursuing his efforts to unite the tribes. Tecumseh, knowing the Indians weren't yet strong enough, warned his brother to evade conflicts until the confederation was properly united and prepared. The Prophet, unfortunately, did not take Tecumseh's wise guidance. He broke a sketchy ceasefire and attacked Harrison's forces. The ensuing engagement is known as **The Battle of Tippecanoe**. The army, after a bloody two-hour engagement, summarily defeated the Indians. The Indians who were able to do so fled the area. Harrison's troops ransacked and burned what was left of the village. Tecumseh, on his return several months later, learned that the village was gone and the tribal coalition, for which he had worked so hard for so long, was destroyed. William Henry Harrison gained the nickname **"Tippecanoe"** which glamorized him for his eventual Presidential campaign.

The **War of 1812** began soon after the destruction of Prophetstown. Tecumseh gathered the remaining force of tribal warriors, who followed him to join the British military. The British were still occupying parts of the Northwest territory and were fighting to protect their assets. They, with the critical support of Tecumseh and his warriors, defeated the American troops at the **Siege of Detroit**.

Tecumseh, after the fall of Detroit to the British, soon joined the forces of British **Major-General Henry Proctor** as they invaded the Ohio territory. The British, with Tecumseh's support, engaged in conflicts and skirmishes with the American troops led by William Henry Harrison. Harrison's command forced the British to retreat back into Canada. Tecumseh, reluctantly, led his warriors to join in the British flight from the Americans. They were pursued to Moraviantown, Ontario, where a final engagement, the **Battle of the Thames**, took place on October 5, 1813. The Americans won decisively. Tecumseh was killed on the battlefield. The loss marked the beginning of the consolidation of the **Northwest Territory**, all falling under the control of the American government.

Tecumseh's death meant the final failure of his noble effort to create a confederation of all the Indian nations and the last hope of the Indians to protect themselves and their homelands. In the years following the death of Tecumseh, most Native Americans soon abandoned their homelands and were moved to **reservations**.

Tecumseh was a highly skilled orator, politician and tribal leader. A favorite quote describing Tecumseh was offered by British General Isaac Brock, who knew him well. Brock said of Tecumseh, "A more sagacious or gallant warrior does not, I believe, exist."

Recommended is a biography by Allen W. Eckert entitled "A Sorrow in our Heart . . . the Life of Tecumseh". The historical novel "Panther in the Sky", by James Alexander Thom is also a very entertaining and educational read.

America in the 1810's

Construction of the **Cumberland Road** was finally started, five years after having been authorized by President Thomas Jefferson, in 1806. Work began in May of 1811, building a road that followed the path of what had been known as **Braddock's Road**. George Washington's troops used Braddock's Road in 1754. The Cumberland Road, which became The **National Road**, the first federal highway, was 128 miles long, beginning in Cumberland, Maryland and finishing in Wheeling, West Virginia. It would eventually extend to Vandalia, Illinois and is now known as U.S. Rt. 40. The Cumberland Road made movement from the east through the Allegheny Mountains much easier, further encouraging American settlements to the west.

The Era of Good Feelings

The period just before and just after the War of 1812 has been called **"The Era of Good Feelings"**. The Federalist party of Alexander Hamilton had fallen into disfavor. They posted a candidate for the presidential election in 1816, who was badly beaten and who became their final presidential candidate. The 1818 Congressional election saw a large victory for Democratic-Republicans, the party of Thomas Jefferson. Remember, Jefferson opposed "big government". Jefferson's party took control of the U.S. Congress, winning 85 percent of all seats. The dominance of this single party was supposed to be the foundation for the "Era of Good Feelings". The basis for the phrase was the opinion that things would be relatively stress-free since one party had substantial political control.

In reality, the Democratic-Republicans were deeply divided within their party. James Madison was followed in the Presidency, in 1818, by James Monroe, who would serve two terms. The party of Jefferson was transitioning and, in many ways, more nearly approximated the policies of Hamilton, leaning toward larger government controls. It may have been the "Era of Good Feelings", but, in reality, much political tension persisted.

The Federalist Party became a non-entity, more or less irrelevant. The Democratic-Republicans, being basically the only functioning party, pursued the significant new economic policies initiated by James Madison. They were policies that Federalist Hamilton would most likely have approved. The changes were to be known as the **"American System"**. The movement was intended to nurture the new nation's critical economic development. There were three basic components of the American System. They included the creation and development of a national bank, one of Hamilton's most important objectives. The Democratic-Republicans were moving toward the old Federalist policies. The American System also provided for protective tariffs designed to boost American businesses and manufacturers. The third component of the American System focused on internal, domestic improvements funded by the federal government.

The comfort of the Era of Good Feelings lasted only a few years. Moving into the 1820s and 1830s, a new pattern for American politics emerged. Political parties became the signature components of the system and coalitions of various groups folded into one party or the other. Allegiance to specific personalities began to fade and allegiance to parties began to drive the political environment.

The Federalists were no longer in the picture. The Democratic-Republican party was in conflict within itself. Future President **Martin Van Buren** rose to a leadership role in a movement to create a new Democrat party, separate from the old Democratic-Republicans. A new two-party system emerged and has survived to our modern times. The Era of Good Feelings passed and has never returned. Modern politics in America are marked by intensely hard feelings and little cooperation between parties. George Washington had warned against a party system. He believed it would lead to paralyzing divisiveness and would prevent positive progress in Congress. Perhaps it would have been smart to have listened to him.

The Creek Indian Wars

The Battle of Horseshoe Bend

Many Native Americans sided with the British during the **War of 1812**. The Indians hoped that a British victory would mean a cessation of the persistent advances of the white settlers. Future **President Andrew Jackson** had a history of conflict with the natives. He led a militia, during the War, in pursuit of a band of **Creek Indians** who were known as **"Red Sticks"**, because they carried bright red war clubs. The Creeks were believers in the teachings of the great **Shawnee Chief, Tecumseh**.

The Red Sticks attacked **Fort Mims**, in the Mississippi Territory, on August 30, 1813. Their attack became a bloody massacre and some 400 people were slain, including women, children and militiamen. Future President **Andrew Jackson** responded a few months later in March of 1814. Jackson, commanding a force of more than 3000 Tennessee regular militiamen and supported by bands of **Cherokee** and **Lower Creek** warriors, attacked Indians gathered in a horseshoe bend of the Tallapoosa River. It was to be known as The **Battle of Horseshoe Bend** or **The Battle of Tohopeka**. Approximately 1000 warriors of the Upper Creek and Red Stick tribes, led by **Chief Me-Na-Wa**, were slaughtered. The Indians were defeated and the **Creek Indian War** was over. The Creek nation was left with little choice but to sign a peace treaty. The treaty mandated that the Creek nation forfeit half of their known homeland, increasing property "owned" by the Americans by twenty-thousand acres of land. Andrew Jackson was later, in 1838, associated with the shameful forced re-location of 15,000 Native Americans that would go down in history as the **"Trail of Tears"**.

The 1810's . . . Continued

The year 1814 was a busy one in historical terms. The War of 1812 continued. On August 24, 1814, British troops, claiming retribution for having seen Canadian public buildings destroyed by American forces, occupied Washington, D.C. and burned the White House. Their attack forced the evacuation and flight of President John Madison. It would be three years before the next President, James Monroe, would be able to move back into a rebuilt White House.

U.S. naval forces, led by the **USS Ticonderoga**, were victorious in **The Battle of Lake Champlain**. Days later, overnight from September 13th to 14th, **Francis Scott Key** wrote the lyrics to our **Star Bangled Banner**. He was, at the time, aboard a British ship, where he was negotiating prisoner releases. Key was inspired by the sight of our flag, **"Old Glory"**, flying over **Fort McHenry**, lighted only by the glow from rockets. The fort, located at the mouth of the Patapsco River, which flowed into Baltimore harbor, was bombarded for 25 hours and our flag was flying still at the end of the siege, motivating Key to write the words to our national anthem.

The Battle of New Orleans

The War of 1812 was winding down. It was 1814 and American and British diplomats were meeting in Europe to create a truce. The British, however, having recently defeated Napoleon in Europe, were able to focus all of their forces on their conflict with the colonies. The Americans had repulsed British attacks at the **Battle of Baltimore** and at the **Battle of Plattsburgh**. Undeterred, the British planned an assault to seize the port of New Orleans, known as the Crescent City. If the British could take New Orleans, it would give them dominion over the mouth of the Mississippi River and they would control all trade into the American south. The **Treaty of Ghent** was signed on December 14, 1814, but news traveled slowly and participants in the war were not aware of the truce for several weeks. The war proceeded in those uninformed areas.

When **American Major General Andrew Jackson** was informed about the British plans to move to New Orleans, he proceeded immediately to New Orleans, where he began to form a defense. Jackson had been busy fighting the Creek Indians and commanding attacks designed to harass and impede British activities along America's Gulf Coast. Jackson was well known as **"Old Hickory",** based on his storied toughness. Andrew Jackson had been, for a time during the Revolution, a British prisoner of war and he harbored deep hostility for the Redcoats. He once told his wife "I owe to Britain a debt of retaliatory vengeance and, should our forces meet I trust I shall repay the debt".

Jackson knew he did not have the numbers among his regular militia to fight off the British. He needed to bulk up his forces dramatically. As word of the British approach reached him, Jackson declared Marshall Law around New Orleans. He ordered that all healthy men and every available weapon be gathered in the defensive effort.

Jackson was successful in bringing together a widely diverse lot of participants. He created a force of 4,500 troops, consisting of army regulars, militiamen, free black men, some representatives of the aristocrats of New Orleans, frontiersmen and **Choctaw Indians**. Overcoming his reluctance, Jackson even accepted the assistance offered by famous pirate **Jean Lafitte**. Lafitte had been managing a very successful and lucrative smuggling and privateering operation based in nearby Barataria Bay.

Pirate Jean Lafitte

The British, in the meantime, were bringing a much larger force, made up of approximately 8,000 regular British troops. They were commanded by **Lieutenant General Sir Edward Pakenham**. Pakenham was an experienced military veteran and was the brother-in-law of the Duke of Wellington. Pakenham had bivouacked (set up camp) several miles South of New Orleans.

Old Hickory, on December 23, 1814, commanded a surprise nighttime assault on the Redcoats. He then withdrew, under cover of darkness and retreated to the Rodriguez Canal. Jackson then gathered local slave laborers to expand the width of the canal. Dirt removed from the canal was used to build a high rampart, behind which Jackson's force could stand, to safely defend against British advances.

The completed defensive line extended more than a mile, forming a blockage that reached from the Mississippi River shoreline to the east, where it terminated at an impassable swamp. Old Hickory was quoted saying "Here we shall plant our stakes and not abandon them until we drive these red-coat rascals into the river or the swamp".

Lieutenant General Pakenham believed that the "dirty shirts", as they called the Americans, in spite of having built their fortifications, would quickly fold when faced with the overwhelming wave of British troops. He divided his troops into two forces. An opening skirmish was engaged on December 28 and was followed by a major duel between artillery forces on New Year's Day. Pakenham then planned an assault that would utilize two separate advances. One, the smaller, was ordered to seize an American artillery battery that rested on the west side of the Mississippi. Once captured, the Redcoats were to use the artillery to fire on American forces on the east bank of the river. Simultaneously, Pakenham would send his much larger force, 5,000 men, to charge directly at the American defensive line along the Rodriguez Canal. He expected to wipe out the American troops.

January 8, 2015, at sunrise, Pakenham launched his attack. British troops charged at the American line. Artillery barrages from both sides were massive. Jean Lafitte's band of pirates manned some of the big guns. British troops commanded by their **Colonel Robert Rennie** successfully overran a remote stand of Americans, who quickly retreated. Colonel Rennie was heard to shout "Hurrah, boys, the day is ours!", only moments before he was shot dead by a barrage of rifle fire from the American troops gathered beyond the canal. Seeing their commander shot down, his men panicked and attempted a chaotic retreat. Most died in a hail of grapeshot and musket balls.

Pakenham had expected early morning fog to offer cover for his advancing lines of troops. Unfortunately for the British, the morning sun very quickly burned off the fog. Redcoats were clearly seen on the field and made easy targets for the highly skilled American frontiersmen, accustomed to hunting in the forests. American cannon fire soon blasted big gaps into the British lines. Redcoats were peppered with American musket balls. The British troops were systematically picked off by the Americans and one British officer was later quoted saying the American rampart resembled "a row of fiery furnaces".

Pakenham's lines were shredded by American rifles and cannon barrages. He was determined to personally lead a group to the front lines and was soon killed in a hail of grapeshot. The British had lost most of their leadership, all dead or wounded and the entire force of Redcoats fell into a chaotic scramble. Pakenham's smaller force had, as directed, taken the American artillery stand on the west side of the Mississippi, but it was too little and too late to have any meaningful impact on the battle.

The British were fleeing the scene, as best they could and the battlefield was littered with the dead and the mortally wounded. Jackson's **Major Howell Tatum** wrote that the enemy casualties "were truly distressing. Some had their heads shot off, some their legs and arms. Some were laughing, some crying and there was every variety of sight and sound".

The Battle of New Orleans resulted in 2,000 British casualties. They lost seven colonels and three generals and it all happened in less than an hour. Andrew Jackson's diversified forces lost less than 100 men. Andrew Jackson was praised by another future President, James Monroe, who said "History records no example of so glorious a victory obtained with so little bloodshed on the part of the victorious". The British went on to attempt a naval assault on Fort St. Philip, but their opportunity to take New Orleans had been lost. They soon packed up their gear, boarded their ships and sailed away.

Andrew Jackson, "Old Hickory", was widely celebrated after the victory at the Battle of New Orleans. He was welcomed by a joyful public celebration as he re-entered New

Orleans, accompanied by local bands playing "Yankee Doodle". Newspapers regaled readers with stories of the battle, calling Jackson a "national savior". Jackson spoke to his troops, after the battle and praised their "undaunted courage". He went on to say "Natives of different states, acting together, for the first time . . . have reaped the fruits of an honorable union". Andrew Jackson would ride the wave of his new-found popularity into a victorious campaign to become, in 1829, the nation's seventh President.

The Second War with the Barbary Pirates

Back in 1805, Thomas Jefferson used the new American Navy to put a stop to privateering and piracy by the pirates of Tripoli. He wasn't able to completely put them out of business, but he was able to stop them from interfering with American merchant ships.

During the War of 1812 and increasingly after the end of the war, the pirates were once again busy. The cities of Algiers, Tunis and Tripoli (Algeria, Tunisia and Libya) were supporting the pirates, who were selling their stolen goods into the economies of those nations. Great Britain also made use of the pirates, by supporting their attacks on American shipping during the War of 1812.

President James Madison was weary of the ongoing threat to America's merchant ships. In February of 1815, Madison asked Congress to declare war against the pirating nations. Congressional leaders convinced him that a declaration of war would be unnecessary and persuaded him to rely on legislation to gain authority to contend with the pirates. Legislators approved the creation of a naval squadron that would fall under the command of American naval **Commodore Stephen Decatur**. The American flotilla included ten warships. There were two sloops-of-war, two schooners, three brigs and three frigates.

The first military encounter occurred on June 17, 1815. Commodore Decatur's ships intercepted an Algerian Navy frigate, the Meshuda, commanded by their Admiral Hamidou. Contact was made off the Coast of Spain. The brief conflict, known now as the **Battle of Cape Gata**, proved that the forty-six guns on the Algerian frigate were easily dominated by the U.S. Navy. The Meshuda turned and ran, attempting to escape to safe ports. The American ships outran and captured the Meshuda and took four hundred and six prisoners. Thirty Algerian sailors died and so did Admiral Hamidou. The U.S. lost only ten sailors.

Only two days later, Commodore Decatur's flotilla, still sailing toward Algiers, observed the Algerian brig Estedio. The Estedio attempted to flee, hoping to find protection in shoals off the Coast of Spain. The Americans sailed four of their smaller vessels, USS Epervier, USS Spark, USS Torch and USS Spitfire, into the shallower waters, in pursuit of the Estedio. A brief battle, now known as the **Battle of Cape Palos**, was engaged. The Estedio soon surrendered their flag and gave up eighty sailors. Twenty-three Algerian sailors died. The Americans lost no one in the battle.

It quickly became clear that the Algerian Navy was not capable of fending off the American vessels. Decatur had secured the two captured Algerian vessels in Spanish ports and then continued his journey to Algiers, where he planned to gain a treaty beneficial to American trade.

Omar Agha was the Dey (ruler) of Algiers. On July 3, 1815, the Dey was brought aboard the USS Guerriere to negotiate terms with Decatur. Omar Agha was allowed to regain possession of the ships that the Americans had captured and almost 500 Algerian prisoners were returned home. The Americans, in exchange, got back ten prisoners and were paid $10,000. The treaty also guaranteed America all shipping rights in the Mediterranean and assured that "tributes" would no longer be demanded of American ships.

In today's world, Somalian pirates continue to operate in the Indian Ocean and the Arabian Sea. Their attacks have decreased in recent years. When they are able to successfully "hi-jack" a vessel, they often hold it for ransom.

James Monroe

America's Fifth President

James Monroe's parents were **Spence Monroe** and **Elizabeth Jones Monroe**. They owned a 600-acre farm property in Virginia and were well-to-do citizens. James was born on April 28, 1758. He was attending, beginning at age 16, the College of William and Mary, when the American Revolution was beginning. James left school, at the age of 22, to join the American forces in their fight for independence.

When George Washington's troops crossed the Delaware, for the **Battle of Trenton**, James Monroe was there, serving as an army lieutenant. A nearly mortal wound in his shoulder caused him to be carried from the battlefield. He was rewarded for his courage, after recovering, with a promotion to the rank of captain. He would go on to participate in the **Battles of Brandywine** and **Germantown** and would ultimately be further promoted to the rank of major. Monroe was with Washington, serving under **General Alexander**, enduring the intense suffering of the winter at **Valley Forge**. At the **Battle of Monmouth**, Monroe served General Washington as a scout.

Following the end of the revolution, Monroe resigned his military commission and studied the law under the tutelage of Thomas Jefferson, who was, at the time, governor of Virginia. The two became close friends and Jefferson was a mentor for Monroe for decades to come. Monroe served in the U.S. Congress from 1783 to 1786 when the nation was still guided by the first constitution, the Articles of Confederation. He became known for his fight to assure the right of the U.S. to navigate and trade along the Mississippi River, controlled at the time by Spain.

James, at age 27, married 17-year-old **Elizabeth Kortright**. The two would have two daughters, Eliza and Maria and lost a son who died in his infancy. As a young woman, her mother, Elizabeth suffered from poor health and Eliza often served as a hostess at political events. Her sister Maria, in 1820, became the first woman to be married in the "President's House", which was what the White House was called at the time.

Elizabeth Monroe was the victim of a persistent "malady" which left her frequently in poor health. While James was President, she often spent long periods away, visiting her daughters, who were by then married. Elizabeth is perhaps best remembered for her voyage to France during the French **"Reign of Terror"**. She became a supporter of the wife of the **Marquis de Lafayette**, who was being held in prison and was likely to be guillotined. Elizabeth, accompanied only by personal servants, went by carriage ride to the prison. Her support is widely believed to be the reason that Lafayette's wife was soon released. The Monroes were very popular in France and Elizabeth became known affectionately as "la belle Americaine". Later, when she had an opportunity to re-decorate the White House, Elizabeth brought many objects over from France. She always, after returning from Paris, which she loved, insisted on dressing in French fashions and on the use of French etiquette at formal gatherings.

Monroe, in 1786, resigned from Congress and returned to Virginia, where he established a law practice. He served as a member of the House of Delegates in Virginia in 1787 and 1788. He was elected to the U.S. Senate in 1790, where he was known as an opponent of the administration of President Washington. Washington, however, recognized Monroe's potential and selected him to be Minister to France in 1794. Monroe was very sympathetic to the cause of the French Revolution, which made him an opponent of Alexander Hamilton's Federalist party. The Federalists believed the U.S. should stay clear of French-English conflicts.

While in France, Monroe became involved in political intrigue. He misled the French about the likelihood of America's passage of **Jay's Treaty**. He also cast doubt on the survival of the Washington administration. Washington began to doubt his effectiveness and had him recalled in 1796. John Jay's treaty was, in fact, passed. The French were not happy to see the agreement made between America and their enemy, Great Britain. Jay's treaty was intended to calm residual tensions which persisted between the U.S. and the British after the revolution. It held little benefit for the U.S. but did solidify peaceful conditions between the two nations.

After he was recalled from France, Monroe was elected governor of Virginia and served in that office from 1799 to 1802.

In 1800, Spain, through the **Treaty of San Ildefonso**, returned Louisiana to the French. The French restricted American trade coming down the Mississippi and Americans were concerned about the French presence. President Jefferson sent Monroe to France to assist in negotiations to attempt to purchase the territory located around the mouth of the Mississippi. Monroe was also directed to assist American **Charles Pinckney** in an effort to get Spain to release territory in Florida to the U.S.

Monroe found, on arriving in Paris in 1803, that American **Robert Livingston** had already made good progress in negotiating with Napoleon. When they realized Napoleon was open to selling the entire Louisiana Territory, an enormous tract of land that would double the size of the U.S., they quickly decided to exceed the authority they'd been granted. They signed a treaty with Napoleon and the **Louisiana Purchase** was accomplished. Monroe left Paris and traveled to Madrid, Spain, where he worked with Charles Pinckney to negotiate clear boundaries for the Louisiana purchase and to continue efforts to gain Florida from Spain. Little was accomplished in Madrid and Monroe was sent to London in 1805. In London, he worked to try to end the practice of English seizures of American merchant vessels and impressment of American sailors. The problem would persist until the War of 1812.

Back in America, Monroe was once again elected to the House of Delegates in Virginia and then was once more elected Governor of Virginia. He gave up the position in 1811 to serve as **Secretary of State** under President James Madison. He held this challenging responsibility through the **War of 1812**. Following the capture of Washington, D.C., by the British, in 1814, Monroe was appointed **Secretary of War** and discharged that responsibility while still being Secretary of State.

James Monroe was elected President in 1816, soundly defeating the Federalist candidate, Rufus King. He was easily re-elected in 1820, as the Federalist party was essentially dying. He received all but one of the electoral votes. His administration, because of the dominance of his party at the time and the prosperous times in America, became associated with the period known as the **Era of Good Feelings**. The Monroe years were marked by the **First Seminole War** in 1817, the acquisition of Florida from Spain in 1819, the **Missouri Compromise** in 1820 and the seminal **Monroe Doctrine**. The Monroe Doctrine originally recognized as **"The Principles of President Monroe"**, maintained a powerful influence on American foreign policy far into the future. The Monroe Doctrine essentially warned European nations that America would not tolerate further "colonization" or invasive adventures into the western hemisphere

James Monroe, after his second Presidential term ended, returned to his estate, **Monroe Hill**, which lies in Northern Virginia and Highland, located near Jefferson's Monticello. He also served the University of Virginia as a regent and he participated in an 1829 convention designed to amend their state constitution. Monroe had spent much money during his many political missions and had necessarily neglected his personal affairs. He was deeply in debt and he went to the U.S. Congress three different times to plead for relief.

James Monroe, like Presidents Thomas Jefferson and Jefferson's old friend John Adams, died on the fourth of July. Jefferson and Adams, incredibly, passed away on the very same day, in 1826. Monroe left this world five years later, in 1831, one year after his wife, Elizabeth, had died.

James Monroe and Slavery

The United States was still a very young nation during the Monroe administration. The institution of slavery had been a source of great tension during the building of our constitution. It was, if anything, becoming the source of a greater and greater conflict between "slave states" and "abolition states".

In 1818, the **Missouri Territory** was attempting to join the union. Slavery had been forbidden in the North. Southern states insisted on defending it. The North wanted Missouri absorbed as a "free state", allowing no slavery. The South, of course, wanted Missouri to be a "slave state". Eventually, an agreement was finalized which admitted Missouri as a slave state, while Maine was simultaneously admitted as a free state, hoping to mollify both forces. The agreement came to be known as the **Missouri Compromise**. It also banned slavery in all of the Louisiana Territory above a specific geographical line.

James Monroe's parents owned slaves. Both of his parents had died by the time he reached the age of 16 and James inherited the property, including the slaves. The census of 1810 records a list of 49 slaves who were living on Monroe's plantation. The slaves practiced numerous roles and kept the plantation working during long absences of Monroe. They served as cooks, livestock caretakers, blacksmiths, household workers and field hands. It should be assumed, that, as with other plantations, very young children were used as laborers, too.

A **slave rebellion** was attempted, led by a slave named Gabriel, during Monroe's tenure as Governor of Virginia. Gabriel had inspired around 150 other slaves to join his attempt to escape their condition. Two slaves informed their owner of the plans and Monroe, on hearing about them ordered up the militia to counter the rebellion. The uprising was quickly quelled. Militiamen spent a few days invading the quarters of slaves all around the Richmond area, terrifying the residents. When it was all over, 72 slaves were prosecuted. Eight were taken to New Orleans, where they were sold. In the slave culture, it was believed that the further "South" they were sent, the worse their quality of life would be. Life was extremely hard for slaves who had to work cotton fields in the deep South. Twenty-six of the slaves, convicted of participating in the rebellion, were executed.

We know that, when Monroe was President, he brought along several of his female slaves to work in the Presidential home. It is believed they worked as cooks, valets, housekeepers and personal servants to the President's family and their guests. After the White House was finished and the Monroes moved in, records show that there were expenses (for shoes and for medical care) for slave women named "Sucky", "Eve" and "Betsey". The financial records also show expenses, for clothing and shoes, for four male slaves, "Daniel", "Tom", "Peter" and "Hartford".

As his career matured, his writings and his behaviors indicated that he developed serious concerns about the institution of slavery and its impact on the union. Monroe was a **"nationalist"**, meaning his greatest interest was in protecting the union. Slavery was a constant irritation and a source of endless tensions between the states in the North and the states in the South and a source of inflammatory divisions between people, often in the same family, who did or did not support slavery. Monroe came to believe that, one way or another, slavery would ultimately have to be abolished. He struggled, as did many others, with arriving at a practical way to eradicate the problem.

There were many complex issues at hand. How would the largely illiterate millions of slaves survive, if freed? Would the process be "all at once" or some form of gradual plan? Would slave owners have to be reimbursed for the loss of their valuable properties, the slaves? How would the employment market be impacted? These questions would continue to plague the American landscape for many years yet to come.

Many Americans, while believing in the abolition of slavery, still did not accept the idea that black people and white people could live together in harmony. Monroe seems to have been one of them. He appears to have reached a point at which he believed the best solution to the "slave problem" would be a gradual transition to freedom, probably some compensation to slave owners and possible "**colonization**" back to Africa.

Monroe knew that the idea of colonizing the slave population back to Africa could not work unless the practice of importing slaves was banned. He worked with the British to enact a policy that declared all slave trade to be an "act of piracy", thereby criminalizing any further trafficking. Unfortunately, the American Senate refused to approve the policy. Monroe continued to work with the **"American Colonization Society"**, (ACS), in their efforts to arrange a process for removing black slaves from America. Their work resulted in the establishment of a new settlement to be located on the western shores of Africa. The settlement was christened **"Liberia"**. The capital city of Liberia was to be known as **"Monrovia"**, in honor of James Monroe. Haiti was the world's first "black republic" and Liberia became the second. The colonization project didn't work out, of course, but Liberia survived as a free nation.

Monroe, later in life, was in possession of 60 to 70 enslaved black people. In spite of his personal philosophy, which recognized the unsustainability of the evil, shameful institution, Monroe made no moves to free his own slaves. He could not overcome his priority of maintaining a profitable business and his business was very dependent on the free labor provided by his enslaved possessions. He made no attempt to re-locate any of his slaves to Liberia. When Monroe died, in 1831, he left documents emancipating only one slave. All of his property was divided between his two daughters, including the slaves. The single slave he freed was Peter Marks, for whom he also recommended employment.

The First Seminole War

The United States was in the middle of the **War of 1812**. A band of **Lower Creek** natives, known by their **Muskogean** language, had migrated, back in the 1700s, to North Florida. That tribe became known as the **"Seminole"**, which word meant "separatist". Florida, at the time, was owned by Spain. American settlers to the north, in Georgia, coveted the rich lands occupied by the **Creek (Seminole band) Indians**. Numerous violent incidents inflamed relations between the Seminole and the United States.

The Seminoles were known to harbor and offer refuge to runaway slaves. U.S. authorities executed incursions into Seminole lands in attempts to re-capture the runaways. The Seminole natives boldly resisted American interference in their homeland. Their resistance ignited the **First Seminole War**.

Major General Andrew Jackson, in 1818, was ordered to march three thousand American troops to North Florida. His objective was to punish and subdue the Seminole. General Jackson wiped out several Seminole villages. He had two British traders executed for encouraging the Seminole in their resistance. Jackson also captured the Spanish fort in Pensacola, Florida and unseated the Spanish government at that location. He did not, however, successfully subdue the Seminole natives. As a result, two additional Seminole wars would be fought in the coming decades. Eventually, the homelands of the Seminole would be confiscated by the U.S. and the land distributed for white settlers to occupy.

Andrew Jackson was the source of an enormous amount of native suffering. Long after the First Seminole War, Jackson would authorize the lethal re-location of the **Cherokee Nation**, which would become known, infamously, as the **Trail of Tears**.

The Missouri Compromise

Residents of the Missouri Territory hoped to be added to the union as the first state west of the Mississippi River. Most Missouri citizens were in favor of allowing slavery in Missouri, which vastly complicated their admission. America was deeply divided between those supporting the institution of slavery and those who were passionately opposed. The spirit of abolitionism was growing rapidly in the North.

There was, at the time, a rough balance between the two factions. Anti-slavery citizens were opposed to bringing Missouri in as a slave state, fearing that it would upset the delicate balance between the pro and the con. Southerners, dependent on slave labor to support their agricultural economy, insisted Missouri should be allowed, as had the original 13 states, to make their own choice about the status of slavery.

The debates in the House and the Senate were lengthy and passionate. New York **Representative Tallmadge** proposed that an amendment be attached to the original statehood bill that was being considered. His amendment would provide for the future end of slavery in Missouri and would eventually free the slaves who were there at that time. The **Tallmadge Amendment** passed in the House. The Senate, though, had exactly the same number of pro-slavery and anti-slavery Senators. The pro-slavery Senators were able to block the Tallmadge Amendment. The House would not pass the original statehood bill without the Amendment. It was a stalemate.

Missouri Territory once again applied for statehood in the latter part of 1819. **Henry Clay** was the **Speaker of the House**. He sought a way to achieve some sort of avenue, agreeable to all or at least agreeable to enough Congressmen and senators, to get Missouri admitted. Clay proposed legislation that would, simultaneously, bring both Missouri and Maine into the union. Missouri would be considered a slave state and Maine would be a free state. (Maine had been a part of Massachusetts). The legislation also provided that in all lands above a certain latitude, which basically ran along Missouri's southern border, slavery would be forever banned. The new state of Missouri was specifically excluded and would remain a slave state. Clay's bill did pass both the House and Senate and would be known as the **Missouri Compromise**. As a result, the states of Virginia, Kentucky and Missouri were left to be slave states. With those three exceptions, all new lands in the Louisiana Purchase which lay above the compromise latitude line were to remain free states, allowing no slavery.

President Monroe signed the Missouri Compromise into law on March 3, 1820. Only weeks later, **Thomas Jefferson** wrote "The Missouri question, like a fire bell in the night, awakened and filled me with terror. I considered it at once as the (death) knell of the Union. It (the slavery issue) is hushed for the moment, but this is a reprieve only, not a final sentence".

The Missouri Compromise was to stay in effect for three decades. It was ultimately repealed in 1854, with the passage of the **Kansas-Nebraska Act**. The Supreme Court decision, made in 1857, in the **Dred Scott** case, made it clear that the Missouri Compromise was unconstitutional. Each decision marked another significant step in the nation's path to civil war.

The Monroe Doctrine

During the 1820s, various global powers continued to try and gain power and influence in North America. Spain continued to test attempts to colonize parts of Central and South America. Russia was trying to spread its sphere of control into the Alaska territory. Great Britain continued to interfere where it could, hoping to retain its position as the prevailing world power.

John Quincy Adams, at the time, occupied the office of **Secretary of State**. He was very worried about the various threats to **American sovereignty** and resources. Adams did most of the heavy work in writing the policies that would become known as the **Monroe Doctrine**.

President Monroe gave his annual address to Congress in December 1823. In the text of that address, Monroe declared a new foreign policy to be practiced by the United States. The Monroe Doctrine did two primary things. One, it declared forbidden any European interference in any part of the Americas, North, South and Central. Two, it declared the United States to be neutral in any future European conflicts. It defined, essentially, a policy of **"isolationism"** for the U.S.

Some historians believe the U.S. would use the Monroe Doctrine to justify what some believe to be U.S. **"imperialism"** in Central and South America in the coming decades. The Monroe doctrine was also used as justification for declaring war against Spain, in 1898, leading to the **Spanish-American War**.

America's policy of isolationism would persist until the two world wars in the 1900s would force them to join other world powers to defend against global threats.

Henry Clay

Henry Clay was born in Virginia on April 12, 1777. He was the seventh of nine children born to **Reverend John Clay** and his wife, **Elizabeth Hudson** Clay. The family was one of modest means. Henry was only three years old when British Troops, during the **Revolution**, entered and ransacked their family home.

As a young man, Clay studied the law. He was admitted to the bar in 1797 and relocated to Lexington, Kentucky, which was, at the time, overwhelmed with lawsuits based on land ownership. New settlers were advancing rapidly and there were many issues with proper legal ownership. Clay was a good fit in his new environment, on the western frontier. He made friends easily and enjoyed drinking alcohol and gambling. Clay was an accomplished horseman and was known to have great affection for his animals.

In 1799, at the age of 22, Clay married the daughter of an affluent businessman, **Lucretia Hart**. They would be together for over 50 years and would be blessed with 11 children.

Henry Clay, in 1803, was elected to Kentucky's General Assembly. He tended to favor the **Jeffersonian** political mindset, resisting a big federal government and supporting state's rights. He was known for having been a strong opponent of the **"Alien and Sedition Acts of 1798"**, which put restrictions on foreign citizens and essentially censored publications criticizing the government.

Henry Clay was popular and his private law practice was very successful. His reputation grew quickly and he soon had many clients. Perhaps the most well-known of his clients was **Aaron Burr**. Burr had been accused of illegally, maybe even treasonously organizing an incursion into Spanish Territory, where it was believed he was hoping to create a personal empire, separate from the United States. When it was determined that Burr was guilty, Clay divorced himself from any further association with Burr. That same year, 1806, Clay, at the tender age of 29 years, was appointed to the U.S. Senate, representing the state of Kentucky.

Henry Clay went on to be elected to the U.S. House of Representatives in 1811. He eventually reached the pinnacle in the House, serving as Speaker of the House. Clay would eventually serve many terms in both the House and the Senate. He was known, early in his career, as a "war hawk", pressuring the government to respond aggressively to the practice Great Britain had of "conscripting" or "impressing" American seamen. America's pursuit of the **War of 1812** surely was partly in respond to Clay's influence. The War of 1812 turned out to be essential in cementing America's true independence from Britain. Clay saw the necessity for the war, but he was also key in negotiating, in Ghent, Belgium, the peace treaty that ended the war.

Clay went on to record one of the most impressive political histories of his time. He pushed for independence for several Latin American republics. He was involved in the negotiations that created the **Missouri Compromise**, which encouraged American growth to the west while stalling bloodshed over the inflammatory slavery issue. Clay's **Compromise Tariff Act of 1833** boosted the nation's economy while cooling tensions between President Jackson and the southern states. When California, in 1850, petitioned to join the Union, the slavery issue once again fired conflict. Henry Clay, once again, coordinated a compromise. His solution brought California into the Union as a "free state", while requiring no simultaneous addition of any "slave state". The compromise also settled a conflict over the boundary lines of Texas, addressed the **Fugitive Slave Act** and abolished the slave trade in the District of Columbia.

Henry Clay, over his many years of service, earned the honored nicknames of **"The Great Compromiser"** and **"The Great Pacificator"**. Abraham Lincoln was known to study his speeches and often included quotes from Clay in his work. Honest Abe called Clay "my beau ideal of a statesman".

Clay hoped, in 1824, to be a candidate in the Presidential election. Unfortunately, there were two other, somewhat stronger, candidates in **John Quincy Adams** and **Andrew "Old Hickory" Jackson**. The Adams-Jackson contest resulted in neither man collecting enough electoral votes. The election had to be decided in the House of Representatives. It was thought that Clay made a deal with Adams, giving Adams his support, in return for a key position in the Adams cabinet. Adams did indeed, when he won, appoint Clay Secretary of State. Much criticism, for "selling out for a job", came to Henry Clay. Andrew Jackson was very bitter about Clay's support for Adams and, going forward, was able to block many of Clay's legislative efforts. The contentious relationships culminated when Clay was challenged to a duel by Congressman **John Randolph**. The duel resulted in no injuries to either party.

Clay's antagonist andrew Jackson, was elected President in 1828. Henry Clay's political party, the **National Republican Party**, was falling apart. It would eventually, fall into the fold of the powerful **Whig Party**. Clay gave up politics and went back to his beloved Kentucky. He was not, however, able to stay away for long and returned to Washington in 1831, where he served in the Senate. He attempted, under the failing banner of the National Republicans, to follow Jackson as President. Jackson defeated him. Clay continued to hold his Senate seat and soon became the leader of the Whig Party. He would go on to unsuccessfully seek another nomination, in 1840, to be the Whig Party candidate for the Presidency. The party, instead, selected **William Henry Harrison**, with **John Tyler** as a running mate. It was a bitter pill for Clay to swallow. He retired from the Senate and once more returned to Kentucky.

The Whig Party brought Clay back one more time, nominating him to be their Presidential candidate in 1844. Their opponent, **James K. Polk**, believed in the "**Manifest Destiny**" of the United States and he wanted the U.S. to annex Texas. Clay feared annexation would cause a bloody war with Mexico and opposed it. He was defeated by Polk.

Henry Clay continued to be an influential player in American politics, almost to his dying day. Tuberculosis spelled the end for Clay and he died on June 29, 1852. He was the first American to lie in state in the rotunda of the nation's capitol and many American cities offered funeral ceremonies.

Henry Clay and Slavery

Henry Clay owned an estate called **"Ashland"** near Lexington, Kentucky. At times he had more than 50 slaves. Records show that he treated his slaves well, giving them unusual freedoms. He is known to have emancipated several slaves over the years. Clay wrote that slavery was "a curse on the master" and "a grievous wrong on the slave". He said that slaves were "rational beings". Still, he never conceded that black people were equal to white people and he never emancipated most of his slaves. His apparent kindness to his slaves, of course, can never excuse his participation in the shameful institution.

In his writings, he expresses support for "gradual emancipation". He was involved with groups who supported plans for "colonization", which meant transporting all black people to Liberia, a nation created primarily to receive emancipated slaves. Obviously, it was a morally flawed and completely impractical solution and never approached fruition.

Henry Clay was one of many landowners of his time who recognized the immorality and cruelty of slavery, but could never make himself suffer the economic penalties of giving up cheap slave labor.

The Erie Canal

America was growing. There was no practical way to move people or goods from the East to the MidWest. There were no railroads. Stagecoach travel took weeks. New York **Governor Clinton DeWitt** promoted the idea of a waterway, a canal, that would carry traffic efficiently. The Governor obtained funding, seven million dollars, in 1817. Construction began.

The Erie Canal would not be completed until 1825. The project was so enormous in scale that many doubted it could be completed and it was sometimes called **"Clinton's Folly"**. In reality, it would become a huge asset for the nation. The completed canal was forty feet wide and four feet deep. It extended for 363 miles, starting at the Atlantic Ocean, passing through the Hudson River and flowing all the way to the Great Lakes. It terminated in Buffalo, New York, where the Niagara River meets Lake Erie. The cost of transporting goods was reduced by 90% and America's expansion, in that part of the country, became far easier.

The Erie Canal quickly became extremely popular and it was necessary, periodically to widen and deepen it. The great success of the canal soon stimulated the creation of "feeder canals". In 1903, New York added the much larger New York State Barge Canal. Eventually, the canal network included the Erie Canal, which connected the Hudson River and Lake Erie, the Cayuga-Seneca Canal, connecting Seneca Lake to Cayuga Lake, the Oswego Canal, connecting the Erie Canal to Lake Ontario and the Champlain Canal, which connects the Hudson River to Lake Champlain. The entire system is now designated a historic district on the National Register of Historic Places.

The Stars and Stripes

Betsey Ross

Our national flag, the stars and stripes, was officially adopted by Congress on April 4, 1818. The thirteen red and white stripes are meant to represent the original thirteen colonies. At that time, there were twenty states in the union. Each state was represented by one star. Since that time, a star has been added for each additional state. The red color was chosen to symbolize hardiness and valor. The white color was chosen to represent purity and innocence. The blue color was intended to represent vigilance, perseverance and justice.

Of course, before the flag was "officially adopted", long after the successful American revolution, there was a prior history. The accuracy of some of the tales is open to question. However, the **"Betsey Ross story"** has been most frequently cited.

Betsey Ross was running a struggling upholstery business. Upholsterers of the time also often did sewing jobs. Betsey told her children and grandchildren that, in May of 1776, three members of the Continental Congress came to her home (and business) to ask her to sew the first national flag. Betsey was well known to George Washington, as her pew was next to his in the church they both attended. The three men who called on her were **George Washington**, **Robert Morris** (probably the richest man in the colonies) and **George Ross**. Colonel Ross was the uncle of Betsey's deceased husband. Washington was known to have visited her home often, both as a friend and for business purposes. Betsey had done embroidery on Washington's shirts and cuffs and he must have been impressed with her work.

As related in family records, Washington illustrated, for Betsey, a rough depiction of a flag that incorporated a six-point star. Betsey showed him a more efficient way to produce a five-pointed star, with a single cut of the scissors. Betsey went on to work on the flag and was finished by May or June of 1776. The new **Declaration of Independence** was delivered aloud, for the first time, in July of 1776, so it's likely the new flag was present for that occasion.

Betsey continued to work in her upholstery shop throughout the revolution and then for decades beyond. During the war, the British occupied her home, but she continued to work. Betsey lost two husbands to the war. When the Redcoats were out of her home, she sewed pouches used by the **Continental Army** to protect their gunpowder.

The Continental Congress, on June 14, 1777, hoping to stimulate national unity, adopted the flag with this resolution: "Resolved: That the flag of the United States be thirteen stripes, alternate red and white; that the union is thirteen stars, white in a blue field, representing a new constellation".

The United States won its independence and a new government was formed. The flag was then, once again, "officially adopted" by the U.S. Congress on April 4, 1818. A new star has been added with the addition of each new state to the union.

The 1810's . . . Continued

The decade of the 1810s was coming to an end. Most notably, in 1819, the **Tallmadge Amendment** was passed in the U.S. Congress. It banned slavery in the new state of Missouri and it became the first vote leading to what would become the **Missouri Compromise**. The compromise, engineered primarily by **Henry Clay**, would over-ride the Tallmadge Amendment, allowing slavery in Missouri, but banning it in Maine.

On February 22, 1819, **the Adams-Onis Treaty**, also known as the **Transcontinental Treaty**, was signed by the U.S. and by Spain. It gave possession of the Florida Territory to the United States. Colonies known then as East Florida and West Florida had remained loyal to the Crown during the revolution. West Florida was a strip of land along the north shore of the Gulf of Mexico. East Florida, the part ceded to the U.S. by the treaty, was most of what we know as today's Florida. Both Floridas were left under Spanish control by the Treaty of Paris, which ended the revolution. American settlers pretty much disregarded the terms of the treaty and began moving into West Florida. The U.S. was able to exploit the weakness of Spain following Napoleon's invasion of their country and soon absorbed all of the Florida territory, either by the Adams-Onis Treaty or by the purchase of the Louisiana Territory.

Robert Fulton had begun experimenting with steam-powered vessels back in 1807, marked by his maiden voyage on his boat, the **Clermont**, on the Hudson River. American builders and investors began to race one another in their efforts to build larger, faster boats that could efficiently haul more cargo. People feared the hazards brought on board by the high-pressure steam engines and the engines had to be so large that they limited the amount of precious cargo that could be carried. Still, the race went on.

The dream was to be able to create vessels that could carry large amounts of goods and large numbers of people all the way across the Atlantic Ocean. **Captain Moses Rogers**, who had substantial financial backing, built the **Savannah** in 1818. She was 98 feet long, 26 feet wide and carried a 90 horsepower steam engine that drove large paddle wheels, which were supplemented by sails. The Savannah was built at a cost, enormous in those times, of $50,000. She completed her first voyage, steaming from New York down to Savannah, Georgia, in 1819. On May 24, 1819, under the command of Captain Rogers and his cousin, Stevens, the Savannah left Savannah, Georgia, to steam to Liverpool, England. The ship held berths for 32 passengers, but no one applied for them, people were still afraid of the hazards of a steam engine. Nor would merchants risk their goods on the initial run, so no cargo was aboard. The plan was to use the steam engine only when the sails could not produce a 4-knot speed (less than 5 miles per hour). The Savannah, even with minimum use of the steam engine, was out of fuel long before Liverpool was seen on the horizon. She started out with 75 tons of coal and 24 cords of wood, all to be used to maintain steam pressure. The Savannah successfully reached Liverpool, where she was an immediate tourist attraction. She had used the steam engine only for about 10% of the voyage. The Savannah continued her voyage from Liverpool to Denmark, Sweden, Russia and then back to Georgia, arriving home on November 30, 1819.

Slavery and The American Colonization Society

In England, in January of 1786, **The Committee for the Relief of the Black Poor** was formed. It was created by religious officials and **slavery abolitionists**. The committee originally focused on feeding, housing and clothing poor black and Asian citizens. Eventually, though, it began to investigate the possibility of establishing a new colony, wherein black people could be truly free to manage their own destiny.

Some members of the British committee were simply altruistic and wished for better conditions for the poor of all colors. Others, though, were motivated by a desire to prevent the mixing of races within their population. The idea of a separate, free colony took hold with enough supporters to initiate an actual movement in that direction. On April 9, 1787, three ships loaded with supplies and with three hundred and twenty black men and women, accompanied by more than seventy white women, sailed for **Sierra Leone**, where they were given full citizenship. Eventually, around four thousand black people were transported from London to Sierra Leone.

The apparent early success of the British colony in Sierra Leone lent credibility and motivation to the movement already started in America. The **American Colonization Society** gained momentum in their efforts to create a larger colony, in western Africa, where American black people could be re-located and could be free. The Society sent members to Africa, where they were eventually, after initial failures, able to purchase land for the purpose of receiving American black people. It would be named **Liberia** and it was located just to the south of Sierra Leone on the southwest coast of Africa. Its capitol city was to be named **Monrovia**, honoring the American President James Monroe.

After America's revolution, the number of slaves in America steadily increased, reaching more than three million by 1850. At the same time, the number of free black people was also rapidly increasing. In 1790, for instance, in Virginia, the total number of free black people was one percent of the population. By 1810, ten percent of Virginia's total population was made up of free blacks. Seven and one-half percent of the entire American population were free black people. Sadly, being "free" and black was not the same as being free and white in America. **Segregation** of the races in most social activities was to be an ugly stain on the American culture for decades yet to come.

The concept of preparing a separate colony, in Africa, for America's black people began to gain credence and support. Observation of the apparent early success of the British colony in Sierra Leone encouraged the movement. The effort to create an African colony for American free black people was preceded by an early experiment. American **Paul Cuffee**, a free man of mixed race and a ship owner, transported thirty-eight black people to Sierra Leone back in 1816. Then, in February of 1820, 86 free black American colonists boarded a ship, the **Elizabeth**, along with three members of the American

Colonization Society and sailed for Freetown, Sierra Leone and then directly south to Liberia.

The original complement of 86 black people was quickly decimated, literally within just a few weeks of their arrival in Liberia, when they were fatally infected with **yellow fever**. Defeated, the remaining people returned to Sierra Leone. Nevertheless, by 1822, more ships with free black people aboard continued to arrive in Africa. A second effort to settle in Liberia began when a U.S. Naval officer, **Robert Stockton**, was able to persuade local tribal chiefs to sell land. Over the next decade, two thousand six hundred and thirty-eight free black souls re-located to Liberia. Throughout the early years of the new colony, local African tribes resisted the new arrivals, but the colony persisted and survived.

Decades later, the Liberians claimed their independence from the American Colonization Society. **Joseph Jenkins Roberts** originally a resident of Norfolk, Virginia, was elected their first black President on July 26, 1847. This is **Article One** of their new **Constitution**:

Article 1: All persons born within the limits of the territory held by the **American Colonization Society** in or removing there to reside, shall be free and entitled to all the rights and privileges of the free people of the United States.

The American Colonization Society boasted of support from some influential Americans, including Daniel Webster, Francis Scott Key, Andrew Jackson, James Monroe, Henry Clay and, early in his career, Abraham Lincoln.

The History of Liberia

The Republic of Liberia lies on the West Coast of Africa, with the Atlantic Ocean along its western coastline. Liberia is a beautiful land marked by rolling hills and a lush rainforest. It was founded by the American Colonization Society in 1821 and was named Liberia in 1824. The capitol city is Monrovia, named for the American President James Monroe, who supported the planned experiment to re-locate America's black population "back to Africa". The idea of transporting all of America's black people was foolish and never had a chance of succeeding. Had it succeeded, the people of America would have suffered the loss of vast potential for greatness. Countless black physicians, authors, inventors, research scientists and so many more invaluable assets, would have been lost to the **United States**.

Liberia today has a population of five to six million souls. Liberia declared its independence in 1847. It is the only African-black state to have never been subject to colonial rule. It is the oldest republic in Africa.

America in the 1820's

The Arikara Indian War

American settlers continued to push westward, acquiring more and more land previously inhabited by Indians. The **Indian Nations** were beginning to feel they were being existentially threatened by the inexorable invasion of white men. The **Arikara** tribe was located along the western flow of the Missouri River, from northern Iowa west to the Dakotas. The tribe also identifies as the **Sahnish**, meaning "the original people from whom all other people have sprung".

Indian tribes along Missouri probably first met white people when French explorers and traders passed through the area as early as the 1770s. The Arikara tribe first met American white men when the Lewis and Clark expedition encountered them along the banks of the Missouri River, which flowed through South Dakota. The white explorers met with the Arikawa, in October 1804 and the interaction, which lasted three days, was peaceful and cooperative. The Arikara were two thousand members strong at the time and could easily have wiped out the entire Lewis and Clark mission. The Indians being located so far west, didn't yet recognize the threat of the tsunami of new white invaders they would soon experience.

The white settlers weren't even the worst threats to the Arikara (Sahnish). Throughout the early decades of the 1800s, they were raided constantly by the **Sioux** and they suffered several rounds of **lethal smallpox infections**.

The fabric of the peaceful relationship with the whites soon began to unravel when an Arikara tribal leader, **Chief Ankedoucharo**, was lost to illness on a trip to Washington, D.C. The Arikara blamed the U.S. for his loss. Chief Ankedoucharo had been among the white people for about a year when he passed away while visiting the Richmond, Virginia area. This is an excerpt from a letter **President Thomas Jefferson** sent to the Arikara, expressing sorrow over the chief's death:

"Chief Ankedoucharo consented to go towards the sea (the Atlantic Ocean) as far as Baltimore and Philadelphia. The Chief found nothing but kindness and good will wherever he went, but on his return to Washington, he became ill. Everything we could do to help him was done, but it pleased the Great Spirit to take him from among us. We buried him among our own deceased friends and relations. We shed many tears over his grave."

Jefferson's missive seemed to have little mollifying impact on the Indians.

Further antagonism was triggered when a fur trader killed the son of an Arikara chieftain. Conflicts between the Indians and fur traders soon became common. Alliances between the Sioux and the French fur traders were another threat to the Arikara.

Fifteen to twenty fur traders were killed in an attack by the Arikara in June of 1823. Survivors stayed in hiding for several weeks, awaiting support from the army. The **U.S. Army**, coming to assist the survivors, first engaged the Arikara on August 9, 1823, marking the onset of the **Arikara Indian War**. It was officially the first army hostile engagement with any Indian tribe in any of the "Western Territories".

The army sent **Lt. Colonel Henry Leavenworth**, commanding the 6th Infantry and leading 230 U.S. Army soldiers, bolstered by 750 **Sioux (Teton Dakota)** Indian allies and by 50 fur company men. On the first day of the conflict, the Sioux cavalry, horse-riding warriors, attempted an attack on the Arikara but were repulsed. The Sioux didn't seem very much committed to the battle, as they had, on occasion, been allies to the Arikara. The Sioux stole corn from Arikara fields and rode away. The army attempted an artillery barrage, on the second day, but was ineffective. It was followed by an attack executed by the army's 6th Infantry, which was also ineffective. Lt. Col. Leavenworth, on the third day, negotiated a peace treaty, with which the Arikara had little confidence.

The Arikara evacuated their village under cover of darkness. The army subsequently burned the village to the ground and then departed the area, returning to Fort Atkinson.

The Arikara War was short, lasting only three days, but it was significant as it marked the first of many conflicts between white settlers, the U.S. Army and the many Indian tribes. Though the war was short, it left very hard feelings between the tribe and the U.S. army and between the tribe and the fur traders. The Arikara, in 1837, after being severely weakened by the Sioux and by smallpox, eventually settled in a peaceful village near Fort Clark. By the 1840s, Arikara warriors had become trusted scouts for the U.S. Army.

Lt. Col. Henry Leavenworth was a lawyer in times of peace. Fort Leavenworth, on the Missouri River, was named for him and was established in 1827. The town of Leavenworth, Kansas, has grown up around the fort. The town is also home to Leavenworth military prison.

America in the 1820's . . . Continued

America continued to expand westward, as more land is occupied and settled by white settlers. The population of the U.S. increased by one-third between 1810 and 1820, reaching a total of 9,638,453 people. Approximately one and one-half million of those were slaves.

The westward growth of the U.S. was spurred, in part, by numerous fur trading expeditions. Most departed from St. Louis and involved reliable trading alliances with many Native American tribes. Some fur traders treated the Indians well and some did not, choosing to exploit the relationships. Complicating the situation was the passage, in 1822, of a law prohibiting the transfer of alcohol to Indians. Alcohol was one of the favored products that many of the Indians valued and would trade fur and other goods to obtain it. Alcohol also rendered the inexperienced Indians vulnerable to unfair trade practices. The law was frequently ignored. Men like **Jim Bridger**, **Zebulon Pike** and **Jedediah Smith** roamed the frontier and westward, mapping out huge segments of American territories.

President James Monroe seems to have been focused on organizing and clarifying American possessions and boundaries. In 1823, the U.S. War Department ordered an expedition north and west to accrue information needed to pursue these objectives. **Stephen Long**, a well-known inventor, civil engineer and explorer, was chosen to lead the expedition. Long would eventually complete five expeditions and would cover more than 26,000 miles before he was done. His work would establish the line along the 49th parallel which would become the formal border between the U.S. and Canada. The work of Long and the other members of his expeditions, would yield vital information about the nature of our western and northern territories. It would also add a great volume of information about the names and populations of a long list of Indian tribes, including the **Yanktonai**, **Osage**, **Ottawa**, **Ojibway**, **Potawatomi**, **Winnebago** and **Menominee** tribes.

President John Quincy Adams

America's Sixth President

Famous patriot and delegate to the Continental Congress, **John Adams** and his wife, also a dedicated patriot, **Abigail Smith Adams**, were the parents of **John Quincy Adams**. He was born July 11, 1767, in the town of Braintree, Massachusetts, which is now Quincy, Mass. His father was America's second **President, John Adams**.

John Quincy Adams grew up through the years of the **American Revolution**. He observed the **Battle of Bunker Hill** from a nearby location known as "Penn's Hill". He often could hear the artillery explosions off in the distance. His town lost their school master, a victim of the war and John Quincy was educated in a series of private schools, including in Paris, France and in the Netherlands. Adams maintained a detailed diary or journal, through the next 60 years of his very eventful journey through life.

John traveled to Russia in 1781, at the tender age of 14, as a secretary and interpreter for U.S. Envoy Francis Dana. Not much was accomplished by Dana in a year in Russia and John Quincy moved on. He joined, after a trip through Scandinavia and the Netherlands, with his father, who was serving as a Minister to the Court of St. James in Paris, France. By 1787, he had returned to America, where he had graduated from Harvard. He then studied the law and was admitted to the bar in 1790.

John Quincy Adams, while practicing law, was busy writing a series of popular articles. He supported the American neutrality philosophy of George Washington during the war between France and England, during 1793. President Washington appointed him **Minister to the Netherlands**, where Adams had experience, in 1794. It was his first political post.

Adams continued to write prolifically, articles and letters back to the U.S. George Washington borrowed some of John Quincy's phrases in his famous **Farewell Address of 1796**. Adams was integrally involved in completing ratifications of the **Jay Treaty of 1794**, finalizing terms of negotiations tying up loose ends after the end of the revolution. He continued to serve at various foreign service postings through the mid-1790s.

John Quincy Adams encountered **Louisa Catherine Johnson** for the first time when he was only twelve years old. She was known to be in poor health and was a victim of migraine headaches, but she was from a very wealthy family. Louisa was very well-traveled and well-educated. She played the harp for visitors and guests and she was familiar with the literature in Greek, French and English languages. Louisa became known as a pleasant and gracious hostess. She married John Quincy Adams in 1797 in London, England. Louisa traveled with John, for many years, to his foreign postings.

John had suffered several previous "love connections" before marrying Louisa. He was much enamored of a French actress. He was interested in marrying another young lady, but his own mother talked him out of the engagement, suggesting he could not afford to support a family. Adams most likely believed that his marriage to the wealthy Louisa would provide him with a financial cushion that would allow him to pursue his love of writing. Unfortunately, within weeks of their marriage, Louisa's family went bankrupt. Adams was known to have periods of great depression and to be a "cold fish" in social interactions. Louisa was rumored to be very regretful about entering marriage with him. The two of them suffered the death of an infant daughter and then the deaths of two adult sons.

One of the young men, their oldest son, George Washington Adams, had earned a reputation as an alcoholic, a gambler and a philanderer. His death, by drowning, was rumored to have been a suicide. A second son, John Adams II, also lost his life to alcoholism. He remains to this day the only Presidential son who was married in the White House.

The third son of Louisa and John Quincy, **Charles Francis Adams**, was much more successful. He was elected to the House of Representatives and he served the U.S. as Minister to England during the years of the American Civil War.

John Quincy Adams returned to America, living in Boston and was elected to the Massachusetts Senate in 1802. The very next year, in 1803, he was elected to the Senate of the United States. A few years later, Adams lost his Senate seat. He became a professor of rhetoric and oratory for several years at Harvard University. The post was appropriate for Adams because his political nickname was **"Old Man Eloquent"**.

John Quincy Adams was serving as America's representative to Russia when the **War of 1812** broke out. In 1814, he was a participant in the negotiations which resulted in the **Treaty of Ghent**, which ended that conflict. The Treaty of Ghent is generally recognized as the final act that solidified the independence of the United States from England. Adams continued to serve the U.S. as ambassador or minister to several nations over the next few years.

President James Monroe appointed Adams **Secretary of State** in 1817. It was the beginning of the period known as the **"Era of Good Feelings"**. It was believed to be a period of unprecedented good relations among America's politicians. Things weren't quite as peaceful, though, as the title might imply.

Adams played the most key role in the negotiations that brought Florida, following the **Louisiana Purchase**, into the union. Adams was able, in 1819, to gain approval from Spain for a treaty that had massive implications for the U.S. Some consider it to be the single greatest diplomatic achievement in American history, up to that time. The treaty, known as the **Transcontinental Treaty**, caused Spain to relinquish all claims to all territories east of the Mississippi River, including the East and West Florida Territories. America agreed to relinquish claims to what we now know as Texas. The Transcontinental Treaty, as the name suggests, also, for the first time, established an American boundary reaching from the Atlantic Ocean to the Pacific Ocean. The treaty provided for the extension of America's northern boundary to the west from the Rocky Mountains all the way to the Pacific Ocean. It was a change that came entirely from John Quincy Adams's work in the negotiations and was considered a brilliant piece of diplomacy.

The Presidential election in 1824 was somewhat chaotic. The **Democratic-Republicans** ran four candidates. They were **William Crawford, Andrew "Old Hickory" Jackson, Henry Clay** and **John Quincy Adams**. Andrew Jackson obtained more electoral votes, 99, than John Quincy Adams. The 99 votes, though, were not the required majority. Electoral votes for Crawford and Clay meant that no candidate held the required majority of electoral votes. Consequently, the House of Representatives voted to select a candidate and they voted to put John Quincy Adams in the office of the President. Adams came to be President while gaining fewer electoral votes AND fewer popular votes, than Andrew Jackson. Henry Clay, a long-time adversary to Old Hickory Jackson, threw his vote to Adams, sealing the win for him.

The "Era of Good Feelings" was quickly drawing to a close. Following the 1824 election, John Quincy Adams appointed Henry Clay to be Secretary of State, an office frequently leading to a future Presidency. Andrew Jackson's supporters were outraged, claiming Adams and Clay had made a "corrupt bargain" which delivered the Presidency to Adams and the Secretary of State position to Clay. Jackson's supporters and they were many, harassed the Adams administration for the next four years. They basically carried out a four-year campaign to get Andrew Jackson elected in 1828.

The nation prospered during Adams' Presidency, but he was not well-liked, in sociability terms and the Jacksonians pursued him relentlessly. He was a hard-working President, rising before the sun and often swimming alone in the Potomac River very early in the morning. One story reports he nearly drowned in one of his morning swims when the billowing sleeves of his blouse filled with water and almost pulled him under in the current. Adams understood that he was not a favorite of the common people, but he focused on national improvements that he could, to some extent, control. Adams first proposed a "national university" and a "national astronomical observatory". He proposed a major expansion of the nation's system of roads. Unfortunately, Congress, dominated by Jacksonians, mostly fought off his proposals, blocking their implementation.

It was probably no surprise to Adams that he was defeated in the 1828 Presidential election. Andrew "Old Hickory" Jackson won the race by a large margin of electoral votes. The supporters of Adams developed into what became known as the **"National Republican Party"**, which later transitioned into the **"Whig Party"**, which eventually transitioned into the **"Republican Party"**. Hard feelings between Jackson and Adams persisted. When Harvard College (later University) presented Jackson with an honorary degree, Adams complained that he would not "be present to witness [Harvard's] disgrace in conferring its highest honors upon a barbarian who could not write a sentence of grammar and could hardly spell his own name."

Following his defeat in 1828, Adams returned to his home base in Quincy, Massachusetts. The **"Anti-Freemasonic"** movement, in 1830, drove Adams back into politics. He was elected, largely based on their support, to the federal House of Representatives, where he served until his death in 1848. He was influential in the Anti-Masonic Party and never gave up hope that he might find his way back into the White House.

John Quincy Adams and Slavery

John Quincy Adams was one of the nation's greatest warriors in the long fight to end slavery. He was, in personal philosophy, an adamant abolitionist. Adams, in 1839, proposed an amendment to the constitution. His amendment would guarantee that every child, of any race, born within the United States on or after July 4, 1842, would be free. It also mandated that, except for Florida, no new state could be admitted to the union if it allowed slavery. It banned the existence of any slave trading in the District of Columbia. Unfortunately, Southern, slavery-supporting, Senators had already managed to pass what were known as the **"gag rules"**. The gag rules forbade any and all discussions of the issue of slavery in the Senate, which blocked any consideration of John Quincy Adams' proposals.

His persistency in fighting for a complete repeal of the gag rules and for the right of the people to petition their Congress to eliminate slavery, became one of the most epic, enduring battles in Congressional history. Adams fought to bring every petition from constituents to the table to be considered, constantly battling against the gag rules. He argued, in the face of great antagonism from Congressional opponents, that the gag rules were a clear violation of the **First Amendment** and he refused to be silenced.

As time passed and Adams continued his eloquent assault on the institution of slavery, earning his nickname "Old Man Eloquent", more and more of his opponents slipped under his influence. Things came to a head in 1837. John Quincy Adams presented a petition, initiated by 22 slaves and was threatened by his Congressional opponents with "censure". His powerful oratory brought even more of the Congressmen over to Adams' side of the debate. Finally, in 1824, his years of persistence paid off. He made a motion to repeal the gag rule. The vote was tallied at 108 for Adams and only 80 for the pro-slavery side. The gag rule was repealed, opening the way for years of intense debate over the shameful issue of slavery.

Adams never stopped working to defend those enslaved in America. In 1841, while still a member of Congress, he defended a group of slaves who had mutinied while aboard the slave ship **Amistad.** Those slaves escaped from their Spanish "owners" and were able to sail the Amistad to a landing near Long Island, New York. The administration of then-**President Martin Van Buren** endeavored to honor the fugitive slave laws and to return the slaves to their Spanish owners. They would, if returned to the Spanish owners, almost certainly be executed for their mutiny and escape from the Amistad. John Quincy Adams represented them before America's Supreme Court, insisting that they were freemen, and he won their freedom.

Adams was also a life-long supporter of the arts, science and of education. He fought to ensure that the wishes of Englishman **James Smithson** be honored and preserved, resulting in the creation and permanent endowment of the **Smithsonian Institution**.

John Quincy Adams was a truly great American. His life was marked by his spartan work ethic, his brilliant orations, his undyingly persistent devotion to public service and his courageously independent stands on divisive issues. He was one of the nation's greatest warriors in the long fight against the institution of slavery. Sadly, his personality was not that of a warm and cuddly uncle. He offered a stern and unapproachable appearance and was never a beloved political character, a characteristic of which he was very much aware.

Adams died on February 21, 1848. He was still actively serving in Congress and was there working on that date. He was busy, as usual, protesting the "honorary grant of swords" to the American generals who carried out what Adams believed was an "unrighteous war" against Mexico. Adams suffered a cerebral stroke and fell to the floor of the House. He was taken to the Capitol building, where, two days later, he passed away.

The primary eulogy for John Quincy Adams was delivered by prominent **Senator Thomas Hart Benton.** Benton said, "Where would death have found him except at the place of duty?"

John Quincy Adams Quotes

- "Try and fail, but don't fail to try".

- "I am a warrior, so that my son may be a merchant, so that his son may be a poet".

- "America goes not abroad in search of monsters to destroy. She is the well-wisher to freedom and independence of all".

- Of the fight to end slavery, he said:

- "Though it cost the blood of millions of white men, let it come. Let justice be done".

- Of future generations, he said:

- "Posterity . . . you will never know how much it has cost my generation to preserve your freedom. I hope you will make good use of it".

- On standing up for righteous causes:

- "Always vote for principle, though you may vote alone and you may cherish the sweetest reflection that your vote is never lost".

- On abuse of power:

- "Power always thinks it has a great soul and vast views beyond the comprehension of the weak and it is doing God's service when it is violating all His laws".

- Another on slavery:

- "If the fundamental principles in the Declaration of Independence, as 'self-evident truths', are real truths, then the existence of slavery, in any form, is wrong".

- On leadership:

- "If your actions inspire others to dream more, learn more, do more and become more, then you are a leader".

America in the 1820's . . . Continued

Aglimpse of America's future modes of transportation was offered in two new developments. **John Stevens**, in New Jersey, in 1825, operated the first experimental **steam locomotive**. Steam locomotives would have a long career and become a key factor in America's expansion and, eventually, industrialization. A year later, in 1826, a patent was granted to **Samuel Morey** for the **internal combustion engine**, which was then called a "gas" or "vapor" engine. Internal combustion engines would eventually drive all kinds of vehicles and tools such as chain saws and lawn mowers. They would impact transportation, industry and, sadly, air pollution.

A remarkable historical coincidence occurred on the fourth of July, 1826, which was the 50th anniversary of America's Declaration of Independence. On that somber day, both **Thomas Jefferson** and **John Adams** passed away. The two giants of American history had often been at odds, politically speaking, in their younger days. As they grew older, they became dear friends and wrote to one another regularly.

Legendary American mountain man, fur trader and explorer **Kit Carson**, as a young man, was "**indentured**" to a man who was to teach him the job of a "saddler". He was apparently not appreciative of the opportunity and he escaped "**bondage**" to run away and join a trading party. Those who ran from their bondage were, legally speaking, fugitives. A one-cent reward was offered, in Franklin, Missouri, to anyone who could capture and return Carson to his bondage. He remained free to establish his image as a great American frontiersman and mountain man. Indentured servants were among the first American settlers, bringing the practice from Europe, where it was common. Many indentured servants were treated more or less as family, while many others were treated little differently than slaves. **Benjamin Franklin** was sold into bondage by his own father and was indentured in service to his brother. Franklin also ran away to establish himself in another town.

Early warning signs of the coming **Texas Revolution** began to show up in December 1826. A collection of American settlers, living in the area which, at the time, belonged to Mexico, made an initial attempt to secede from Mexico. They established what they called the **"Republic of Fredonia"**, which was to endure for only one month. The government of Mexico responded by restricting any further immigration into Mexico of American settlers. The settlers were, for the moment, defeated, but their intentions were not dampened and their desire for freedom from Mexico would eventually lead to the Texas Revolution.

The first functional, operating railroad system was created, in February 1827, when the **Baltimore and Ohio Railroad** was incorporated. It would turn out to be the first regularly operating railroad to transport people and commercial products. It would be followed by a vast system that would ultimately crisscross the entire United States. The Baltimore and Ohio Railroad first carried paying passengers on July 4, 1828.

The **abolition movement** continued to make gradual progress. New York State, on July 4, 1827, legally abolished all forms of slavery. Much was left to be done, but pressure for abolition was building across the nation.

In September of 1827, **Joseph Smith, Jr.**, revealed his claim that **golden tablets** bearing ancient records had been delivered to him by the **angel Moroni**. The plates could be seen as reminiscent of the tablets carrying the ten commandments, which the Bible teaches were given to Moses by God. Joseph Smith would go on to be the founding leader of the **Mormon Church** or the **Church of Latter-Day Saints**, which he initially called the "Church of Christ". He published the **"Book of Mormon"** at the age of 24. Members of other religions were antagonistic to the Mormons, especially regarding the Mormon practice of **"polygamy"**. Smith and a gathering of Mormon followers established a settlement at Nauvoo, Illinois, along the Mississippi River. Smith, himself, was shot to death by a mob after being jailed in Carthage, Illinois, in June of 1844. The remaining Mormons were driven out of Illinois and moved to Utah, under the leadership of **Brigham Young,** where they created a successful community.

Andrew "Old Hickory" Jackson soundly defeated **John Quincy Adams** in the **Presidential Election of 1828**. Jackson won easily in both the popular and electoral vote tabulations.

Andrew "Old Hickory" Jackson

America's Seventh President

The states of North and South Carolina have a long-standing dispute over which state was the birthplace of **Andrew Jackson**. He was born, on March 15, 1767, in an area where boundaries were not yet clear and there is no definitive answer to the question. Jackson, himself, always described himself as a South Carolinian. Andrew was born to struggling Irish immigrants. He benefited from very little formal schooling and was primarily self-educated.

When the **American Revolution** began Andrew Jackson was around ten years old. The Redcoats assaulted the Carolinas in 1780 and Andrew saw his mother and two brothers killed by the British. Andrew joined the local rebel militia at the age of 13 and served as a courier to the American patriots. Young Andrew was taken prisoner by the Redcoats. One of their officers demanded that he shine the officer's boots. Andrew refused and received a saber slash across his face, which left permanent scars. Antagonism toward the English would stay with him throughout the remainder of his life.

Jackson, as he neared the age of 20, studied the law. He became well enough educated to pass the bar in 1787. Andrew soon relocated to the west side of the Appalachian Mountains, to reside in what was then the Tennessee Territory, not yet a state. He was successful enough to become a prosperous prosecutor in the area that is now Nashville, Tennessee.

As he became better known and more prosperous, he opened a private law practice. The daughter of a local military colonel, **Rachel Donelson Robards**, caught Andrew's eye and romance ensued.

Rachel was described as a friendly, vivacious young woman. She had been previously married, at age 17, to a man who became violently abusive and extremely jealous. The marriage ended after a separation and several unsuccessful attempts at reconciling. Rachel was aided by lawyer Andrew Jackson, who was boarding with her family. She left Robards for the last time in 1790. Rachel and Andrew Jackson heard, erroneously, that Robards had finally divorced her. Andrew and Rachel were married. Two years later, they learned that the divorce hadn't been finalized, meaning their marriage was not legitimate. The divorce did finally go through in 1793 and Rachel and Andrew were married for a second time. Jackson's passions ran high and, in 1806, he killed a man, in a duel, for slandering Rachel's character.

Time passed and Jackson continued to do well in his law practice. He grew wealthy enough to build a mansion, which would be known as **The Hermitage**, located near Nashville. He also began to purchase slaves.

192

The couple lived the rest of their lives at the Hermitage. Rachel was the subject of much bad press, which depicted her as being poorly educated and lacking social refinement. She was the object of ongoing rumors of adultery, following her mistaken early marriage to Jackson. She was described in the papers as "a fat dumpling". Still, over the years when Andrew was frequently away for extended time periods, she seems to have successfully managed the operations of the plantation. She was very religious and, perhaps, somewhat eccentric. On orders from her doctor, to treat chronic shortness of breath, Rachel famously smoked a corncob pipe daily. When Andrew was elected President, in 1828, Rachel was not happy about the situation. She did not want to move to Washington, D.C. and remarked that she would "rather be a door-keeper in the House of God than to live in that palace in Washington". Sadly, Rachel had a heart attack and died before having to move to the White House. She was buried at the Hermitage on Christmas Eve, before making the dreaded trip. She was buried in what would have been her inaugural gown.

Tennessee called together a convention of leaders with the objective of drafting a state constitution. Andrew Jackson was a contributor to the effort. He became the state of Tennessee's first representative in the federal House of Representatives. His noteworthy political career had begun. Jackson returned home after declining to run again for Congress. He was quickly elected to the U.S. Senate, where he served for only a year before being elected judge in the superior courts of Tennessee. This position he held until the emergence of the War of 1812.

Jackson was the head of Tennessee's state militia when the War of 1812 broke out. He was appointed Major General in that conflict. His most significant contribution was seen in a campaign, lasting several months, against the **Creek Indian** nation, who were in the fight on the side of the British. That campaign ended with the crushing victory for the Americans in the **Battle of Tohopeka**, also known as the **Battle of Horseshoe Bend**. Jackson would become a primary figure in the relentless pursuit of the Indian tribes over the coming decades. Jackson then led an American force that achieved a remarkable victory over British troops who held control over much of what was then the Louisiana Territory. The victory, known as the **Battle of New Orleans**, under the circumstances, was deemed extraordinary. Andrew was quickly elevated to the level of a national military hero. It made no difference that it turned out that the war was actually formally ended, with the **Treaty of Ghent**, weeks before the battle actually occurred. He was loved and admired by his troops. They said he was "tough as an old hickory", which led to his gaining the nickname **"Old Hickory"**.

In November 1814, Jackson moved his troops south, occupying Pensacola, Florida. He had no federal instructions to do so, but had heard the British had moved into the city. He most likely hoped that his occupation of the Florida city would smooth a more thorough American effort to take possession of Florida, which was owned, at the time, by the Spanish government. The British troops evacuated Pensacola, avoiding conflict with Jackson's force and Jackson took possession of Pensacola and the Spanish fort at St. Mark's. Jackson's move on Florida and his claim of American ownership of the area, led to much political debate. Ultimately, Secretary of State John Quincy Adams gave his approval and Jackson's moves expedited America's full ownership of the Floridas, accomplished in 1821.

Jackson claimed to have no interest in the Presidency, but his supporters, and they were many, in 1824, got him a seat in the U.S. Senate. They also got him nominated for the Presidency. The 1824 election was complicated, involving four main candidates. One candidate, Secretary of the Treasury **William H. Crawford**, suffered a critical cerebral stroke. He was out of the running. The election resulted in no one candidate having a majority of electoral votes. The result was decided in Congress, where the Speaker of the House, **Henry Clay**, delivered his support and the election, to **John Quincy Adams**. Andrew Jackson never forgave Clay for what he considered a betrayal. Henry Clay had finished fourth in the election, but when Adams took the White House, he appointed Clay in the critical position of **Secretary of State**. Jackson and his supporters considered the move a "corrupt pay-off" by Adams, rewarding Clay for throwing the election to Adams. The hostilities would be long-lasting.

The Presidential election campaigns for 1828 were hard-fought, bitterly contested battles. In the end andrew Jackson defeated John Quincy Adams decisively. He became the first American President who lived on the frontier and the first President not from either Virginia or Massachusetts. Jackson was the first incoming President to issue a general invitation to the public to come to the inaugural ball. It was held in the White House and the move was very popular. Furniture and dinnerware were destroyed, but the event was well received.

Hard feelings persisted between the supporters of John Quincy Adams and Andrew Jackson. Their followers began to split into two new divisions by political party. The old "Republican" party was transformed into the "Democrat-Republicans", who were the supporters of Andrew Jackson and the "National Republicans" or "Whigs", who opposed Jackson. The Whigs were led by Henry Clay and Daniel Webster and they believed Jackson was taking too much power for the Executive Branch. Jackson used the Presidential power of veto liberally and the Whigs accused him of trying to make himself King. They called him "**King Andrew the First**" and gave him the nickname "jackass". Jackson decided he liked the appellation and the donkey (jackass) became the national symbol for the Democratic Party.

Andrew Jackson never forgot the way John Quincy Adams became President, having neither the most popular votes nor the most electoral votes. As a result, while President, he unsuccessfully attempted to dismantle the electoral system.

When he became President Andrew Jackson quickly replaced many government officeholders with his friends and supporters. He was the first President to take such actions to such an extreme and the practice became known, thereafter, as the **"spoils system"**, after a pundit described the situation as "To the Victor go the Spoils". It is a system that continues, unabated, to modern-day government. It is unlikely that it does much to improve government services. In present-day, the "spoils system" has become the more sophisticated sounding **"Patronage system"**, which means the friends of newly elected officials are given government positions, called **cronyism**, or the relatives of newly elected officials are given similar positions, called **nepotism**.

Jackson's administration was perhaps best known for the **"central bank issue"**. America had struggled with the idea of a strong, national, central bank since the days of **Alexander Hamilton**. Jackson opposed the **Second Bank of the United States**, which was ostensibly privately owned, but actually operated as a government-run monopoly. Jackson believed the national bank was run by wealthy elitists who manipulated the money market to their own advantage. He was probably right. His position was that the bank was an enemy to the common man. Jackson's position on the electoral college was also sold as a stand for the common man and he became known, by his supporters, as the **"People's President"**.

While Jackson opposed the Second Bank, **Henry Clay** and **Daniel Webster**, who served as lawyers for the bank, were strong supporters. Clay and his supporters attempted to pass a bill that would renew the charter for the bank. It passed in Congress, but when it reached Jackson's desk, he exercised his power of veto, killing the legislation. He justified his action by saying the bank protected "the advancement of the few at the expense of the many". The central bank issue faded and the bank was dead.

Jackson's next big conflict was initiated by his own Vice President, **John C. Calhoun**. Major tariff legislation had been passed, in 1828 and in 1832, which Southerners believed worked to their detriment and to the advantage of Northerners. Tensions that would eventually lead to America's Civil War were already beginning to fire up hostilities. South Carolina passed legislation nullifying the tariff acts in their state, attempting to void the federal laws. They claimed to be following the **"Principle of Nullification"**. South Carolinians threatened to secede from the union. Jackson did not believe individual states had the right to nullify federal laws.

The conflict over the tariffs was severe enough to cause Jackson to replace Calhoun on the next election ticket and Calhoun responded by becoming the only Vice President to resign his position. Jackson made it clear he would use federal military forces to enforce federal laws and sent an armed expedition to South Carolina. It was said that he also threatened to hang Calhoun. Jackson was not a big fan of the high tariffs, but he felt the issue of whether states could or could not, disregard federal law was much more important.

The situation between Calhoun and the South Carolinians versus the federal government has highly inflammatory. It seemed that a violent conflict might soon flare up. Henry Clay, a great negotiator, formulated a reasonable compromise. As a result, South Carolina dropped their attempt at nullification and the tariffs were somewhat lowered. Violence was averted, in this case, but the critical **"states' rights"** issue would continue to inflame political rhetoric for a couple of more decades and would lead inexorably to civil war.

Following the resignation of Calhoun from the office of the Vice Presidency, the Senate rejected Jackson's nomination of **Martin Van Buren** to be Minister to England. Jackson was furious. He selected Van Buren to be his Vice-Presidential partner in the Presidential Election, which they won handily. Martin Van Buren would then follow Jackson in the Presidency.

The first-ever attempt to assassinate an American President took place on January 30, 1835. **Andrew Jackson** was exiting the Capitol, following a memorial service for a deceased Congressman, when an unstable attacker rushed from the crowd. He was **Richard Lawrence**, a mentally deranged Englishman who believed the U.S. owed him a huge amount of money. Lawrence aimed and pulled the trigger on a handgun, which misfired. He quickly drew a second gun and, once more, attempted to fire. His second weapon also misfired. "Old Hickory", furious at the attempt, personally charged at the shooter and began beating Lawrence with his cane. Other bystanders jumped in and helped subdue the man. Lawrence was tried, found innocent by reason of insanity and spent the rest of his life locked up in mental institutions. Some believe that placement may have been more unpleasant than going to a regular prison.

Andrew Jackson was a very popular President. It was not, however, an administration without fault. Jackson's treatment of American Indians was disturbing, at best. He signed and then pursued the **"Indian Removal Act"**. It gave the government the power to make treaties with various Indian tribes which exploited them and which allowed the federal government to "displace" them to undesirable lands west of the Mississippi. Native Americans had little choice, by then, to do anything but comply. The treaties generally claimed to repay the tribes for the loss of all of their ancestral homelands by replacing those territories with lands somewhere west of the Mississippi. Meantime, Jackson was quiet as the state of Georgia forcibly seized nine million acres of Indian land. The land had been promised to the **Cherokee** nation as part of a separate federal treaty. America's

Supreme Court twice ruled that the property could not be taken from the Cherokee, but Andrew Jackson refused to honor those decisions. He negotiated a deal that offered the Cherokee lands west of Arkansas in return for the Georgia real estate.

Jackson's actions, based on the Indian Removal Act would lead directly to the horrors of the **Trail of Tears**. He was no longer President when the actual displacement occurred, but he certainly created the environment in which it would happen. The forced relocation of 15,000 Cherokee resulted in the deaths of more than 4,000 Indians, succumbing to starvation, exposure to the elements and disease. Along with the institution of slavery, it marks one of the most disgraceful events in American history.

Yet another black mark on Jackson's history followed his nomination of **Roger Taney** to the Supreme Court. Taney's career on the court was best remembered for the **Dred Scott** Decision. It was a case that resulted in a declaration that black Americans were not legal citizens of the U.S. and were not eligible to file lawsuits for any purpose. The decision also declared that the federal government had no authority to forbid slavery in U.S. territories. Ironically, Taney would be the Supreme Court Justice who would swear in Abraham Lincoln, the man who would end slavery, as President of the United States.

In still another ironic turn Andrew Jackson and his wife Rachel actually, having no children of their own, adopted two Indian children. Jackson encountered the infants during his part in the **Creek Indian Wars**. One of them, Lyncoya, was discovered being held in the arms of his dead mother, who had been killed on a battlefield. The other child, Theodore, died as a child in 1814. The Jacksons also adopted the son of Rachel's brother and named the child Andrew Jackson, Jr.

When his Presidential term ended, Jackson returned to his plantation, the Hermitage. His dear wife had passed away almost twenty years earlier and was buried on the plantation. Andrew Jackson died on June 8, 1845, as a consequence of lead poisoning from two bullets that had rested in his chest for many years. He is buried on the plantation, resting beside the grave of his beloved Rachel.

Andrew Jackson and Slavery

Andrew Jackson's plantation, the Hermitage, located in Tennessee, was operated with the benefit of free labor provided by numerous enslaved workers. They worked in the fields and they worked in the household. Historical records indicate that Jackson never declared any rejection of the shameful institution of slavery. Records also indicate that he subscribed to a "paternalistic" view of ownership of other human beings. In this view, slavery was an acceptable condition, if owners provided a good environment for those enslaved. He objected to the harsh treatment of slaves and wrote that he supported a policy that offered authority without cruelty and discipline tempered by patience.

Andrew Jackson grew wealthy during his working lifetime and the exploitation of slave labor is the most important reason for that wealth. Jackson employed an "overseer", Graves W. Steele, who was accused of fatally disciplining one of the slaves at the Hermitage. Jackson, away on government business, wrote to Steele and demanded "a full account of your guardianship with the loss of my property". His words suggested that Jackson was most likely more disturbed about the loss of a working asset than about the humanitarian side of the issue. In the minds of many slave owners, the enslaved workers were considered valuable in the same way a farmer today would value his tractor or combine. It was not wise to mistreat that asset to an extent that diminishes its value as a working "tool".

Records indicate that Jackson, in daily life on the plantation, did not live up to his public declarations of "paternalism". Not many fathers would treat their children as they treated their slaves. When one of his female slaves, Betty, was accused of "improper conduct", he instructed his overseer to "rule with the cowhide", meaning he should use a whip. Jackson ordered that, should Betty misbehave again, she should receive 50 lashes. When one of the male slaves tried to run away, Jackson offered a reward for the return of the "fugitive". He added to the reward if the people who captured the run-away would give the man 100 lashes and an added ten dollars for each additional 100 lashes, up to a maximum of 300 lashes. Such an assault would almost certainly have killed the man. Furthermore, on a daily routine basis, Jackson forbade his slaves from leaving the property, he did not believe in educating slaves and his slaves worked long, hard days with no pay. Slave owners generally wanted slaves to remain educationally ignorant, making it difficult for them to survive on their own.

In the months before he became President, in 1829 Andrew Jackson had an "inventory" or census, of his slave property. The result showed that a total of 95 slaves worked and lived at the Hermitage plantation. One year later, living as President in the White House, Jackson listed fourteen enslaved people whom he had brought with him to serve the family and himself. Eight female and six male individuals were listed by name and by familial connections. Jackson ordered the completion of a new North Portico to the White House, built a new stable and had running water service to the house. It is very probable that much free slave labor was involved in those projects. Black people have provided the labor foundation for many American developments and improvements.

A glimpse into the daily life of Jackson's slaves is offered by interpretation of his letters and personal notes. A slave named George, for instance, was the son of a venerable slave cook known as "Old Hannah". George was selected to be Jackson's "man-servant". George was required to be available to respond to Jackson's needs at all times. He slept on a pallet on the floor near Jackson's bed. He stayed with Jackson for many decades and was at Jackson's bedside when he died.

The slave known as "Charles" had served Jackson through his military campaigns and was a carriage driver for the family. He was brought along when Jackson went to the White House. Charles had a wife and three children at the Hermitage and the family was separated for years as Charles was taken along with Jackson. Charles apparently lost his connection to the family, as Jackson requested his approval to sell the wife and children and Charles approved the sale. While the sale appears to have never happened, the intent was clear. Jackson had offered the wife, Charlotte and the three children, all to be sold together, for $800. Years later, they were still at the Hermitage. Jackson described Charlotte, to the proposed buyer, in this manner: "one of the best servants I ever saw, were it not for her ungovernable temper and tongue".

While Jackson seemed to have some concern about splitting up the family of Charles and Charlotte, he didn't let those concerns prevent him from buying individual children. He bought a slave boy, Adam, who worked in the White House. He bought an eight-year-old girl, Emeline, to be a gift for a grandniece. Emiline never saw her own family again. Jackson also purchased, while in the White House, a slave girl named Gracy Bradley and Gracy's sister Louisa. Gracy served as a lady's maid and as a seamstress, while Louisa served as a nurse for Jackson's grandchildren.

At the time of his death andrew Jackson "owned" approximately 150 slaves. There is no indication he set any of his slaves free and he made no arrangement to free any of them at his death. He owned, used and exploited slaves, separated enslaved family members and he resisted abolitionists. Jackson achieved some remarkable things and contributed significantly to the development of the new nation, but his adherence to the exploitation of black people and his part in the abuse and exploitation of Indian nations, leaves a dark stain on his history.

The Oregon Trail

Americans living in the East were hearing and reading about the passage of pioneers into America's West. They read "dime novels" glorifying heroes such as Jim Bridger and Kit Carson. They were tempted by the ability to "homestead" one hundred and sixty acres of land for the price of only an $18 filing fee. They had heard about the glorious adventures of the Lewis and Clark expedition. Everyone was looking for the easiest pathway to cross the formidable Rocky Mountains to reach the west coast.

The Oregon Trail was discovered during the trial-and-error process of attempting various possible crossings. It was a route more easily and safely traveled than the original Lewis and Clark route, though the Oregon Trail actually followed the path of the final miles of the Lewis and Clark expedition.

An expedition organized by the **Pacific Fur Company**, owned by **John Jacob Astor**, is credited with being first, in 1810, to travel the Oregon Trail. They started at Fort Astoria, on the West Coast and traveled east to St. Louis. The trip covered 2,170 miles and extended from Astoria oregon, back to Missouri. As the trip became more familiar and safer, more and more Americans succumbed to the temptations of the western frontier. Caravans made up mostly of covered wagons, often called "Schooners", began to form. The canvas covers were soaked in linseed oil to make them waterproof. The wagons were pulled by teams of four to six horses. The wagon's driver usually walked alongside or rode on one of the horses at the back of the team. The wagons could travel as much as 14 miles a day, in good conditions.

Prairie Schooner Travel

As more and more Americans chose to emigrate westward, the typical process began in St. Louis, where travelers were organized into "wagon trains" and vital supplies were gathered for the long trip. The journey often began for the wagon trains in Independence, Missouri, which is now a township in Kansas City. The trip passed by Fort Kearney, near

Omaha, Nebraska and followed the Snake River through Idaho into what is now Washington State. In Washington, the settlers reached Fort Vancouver and then drove into the Willamette Valley in Oregon. The journey generally took more than six months, when things went well. They passed through very rough lands and sometimes had to cope with hostile Indians. Bad weather could trap them in the mountains. Wagons broke down. Livestock died. They ran out of food and water at times. Yet, the number continued to increase of Easterners who wanted to be Westerners.

The earliest travelers along the Oregon Trail route left markers for future voyagers. The first fur traders used the trail in pursuit of their fortune in the 1830s. **Marcus Whitman**, with his wife **Narcissa**, used the South Pass of the trail and reached Walla Walla, Washington, in 1836. Together they established a Mission, a religious settlement,". that would serve many future travelers. The first wagon train to successfully reach Oregon arrived there in 1841. The beginning of what would become a mass migration was in 1843. A wagon train made up of one thousand settlers left Independence, MO. and utilized the South Pass to successfully reach Oregon. Thousands more would follow and the wagon trains continued into the 1860s.

America in the 1830's

Jedediah Smith

In 1799, in what is now Bainbridge, New York, **Jedediah Strong Smith** was born. He was an avid reader as a child and was fascinated with the history of the Lewis and Clark expedition. He responded, as a young man, to an advertisement for **"Ashley's Hundred"**, which was a recruiting effort for the company that would later become the **Rocky Mountain Fur Company**. Jedediah wanted to explore the new country and he needed to make money for his struggling family. Jedediah was a big man for his time, standing six foot three inches tall. He was hired quickly by Ashley and assigned to be a hunter for the company. Jedediah quickly proved his value, working for the fur company and displayed courage and competence in battles during the **Arikara War** in 1823. Ashley made Smith a Captain in his organization.

It wasn't long before he began to build a reputation as a fur hunter and American explorer. The Rocky Mountain Fur Company did not survive competition from Great Britain's **Hudson Bay Company** and John Jacob Astor's **American Fur Trading Company**, but Jedediah Smith went on to expand on his legendary reputation. Smith ultimately survived mauling by a bear and lived through three Indian massacres. He wrote that he "wanted to be the first to view a country on which the eyes of a white man had never gazed and to follow the course of rivers that run through a new land". He became the first white man to traverse the Mojave Desert and the Great Salt Lake frontier and to navigate the Colorado River.

As one of the fur company's leaders, Jedediah Smith was given responsibility for leading seventeen men on an expedition to open up avenues of trade between the east Coast and the west coast, focusing on Oregon and California. The expedition, leaving in 1826, was traveling the wilderness for two years and soon reached the area around today's Los Angeles, which was then owned by Mexico. The Mexicans discouraged his efforts to establish a trade center there and Smith took his group east and then north to search for beaver in Oregon.

In their trek North to Oregon, Smith's group, which had grown to nineteen men, was attacked by **Klawatset Indians**. The Klawatset killed fifteen of Smith's men and Smith, along with the other remaining three survivors, fled to Fort Vancouver. Fort Vancouver was the possession of fur trading competitor, Britain's Hudson Bay Company.

By 1830, Jedediah had collected a large store of furs and returned to St. Louis to market his product. His brothers Austin and Peter beseeched him to let them join him in hunting for furs. Jedediah recognized that the fur trade was being dominated, while the furs were still available, by the two large fur trading companies. He encouraged his brothers to forget about hunting and join him in following the Santa Fe trade routes that were already available and sell necessary goods to hunters and settlers and even to some Indians. The three Smith brothers joined the **"Commerce of the Prairies"** wagon train, which left from St. Louis in April of 1831. The train was made up of twenty-two covered wagons worked by seventy-four men. Prior to departing with the wagon train, Jedediah Smith warned the U.S. Secretary of War under President Jackson, John Henry Eaton, of the militarily dangerous occupation, by the British, of parts of the Oregon Territory. Smith suspected the British planned to establish permanent ownership of the area.

Several weeks later, the wagon train, crossing the desert, ran out of water for several days. Men from the wagon train went searching, in different directions, for fresh water. Jedediah struck out in the direction of the Cimarron River, which is near the town of Ulysses in today's state of Kansas. He encountered, near a spot known as Wagon Bed Spring, a hostile war party of about twenty Comanche Indians. He failed in an attempt to negotiate with them. They ran his horse off and shot him in the shoulder. Reports indicated he returned fire and, in a short skirmish, killed their Chief and some others of the band of Comanche. He was insurmountably outnumbered and was fatally assaulted with Comanche spears.

Jedediah's brothers, Austin and Peter, had no way of knowing what had happened to him. They reached Santa Fe on July 4th, 1831, where they found his possessions, including his guns, being traded on the city's streets. They later learned the details of his death from Mexican traders, who had heard reports from the Comanches.

Nat Turner

Nathaniel Turner was a black slave who was born, around the year 1800, on the plantation of Benjamin Turner in Virginia. It was not uncommon for slaves to be given the last name of their "owner". "Master" Turner allowed Nat to be educated in the academic areas of religion and of reading and writing. Nathaniel was sold three times during his younger years and was "hired out" to other owners, as well. On Turner's plantation, during the 1820s, Nat became known as a passionate preacher of religion and a leader of enslaved Africans.

Nat Turner, via the underground communications of the enslaved, gained a reputation as a gifted leader and was able to exert some influence over the enslaved population. He was, as were many black people, a spiritual man. He was convinced that God was offering him signs and visions and that he was meant to lead all the black people out of their bondage.

In 1831, there was a solar eclipse. Nat believed it was the sign that the moment had arrived when the enslaved would rise up and free themselves. He persuaded four other slaves to assist him and others soon joined their mission. On August 21, 1831, Nat and six other slaves killed a family named Travis. They gained control of some weapons and horses. Joined by seventy to eighty other slaves, they engaged in a poorly organized **"insurrection"**. They murdered, by the time it was all over, fifty to sixty white people.

Nat Turner, after the failed insurrection, was able to hide out from authorities for several weeks. He was ultimately found, tried and convicted. He was hung, in Jerusalem, Virginia, by the neck until dead. Sixteen of his co-conspirators were also hung. More than 200 other black people were severely beaten, many being killed.

The result of the **Nat Turner Rebellion** was the enhancement of long-time fears, among Southerners, of a general slave uprising. Black people were subjected to even harsher treatment. Laws were passed prohibiting the education of African slaves. The growing movements supporting emancipation and abolition of slavery were suffocated. Tensions between the supporters of slavery and the abolitionists were even more divisive and the nation continued to edge closer and closer to civil war.

The Black Hawk War

Black Hawk was a **Sauk Indian** warrior. He was born, in 1767, in what is now known as the state of Illinois, in a village called Saukenuk. His Sauk name was Ma-ka-tai-me-she-kia-kiak. As a young man, he gained a reputation as a brave and fierce warrior. He participated in the frequent conflicts between his Sauk tribe and their enemies, the **Osage**.

As time passed, the tribes began to realize that the real threat to their existence was not the other Indian tribes but the every-encroaching settlements of white people. The **Sauk** and **Fox** or **Mesquakie**, Indians agreed to a treaty in 1804 that surrendered a vast section of Indian property to the United States. The treaty relinquished all of the Indian territory lying to the east of the Mississippi River. Black Hawk objected to the treaty and argued that Indians were given alcohol and were not responsible for the signing. Eventually, though, he was unable to fight the inevitable and did sign the treaty. He was quoted much later saying that he did not understand that the treaty would require Indians to surrender their homelands. Black Hawk's own village, **Saukenuk**, was located where we now see Rock Island, Illinois.

The U.S. Army continued to move westward, building forts and protecting more and more settlers. By 1831, white settlers were moving into the area in and around Saukenuk. The army, citing the treaty signed 15 years earlier, in 1804, pressured the Indians to leave the area. Black Hawk was furious. He refused to evacuate his home. He began to gather forces to prepare for battle.

The U.S. Army, led by **General Edmund P. Gaines**, in 1832, moved a large number of army troops, plus some Illinois militiamen, into the area around Saukenuk. Black Hawk had organized a substantial band of Indian warriors. He withdrew his war party and their women and children, to the far side of the Mississippi River. Black Hawk was led to believe he would have the support of the British, who still resided to the north and of other Indian bands. On the fifth of April, 1832, he brought his people back into the Saukenuk village area.

The Americans came forward to pursue Black Hawk and his followers. They came face-to-face near the Rock River, in the locale of Northern Illinois. Black Hawk soon learned that he would be abandoned by both the British and the other bands of Indians. Seeing the futility of his mission, Black Hawk attempted to surrender. Luck had left his side and a truce messenger was killed by the Americans. **The Black Hawk War** then began in earnest.

Black Hawk's people were inspired by a victory over American forces in the month of May. The Americans were demoralized and the war continued. It wasn't long, though, before the overwhelming forces and resources of the U.S. Army brought the conflict to its inevitable conclusion. U.S. soldiers caught up with Black Hawk on August 2, 1832. The Indians were nearly wiped out as they tried to flee to the west across the wide Mississippi River. Black Hawk was finally left with no option but to surrender. The war had lasted nearly four months. Different reports record that somewhere between 442 and 592 Indians were killed, while only about 70 U.S. soldiers died. Black Hawk himself was captured and imprisoned at Fortress Monroe, in the state of Virginia. The American government, in an effort to demonstrate the power of the United States, took Black Hawk on a tour of American cities in the East, hoping to discourage any future resistance. Black Hawk was then allowed to live out the final six years of his life in an Indian Agency in the state of Iowa. He was supervised by another Sauk chieftain who had once been his opponent.

We can now visit the site of the village of Saukenuk on the high bluffs over the Rock River, near Rock Island, Illinois.

The Trail of Tears

Trail of Tears

The administration of **President Andrew "Old Hickory" Jackson**, in 1830, passed legislation known as the **"Indian Removal Act"**. It was intended to expedite the re-location of Native American tribes from areas being settled by white people. It was an exercise in the utilization of governmental power to disenfranchise an entire culture and is the foundation for one of the most shameful chapters in American history.

The government, on passage of the Indian Removal Act, was quick to send its Indian Commissioners out to begin persuading the many Native American tribes to cooperate. The Indians had little choice but to comply with the new treaties. The **Cherokee**, especially, exercised all available options in their efforts to resist their removal but still experienced a very bad outcome. The **Seminole**, in the Florida area, also fought persistently to remain on their homelands.

There were, at the time, five major tribes that had been designated "civilized". The **Choctaw** was one of them. The Choctaw agreed, on September 27, 1830, to the **Treaty of Dancing River Creek**, which was to take effect in February 1831. The initial phase of "Indian Removal" was begun in November 1831, as the Choctaw began to move away. The treaty gave the Choctaw 15 million acres of land in Oklahoma territory, while the Choctaw ceded 11 million acres of tribal lands in the state of Mississippi. The environment in Oklahoma was vastly different from the environment of their original homelands. Choctaw who wished to remain in Mississippi was supposed to be given the right to retain 640 acres of land and a couple of thousand elected to stay in Mississippi.

Three famous Americans, the well-known author **Washington Irving**, **Henry Levitt Ellsworth** and **Captain Jesse Bean**, probably without understanding the eventual consequences, traveled, beginning at the Arkansas River, through much of the remaining Indian territory. Their journey amounted to one of the early steps in choreographing the ultimate removal of all tribes from America's eastern territories. The three men, in their individual travels, met with and discussed the pending plan to accomplish the relocation of the Indians to the West. The Indians were told that they would be led to a land where they would be free of white interference and would be able to farm and hunt as they wished. They weren't told that the land they would be given was largely dry and barren and the wildlife had already been hunted to scarcity. Irving, Ellsworth and Bean would play key roles in gaining Indian compliance with the Indian Removal Act.

The winter of 1831 – 1832 was harsh, but the Choctaw had to begin their awful journey away from their sacred homelands to the West, to go to the Oklahoma territory. A Choctaw Chief was the originator of the term **"Trail of Tears"**. **French philosopher Alexis de Tocqueville** wrote: "In the whole scene there was an air of ruin and destruction, something which betrayed a final and irrevocable adieu; one couldn't watch without feeling one's heart wrung. The Indians were tranquil but somber and taciturn. There was one who could speak English and of whom I (Tocqueville) asked why the Choctaw were leaving their country. 'To be free', he answered. We watch the expulsion of one of the most celebrated and ancient American peoples".

Twelve thousand Choctaw would finally make the journey westward, though thousands would not make it to the final destination. An estimated six thousand took the option of remaining in Mississippi to become American citizens. Most of the Treaty promises made to them by the government would not be honored.

The **Creek Indian Nation**, following the example of the Choctaw, agreed to the **Treaty of Cusseta** in March of 1832. They gave up their homelands east of the Mississippi River and 19,600 of them began the perilous walk to Oklahoma. The **Chickasaw** tribe, in October 1832, was compelled to sign the **Treaty of Pontotoc Creek**, which put 4,000 Chickasaw on the long trail west. The **Cherokee** tribe, in December 1835, signed the **Treaty of New Echota**, which led, after much resistance, to their eventual forced removal from their own homelands in the area around today's state of Georgia. It is likely that the fact that gold had been discovered on Cherokee lands was a factor in motivating the Americans to expedite the removal of the Indians.

The Cherokee soon began to understand that they would be expected to leave their homes and, for a couple of years, they resisted the government's direction. **President Martin Van Buren** sent **General Winfield Scott** to enforce the terms of the Treaty of New Echota. The painful process would continue from 1836 to 1839.

General Scott was perhaps the best-known American military officer in the period between the Revolution and the Civil War. He was known as **"Old Fuss and Feathers"**.

Scott delivered his **Order No. 25** in the spring of 1838, declaring that the Cherokee would move or be moved by the American military. He brought a force of 3,000 troops to enforce the removal of the stubborn Cherokee.

The Cherokee, under the leadership of their **Chief John Ross**, resisted the order. They appealed to the U.S. Supreme Court for relief, asking that their rights to property ownership of their homelands be respected. The court offered them no relief. General Scott's troops began, often at gunpoint, forcibly evicting the Cherokee from their homes and holding them in internment camps. Some were in the camps for several weeks, with very little food, water or medical care. Many became so ill that, once the journey westward began, they soon became fatal victims. An estimated 4,000 Cherokee passed away during the evacuation.

While the Cherokee are most often cited as the primary victims of the Indian Removal Act, several other tribes were also forcibly relocated. America's native **"Eastern Woodland Indians"** included the Cherokee, the Seminole, the Choctaw, the Chickasaw and the Creek tribes. They were all involved and all were victimized.

Modern estimates report that around 100,000 Indians were "removed" westward to live on reservations. Some 15,000 died on the long walk. The overland trail route of the "Trail of Tears" extended more than 5,000 miles and most had to walk. Indians living in nine eastern states were made to move out of their homelands. Many previous treaties, which had promised the Indians various large tracts of land between the Mississippi River and the east coast, were ignored and broken by the Americans.

President Andrew Jackson's Indian Removal Act, leading to the Trail of Tears, represents a shameful and unfortunate chapter in our history. Native Americans, in many cases, still live in conditions of destitution, some in extreme poverty.

America in the 1830's . . . Continued

The 1832 Presidential election was won decisively by Andrew "Old Hickory" Jackson. John Calhoun resigned the Vice Presidency, in December, 1832, and he was replaced by Martin Van Buren. Jackson and Van Buren defeated candidate Henry Clay, winning both the electoral and the popular vote. Calhoun had voiced his opposition to some Jackson policies and resigned to return to a Senate seat in his home state of South Carolina. He hoped to mount a run for the Presidency in 1844, but found little support, even in his own state.

The USS Constitution

(Old Ironsides)

The famous American frigate, **"USS Constitution"**, known better as **"Old Ironsides"**, was retired on June 24, 1833. She was launched in 1797 and is now the oldest commissioned vessel in the American Navy.

The USS Constitution was a key player in the War of 1812. The British were harassing American shipping, "impressing" American sailors and interfering with American commerce. The British may have been hoping that, by triggering another war with America, they might regain possession of America. The English had the world's greatest navy, putting more than 600 ships on the sea. America had only twenty. Nonetheless, in early 1812, America declared war on Great Britain.

A ship designer and builder named **Joshua Humphreys** was constructing ships for America. He recognized the fact that the United States would not be able to compete with British navy numbers. He built ships, therefore, that were bigger frigates than the British frigates and were faster and stronger. He created streamlined hulls and he put the critical ribs in the infrastructure much closer together and he used American oak, which it turned out, was harder and stronger than English oak.

In spite of the tremendous odds against them, the Americans won the war. The Constitution was a big part of the victory. She got her nickname, Old Ironsides, after a naval battle. The Constitution was in battle with a British frigate named "Guerriere", which means "warrior" in French. The battle was fierce and, when a British sailor observed 18-pound English cannonballs bouncing easily off the Constitution's hull, he famously declared "Huzza! Her sides are made of iron". Of course, the sides were actually just made of solid American oak. The Guerriere had to drop her flag and surrender to the Constitution.

Sea travel, by 1830, was quickly transitioning from the **"Age of Sail"** to the **"Age of Steam"**. The Navy was, more or less, just letting the sailing ships rest and deteriorate, as they were no longer competitive. **Oliver Wendell Holmes**, as an unknown young law student, wrote and published a poem that bemoaned the loss of the Constitution, which he considered a national treasure. His poem included the lines: "The harpies of the shore shall pluck . . . The eagle of the Sea!" The poem and the sentiment, became popular across the nation. It triggered a public movement to save the old girl. Consequently, the government responded and the USS Constitution is still a Navy vessel today. Perhaps the only potentially mobile national monument, she is now a drydocked exhibit at the Charlestown Naval Yard, near Boston and the Bunker Hill Monument. She still sails through the Boston Harbor for certain anniversaries and celebrations.

America in the 1830's . . . Continued

Oberlin College was founded in September of 1833. It is located in Oberlin, Ohio and it still serves students today. Oberlin opened its doors to welcome students of all races, at a time when black people were still forbidden any education in some states. Oberlin also holds the distinction of being the first American college to enroll students of both sexes, making it the first co-educational campus.

Stephen F. Austin, whom we now know as the **"Father of Texas"**, was arrested and imprisoned by the Mexican government. It was January of 1834 and Texas was still a property of Mexico. Austin was an early seeker of independence for Texas and the Mexicans charged him with insurrection. He was ultimately released without standing trial in Mexico. The path leading to the **Battle of the Alamo** was being laid.

The **institution of slavery** was banned in Great Britain on August 1, 1834.

The Great Fire of New York burned for three days in December of 1835. Large sections of the city burned to the ground. Manhattan was devastated. Seventeen blocks were all burned to the ground and even the East River was aflame. The massive destruction led to improvements in the city's water system and basic infrastructure.

African-American **Henry Blair**, of Glen Ross, Maryland, apparently born a "freedman" in 1807, obtained the second **U.S. Patent** ever granted to a black person. Blair was a successful farmer and generated several inventions. He patented a **"corn planter"** or **"seed planter"** in October 1834. It had the appearance of a wheelbarrow but had a compartment which held seed and had attached rake-like instruments which followed the planter and covered the seed. It was a boon to all farmers, as it allowed them to complete more work in less time, increasing efficiency for all. Later, in 1836, Henry Blair obtained a second patent, this time for a **"cotton planter"**. It was horse-drawn and involved a pair of plow-like blades that opened the ground and carried a cylinder that deposited cotton seeds into the new openings. Blair was listed on the patents as a "colored man" and, as he was illiterate, carried the "X" mark he used as a signature. The first patent given to a black man went to **Thomas Jennings**. Jennings was a launderer who invented processes that would develop into modern methods of dry cleaning fabrics. Jennings obtained the first patent ever given to a black man back in 1821. It was a controversial accomplishment, as slaves were not allowed to patent inventions at the time. Jennings, however, like Henry Blair, appears to have been a "freedman". It wasn't until 1861 that laws were passed that made the patent process available to all races.

The Revolution of Texas

The Battle of Gonzales

Four hundred Americans, under the leadership of **Green DeWitt**, had settled in the Mexican territory of Texas, basically establishing a colony. A settlement called Gonzales was their "capital". The people there were known as **"Texians"**. Gonzales had been repeatedly attacked by various Indian tribes, including the Comanche. Concerned for the safety of his people, DeWitt requested assistance from the Mexican government. The Mexicans delivered to him, in 1831, a small, "six-pounder" cannon for the Texians to use in defending against attacks. In 1835, after **Mexican General Antonio Lopez de Santa Anna** had overthrown the Mexican government, making himself the dictator, the tolerance of the Mexicans for the intrusion of the American colony at Gonzales was fading quickly.

The little cannon "loaned" to the Texians became a focus of conflict when Mexican General Santa Anna demanded that the settlers be disarmed. Mexican soldiers were directed to Gonzalez to relieve the Americans of their weapons, especially the cannon. One hundred Mexican "dragoons" were dispatched to Gonzalez. They expected to easily disarm the Americans.

The Texians had established a local militia, which resisted the efforts of the Mexicans, refusing to give up the cannon and their other weapons. At the initial approach of the Mexican army, the Texians numbered only eighteen militiamen, who came to be known as "the old 18". On approaching Gonzales, it was obvious that the river between the Mexicans and the Americans would be an obstacle for the Mexicans. The Texians managed to stall off the conflict for a few days, as other Americans nearby rushed to assist those resisting the Mexicans.

On October 1, 1835, the Americans, by then numbering 170 men, dragging the little cannon, quietly approached the Mexican army camp. They were a motley group, dressed in homemade buckskin outfits, moccasins and raccoon-skin hats. They were led by **John Henry Moore** and they crossed the river and moved upstream to carry out a surprise attack on the resting Mexicans. **The Battle of Gonzales** erupted between the two groups, on October 2, 1835 and the **Revolution of Texas** was begun.

The Mexicans, in the early morning fog, were unaware of the oncoming Americans until a barking dog delivered a warning. The two forces exchanged a short volley of gunfire. Then, the two commanding officers, Moore and Mexican officer **Castaneda**, consulted one another. They failed to reach a peaceful solution to their conflict and each retreated to the positions of their respective forces.

The Americans quickly posted a hastily conceived banner. It depicted a cannon and a lone black star, both resting on a white field. Below the cannon were inscribed the words **"Come And Get It"**. It was a phrase that had been used by American rebels during the Revolutionary War. It was reported, at the time, that the banner had been constructed using material cut from the wedding dress of **Naomie DeWitt**. Naomi was the daughter of the founder of the American settlement at Gonzales, Green DeWitt.

The upstart Americans proceeded to fire the six-pounder cannon at the Mexican force. It was armed with pieces of scrap iron and sections of chain. The Mexican commander, Castaneda, had been given orders to disarm the Americans, but to do so without armed confrontation. Following that direction, Castaneda withdrew his forces from the little battle.

Castaneda's own commander persisted, though, in demanding the surrender of American arms, including the cannon. In the meantime, in ensuing weeks, more American Texian volunteers or Texans, continued to gather around Gonzales. **Sam Houston** himself brought 300 more men. He wrote that "War is declared". Houston was quickly chosen commander-in-chief of what became the **"Army of Texas"**.

Only two Mexican soldiers were killed at Gonzales, but the little conflict is recognized as the opening volleys of the Texas Revolution. It was only six months later that the much more significant battle at the **Alamo** would inspire Texas independence. A group from Gonzales, called by some the **"Immortal 32"**, would join the doomed defenders of the little mission in San Antonio.

The Battle for the Alamo

The Alamo was originally established in 1718. The "Long Barrack" building was started in 1724 and the mission church itself was constructed in 1744. Franciscan missionaries built the mission. The mission was known as Mission San Antonio de Valero and it was the first of the San Antonio missions created to provide a home for the Franciscan missionaries as they worked to convert American Indians to Christianity. It became a base for a small community of Catholics and served Spanish, American Indian and Mexican believers. The Alamo had been neglected, though and was unoccupied by the time of the Battle of Gonzales in October 1835. The Battle of Gonzales fed the fire of the Texas Revolution.

On October 9, 1835, the Alamo was used as a gathering point for 1200 Mexican soldiers, led by Mexican **General Cos**. A group of Texan volunteers attacked the mission, in December and drove General Cos out, along with his troops. Other Texans, dreaming of independence and hoping to make Texas an independent nation, began to arrive to support the group holding the old mission. American frontiersman **Jim Bowie** was sent to the Alamo by **General Sam Houston**, who was not on the site. Bowie arrived in January 1836. Another famous American frontiersman (and politician), **Davy Crockett**, made his way to the little church in February and he brought twelve additional volunteers, mostly friends and relatives of his. **Colonel William B. Travis** was in charge of the volunteers.

Sometime in January 1836, the Texans learned that the Mexicans had dispatched a large group of soldiers to regain control of the Alamo. The American government was not able to organize reinforcements to send to assist the approximately 200 defenders of the Alamo. Inside the Alamo was a diverse group of volunteers. No help was coming and they were on their own.

Mexican General Antonio Lopez de Santa Anna led 5000 Mexican soldiers. They arrived at San Antonio on February 23, 1836 and immediately laid siege to the little fort. The Mexican army isolated the mission for 13 days, allowing access to no food, water or other resources. They attacked the Alamo repeatedly. No one got in or out.

The Mexican General ordered his troops to "take no prisoners", meaning he wanted everyone in the mission killed. March 6, 1836, marked the final day of the battle. The intense fighting that day lasted less than two hours and was marked by furious combat. 187 defenders of the mission were killed, including the leaders **Colonel William B. Travis**, **Davy Crockett** and **Jim Bowie**. Among the dead were 41 immigrants who had been born in European countries and 13 native Texans and "Tejanos" or Texans of Mexican descent. All the rest were volunteers who had come from several American states. A small number of survivors were mostly wives, slaves, servants and children, who had hidden and not participated in the battle. Santa Anna's troops lost 1,544 men in **The Battle for the Alamo**.

The Texans courageously held off the Mexican army for days, before their inevitable defeat, but, for them, the battle was lost. In the days following the defeat, word of the battle spread through Texas and the United States. Texans and Americans from the states were inspired to support the drive for Texan independence from Mexico. Texas declared its independence on March 2nd, 1836.

The Mexican Army was joined in battle with the Texan Army, led by **James Walker Fannin**, on March 19th and 20th, 1836. The location was near the town of Goliad and the engagement was known as the **Battle of Coleto Creek**. The Mexican Army, under **General Jose Urrea**, was too strong for the Texans and Fannin had to surrender. Days later, General Urrea had Fannin and more than 300 Texan troops executed. The brutality of the mass execution prompted residents of Texas to begin to evacuate the area and inspired more resistance to Mexican rule.

The Texan army grew and the motivation of all Texans to gain their freedom grew. General Sam Houston led the Texan army on April 21, 1836, when they attacked the Mexican force, still led by Santa Anna, on the banks of the San Jacinto River. Houston led his troops with loud calls of **"Remember the Alamo!"**. The **Battle of San Jacinto** was devastating for the Mexicans. After less than twenty minutes of battle, the Texans had defeated Santa Anna and his army.

Santa Anna had no choice but to surrender Texas to the Texans. By the arrival of June, the Mexicans had abandoned San Antonio, the home of the Alamo.

Texas remained an independent country for nine years. It worked to gain annexation to the United States, but issues related to slavery made the process difficult. Ultimately, though, on December 29, 1845, Texas joined the union as the 28th state. It would, sadly, turn out to be the last state, after the Civil War, to eliminate all forms of slavery.

Sam Houston

Sam Houston was born in the state of Virginia in March of 1793. His parents were Major Samuel Houston and Elizabeth Houston. He was born, the fifth of nine children, in a log cabin located on a plantation owned by the family. Sam's father died in 1807 when he was thirteen years old and his family soon moved to Maryville, Tennessee, where they opened a general store and farmed 419 acres of land near the Great Smoky Mountains.

It turned out Sam didn't love farming or store management and he ran away from home when he was sixteen. He went, on his own, to live with the Cherokee, where he remained for the next three years. Sam was welcomed by a Cherokee clan which was led by Chief Oo-loo-tek-a. Oo-loo-tek-a became Sam's Indian father. The Chief was well known to white people, who knew him as John Jolly. The Cherokee taught Sam their language and their customs and they assigned him a Cherokee name, Colonneh, which meant "the Raven".

When the War of 1812 was beginning, Sam Houston joined the U.S. Army. He soon found himself serving in the Battle of Horseshoe Bend, led by General Andrew "Old Hickory" Jackson. An arrow pierced Houston's thigh early in the battle against the Red Stick Indians. The arrow was pulled free and he continued to fight. Sam was shot two more times during the battle, these times with musket balls. He would carry fragments of musket balls in his body for the remainder of his life. His wounds were very serious and he did not heal in time to return to serve again in the war. His performance was noticed, though, by Andrew Jackson.

General Jackson was much impressed with the courage of young Houston and soon became a kind of father figure and protector for Sam. Jackson brought Houston onto his personal staff after the war. It wasn't long, though, before Houston resigned his military position, in 1818, in hopes of launching a new career as an attorney. Jackson persuaded Sam to give up that dream and rejoin the army as a General of the Tennessee militia.

Houston continued to follow Andrew Jackson's path through American politics. He served, while in Nashville, as Attorney General. This led him to candidacy for the Tennessee House of Representatives, as Jackson occupied a Tennessee Senate seat. Sam Houston served two terms as a Congressman and was then elected Governor of Tennessee in 1827 when he was 34 years old.

Things looked good for Houston, as Andrew Jackson won the Presidency and took office in January 1830. Houston, being so close to Jackson, appeared to be in a good position to further his own political career.

Sam, in 1829, married **Eliza Allen**. Details are murky, but some sort of scandal was generated and Eliza left Sam to return to the home of her father, after only three months of marriage. Consequently, Sam Houston resigned from his position as Governor. He quickly retreated, returning to the Cherokee, in the Arkansas Territory, who welcomed him back. They formally adopted him into their clan.

Houston took himself, at least two times, to Washington, D.C., to argue on behalf of Indians. His efforts were focused on the exposure of frauds being perpetrated on Indians by U.S. government Indian agents. President Jackson sent Houston to Texas, which was, at the time, a Mexican territory. He had the objective of negotiating Indian treaties for the protection of trade and the encouragement of peaceful relations.

Meanwhile, Houston kept active in assisting peaceful arrangements between various Indian tribes and clans. In 1830, Sam married a Cherokee woman named **Tiana Rogers**. Together, they opened and operated a trading post. He was a regular delegate in the representation of the Cherokee, traveling frequently to Washington to fight for fair treatment of his adopted tribe.

Congress was debating the activity of Andrew Jackson's Indian policies in March of 1832 Ohio **Representative William Stanbery** implied that Sam Houston was involved in defrauding the government. A few days later, Houston encountered Stanbery on the sidewalks of Pennsylvania Avenue in D.C. Houston, enraged by Stanbery's insult, approached Stanbery and beat him fiercely with a hickory cane. After his arrest for the beating he gave Stanbery, Houston was put on trial in the House of Representatives. His attorney, representing him in the proceedings, was **Francis Scott Key**, who would one day write The Star Spangled Banner. Houston was reprimanded and had to pay a fine, but not everyone was unhappy about his actions. The incident seems to have inspired him to pursue further political ambitions.

It wasn't long before Houston, with the support of President Jackson, left his life and wife Tiana, with the Cherokee. He traveled south to cross into the Mexican province of Texas. He took up residence in Nacogdoches. He was, in keeping with Mexican laws at the time, baptized into the Catholic Church. He opened a law office. He quickly obtained a divorce from his first wife, Eliza. The legal implications of his multiple marriages were foggy.

Stephen Austin, a leader of American-Texian settlers and Sam Houston, representing Nacogdoches, were both at the Convention of 1833. In the course of the convention, Austin petitioned the Mexican government to grant independence to Texas. Austin went to Mexico to deliver the petition. The Mexican government took great offense and arrested Austin. He would remain in custody until the middle of 1835. **General Antonio**

Lopez de Santa Anna controlled the Mexican government and would be a key player in later American conflicts.

Mexican soldiers fought Texan, also called Texian, forces in the **Battle of Gonzales**, which marked the beginning of what would be known as the Texas Revolution. Houston had been named commander of the Texan army. The Texans retreated to the old mission now known as **the Alamo**. **General Santa Anna** laid siege to the mission and attached barracks. On the thirteenth day of the siege, Santa Anna attacked in force. 1500 Mexican soldiers were killed by the Texans, but, in the end, every Alamo defender was killed. At the time of the battle, Houston was participating in a convention at Washington-on-the-Brazos, where Texans voted for their independence.

Shortly after the massacre at the Alamo, Sam Houston led a command of around 900 Texans. They surprised Santa Anna, leading about 1300 Mexican troops, at the **Battle of San Jacinto**. Santa Anna was thoroughly defeated. Independence was secured for Texas.

Sam Houston was soon elected President of the Republic of Texas. He served a term as President, followed by a term as Senator and then regained the Presidency. He was an integral player in obtaining the admission of Texas, as a new state, to the United States. It was 1845. Houston was subsequently elected U.S. Senator, representing the state of Texas in the U.S. Senate. Sam Houston was an advocate of saving the union, as the Civil War appeared on a dark horizon. His opinions were not popular among supporters of slavery, who were many in the South, not excepting Texas. He was not re-elected Senator but was able to regain his position as Governor of Texas. Having been governor of Tennessee, Houston became the only person to be elected governor in two states. He worked to resist the secession of Texas as the war began, but was unsuccessful. He refused to swear allegiance to the new **Confederate States of America** and was then thrown out of office. He remarked, on losing his office, "I love Texas too well to bring civil strife and bloodshed upon her".

Sam Houston and Andrew Jackson were close friends throughout their lives. Houston, in June of 1845, learned that Jackson was dying. Sam attempted to reach the Hermitage, Jackson's famous home, in time to speak with Jackson one last time. Sadly, he was late and Jackson succumbed shortly before Houston's arrival. Observers reported that the tall Texan fell to his knees and cried openly at the dead former President's bedside. Houston stayed for the funeral and acted as one of the pallbearers.

Sam Houston, who had married once again, this time to **Margaret Lea**, retired to Huntsville, Texas. They had eight children together. Sam died, almost without notice, on July 27, 1863. He expired in a downstairs bedroom in the home known as **Steamboat**. The war was demanding all attention and his funeral was sparsely attended.

The city of Houston, Texas, was named in his honor.

Sam Houston and Slavery

Sam Houston was born into a society in which slavery was pervasive. His behavior was, as was true of many Southerners at the time, in conflict with his stated beliefs. He owned, according to records, twelve slaves.

His record, in the words of his own slaves, was one of kindness and consideration for his slaves. At a time when it was illegal to allow slaves to be educated, he insisted that his own slaves be taught reading and arithmetic. Houston believed that black people were inherently as intelligent as white and should all be educated. When his slaves worked, for him or when "rented out" to other farmers, they were paid and they were allowed to keep their wages.

One of Houston's former slaves, **Jeff Hamilton**, wrote a book entitled "My Master – The Inside Story of Sam Houston and his Times".

Jeff Hamilton wrote that Houston treated his slaves as though they were blood members of his family. They were allowed to take outside jobs to earn and save money. Jeff said, "The slave cabins were comfortable and nicely furnished, the slaves were treated with kindness and they spoke in glowing terms of the plentiful supply of good food given to the slaves."

Jeff Hamilton was born, in 1840 in the state of Kentucky, into a slave-owning family. He shares, in his book, this story:

Jeff was "owned" by a family named Gibson. They moved to Texas, taking their slaves along, including Jeff. Gibson was killed in Texas. His widow then married a cruel man named McKell, who was a servant of alcohol. McKell owed a past-due debt for the purchase of two barrels of whiskey. Jeff was, at the time, in 1853, thirteen years old. McKell decided to sell Jeff to pay off his whiskey debt.

A slave "auction block", located in front of a local general store, was where slaves were being sold and traded almost daily. On the day Jeff was to be placed on the block, a large crowd had gathered to watch the awful spectacle of human beings being treated as property. Jeff writes that, as the auction proceeded, he began to cry. As a man known to be very hard on slaves, an "evil" man named Moreland, according to Jeff, made a claim on him, Sam Houston was seen pulling up in a carriage. Moreland offered $500 for Jeff and went to get the money to close the deal.

Sam Houston asked, "What is all the excitement about?" Someone responded "Nothing going on, General. Just a little n----r boy being sold." Houston immediately offered McKell $450 for Jeff, but only if McKell would also sell the rest of Jeff's family to him". McKell agreed but later sold Jeff's mother and his siblings to other slave owners. Jeff Hamilton didn't see his mother again for twenty-five years.

Jeff continued: "My new master then lifted me off the block and took me into the Gibbs store. Tom, he said to the store owner, give this little rascal something to eat. After Sam was certain Jeff had enough to eat, he bought Jeff a bag of candy and a nice new hat. He said to Jeff 'I have a little boy almost as old as you with whom you will play'. I could not then know that on that day fate had taken "a little n----r from the auction block" and would make him "the trusted servant of a great leader, one who believed in the just and humane treatment of my people".

More evidence that Houston was a beneficent slave owner comes from his former slave **Joshua Houston**. (Joshua voluntarily took the name "Houston" when he was freed). Joshua said that Houston didn't free his slaves before the end of the Civil War because it is most likely they would have been quickly captured by other deep South slave owners and sent to work in the cotton fields. Cotton field labor was known to be a very bad existence for slaves.

Much has been written about the close relationship between Joshua and General Houston. Joshua, who served, among many other things, as Houston's carriage driver, eventually carved out his own impressive history. One biographer, Marquis James, described him as "the gigantic Joshua" and described his skills as a carriage driver, blacksmith, carpenter, architect and most trusted servant.

When Sam Houston died, Joshua, whom Houston had encouraged to take work and save his money, came to Houston's widow, Margaret. He dropped a leather bag of money worth $2000 on her kitchen table. The amount would be, in today's value, worth approximately $150,000 dollars. The money was heavy in the bag and had been earned by Joshua working as a blacksmith and other jobs. He wanted Margaret to have the money for the welfare of the Houston family. After the fall of the Confederacy, Southerners were suffering and were financially crippled. Confederate dollars were worthless. Margaret refused the generous offer, telling Joshua to spend the money on good education for his children, but the story illustrates how Houston's former slaves felt about him.

Joshua Houston, during the post-Civil War Reconstruction period, made an impressive mark on his world. He purchased tracts of land, served as a County Commissioner, was a City Councilman, served as a trustee to three churches and even founded a college. He was well known as, according to one biographer, "a tireless worker for the cause of peace between the two races. His many accomplishments, he surely would readily concede, were, in part, attributable to the kindness and concern of Sam Houston.

While Houston was President of the Republic of Texas, in 1837, he had a law passed to make the importation of slaves into Texas illegal. Violators were to be summarily executed. He blocked any entrance of slave ships to Texas shores. He refused to allow permits to be issued to fugitive slave "bounty hunters" and he blocked any payments to them. Houston served as a U.S. Senator for thirteen years. He voted repeatedly to stop the spread of slavery to new states. He voted against the notorious **Kansas-Nebraska Act**, which would permit slavery to be introduced in new Western states. He was the only Southern governor to vote against secession from the Union. When he refused to pledge his allegiance to the Confederacy, he was removed from office.

His behaviors and his political record show that Sam Houston was adamantly opposed to the institution of slavery. Houston lived in a world where slavery was the primary foundation for the Southern agrarian economy. He grew up in America's pre-Civil War South and slavery was woven inexorably throughout both the genteel society and the business environment. The awful institution, though, can never be excused or forgiven. Houston was, by all accounts, a kind and beneficent slave owner and a political supporter of ending the practice. Still and inescapably, Houston was a lifelong participant in the sickness that was slavery. He was a man of his times, a product of his culture and must share the guilt of that culture.

Davy Crockett

American Frontiersman, Pioneer, Soldier and Politician

John and **Rebecca Crockett** lived in East Tennessee when David was born on August 17, 1786. The family moved many times, as John had difficulty finding work that would pay the family bills. Davy was the fifth born of nine children in the family. As he grew older, he was frequently hired out as a laborer, to assist in payment of family debts.

Davy, living on the Western frontier of the new nation, gained much of his education in the realm of hunting and surviving in the hills and forests of Tennessee. He developed great skills as a scout, a hunter and a woodsman.

Davy was hunting, with a rifle, by the time he was **eight-years-old**. When he was thirteen, he was enrolled, apparently against his wishes, in a local school. He was very quickly involved in a fight with the school bully and refused to attend to continue his education. Davy's education seems to have been entirely gained in about a hundred days of "tutoring" obtained from a neighbor. Rather than returning to a classroom, Davy ran away from home. He lived, on his own, on the frontier, where he continued to enhance his hunting and scouting skills, before eventually returning to his family.

Davy experienced an early romance and was engaged to be married, but was abandoned by his first fiancée. He soon moved on to marry **Mary (Polly) Finley**, in August of 1806. Polly and Davy were blessed with three children. They moved together to a farm, located in Franklin County, Tennessee, which they named "Kentuck". Sadly, Polly died in 1815. Davy then married **Elizabeth Patton**, a widow who came to him with two children. Polly and Davy added three additional children to the family.

Another family move, going further West in Tennessee, brought Davy near the area of the Creek War. He was about 25 years old when he volunteered to serve, in 1813, in that conflict. His role in the **Indian Wars** included his participation in the massacre of **Creek Indians** that took place, in 1813, at **Tallushatchee**. His performance during two years of participation in that war brought his name into the public arena, building popularity based on his "frontiersman" image.

The **War of 1812** was continuing. Davy, after the **Creek Wars**, enlisted as a Sergeant to serve under Captain John Cowan in what was then Spanish Florida. He was engaged there in the effort by Andrew Jackson to clear out British forces in Florida, which were aided by regional Indians, whom the British had trained.

Crockett, having been discharged, returned to Tennessee in 1815. He engaged in several business ventures and began to focus on his political interests.

He was a County Commissioner in 1817 and was then elected Justice of the Peace. He became a Lieutenant Colonel in the Tennessee militia. Davy was elected, in 1821, to the Tennessee legislature. His campaign focused on speeches in which he relied on homespun tales of his adventures on the frontier and in the Indian wars. He became known as the resourceful, courageous, noble bear hunter who mastered the "wild frontier". During this time period, Crockett's businesses were wiped out in a flood. His attention to politics became more focused.

Crockett's political career was a roller-coaster ride in and out of office. He served two terms in the Tennessee state legislature, beginning in 1821 and 1823. He lost the seat in 1825, won it back in 1827 and again in 1829, lost it in 1831 and regained it, by a very slim margin, in 1833. His final loss came in the race in 1835. Crockett was a **Whig** and was aggressively opposed by the **Jacksonians**, the party of **Andrew "Old Hickory" Jackson**.

After his final loss in 1835, Crockett was quoted saying "I told the people of my district that I would serve them faithfully as I had done; but if not, they might go to hell and I will go to Texas". And, so he did. Davy left politics. He went south to assist in the pursuit of Texan independence. He, along with a gathering of 30 other volunteers, headed for San Antonio. Some were offered tracts of land in Texas as a reward for joining the battle. They entered the old mission known as **the Alamo**, where they endured 13 days of siege by the Mexican Army led by **General Santa Anna**. On the 13th day, a series of attacks ended with the killing of every Alamo defender, including the legendary Crockett. Later, a Mexican officer who had been at the Alamo, wrote that Crockett and a handful of others were still alive when the battle ended and were captured. His account claims they were quickly executed and he said the group "died without complaining and without humiliating themselves before their torturers". The truth of the matter remains undetermined.

Daniel Boone

Daniel Boone was born into a Quaker family, on October 22, 1734, in a one-room cabin in Berks County, Pennsylvania. His parents were **Squire Boone** and **Sarah Morgan Boone**. He was the sixth of their eleven children. His father, Squire, was a weaver and a blacksmith by trade.

During his time in Pennsylvania, Daniel spent much of his time on the nearby western frontier. He learned hunting and scouting from the settlers and from his encounters with local Indians. One story about his frontier exploits describes an episode when a panther attacked Boone and his boyhood companions. All scattered and fled, except Daniel, who courageously stood his ground, cocked his rifle and shot the panther, right through the heart, dead. The tale may be apocryphal folklore but is part of the Boone legend.

The Quaker Boone family loaded up their wagon and relocated to North Carolina in 1750. Daniel had very little formal education but did pick up reading and writing basics. He was known, later in life, to carry the Bible and the book Gulliver's Travels with him on fur hunting trips and to enjoy reading aloud, around the campfire, to his hunting companions. He continued his love of hunting and exploring after his family moved to the Carolinas. Daniel traveled, mostly on foot, throughout the known states, colonies and territories. He is known to have ventured as far north as Nebraska, as far south as Florida and as far west as Missouri.

Daniel joined a North Carolina militia company during the French and Indian War. He served as a blacksmith and a teamster. Records appear to indicate he served away from the front lines and saw little or no combat action. He returned home to marry **Rebecca Bryan** in 1756. The pair had ten children and also took on the burden of raising eight additional children of relatives who had died.

As Boone's family grew, even though the frontier was unsettled and Indian relations were unpredictable, Daniel would leave home late each summer to embark on long hunting trips. He supported his family as a hunter and trapper, collecting large accumulations of pelts to sell to the fur trading companies. He was often in debt and had to sell fur pelts and pieces of family land to settle those debts.

As he wandered the wilderness, hunting and exploring, Boone often carved his name or initials into trees and some of those "tags" are still found. One reads "D. Boon cilled a. Bar on the tree in 1760". (Daniel Boone killed a bear on this tree in 1760). Some such remembrances are undoubtedly authentic and some are probably fakes, produced by pranksters.

Boone attempted to lead a small group of families to the Kentucky territory in 1773. The group was attacked by **Cherokee Indians** as they continued past the last established settlement. Two members of Boone's party were captured by the Cherokee, tortured and killed. One of those killed was Boone's son, James. The travelers returned to the Carolinas.

In 1775, Boone gathered a number of Cherokee leaders to meet with a man named **Richard Henderson**. Henderson persuaded the Cherokee to sell him their rights to the Kentucky territory. (The deal was later invalidated). Boone then was hired, by Henderson, to take a group into Kentucky to establish a settlement, to be known as **Transylvania**. Boone then led a group to open a new trail leading from the east to the Appalachian Mountains, proceeding along **"Boone's Trace"** westward through the **Cumberland Gap**. The pathway would be known as the **"Wilderness Road"**. Among Boone's party was a slave owner and a slave known as Sam. During an Indian attack, both Sam and his "owner" were killed. It is likely other enslaved black servants also accompanied the group. The attempt to form a colony, Transylvania, failed. Kentucky was made a part of Virginia.

Daniel Boone founded a settlement named **Boonesborough** later in 1775. Boonesborough was a fort-like compound and was located along the Kentucky River in central Kentucky. Indian attacks were still fairly common, but Boone brought his wife and family to Boonesborough in late 1775. A few white women had previously been captured by Indians, but it is likely Boone's wife Rebecca was the first female white settler that far west on the frontier.

The American Revolution, beginning in 1776, soon impacted the frontier. Boone was made a captain in his county's militia and led multiple defenses of Boonesborough, as Indians affiliated with the British attacked periodically. One of Boone's daughters, Jemima and two other girls, were captured by hostile Indians in July 1776. Daniel led a party of Boonesborough men who pursued the Indians. They were able to locate and successfully ambush the Indians. The three girls were rescued, all unharmed. The incident enhanced Daniel's "wild frontiersman" image. The story became an episode in a **James Fenimore Cooper** book entitled **"The Last of the Mohicans"**, now a popular movie.

The **Shawnee Indians** captured Boone in Kentucky in the winter of 1778. He was taken to a Shawnee village back in Ohio. Daniel was "adopted" by the Shawnee tribal **Chief Blackfish**, who meant Daniel to be a replacement for one of his sons who had been killed. The Indians named Daniel "Sheltowee" or **Big Turtle**. It is said that he took a Shawnee wife and was well treated. He was with the Shawnee for several months before finally escaping to find his way back to Boonesborough. He warned the settlers there that the Indians were planning a major assault. A group of Shawnees, supplemented by other tribal warriors, attacked Boonesborough for eleven straight days in September 1778. The defenders at Boonesborough, though highly outnumbered, fought off the series of attacks and the Indians retreated. The episode boosted the confidence of fearful new settlers and

Boone began to lead more of them through the Cumberland Gap or Wilderness Road, to Kentucky.

As the settlement in Kentucky grew, Boone attempted numerous business endeavors. He tried working in the real estate market, but the territories had little legal foundation or structure and he lost money. Daniel tried running a combination store and tavern but was unsuccessful. He began selling ginseng root, but that market collapsed. Daniel obtained a number of horses, hoping to sell them for profit, but many escaped and he was once more left in debt. He finally gave up on the business experiments and left Kentucky in the late 1790s. When the revolution ended, Daniel Boone worked as a surveyor for a few years. He settled in what is now West Virginia.

In 1799, Daniel followed a couple of his sons to Missouri, then part of the Louisiana Territory and owned by Spain. The Spanish, at the time, were actually trying to draw settlers to Louisiana. They were happy to see the celebrated Boone come to their land. They gave him 850 acres of land and they made him a local magistrate. There, he continued to hunt and trap through his later years. Daniel died at the home of Nathan, one of his sons, on September 26, 1870, in St. Charles, Missouri.

Jim Bowie

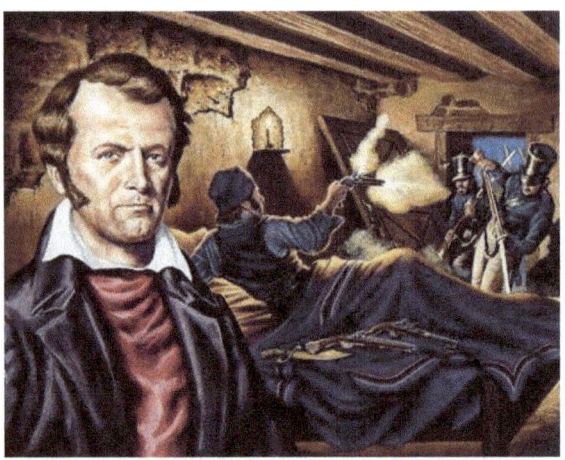

Jim Bowie

James (Jim) Bowie was born, by reports of his brother, John, on March 10 in 1796, just after the end of the Revolutionary War. Jim was the ninth of ten children born to his parents, **Reason** and **Elvira Catesby Jones**. Reason Bowie was wounded while fighting in the revolution and eventually married Elvira, who nursed him back to health. When Jim was born, the family was living in Kentucky, but moved to Missouri in 1800 and then to Spanish Louisiana in 1802. The children in the Bowie family grew up on the frontier, where they labored to clear land, plant crops and harvest produce. Living in Spanish Louisiana, all of the kids learned to speak English, but James and his older brother, Rezin, also learned Spanish and French languages and to read and write in all three.

The Bowie children learned a wide array of skills while surviving on the hazardous frontier. They hunted, fished, cleaned and butchered animals they killed and they became proficient farmers. Jim Bowie developed a reputation as a skilled shooter with a pistol and rifle and was known to be adept with a knife. As a young boy, a Native American friend taught Jim to "rope" alligators.

The **War of 1812** was well underway when **General Andrew "Old Hickory" Jackson**, in 1814, requested volunteers to support the fight against the British. Both Jim and his big brother Rezin joined the Louisiana militia. They were off to New Orleans to join up with General Jackson's forces. By the time they arrived, though, the **Battle of New Orleans** had ended, with a decisive victory for General Jackson.

Bowie left the militia and returned home to work in the lumber business. He labored at sawing rough planks and cutting wood, which he then floated down the bayou to take to market. **The Long Expedition** was organized in 1819, with the objective of liberating Texas from Spanish possession. Bowie joined the expedition, which successfully captured Nacogdoches and then declared Texas an independent republic. The "independence" never took effect and the invasion of the Long Expedition was quickly terminated and rejected when forces of Spanish troops arrived to put an end to the doomed effort. Jim Bowie had returned to Louisiana before the Spanish troops showed up.

The Bowie's were involved in a series of land speculation activities. They purchased, improved and sold properties. Jim and his brother Rezin, at one point, bought and operated a sugar plantation. The family was well known and was deeply involved in "society life". Jim Bowie was elected to serve as a Louisiana State Representative.

In 1827, reports spread across the nation of a **"Sandbar Fight"**, which took place near what is now Vidalia, Louisiana. The episode featured a duel between two men, neither being Jim Bowie, which soon turned into a brawl between all those in attendance. Bowie was both shot and stabbed during the fighting, but still managed, using a large knife, to kill the sheriff of the parish. The incident, well-publicized, was the birthplace of the legend of Jim Bowie and his **"Bowie Knife"**.

Jim left Louisiana again in 1828, moving to Bexar in Spanish-owned Texas. Bexar became San Antonio and is the home of **the Alamo** mission. Bowie became close friends with Mexican government officials and soon had Mexican citizenship. He purchased parcels of land. He married the Mexican Vice-Governor's daughter, **Marie Ursula**, in 1831. They would have two children.

Bowie led an expedition, in 1831, of 14 men, including his brother Rezin, to try to find a legendary silver mine. The supposed location of the mine was deep in Indian territory. The group was intercepted by a large band of **Waco**, **Caddo** and **Tawakoni Indians**, numbering about 120 warriors. Bowie attempted to negotiate with the Native Americans, but the effort was fruitless. The Indians attacked and the fight lasted 13 hours, by which time more than 40 Indians had died. Bowie's group lost only one man but was persuaded to end their expedition. The episode was graphically described and widely distributed in the press of the times and Bowie's fearsome reputation was further enhanced. Bowie was notoriously silent about his own exploits. A former traveling companion, **Capt. William Y. Lacey**, who lived in the wilderness for long periods with Bowie, described Bowie as "a humble man who never used profanity or vulgarities".

It wasn't long before Mexican-owned Texas was inundated with American settlers. Tensions were building as Mexico tried to restrict the influx of Americans. A movement to "liberate" Texas from Mexico was building rapidly. Bowie became a supporter of the revolutionary wave. He joined the army of Texas and was a fighter in a series of battles during that revolution. He became a colonel in the army and, battling an illness, went to Bexar to join **Col. William B. Travis**. Travis was in command of a diverse group who had come to an abandoned mission called **the Alamo** and Bowie was assigned to share the command.

Jim Bowie, working at building up the defenses of the old mission, trying to position a cannon, fell from atop a wall. He broke several ribs and was disabled by the fall. Several days later, on March 6th, 1836, while lying on a cot in a back room, too wounded to fight at the mission's walls, Bowie died with all of the other defenders of the Alamo. He and less than 200 others fought off thousands of Mexican soldiers for thirteen days before finally being defeated and then massacred, by Mexican General Santa Anna's troops.

Jim Bowie and Slavery

Jim Bowie's father, Reason, owned black slaves. Sometime around 1820, just before he died, Reason gave ten slaves, along with other assets, to Jim and his older brother, Rezin. Those "assets" permitted the brothers to spend the next few years speculating in land deals and managing a sugar plantation that Jim had acquired. Records are sparse, but it is known that being a slave on a southern plantation, sugar or cotton-based, was a very hard way to live.

The Bowie brothers had some sort of relationship, perhaps even a formal partnership, with the notorious pirate, **Jean Lafitte**. Lafitte had a complicated history. He was a land-based businessman, an importer-exporter, a privateer and a smuggler. One of the products he smuggled was black slaves. The import of slaves had been forbidden in Louisiana, but the plantation owners needed the free labor provided by slaves. Lafitte smuggled slaves in and sold them to the plantation owners, including the Bowie brothers. Lafitte double-crossed the British in the War of 1812 and assisted General Jackson in the critical victory in the Battle of New Orleans.

Southern states, after the importation of slaves was banned, were paying "incentives" to those who informed on slave smugglers. In a bizarre legal environment, the Bowie's engaged in a complex arrangement that worked to their financial advantage. They went to the pirate Lafitte's property on Galveston Island, where they purchased slaves. They then immediately took themselves and the newly acquired slaves, to the "customhouse", where they "informed" on themselves. The laws provided that informers would receive one-half of the amount paid for the slaves when sold. The Bowies purchased the very slaves they had reported to the customhouse and were then paid back half of the cost of the slaves. They basically obtained the valuable slaves for half their value, then took them up the river and sold them for full value. The Bowies were known to earn at least $65,000.00 running this scheme. It worked pretty much as though they were bank robbers and turned themselves in to the sheriff to collect the rewards, but never had to go to jail!

Jim and Rezin Bowie and another brother, Stephen, purchased a property known as **Acadia Plantation**, near Thibodaux, Louisiana. It was 1825. They built there the first **steam-driven mill** in Louisiana, where sugar cane was ground to make granular sugar. It was well done and successful and was perceived to be a model for that type of operation. The brothers proceeded to sell the whole business, including 65 slaves, for $90,000.00. They then purchased another plantation, this one in Arkansas. It is safe to assume that the new plantation was also worked with the benefit of free slave labor.

The Panic of 1837

An unprecedented high level of unemployment and the failure of some New York banks, in May of 1837, signaled the beginning of what became a global economic crisis. It would be known as the **Panic of 1837** and it led to a financial depression that would last for five years. The panic was the result of a combination of many factors.

A huge cotton brokerage firm, **Herman Briggs and Co.**, failed due to dropping cotton prices. The value of assets, including cotton, land and human slaves, was falling dramatically. New York banks failed and more than $100 million was lost. Almost half of all American banks failed and closed. In many parts of America, unemployment reached 25% of all workers. Nearly 40,000 American families went bankrupt, losing everything. Some states defaulted on their bonds. Farmers lost their land. Tradesmen could not pay their debts. In urban areas, there were "food riots", as families lost their incomes and food prices soared. People working for manufacturers lost their jobs. Texas was still an independent republic at the time and some people fled to Texas to avoid their debts. Stock values dropped dramatically. Some previously wealthy businessmen committed suicide, unable to cope with their losses. Nutritional deficits led to low birth weights for children born at the end of the panic.

Southern states Mississippi, Arkansas and Florida completely defaulted and repudiated their debts. Southern properties were sold off in a massive redistribution of wealth. In one of the ugliest consequences of the panic, surviving investors from Europe and northern U.S. banks found themselves, perhaps without intention, in possession of large numbers of black slaves. The slaves had been sold off to attempt to obtain money for survival during the Depression. African-American slave families were cruelly separated and sold and then sold again. Some never regained contact with beloved family members. Some records indicate that human slaves were among the most highly valued assets being "re-distributed". The huge slave trading company, **Franklin and Armfield** and equally huge merchant bankers, such as the **Brown Brothers**, added vast new amounts to their fortunes. It would be another 25 years before the enactment of the **Emancipation Proclamation**.

The Panic of 1837 persisted until 1842. Presidents Jackson and Van Buren, based on their monetary policies, were widely blamed for the depression in America.

Elijah Parish Lovejoy

American Abolitionist

Elijah Parish Lovejoy was murdered by a pro-slavery mob on November 7, 1837. He was born, in what is now Albion, Maine, in 1802. His father was an activist preacher and a farmer. He graduated cum laude from what is now Colby College. Elijah then moved west to St. Louis, where he ran a private school. By 1829, he had left the school and had become an editor of the St. Louis Times newspaper.

Many of his co-workers at the newspapers were enthusiastic about the **Liberia Project**, which planned to relocate American slaves to Africa. Lovejoy sometimes "leased" slaves, in order to remove them from their ugly situation and paid them for their labor. Among those slaves was **William Wells Brown**, who eventually escaped from slavery and became a well-known abolitionist and writer.

Lovejoy returned back East, where he became an ordained Presbyterian minister in 1832. Protestants out west in St. Louis pleaded with Lovejoy to come back to Missouri and serve as editor of a religious newspaper, an invitation he enthusiastically accepted. He ran the **St. Louis Observer**, which was boldly abolitionist in its content. The paper attacked slavery, with Lovejoy, early on, promoting the idea of gradual emancipation of slaves. He soon graduated, though, to a belief in the full and immediate emancipation of all American slaves. He began receiving threats of violence from pro-slavery factions. Some promised to have Lovejoy "tarred and feathered". He moved the newspaper from St. Louis, Missouri, across the Mississippi to Alton, Illinois. The relocation took the paper out of a "slave state", but kept it within easy access to the river. Alton was known to be a common destination for "slave fugitives".

After his move to Alton, a notorious legal case was decided. **Judge Lawless** ruled on the infamous case of **Francis McIntosh**, a free black man, who was burned and lynched by a racist mob. Judge Lawless ruled that the mob acted out its brutality as a mob. He decided that individuals in the mob could not be held responsible. Elijah Lovejoy was outraged by the decision and expressed his outrage in the newspaper. A pro-slavery mob promptly destroyed Lovejoy's offices. It was not the first time pro-slavers had destroyed his printing press. He began hiding his offices and press in a warehouse owned by one of his supporters. Pro-slavers discovered his hide-out and gathered to fire on the warehouse. Lovejoy and his co-workers fired back and their shots killed a pro-slaver named Bishop. After the shooting stopped, when Elijah thought the incident had ended, he left the warehouse. The pro-slavers were still in the area and quickly resumed firing at him. He suffered five bullet wounds and died on the spot. Elijah was buried in secret to protect his grave from desecration by pro-slavery vandals.

America in the 1830's . . . Continued

John Quincy Adams was one of our nation's earliest and most vocal, abolitionists. While serving in Congress, after being President, Adams presented a series of petitions on behalf of the enslaved. His propositions angered Southern Democrats and Northerners who supported slavery. His ideas would grow in popularity, over the years, but in the early 1830s were inflammatory. Southern Democrats, furious over Adam's contributions, introduced legislation to ban any discussion of the issue of slavery in Congress. The legislation passed and would become known as the **Gag Rule.** Adams led opposition to the Gag Rule, but it was renewed every year for the next eight years and wasn't rescinded until 1844.

King William IV, of Great Britain, passed away in Windsor Castle, in London, on June 20, 1837. On that same date, **Victoria** was installed as the **Queen of Great Britain**. She was eighteen years old.

Martin Van Buren was sworn in as President of the United States on March 4, 1837.

An unknown young lawyer, **Abraham Lincoln**, 28 years old, in January of 1838, addressed a Lyceum gathering of citizens of Springfield, Illinois. It is recognized today as Lincoln's first significant speaking engagement. (A "lyceum" is a place designated for educational and political discussions). Lincoln's speech covered many topics, but seems, in part, to have been stimulated by the killing, a couple of months earlier, about 80 miles from Springfield, of abolitionist newspaperman **Elijah Lovejoy**. The title of Lincoln's speech was **"The Perpetuation of our Political Institutions"** and is known now as **Lincoln's "Lyceum Speech"**.

The Mutiny on the Amistad

The Spanish **slave ship Amistad** sailed near the coast of Cuba in July of 1839. It carried 53 slaves who had been captured by Portuguese slave hunters in **Sierra Leone** in Africa. Among the slaves were 49 adult men and four children, three of whom were girls. Two Spanish sugar plantation owners purchased the slaves when the Amistad came to Cuba. They put the slaves on the Amistad to move them to another part of Cuba, where their plantations were located.

The slaves revolted in mutiny, killing the captain and the ship's cook. The cook had gained their anger by teasing them that they would be killed and cooked on the plantations. They wisely preserved the life of the Amistad's navigator, hoping he could help them sail back to their home in Sierra Leone. The navigator betrayed the slaves and sailed the Amistad to the North, where, two months later, the ship was seized by the **U.S. Navy**. It was towed to New London, Connecticut, where the slaves were jailed.

Slavery was, at the time, legal in Connecticut. The importation of slaves, though, had been banned. The black mutineers were tried in 1841 and former **President John Quincy Adams** argued eloquently on behalf of the Africans. The court agreed with the argument that the slaves had been kidnapped and so had a right to escape their captors. The Africans, unexpectedly, were set free by the U.S. Supreme Court. Pro-slavery Americans were furious about the outcome and the Amistad incident added to the tensions that were building before the Civil War.

The slaves were defended, in part, by a group that became the **American Missionary**. Only 35 of the abducted Africans had survived the mutiny and subsequent travels, 18 died during the mutiny or while in prison. Donations from American citizens made it possible for those 35 to return, in January 1842, to Sierra Leone. The ship on which they were carried home was the **"Gentleman"**.

Martin Van Buren

America's Eight President

Martin Van Buren, the eighth President of the United States, was born in Kinderhook, New York, on December 5, 1782. He was the first American President to be born a citizen of the United States, the preceding seven **Presidents** all being born as subjects of Great Britain. His parents were of Dutch descent and were **Abraham** and **Maria Van Buren**. Martin was the third of five children born to the pair. The family was not affluent, but Abraham owned a tavern and worked a farm. The tavern was a local gathering place for active citizens and provided Martin's early exposure to political discourse. **Alexander Hamilton** and **Aaron Burr**, future contestants in a fatal duel, were frequent visitors to the Van Buren tavern.

Martin's parents were not financially able to send him to college, but his father obtained him an apprenticeship with a local lawyer. Martin studied the law for several years and was admitted to the bar in 1803. He argued his first legal case and won, at age 15. He married **Hannah Hoes**, a cousin, in 1807. They would have four children. Much later, when Martin became President, two of his children would serve in his cabinet.

As Van Buren settled into married life, he became more active in politics. He was associated with a segment of the **Democratic-Republican Party** known as the **"Bucktail"** faction. The group was devoted to a belief in a limited federal government, a **Jeffersonian** philosophy. He was elected to the New York State Senate in 1812 and served two terms. His wife, Hannah, died from tuberculosis during his second term in the Senate, leaving Martin to care for their four children. In 1815, Martin was appointed Attorney General for the state of New York. He was elected to the U.S. Senate in 1821.

Van Buren was adept in political maneuverings and was effective in his various roles. He joined a group of **Jeffersonian Republicans**, supporters of Andrew Jackson and they formed what would become the new **Democratic Party**. It was to be a party dedicated to minimal federal government. In our world today, the Democrat party is very much different and often supports more and bigger government.

As President Andrew Jackson appointed Van Buren his Secretary of State. Van Buren also served as American Ambassador to Great Britain. He was, in 1832, nominated to be the new Democratic party's Vice Presidential candidate, under Jackson. They won the election, defeating Henry Clay and the Whig Party.

President and military hero andrew "Old Hickory" Jackson favored Van Buren and Van Buren was elected President in 1836. His administration was severely impacted by the **Panic of 1837** and the attendant depression and recession. The "panic" lasted several years, the citizens suffered its consequences and Martin Van Buren was not re-elected for a second term. One of his last acts as President was to order that no one working on federal public works jobs was to work more than ten hours per day.

Adding to the problems caused by the economic panic, a long and costly war with the **Seminole Indians** made the administration more unpopular. Van Buren supported Andrew Jackson's harsh policies related to American Indians, which gained him more opposition. He tried again in 1844, to run for President, but was unsuccessful when he lost the party's nomination to **James K. Polk**, a supporter of Southern culture. Anti-slavery Democrats, known as **"Barnburners"**, supported Van Buren. He tried one more time, in 1848, running as a representative of the anti-slavery **Free Soil Party**. Once again, he was defeated, failing to gain a nomination.

After the defeat of Van Buren and the Free Soilers, he retired to his estate in Kinderhook, N.Y. He remained, from the sidelines, active in politics, supporting anti-slavery positions and arguing against Southern Democrats. He threw his support to more moderate Democrats, including **Stephen Douglas**.

Martin Van Buren died in July 1862. The Civil War had begun and the battle over slavery was in full force. He would, no doubt, have been pleased with the outcome.

Martin Van Buren was only 5 feet 6 inches tall. He was known to many as **"The Little Magician"**. His skills at manipulating political situations brought others to refer to him as **"The Sly Fox"**.

Some favorite Martin Van Buren quotes:

"It is easier to do a job right than to explain why you didn't."

"As to the presidency, the two happiest days of my life were those of my entrance upon the office and my surrender of it."

The Antarctic Treaty

American **Captain Charles Wilkes** led an expedition of six sailing vessels that sailed all the way around the world. Along the way, the expedition sailed to Antarctica, where they mapped out almost 2000 miles of shoreline. An American, seal hunter **John Davis**, may have previously landed on Antarctica in 1821 but the episode can't be confirmed. It is known that the icy continent was visually sighted by previous visits by a Russian Navy ship and by a British ship.

On January 19, 1840, Wilkes "claimed" Antarctica for the United States, naming it **"Wilkes Land"**. The legalities of "claiming" new lands have always been dubious, at best. Over the decades, several nations have sighted various parts of the Antarctic shoreline and some have even claimed ownership.

The United States, in the 1930s, established a policy promising to claim no new lands and to recognize no efforts by other nations to claim new lands. The hope was to discourage **"colonialization"** around the globe. In today's world, the legal status of the Antarctic remains clouded. Australia still claims part of "Wilkes Land", but its signature on the Antarctic Treaty seems to negate their claim. The **Antarctic Treaty of 1959**, signed by both the U.S. and Australia, designates Antarctica to be an international nature preserve, open to scientific studies, but with no military presence. As of 2016, 53 nations had signed the treaty.

William Henry Harrison

America's Ninth President

William Henry Harrison was born in Virginia, on February 9, 1773, at the family's home on the James River, known as the **Berkeley Plantation**. His parents were **Benjamin Harrison V** and **Elizabeth (Bassett) Harrison** and William was their seventh child. Benjamin was a planter who served in the Virginia legislature, was a delegate to the **Continental Congress** and was a signer of the **Declaration of Independence**.

William thought of himself as "a child of the revolution" and grew up in a home located just thirty miles from the site of the definitive **Battle of Yorktown**, where **General Washington** won the revolutionary war against the British.

William Henry Harrison was home-educated until he went to a Presbyterian college at age 14. He studied Latin, Greek, French, logic and debate. He moved to Philadelphia with an older brother in 1790. William's father died in 1791, when he was 18, at which time he was placed in the care of close family friend **Robert Morris**, for whom present-day Robert Morris University is named. William began the study of medicine at the University of Pennsylvania but soon withdrew. His oldest brother inherited all of his father's assets and William could no longer afford the university.

Another friend of his father's, **Governor Henry Lee III**, persuaded William to pursue a military career. The very day after he met the Governor, William was given a military commission, making him an officer and had joined the Army. Ensign Harrison was assigned to Fort Washington, in Cincinnati, where the Indian wars were being engaged. Ensign Harrison's first activity, as an Army officer, was to corral a group of about eighty men who were hanging about on the streets of Philadelphia and to persuade them to enlist in the Army. He then proceeded to march the "volunteers" off to Fort Washington.

By 1793, Harrison had been promoted to Lieutenant and had become an aide to **General "Mad Anthony" Wayne**. Wayne was aggressively pursuing the Indian wars and Harrison learned the skills of an Army commander on America's frontier. General Wayne's forces ended the **Northwest Indian War** with a decisive victory, on August 20, 1794, at the **Battle of Fallen Timbers**. Wayne wrote a commendation for Harrison after the battle, giving him credit for his bravery in communicating Wayne's orders to various units during the battle and for "exciting the troops to press for victory". Harrison signed, as General Wayne's witness, **The Treaty of Greenville of 1795**. The treaty forced a coalition of Native Americans to give up a huge section of their lands to the U.S. and to open those lands up to American settlers.

William Henry Harrison's mother died in 1793, at which time he inherited a portion of the wealthy family's land, along with several slaves. He was still active in the Army and sold the property to his brother. Harrison, having reached the rank of Captain, resigned from the Army in June of 1798.

In 1795, while still in the Army, Harrison was romantically smitten by **Anna Tuthill Symmes**. Her father was a judge who had served in the Revolution as a colonel in the Army. The judge rejected Harrison's request to marry Anna. The couple was undeterred and, waiting until the judge was out of town, they eloped. They were married on November 25, 1795 and, because William was still an Army officer, enjoyed their honeymoon at Fort Washington. Judge Symmes caught up with the couple two weeks after the wedding. He confronted William, insisting that William explain how he intended to care for and support a family. William responded, "By my sword and by my own right arm, sir". The judge was unconvinced and told a friend, about William, "He can neither bleed, plead or preach and if he could plow I should be satisfied". The relationship between the two would eventually mellow and the judge later sold the couple 160 acres of land, on which they built a home and began farming. William and Anna would have ten children.

William enlisted the assistance of influential friends, such as Secretary of State Timothy Pickering, to campaign for a position in the Northwest Territorial Government. He was appointed, in 1798, the post of Northwest Territorial Secretary by President John Adams. It was tedious work and William was soon campaigning for a Congressional office.

Harrison had earned a solid reputation through his Army career and his very successful horse breeding business, which was known throughout the territory. He gained support through his efforts to lower land prices. The Northwest Territory had become eligible to have its own Congressional delegate. Harrison campaigned on promises to work to facilitate settlement in the territory and to seek statehood. He won the Congressional election by a single vote and became the territory's first Congressman, at age 28.

President Adams made Harrison the Governor of the Indiana Territory in May of 1800 and he would serve in that position for twelve years. As territorial governor, Harrison was expected to work to take control of more land occupied by Native Americans. Meanwhile, he founded Vincennes University in 1806. He kept busy in various land speculation efforts, so gaining statehood for the territory was important to him, in terms of his financial interests. The Harrisons built a home near Vincennes in 1805. It was one of the first brick homes in the territory, included 26 rooms and was built in the style of plantations of the times. When the territorial capitol was moved in 1813, the Harrisons built a second home in "Harrison Valley". He continued to serve as Governor and to buy and sell land and he built two milling businesses. Harrison was credited with being a good territorial administrator and with making critical improvements in the territory's infrastructure and public roads.

As mentioned, in his job as governor, Harrison was given substantial authority to negotiate and treaty with Native Americans. He oversaw, in 1804, the **Treaty of St. Louis**. **Sauk tribal Chief Quashquame** (Jumping Fish) negotiated on behalf of the **Sauk** and **Meskwaki** tribes, which had large settlements near Nauvoo, Illinois and Montrose, Iowa and a smaller village in Cooper County, Missouri. The treaty effectively surrendered the entire area to the United States. Many of the Sauk Indians bitterly resented the sacrifice of their lands and repudiated the authority of Quashquame to represent them. Sauk tribal **Chieftain Black Hawk** led the resistance. Tensions were very high along the frontier.

Harrison also negotiated the **Treaty of Grouseland**, which took great parts of Indiana and Ohio from the Indians. Historians argue that the Indians had no real understanding of the concept of "owning" land, believing that the land is like the air we breathe and that their Mother Earth was to be shared by everyone. It would have been very easy to exploit their vulnerability. Harrison was able to acquire, in 1805 alone, 51 million acres of Native American land. It included large sections of Illinois, Wisconsin and Missouri. The United States paid one penny per 200 acres and the agreements were negotiated, with the assistance of generous gifts of alcohol, with five Indian Chiefs.

Many promises were made to the tribes, including large financial subsidies. Harrison continued his work to acquire Indian lands through 1809, when he negotiated the **Treaty of Fort Wayne,** by virtue of which he purchased 2.5 million acres of land from the **Potawatomi**, **Delaware**, **Miami** and **Eel River** Native American tribes.

In August of 1810, Harrison requested that the great **Shawnee Chieftain Tecumseh** come to Vincennes to meet with him. Tecumseh, along with several hundred warriors came down the Wabash River. Tecumseh insisted to Harrison that the many treaties were illegal and worthless. He said the various tribal chiefs who signed the treaties did not have the authority to sign for all Indians. Harrison argued that each tribe could sign for itself and, if the Great Spirit meant them to be all one tribe, they would all speak the same language. Tecumseh was reported to berate Harrison harshly and call him a liar.

Tecumseh left the tense meeting angry and soon began his journey to attempt to bring all the Indian nations together to resist the white settlers and the U.S. Army. Tecumseh was traveling in 1811 and Harrison persuaded President Madison to allow him to take a force of 950 soldiers to try and intimidate the tribes, led in Tecumseh's absence by his brother **"The Prophet"**. Harrison thought his force would frighten the Indians into a peace agreement.

The Americans traveled to near the location of the Indian settlement known as **Prophetstown**, at the intersection of the Wabash and Tippecanoe rivers. A meeting was planned for the next morning. The Indians, instead, attacked the American troops early. The **Battle of Tippecanoe** followed and the Indians attacked for hours. The soldiers stood their ground. After the Indians departed the area, Harrison's troops destroyed the village of Prophetstown. They burned the homes and 5,000 bushels of corn and beans. They dug up Indian bodies and left them scattered on the ground. Harrison claimed a decisive victory, though the battle seems to have been more of a draw. He was, however, celebrated in the press for the victory and gained the nickname **"Tippecanoe"**.

Harrison's work was leading to increased tension between settlers and Indians, which led some settlers to be less than happy with him. At the same time, pro-slavery and anti-slavery contingencies were becoming more and more hostile to one another. Harrison was a pro-slavery plantation owner and not a favorite of Indiana Territory's large abolitionist movement. He argued, in 1803, to have **Article VI** of the **Northwest Ordinance** suspended for ten years. It is the Article that prohibited slavery in the territory. His effort was unsuccessful, but he did succeed in enacting laws that authorized indentured servitude and gave "masters" of indentured servants the right to establish the required length of indentured service. Anti-Slavery factions gained control of much of the territorial Congress in 1809, though and repealed the indenturing laws supported by Harrison.

The War of 1812 broke out between the U.S. and Great Britain. Some Indians sided with the Americans, but many took up the cause of the British. Certainly, Tecumseh and his followers were no friends of the Americans, after his previous conflicts with Harrison. Harrison was commissioned to serve as commander of the Army of the North West. He was eventually to lead his forces north to fight the British, who had occupied Detroit. Harrison was victorious in battles in the Indiana Territory and in Ohio and he re-captured Detroit. Harrison led Americans in the **Battle of the Thames**, where his old adversary, Tecumseh, was killed while fighting for the British. His adventures in the war enhanced Harrison's national reputation. Congress awarded Harrison a gold medal for his service.

Harrison held a series of political offices, including a Senate seat in Ohio and then a seat in the United States Senate. He went to Columbia, South America, as an American minister and entered an antagonistic relationship with **Simon Bolivar**. He opposed the militaristic regime and was not to remain long in the position. After being called back by President Jackson, his political light dimmed and he returned to his farm.

Harrison had accumulated many debts during his decades of service and was no longer a wealthy man. One biographer described him, at this time in his life, as "poor, with a numerous family, abandoned by the government, yet vigorous and with independent thinking". He worked as Clerk of Courts, from 1836 to 1840, for the county where he lived. He continued to manage his farm. He built a distillery, using corn he grew himself to make whiskey, but, not liking the effect it had on his customers, soon closed it down. He wrote that he regretted his sin in producing the intoxicating liquid.

George DeBaptiste lived in a nearby town. He was a well-known abolitionist and a conductor of the **Underground Railroad**. Harrison, historically pro-slavery, met DeBaptiste, who appears to have had a great impact on Harrison. DeBaptiste became Harrison's valet and would follow him to the White House. Harrison wrote, "We might look forward to a day when a North American sun would not look down upon a slave".

Harrison still had many influential friends in the government. In 1836, when Van Buren was still very popular and running for re-election as a Democrat, the Whig party ran four candidates. One was Harrison. Van Buren won the election, but Harrison was brought into the public domain again.

In 1840, the Whig Party ran William Henry Harrison in opposition to Martin Van Buren, the incumbent President. John Tyler was his running mate. The slogan **"Tippecanoe and Tyler, too"** was popular. Van Buren was hurt by the Panic of 1837. The Whigs framed Van Buren as a wealthy, aloof elitist. They positioned Harrison as a common man of the people. Harrison won and became the nation's ninth President.

The new President went to Washington to be inaugurated. He took office on March 4, 1841. It was bitterly cold and it was raining. He mounted his horse, wearing no coat or hat and rode to the ceremony. His inaugural address was the longest in history and he stood in the cold rain for two hours delivering it. In his speech, he confirmed his resistance to "big government", downplayed the power of the Presidency, conceded the authority of Congress and the supreme court and emphasized state's rights. His support of state rights extended to his belief that each state should make its own rules regarding the institution of slavery. He promised he would not run for a second term, confirming his belief that the Presidency should not be too powerful.

After his lengthy speech, Harrison stood in line for three hours receiving guests and then attended three inaugural parties. In the following days, he was overwhelmed with petitions from thousands of citizens who wanted government jobs. He became ill on March 28th. Doctors treated him with bloodletting, applications of heated cups, medicines to induce vomiting, castor oil, laudanum, opium and camphor. He was administered both wine and brandy. His wife, Anna, was in Ohio, suffering her own illness. Harrison was failing and cabinet members had been summoned to be nearby. He spoke his last words on Saturday evening: "Sir, I wish you to understand the true principles of the government. I wish them carried out. I ask nothing more". He was speaking to his Vice President and physician, John Tyler. William Henry Harrison died on April 4, 1841. It was exactly one month since he presented his inaugural address. He became the first American President to die in office.

While it was assumed, at the time, that he had died of pneumonia, modern clinicians discovered that the White House water supply was most likely contaminated with public sewage. They believe his death was due to septic shock caused by typhoid or paratyphoid fever.

Harrison was nearly penniless when he died. Congress voted for his wife a $25,000 annual pension and declared she could use the postal system free of charge.

William Henry Harrison and Slavery

William Henry Harrison was born into a wealthy, slave-owning family in Virginia. When his mother died, in 1793, Harrison inherited land and several slaves. Records indicate he owned, bought and sold slaves.

While Governor of the Indiana Territory, he argued for the repeal of the portion of the **Northwest Ordinance** which blocked expansion of slavery into the territory. He was successful in getting it suspended for ten years. "Indentured Servitude Laws" were enacted, though, in place of allowing slavery and kept many black (and white) people held in bondage for years.

Harrison attempted, in both 1805 and 1807, to have slavery fully legalized. While serving in Congress, he consistently opposed any efforts to curtail or restrict the institution of slavery. Anti-slavery forces gained control of the Indiana legislature in 1809 and immediately blocked all of Harrison's efforts to maintain slavery in the territory.

Harrison, in 1831, met well-known black abolitionist **George DeBapiste**, who seems to have had some impact on Harrison's beliefs about slavery. DeBaptiste was a free black man who was an important "conductor" of the Underground Railroad. DeBaptiste became a close friend to Harrison and became Harrison's valet. DeBaptiste later became Harrison's White House Steward. Some believe that Harrison was unaware of DeBaptiste's abolitionist activities. Harrison, however, wrote: "We might look forward to a day when a North American sun would not look down upon a slave."

There is no doubt that, in the early part of his career, William Henry Harrison was a big defender of slavery. He openly repudiated any association with abolitionists. In his private life, he most definitely exploited the institution in managing his properties. There are rumors that he fathered a child or children, with at least one of his female slaves. There are some indications that his attitude about slavery changed, particularly after befriending George DeBaptiste. Some records indicate that DeBaptiste was at Harrison's bedside when the President passed away.

George DeBaptiste

American Abolitionist

In 1815, in Fredericksburg, Virginia, **George DeBaptiste** was born. His parents, **John** and **Frances "Franky" DeBaptiste**, were most likely both born into slavery. Records for black citizens are sketchy, at best and other historians have suggested different names for George's parents. Sources are conflicted as to whether or not young George was born free, but the favored opinion is that his parents had gained their freedom before George was born, making George a free man at birth. One report has both George and his mother being slaves, owned by his father, who gave them both their freedom in 1823. George would have been, at that time, about eight-years-old.

George DeBaptiste, as a teenager, learned the barbering profession while living in Richmond, Virginia. He married a slave named **Marie Lucinda Lee**, who went by "Lucinda" and soon purchased her freedom. As a free black man, George was allowed to keep his own earnings. Black slaves were not so fortunate.

In 1835, George obtained, as a free black man, a **"Free Movement Pass"** for travel in the state of Virginia. Slaves were allowed only very limited travel and only with permission of their owners. The paperwork for the free movement pass described George in this way: "A mulatto boy, about five feet seven and a half inches high and about twenty years of age, who was born free". George wrote, later, that he used that pass more than thirty times to aid fugitive slaves to escape from their owners. It is likely that George assisted more than a hundred fugitives slaves in their journey to freedom.

George, along with his wife Lucinda, relocated to Madison, Indiana, so that they would live in a "free state". Madison is near the Ohio River, between Cincinnati, Ohio and Louisville, Kentucky. It became a favored destination for black slaves in their efforts to escape their bondage.

The Underground Railroad was a clandestine system of people who were willing to risk everything to assist slaves. The "railroad" offered a path to freedom. Slave hunters, men who hunted fugitive slaves, captured them and returned them to their owners, were common. The slave hunters labored to interfere with the work of the underground railroad. DeBaptiste became an active "conductor" on the railroad, doing what he could to assist in safe passage for the fugitives.

A fugitive slave named **Robert Cromwell**, in 1840, in Detroit, was being tried for his unsuccessful attempt to flee his owner. DeBaptiste, with the aid of white abolitionists, was able to rescue Cromwell and take him to safety. DeBaptiste continued his work on the underground railroad, bringing fugitives, by ferry, across the Detroit River and then directing the escapees northward to Canada. DeBaptiste gained the enmity of slave owners. There was, at the time, a law that required free black people to pay a "bond" of $500. The slavers demanded DeBaptiste be arrested for failure to pay the bond. $500 at that time was worth far more than it is today and many free black people were not able to raise the money. **Judge Stephen C. Stevens** ruled that the "$500 bond" law was unconstitutional. DeBaptiste was declared innocent, but the threat from the slavers in southern Ohio was great enough to convince him to leave the area.

DeBaptiste was 34 years old in 1846 and was working in his trade as a barber and also working as a clothing salesman, in Detroit. He was very active in the underground railroad and was considered the "President" of the railroad's activities in the area. George worked as a steward on a steamship in 1848 and learned the skills of a boat operator. He was a successful businessman. He purchased a steamship, the **"T Whitney"**, in 1859, along with a business partner. Black men could not earn a captain's license, so DeBaptiste had to hire a white captain. The T Whitney worked a route, through the Great Lakes, that went north to Ontario, Canada and back south to Detroit, Michigan and to Sandusky, Ohio. It is almost certain that the boat was carrying, along with its legitimate cargo, fugitive slaves, commonly called **"black wool"** in the vernacular of the time.

George DeBaptiste was also a frequent contributor to anti-slavery, abolitionist print media. His writings were published in abolitionist journals such as the **"North Star"** and the **"Liberator"**. In 1859, George met, at the home of abolitionist **William Webb**, with the notorious **John Brown**, the famous black abolitionist **Frederick Douglass** and other anti-slavery citizens. They gathered to discuss ways to promote the emancipation of all African-Americans.

In the course of his work on the rivers and lakes, DeBaptiste met the American **General William Henry Harrison**, who would one day be President. The two struck up a friendship and Harrison hired DeBaptiste to serve as his valet. Historians think it is unlikely Harrison, who supported slavery at that time, was aware of DeBaptiste's abolitionist activities. As a valet, DeBaptiste would have managed all of the personal needs of Harrison, including shaving and dressing the General and organizing his clothing and other belongings. One writer described DeBaptiste as the General's "bright and intelligent servant". Harrison took DeBaptiste along with him to the White House, when he became President. Harrison's term was brief, as he succumbed to illness soon after taking office and George returned to his home.

When the Civil War broke out, DeBaptiste was still working on the civil rights of African-Americans. Frederick Douglass had been working to convince President Lincoln that engaging the black community to serve on the side of the Union could actually save the victory for the North. Lincoln was skeptical but eventually came to agree with Douglass. DeBaptiste was a key player in the creation of Michigan's first black regiment of Union soldiers, to be known as the **"102nd U. S. Colored Troops"**. He also worked as a "sutler" during the war, offering support to the 102nd regiment. A sutler was a businessman who often had a shop inside military facilities or who followed the troops to sell various provisions.

Late in the 1860s, George DeBaptiste continued his work on behalf of civil rights for African-Americans and he served on the **"Freedmen's Bureau"**. He opened an ice cream store. He became a caterer and his wedding cakes won first prize at the 1873 Michigan State Fair. He campaigned for the rights of African-American students to attend "white" schools in Detroit. DeBaptiste became the first black man to be elected to be a delegate to the Republican nominating convention. It was a time when southern American Democrats were engaged in creating the racist **"Jim Crow"** system, designed to keep African-Americans from participating in the white culture.

George DeBaptiste passed away at his home, a victim of cancer, on February 22, 1875. The home is now commemorated by a Michigan Historical Marker.

America in the 1830's . . . Continued

Samuel Morse was an American portrait painter. He became interested in electricity after hearing early discussions about it while at Yale University. He was on a ship returning to America, after studying art in Europe, when he heard a conversation about the new discovery of **electromagnetism**. Morse and his friend Alfred Vail began studying models of **telegraphic systems**. By 1838, they had produced equipment that would send messages, over the wire, distances exceeding ten miles. They had also developed the "dots and dashes" **Morse Code**, which made telecommunications possible. Their first telegraph line ran from Washington, D.C., to Baltimore. The first message sent, on May 24, 1844, was **"What hath God wrought"**. Telegraph lines would soon connect all parts of the United States and would create an information system that would take important news stories instantly over long distances. It would provide a lifeline from the frontier back to civilization. It would facilitate the settlement of new lands and would be an essential tool in the coming Civil War.

Frederick Douglass was an American black man. He was born into slavery. On September 3, 1838, Douglass boarded a train in the state of Maryland. He carried identification papers and a seamen's apparel, borrowed from a courageous free black sailor. Frederick Douglass was running away from enslavement and was now a fugitive. He would become one of America's greatest abolitionists and a close friend of Abraham Lincoln. We will have much more to say about him.

Two hundred years after Harvard University was established, the first University west of the Mississippi River was founded. **The University of Missouri** was created by Missouri's General Assembly in February of 1839. It was to be located in Columbia, Boone County, Missouri. Boone County residents contributed a $117,900 "bonus" to convince legislators to select Columbia.

Women in America were not able to legally own land, as they had no property rights. The first state law granting **women the right to own property** was passed on **February 15, 1839**, in Jackson, Mississippi. It seems incongruous that the American Deep South would be the location for this action. Years before, in Maine, a law had been passed that allowed women who had been abandoned by their husbands to own their property. The Mississippi law, while being more liberal than any preceding legislation in America, did still limit the right to property ownership to married women. In practice, men were still involved, so much work remained to be done.

America in the 1840's

The first organized, civilian "**wagon train**" gathered in Independence, Missouri, now part of the Kansas City metro area. The challenging and treacherous journey began on May 1, 1841 and would not be completed until November. It included sixty-nine adults and several children. The wagons followed the **Santa Fe Trail**. A second civilian wagon train would depart from Missouri in 1843 but would follow the **Oregon Trail**. Previously, a military wagon train, in 1832, traveled along the Missouri and Platte Rivers to eventually reach Wyoming. We'll learn more about wagon travel in the biography of **Narcissa Prentiss.**

European nations, on November 28, 1843, recognized the **Kingdom of Hawaii** to be an independent nation. The date signified **Hawaiian Independence Day**. Hawaii would not become an American state until August 1959.

William Henry Harrison's presidency was cut short when he died shortly after his inauguration. **John Tyler** became the nation's 10th President. He would serve from 1841 to 1844.

Henry Clay was defeated in the Presidential election of 1844 by Democrat **James K. Polk**.

John Tyler

America's Tenth President

John Tyler became the tenth President of the United States by default after William Henry Harrison died only a month after taking office. John was born, on March 29, 1790, to his father, **John Tyler, Sr.** and his mother, **Mary Armistead**. The family was well-known and prosperous. John grew up on their plantation in Virginia. His father served in the Virginia House of Delegates during the **American Revolution** and later became the Governor of Virginia. Young John Tyler attended the College of William and Mary, graduating in 1807 and he gained admission to the bar in 1809.

John married **Letitia Christian**, his first wife, in 1813, on his 23rd birthday. The couple would be blessed with eight children. Letitia suffered a stroke in 1839. The after-effects of the stroke made her incapable of managing the responsibilities of a national **"First Lady"** when her husband won the office of the Presidency. Letitia's daughter-in-law, who had been a popular actress, stepped up to serve as a substitute "First Lady", officiating as hostess of White House social events. Letitia, sadly, suffered a second stroke in 1842. The episode caused her death, at the young age of 51 and made her the first President's wife to pass away while still living at the White House.

President John Tyler, while still in the White House, remarried in 1844. His second bride was **Julia Gardner**, thirty years his junior, who was the product of a wealthy New York family. Julia was well-known in high society and was known as **"the Rose of Long Island"**. Julia and John would go on to have seven children, which, added to his children born to Letitia, made John the father of a total of 15 children, more than any other American President.

John Tyler's political career began when he was elected to the Virginia legislature in 1811. He then served in the U.S. House of Representatives, elected as a member of the Democratic-Republican party, the party of Thomas Jefferson and James Madison. Tyler was a strong advocate of states' rights, strict adherence to the Constitution and limits to a larger government. He considered himself a political maverick, an independent thinker who fell cleanly into no political stereotypes.

John went on to serve again as the Governor of Virginia and then as a U.S. Senator. He was on the ballot as William Henry Harrison's Vice President and they won the 1840 election. When Harrison very promptly passed away, one month after taking office, John Tyler fell into the Presidency. He was the first President who took office due to the death of the elected President. He was elected as a Whig, but he balked at the constraints of party political policies. He was, consequently, while in office, rejected by both the Democratic and the Whig parties. He administered his presidency as a political independent. Tyler carried the nickname **"His Accidency"** because of the unique way in which he became President.

John Tyler considered himself a political outsider or outlaw and he named his Virginia plantation **"Sherwood Forest"** because he saw himself as a political Robin Hood. The plantation home still remains with the Tyler family and can be toured by the public.

Tyler was basically a President with no party. After Harrison died, there were questions about whether the Constitution intended the Vice President should advance to the open presidency. John Quincy Adams argued that the appropriate move was to allow the VP to govern as a "Vice President serving in place of the President". Tyler put an end to the debates by simply moving into the White House and beginning to serve as President.

Tyler's administration, even though he had no reliable support from either party, managed to achieve many of his objectives. He had the **U.S. Navy** re-organized. He created the **U.S. Weather Bureau**. He brought the **Second Seminole War** to a close. He shut down a rebellion **(Thomas Dorr)** against the government of Rhode Island. In 1841, John Tyler signed the **Pre-Emption Act**, which made it possible for American settlers to stake claims on 160 acre tracts of land and then to purchase that land from the American government. As President Jackson's policies designed to relocate Native Americans westward proceeded, including the shameful **Trail of Tears**, more and more land became available to Americans. President Tyler signed, in 1841, the **Treaty of Wanghia** with the Chinese government. The treaty gave American businesses access to Asian ports. A year later, in 1842, he signed the **Webster-Ashburton Treaty**, which settled a series of disputes over the boundaries between the U.S. and the British North American (Canadian) colonies. In 1845, Tyler signed the legislation which annexed the **Texas Territory**. Texas became the 29th state late in 1845. President Tyler signed the bill which made **Florida** the nation's 27th state on his last day in office.

John Tyler, after leaving the presidency, remained active in public affairs. He was a Southerner and he defended Southern interests. When the Civil War was imminent, he stood strongly against secession from the Union. He led the **Washington Peace Conference**, which represented an unsuccessful effort to maintain the peace between North and South. When the peace conference failed, Tyler returned to Virginia, where he reluctantly supported the secession. Once all hope of avoiding the war between the states was exhausted, Tyler went back to Virginia where he acted as a delegate to the Virginia Secession Convention. He was elected to the Confederate House of Representatives, but he did not live to see the war.

John Tyler died in Richmond, Virginia, the capital, at the time, of the Confederacy. He passed away on January 18, 1862. Abraham Lincoln was President and Lincoln did not allow the government to recognize the loss of the Tyler, a former President, because Tyler was considered a traitor to the Union.

John Tyler and Slavery

John Tyler's father was a politician, a District Judge and owner of a plantation known as **Greenway**. He "owned", in 1810, twenty-six enslaved humans. When Judge Tyler passed away, he left Greenway and thirteen slaves to his son.

John soon purchased his own plantation, **Woodbourne**, on which he held twenty-nine slaves. More than half of those slaves were children. The enslaved children most likely assisted their parents with work tasks and were companions and caretakers for the many Tyler children.

Over the years and through ownership of plantations named Greenway, Woodbourne and Sherwood Forest, John Tyler owned varying numbers of enslaved humans. At the lowest point, he held 14 and at the highest point, he held between 60 and 70.

President John Tyler owned slaves throughout his adult life. He was a staunch advocate of "states' rights", including the right of a state to legalize slavery. He did oppose the introduction of slavery to Washington, D.C., but he worked to protect the "right" of new states to allow slavery.

In his personal life, records show he was a relatively kind "master", forbidding cruel treatment by his overseers and refusing to split up slave families. Tyler was aware of the moral problems with slavery and he was disturbed by harsh treatment of slaves, which was illustrated by his refusal to ever personally attend "slave auctions". He had his agents manage the purchases and sales of slaves. He was chronically in financial trouble and was once reported to be very upset when forced to sell off a favored slave. Many would argue that there is no "kind" way for one human to claim ownership of another human.

James K. Polk

America's Eleventh President

A small log cabin in Pineville, North Carolina, was the birthplace of **James K. Polk**. His parents were **Samuel** and **Jane Polk** and James was the first of their ten children. The Polk family was of Scots-Irish heritage and arrived on America's shores in the late 1600's. James's mother was a dedicated **Calvinist.** It is likely that it was her influence that instilled in James his characteristics of hard work, piety, self-discipline and individualism. His father, Samuel, was a surveyor, a farmer and a slaveholder.

Samuel moved his family, in 1803, to the town of Columbia in Tennessee. They were prosperous and operated a successful farm. Samuel soon became a County Judge. The Polk home entertained many prestigious visitors, including Andrew Jackson, who had also served as a judge.

James suffered poor health through his childhood, making his education challenging as he was not able to take advantage of formal schooling. He was, though, a hard worker and was able to pass the exams necessary to enter the second-year class at the University of North Carolina. James graduated in 1818, salutatorian of his class and a high-ranking scholar in the areas of mathematics and the classics of literature. The university, at that time, had about 80 students.

James returned to his home in Tennessee after graduating from the university. He was admitted to the bar in 1820 and established a law practice in Nashville, Tennessee, where he began to nurture his own fascination with politics. His first case as an attorney was a defense of his father, who was charged with **"public fighting"**. James was a solid **Jacksonian Democrat**. He turned out to be an excellent orator and was later described as the **"Napoleon of the Stump"**.

James K. Polk was an energetic, likeable, articulate candidate and was elected to the Tennessee House of Representatives. He worked hard in his campaign and served alcohol at his speeches. He won.

After being elected to the state House of Representatives, James married **Sarah Childress Polk** on January 1, 1824. Sarah came from a locally prominent family and she was no wallflower. She was much better educated than most women of those times. She was politically astute, she was charming and she displayed an aristocratic aura. Sarah was described as "high-spirited" and ambitious. She and her sister famously rode horseback more than 500 miles so they could attend the most prestigious of southern schools, the **Moravian Female Academy**, located in Salem, North Carolina. James and Sarah had no children and Sarah had no love of housekeeping chores. She kept busy tracking her husband's health and serving as a charming and entertaining hostess for formal gatherings. Her strict Presbyterian beliefs caused Sarah to oppose gambling, horse racing, dancing and, on Sundays, music. Many influential and powerful Americans were influenced by Sarah. She was, when James was eventually elected President, known as the **"Presidentress"** and he valued her advice. Sarah supervised the first installation of **"gas lights"** in the White House.

Polk was elected to the U.S. House of Representatives, in 1826, at the tender age of 29 years. He continued his position as a Jacksonian Democrat, often opposing the policies of President John Quincy Adams. He was re-elected several times and rose to become Speaker of the House. Polk was a Southerner, but steadfastly resisted a movement for southern states to secede from the Union. While in Washington, his wife, Sarah, brought James and herself to a position of dominance in Washington D.C.'s "high society".

James was an adamant supporter of **"the Gag Rule"**, which forbade any discussion of slavery in the House. **President John Quincy Adams**, an abolitionist, frequently engaged in passionate debate with Polk.

In 1839, James left the House to return to serve as Governor of Tennessee. He would eventually be elected President of the United States. In his presidential campaign, Polk supported the annexation of Texas to the United States and he supported having America claim the entirety of Oregon. The concept of **"Manifest Destiny"** was popular and declared that ALL land between the Atlantic and the Pacific, south of Canada and north of Mexico, should be part of the inevitable spread of the United States to occupy the entire, vast area. Polk's declared policies supported that concept.

James K. Polk is acknowledged to have been one of America's most effective Presidents. He worked very well with Congress and he achieved most of the goals he defined during his candidacy. The railroads were expanded and the use of telegraph was increased. Texas was annexed, which led to the war with Mexico. The war was won and led to the acquisition of territory to the Southwest and far West, including California. He choreographed the peaceful settlement of disagreements with England which resulted in American ownership of the Oregon Territory. The **United States Naval Academy** was established at Annapolis. His administration authorized creation of the **Smithsonian Institution**. The amount of territory included within the boundaries of the United States increased by one-third during Polk's presidency.

In his inaugural address, Polk addressed growing tensions between Northern and Southern states. Though he was a slave owner, he insisted the union must be preserved. He said: "Every lover of his country must shudder at the thought of the possibility of its dissolution and will be ready to adopt the patriotic sentiment, 'Our

Federal Union—it must be preserved.'" He also addressed the issue of slavery, in a sideways kind of manner, by stating his opposition to any form of secession from the Union. His opposition to secession did not stimulate him to free his numerous slaves, whom he needed to provide the labor for his farm. While living in the White House, some of his slaves served his family in the residence.

During his campaign for the presidency, Polk made a promise to the people, stating that he would not run for a second term. He kept that promise, probably due to his opposition to any form of **"Monarchy'** in America. Polk was known for working very long hours throughout his Presidency. He had an aversion for delegating important responsibilities and took pride in personally managing every issue. His work habits, though, may have been his doom.

When he entered the White House, his health had improved markedly and he was robust and enthusiastic. After four years in the job, he was thoroughly exhausted. He and Sarah left for a long tour of the southern states. They returned to their new home, **Polk Place**, in Nashville. There he died on June 15, 1849. James was only 53 years old. His last words were reportedly "I love you, Sarah, for all eternity, I love you".

James K. Polk and Slavery

Samuel Polk, James K. Polk's father, established a plantation-type farm near Columbia, Tennessee. He purchased slaves and used them to provide free labor (but not 'free' laborers) on his plantation. When Samuel died, in 1827, he bequeathed, to his ten children, the 8,000-acre plantation and at least 53 enslaved African-Americans.

James K. Polk grew up living in an environment in which slavery was a constant, always there in the background of Southern society. As Polk grew more influential and more affluent, he steadily increased his property holdings. He established, in 1831, in the south of Tennessee, a plantation named **Somerville**. He held "ownership" of slaves who worked the plantation.

Polk was an enthusiastic supporter of Andrew Jackson. Jackson engineered the **Indian Removal Act** which led to the infamous **Trail of Tears**, which was the forced removal of Native Americans from their homelands west to reservations. The land surrendered by the Indians was "gold" to investors and land speculators. Many of America's wealthy and influential citizens took advantage of the sudden availability of the precious land. Polk was one of the privileged many who purchased land taken from the **Choctaw Indian** tribe. He put his Tennessee property on the market and declared he was moving his future to the South. He established a new plantation in Mississippi.

The American attitude toward the institution of slavery was changing. Many opponents to the shameful practice became more visible and vocal. Polk chose to keep his public image clean as possible and he carried out many of his transactions through proxies, holding his own name hidden from the public eye.

His "overseers", who ran the day-to-day operations on the plantation, had a series of problems with the enslaved workers. Polk felt that it would be easier to manage them in America's deep South, where plantation activities were far from the public eye and where more abusive practices were accepted. He thought escapes would be more difficult in Mississippi than in Tennessee. When Polk transferred his operations to the South, he intentionally kept the move secret from his slaves. He wrote: ""The negroes have no idea that they are going to be sent to the South and I do not wish them to know it and therefore it would be best to say nothing about it at home, for it might be conveyed back to them." It was common knowledge that the further south you went in the U.S., the worse the conditions became for the enslaved. Polk was known to have fired one of his overseers who had too severely beaten one slave and had shot "birdshot" into another.

James K. Polk served as President, in the White House, from 1845 through 1849. He brought some of his slaves to serve his family in the residence. While in the White House, Polk purchased at least 19 negro slaves, of whom 13 were children. The youngest among them was a ten-year-old boy named "Jerry". Records indicate all of these children were torn from their own families when sold to Polk. Polk wrote that he preferred buying children, as they were less expensive, would last longer and would grow up to have children of their own, expanding his holdings.

Historians have written that approximately 46% of enslaved children who worked on plantations died before age 15 and the figure for Polk's plantation appeared to be at least 51%. After James died, his wife continued to operate under the same conditions that James had established. We know now that 40% of slave owners were females. Parents often left slaves to their female children, knowing that the slaves were valuable property, which would make the girls more "marriage-able".

Polk tried to minimize the appearance of being a slave holder by using surrogates to make purchases and transfers for him. The slaves purchased were then taken south, to Mississippi, to work on Polk's cotton plantation.

Polk steadfastly resisted efforts to block the allowance of slavery in new states and territories. He fought to preserve the "rights" of slaveowners to own black slaves and to take those slaves anywhere they chose to take them.

When the Civil War began, Union soldiers visited the Polk Mississippi plantation. Sarah Polk entertained them in the genteel manner of Southern society. Ten slaves left the plantation with the Union soldiers and seven of them went on to fight with the Union troops.

Samuel Polk "gifted" a slave named Elias to James and Sarah Polk when they married. **Elias Polk** served the family for decades and it is most likely that he accompanied the family to the White House. James Polk hired Elias out to another white man for one year, but Elias was brought back to the Polk household to accompany them to Tennessee when they left the White House. Elias Polk gained his freedom as the Civil War drew to a close. He became, surprisingly, a political leader in the Tennessee post-war culture. Elias oddly allied himself with prominent Southerners within the Democrat Party.

Narcissa Prentiss Whitman

American Pioneer and Missionary

Stephen and **Clarissa Whitman** built a small frame house in Prattsburgh, N.Y., in 1805. **Narcissa** was born there in 1808. The family was deeply religious and supported provision of a good education for their daughter. Acquaintances wrote of Narcissa's beautiful singing voice, as she performed with the church choir.

Narcissa had early aspirations to become a religious missionary. She did well in school and became, herself, a teacher. She taught older kids in one location and kindergarten in another. One of the children who attended her classes later wrote "The lovely young teacher, in the pedagogical method of that day, used cards with letters on them in teaching the alphabet. She kept a cradle in the school room in case any child got sleepy or seemed not well".

When, in 1835, Narcissa heard **Mr. Samuel Parker** speak about the need for missionaries in the American West, she asked whether single females would be allowed to join the good works. The **American Mission Board** refused her request. **Dr. Marcus Whitman** heard about Narcissa and her frustrated dream of serving as a missionary. Dr. Whitman and Narcissa were quickly engaged and then married in February of 1836. They began their journey westward on the very next day.

Narcissa and Marcus Whitman

The trek to Oregon would cover more than 3,000 miles. A group of fur company traders and indigenous Americans led the group, on July 4, 1836, across the heights of the Continental Divide. It was the 60th Anniversary of American Independence. Narcissa, and one other white woman, **Eliza Spaulding**, would become the first white women to cross over the Rocky Mountains. Their successful passage would open the door to future mass crossings, all including women settlers.

Once the peaks of the mountains were crossed, the fur traders turned back eastward. The travelers met with the **Nez Perce Indians**, who worked out passage for them down the west side of the Rockies, along the Snake River, leading to Oregon. Agents from Britain's **Hudson Bay Company**, fur traders, eventually joined them and led them through the remainder of their journey.

The column of travelers was engaged, going down the mountain sides, by a troop of Indians on horseback, hollering and shooting off rifles. The white people were frightened by the loud display and set up to defend themselves. They soon understood that the riders were not a hostile band, but, instead, a welcoming committee. They led the caravan to a clearing where people had gathered to see the new arrivals. The tale of white women soon drew a crowd of Indians and 'mountain men', all in awe of the two ladies. While they stayed with the **Nez Perce**, Narcissa was reported to have spent much of her time with the fur trappers, laughing and sharing stories. Eliza, on the other hand, was more reserved and spent much of her time learning the Nez Perce language. Both women wrote of their appreciation of the kindness and hospitality of the Indians.

Narcissa and her husband established a mission near what is now Walla Walla, Washington. It was then part of the Oregon Territory and was claimed by both the United States and Great Britain. Marcus was a physician, Narcissa was a teacher and between the two they served the physical, educational and spiritual needs of the **Cayuse Indians**.

Marcus and Narcissa, while serving at their mission, had a daughter, Alice. Alice would be the very first white child born west of the Rocky Mountains. Sadly, Alice drowned at the age of two in the Walla Walla River. The Whitman's endured the tragedy of their loss and continued to serve Indians and white settlers. They offered food, shelter, provisions and medical assistance to all arrivals. Marcus and Narcissa also took in a series of orphaned children, including the seven **Sager children**, whose parents had died in the journey from Missouri.

As the 1840s passed, the Indians became more concerned about the growing numbers of white people invading their lands and taking their wildlife for the furs. In 1847, white settlers brought a measles epidemic to Oregon. Many, especially children, died. The Cayuse Indians then attacked the mission, killing thirteen missionaries, including Marcus and Narcissa.

Americans today can see the **Narcissa Prentiss House** in Prattsburgh, New York and the **Whitman Mission National Historic Site** in Walla Walla.

Note:

The Sager Family, led by parents **Henry** and **Naomi**, attempted the journey from their home in Missouri to Oregon in 1844. Their daughter, **Catherine**, wrote that the wagon ride, swaying and bouncing, "made us all sick and the uncomfortableness of the situation was increased from the fact that it had set to rain, which made it impossible to roll back the wagon cover to let in fresh air. It caused a damp and musty smell that was very nauseating".

During the long journey, long before reaching the Rocky Mountains, Naomi gave birth to a daughter, their seventh child. The rains continued in such force that water was running freely through the wagon, drenching their belongings. Soon, in the mud from the soaking rains, their wagon overturned. Naomi was nearly killed in the accident.

Naomi recovered enough to continue the journey. Along the way, the children would sometimes climb down to the wagon tongue to jump off and play or run alongside, doing so allowing their father to continue without stopping the progress of the wagon. Catherine one day attempted to climb down and jump off, but her dress was caught and she was pulled down. Both wheels of the wagon ran her over and her left leg was crushed. Her father did his best to set and split the break in the leg and Catherine grew up with only a slight limp as a reminder.

More tragedy, though, was to follow the Sager family. The father, Henry, was killed when he turned a buffalo stampede away from their charge toward the family's wagon. He was overrun and died quickly from his wounds. Naomi, still suffering from her own injuries, following the overturning of their wagon, found strength enough to continue the journey. Naomi was able to find a man who, for pay, was willing to drive their wagon on westward. His real intentions seem to have been suspect, as it wasn't long before he stole their only gun and ran away to catch up with another wagon train, in which rode his female love interest.

Naomi's sufferings built as she grieved for her dead husband and was weak from the birth of her daughter. Her overall health declined seriously and she began to display the delirium common to those sick with **"camp fever"**. Other travelers cared for her children. Naomi passed away and was buried in a grave beside the trail. Her seven children, aged from 14 years down to only a few weeks old, had become orphans over a span of only twenty-six days.

Companions on the wagon train cared for the Sager children. When the group reached the Oregon Territory and encountered the Whitman Mission, Marcus and Narcissa Whitman took all seven children into their homes. Things went well for them for the next three years, but, when Cayuse Indians attacked the mission, the two male Sager children were killed, along with both the Whitman's and several others. The female children were spared.

America in the 1840's . . . Continued

In October of 1845 the newspapers in New York began publishing mentions of the new game of **Baseball**. The **New York Knickerbockers** was the first named team discussed. The Knickerbockers seem to have created the first set of baseball rules. There were to be nine players on each team, though different numbers of players had engaged in early games. Games sometimes yielded scores of thirty to forty runs for each team, so defense must have been pretty sketchy. By 1848, the Knickerbockers had introduced a system of fines for bad behaviors on the playing field. If a player used bad language or argued with the umpire, he was to be fined twelve and one-half cents. Players who refused the instructions of the team captain were to be fined fifty cents. Fines had to be paid on the spot, before leaving the field. In 1849, the first uniforms worn by baseball players, actually "cricket" uniforms, were introduced by the Knickerbockers. The uniforms were blue and white.

The **Republic of California**, on June 10, 1846, declared its independence from Mexico. The flag of the Republic of California, with its signature bear, was raised to celebrate their independence.

The American war with Mexico was already brewing.

The Mexican-American War

America's **President James K. Polk** promoted a belief in the **"Manifest Destiny"** of America to inevitably expand to include all the land between the Atlantic and Pacific oceans, north to Canada and south to Mexico. His objective was complicated because boundaries in all directions were at issue. America had recently taken claim to the Oregon territory, which had previously been "shared" by the U.S. and the United Kingdom. In that move, a new boundary was established between the U.S. and Canada in the American Northwest.

Texas had already, in 1836, gained their independence from Mexico. The Mexican government was in disarray and their military was in a state of disorganization and was not prepared for a major war. America was also experiencing tension and divisiveness based on questions about slavery. Northerners were reluctant to make Texas a state if it meant adding another state which would allow and support slavery.

President Polk, following his dream to fulfill our Manifest Destiny, wanted Oregon occupied by Americans and wanted to gain control of the American Southwest. President Polk wanted to "annex" Texas, bringing it under American control, but without making it a "slave state". He attempted a series of unsuccessful moves to obtain Texas. He then sent troops to an area of land between the Rio Grande River and the Nueces River, which was a location that all parties had previously recognized as the Mexican state of Coahuila.

The Mexican government reacted to Polk's move by sending Mexican Army cavalry to attack American soldiers between the two rivers. Several American soldiers, under the command of **General Zachary Taylor**, a future President, were killed in the skirmish. The Mexican Army proceeded to attack the American Fort Texas, located along the Rio Grande.

General Taylor called in reinforcements. His troops were better trained and were armed with superior weaponry. Taylor's military force soon dominated the Mexican army at the **Battle of Palo Alto** and then at the **Battle of Resaca de la Palma.**

American troops led by **Col. Stephen Watts Kearny** and **Commodore Robert Field Stockton** easily conquered and occupied the land in Texas between the Rio Grande and the Nueces. Around 75,000 Mexicans were living in the area. Soon after, General Taylor occupied the Mexican city of Monterrey. American **General Winfield Scott** landed a force at Veracruz and quickly occupied the city. He then began a march toward Mexico City.

The Mexicans enlisted the aid of their **General Santa Anna**, who had been living in exile in Cuba. Santa Anna was known best for his attack on **the Alamo** mission, where his men had killed all of the American volunteers inside. Santa Anna negotiated an agreement with President Polk that, if he were to be allowed back into Mexico, he would arrange a treaty "favorable to America". He was allowed to return, based on the agreement that he would quickly negotiate a peace.

Santa Anna double-crossed the Americans and led the Mexican army into the **Battle of Buena Vista** in February of 1847. The Mexicans suffered another decisive defeat, endured heavy casualties and had to retreat from the field of battle. The Mexicans continued to offer resistance at the **Battle of Cerro Gordo** and at a few other skirmishes, but were defeated in every effort. American General Scott attacked and successfully laid siege to the **Chapultepec Castle** in Mexico City. It was reported that a small "force" of military school cadets, to be known as the **"ninos heroes"**, committed suicide there rather than surrender.

As the war wound down, Santa Anna had been made President of Mexico. When it became clear that the Americans would win the war, Santa Anna stepped down. The Americans had to wait for a new Mexican government to be organized before peace negotiations could be concluded.

The **Treaty of Guadalupe Hidalgo** was finally signed on February 2, 1848, formally ending the **Mexican-American War**. The Rio Grande River was designated the American southern border. Texas was annexed as a territory, not yet a state. America agreed to pay Mexico fifteen million dollars for California and all of the territory north of the Rio Grande. It was a very, very good deal for the United States. America acquired 525,000 square miles of new land. Salt was rubbed into Mexican wounds as large deposits of gold were discovered in California at just about the same time as the treaty was signed.

The Mexican-American War lasted from 1846 to 1848. It was the first American war fought on foreign soil. President Polk's opponents suggested that the war was engineered by President Polk as an aggressive "land grab". When it was all over and the Mexicans had decisively lost the conflict, Mexico had given up nearly one-third of its previously owned property. The loss to Mexico, or the gain to the U.S., included all of the lands associated with Utah, Nevada, Arizona, New Mexico and California. The massive addition of land to American control was almost as significant as the Louisiana Purchase.

America in the 1840's . . . Continued

In December of 1845, President Polk declared the validity of the concept of **"Manifest Destiny"** as he applied it to the U.S. The idea was that the ultimate extent of the land owned by the U.S. would inevitably stretch from the Atlantic to the Pacific and from Canada to Mexico. The reasoning behind Manifest Destiny was that the nature of the geography of North America made it obvious that all of the land within those boundaries should be part of one large, un-interrupted expanse of property. President Polk, at the same time, re-affirmed the importance of the **Monroe Doctrine**, which declared that nations in the Western hemisphere must defend against encroachment from European or Asian nations. The Monroe Doctrine held that nations in the Americas would resist any new efforts by European nations to interfere with, invade or attempt to colonize anywhere in the Americas.

The Oregon Treaty was signed, by the United States and the United Kingdom, on January 5th, 1846. America and England had been working under a sort of truce, with neither having legitimate ownership of the Pacific Northwest. Residents included many involved, one way or another, in the lucrative fur trade. **The Oregon Treaty** established, once and for all, that the United States was the owner of the Territory. The northern border of the United States was determined to be the 49th parallel, stretching from the Straits of Juan de Fuca to the Rocky Mountains. The Straits of Juan de Fuca run between Victoria, in Canada and the Olympic National Forest, which is now the western part of the state of Washington.

Cape Girardeau, Missouri, was struck my a **meteorite** on August 14, 1846. It gained national attention as the collision between meteorite and earth created a loud bang and shook the ground. The meteorite weighed just over five pounds and was graded an **"H6 Meteorite"**. It consisted of high-iron chondrite and homogenized mineral composition. Twenty-four meteorites have been recorded as having fallen somewhere in Missouri.

The first **postage stamps** with adhesive backs went on sale in the United States on July 1, 1847. The 5-cent stamp featured a portrait of Benjamin Franklin and the 10-cent stamp was graced with a portrait of George Washington.

Mormons led by **Brigham Young,** fleeing persecution, came to rest and settled near the Great Salt Lake in Utah. They had been driven out of Illinois, where they had settled at Nauvoo, on the Mississippi River. Citizens of Illinois persecuted the Mormons because of objections to some of their beliefs, most notably the **practice of polygamy**. One hundred and forty-eight Mormons, on July 24, 1847, established their permanent base at Salt Lake City, where their central temple resides still today. The founder of their church, **Joseph Smith**, renamed their organization **"The Church of Latter Day Saints"** in 1838. Smith was killed during anti-Mormon confrontations in Carthage, Illinois.

Gold was discovered, in California, tiny flecks in the water, in January of 1848. **John Sutter** had arrived in California in 1841 and proceeded to build a small fort and a ranch. Another man, **James Marshall**, had arrived by way of the Oregon Trail. Marshall was hired by Sutter with a plan to build a sawmill. They created a small canal or drainage ditch, to run from the American River to provide power for the mill. As the water flowed into the ditch, tiny flecks of gold were visible. In no time at all, rumors of easily available gold spread across the country. Dreams of riches stimulated a huge increase in travelers from the East to the West. The need for roads and railroads to carry the load of gold miners incentivized further development westward. The town of San Francisco, which was home to about a thousand citizens, quickly grew its population to twenty-five thousand souls. More than 80,000 hopeful gold seekers passed through the area around **Sutter's Mill** in 1849, giving rise to the term **"Forty-Niners"**. The **"Gold Rush"** created much pressure to further develop the infrastructure of the United States. The Gold Rush ended in 1855, but, by then, three hundred thousand people had come to California, all seeking the shiny metal.

One hundred men and women met in **Seneca Falls, New York**, on July 20, 1848. They gathered in sympathy for the **rights of women** in America. They were led by early **"suffragettes" Lucretia Mott** and **Elizabeth Cady Stanton**. The group's members all signed a document they titled **"The Declaration of Sentiments"**, which demanded equal rights for women, meaning rights equal to those of white men. An actual **Equal Rights Amendment**, specifying equal rights for women, would not be passed until 1972.

Elizabeth Blackwell, in January, 1849, was granted a degree by the Medical Institute of Geneva, New York. She became the **first certified woman physician** in the United States.

The need for creation of a reliable path to **carry mail and freight** from the East Coast to the West Coast was the impetus for proving a **water route** could be practical. Merchants in New York created, in 1848, the **Pacific Mail Steamship Company**. A government contract paid for the construction of their first ship, which cost $200,082. She was a steamship named the **SS California**. The original plan was for the California to steam south around Cape Horn, then north to Panama, where mail would be collected, then on north to San Francisco. There were several stops in ports along the way. The first voyage launched on October 6,1848. Meanwhile, the gold rush was just beginning. President Polk had announced that the first deposit of gold into the treasury amounted to $3000 in value. People took notice. Gold was being found in California. As the SS California proceeded south and came around Cape Horn, dreamers of riches in gold came to each port, hoping to gain passage on the steamship. By the time she reached California, she was loaded to her maximum capacity with **"Forty-Niners"**, all hoping to find their own pot of gold. The SS California was constructed to carry two-hundred and ten passengers, but she unloaded three-hundred sixty when she docked in San Francisco on February 28, 1849. The voyage began as a mail run, but became a vessel for the gold rush. Once in California, almost all of the California's crew abandoned the ship, hoping to find their own gold.

The man who would become one of our Native American's greatest heroes, **Crazy Horse**, was born on December 4, 1849. He would become the powerful **War Chief** of the **Oglala Sioux Nation**.

Elizabeth Cady Stanton

Abolitionist and Women's Rights Activist

Elizabeth Cady Stanton

On November 12, 1815, a female child, **Elizabeth Cady Stanton**, was born to **Daniel Cady** and **Margaret Livingston**. Elizabeth's father was a prominent citizen. Daniel was a successful lawyer, a judge and a Congressman. He owned slaves, which may have had an impact on his young daughter.

Daniel, unlike many of his time, encouraged his daughter to engage activities generally pursued only by men. She studied the law and became aware of the prejudices against women ingrained in the legal system. When Elizabeth graduated from the Johnstown Academy she was sixteen years old. Women were not allowed to enroll in college and she took the next best option, beginning her advanced studies at the rigidly religious Troy Female Seminary. The curriculum there featured religious instruction highlighted by terrifying depictions of the hellfire and damnation sinners would experience. She was said to have had suffered an emotional breakdown and held deep reservations about religion for the remainder of her life.

By 1839, Elizabeth was residing with a cousin, **Gerrit Smith**, who would one day support the **John Brown** raid on **Harper's Ferry**. There, she was introduced to **Henry Brewster Stanton**, a well-known journalist and abolitionist. Stanton was a member of the **American Anti-Slavery Society**. It wasn't long before marriage was proposed and

Elizabeth became the wife, in 1840, of Henry Stanton, though she had the word "obey" removed from the wedding vows.

While still on their honeymoon, traveling to London, England, the couple intended to attend, as delegates, the **World Anti-Slavery Society Convention**. Ironically, Elizabeth and fellow activist **Lucretia Mott**, were refused entry to the meeting, wherein the focus was freedom and equality for black people, because they were females.

Returning to America, Henry studied the law and the couple, by 1848, had moved to Seneca Falls, NY and produced their first three children. Elizabeth would eventually, by 1859, deliver a total of seven children. Her household duties were extensive, but she remained active in the movements to gain women's rights.

In 1848, Elizabeth joined other activists, including Lucretia Mott, to organize the **"First Women's Rights Convention"**, also known as the **Seneca Falls Convention.** She was one of the authors of the **"Declaration of Sentiments"**, which was roughly modeled after America's **Declaration of Independence**. They believed that the fight for women's rights was justified by the same reasons that justified America's Revolution. The Declaration of Sentiments defined many ways that women were oppressed by men in American society. Some of those complaints:

- Women were not allowed voting rights.

- Women had to submit to laws created without any representation by women.

- Women were forbidden to own land.

- Women, in many instances, were not allowed to earn or keep wages.

- Men were given authority in child custody and divorce hearings.

- Women were not allowed to seek a college.

- A double standard existed which allowed men much more. "behavioral" freedom than women . . . women were subject to a much stricter moral code.

- Women were banned from many church proceedings.

- Women were expected, in American society, to take a dependent and submissive role, subject to male domination.

Elizabeth, in addition to reading the Declaration of Sentiments, also proposed that women be given the fundamental right to vote. Famous black abolitionist **Frederick Douglass** was a signer of the document. Douglass and others, would withdraw support when it later became clear that Elizabeth believed that women should come before black people in gaining civil rights.

Elizabeth was introduced to the famous **Quaker** social reformer **Susan B. Anthony** in 1851. Anthony was focused on the rights of women to vote, or **suffrage**, and on the **Temperance Movement**, which attempted to eliminate alcoholic beverages. Elizabeth Stanton focused more broadly on all women's civil rights.

Elizabeth was able to deliver her **"Address to the Legislature of New York"** in 1854. It led to the eventual, in 1860, passage of reform laws which delivered to women the right to gain joint custody of children following divorce proceedings and to participate in business transactions and to own property in their own names.

The "**Women's Loyal National League**" was created by Elizabeth and **Susan B. Anthony** as the Civil War broke out in the United States. They worked for passage of the **13th Amendment**, which abolished slavery. Soon, though, they began to lobby AGAINST the 14th and 15th Amendments, which granted black men the right to vote. For many observers, their resistance amounted to a form of racism. The reason they wanted those Amendments blocked was because, while granting black men the right to vote, they did NOT grant women the same rights. In those times, many citizens still believed that it was more important that all MEN, black and white, be given the right to vote, than that women be assured the same right.

Stanton lost support from many abolitionists, including **Frederick Douglass**, after making statements such as this one: "We educated, virtuous, white women are more worthy (than black men) of the vote."

Elizabeth persisted, though, in her struggle to advance the cause of women's rights. She began, in the later 1860's, to promote measures that women could pursue in trying to avoid pregnancies. She led movements to drive for divorce laws more fair to women and to support reproductive self-determination and to advance more liberal sexual freedoms for women. Some perceived her ideas to be too radical for the times and she lost some of the power of her influence and voice.

After the Civil War, Elizabeth Cady Stanton and Susan B. Anthony carried on with their fight for women's rights. They formed the **National Woman Suffrage Association** in 1869, bringing the focus more on national level efforts. Not long after, their old friends from the abolitionist movement joined the in forming the American Woman Suffrage Association. Anthony was able to unite those two organizations in 1890, creating the **National American Woman Suffrage Association** (NAWSA). Four states, by 1896, had passed laws allowing women to vote.

It would be not until 1919 that the **19th Amendment** would gain passage, finally giving women voting rights.

America in the 1850's

The 1850's marked the tension and divisiveness that led, ultimately, to America's Civil War. Our westward growth meant that new territories were hoping to be added to the United States. The most challenging element in their efforts was the question of slavery. Some hoped that slavery would be allowed in new states and others hoped to terminate the spread of the shameful institution. Annexation of new territories was often blocked, at least temporarily, as disagreements over slavery were worked out. Threats of a "North vs. South" civil war were already in the air.

The Compromise of 1850

Henry Clay, "the great compromiser", took the floor of Congress, January 29, 1850, to introduce his **"Compromise of 1850"**. Fellow **Senator Daniel Webster** supported the legislation, hoping it might avert the threat of civil war. The Compromise of 1850 came when America was trying to manage the acquisition of large amounts of new territory, the result of the Mexican-American War. There was, at the time, a precarious balance of free states and slave states. When new territories applied for statehood, free state leaders did not want additional slave states added and slave state leaders did not want additional free states added. It was a stand-off of sorts.

Back in 1820, the **Missouri Compromise** was passed. It brought in two states. Missouri came in as a slave state and Maine, at the same time, was brought in as a free state. The Missouri Compromise found a way to keep both sides of the conflict satisfied.

In 1849, California territory petitioned the United States for entry to the union as a "free state". Slave staters obviously were opposed, as adding another free state would upset the Congressional balance in favor of the free staters.

Henry Clay's **Compromise of 1850** included five basic resolutions, listed below, all designed to address areas of conflict. Months of debate followed introduction of the compromise proposal. When it was all over and the legislation passed, there had been many modifications.

1. Creates a free state of California. No slavery.

2. It amends the Fugitive Slave Act. It made the slavers happy because it made it easier for them to re-capture and re-enslave runaway slaves.

3. It ends the business of trading slaves in Washington D.C., the location of the biggest slave trading market in America. Slavery itself was still permitted in D.C., but slave trading was forbidden.

4. It establishes a territorial government in Utah and it leaves Utah and New Mexico with the right to decide for themselves whether they would or would not tolerate slavery.

5. It settles a territorial boundary dispute between New Mexico and Texas.

The Compromise of 1850 was an acknowledgement by Northerners that, while they despised slavery, they didn't have the power to force slave states to change. The wealthiest and most influential citizens in slave states were not about to give up the free slave labor that made their plantations profitable. Senators Stephen A. Douglas and Daniel Webster supported Clay's compromise. Senator Webster was forced to resign his seat, after 20 years of service, because his New England constituency was infuriated by his support of the compromise.

The Compromise of 1850 served the purpose of delaying the threat of armed conflict between slave and free states. Tensions remained, though and continued to build. It is important to note that in northern "free states", while they did not generally use slaves for the hardships of plantation field laborers, many did permit the ownership of slaves. Slave trading was often forbidden, but household slaves, in some northern states, were still "possessed" by "masters". The states of Rhode Island, Connecticut, Massachusetts, Vermont and Maine, in New England, all had some history of permitting slavery. Maryland, Delaware, Missouri and Kentucky all permitted slave ownership but were "Northern" states in that they did not join the rebel confederacy during the Civil War.

Zachary Taylor

America's Twelfth President

Richard Taylor and his wife, **Mary Strother**, moved to Kentucky from Virginia not long after the third of their nine children, **Zachary**, was born on November 24, 1784. The Taylors ran a tobacco plantation, known as **Springfield**, on the Kentucky frontier near today's Louisville. The plantation was worked by slaves. Zachary was exposed to only very basic education but learned a great deal about hunting, horsemanship, farming and the use of a musket.

Zachary, at the age of 22, joined the army in 1806. He returned to Kentucky, in 1810, to marry **Margaret Mackall Smith**, with whom he would have six children. One of their daughters, **Sarah Knox Taylor**, would eventually marry **Jefferson Davis**, who would be President of the Confederacy.

Over the next two decades, Zachary Taylor led various American Army forces in efforts to manage and police the borders of America's frontier. He was in charge of units assigned the unpleasant and often shameful, task of controlling and re-locating Native American Indians.

Taylor also would become, over time, the owner and operator of plantation farms in Baton Rouge, Louisiana and in Rodney, Mississippi. On those plantations lived and worked hundreds of enslaved black people.

In the course of his army career, stretching nearly 40 years, Taylor reached the rank of Major General by 1846. He led forces in combat in the **War of 1812** and in the **Black Hawk War of 1832**. He also commanded forces in the **Second Seminole Wars** in Florida, which lasted for several years. His leadership during the **Battle of Lake Okeechobee** led to his promotion to the high rank of Brigadier General.

Taylor's series of well-publicized successes achieved during the **Mexican-American War** led him to national popularity. His troops won solid victories at the **Battle of Palo Alto** and then again at the **Battle at Resaca de la Palma**. After capturing the Mexican city of Monterey, Taylor offered the Mexican army an eight-week armistice, which angered President Polk. Polk re-assigned many of Taylor's troops and told Taylor to restrict his activities to those necessary for defense. Zachary Taylor disobeyed Polk's orders and led his troops south to engage the Mexican Army in the **Battle of Buena Vista**. Taylor's command won a brilliant victory, even though, after Polk stripped his forces, he was outnumbered four to one by the Mexicans. His victories during the Mexican-American War brought him a wave of popularity that stimulated the Whig Party to begin staging him as a potential Presidential candidate.

The Whig Party nominated Taylor to represent them in the Presidential election of 1848. His Vice-Presidential running mate was **Millard Fillmore**. They won the election and Zachary Taylor became our twelfth President.

The administration of Zachary Taylor was beset with sticky problems related to the annexation of new territories and whether or not those territories and states would be accepted as free or slave entities. Taylor, though he still owned slaves who were working his plantations, had come to believe it would be a bad thing to allow the institution to be carried over into new states. In late 1849, President Taylor called for immediate statehood for California, which would, if admitted, be a "free state", allowing no slavery. Southerners, not wanting the balance of power to shift to the "free staters, fought bitterly to resist the admission of California. The issue remained unresolved until the passage of the Compromise of 1850. President Taylor, by that time, was dead.

President Zachary Taylor was the victim of stomach problems caused by a sudden and severe attack of cholera and died on July 9, 1850. He had served only 16 months in office.

President Zachary Taylor and Slavery

Zachary Taylor's father was a plantation owner. He owned, in the early 1800s, 26 enslaved workers. Their home in Kentucky was built, and then maintained, using slave labor. When Zachary's father, Richard, died, he left two slaves, named Charles and Tom, to Zachary. Charles and Tom both remained with Zachary until his death in 1850. Zachary eventually owned at least three plantations, one being in Kentucky, another in Mississippi and yet another in Louisiana. When he purchased the plantation in Mississippi, **Cypress Grove**, he also purchased eighty-one enslaved men, women and children. Each of their names is still on record.

Taylor would ultimately "own" hundreds of slaves. In his political career, he was known to be opposed to the spread of slavery to newly admitted states. He was a "fence-sitter" on the **Wilmot Proviso**, which would have allowed slavery in new lands gained from Mexico, but he pushed for admission of California as a free state.

Twelve years after Zachary's death, during the Civil War, in 1862, Union troops occupied one of his plantations. Most of his books and records were destroyed, which makes tracking exact information about his slave ownership difficult. He was in the White House for such a short time that not a lot of information was left behind. We know that he was the last President to bring slave labor into the White House, but we don't know much about how many or exactly who those slaves were. One of the slaves who accompanied him to the White House was his long-time personal servant Charles. Charles died suddenly, shortly before the unexpected death of the President.

Records show that slaves named **Charles**, **Tom**, **Dicey**, **Jane**, **William** and **Caroline** seemed always to be with Zachary, even when he went to war. On his death, he left those same six to his wife. Some of them eventually became the property of some of Zachary's children. His daughter Ann wrote of the slaves: "They have been first class family servants, always having employed in that capacity. Jane is an excellent cook. Three are good seamstresses."

Even while President, Taylor visited his plantations and wrote to his overseers regularly. One of his letters directs his overseer "Let your first consideration be the health of the servants." He instructed the overseer to deliver five dollars to each slave laborer at Christmas. As a plantation owner, it was only good business to maintain the good condition of his slaves, enabling them to produce long days of hard labor.

Just prior to his early death, in 1850, Zachary bought a plantation for one of his sons. It was in Louisiana and was known as **"Fashion"**. Along with the plantation, Taylor purchased an additional sixty-four slaves.

On his death, Zachary Taylor bequeathed more than 130 slaves to members of his family. His will instructed that they be **"slaves for life"**. He wrote this direction: "I wish the servants only moderately worked and kindly treated and the old men took good care of and made comfortable."

His tone seemed kind and paternalistic, but the fact is that Taylor freed none of his slaves and continued his active participation in the slave culture through to his death. Some of his slaves were eventually freed through emancipation and many of them escaped during the confiscations and ransacking of the plantations by Union troops.

Millard Fillmore

America's Thirteenth President

Many Presidents claimed "humble origins", but Millard Fillmore was one who actually was born, on January 7, 1800, in a log cabin. The cabin was in New York state and served as the family home while Millard's father labored as a poor tenant farmer. Millard was blessed with very little formal education, but managed, at age 18, to put together six months of continuous schooling. He was "apprenticed" to a "wool carder" in his early teens. When he fulfilled the terms of his apprenticeship, Millard took work in a law office. He was known to be a hard and reliable worker. Millard was himself admitted to the bar when he was 23 years old. Once Millard had established stable employment and gained security, he married, in 1826, the girl he had loved for several years, a teacher named **Abigail Powers**.

Abigail Powers Fillmore was the first "First Lady" to hold a job while living in the White House, as she continued teaching. She added a music room and three pianos to the White House furnishings. She expanded the White House library. Their first child, a son named Millard Powers Fillmore, was born in 1828, to be followed by his sister, Mary Abigail, in 1832. Abigail Fillmore, Millard's wife, died, as a victim of pneumonia, in 1853. Five years later, Millard re-married. His second wife was **Caroline Carmichael McIntosh**, a wealthy widow.

Millard Fillmore became a successful attorney and politician in the area around Buffalo, New York. In 1828, he was elected to the New York Assembly and then, in 1832, to the House of Representatives. Along the way, he was an early member of the Whig party. The Whig Party eventually was transformed into the new Republican Party and was dominated by anti-slavery forces.

Fillmore served four terms as a Congressman. He attempted an unsuccessful run, in 1844, to be Governor of New York. In 1848, he was serving in the office of comptroller of New York. He was selected, by the Whig party, to run for Vice President, on the ticket on which Zachary Taylor was running for the Presidency. They won, but Taylor died only weeks into his term, moving Millard Fillmore, by default, into the Presidency. Taylor was a slaveholder from Louisiana, though he didn't favor the expansion of slavery into new states. Fillmore was a Northern businessman and the Whigs thought his antagonism to slavery would add balance to their ticket.

The **"free state vs. slave state"** conflict, at the time, was intense. Zachary Taylor supported the entry of California and New Mexico as states in which slavery would be banned. The move was passionately resisted by Southern Democrats. Taylor was not a supporter of **Henry Clay's Omnibus Bill**, which became the foundation for his

Compromise of 1850. Millard Fillmore, though, did support Clay's Compromise. After Taylor unexpectedly died and Fillmore became President, Fillmore dismissed Taylor's Presidential Cabinet and filled the positions with his own selections.

Fillmore pressed for the passage of the Compromise of 1850 and it was passed. The Compromise was far from perfect, but it served the immediate and much-needed purpose of delaying the Civil War for another ten years. Fillmore was firmly anti-slavery. The Compromise was the best available way to manage the growing anger and tension around the slavery issue. It was comprised of five separate bills. One brought California into the Union as a free state. Another left Utah and New Mexico in limbo, allowing them to make their own decisions about how to address slavery. Another banned the 'slave trade' in Washington, D.C., though it allowed the continuation of slavery as it existed at that time. The Compromise also redefined the boundaries of Texas, following the Mexican-American War. Finally and most damaging to Fillmore, the Compromise provided that **The Fugitive Slave Act** was to be honored. Northerners and the government were to be bound by the law to return run-away slaves to their "owners". This condition had to be added or no Southern state representatives would vote to support the Compromise.

Millard Fillmore was no supporter of slavery. He was faced with the imminent dissolution of the Union if some sort of compromise couldn't be reached. He believed Clay's Compromise of 1850 was the best avenue to keeping the Union altogether. Unfortunately, the anti-slavery, abolitionist movement was growing more and more powerful and they deeply resented the part of the Compromise that required compliance with the Fugitive Slave Act. They blamed Fillmore. He made the situation worse when, reluctantly, he announced that, if necessary, the American military might be used to enforce the Fugitive Slave Act. The issue probably doomed Fillmore's chances of ever being re-elected.

Millard Fillmore, indeed, was not re-elected for a second term. He took another run at the Presidency in 1852. It was the final campaign for the Whigs. Fillmore, one more time, representing the **"Know Nothing Party"**, tried for the Presidency in 1856. It would be his final attempt and it was unsuccessful.

The "Know Nothing Party", also known as the **"American Party"**, was formed by an assembly of religious Protestants who were in fear of what they perceived to be a dangerous expansion of the Catholic Church. The "Know Nothings" must have been a little paranoid and gained the name because insiders were required to answer "I know nothing" anytime they were asked about the details of their organization. The Know Nothings supported the rights of laborers, the expansion of civil rights for women, a bigger government and more government regulations applied to business and industry. The party was an ancestor of the American temperance movement.

Fillmore, after his final Presidential campaign failure, returned to his home in Buffalo, New York. He remained active in civic affairs and local politics. He was one of the founders of the University of Buffalo, back in 1846. Millard also was a founder of Buffalo General Hospital. His beloved wife, Abigail, died in 1853 and he remarried in 1858.

Fillmore is frequently listed as one of America's worst Presidents. His reputation was stained by the attacks on him, based on the old anger over the Compromise of 1850 and because he supported the Reconstruction activities of President Andrew Johnson, now considered to be racist and characterized by the "Jim Crow" era.

America in the 1850's . . . Continued

The **census count** of 1850 revealed that the population of the United States had grown by 35.9% since the count was done one decade previously. There were now 23,191,876 people within the boundaries of the United States. Among those were 3,204,313 enslaved human beings, which reflected 716,958 more slaves than were in the U.S. in 1840, just ten years earlier. In 1850, the Union included 30 states. The city with the highest number of occupants was New York, which was home to more than 500,000 citizens.

American showman and entrepreneur **P.T. Barnum** brought **Jenny Lind**, "the Swedish Nightingale" to America in September of 1850. He introduced her at the Castle Garden, formerly a fort on Manhattan Island, where 6,000 people paid the high price of $3.00 each to see the singing phenomenon. Her performance was a rousing success. Jenny Lind was paid $187,000, the equivalent in today's money of more than six million dollars and she delivered 150 concerts in cities all across the United States.

P. T. Barnum

Jenny Lind

Harriet Beecher Stowe's book "**Uncle Tom's Cabin or, Life Among the Lowly**" was published in March of 1852. The nation was, at that time, deeply divided over the issues surrounding the institution of slavery. Many Northerners were passionate abolitionists, but slavery existed in many northern states. "Uncle Tom's Cabin" brought the misery of life as an American slave, the fear, the cruel brutality and the immorality of the very idea of one human "owning" another, all into clear view. The book was immensely popular and is often credited with bringing opposition to slavery into the open, forcing acknowledgment of its existence and fueling the fire that would soon build into the tragic flames of the Civil War.

The intensity of the struggle between abolitionists and slave supporters, between northern and southern states, continued to increase throughout the 1850s. Most events occurring during that time frame were flavored, one way or another, by the slave question. In September 1851, a fugitive slave hunter, **Edward Gorsuch**, was in Maryland to capture four black seekers of freedom. His efforts resulted in what came to be known as **"The Christiana Riot".** Gorsuch was soon engaged by persons on the farm where the black fugitives had been staying and he was shot to death. The incident drew a lot of attention, which became focused on Northern resistance to the **Fugitive Slave Act**, which required Northerners to return fugitive slaves to their owners. Following that law, a manhunt was organized to pursue the four fleeing slaves. The fugitives were aided by the **Underground Railroad** and benefited from the intervention of the famous black abolitionist, **Frederick Douglass**, who had himself been a fugitive from slavery. The four made it safely to freedom in Canada. Some of those who defended the escaped slaves were then arrested for violation of the Fugitive Slave Act. A white man, **Castner Hanway**, a Quaker, was arrested for treason. His trial became a trial of the Fugitive Slave Act and Hanway was found innocent and released. While the Christiana Riot is not well known today, it marked another spark in the fire building toward the Civil War. Other incidents would soon follow.

On December 30, 1853, **the Gadsen Purchase** brought an additional 30,000 square miles into the United States. The area was located between the Southern borders of Arizona and New Mexico and the Northern border of Mexico. The land was desired by **James Gadsden**, who was President of the South Carolina Railroad and the purchase was pushed by **Jefferson Davis**, who was the American Secretary of War at the time. Gadsden had been involved in the **"Trail of Tears"**, the forced relocation of the **Seminole Indians**. He hoped to build a **transcontinental railroad** that would pass through the area included in the **Gadsden Purchase**. The United States paid ten million dollars for the 29,640 square miles given up by Mexico. The purchase characterized the continuing rapid expansion of the United States. It marked the completion of the final borders of the continental United States.

The Kansas-Nebraska Act

Illinois **Senator Stephen A. Douglas** proposed the **Kansas-Nebraska Act** in 1854. It followed the passage of the **Compromise of 1850** and it reversed some of the terms of the **Missouri Compromise of 1820**, which banned slavery above a designated boundary. Much of the **Nebraska Territory** was located north of that line and therefore permitted no slavery. Douglas hoped to gain entry into the area, perhaps because he wanted to run a railroad across it. The Nebraska Territory included Kansas, Nebraska, Montana and the Dakotas. The Compromise of 1850 provided that each of these territories could determine their own decisions related to becoming slave or no-slave states.

California had just entered the Union, under the terms of the Compromise of 1850, as a free state. The balance of power between slave states and free states was precarious. Stephen A. Douglas needed the support of slave states to get his Kansas-Nebraska Act passed. The terms of the Missouri Compromise of 1821 made much of the Nebraska Territory bound by the ban on slavery. Southern states were opposed to the passage of the Kansas-Nebraska Act because they did not want additional free states brought into the Union. It would disturb the free state-slave state balance of power in favor of the free states.

In order to bring the southern 'slave' states on board with his proposal, Stephen A. Douglas added to his Kansas-Nebraska Act amendments to repeal the Missouri Compromise and to create new territories. The new territories would be Kansas and Nebraska and they would each be allowed to vote for their own decisions about slavery status. The concept of allowing each area to vote to establish its own conditions was known as "**popular sovereignty**". Repeal of the Missouri Compromise opened up the possibility of the introduction of slavery to new territories and states, which gained Douglas the critical support of southern slave states.

Abolitionists passionately opposed the passage of the Kansas-Nebraska Act or Nebraska Act. In spite of their adamant resistance, the Nebraska Bill was passed and it was signed into law, on May 30, 1854, by then-**President Franklin Pierce**. The anger of abolitionists over Douglas's legislation may have done irreparable harm to his hope of becoming President.

While the Kansas-Nebraska Act created new conditions to manage the additions of new territories, it reflected the continuing abuse of **Native Americans**. Many American Indians had been given no real option but to sign a long series of treaties with the American government. Those treaties forced the Indians to accept terms that gave up more and more of their original homelands and to agree to accept, in return, re-locations to various western tracts of land. As white settlers continued to move westward and pressure was increased to push roads and railroads westward, the treaties were repeatedly broken by the American government and the Indians were forced further west. Many in the Nebraska area were eventually relocated to the barren lands of Oklahoma.

Abolitionists and "free staters" were furious about the passage of the Kansas-Nebraska Act. They believed that their movement to eliminate slavery completely was back-stabbed by Stephen A. Douglas's legislation. They perceived it to be equivalent to opening a door wide to further the institution of slavery, while they were fighting to put a stop to it.

Nebraska was firmly anti-slavery and would enter as a free territory. Kansas, however, was a hotbed for conflict between the two forces. Groups of advocates for both pro-slavery and anti-slavery poured into the territory. Conflicts between them quickly escalated. Kansas became known as **"Bleeding Kansas"**. Pro-slavery **"border ruffians"** periodically invaded Kansas to deal violence and destruction to anti-slavery establishments. Anti-slavery raiders from Kansas, called free soilers, crossed the river to do the same sort of things in Missouri

Tensions across the country were amplified. Political parties were torn apart, as groups within the parties split on the issue. The **"Whig Party"** was basically killed off in the conflicts and would essentially be replaced by the new **"Republican Party"**. The Republican Party was formed around the objective of completely eliminating slavery. It had virtually no support in the South. Young **Abraham Lincoln** began to make his name while being drawn into the new Republican party. His eloquent arguments in opposition to any extension of slavery into new territories were widely shared.

The Democrat Party was also torn asunder by conflicts between Democrats living in different regions of the U.S. **Stephen A. Douglas** would become the Democrat who represented Democrats in the Northern states. His debates with Abraham Lincoln would become legendary.

The antagonism between the pro- and anti-slavery sentiments was tragically illustrated in an act that would live in infamy in the history of our Senate and House of Representatives. **Senator Charles Sumner** of Massachusetts, very much anti-slavery, had delivered a speech on the Senate floor which addressed what he called the "crime against Kansas". His speech argued that anyone who supported permission for slavery in Kansas was committing a crime against the territory and the nation.

Senator Sumner specifically pointed out two Senators as being the principal perpetrators of the "crime". He named Stephen A. Douglas, of Illinois and **Andrew Butler**, of South Carolina, as the drivers of the legislation, which he said would encourage the spread of slavery. Sumner openly described Stephen A. Douglas, right to his face, as a "noise-some, squat and nameless animal". He further mocked Senator Andrew Butler, who was not present at the time, by making fun of Butler's status as a "chivalrous" man.

284

Sumner claimed that Butler had taken "a mistress who, though ugly to others, is always lovely to him; though polluted in the sight of the world, is chaste in his sight." "I mean", Sumner added, "that harlot, Slavery".

Three days after Sumner's speech, on May 22, 1856, a member of the House of Representatives entered the Senate Chamber. He was **Representative Preston Brooks**, who was a friend and kinsman to fellow South Carolinian Andrew Butler. Brooks, in tune with Southern culture, would have challenged Sumner to a duel, but he did not do this as it would lend credence to Sumner being a "gentleman". Instead, to illustrate his disdain for Sumner, he brought along a light cane, typical of an instrument that would be used to discipline a mangy, mean dog.

The Senate had adjourned and the chamber was mostly empty, but Sumner was there, busy putting postage on copies of his "Crime Against Kansas" speech. Preston Brooks approached him briskly. Brooks brought his cane, with its metal top, down hard on Sumner's head. He struck Sumner repeatedly. Sumner gained his feet but was blinded by blood and he lurched about aimlessly as Brooks continued to strike him. It became, unquestionably, a savage beating. Sumner was beaten into unconsciousness.

Brooks, after the beating was ended, walked nonchalantly out of the chamber, with no effort made to detain him. Sumner was lifted and carried away for medical attention. Brooks was censured by the House and then resigned. His actions were actually celebrated by pro-slavery factions and he was immediately re-elected. He died at the young age of 37. Sumner slowly recovered from his wounds and would serve in the Senate for many more years. Just as Brooks was glorified by pro-slavers, Sumner was a hero to abolitionists.

Franklin Pierce

America's Fourteenth President

Franklin Pierce was born in Hillsborough, New Hampshire, on November 23, 1804. His father was a hero of the **American Revolution**, **Benjamin Pierce**, who was a farmer, a tavern owner and a politician who had served two terms as Governor of New Hampshire. Franklin grew up in a well-to-do, prosperous, prominent family environment. His mother, **Anna Kendrick** Pierce, made the education of her children her highest priority. Anna would eventually give birth to eight children, of whom Franklin was the fifth.

Franklin attended public schools until age 12, at which time he began to attend private facilities. Franklin then attended Bowdoin College, located in Maine, where he met his future wife, Jane. He enrolled at Bowdoin at the age of 15. While at Bowdoin, Franklin established a reputation as an excellent public speaker. He proceeded, on leaving Bowdoin, to the study of law and was admitted to the bar in 1827.

As a member of the Democratic Party, Franklin was first elected to the New Hampshire state legislature at the age of 24 years. Only two years later he was elected Speaker of the House. His father, at the time, was serving as Governor. Franklin was a solid supporter of President Andrew "Old Hickory" Jackson, which led to his being nicknamed **"Young Hickory"**. Franklin began serving in Congress in 1833. He married **Jane Means Appleton**, who was the daughter of the President of Bowdoin College, in 1834. Jane was a shy and quiet woman, quite religious, who was a supporter of the temperance movement, fighting the use and effects of alcohol. She suffered illnesses, including tuberculosis and depression, throughout her life.

The personal and family life of the Pierces was peppered with unhappy episodes. Franklin and Jane produced three children. None of their three sons would survive. Their first son died at the age of three days. Their second son died at the age of four, a victim of typhus. Their third son died in a train accident, only weeks after Franklin's Presidential election. While traveling to Boston, early in January 1852, their train left the rails and rolled down a hillside. Franklin and Jane were not seriously injured, but their son, Benjamin, was crushed and nearly decapitated in the wreckage. Franklin was not able to prevent Jane from viewing the carnage. Jane never recovered from the loss of her three sons.

While at Bowdoin College, Franklin organized an intramural sort of militia, known as the Bowdoin Cadets. Their drills were shut down when the President of the college complained about the noise made by their drilling exercises. Later, Pierce joined the New Hampshire militia, as nearly all white males did, and would serve for many years. He was chosen to serve **as "aide de camp"** to the Governor in 1831 and he would continue to serve in the militia until 1847, by which time he had reached the rank of colonel. He would be promoted to brigadier general in the U.S. Army during the **Mexican-American War**. In 1832 he was nominated to serve New Hampshire as a member of the U.S. House of Representatives, an election he won easily. At the time, he had become recently engaged to Jane and had purchased his first house. President Jackson visited New Hampshire in 1833, where he was welcomed by Franklin Pierce and his father, Benjamin.

Franklin Pierce served two terms in the U.S. House of Representatives and then one term as a U.S. Senator, always representing New Hampshire. His reputation was that of an intelligent man, popular, likable and outgoing. He left the Senate due to family issues, believed to be his wife's poor health and returned home to resume his law practice. As an attorney, he was known for his skills in the courtroom and for representing people who had few or nor resources with which to pay for his services, **"pro bono"** work.

Pierce served in the Mexican-American War (1846-1848) as an officer. As a brigadier general, he led his troops through several battles. At the **Battle of Contreras**, his horse went down, severely injuring Pierce's knee. In spite of excruciating pain, he had himself tied to his saddle and continued to lead his forces through several more battles, fighting through the end of the war.

Pierce was politically quiet until the 1852 election. The Democratic Party reached a deadlock among the three most popular contenders for their nomination and were at a standstill. Pierce was put forth and was nominated, as a solution to the impasse. He won the election and became America's fourteenth President. The campaign was focused, in large part, on issues around slavery. The **Compromise of 1850** and the **Fugitive Slave Act** provided fuel for the fires of contention.

The nation was stable economically during Pierce's administration and it was the issue of slavery that continued to create conflict and tension. The Compromise of 1850 was followed by the **Kansas-Nebraska Act**, proposed by **Stephen A. Douglas** and supported by Franklin Pierce. Pierce signed off on the Kansas-Nebraska Act, primarily because he believed it would facilitate travel to the West and Northwest. One of his main objectives was to expand the holdings of the U.S.

The **Kansas-Nebraska Act,** though, inflamed the anger of abolitionists, as it repealed the **Missouri Compromise** and opened the Kansas territory to slavery. It called for the support of Northerners for the Fugitive Slave Act, infuriating abolitionists. The Kansas-Nebraska Act provided for what Pierce called **"popular sovereignty"**, which was a states' rights concept leaving the decision as to whether or not to allow slavery in a new state up to a vote of the residents of that state. Pierce tried to straddle the fence between pro-slavery and abolitionist forces, without a great deal of success. Passage of the Kansas-

Nebraska Act angered abolitionists, former Whigs and a group known as the **"Free-Soilers"** so much that they began, in response to what they considered a pro-slavery trend, to organize the new **Republican party**. The Republican Party would become the home for the anti-slavery forces in America. The **Democratic Party** went forward as the home for pro-slavery forces.

Unfortunately, when Franklin Pierce signed the Kansas-Nebraska Act, the result was the creation of a battleground in Missouri and Kansas. The Act allowed for the residents of Kansas territory to determine their own status as a **"slave state"** or a **"free state"**. Kansas became known as **"Bleeding Kansas"**. Anti-slavery and Pro-slavery forces gathered in the area to fight out the destiny of the new state. Anti-slavery forces considered the Kansas-Nebraska Act to be to the benefit of slavers. Pierce's support of the Act, and his handling of the issue, caused the loss of many of his supporters. It undoubtedly cost him the next Presidential nomination and election.

Pierce added to the perception that he was pro-slavery when he sent federal troops to break up meetings of a group of **"Free-Soilers"** who had set up a government in Kansas. The group drafted a constitution, the **Topeka Constitution** and intended to rule the territory as an anti-slavery region. Pierce declared their actions **"an act of rebellion"**, justifying his use of troops. At around the same time, in Boston, an escaped slave named **Anthony Burns** was captured. Under terms of the Kansas-Nebraska Act, Pierce insisted the **Fugitive Slave Act** be honored. He sent federal troops to take Burns and forcibly return him to Virginia, where his "owner" resided. The use of federal troops in these instances, perceived to be support of slavers, cost Pierce many supporters.

Pierce's administration, meanwhile, worked to further expand the boundaries of the United States. He attempted, unsuccessfully, to find a legal way for the U.S. to acquire the island of Cuba. He worked toward preparing the groundwork for a **transcontinental railroad**. In 1853, Pierce's Minister to Mexico, **James Gadsden**, successfully negotiated the **Gadsden Purchase**. The deal brought 30,000 square miles of Mexico into the United States. It cost only ten million dollars.

His administration was unique in that his Vice President, **William R. King**, a man with whom he had little contact, died of tuberculosis only a few days into his service. He was never replaced and the Vice Presidency remained vacant for the remainder of Pierce's administration. Our constitution, at the time, made no provisions for dealing with such a circumstance.

Franklin Pierce believed in restricting powers of the federal government. He worked to grow the nation by acquiring new territories and by expanding the nation's boundaries. His efforts to appease pro-slavery forces and the violent impact of the Kansas-Nebraska

Act, would render him politically too weak to go forward. As his administration ended, the nation had grown closer to a civil war.

After leaving the Presidency, Franklin Pierce argued for avoiding a civil war at all costs. He denounced **Lincoln's Emancipation Proclamation**, believing it would cause the permanent destruction of the union. He and his wife traveled extensively until her death in 1863. His penchant for alcohol was damaging his health and he eventually became what he called "an old farmer". He became more spiritual and reduced his drinking habit. He worked to encourage good treatment of **Jefferson Davis**, the imprisoned President of the failed Confederacy. He farmed and enjoyed visits from friends and relatives. His health turned for the worse in the late 1860's and he quit drinking. Franklin Pierce died in Concord, Massachusetts, on October 4th, 1869. A caretaker had been hired, but none of his family members were present at his death.

Franklin Pierce and Slavery

Franklin Pierce was another example of an American leader who knew that the institution of slavery was immoral and barbaric, but who did not fight to gain its elimination in the United States. Pierce said "I consider slavery a social and political evil and I most sincerely wish that it had no existence upon the face of the earth". He owned no slaves.

Pierce was more concerned with avoiding civil war and with preserving the union of all of the states, Northern and Southern. He believed that, left alone, the Southern states would eventually put an end to slavery. Pierce was very much opposed to the abolitionist movement because he believed it would lead, inevitably, to civil war. He once said "This abolition movement must be crushed or there is an end to the Union". It turned out that he was right. The Union was shattered by the slavery issue and civil war was the sad result. Ultimately the war did end slavery. It doesn't seem likely that slavery, an important brick in the foundation of the Southern economy, would have been ended any time soon, had there been no war.

Pierce also was opposed to the more aggressive abolitionists because he believed in state's rights. Abolitionists, of course, were demanding federal legislation to ban all forms of slavery and slave trade. Pierce believed each state should have sovereignty over decisions about slavery within their own borders and the federal government should stay out of it.

When Southern legislators tried to block efforts to bring anti-slavery petitions to Congress, though, Pierce fought for their right to petition Congress. On the other hand, though, Pierce supported passage of what was to be known as **"the Gag Rule"**, which stated that petitions could be "received" but could not be "read or considered".

His objective was to do those things that would preserve the union and avoid civil war. He believed slavery would eventually be eliminated, but he didn't want the issue to be the cause for dividing the nation in a bloody civil war.

Newspapers attacked Franklin Pierce, saying he was "a Northerner with Southern sentiments". Pierce once accused **Abraham Lincoln** and the new, but quickly growing, anti-slavery **Republican Party**, of "reckless conduct". He meant that the aggressive abolitionists, including the Republicans, were forcing the nation into civil strife, which he believed to be very dangerous and a threat to the survival of the United States.

Pierce's fears were realized when the Civil War began. The slavery issue was to be decided in the most passionate form of violence, dividing not just the states, but the nation's families. **Lincoln's Emancipation Proclamation**, which Pierce opposed, ended any legal support for slavery in the United States. We will never know whether America's

Southerners would have, on their own, ended slavery. It surely would have taken much longer and millions would have suffered their chains for more generations.

Franklin Pierce was right that slavery was wrong and should not exist on earth. He hoped it could be ended without a civil war. His concern for preserving the union overcame his opposition to slavery.

America in the 1850's . . . Continued

President Franklin Pierce officiated at the opening of the first **World's Fair** to be produced in the United States. It was called **"The Exhibition of the Industry of All Nations"**. The date was July 14, 1853. Twenty-three foreign nations and colonies took part in the grand exhibition. It was located in a large "palace" on 6th Avenue in New York City, on which site is now located the **New York Public Library**. The World's Fair would be extended for a second season, which was performed under the guidance of **Fair President P.T. Barnum**, the famous showman. The Fair closed after 393 days of exhibition and more than a million visitors would attend.

The United States, in the 1850's, counted more than twenty-three million residents. Almost four million of those lived in New York state. There were thirty states already in the union and more territories pending statehood. There were between three and four million enslaved humans in America. America was steadily increasing in land size, as new territories were acquired or admitted and the numbers of people immigrating to the United States was increasing every month.

Immigrants came to America seeking better lives and personal freedoms. A potato famine in Ireland stimulated greater numbers of Irish immigrants. On the East Coast, most immigrants came from the German states, from Scandinavia and from England. On the West Coast oriental immigrants, primarily Chinese, came in huge numbers. Employment was easily available to them as gold mining and building of roads and railroads were proceeding at feverish paces.

The time period around the 1850's marked a cultural era known as the **Post-Romantic Period**. As Americans became more secure and safely established and their primary survival needs were generally satisfied, they had more time for music, art and literature. Jenny Lind was touring in America and drawing huge crowds. The music of composers of the time, Richard Wagner, Johann Strauss and Franz Liszt came over from Europe and was shared with Americans at popular concerts. Works of literature being enjoyed are still popular today. Charles Dickens wrote "David Copperfield". Harriet Beecher Stowe wrote "Uncle Tom's Cabin". Herman Melville wrote "Moby Dick". Henry David Thoreau wrote "Leaves of Grass". Charles Darwin wrote "The Origin of the Species", which led to controversies over to what extent God contributed to the development of plant and animal species and to what extent nature, on its own, created a process of "evolution". Black abolitionist Frederick Douglass published his autobiography "My Bondage, My Freedom". The first issue of the nation's preeminent newspaper, "The New York Times" was published in 1851.

Inventors and entrepreneurs were very busy in America and around the globe, in the 1850's. **Henry Bessemer** gave industry a big boost when he invented the **Bessemer**

Process. It was a more efficient, less expensive method of mass-producing steel. The **first elevator** was invented by **Elisha Otis**. The availability of elevators was a crucial step toward building of safe "high-rise" buildings. Many Americans still made most of their clothing at home. **Isaac Singer** manufactured the **first sewing machine** for home usage, a great convenience for all the home seamstresses. The beginning of the petroleum industry was marked when the **first productive oil well** was drilled in Titusville, Pennsylvania. The first steps were being taken toward what would become **the Industrial Revolution**.

The United States, in the 1850's, continued the process of taking lands from Native Americans, in exchange for cash and reservation agreements. One of the last such treaties was signed July 1, 1855. It gave the **Quinault**, **Quileute** and **Hoh** tribes $25,000 and land for reservations, in exchange for many miles of coastal property on the Olympic Peninsula, just west of Washington state. It was a great deal for the United States, but not so much for the Indian tribes. The three tribes were consolidated and the treaty allowed for the American President to change the boundaries of the reservations at any time, for any reason. Fortunately, the reservation, today, is very large. It occupies a beautiful two hundred thousand acres of property on the peninsula, as well as more than twenty miles of Pacific shoreline. The Quileute and Hoh tribes resisted the treaty from the outset and refused to move onto the Olympic peninsula. They now each occupy their own, smaller, reservations.

The Lecompton Constitution

Kansas, in the late 1850's, was the focus of the increasingly heated debate over how new states should be admitted to the union. Slavery supporters, mostly Southern Democrats, were fighting to designate new territories and states as being open to slave ownership and slave trading. The Kansas-Nebraska Act brought more intensity to the arguments, as did the Fugitive Slave Act. "Bleeding Kansas" was the location of much of the actual conflict. "Border Ruffians" from pro-slavery Missouri were crossing into Kansas to harass and attack anti-slavery citizens and towns. Anti-slavery "Free Soilers" were crossing the river in the other direction, from Kansas into Missouri, to do the same things. Kansas was still a Territory, petitioning for entry to the union.

The Lecompton Constitution, formally proposed to be the constitution of Kansas in 1859, was very heavily weighted with pro-slavery conditions. **President James Buchanan** was supportive of the document and of other pro-slavery activities, because he believed antagonizing the pro-slavery community would lead to a civil war. The Lecompton Constitution was named for the Kansas town where it was composed.

It's inflammatory content led to further increases in the tensions between pro- and anti-slavery forces. The Lecompton Constitution provided a litany of protections for the institution of slavery. It protected the right to ownership of slaves. It excluded black people from being protected by the American Bill of Rights. It prohibited any efforts by the government to emancipate individual slaves without the consent of the slave's "owner".

Democrats in the American South supported the Lecompton Constitution, while many Democrats in the North, who were represented by **Stephen A. Douglas**, were opposed. The Lecompton Constitution was initially voted on and passed, in an election that was widely considered "rigged" and fraudulent. It was voted on a second time, in a more traditional election format and was overwhelmingly rejected. 10,226 citizens voted to reject it, while only 138 voted in support of it. The citizens in Kansas territory, by a wide margin, were **"free staters"** and the Lecompton Constitution had no realistic chance of ever being approved.

Kansas was soon, in 1861, admitted to the Union. It was admitted as a free state. A new state constitution, the **Leavenworth Constitution**, was proposed and it did not condone slavery. Kansas was admitted to the Union as a free state very quickly after Senators who were pro-slavery exited the U.S. Senate. They represented states that were in the process of seceding from the Union and were no longer active members of the U.S. Senate.

The Lecompton Constitution, designed to protect slavery, was never likely to take effect, but it was the reason for passionate, angry debates between slavery and anti-slavery groups. It undoubtedly hastened the nation's progress toward civil war.

Bleeding Kansas

The years between the early 1850's and 1860 saw the battle to admit Kansas as a new state marked by violence. Kansas was initially expected to enter the Union as a free state, but proslavery forces emphatically resisted. Admission of Kansas would add two senators to the national legislature and would tilt the balance of votes in the senate in favor of the abolitionists.

America's government and citizens were bent on creating a **transcontinental railroad**, connecting the Eastern states with California. Both the abolitionists, or "free staters", and the proslavery forces were deeply concerned about how the territories between the East and the West would be integrated into the Union. Would they be "free states" or would they be "slave states". Each new state would add two new senatorial votes to the federal legislature and, based on population, more representatives, as well. Both sides were willing to fight to preserve their own leverage in the government.

Proslavery forces feared that, if free staters gained enough votes, slavery would be banned. It would wreck their Southern, agricultural economy, which depended on free slave labor.

Missouri had been a state for years and was friendly to slavers. Most new residents of Kansas were free staters. Kansas was, however, split between the two groups, as proslavers moved in to establish a position.

In 1854, the Kansas-Nebraska Act, dividing up lands previously owned by Native Americans, into two new territories. One would be the Kansas Territory and one would be the Nebraska Territory. It killed the impact of the Missouri Compromise of 1820, which had declared slavery forbidden in a vast area of territory that would one day achieve statehood. Senator Stephen A. Douglas, of Illinois, was the primary driver of the Kansas-Nebraska Act. Douglas hoped that the Act would serve as a compromise between slavers and abolitionists and would hold off initiation of a civil war.

Stephen A. Douglas believed that, by adding two new territories at once, he might preserve the balance between slave states and free states. He anticipated that the more Northern of the two new territories, Nebraska, would ultimately enter as a free state. He assumed that the more Southern new territory, Kansas, being adjacent the slave state Missouri, would choose to enter as a slave state. The Kansas-Nebraska Act declared that the new territories would enjoy "popular sovereignty", meaning the citizens of each territory could vote to determine their own fates in terms of the slave controversy. In general, Southerners were happy about the Kansas-Nebraska Act, while Northerners saw it as a threat to their efforts to forbid slavery in all new states. Most Northerners wanted to see slavery forbidden in all states.

Douglas's hope of avoiding violence was completely disappointed, as advocates of both sides of the slave issue invaded Missouri and Kansas. He was right about Nebraska, as the sentiment there weighed heavily in favor of becoming a free state. This only served to inflame the anger of proslavery forces, who feared losing influence in Congress by the addition of another slave state. Both abolitionists and proslavers came to Kansas, hoping to add weight to their own sides in the coming votes to decide the slavery issue in the territory.

The area in Western Missouri and the Kansas Territory quickly became the site of a long series of very violent confrontations. **"Border Ruffians"** were gangs of citizens who crossed the border into Kansas to carry out activites that would be described today as "terrorism". Anti-slavery "Free Soilers" were crossing the river in the other direction, from Kansas into Missouri, to do the same things. Both proslavery and anti-slavery citizens moved into Kansas to masquerade as Kansas residents, leading to election fraud on a large scale. Kansas Territory became the home of what would become a preview of the coming civil war. At least 56 people were killed, but historians believe the actual total might be more near 200 fatalities. Kansas soon suffered creation of two state capitols. One, powered by proslavers, was in Lecompton and the other, powered by free staters, was in Lawrence, near Topeka. Each had its own constitution.

The proslavery forces in Kansas and Missouri gained support from the American government in the persons of Presidents Franklin Pierce and James Buchanan. As the fighting went on, with confrontations continuing in Western Missouri and Eastern Kansas, it began to become more and more clear that the large majority of Kansas residents would vote to become a free state.

The fighting increased. Southerners in the government blocked legislation to bring Kansas in as a free state. The border confrontations would continue even after the Civil War began.

The **"The Sacking of Lawrence, Kansas"** occurred on May 21, 1856. Lawrence had been settled by anti-slavery free-staters from Massachusetts. **Sheriff Samuel J. Jones** gathered a large force of pro-slavery supporters and surrounded Lawrence. Jones brought along a cannon and fired down on the town from a nearby hilltop. His men entered the town and destroyed two anti-slavery newspapers. They destroyed the Free State Hotel and they burned down the home of **Charles L. Robinson**, who would one day be governor of free Kansas. One of Jones's men died in the attack when part of the crumbling hotel fell on him.

Three days later, May 24, 1856, the notorious abolitionist, **John Brown**, reacted with force to the attack on Lawrence. He gathered his five sons and a small force of anti-slavery settlers, some of whom belonged to a local militia group known as the **Pottawatomie**

Rifles. Brown led the group to a location near Pottawatomie Creek in Franklin County, Kansas territory. Angered by the attack on Lawrence and the physical beating of anti-slavery Senator Charles Sumner, Brown's group attacked and killed five pro-slavery settlers, as their families looked on. The episode would become known as the **Pottawatomie Massacre**.

The attack would be, judged by his supporters and his enemies, the most shameful of John Brown's activities. He would become far more famous or infamous, for his attack, during the Civil War, on the Union armory at Harper's Ferry. Frederick Douglass, who knew of **John Brown** and would later become a friend to him, said of the killings: "It is a terrible remedy for a terrible malady".

Years later, in 1863, during the Civil War, Lawrence, Kansas, would be the site of another attack by pro-slavers. The attack would be known as the **Lawrence Massacre** and many would die.

On August 21, 1863, a guerilla force led by **Confederate William Quantrill** attacked the Unionist, anti-slavery town of Lawrence, Kansas. The gang, known as **Quantrill's Raiders**, attacked Lawrence because it was known to be a stronghold for free staters and a center for "**Jayhawkers**". The Jayhawkers, free state vigilantes and militia groups, were believed to have attacked plantations in pro-slavery Western Missouri and Quantrill's Raiders meant to punish the town for harboring them. Lawrence was nearly destroyed in the attack. The raiders murdered between 160 and 190 anti-slavery citizens of Lawrence and nearly burned the entire town down.

The reaction to the horrible attack on Lawrence by Quantrill led to the delivery of **General Order No. 11** was issued, on August 25, 1863, by Union Army **General Thomas Ewing, Jr**. It was a reaction to the Lawrence massacre and it ordered that Union officers investigate the residents of several counties in western Missouri, mostly south of the Missouri River. Ewing wanted pro-slavery residents in the towns and farms in the area to be driven from their homes and driven out of the proximity of that area. Pro-slavers were given an opportunity to evacuate the area within 15 days or be driven out by the Union Army. Order No. 11 also ordered all farmers to deliver their hay and grain to army depots, meaning to remove it from any access by Southerners. The order infuriated not only the pro-slavers, but also some of the free staters. Ewing's order forced farmers and residents, regardless of their status on the slavery issue, to vacate their homes and re-locate to areas very near Union Army forts. Those who could not do so were ordered to leave the area entirely, even if they were anti-slavery residents. General Order No. 11 was meant to remove any material or human support for the Confederate Army from Western Missouri. The order so angered many citizens that it resulted in the opposite effect from the one wanted by General Ewing. Missouri was considered a slave state and the citizens of Missouri carried their anger and resentment about the order for many years after the war. The Confederate guerrilla fighters probably actually gained support because of General Order No. 11. A new General was appointed in 1864 and the order was quickly repealed.

On the very day that several Southern senators left the Congress, as their states seceded from the Union, Kansas Territory was admitted to the Union as a free state. The exit of the Southern senators gave free state senators the numbers they needed to vote Kansas into the Union. The action contributed to the "final straws" that ignited the Civil War. Once admitted, Kansas was never again realistically threatened by proslavery forces.

Frederick Douglass

Former Slave and Great American Abolitionist

Frederick Douglass

Frederick Douglass was born into slavery on **Holme Hill Farm**, located in Talbot County, Maryland, on the shore of Chesapeake Bay. He was "owned" by Thomas Auld, who was represented by Aaron Anthony, who was chief overseer for Colonel Edward Lloyd V. Colonel Lloyd was a wealthy owner of land and slaves in Maryland. Maryland was a slave state.

Frederick's father, perhaps his mother's "owner", was white and was of European descent. Frederick's mother was an enslaved black woman whose name was **Harriet Bailey**. His name, at birth, was **Frederick Augustus Washington Bailey** and he was born, as closely as can be determined, in February of 1818. Frederick, as an adult, celebrated his birthday on February 14th. He took the last name "Douglass" only many years later, when he escaped the bonds of slavery. Frederick would return many years later, as a free citizen, to purchase land in Talbot County that "was important" to him.

Frederick was separated from his mother as an infant, not unusual in slave families in those times. Later in life, Frederick wrote of his birth mother: "I do not recollect of ever seeing my mother by light of day. She was with me in the night. She would lie down with me and get me to sleep, but long before I waked she was gone". He lived for a few years with his maternal grandmother, a lady named **Betty Bailey**. Betty was a slave on the farm and was in charge of caring for enslaved children. His maternal grandfather was a free Black man named **Isaac Bailey**. Frederick was taken from them at the age of six years and sent to the **Wye House** plantation in Maryland.

Frederick's mother, Harriet, was an enslaved field worker on a plantation located twelve miles from the plantation where Frederick lived with his grandparents. She would, on very rare occasions, be allowed to walk the twelve miles for very brief visits with her son. He saw her only a few times before her death, which occurred when he was seven years old. Later in life, Frederick learned that his mother had been the only Black person in Talbot County, at that time, who could read. It was a rare achievement for a field slave. Frederick remembered her as being "Tall and finely proportioned, of dark, glossy complexion, with regular features and amongst the slaves was remarkably sedate and dignified."

On the death of Aaron Anthony, while living on the Wye Plantation, owned by Thomas Auld and overseen by Colonel Lloyd, Frederick was delivered to Lucretia Auld. Frederick was sent, by Lucretia's husband Thomas, to live in Baltimore for the purpose of working for Thomas's brother, Hugh. Frederick later wrote that Hugh's wife, Sophia, was the first to help him learn to read, teaching him the alphabet.

Those were times when many white people were adamantly opposed to allowing slaves to be educated in any way. In some states, it was illegal to teach slaves to read and write. The fear was that educated slaves would be much more likely to rebel against their lowly condition. Sophia defied the common belief and proceeded to teach Frederick, just as she taught her own son. Before long, Hugh discovered what his wife was doing and was furious. He insisted that literacy would "spoil" a slave and forbade her to continue. Frederick, however, persisted, in secret, on his own, in pursuit of reading skills. He wrote later that he persisted in observing written work where he could, tracing letters on any documents he found and trading bread to poor white children in the neighborhood for helping him learn reading skills. He later would write "Knowledge is the pathway to freedom from slavery".

Hugh Auld, angered at finding Frederick was learning to read, sent Frederick to work for William Freeland, where Frederick was soon engaged in surreptitiously teaching other enslaved black people to read. He used, primarily, the Bible as a teaching tool. As many as thirty male slaves would gather on Sundays to learn reading skills from Frederick.

In Maryland it was illegal to teach slaves to read and write. When word got out that Frederick was somewhat educated and was teaching other slaves, Thomas Auld, very much angered, took Frederick back to the plantation. He transferred Frederick to **Edward Covey**, a landowner known for his cruelty to slaves and who was called a **"slave breaker"**. Frederick was, indeed, treated brutally by Covey, who whipped him numerous times. Frederick would have been around sixteen years old during this hard time in his life as a slave. Frederick was whipped so often that his wounds had no time to heal between the beatings and he would be left with permanent scars. Eventually, in desperation, Frederick confronted Covey. He fought back, physically and won the brawl. Covey, after that confrontation, pretty much left Frederick alone. Douglass wrote, later in life, that the brutal beatings "broke him body, soul and spirit". He said that he used the Covey episodes to explain that he was transformed "From a man into a brute". He said, in the introduction to his autobiography, about the physical fight he won over Covey:

"You have seen how a man was made a slave; you shall see how a slave was made a man".

In 1837, Douglass, while still enslaved and still working for Covey, met a free black woman named **Anna Murray**. Her status as a free woman stimulated Douglass to work harder toward his own freedom. Anna Murray supported him with aid and money.

Frederick attempted, unsuccessfully, to escape Covey's farm several times. Finally, in 1838, he found a way off the farm and boarded a northbound train to Havre de Grace, Maryland. He became a run-away slave, a fugitive. If slave-hunters caught him, he could be sold into enslavement in the brutal southern plantations. Maryland, being a slave state, was not the place to settle. He traveled on, though and made his way through Delaware, another slave state.

Anna Murray helped him obtain "identification and protection papers" and a sailor's clothing, from a free black sailor, to assist him in his flight. He made it to New York, where he rested in the home of **David Ruggles**, an abolitionist who provided a safe house for run-aways. Ruggles had courage enough to make his home a "station" on the **Underground Railroad**.

On his arrival at the Ruggles safe house, Frederick sent for Anna Murray. She came to New York, bringing along with her the basic needs to set up a home. They were married only eleven days after Frederick reached New York, on September 15, 1838. They used the name Johnson, initially, to protect Frederick from slave hunters.

Frederick and Anna made their first home in New Bedford, Massachusetts. It was a stronghold for abolitionists and there were many former slaves or fugitive slaves, in the area. The couple moved to Lynn, Massachusetts, in 1841. Frederick used several surnames in his progress through life, including his mother's last name, Bailey. He progressed through Stanley and Johnson and settled, finally, at the suggestion of friends, on the last name Douglass.

The Douglass's, after learning a white Methodist church was segregated, joined the African Methodist Episcopal Zion Church. The church enumerated among its members the legendary abolitionists **Sojourner Truth** and **Harriet Tubman**, the famous "conductor" on the underground railway. Frederick became a leader in the church and became a licensed ordained preacher in 1839. His activities in the church gained him great growth in his public speaking skills, presaging his future as a great orator.

Frederick became a regular attendee at meetings of abolitionist groups. He soon met the famous **William Lloyd Garrison**, who ran the abolitionist bible, his newspaper **The Liberator**. Garrison was a tremendous influence over Douglass, who wrote of him: "No face and form ever impressed me with such sentiments of the hatred of slavery as did those of William Lloyd Garrison."

Garrison encouraged Douglass to become more active as a speaker, recognizing that Douglass's personal history made a powerful story in opposition to slavery and in support of abolition. Frederick Douglass was a tall and handsome man, dark complected and possessed of a piercing, confident gaze. Douglass began to travel through the northern states, joining other speakers as the fight against slavery gained power. He was thrown off a train in 1841 for refusing to be seated in a segregated section.

By 1843, Douglass was touring, with other speakers, the eastern and midwestern states, speaking out against slavery. Douglass was a powerful and passionate speaker and he became well-known. Pro-slave supporters frequently accosted the speakers, most often verbally, but sometimes physically. In Pendleton, Indiana, a mob of angry pro-slavers chased Douglass and beat him badly. His hand was broken and never properly healed. He was rescued by a local Quaker family with the name of Harvey.

Frederick Douglass's friends were worried that all of the attention he was drawing might alert his "owner", **Thomas Auld**, who could pursue Frederick to regain what Auld still considered his own "property". They advised him that a trip abroad might be a good plan to keep him free. He boarded ship and set sail for England and Ireland on August 16, 1845.

Douglass was, at times, shocked by the poverty he observed in Europe, but he was mesmerized by the way he, as a black man, was treated. He wrote of his first experiences in Ireland: "Instead of the bright, blue sky of America, I am covered with the soft, grey fog of the Emerald Isle [Ireland]. I breathe and lo! the chattel (slave) becomes a man. I gaze around in vain for one who will question my equal humanity, claim me as his slave or offer me an insult. I employ a cab and I am seated beside white people. I reach the hotel where I enter the same door and am shown into the same parlor and I dine at the same table. . and no one is offended. I find myself regarded and treated at every turn with the kindness and deference paid to white people. When I go to church, I am met by no upturned nose and scornful lip to tell me, 'We don't allow niggers in here!'"

Douglass ultimately stayed in Europe for two years. He spoke in many venues and his appeal was so great that the halls were often said to be "filled to suffocation". He spent time in Scotland, where they declared him **"Scotland's Anti-Slavery Agent"**.

While he was traveling and speaking in Europe, friends in America raised enough money to "buy" Douglass his freedom from Ault and he became truly a free black man. America saw his return in the spring of 1847.

When Douglass returned to his wife, Anna, in America, he found that English supporters had raised enough money for him to begin publishing his own newspaper. He called it **The North Star**, reflecting the importance of the North Star to fugitive slaves, who were told always to follow it to freedom.

His paper's motto was "Right is of no sex . . . Truth is of no color . . . God is the Father of us all and we are all brethren". His writings in the paper voiced his opposition to the futile plans of the **American Colonization Society**, which believed everyone would be better off if all free black people could be sent to some new country, back in Africa. Their efforts eventually resulted in the creation of the African nation **Liberia**. Some black people actually did choose to move to Liberia, but the idea of re-locating millions of well-established black people back across the ocean was never remotely realistic. Douglass and his wife were also active conductors in the Underground Railroad. They would provide resources and safe harbor to more than 400 fugitive black slaves.

Douglass continued to publish the North Star, but he split from his old mentor, William Lloyd Garrison, the publisher of The Liberator. Garrison came to believe that the American Constitution should be burned, while Douglass firmly believed the Constitution could more effectively be used to fight slavery.

By 1848, Anna and Frederick had four children. Looking upon his children, he was overcome with emotion, knowing how different their lives were from what had been in his own childhood. It was the tenth anniversary of his escape from slavery. He decided to publish an open letter to Thomas Auld, his former "owner". He wrote this:

"Oh! sir, a slaveholder never appears to me so completely an agent of hell, as when I think of and look upon my dear children. It is then that my feelings rise above my control. The grim horrors of slavery rise in all their ghastly terror before me, the wails of millions pierce my heart and chill my blood. I remember the chain, the gag, the bloody whip, the deathlike gloom overshadowing the broken spirit of the fettered bondman, the appalling liability of his being torn away from wife and children and sold like a beast in the market."

Douglass went on, in the letter to Auld, to ask Auld how he would have felt had Douglass come to take away Auld's own daughter, Amanda, to be sold into slavery and to see her treated the way Auld had treated him and his family. Douglass ended his message by telling Auld that he held no personal malice toward him, adding: "There is no roof under which you would be more safe than mine and there is nothing in my house which you might need for comfort, which I would not readily grant. Indeed, I should esteem it a privilege, to set you an example as to how mankind ought to treat each other".

The **Seneca Falls Convention** of 1848 was the first large convention of women's rights supporters. The meeting was led by famous suffragette **Elizabeth Cady Stanton**. Frederick Douglass was the only Black person in attendance. He spoke eloquently on behalf of **women's suffrage** or the woman's right to vote. He suggested that Black people or at least he, as a Black man, should not accept the right to vote unless women shared the same privilege. Douglass believed America would be better governed if women participated. He said: "In this denial of the right to participate in government, not merely the degradation of woman and the perpetuation of a great injustice happens, but the maiming and repudiation of one-half of the moral and intellectual power of the government of the world". He went on to regularly offer support for women's suffrage in his newspaper, the North Star. He wrote: "A discussion of the rights of animals would be regarded with far more complacency than would be a discussion of the rights of women. We hold woman to be justly entitled to all we claim for man."

As his fame grew, Douglass became acquainted with and often friends with, many famous people. On March 12, 1859, Douglass met with the passionate abolitionist **John Brown**. **George DeBaptiste**, a black abolitionist, was also at the meeting. John Brown explained his plan to raid the U.S. armory at **Harper's Ferry**, in Virginia.

Brown, not long after, visited at Douglass's home, where he played with the Douglass children. Brown was counting on Douglass's participation in the Harper's Ferry raid or at least his support. Frederick Douglass correctly believed the raid would be suicidal and declined to participate. Douglass had been harboring, for several months, a fugitive slave named **Shields Green**, who called himself **"the Emperor"**. Green surprised Douglass by agreeing, after a second meeting, to follow John Brown.

John Brown would be captured at Harper's Ferry and would be hanged for his efforts. Most of Brown's followers, including "the Emperor" died in the fighting at the armory. The Harper's Ferry raid failed in its primary purpose, but certainly served to further inflame tensions between the North and the South.

Supporters proposed that Frederick Douglass run for the Congressional seat of **Gerrit Smith**, who was a friend and supporter of Douglass and who was stepping down. Gerrit Smith wisely advised Douglass not to run. Smith knew that, should Douglass be elected or if Douglass was even allowed to run for the office, all of the Southern Congressmen would bolt and civil war would be the result. Douglass declined the offer. No black man would serve in Congress until after the passage of **the Fifteenth Amendment**, in 1870.

There was a time, in the years before the Civil War, when Frederick Douglass was better known and more famous than **Abraham Lincoln**. Later, after the war began, Douglass pressured Lincoln to allow black men to fight on the side of the Union Army. The war was not going well for the North and Lincoln was finally persuaded, largely through Douglass's efforts, to bring black troops into the fray. The decision paid off enormously, as the **First Kansas Volunteer Colored Infantry** was formed and became the home of the first black troops in the Union Army. The **54th Massachusetts Infantry**

Regiment was formed soon after and Douglass's sons, **Charles** and **Louis**, both served in it. The black regiment became known for its extraordinary courage and aggression in the fight against the pro-slavery Confederacy. Frederick Douglass supported Lincoln by assisting with recruiting efforts, believing that no one would fight harder for the freedom of black people than would black men.

Douglass first met Abraham Lincoln in person in 1863. Douglass was concerned about the treatment of black troops and the fact that black troops were paid half what white troops were paid. He traveled to Washington, hoping to gain an audience with the President. In those times, citizens could walk in off the streets, unhindered and request a meeting with the President.

Douglass, early in the morning, approached the White House. He saw a long line of applicants waiting to see Lincoln. He assumed he might have to wait all day. He wondered if a black man would even be permitted in the inner sanctum. Douglass offered a card or note to a staff worker, asking that it be delivered to the President. He is stunned when, only minutes later, the staffer returns, only to personally escort Douglass directly to the President's office. As he passed by the long line of impatiently waiting white people, one was heard to say "I see how it is . . . they let the *nigger* through".

Lincoln and Douglass would meet again in 1864, under different circumstances. This time, Lincoln telegraphed an urgent invitation, offering an all-expense paid trip to Washington for Douglass. Douglass met with Lincoln and learned that Lincoln was worried about how the war was going for the North. He encouraged Douglass to increase his efforts to recruit black troops from the South, meaning they would have to run away from their owners to participate. Lincoln also worried that, if war conditions didn't improve, he would not be re-elected. Douglass knew that, should Lincoln be voted out, any hope of freedom for all black people would most likely die. The two men needed each other if they were to achieve their separate goals. They understood that, if enough fugitive slaves enlisted in the army of the North, there was a much better chance of winning. They also understood that, even if the war were lost, the fugitives, now being Union soldiers, would at least be free men. In the field of war, **General Ulysses S. Grant** had let it be known, though he had no proper authorization to do so, that fugitives who made it to his army would be allowed to fight. Thousands of fugitive black men responded. Lincoln, when he learned of them, heartily approved Grant's actions.

Douglass wrote, after the second meeting between himself and Lincoln, that he had never realized how very much Abraham Lincoln hated slavery in the South. Lincoln's attitude toward slavery had always been in terms of practical solutions. At one time, he supported the idea of allowing Black people, should they choose to do so, to be transported back to Africa (The Liberia project). He was morally deeply opposed to slavery, but he was more concerned with his personal responsibility to prioritize saving the Union. The second meeting between Douglass and Lincoln lasted more than two hours, as white governors, Congressmen and regular citizens waited impatiently. The two came to understand one another's beliefs and political positions and to respect one another deeply. There were times when Lincoln made decisions based on trying to re-unite the country, rather than on what might more quickly eliminate slavery. Douglass at first was angered at Lincoln's actions, but, later in life, came to understand that the Union had to be preserved, at any cost, or there would never be an end to slavery.

The third meeting between Douglass and Lincoln took place at Lincoln's second inaugural address, only a short time before Lincoln's assassination. Douglass was assigned a front row seat, directly in front of Old Abe. Lincoln invited him to the reception following the speech. On approaching the White House, a white policeman stopped him, saying no black people were allowed in the White House. Douglass told him he was mistaken and went to the East White House entry. Surrounded by white supporters, Lincoln saw Douglass at the entry. Lincoln said, from all the way across the room "Here comes my friend, Frederick Douglass. It's good to see you." Lincoln took Douglass's hand. He tells Douglass "I saw you in the crowd today. What did you think of my inaugural address? There is no man in these United States whose opinion I value more than yours." Lincoln gave Douglass, as a token of their friendship, his most favored walking stick. Douglass treasured it and often used it, through the rest of his life.

Lincoln's Emancipation Proclamation, delivered on January 1, 1863, was a "war measure", meaning it could only apply to black people in the South. As a practical measure, it meant little to southern black people because their owners did not recognize the Proclamation or the United States government. It did not apply to black people in northern states, though many were still enslaved. Northern black people were emancipated by The **13th Amendment**, passed on December 6, 1865. **The 14th Amendment** codified birthright citizenship and prohibited violation of basic American privileges and immunities or denying "due process" of any citizens, including Black citizens. **The 15th Amendment** finally prohibited any kind of discrimination based on race.

After the Civil War, Frederick Douglass continued to work to implement the national equality of races that he and Lincoln had planned. Unfortunately, after Lincoln was killed, the President who took over was not friendly to Black causes. **The Reconstruction Period** began. Pro-slavery, anti-Black Southerners gained control of politics in every southern state. The **Ku Klux Klan** was organized. **"Jim Crow laws"** and **"Black Codes"** subverted the intentions of the emancipation. It would be many years before great progress in the plight of black Americans could be seen. The struggle to advance the civil rights of ALL citizens continues today.

Frederick Douglass, born to slavery, became **President of the Freedman's Savings Bank**, which was meant to support the struggles of Black citizens who were learning to cope with American society as free Black people. In the South, the struggle was brutal.

In 1868, Douglass, then about 54 years old, supported the Presidential campaign of **General Ulysses S. Grant**. Grant hoped to do his best to promote the goals that Douglass, Lincoln and himself had defined in terms of helping Black people transition successfully to their new state of freedom. Millions of black people, overwhelmingly illiterate, with only the skills they learned in their slave labors, were now faced with managing all of the responsibilities and privileges of free citizens. Grant and Douglass were bent on making it all work. There was tremendous resistance from former slave holders. Many Black people were left with no realistic option except to return to work on the plantations and farms, some having to go back to work for their previous "owners".

Victoria Woodhull, a popular advocate of women's rights, ran for President in 1872. Frederick Douglass became the first black man to be nominated to run for Vice President of the United States. He was nominated without his knowledge or approval and he did not campaign. The pair had no hope of winning. Douglass did, however, serve as presidential **'elector-at-large'** for the State of New York and did deliver the electoral votes of New York to Washington, D.C.

June of that same year, 1872, saw Douglass's home burned down. The cause was suspected to be arson. Many of his writings and memorabilia were lost.

President Rutherford B. Hayes appointed Frederick Douglass **United States Marshall** for the District of Columbia. Another "first" for black citizens. Douglass had many "firsts". The appointment, in 1877, made Frederick financially secure.

During that same year, 1877, Frederick chose to visit his former "owner", slave-master Thomas Auld, who was dying. Douglass had become acquainted with Auld's daughter, Amanda Auld Sears, several years previously. She became a supporter and attended some of his speeches. Douglass and Auld, on his death bed, reconciled and Douglass seemed to find some closure as a result of their brief meeting.

Douglass purchased his final home in that year, too. After residing for many years in homes in Rochester, New York, he and his beloved Anna bought a permanent home in Washington, D.C., which rested on a hill above the Anacostia River. They called the home **Cedar Hill**. It has been preserved and is now an iconic American landmark, open to visit for today's travelers.

Douglass was appointed **Recorder of Deeds** for the District of Columbia in 1881.

In 1882, after 44 years of marriage, Anna Murray Douglass died. Frederick was devastated by his loss. He returned to a focus on social activism and continued the battle for women's rights. He married again, in 1884, to a white woman who was also an activist, **Helen Pitts**. Their marriage led to popular controversy, partly because Helen was white and partly because she was twenty years younger than Frederick. He responded affably to the criticisms, saying that his first marriage had been to someone the color of his mother and his second to someone the color of his father.

Frederick and Helen traveled Europe during the years 1886 and 1887. He spoke frequently in support of civil rights for all citizens. In 1888, at the **Republican National Convention**, Douglass became the first black man to receive a vote for President of the United States in the roll call vote of a major party.

In 1892, Douglass built rental housing for Black people. It was located in Baltimore, near Fells Point and the complex still exists today.

During his later years, Frederick was a proud and enthusiastic gardener. He loved nature and frequently strolled around his property, taking in the beauty of nature.

Douglass attended a meeting of the **National Council of Women** on February 20, 1895. He spoke briefly and received a standing ovation from the grateful attendees. He had supported their causes for many decades. Returning to Cedar Hill following the meeting, Frederick suffered a massive and fatal, heart attack. He was dead at the age of 77. Thousands attended his funeral, including United States Senators and Supreme Court Justices, who served as pallbearers. Leaders of other nations sent their condolences. Frederick Douglass had become a citizen of the world.

Back in 1883, Frederick Douglass had been back in Talbot County, where he had begun life in slavery, because he wanted to purchase some land. He felt it was important to him to own some land where he used to be, himself, "owned". He was invited to speak to children there who were attending a **segregated school**. His speech there seems to be a fitting summary of his life. He told those Black children:

"I once knew a little colored boy whose mother and father died when he was six years old. He was a slave and had no one to care for him. He slept on a dirt floor in a hovel and in cold weather would crawl into a meal bag head foremost and leave his feet in the ashes to keep them warm. Often he would roast an ear of corn and eat it to satisfy his hunger and many times has he crawled under the barn or stable and secured eggs, which he would roast in the fire and eat."

"That boy did not wear pants like you do, but a tow linen shirt. Schools were unknown to him and he learned to spell from an old Webster's spelling-book and to read and write from posters on cellar and barn doors, while boys and men would help him. He would then preach and speak and soon became well known. He became Presidential Elector, United States Marshal, United States Recorder, United States diplomat and accumulated some wealth. He wore broadcloth and didn't have to divide crumbs with the dogs under the table. That boy was Frederick Douglass."

Frederick Douglass Quotes

"Once you learn to read, you will be forever free."

"Knowledge makes a man unfit to be a slave."

"I prayed for freedom for twenty years, but received no answer until I prayed with my legs."

"Without a struggle, there can be no progress."

"The white man's happiness cannot be purchased by the black man's misery."

"To suppress free speech is a double wrong. It violates the rights of the hearer as well as those of the speaker."

"People might not get all they work for in this world, but they must certainly work for all they get."

"Power concedes nothing without a demand. It never did and it never will."

"I would unite with anybody to do right and with nobody to do wrong."

"Slaves sing most when they are most unhappy. The songs of the slave represent the sorrows of his heart; and he is relieved by them, only as an aching heart is relieved by its tears."

"No man can put a chain about the ankle of his fellow man without at last finding the other end fastened about his own neck."

The Women's Rights Movement

It was 1776 and **John Adams** was one of the primary authors working on **America's Declaration of Independence**. **Abigail Adams**, who had great influence on her husband's opinions, wrote to John, who was off in Philadelphia working on the Declaration, saying to John: "Remember the Ladies". Adams responded, jokingly: "The Declaration's wording specifies that 'All MEN are created equal'". While John Adams was teasing his devoted wife, his words did not portend well for the rights of American women.

Decades later, by the mid-1800's, the pathway to women's rights was still largely undeveloped. The American Revolution, fought for the human rights of citizens, was seventy years in the past. The institution of slavery had not yet been eliminated in America and was the focus of growing violence. The lack of fundamental rights for American women, however, remained in darkness in the social background.

America's women's rights movement probably began in London, in 1840, at the **World Anti-Slavery Congress**. Two American women who supported the abolitionist movement in America attempted to attend the conference. They were not allowed to enter or participate. Women were not taken seriously as activists by most of the males of those times. The two women, **Elizabeth Cady Stanton** and her friend, **Lucretia Mott**, were angered by their treatment at the conference. Their anger was their inspiration to begin their work, back in America, for women's rights, including a persistent pursuit of the right to vote.

On a hot summer day, July 13, 1848, a small gathering of women, drinking tea around the table of **Jane Hunt**, a Quaker activist, marked the beginning of America's **Women's Rights Movement**. It would also be known as the **"Women's Suffrage"** movement. During that gathering, Elizabeth Cady Stanton, a young wife and mother, expressed her anger about the status of women in American society. The women noted that America's women played an essential role in the fight for American independence, but then were not beneficiaries of the same rights American men gained by the war.

In just two days, Elizabeth Cady Stanton and her friends put together a plan for a larger meeting. They arranged a date and location for a convention. They publicized the meeting, announcing the date, July 19 and 20, 1848 and the location, the Wesleyan Chapel in Seneca Falls, New York. The convention was promoted as **"A Convention to Discuss the Social, Civil and Religious Condition and Rights of Woman"**. The meeting would be known as the **"Seneca Falls Convention"** and it was the first such meeting in history.

Elizabeth Cady Stanton, along with her four friends, wrote up a document titled **"A Declaration of Sentiments"**, to be delivered at the Seneca Falls convention. Stanton opened their Declaration of Sentiments with these famous words from the Declaration of Independence: "We hold these truths to be self-evident; that all men and women are created equal; that they are endowed by their Creator with certain inalienable rights; that among these are life, liberty and the pursuit of happiness." She wrote "The history of mankind is a history of repeated injuries and usurpations on the part of man toward woman, having in direct object the establishment of an absolute tyranny over her. To prove this, let facts be submitted to a candid world."

Stanton and her friends then listed the conditions in which American women were unjustly treated, given the absence of legislation to protect them. Among those injuries to women, the friends listed these:

The failure of legal protections for women, saying the law treated women as dead people.

Women had no property rights, though they were obligated to pay property taxes.

Women were not allowed to vote.

Women were subject to punishments by laws in which they had no voice.

Husbands were legally given total responsibility for their wives and could legally imprison and physically beat their wives, with impunity.

Men were favored over women, by the law, during divorce and child custody court hearings.

Women, if they were "allowed", by their husbands to work, were legally bound to turn over their wages to their husbands. "Work" for women, in those times, generally referred to housework, cooking, sewing and gardening.

Women were obligated to be obedient to their husbands.

Many colleges and universities refused admission to women, blocking their access to education.

Some professions, such as law and medicine, were not available to women.

Women were not allowed, in most cases, to participate in the affairs of the church. The churches were the foundations for family lives in many American families of the times. Women were expected to attend, but to refrain from interfering with the "business of the church".

Most occupations were closed to women and when they could work, they were paid far less than men.

Altogether, Elizabeth Cady Stanton and her four friends listed 18 specific grievances in her Declaration of Sentiments. It was probably no coincidence that our national Declaration of Independence also listed exactly 18 specific grievances against the royal crown and England.

More than 300 citizens showed up for the Seneca Falls Convention, which had originally been called The Women's Rights Convention. Most of the attendees were women, but many men also attended. There were other activist movements at the time, abolition of slavery and anti-alcohol advocates included and many members of those groups also attended.

The women's rights movement, the **"temperance movement"** in opposition to alcoholic drinking and the **abolitionist movement** to end slavery all shared some common objectives and often worked together.

On the first day of the Seneca Falls Convention, July 19, 1848, only women were allowed to participate. Elizabeth Cady Stanton and her friend, another activist, Lucretia Mott, were the leaders of the new movement. Elizabeth opened the convention with these remarks:

"We are assembled to protest against a form of government, existing without the consent of the governed, to declare our right to be free as man is free, to be represented in the government which we are taxed to support, to have such disgraceful laws as give man the power to chastise and imprison his wife, to take the wages which she earns, the property which she inherits and, in case of separation, the children of her love."

The attendees at the convention proposed and passed, eleven **women's rights resolutions**. The final resolution, the woman's **right to vote**, was not initially passed. Some activists of the time believed that, while they were fighting passionately to gain black people the right to vote, it may be asking too much of traditional males to expect them to simultaneously accept the right of women to vote.

The famous black abolitionist, **Frederick Douglass**, whom we might have expected to be motivated solely by the voting rights of African-Americans, delivered an eloquent and impassioned speech in support of women. The resolution passed.

Note that the famous "women's suffragette" **Susan B. Anthony** was not in attendance at Seneca Falls. She would meet Elizabeth Cady Stanton a couple of years later and the two of them would carry the women's rights battle forward, together, for fifty more years. It would be seventy-two more years before American politicians granted American women the right to vote. The **Nineteenth Amendment** to the Constitution would finally be passed in in 1919 and ratified 1920.

313

Following the Seneca Falls Convention, **Horace Greeley**, the well-known and very influential editor of the New York Tribune, wrote in support of the resolutions declared at the meeting. He was, however, still skeptical of whether it would be responsible to grant women the right to vote. Greely wrote that, if Americans really believed in the Constitution, then they would have to concede to the rights of American women.

The publication of "The Declaration of Sentiments" quickly drew heavy fire from most of the American press and, probably, most American men. Newspapers printed the list of declarations written by Stanton and her friends, but offered nothing but ridicule, most notably for the item demanding that women have the right to vote.

As the nation began to focus all of its attention on the Civil War, the women's rights movement was pushed aside. The attention of the nation's activists was directed at freeing the slaves. When the war ended, the **14ᵗʰ Amendment**, in 1868, was passed. It gave constitutional protection to "all citizens", but it defined "citizens" as "males". The **15ᵗʰ Amendment** was passed in 1870. It guaranteed Black men the right to vote. Women were excluded and were still invisible as voting rights were concerned. Some women joined forces with racist Southerners who were supporting the right of white women to vote. Those Southerners hoped the votes of white women would cancel out the votes of Black men, reducing the impact of Black votes.

Elizabeth Cady Stanton and Susan B. Anthony persisted in their life-long battles for women's rights. In 1869, the two formed a new group, which was called the **National Woman Suffrage Association**. The group would lead the 'women's rights fight' for decades into the future. In 1890, the two largest women's rights groups merged to form the **National American Woman Suffrage Association**. Elizabeth Cady Stanton was the new organization's first President.

The Seneca Falls meetings lit the fire for widespread women's rights activities. The women involved, and others, would campaign ceaselessly for decades afterward. Some of the most prominent and hardest working "suffragettes" were Elizabeth Cady Stanton, Lucretia Mott, Susan B. Anthony, Lucy Stone, Alice Paul and Sojourner Truth.

African-American women also became important players in the movement for women's rights. They had far greater problems, of course, as they had been suffering through the **"Jim Crow"** era of violent racism in America's **'Reconstruction'** South. Still, some were also able to join the fight for the right of women to vote.

Perhaps the most famous African-American suffragette was **Ida B. Wells**. Ida was born a slave but worked her way to freedom and had become a country school teacher by the age of 14. She would eventually be successful enough to buy part ownership of a newspaper.

Ida B. Wells fought against racism in post-civil war America, campaigning courageously against the practice of lynching black people who violated "Jim Crow" regulations. Three of Ida's supporters were lynched. She was the recipient of serious death threats and her office was destroyed. Ida moved north and continued her crusade. She joined the movement to gain women's rights, but continued her other missions, as well.

Mary Church Terrell, also African-American, was a friend and co-worker with Ida. The two successfully engaged and organized large numbers of African-American women in the causes of ending lynching and obtaining basic rights for women of all colors.

Sojourner Truth, another African-American voice in the battle for women's rights, delivered a speech to the 1851 Women's Rights Convention, held at the Old Stone Church in Akron, Ohio. The speech would be known as the **"Ain't I A Woman?"** speech. It will be covered in more detail in our Sojourner Truth biography.

In December of 1868, a Liberal Republican named **George Washington Julian** introduced the first proposal to enfranchise women in America. His **"Women's Suffrage Constitutional Amendment"** would have guaranteed citizens the right to vote "without any distinction or discrimination whatever founded on race, color or sex." Julian's resolution, though, was never brought to a vote.

Long before the 19th Amendment was passed, many territories and states had already granted women the right to vote. That right applied only to the women who resided within those states and territories. Women could still not vote in federal elections and so could not vote for a Presidential candidate or for other federal political offices.

Ulysses S. Grant was running for President in 1874. Suffragette Susan B. Anthony supported Grant, who was trying to follow the plans of Abraham Lincoln and Frederick Douglass to make easier the transition of black slaves into a "free society". She registered to vote and then she actually voted. Anthony was quickly arrested, put on trial and summarily convicted for voting illegally. Women were put back in the "no voting rights" box.

Senator Aaron A. Sargent, a Republican, wrote the first women's voting rights, or women's suffrage, amendment in 1877. He proposed it in the federal Congress in 1878. The words he wrote would provide the basis for the **19th Amendment**, which would not be passed for another forty years. Sargent presented the amendment and hoped to see it passed. It was tabled by Congressional leaders, meaning nothing was done and no vote was taken. The proposal was ignored until 1887 when it was voted down.

Sargent wrote these words in his proposal for the right of women to vote in America: "The right of citizens of the United States to vote shall not be denied or abridged by the United States or by any State on account of sex."

After Republicans could not garner enough support and the proposal was finally voted down in 1887, the bill was once again proposed in 1914. It was, once more, voted down.

Wyoming, under **Republican Governor John Campbell**, was the very first territory to afford women the right to vote within their boundaries. Women were first given the right to vote in **Wyoming Territory** in December of 1869. Newspapers wrote that "a gentle white-haired housewife, 69-year-old **Louisa Swain**" was the first woman to cast a ballot under the new law. With her vote, Wyoming Territory became the first U.S. state or territory to grant suffrage to women. Famous women's rights leader Susan B. Anthony declared "Wyoming is the first place on God's green earth which could consistently claim to be the land of the free!" Wyoming Democrats, a couple of years later, would try to rescind the right of women to vote, but could not generate enough votes to pass their effort.

Utah Territory had passed a suffrage law, giving women the right to vote, AFTER Wyoming passed their law. Utah, though, had a couple of elections prior to the first election in Wyoming after Wyoming law passed. Women in Utah, then, while their law was changed after Wyoming's law, actually voted before Louisa Swain voted in Wyoming Territory. The first woman to vote in Utah, which was actually the first vote cast by a woman, was Seraph Cedenia Young. Wyoming was the first to grant women the right to vote, but Utah was the location where the first vote was cast by a woman.

Two decades later, when Wyoming sought statehood, its citizens approved a constitution that maintained the right of women to vote. The federal Congress demanded that Wyoming Territory kill the right of women to vote or be shut out of statehood. Wyoming stood its ground, refused to give up women's right to vote and declared "We will remain out of the Union for one hundred years rather than come in without the women." Congress eventually and reluctantly relented and Wyoming, when it became a state in 1890, became the first state to give women the right to vote.

America's West became the nation's leader in granting rights to women. Wyoming was first, but Colorado gave women the vote in 1893, Idaho in 1896 and Utah in 1897. The 19th Amendment, guaranteeing all American women the right to vote would not be passed until 1920. Long before it was passed in 1916, Montana elected a woman, **Jeannette Rankin**, to serve in the U.S. House of Representatives. Also before the passage of the 19th Amendment, in 1919, fifteen states had already given women the right to vote in local elections. All but two of those states were located West of the Mississippi River.

The **National Association of Colored Women** was formed in 1896. It merged the efforts of more than 100 independent groups for African-American women. They would add their strength to the growing women's rights movement.

The movement for women's suffrage was lost in the chaos of the Civil War and was blocked, largely by Southern Democrats in Congress, for many decades. The movement never softened, though, and its leaders persisted indefatigably, decade after decade. In 1912, leading up to the Presidential election, the impact of their continuing struggle was evident when **Theodore Roosevelt** and his Bull Moose/Progressive Party", made women's suffrage one of his campaign planks.

World War I came along in 1917. America's women served in many ways on the homefront. Some women served, in specific roles, in the military. Women became an essential element in the home-based support of American troops. Their performance added much leverage to their ongoing fight for voting rights.

Their valiant efforts were finally rewarded on August 18, 1920, when Congress ratified the **19th Amendment**: "The right of citizens of the United States to vote shall not be denied or abridged by the United States or by any State on account of sex." (Remember Senator Sargent?)

Only months later, more than eight million American women voted in the Presidential election.

The 19th Amendment locked in the right of American women to vote in federal elections. Discrimination, though, continued unabated on many levels. Opportunities in education and employment still were limited for women. Men still held many legal advantages over women. The **National Woman's Party**, in 1923, proposed another **"rights amendment"** which would prohibit ALL DISCRIMINATION on the basis of sex. It was to be called the **Equal Rights Amendment**. It did not pass to become law.

Hattie Ophelia Caraway was a schoolteacher in Tennessee who married **Thaddeus Caraway** in 1902. The couple moved to Arkansas, where Thaddeus served first as a Congressman and then as a U.S. senator. Thaddeus Caraway passed away in late 1931 and the governor of Arkansas appointed Hattie to serve in the seat of her deceased husband. She was then re-elected in a special election, to complete her first term and then was elected two more times. Hattie was the second American woman to serve in the U.S. Senate, the first having been **Rebecca Felton**, who had been seated in 1922. Hattie was the first female to chair a Congressional committee and to preside over a Congressional session. One of her actions as a U.S. Senator was to co-sponsor, in 1943, another attempt to pass the **Equal Rights Amendment**. Still, it did not pass. To this day, it has never been ratified.

Jeannette Pickering Rankin became the first American woman to hold a federal office when she was elected to the U.S. House of Representatives in 1916. She was a life-long, dedicated pacifist and women's rights activist. She already had a history of lobbying in support of women's suffrage in several states. Jeannette represented the state of

Montana in Congress. While engaged in her first Congressional term, Jeannette introduced legislation that would eventually become the **19th Constitutional Amendment**. She served a single term at that time, but ran again in 1940 and was elected again. During her first term, Jeannette was one of fifty representatives to vote against declaring war against Germany. Then, decades later, as the fires still burned at Pearl Harbor, Jeannette was the only member of Congress to vote against declaring war on Japan. Following the session, bystanders angered by her vote pursued her until she had to take refuge in a telephone booth. Her stand was unpopular but reflected the courage that had marked her many decades of activism.

As the twentieth century rolled on, women like Eleanor Roosevelt, Betty Friedan, Gloria Steinem, Angela Davis, Coretta Scott King, Maya Angelou and Ruth Bader Ginsburg would continue to battle for women's rights and equal treatment of women.

Sojourner Truth

Former Slave, American Abolitionist, Women's Rights Activist

Sojourner Truth

Isabella Baumfree was born in 1797 in Dutch-speaking Ulster County, New York. Both of Isabella's parents were slaves. She would later become a famous abolitionist and women's rights advocate and would take the name **Sojourner Truth**. Isabella, at age nine years, was sold at auction, along with a number of sheep, for one hundred dollars. Her new "owner" was a cruel man named John Neely. Neely was a brutal master and beat Isabella frequently.

Isabella would be sold three or four times and, around 13 years of age, became the property of John Dumont and his wife Elizabeth. She was again subjected to violent punishments and forced into harsh physical labor.

At the age of 18, Isabella found herself in love with a slave named Robert. Robert worked on a nearby farm and the two were not allowed to pursue their relationship. She was united, instead, with a male slave named **Thomas** and records show the two had five enslaved children. The first of the children was born in 1815. John Dumont verbally promised that he would, if Isabella behaved and worked properly, grant her emancipation on the fourth of July, 1826. When the time came, though, he refused to honor their agreement.

Isabella reacted to what she perceived to be the unfair treachery of John Dumont by walking away. She was twenty years old. She believed she had properly fulfilled her obligation to Dumont. She escaped, taking her infant child Sophia along, running to the nearby home of a known abolitionist family, the Van Wageners. She was forced to endure separation from her other children, all of whom were the legal property of John Dumont or had been sold away. The Van Wageners purchased Isabella's freedom.

They also assisted her in legal efforts, which were ultimately successful, to gain return of Isabella's son Peter. Peter, five years old, had been illegally sold into slavery in Alabama. John Dumont, after passage of the New York Anti-Slavery Law, disregarded the law and illegally sold Peter, five years old at the time, to another slave owner. Isabella, with the assistance of the Van Wageners, eventually won her lawsuit and regained custody of young Peter. The case marked the very first time a black woman filed suit against a white man . . . and won.

Isabella's time with the Van Wagenens, who were devoutly religious, inspired her spirituality. She soon became a devoted Christian. She took her son Peter and moved to New York City, where she worked as a housekeeper for an evangelist preacher, Elijah Pierson. Three years later, she took a position working for Robert Matthews, another Christian preacher. Records show that when Elijah Pierson died, Robert Matthews and Isabella were charged with having poisoned him and stolen from him. Both of them were acquitted of the charges.

Her experiences with the Van Wageners, Elijah Pierson and Robert Matthews so moved Isabella that she felt she had received a calling, herself, to spend her life spreading the Christian word. In 1843 Isabella formalized her new mission, changing her name to Sojourner Truth. She proceeded forward from that time, becoming an effective public speaker and a hard-working campaigner. She joined the causes of the abolition of slavery, the end of oppression of black people and women and the movement toward women's voting rights.

Sojourner Truth became a charismatic itinerant preacher. She would soon be interacting with nationally known abolitionists, including **Frederick Douglass** and **William Lloyd Garrison**. While Sojourner never did learn literacy and could not read or write, she spoke in devastating terms of the evils of slavery. She had to dictate her autobiography, written with her direction, by **Olive Gilbert** in 1850. It was **titled "The Narrative of Sojourner Truth"**. Sales of the book provided financial support for her and made her nationally famous. She met **Elizabeth Cady Stanton** and **Susan B. Anthony**, both of whom were heavily engaged in battles to obtain basic rights for America's women and against the use of alcohol. Sojourner became active in both causes, while continuing her fight for the abolition of slavery.

In Akron, Ohio, in 1851, Sojourner spoke passionately for women's rights. Her speech would become a milestone and would be known as her famous **"Ain't I A Woman?"** speech. The prevailing cultural beliefs about the inferiority of black citizens and of all women were challenged in her address. Sojourner was nearly six feet tall, unusual in those times for a woman. She spoke of her strength and challenged any assumption that, being black and female, she was somehow "inferior". A newspaper reported that she remarked "I have plowed and reaped and husked and chopped and mowed and can any man do more than that?"

Sojourner eventually separated her objectives from those of Frederick Douglass. Douglass believed that the focus on women's rights, even those of black women, was a distraction that interfered with his main focus, which was elimination of slavery and gaining fundamental rights for black men. He believed in the struggle for women's rights, but he felt the rights of black men would have to be obtained first. Sojourner believed both objectives could be simultaneously pursued.

During the Civil War, in the path of **Harriet Tubman**, another escaped slave woman, Sojourner assisted in recruitment of black soldiers. She rallied movements to collect and provide clothing and supplies to black fugitives. She continued her support, like Tubman, of the underground railroad. She continued to speak out against oppression of black people and women.

Her actions in the movement to abolish slavery and to support black troops drew the attention of **President Abraham Lincoln**. He invited her to join him at the **White House** in October of 1864, where he personally showed her a Bible that had been a gift to him from African American citizens. While visiting in Washington, D.C., Sojourner showed her continuing courage and her dismissal of racist segregation by insisting on riding on "white people only" streetcars. When a streetcar conductor attempted to physically throw her off the car, Sojourner pressed charges against the man and won her case in court.

After the Civil War, Sojourner Truth worked to find freed slaves ways to escape poverty. She continued her fight against segregation. She worked, unsuccessfully, for passage of legislation intended to give freed black people land on which they could live and build farms.

Sojourner grew nearly deaf and blind in her later years. She settled in Michigan, near the homes of three of her daughters. Sojourner died at her home on November 26, 1883. She was 86 years old. Her life was dedicated to the preaching of Christianity and the battle for equal rights for all Americans.

Sojourner Truth said, in 1863: "Children, who made your skin white? Was it not God? Who made mine Black? Was it not the same God? Am I to blame, therefore, because my skin is Black? Does not God love colored children as well as white children? And did not the same Savior die to save the one as well as the other?" These words, her own, seem to offer a perfect eulogy for this amazing woman.

James Buchanan

America's Fifteenth President

On April 23, 1791, **James Buchanan, Jr.**, was born. His parents were **James** and **Elizabeth (Speer) Buchanan** and they lived in a log cabin near Cove Gap, Pennsylvania. His father had emigrated to the United States from Ireland. The family, shortly after James, Jr., was born, moved to a farm and then moved once more, this time into the town of Mercersberg, Pennsylvania. The elder Buchanan worked successfully as a farmer, a merchant and a real estate broker and he became the wealthiest resident of Mercersberg.

James attended the Old Stone Academy in Mercersberg and then enrolled in Dickinson College (Carlisle, Pennsylvania). At Dickinson, Buchanan exhibited some behavior problems and was nearly expelled. He pleaded for leniency and a second chance and he was eventually, in 1809, graduated with honors. He then studied the law and was admitted to the bar in 1812. He opened a law practice in Lancaster, Pennsylvania, where he would make his home for the remainder of his life.

Buchanan operated a successful law practice. In 1821, he earned more than eleven thousand dollars, which in 2021 would be the equivalent of $220,000.

Buchanan was engaged for marriage only one time in his life. He courted and was engaged to **Ann Coleman** in 1819. Ann was the child of a wealthy iron manufacturer. There were rumors that Buchanan was only interested in her money and that Buchanan was seeing other women. Later in life there was speculation that Buchanan was less than fully committed to a heterosexual lifestyle. Historians found that, in her letters, it was apparent that Ann was aware of the unpleasant rumors. Their engagement was terminated during that same year and the wedding never happened. Ann Coleman died soon after the break-up and rumors circulated in society that her death was a result of suicide. Buchanan requested permission from Coleman's father to attend her funeral. He was refused and did not attend. He was quoted to have declared "I fear that happiness has fled from me forever". Buchanan is the only American president who never was married. Buchanan's niece, **Harriet Lane**, assumed the social duties of the lady of the White House during his presidency.

Buchanan rapidly gained fame and social prominence. He was elected to the Pennsylvania House of Representatives in 1814, as a representative of the Federalist party. In 1820, he was elected to the U.S. House of Representatives and he would pursue a long political career from that point on in his life. The Federalist party died out in 1824 and Buchanan became a Democrat. He served as Chairman of the House Judiciary Committee, then as a Minister to Russia in 1831. He was elected to the U.S. Senate, where he was re-elected twice. He served under President Polk as Secretary of State. After being passed over a couple of times, Buchanan was nominated for the Presidency, which he won, in 1856. His victory address was less than unifying, as he loudly denounced the Republicans, claiming they were "unfairly attacking the South".

His presidency was marked throughout by the inflammatory issues of states' rights and slavery. Buchanan, being a **Democrat**, was generally supportive of Southern demands. He believed the federal government should stay out of the politics, including the slavery issue, of individual states. He had, in 1846, taken the side of Southerners when they blocked the **Wilmot Proviso**, which would have banned slavery in all territory gained in the Mexican-American war. He supported the **Compromise of 1850**, which granted each new state **"popular sovereignty"**, meaning each state could decide for themselves whether or not to admit slavery.

When he assumed the presidency, Buchanan appointed both Northern and Southern sympathizers to his cabinet, hoping to maintain peace. It did not work. The intensity of the tensions between slavery and anti-slavery forces continued to increase. Buchanan was seen by Northerners to be more sympathetic to the slavers. Only two days after he took office, the Supreme Court handed down its notorious **"Dred Scott"** decision, believed by many to be the worst of all Supreme Court decisions. It determined that the federal government had no legal right to regulate slavery laws in the territories and it denied African Americans the fundamental rights of American citizens. There is strong evidence that President Buchanan had pressured a "Northerner" SCOTUS justice to cross over to vote with the Southerners. He hoped the Dred Scott decision would settle the monolithic slavery issue, but it did just the opposite, adding much fuel to the burning fire. The nation was further and more intensively, divided.

Buchanan went on to support the **Lecompton Constitution**, which would have made Kansas a new state allowing slavery. The document was never voted into effect and Kansas joined the Union, in 1861, as a free state. During his administration, little was accomplished as Republicans blocked much of his proposed legislation and he vetoed much Republican legislation. Governmental activity was logjammed. Things got worse when, in October of 1859, super-abolitionist **John Brown** carried out his attempt, by attacking the federal armory at **Harper's Ferry**, Virginia, to incite a massive slave uprising. Brown was unsuccessful and was hanged for his efforts, but his activities furthered exacerbated the growing movement toward civil war.

James Buchanan's administration was further plagued by the **"Panic of 1857"**, which was financially devastating, especially to northern states. Unemployment rose drastically and the nation's economy spiraled downward.

In the presidential election of 1860, Buchanan abided by an earlier promise to be a "one term president". He did not run. He generally supported candidates with leanings to the South. After the election was over and **Abraham Lincoln** was elected, Buchanan attempted to order the reinforcement of southern military facilities with provisions, weapons and troops. He was convinced to rescind his order.

In his final address as President, Buchanan blamed the Northerners for interfering with the slavery issue in the southern states. He warned that, if Northerners didn't withdraw their interference, Southerners would be justified in **"revolutionary resistance"** to the Union. He encouraged confirmation of the constitutional legality of slavery and he advocated support for fugitive slave laws. Some citizens, as southern states seceded and the Civil War began, called the war **"Buchanan's War"**.

Only two months after Buchanan left office, Southerners shelled **Fort Sumter** and the **Civil War** was launched. Many Northerners blamed Buchanan for the nation's descent into war. He supported, as a civilian, the Union. He declared that the attack on Fort Sumter left the North no alternative but to prosecute the war. He wrote a letter, widely published, encouraging his fellow Pennsylvanians to join the Union Army. Nevertheless, Buchanan was commonly believed to be a supporter of the South and of slavery. He was routinely condemned by the press.

The state of his reputation became a great concern for Buchanan. He wrote a book attempting to justify his political positions. He became depressed and lost his physical health. James Buchanan died at the age of 77, at his home at **Wheatland**, the family estate near Lancaster in Pennsylvania.

Historians have been harsh on Buchanan, generally listing him among the least effective of all presidents.

Wheatland, a beautiful "federal style" home, still stands. It can be visited in Lancaster and has been designated a National Historic Landmark and has been added to the National Register of Historic Places.

James Buchanan and Slavery

Buchanan's biography makes it clear that he believed that slavery was an issue to be defined and regulated by each individual state. His sympathy for Southern, pro-slavery, causes seems to have been pervasive. In his personal life, historical records seem to indicate he had little affection for the evil institution, but also didn't support federal intervention to limit it. The big question, did he actually OWN slaves, is a little more foggy.

Among American presidents, preceding Abraham Lincoln, all owned slaves, with the only exceptions being John Adams, John Quincy Adams, Millard Fillmore and Franklin Pierce. Buchanan is generally listed among the slave owners. The story is complex.

James Buchanan, in 1834, while running for the U.S. Senate, discovered that his own sister's husband's family owned two slaves, located in Virginia. Buchanan, hoping to escape the political blowback, purchased both of them. He did so under the auspices of what was known as **"a deed of emancipation"** (Virginia) and **"a deed of conditional manumission"** (Pennsylvania). Under these legal terms, the two slaves became **"indentured servants"** and therefore "bound" to Buchanan. One was **Daphne Cool**, 22 years old at the time and the other was Daphne's daughter, **Ann Cool**, who was only five years old and would be, under the terms of the 'purchase', indentured for another twenty-three years. Technically, Daphne and Ann were not legal "slaves", but certainly they were not free. They served out their time as house servants, under the direction of Esther Harper, the supervising housekeeper known as "Hetty", for the Buchanan home.

Some historians have noted that there is a piece of paperwork, related to the transfer of Daphne and Ann to Buchanan, which has written on its backside, a note written by James Buchanan. It is said to state that Ann died in 1835 and that Daphne "ran away" not long after. If true, it would certainly imply that Daphne was not loving the conditions of her indenturement. Or, it may have been simply a way for Buchanan to create a record showing he no longer held indentured servants.

Slavery became illegal in Pennsylvania in 1847. Ann Cool's indentured contract did not end until 1857, when Buchanan was already President. The question of whether she was or wasn't illegally enslaved after the year 1847 is legally obscure. She may have been, as Buchanan's note implied, already dead. Buchanan would undoubtedly have claimed that he owned no "slaves". Daphne and Ann may have emphatically objected.

Some historians report that Buchanan also purchased other slaves and brought them to Pennsylvania, where they were freed and were "left to decide for themselves how to 'pay Buchanan back'". It's unknown whether they were released into true freedom or released into the same indentured conditions endured by Daphne and Ann Cool.

The First Oil Well

The 1850's saw the infancy of the coming, life-changing **Industrial Revolution**. There was a surge in the invention and introduction of many new types of machinery. The machines often required oil to allow them to function efficiently. In those days, whale oil was used for many purposes and oil from the ground was collected from "seeps", where it seeped through to the surface. Blankets were used to soak up the seeped oil. Only small amounts of oil could be accumulated from the seeps on the ground.

In 1859 a railroad conductor, **Edwin L. Drake**, was in position to see the need and utility of oil, as the big locomotives and train cars required substantial amounts of the lubricant. Two executives from the new **Seneca Oil Company** met Drake, who had retired from the railroad due to health problems. They hired him to travel the region and inspect their various operations, through which they collected oil from seeps. He was a good choice for them because, due to his railroad career, he could ride the railroads free of charge. Drake quickly realized the futility of collecting significant amounts of oil from the seeps.

Drake wanted to find a better way to collect more oil from the ground beneath him. At first, he tried to dig a mine in search of the precious fluid, but the mine shaft flooded and the effort failed. Drake had observed the way that salt was sometimes collected by drilling down into the earth. He began to experiment with attempts to drill for oil. Observers described his efforts as **"Drake's Folly"**. Nevertheless, Drake persisted.

Drake selected a location in Titusville, Pennsylvania to sink his first well. His experiments led him to discover that he could drive iron pipes down through layers of shale and he hoped the process could reach deep enough to access oil reserves. Drake hired a local man, **William "Uncle Billy" Smith**, who was a successful blacksmith. They began to drill their pipes, a painfully slow process. They were able to sink the pipes about three feet deeper each day. The well reached a depth of nearly seventy feet on August 27, 1859. When Uncle Billy arrived on the scene the following day, he was excited to find that oil had actually risen to the surface.

The Drake oil well was an instant success. Edwin and Uncle Billy began collecting oil in whiskey barrels. They were soon steadily collecting 400 gallons of pure oil every day. Drake never patented his plans, so others were soon imitating his efforts. Newer oil wells produced even more petroleum than Drake's first well and his well was shut down about two years after being created. By that time, the early 1860's, Pennsylvania was experiencing a full-blown oil boom. Wells were producing thousands of gallons daily and the sudden availability of such large amounts soon drove the price of oil very low.

Drake and the two executives of Seneca Oil, were driven out of the business. Drake lived for many years in poverty, while others grew very wealthy using the process he invented. The Pennsylvania government, in recognition of his contributions, awarded him a pension in 1870, which allowed him to live comfortably until his death in 1880.

Edwin's process for extracting oil from the ground was very successful. It was the foundation for creation of a completely new industry and would make businessmen like **John D. Rockefeller** very, very wealthy. The new abundance of oil made possible the effective functioning of a long series of new machines. Oil was the lubricant that made much of the industrial revolution possible.

The Dred Scott Decision

Dred Scott

Dred Scott's parents were slaves and Dred was born a slave. His exact birthdate, as was true of many slaves, is unknown, but it is most likely he was born sometime in 1799. He was owned by **Peter Blow**, who resided in Virginia. Blow moved to Alabama first, in 1818 and then to St. Louis, MO., in 1830, taking Dred with him. Virginia, Alabama and Missouri were all "slave states" at the time. In St. Louis, Peter Blow ran a boarding house and Dred Scott was probably a servant.

In 1832 Peter Blow died. Dred Scott was purchased by an army surgeon, **Dr. John Emerson**. Dr. Emerson took Dred to Illinois and then to Fort Snelling in Wisconsin Territory. Illinois was a free state and the **Missouri Compromise** had outlawed slavery in Wisconsin. While in Wisconsin, Dred married a slave, **Harriet Robinson**, whose owner transferred ownership of Harriet to Dr. Emerson. Harriet's owner had been Major Lawrence Taliaferro, who was the Indian Agent stationed at Fort Snelling. The marriage was an unusual civil ceremony and may suggest that Dred and Harriet were treated with more respect and compassion than was the lot of many other enslaved people.

Dr. Emerson returned, in 1837, to St. Louis, but he left Dred and Harriet in Wisconsin. He hired them out to work for others in his absence. Emerson married Eliza (Irene) Sandford in 1838 and they moved to Louisiana, a confirmed slave state. He had Dred Scott join him in Louisiana. The group, after a series of moves, eventually moved back to St. Louis, also a slave state. Emerson died in 1843 and Dred and Harriet became the property of Irene. By this time, Dred and Harriet had two young daughters.

Over the years, Dred attempted to purchase his freedom and that of his family, but Irene refused. There is no indication that Dred or Harriet ever attempted to escape their bondage. They would have had the legal right to take their freedom, while living in the free territory of Wisconsin and the free state of Illinois, but, for whatever reasons, never did so. It's possible they were never informed of their rights or that they knew their rights, but were prevented from exercising them.

Dred and Harriet, in April of 1846, with the assistance of anti-slavery lawyers, filed separate lawsuits for their freedom. Dr. Emerson's wife, **Irene Sandford**, chose to oppose the lawsuits. The case would be known as **"Dred Scott v. Sandford"** and would go all the way to the Supreme Court.

The original lawsuit was based on two statutes that were active in Missouri at the time. One statute allowed that any person, of any color, could sue for "wrongful enslavement". The second statute declared that any person taken to any free territory automatically became free and could not be re-enslaved upon being returned to a slave state. Dred and Harriet's lawsuits were filed on grounds that, as they had resided in both Wisconsin and Illinois, a "free" Territory and a "free" state, they were legally freed from slavery. The court decided to hear only Dred's lawsuit, but the outcome was to apply to both Dred and Harriet.

The Dred Scott case is sometimes perceived to be the first of its kind, but historians have determined that hundreds of slaves, in various situations, had previously attempted to sue for their freedom. Dred and Harriet both were illiterate and were not able to serve themselves adequately through the legal process. They received assistance from abolitionists, from their church and from, surprisingly, the relatives of the family that formerly owned Dred, the family of Peter Blow.

The case first went to trial in Missouri in June of 1847. The judge ruled against the Scotts based on a legal technicality. The case returned to trial in January of 1850 and ruled the Scott's to be free. They were no longer legally enslaved. Irene Sanford appealed the decision and the case ended up back in the lap of the Missouri Supreme Court, which reversed the earlier decision. Dred and Harriet were once again, in 1852, slaves.

Irene Sanford left Missouri, leaving Dred and Harriet under control of her brother, John F. A. Sanford, who lived in New York. (Note: the correct spelling of the surname is 'Sanford', but it is incorrectly listed as 'Sandford' in many documents). The case was continued to a federal court, which ruled in Sanford's favor and against the Scott's, leaving them enslaved. Yet another appeal led to consideration by the U.S. Supreme Court. It announced its decision in March of 1857 and it ruled against Dred Scott. The Scott's were locked in slavery.

The **Chief Justice** of the Supreme Court, at the time, was **Roger Taney**. Taney wrote the majority opinion in the Dred Scott case and it pretty much defined his term on the court. His opinion declared all people of African heritage, whether free or enslaved, were not citizens of the United States and therefore had no right to sue in federal courts. He added that the Fifth Amendment protected the rights of slave owners because the enslaved were the legal property of their owners. Furthermore, the ruling declared the Missouri Compromise unconstitutional, which had the practical effect of taking away any power Congress might have to limit the spread of slavery. The decision has been widely condemned as the worst ruling in Supreme Court history.

There were many problems, based in constitutional law, with Roger Taney's written opinion. Two of the other Supreme Court justices wrote scathing criticisms of the ruling. The public reaction to the Dred Scott decision was immediate and was explosive. Anti-slavery forces were enraged. Pro-slavery forces were elated and celebrated the decision. Tensions between the North and the South were instantly amplified. A giant step was taken in the direction of Civil War.

The Dred Scott case wandered through the American judicial system for a decade. When the U.S. Supreme Court handed down the final decision, Irene Sanford had remarried. Her new husband, **Calvin Chaffee**, was an abolitionist and a U.S. Congressman. He was not happy when he learned his wife was the current owner of the most notorious slave in America. He sold Dred Scott and his family, to **Taylor Blow**. Taylor was the son of Peter Blow, who had been Dred's original owner.

Taylor Blow emancipated Dred Scott and his family, on May 26, 1857. It was ten years after the original lawsuit was filed and it was only three months after the Supreme Court decision had declared him a slave. Dred Scott took a job as a porter at a St. Louis hotel. His life as a free man was, sadly, very short. Dred died of tuberculosis on September 17, 1858. Dred's wife, Harriet, would live on to see the Emancipation and the end of the Civil War. She passed away in 1876.

In a bit of historical irony, Supreme Court Justice Roger Taney, in 1861, would swear in "the Great Emancipator", Abraham Lincoln, as President of the United States.

John Brown

American Abolitionist

The Attack on Harper's Ferry

John Brown, abolitionist

On May 9, 1800, **John Brown** was born in Torrington, Connecticut. His parents were **Owen Brown** and **Ruth Millss**. His grandfather, **Captain John Brown**, died fighting in **America's Revolutionary War**. Ruth's father, **Gideon Mills**, also fought in the Revolution. Owen Brown was in the tannery business and the family was reported to be respectable, but poor. Owen became a successful businessman and the family gained wealth. Jesse Grant, the father of future president **Ulysses S. Grant**, worked for Owen and, for a time, lived with the Brown family.

The family relocated a couple of times and young John Brown spent most of his younger years at their home in Hudson, Ohio. This may have been significant in John's development, as Hudson was an important stop on the **Underground Railroad**. John's father, Owen, became an active supporter of the effort to bring enslaved people to freedom. Their home became a **"safe house"** where fugitive slaves could find sanctuary.

David Hudson was the original founder of Hudson, Ohio. The region, at the time, was mostly untamed wilderness. David was a fervent abolitionist and the area around Hudson became one of the most aggressively anti-slavery areas in the country. David was an advocate of using force to fight slavery, while many other abolitionists were pacifists. Hudson's beliefs very likely impacted young John Brown.

No schools that reached beyond lower grade levels were available in the Hudson area. John Brown studied at the country school of well-known abolitionist **Elizur Wright**. Elizur was the father of a much more famous abolitionist, who was also named **Elizur Wright**. John's mother, Ruth, died in 1808. His father remarried, but John seems to have never grown attached to his new mother.

John sometimes shared a story, passed down by his family, about being away from home, working for a man who was moving cattle. The man owned a black boy and, when the boy didn't satisfy the man's work demands, the man beat the child with a shovel. John asked the man why he abused the child and the man responded "Because he is a slave". Brown later declared that this was the moment when he determined to spend his life improving the condition of America's black people.

John Brown left his home and family at the age of sixteen. He went to Massachusetts and, later, to Connecticut. He attended schools and became an ordained minister. His education was always combined with a strong dose of religious instruction. When a chronic eye condition put an end to his formal education, he returned to Hudson, where he opened a tannery on the other side of town from his father's business. He studied books to become a professional surveyor.

A housekeeper, Mrs. Amos Lusk, a widower, moved into John Brown's log cabin. She managed household chores and did some cooking and she brought with her a daughter, **Dianthe**. In 1820, Brown married Dianthe. He wrote of Dianthe that she was "A remarkably plain, but neat, industrious and economical girl, of excellent character, earnest piety and practical common sense". John and Dianthe would produce seven children before Dianthe died, in childbirth, in 1832.

John Brown became a master of the contents of the Bible and would point out the smallest of errors made by others. He lived a spartan life, never using tobacco, tea, coffee or alcohol. He loved to read and studied "Plutarch's Lives" and biographies of Napoleon and Cromwell.

Brown moved his family, in 1825, to Pennsylvania, seeking a location that would be more safe and secure for his abolitionist activities. He built a cabin, a tannery and a barn. In the barn, he created a well-ventilated, secret room, in which he could hide fugitive slaves. His home became an important stop on the Underground Railroad. Historians believe he assisted some 2,500 fugitives in their escape to the North. Most made their way to Canada.

John was paid to survey new roads, he recruited a preacher for the town and he erected a school. Students met in his home until the school was built. **President John Quincy Adams**, another abolitionist, appointed John Postmaster of Randolph, Pennsylvania. He carried mail for several years.

A group of white farmers asked Brown to assist them in driving out **Native Americans** who still roamed the area hunting for fur and food. Brown refused their request, calling their effort "a mean act". Brown grew up in the wilderness around Hudson and was a friend to some of the Indians. He was able to communicate with them, to some extent, in their own languages. He hunted with them and they took meals in his home.

John's son Frederick died in 1831. He was four years old. Brown fell ill himself and his businesses were failing. His first wife, Dianthe, died in 1832 and a newborn child did not survive. John was left with five remaining children. He remarried, in 1833, to **Mary Ann Day**, who was seventeen years old and was his housekeeper's younger sister. Mary and John would go on to have thirteen children. Several would eventually join John in his fight against slavery.

John's businesses and his financial status, ranged up and down, from successes to failures. He was, at one time, a bank director. He lost a lot of money in the **Panic of 1837**. He was jailed for refusing to leave a farm on which he'd been foreclosed. John and three of his sons, were expelled from their church because they brought a black man into their pew.

John, in the early 1850's, moved his family once again, taking them to a community known as Timbuctoo, located in the Adirondack region in New York state. Famous abolitionist **Gerrit Smith** was giving plots of farm land to black men. Black men who were owners of land or of a house were allowed, in that area, at that time, to vote in local elections. John Brown purchased a farm nearby in Lake Placid, New York. He remained engaged in efforts to advise and assist black people in the community.

In November, 1837, a well-known newspaper editor, minister and abolitionist was attacked and killed in Alton, Illinois. He was **Elijah Parish Lovejoy** and his murder lit a fire of outrage in abolitionists across the country. John Brown responded with this declaration: "Here, before God, in the presence of these witnesses, from this time, I consecrate my life to the destruction of slavery".

Two of John's sons, by 1855, had moved to Kansas Territory and both were very active abolitionists. They invited their father to join them, as they feared attacks from pro-slavery **"border ruffians"** out of Missouri. John Brown believed that he and his family could fight off the slavers and could help bring Kansas into the Union as a free state. They were living in the middle of the border fighting that was to be known as "**Bleeding Kansas**".

There were numerous incidents of attacks back and forth across the Kansas-Missouri border. Pro-slavers came from Missouri to attack free- staters in Kansas and free-staters crossed from Kansas to attack pro-slavers in Missouri. After the notorious **"sacking of Lawrence, Kansas"**, in 1856, John Brown planned retaliation. Brown, along with his sons and other abolitionists, most from a group of raiders called the **Pottawatomie Rifles**, gathered to exact revenge. The Pottawatomie Rifles numbered several dozen free-staters and were led by John Brown's son, John, Jr. They were angered by the attacks on Lawrence, by the establishment of pro-slavery forces around LeCompton, Kansas and by the beating of **Senator Charles Sumner** on the floor of the U.S. Senate.

On the night of May 24, 1856, John Brown, several of his sons and a supporter named **Theodore Weiner**, were camped near the small pro-slavery town of Pottawatomie Creek. Under cover of darkness, Brown's small band sought out the homes of settlers they believed to be pro-slavers. They first approached the rural home of **James P. Doyle**. They ordered James and two of his sons, out of the house. Brown accused them of belonging to the pro-slavery **"Law and Order"** political party. Two of Brown's sons, Owen and Frederick, slashed the three Doyles to death with broadswords. John Brown himself fired a shot into the head of John Doyle to make sure Doyle was dead. Doyle's wife begged for the life of her sixteen-year-old son, John, whom she promised was not involved in politics. The boy was spared.

Brown then led his group to the home of **Allen Wilkinson**, who was also forced from his home. In the darkness, Wilkinson was slashed and stabbed to death. Not finished with their bloody mission, Brown's group proceeded to the cabin of **James Harris**. Their primary target, a man called **"Dutch Henry"**, was not at home. Three others, however, were staying at the cabin. They were all interrogated fiercely by Brown and his men. Two of the men were allowed to return to the cabin. The third, though, **William Sherman**, Dutch Henry's brother, was hacked to death by broadswords.

John Brown and his sons and followers had brutally murdered five pro-slavery settlers in just that one night. The reaction to their raid would be rapid and violent. The **"Pottawatomie Massacre"** is considered the trigger event that led to **"Bleeding Kansas"**, which amounted to a local civil war along the border between Missouri and Kansas. "Bleeding Kansas" featured several months of raids and counter-raids that ultimately brought the deaths of nearly thirty settlers. They marked the series of events that made up to the first real violence of America's Civil War.

The Pottawatomie Massacre enraged the pro-slavery forces. Several skirmishes between the groups occurred in the following months. Brown's men took pro-slavery prisoners at an engagement known as the **Battle of Black Jack**. They also attempted, unsuccessfully, to protect the town of Osawatomie from an attack by pro-slavers. The town was sacked and burned and Brown's son, Frederick, was killed at the **Battle of Osawatomie**.

Brown became, with the loss of his son, even more dedicated than ever before to the abolitionist movement. He traveled the country raising money and resources to support the cause. In 1858, Kansas held elections and voted to enter the Union as a free state. Brown, by 1859, was seeking out locations where people were enslaved and carrying out raids to try and free them. During this time period, John Brown met the famous Underground Railroad conductor, **Harriet Tubman**. He also encountered **Frederick Douglass**, with whom he became friends. Douglass and Brown visited one another's homes, where their children played together.

John Brown, with assistance from **Harriet Tubman**, whom Brown addressed as **"General Tubman"**, began planning a military-like attack on slaveholders. Brown meant to overcome the guards at the United States military arsenal at **Harper's Ferry**, thereby gaining a large cache of weapons to serve his cause. Harper's Ferry was located in what is now West Virginia. Brown hoped to use freed slaves and his own men to take over the armory and trigger a massive revolt of southern slaves. He laid the groundwork by using the word-of-mouth gossip communications system that passed information from slave to slave and plantation to plantation. Brown expected that, on hearing about his capture of the arsenal, black slaves would revolt in mass and join his battle to bring freedom to all black people. He brought together a dedicated group of twenty-two men, including several freed slaves and two of Brown's sons, Owen and Watson. Brown drew on the expertise of friendly experts from the abolitionist movement to bring military training to the small force.

The raid on Harpers Ferry began when Brown rented a small cabin, the Kennedy Farmhouse, four miles north of the arsenal. He used the name Isaac Smith for cover. His group numbered 16 white men and five black men. Abolitionist friends to the North sent Brown 198 Sharps carbine rifles. They also were given 950 "pikes", which were meant to be used by untrained black men who had no experience with firearms. The pikes were never used, but, after the event, were widely distributed as souvenirs. One was given to Harriet Tubman.

The first action taken by Brown's men was to capture **Colonel Lewis Washington**, a distant relative to **George Washington**, who owned slaves. Owen Brown kidnapped Washington, while the rest of the band, led by John Brown, began the raid on the arsenal at Harpers Ferry. Knowing he had to take the arsenal before the government learned of his raid, Brown's men cut telegraph lines and stopped a train that was headed for the nation's capitol. He eventually allowed the train to continue its trip and a conductor on the train was able to notify authorities about what was happening at the arsenal. Sadly and ironically, the first death caused by Brown's raid occurred when Brown's men shot a black man, **Heyward Shepherd**, who was a baggage handler at the train station. They killed a free black man who was exactly the type of person Brown was desperate to help.

The United States Armory at Harpers Ferry was a compound of buildings where the army manufactured small arms. There were around 100,000 muskets and rifles at the weapons storehouse. Brown hoped to put the weapons in the hands of revolting slaves. He had the assistance of Harriet Tubman in planning his mission. He tried, unsuccessfully, to enlist the service of **Frederick Douglass**. Douglass told him the mission would be suicide and, even if successful, would cause many Americans to repudiate their cause. One report indicates that Douglass later said, of Brown, "The Old Captain (Brown) told us, we stood nine chances to one of being killed, but there are moments when men can do more dead than alive". Brown meant that a martyr can sometimes bring about more change than a live soldier. A man who joined Douglass in that last clandestine meeting with Brown, a former slave known as **"Emperor" Shields Green**, did decide to proceed with Brown, rather than returning to the home of Douglass.

Brown and his men were able, with relative ease, to occupy the armory. Workers began to arrive to begin their day and were captured. The captives were divided into two groups. It was Monday, October 17, 1859 and the local townspeople began to learn of the raid. They organized to fight back. Several military groups from towns in the area began to arrive. The compound was surrounded. Harpers Ferry is on a peninsula and bridges leading away from it were occupied by militia, blocking any hope of escape for Brown's group. Gunfire was sporadically exchanged and four local citizens, including the mayor of Harpers Ferry, were killed. Brown's attack was doomed when slaves in the area, contrary to his imagination, did not revolt and join his cause. Word about Brown's plans may not have reached the slaves or they may have been too fearful of the consequences, had they been caught by their "owners".

John Brown's raiders were surrounded and numerically overwhelmed. He had to move his men and their small group of captives, to a small, stone building, which was the armory's engine house. It became Brown's fort. They barricaded themselves in the engine house. Attacks by militia resulted in the escape of several of the captives. Eight railroad men or militiamen were killed in the fighting. John Brown sent one of his sons, Watson, out to surrender. Watson was shot and mortally wounded, dying a day later in agony. Another of Brown's men, William H. Leeman, was shot to death while trying to escape by swimming across the river. John Brown's son, Oliver, was shot during the fighting. He died while lying on the floor next to his father. Reporters wrote that many of the local militia were "disorderly and unreliable . . . most got roaring drunk". One local newspaper called the event a "broad and pathetic farce". The Governor was outraged at the performance of the militia.

Robert E. Lee, who would later command the Confederate Army, was in charge of a company of U. S. Marines. They received orders from **President James Buchanan** to "put an end" to the episode. Next day, the morning of October 18, 1859, Colonel Lee proposed that John Brown surrender. Lee sent **J.E.B. Stuart**, an aide, under a white flag of truce, to negotiate Brown's surrender. Stuart would also later play a big role in the Civil War. Brown was told that his men would be spared if he would put an end to the occupation. Brown refused.

Lee's Marines, led by **Lt. Israel Greene**, quickly stormed Brown's little stone fort, battering down the doors, taking Brown, all of Brown's surviving men and all of their remaining captives alive. Greene was the first man through the door. He later wrote:

"Quicker than thought I brought my saber down with all my strength upon Brown's head. He was moving as the blow fell and I suppose I did not strike him where I intended, for he received a deep saber cut in the back of the neck. He fell senseless on his side, then rolled over on his back. He had in his hand a short Sharpe's cavalry carbine. I think he had just fired as I reached Colonel (Lewis) Washington, for the Marine who followed me into the aperture made by the ladder received a bullet in the abdomen, from which he died in a few minutes. Instinctively, as Brown fell, I gave him a saber thrust in the left breast. The sword I carried was a light uniform weapon and, either not having a point or striking something hard in Brown's accouterments, did not penetrate. The blade bent double."

John Brown survived his gory wounds and was interviewed by several people, including the governor, as he lay bleeding on the floor of the paymaster's office. Interviewers described him, in spite of his wounds, as being "courteous and affable" and "the gamest man we ever saw". Brown was imprisoned, tried and found guilty of treason. He was hanged, at age 59, on December 2, 1859. Among the witnesses to his hanging was Robert E. Lee and the man who would kill Lincoln, **John Wilkes Booth**.

In one sense, Brown's attack on Harpers Ferry was a monumental failure. In another, though, considering that his goal was to incite a revolution against slavery, he was somewhat successful. His actions were considered by many abolitionists to be the extreme to which they must go to achieve their objective, the ultimate end to slavery in America. The raid on Harpers Ferry was most definitely a significant episode in the path to the civil war.

Harriet Tubman

"The General" on the Underground Railroad

Harriett Tubman

Ben Ross was an enslaved man who lived on a plantation owned by **Anthony Thompson**. Ben was an expert woodsman and was in charge of timber operations on the plantation. The Thompson plantation was located in Dorchester County, Maryland, near the Blackwater River.

Harriet Green, known as **"Rit"**, was an enslaved woman who was owned by **Mary Pattison Brodess**. Harriet's mother, **Modesty**, arrived in America aboard a slave ship, but little else is known about the family's background. Mary Brodess became the second wife of Anthony Thompson. Records suggest "Rit" probably had a white father. "Rit" served as a cook on the Thompson plantation, while Ben worked in the field.

The best historical records indicate that Ben and Rit were married around 1808. The couple produced 9 children. The fifth among those children was **Araminta Ross**, who was called **"Minty"**. Best estimates indicate that "Minty" was born in 1825, though it may have been as early as 1822.

Mary Brodess's son, Edward, sold three of Minty's sisters, separating the family forever. Later, Rit learned that a slave trader from Georgia was coming to the plantation with plans to purchase her youngest son, Moses. Assisted by other slaves, Rit managed to hide Moses for several weeks. Eventually, Edward Brodess and the Georgia slaver approached Rit's cabin, planning to take Moses by force. Rit met them at her door and declared "You are after my son, but the first man that comes into my house, I will split his head open. Brodess decided to cancel the sale and walked away. It's likely that seeing her mother, Rit, stand up to resist her "master" was an image that stayed with young "Minty". Araminta later changed her first name to **"Harriet"** to honor her courageous mother.

Young Minty's mother, Rit, worked as a cook in the "big house" of the Thompson plantation. Minty was left to care for younger brothers and sisters. At the age of five or six, she was "rented out" to serve as a caretaker for a "Miss Susan's" infant child. Minty was assigned to keep the baby quiet. When the baby cried, Minty was whipped. She later wrote that, on one occasion, she received five lashes before breakfast. She carried scars from the whippings for the remainder of her days. She tried to resist. She attempted to run away. She wore extra layers of clothing to absorb the blows. Her resistance led to additional punishment.

As an older child, seven or eight years, Minty was rented out to James Cook, who gave her the job of wading into the marshes to set and clear muskrat traps. She became ill, though and was sent back to the Brodess's. When she recovered sufficiently, she was hired out again. She was sent to work in the fields, where she learned to drive oxen, plowing fields and hauling logs out of the forest. She would, later in life, say that she much preferred "field labor" rather than "house work".

A few years later, Minty was working in the fields when she saw another slave attempting to run from the overseer. The overseer grabbed a two-pound weight and prepared to throw it at the fugitive. Minty jumped between the two, probably hoping to discourage the overseer from throwing, but the weight was thrown. It hit Minty in the head. She would describe the incident, saying "the weight broke my skull" and saying that, as she fell in and out of consciousness, bleeding profusely, she was carried to a resting place. She lay on the seat of a loom for two days, receiving no medical treatment. Forever after she would experience terrible headaches and she began to have some sort of seizures. Minty soon began having what she believed to be "visions", which she came to believe were messages from God. She had no education and was illiterate, but she went to church as a Methodist and she listened intently to stories from the Bible. Her faith in God was deep and passionate.

It would be a reach too far to claim that Minty's severe head injury could be a "blessing", but it may have been a benefit to her in one way. Her "seizures" sometimes looked much like narcolepsy. She would fall, without warning, into a long period of unconsciousness. The impediment probably made her unattractive to slave traders.

Anthony Thompson had promised to free or **"manumit"**, Ben Ross, Minty's father, when Ben turned 45 years old. He became 45 in 1840 and Anthony's son followed through on the promise. Ben was freed, though he chose to continue to work for the Thompson family as a timber foreman.

As she grew older, "Minty" changed her name to "Harriet", honoring her mother. She met **John Tubman** around 1844, who was a free black man. The two were soon married, making her Mrs. Harriet Tubman. Still living in Maryland, the two had a "blended" marriage. A freedman and a slave. By law, if they had children, those children would be slaves, owned by Harriet's owners, Mary and Edward Brodess. It was a time in Maryland when nearly half of the state's Black people were free and many black families consisted of mixtures of free and enslaved members.

"Minty", daughter of "Rit", was now Harriet Tubman, wife of a freedman. She spent five dollars to hire an attorney. She wanted to investigate the free vs. enslaved status of Rit. Harriet learned that the grandfather of Mary Brodess had stipulated in his will that Rit, and all of her children, were to be manumitted, freed, once Rit reached age 45. Rit and her nine children were legally free, but the Brodess family, with far greater resources, refused to acquiesce to the law. The family remained enslaved.

Harriet's health declined again in 1849. She learned, during that time, that Edward Brodess was planning to sell her and two of her brothers. Harriet later described her prayers at the time. She said she prayed, first, that their owner would have a change of heart and would choose not to sell them. As Brodess continued his efforts, she changed her prayers. She prayed that Brodess would die before he could sell her family members. Within days, Brodess did, indeed, die. Harriet was ever after remorseful for her prayers wishing for his end.

Edward Brodess's widow, Eliza, continued with plans to sell the slaves. Harriet decided not to wait longer to see what might be their fate. She made plans to run. Her husband, John Tubman, tried to change her mind, fearing the consequences should she be apprehended. Harriet later explained her position: "There was one of two things I had a right to . . . liberty or death; if I could not have one, I would have the other".

Harriet and two of her brothers had been hired out to work in a nearby county for another plantation owner. They escaped on September 17th, 1849. Harriet would have been in her early twenties. It worked to their advantage that they were living away from the Brodess plantation, because it was probably several days before Eliza learned that her slaves had run. She posted a reward of one hundred dollars each for their capture and return to her. One of Harriet's brothers, Ben, developed enough fear or remorse to make him decide to return to his bondage. Harriet and the other brother felt compelled to accompany him, giving up their escape attempt. Ben may have been feeling guilty about leaving his wife and children behind in slavery.

A couple of months later, Harriet ran again. This time she went alone, after singing, to another slave, Mary: "I'll meet you in the morning, I'm bound for the promised land". Little is known about Harriet Tubman's specific route in her journey to freedom. She utilized assistance from members of the **Underground Railroad**. She traveled in darkness, always following the **North Star**. Her fearful trek took her out of Maryland, probably with the assistance of Quakers, through Delaware, on northward into Pennsylvania. She fled a distance of approximately 90 miles and her trip most likely took several weeks. Throughout her time on the run, she would have been peering over her shoulders, watching constantly for the dreadful slave catchers.

"Conductors" on the Underground Railroad helped to hide fugitive slaves during daylight hours or to engage in various "ruses" to help the run-aways avoid capture. On one of her stops, a woman of the house had Harriet take up a broom and stay busy sweeping the family yard, lending the impression that Harriet was a legitimate employee of the family. When the sun went down, the same lady loaded Harriet into the back of a cart, covered her up and drove her to the next stop on the "railroad". On finally crossing over the border into Pennsylvania, Tubman said "When I found I had crossed that line I looked at my hands to see if I was the same person. There was such a glory over everything; the sun came like gold through the trees and over the fields and I felt like I was in Heaven".

Harriet found herself in Philadelphia, where she began working at whatever odd jobs she could find. She saved her money, always worrying about how she might be able to help the rest of her family escape slavery. Her situation became more serious in 1850 with the passage, by the United States Government, of the **Fugitive Slave Act**. The Act was an attempt by the federal government to mollify Southern states, who were growing aggressive in their insistence that the institution of slavery remain intact.

The Fugitive Slave Act declared that all run-away slaves remained the property of their original owners and that states to which slaves had run must assist in returning those slaves to their rightful owners. Suddenly, it was no longer so safe in Pennsylvania. Run-aways who had believed they had reached freedom began to move further north, into Ontario, Canada. Slavery had already been abolished in Canada. Conditions in Philadelphia were deteriorating for the black fugitives, anyway, as thousands of Irish immigrants, running from the **"Great Hunger"** in Ireland, were flooding in and were competing for labor jobs.

Harriet Tubman went back to Maryland in December of 1850, after learning that several of her relatives, including small children and an infant, were to be sold on the auction block. One of the women, Kessiah, was purchased by her own husband, John

Bowley, a black freedman. Several of the other relatives managed to slip away and into hiding. Overnight, Bowley spirited the family away, loading them onto a log canoe on which they floated for sixty miles. There they met Harriet Tubman and Harriet led them safely to Philadelphia.

Early in 1851, Harriet made another trip back to Maryland, where slave catchers were always watching for her. She was able to find and extract her younger brother, Moses, as well as two other slaves. Slaves utilized an efficient "word of mouth" communications network and word was getting around about Harriet's trips to freedom. She was almost certainly, by then, working with other abolitionists. One was the Quaker **Thomas Garrett**, who owned a hardware store in Wilmington, Delaware. Garrett was one of the busiest of the Underground Railroad "station-masters".

Later that same year, Harriet found the courage to return to Dorchester County. She hoped to find and free her husband, John Tubman. She was angered to find that John had married another woman. He told Harriet he was happy right where he was. He refused to accompany her North. Swallowing her bitterness, Harriet turned the fearful trip into a success by assisting several other slaves back North to freedom.

Historians suggest that, on one of her trips guiding fugitive slaves north to Canada, Harriet made a stop at the home of another former slave, the famous abolitionist **Frederick Douglass**. The two were certainly well aware of one another and each had great respect for the other. Douglass would later write of Harriet Tubman:

"Most that I have done and suffered in the service of our cause has been in public and I have received much encouragement at every step of the way. You, on the other hand, have labored in a private way. I have wrought in the day. You in the night. The midnight sky and the silent stars have been the witnesses of your devotion to freedom and of your heroism. Excepting **John Brown,** of sacred memory, I know of no one who has willingly encountered more perils and hardships to serve our enslaved people than you have."

Harriet worked for more than a decade, through 1862, journeying back and forth through Philadephia and Canada and eastern Maryland, finding those who were crying out for their freedom and conducting them to safety. She became the most famous of the Underground Railway "conductors". She made at least thirteen trips and rescued at least 70 slaves, though some estimates run as high as 300. She was able to rescue three more of her own brothers, along with their families. As her reputation spread, more of the enslaved grew to trust her enough to make the journey with her. Besides those she personally led out of bondage, she left instructions that were followed by many others. Somewhere along the line, Harriet gained the nickname **"Moses"**, comparing her to the biblical prophet who led the Hebrews to freedom out of Egypt.

Harriet's father had purchased her mother, in 1855, for $20 (worth about $600 in the present day). The two were "free", but certainly, where they lived, not safe. Harriet found out her father was under suspicion for harboring fugitive slaves. On one of her last missions, Harriet returned to Maryland to find and extract her parents. She was able to locate them and lead them north to Ontario, where they were able to rejoin many of their relatives, including Harriet's brothers.

Those who worked with Harriet often commented on her faith in God. She talked of "consulting with God". She sometimes manipulated the words in common gospel songs so that they could be used to communicate information. They might warn fugitives that a movement was too dangerous or inform them that it was safe to proceed. She was known to sing out joyously, as she crossed a state border leading run-aways to freedom, "Glory to God and Jesus, too! One more soul is safe!"

Tubman would go to any lengths to preserve the safety of her groups of run-aways. She was known to have drugged infants to make them quiet, so the slave catchers wouldn't hear them. Harriet carried a loaded revolver on her journeys, in part to protect from the dogs of slave catchers and in part to threaten any of her "passengers" who might consider returning to their owners. She knew that if one slave separated from her group, the whole group would be endangered, as would anyone who was assisting them in their journey. She said that, when one slave threatened to go back, she put the gun to his head and told him "Go on (with us) or die). He continued and was grateful to reach Canada.

Harriet "Minty" Tubman, herself a tiny black woman, carrying the burden of a debilitating disability, was so successful that groups of white slave owners began to take notice. They couldn't understand the sudden increases in losses of runaway slaves. They put the blame on white abolitionists like Thomas Garrett and John Brown and on black freedmen like Frederick Douglass. Neither Harriet nor any of her "passengers" were ever apprehended. Frederick Douglass took to calling her "General Tubman". Later in life, she told a group: "I was conductor of the Underground Railroad for eight years and I can say what most conductors can't say. I never ran my train off the track and I never lost a passenger". When John Brown was hanged, after his failed attack on Harper's Ferry, Tubman said of him "He done more in dying than 100 men would in living".

The Civil War began in 1861. Harriet Tubman continued to support the fight against slavery. She was recruited to serve as an aide to fugitive slaves living at **Fort Monroe**. She served by doing laundry, cooking and offering nursing care. Her skills with herbal medicines helped in the treatment of both soldiers and slaves. During an assault on **Fort Wagner**, in 1863, Harriet served **Colonel Robert Shaw**, who was wounded, his last meal. She would later say of the battle:

"We saw the lightning and that was the guns and then we heard the thunder and that was the big guns; then we heard the rain falling and that was the drops of blood falling; and when we came to get the crops, it was dead men that we reaped."

Harriet nursed soldiers suffering from smallpox and typhoid but did not get infected herself, for which she credited God. She began receiving government rations, in recognition of her services, but declined them, not wanting to appear to be getting special treatment. She sold homemade root beer and pies to gain money.

By 1863, Harriet Tubman was a recognized Union Army asset. She led a group of scouts and spies who delivered critical information about rebel troop movements and supply routes. She guided Union gunboats around Southern artillery emplacements. She helped to liberate Southern slaves who were ultimately allowed to form Black Union regiments in the United States Army. She was present at several military engagements. She was barely five feet tall, but she cast a long, long shadow.

Following the end of the Civil War, the U.S. government was not prompt in recognizing her service. She finally received $200 for her three years of dangerous service. She was promised a nursing position with the military, but it never materialized. She decided to move back to her home in New York, where her constant charitable activities kept her living in poverty.

Harriet was given a half-price ticket which allowed her the luxury of a train ride back to New York. Harriet was ordered, in a stroke of bitter irony, by a train conductor, to relocate from a regular passenger car to a much less pleasant smoking car. Harriet refused to move. The conductor took hold of her, cursing her in anger. Several white men assisted the conductor, injuring Harriet in their actions. Other white passengers cursed at Harriet, demanding that she be kicked off the train. "General Tubman", the greatest of the Underground Train conductors, was learning in the worst way that the Civil War was not going to bring immediate change to a well-established culture of racism.

In 1869, Harriet Tubman married **Nelson Davis**. Davis was a former slave and a Civil War veteran. The couple adopted a young girl whose name was Margaret and whom they called Gertie. Harriet was an easy touch for anyone in need. She became a philanthropist and she supported her charitable efforts by selling garden produce, raising hogs and accepting donations from friends. She never learned to read, but she became an effective speaker. Harriet met **Susan B. Anthony** and was in demand to speak in support of the new **"women's suffrage"** movement.

Harriet opened her **"Harriet Tubman Home for Aged and Indigent Colored People"** in 1896. She was never relieved of the effects of the brain injury she suffered as a young slave and she underwent brain surgery to try to minimize the pain. The surgery was not particularly successful. Harriet's general health began to deteriorate. She ultimately had to move into her own nursing home and she passed away, a victim of pneumonia, on March 10th of 1913.

The Lincoln-Douglass Debates

August to October 1858

Stephen A. Douglas was a well-established, well-known U.S. Senator in 1858. Douglas was a Democrat. Lincoln was the best-known and most popular representative of the new Republican Party in Illinois. Douglas was the prime driver behind the **Kansas-Nebraska Act**, which repealed the **Missouri Compromise** and established the **"doctrine of popular sovereignty"**, which determined that each new territory would vote to decide for itself whether to become a slave state or a free state.

His disapproval of the Kansas-Nebraska Act motivated Abe Lincoln to rejoin the political struggle. He had initiated a run for the U.S. Senate back in 1855 but decided to step aside for another candidate. His popularity in the Republican party made Abe the best choice to run for the Senate in opposition to Stephen A. Douglas.

The two represented dramatically different personal images. Douglas was dressed in expensive, well-tailored suits and presented an eloquent, finished appearance. Lincoln was an unusually tall, lanky, homely man, wearing wrinkled and rumpled suits. Lincoln and Douglas traveled more than 4,000 miles throughout the course of their seven debates. Lincoln traveled by boat, carriage or railroad. Douglas was more impressive, traveling in a custom private train. Each time he arrived at a new debate site, a cannon installed on Douglas's train fired a welcoming blast.

There were seven debates during the campaign. Each debate was held in a different Congressional district in Illinois. The rules for the encounters gave each contender one hour to present his case. After each gave his initial presentation, the first candidate was given thirty minutes to respond to his opponent's effort. The weather was often unpleasant and the length of the debates extensive, but, nevertheless, they became an enormous attraction. They drew, at times, more than 20,000 people. The press was heavily represented. Distribution of news exceeded any previous events, as the new technology of the telegraph and the availability of railroad travel made access to information easier and more complete than ever before. The Lincoln-Douglas debates would crystallize and illuminate the nation's differences over the slavery issue in a way that would define the future.

Lincoln's position was established prior to the Douglas debates. Earlier in 1858, in June, Lincoln delivered a speech in Springfield, Illinois. In that first speech of his campaign for the U.S. Senate, referring to the threat of civil war, Lincoln said "A house divided against itself cannot stand. This government cannot endure, permanently, half-slave and half-free". It would become historically famous as his **"House Divided"** speech. (You can still tour Lincoln's long-time residence in Springfield).

The first of the seven debates was held in Ottawa, Illinois. Douglas set the tone by accusing Lincoln of being radically antislavery, calling Lincoln the **"Black Republican"**. Douglas linked Lincoln with the nation's leading abolitionists, including **Frederick Douglass**, though Lincoln, at that time, had not yet met Douglass.

Lincoln, on the other hand, emphasized Stephen A. Douglas's support of the Supreme Court's **Dred Scott decision**, which summarily deprived all black people, free or enslaved, of any form of citizenship. Lincoln framed Douglas's position as being one of making slavery the law of the land, both North and South. At the debate in Freeport, Illinois, Abe asked Stephen whether settlers in a territory could vote to exclude slavery before it joined the Union. Douglas replied in the affirmative. Lincoln undoubtedly knew what the answer would be and knew that it would be problematic for Douglas, among his pro-slavery followers. Douglas tried to soften the impact by adding that popular sovereignty would allow local citizens to make laws choosing not to enforce the Dred Scott decision, which would eliminate legal protections for slaveholders. His argument would be known as the **Freeport Doctrine** and it would bring hard feelings from a large segment of his pro-slavery supporters. It would come back to hurt him in his 1860 campaign for the presidency.

Lincoln professed his belief that only the federal government had the power and authority to abolish slavery. Douglas believed in popular sovereignty and the ability of each territory or state to determine its own rules.

Douglas, a Democrat, persistently attacked Lincoln about what he considered Abe's radical views on racial relations. He threatened that Lincoln would make drastic changes in the fabric of society, granting citizenship rights to freed slaves and even allowing black men to marry white women. His tactics were meant to alarm white citizens. Douglas warned that Lincoln's liberal notions would put the nation on an inevitable path to civil war.

Lincoln replied to Douglas's attacks by indicating his ideas implied "no purpose to introduce political and social equality between the white and black races". At that time in his life and his evolution, Lincoln believed that "a physical difference between the two" might make it improbable that the two races would ever exist in "perfect equality". Lincoln was convinced that slavery was an evil and disgraceful institution, but, like most white people of that era, he believed the white race was, in some ways, superior to the black race. His beliefs would change with the events of the civil war and with his interactions with people like Frederick Douglass.

Stephen A. Douglas believed that the Declaration of Independence and the Constitution had been written by white men and for white men. He excluded women and negroes from the rights and protections offered by those essential documents. Lincoln countered that "there is no reason in the world why the negro is not entitled to all the natural rights enumerated in the Declaration of Independence". Lincoln, considering his campaign effort and trying not to antagonize too many voters, made it clear he had no intention of interfering with the institution of slavery where it was already well-established. Of course, his behaviors during the Civil War, especially the **Emancipation Proclamation**, would prove to contradict that promise markedly.. Lincoln also made it clear that he believed that our nation's founding fathers, though many owned slaves themselves, did regard the awful institution as a shameful moral evil that would eventually, inevitably, have to be eradicated.

In the Senate election of 1858, held just as the seven debates ended, Republican Lincoln gained 53% of the popular vote. The distribution of electoral districts, though, favored Democrats. Stephen A. Douglas won the election and kept his seat in the Senate. The two would face one another again in the 1860 Presidential election and the outcome would be different.

Causes of the Civil War

America's **Civil War** began with the writing of the original **Declaration of Independence** and our **Constitution**. The colonies were, to some extent, united in their resistance to being governed, going forward, by the English crown. Americans were frustrated with being burdened by laws, especially tax laws, that were imposed on them by an English government in which American colonists had no voice or vote.

The colonies had no hope of obtaining their independence from England, though, unless all of the colonies, unanimously, supported a revolution. Several Southern colonies were already, by that time, supported largely by an economy highly dependent on free slave labor. Our Founding Fathers, while several of them owned and utilized enslaved workers, almost universally understood the evil and immoral character of the shameful institution of slavery. They knew that slavery would have to, at some point in time, be erased from our nation. At the same time, though, they realized that, if they were to be successful in revolting against England, it would be necessary to have the support of all of the colonies. They knew that, if terminating slavery was to be included in the Declaration of Independence, the Southern colonies would refuse to join in the revolution. The Founding Fathers understood that, if they were to gain independence and freedom for America, the slavery issue would have to be avoided until after the war.

Following the successful Revolution, the issue of slavery continued to be a primary divider between the "Southern slave states" and the "Northern free states". In reality, the division was never as clear as a simple "North-South" demarcation. There were slaves in many Northern states. Most people in the South were never slave owners. Northern slaves tended to be "house servants", while Southern slaves were more often workers in the tobacco or cotton fields. While most Southerners could never afford to own slaves, they were all dependent on the Southern, agrarian culture and economy.

The issues between the North and South were often expressed in terms of support or opposition to "states' rights". In the South, citizens claimed that each state was "sovereign", to the extent that each could create their own laws, especially as slavery was concerned. Northerners, especially abolitionists, often believed that a strong federal government should be able to make laws that applied to ALL states. Many Southerners adopted the policy of "**Popular Sovereignty**", which held that each state should be able to create its own laws concerning slavery.

A relatively equal balance between slave states and those opposed to slavery meant that the issue was never resolved. As new territories applied to become states, both sides were worried that they could lose their balance of power in the federal government if too many new slave states or too many new anti-slavery states, were added to the roster. Legal battles broke out whenever a new state was added.

The **Missouri Compromise** made slavery illegal in any new territories north of Missouri's southern border. It was supposed to solve the problem, but, in reality, it served to inflame tensions. The **Kansas-Nebraska Act** passed in 1854, replaced the **Missouri Compromise** and established the rule of **"Popular Sovereignty"**. It meant that each new state, as it was added to the Union, could vote to determine whether or not slavery would be a part of their culture. The Kansas-Nebraska Act, leaving the decisions about slavery to the individual states, had the impact of creating a "little civil war" in each potential new state. Nebraska, being so far north, was certain to join the Union as a free state, which threatened the legislative balance of power in favor of the "free staters". This made the battle for power in Kansas more important to the pro-slave forces.

At about this same time, the historic **Whig** political party, which went all the way back to the **Revolution**, was slowly losing power. It was replaced when the new **Republican Party** was formed. The Republican Party was founded around a core belief opposing slavery. It would make **Abraham Lincoln** its Presidential candidate. The primary opposition to the Republicans would be **the Democrat Party**, which was heavily represented by Southern supporters of slavery.

Kansas Territory was, at the time, the most visible and most incendiary location for the focus of the conflict between the two sides. It became the center of the growing conflict over the issue of slavery. Pro-slavery **"Border Ruffians" "Free-Stater Jayhawkers"** crossed back and forth across the line between Missouri, a slave state and Kansas, where most of the settlers were in favor of banning slavery. Vicious fighting ensued, earning the area the title of **"Bleeding Kansas"**. The fighting lasted from 1854 through 1859.

Pro-slavery forces settled around Lecompton, Kansas and created the **Lecompton Constitution**, which legislated support of slavery. It never became law. Abolitionists sent anti-slavery settlers to Kansas, hoping to gain voting support for their cause. At the same time, thousands of pro-slavery Missourians came to Kansas to vote for their own side. The elections were characterized by illegal voting and sheer intimidation. Violence was common. Pro-slavery forces elected the first Kansas territorial representative to Congress, though only half of the votes were legitimate.

In May of 1855, pro-slavery forces attacked Lawrence, Kansas, a town populated almost entirely by **"free staters"**. The attack would be known as **"The Sacking of Lawrence"** and it further increased tensions between the groups. **Abolitionist John Brown**, along with his sons, responded to the attack on Lawrence by executing a midnight raid on settlers they believed to by pro-slavery. They brutally executed five settlers, slashing them with broadswords before shooting them, some murdered right before the eyes of their wives and children.

The growing battle was further intensified when, on the floor of the federal Congress, pro-slavery **Representative Preston Brooks** of South Carolina attacked and severely beat **Senator Charles Sumner** of Massachusetts. Brooks beat Sumner senseless, with a cane, in response to Sumner's angry speech denouncing pro-slave forces in Kansas.

Brooks Caning Sumner

In 1857, the Supreme Court ruled on the **Dred Scott** case. The judgement confirmed the legality of slavery and forced anti-slavery people to assist in returning fugitive slaves to their owners. Abolitionists were infuriated. Then, in 1859, abolitionist John Brown carried out his unsuccessful raid on the federal arsenal at **Harper's Ferry**, in Virginia. Brown had believed that masses of slaves would revolt in support of his raid, but they did not. The Harper's Ferry raid served to add to the fears of Southerners that their fellow citizens to the North were planning to destroy the institution of slavery.

Abraham Lincoln was elected President in November of 1860. It was the straw that broke the Southern camel's back. Southerners were convinced Lincoln was going to free their slaves. Southerners believed that they should each have the **"states' right"** to determine their own destinies. Lincoln, in reality, was more concerned about preserving the Union than he was in freeing the slaves. He believed that managing the slave issue could only be done successfully by preserving the Union. His hopes were quickly dashed.

By the time Lincoln had been in office for three months, seven Southern states had seceded from the Union. They were South Carolina, Mississippi, Texas, Louisiana, Florida, Alabama and Georgia. Kansas, meanwhile, finally entered the Union, as a free state, in 1861. Three months later, the Civil War began.

As the Civil War started, the Northerners, the Union, had many important advantages. They had more than twice the population, meaning they could draw troops from their population and still be able to keep their industrial resources working. The North had 22 million residents. The South had only nine million residents and one-third of those were slaves. The Union would put 2.1 million troops in the field, while the South could field only 1.2 million.

The North had a much larger industrial manufacturing base, meaning they could manufacture their own military necessities much more easily and in much greater quantities. The South, which became the Confederacy, had only one-ninth the industrial resources, when compared to the North. In 1860, the North controlled almost all of the manufacturing of weapons and ammunition. They also controlled more than 90% of the making of cloth materials, the making of shoes and boots and the manufacturing of iron products. All of these were essential to the war.

The North had far more major banking institutions and superior economic resources. While the South was more of an agrarian society, the North actually had more farms, which meant more nourishment for the population, including troops. The North also had 21,000 miles of railroad, a much greater network than in the South. It meant the North could more easily and more rapidly move supplies and troops from place to place. The North, at the beginning of the war, had possession of all of the vessels of the U.S. Navy. This allowed them to effectively blockade Southern ports, preventing Southern access to essential supplies coming from Europe.

As the war progressed and fugitive slaves began to approach the Union Army for sanctuary, Northern **General U.S. Grant** began allowing them to participate as troops. The North would eventually begin to allow Northern Black people to join the Union Army. These Black troops would prove to be very highly motivated, as they were fighting for the freedom of their own people. Their military performance was exemplary.

The North also had an advantage in that most of the war would be fought on the soil of the South. Resources in the Northern part of the country were not damaged with the frequency and the massive amount of destruction suffered by the South. On the other hand, the South may have had a military advantage because they were fighting, much of the time, on their own property and were passionately defending the homes and farms of their friends and families.

The Confederacy also was hurt by its insistence on basing the conflict on "states' rights". Their focus on the rights of states to determine their own destinies prevented their own federal government, the Confederacy, from taking certain essential actions. Their own policy handcuffed them. The Confederacy could not force their states to do anything. They could not make their Southern states provide critical resources, make their states free slaves to fight in their army, make their states "draft" troops for the army or make their states levy taxes for funds to support the war. "States' Rights" became a major military handicap for the Confederacy.

The South, the Confederacy, also had some advantages. The Confederate troops were fighting to defend their homes, farms and towns. The Union troops were fighting to preserve the Union and were not likely as enthusiastic about fighting. The South was able to stay home and play defense, hoping to persevere in their survival until the North grew fatigued with the fight and gave up their cause and went back home. Slavery, as a moral factor, didn't really enter the equation for Northerners until Lincoln signed the **Emancipation Proclamation** in 1863.

When Lincoln signed the Emancipation Proclamation, it changed the nature of the war. Instead of having the objective of saving the Union, the war became focused on the elimination of slavery. The South, where they hoped their ability to ship out cotton and tobacco would earn them the support of European nations, lost the moral high ground. In terms of political optics, the South was no longer fighting to defend their homeland, they were fighting to defend slavery. No European nation wanted to appear to be supporting preservation of the shameful institution. The Emancipation Proclamation undoubtedly served to incite the Southern troops, but, overall, the Proclamation hurt the South.

The South was the location of all but one of the major military academies. This gave them a wider selection of well-trained military officers, a big leadership advantage. Lincoln would suffer through some very ineffective Generals before he found the man who would lead the Union to victory. Military experts generally credit **General Robert E. Lee**, of the South, with being the greatest leader of the Civil War. He was able to come very near to defeating a Northern army that had all the obvious advantages.

The South had the advantage of fighting a primarily defensive battle. They did not have to move troops North to invade and occupy defended territories. The Union had to move large masses of troops greater distances, which stressed supply lines and exhausted soldiers. The South was able to produce large amounts of food, but it had challenges in transporting the food to the locations of their troops.

In the beginning, Northern Americans expected the Civil War to very brief and would result in a definitive Northern victory. The South would prove them wrong and the war would go for four long, brutal years. The cost to the nation would be enormous. More than 600,000 Americans would die, more than in the Revolutionary War, The War of 1812, The Mexican War, The Spanish-American War, World War I, World War II and the Korean War, all combined. Some historians believe the actual total of Civil War deaths most likely exceeded 800,000.

America's Civil War

The Most Important Personalities

Many important Americans, North and South, played key roles in the Civil War. Detailed, lengthy biographies have been written about all of them. We can't offer complete biographies in this 'true history', as it would require many hundreds of pages of information. We will, however, attempt to provide the most essential and relevant facts about each of the most noteworthy players. We'll begin with the man who played the most important role, Abraham Lincoln.

Abraham Lincoln

America's Sixteenth President

Abraham Lincoln came from the most humble of beginnings. His parents were **Thomas Lincoln** and his wife, the very religious **Nancy (Hanks) Lincoln**. They lived in Hardin County, Kentucky. When Abe was born, February 12, 1809, the family was living in a rustic, rural, one-room log cabin. When Abe was two the family moved to a small farm near Knob Creek, Kentucky. Together, Nancy and Thomas had three children. They were Sarah, Abraham and Thomas, all given biblical names. Thomas did not survive infancy.

Abraham's father, Thomas, was a hard-working, sturdy America pioneer, but he never was able to find financial success. Abraham enjoyed very little formal schooling, though he did very briefly attend local schools at three different times. Abe was obliged to work throughout his childhood, helping to support their family. When Thomas faced a lawsuit, in 1816, which placed doubt on the title to his land, the Lincoln family moved to Southern Indiana. There, the family "squatted" on public land. They put up a primitive structure made with logs and branches, leaving one side open to the harsh Indiana weather. Thomas eventually was able to purchase the plot of land and the family built a small, but permanent, cabin. Abraham later wrote of these times about helping to clear fields of trees and rocks and helping to plant and reap crops. He didn't enjoy hunting or fishing, but he recalled the sound of "the panther's scream" and spoke of the "bears that preyed upon the swine". He described the poverty the family endured on the small frontier farm.

When Abraham Lincoln was nine-years-old, in the fall of 1818, his mother, Nancy, died. After seeing his mother buried in the forest, Abe's family was to endure a harsh winter, with no motherly warmth to bring comfort. Thomas Lincoln was not a man to live without the support of a good woman, though, and before another brutal winter set in, he went back to Kentucky to obtain a new wife and a new mother for Sarah and Abraham. She was a widow named **Sarah Bush Johnston Lincoln**. She brought along two girls and a boy child of her own. Lincoln later said of her that she treated all the kids as her own and treated all with a fair and even hand. Sarah became especially close to Abraham, who frequently referred to her as his "angel mother".

Abe's stepmother, Sarah, stimulated his love for reading, but there is little record to explain his motivation to be educated. Both of his parents were functionally illiterate. It is likely that the only book they owned was a Bible. His very brief exposure to formal education seems to have had little to do with his accumulation of knowledge. He said that he went to school "by littles" . . . a little bit here and a little bit there. The total of all of his formal education would not add up to one year of regular attendance.

It isn't likely he had experience with very many books, but he was known to borrow books at every opportunity and to fully immerse himself in the contents. Acquaintances would tell stories about Abe traipsing many miles, walking through mud, rain and snow, just to borrow a single book. Biographers tell of him lying on the dirt floor of the cabin, by light of the fire, scratching notes from books on the blade of a shovel. Abraham, himself, would tell friends that he did not know much when he came of age, yet, somehow, had learned to "read, write and cipher".

Some of the literature we do know that Abe read included Parson Weem's 'Life and Memorable Actions of George Washington', Daniel Defoe's 'Robinson Crusoe', John Bunyan's 'Pilgrim's Progress', Aesop's 'Fables' and, of course, the Bible.

Abraham was 21 years old in 1830 when his family relocated to Southern Illinois. He took a job working on a flatboat on the Mississippi River. They hauled cargo down the river to New Orleans and then worked their way back North. His flatboat trips carried him through the South, where he was exposed to images of slavery which impacted him throughout the rest of his life.

Abe settled in Salem, Illinois, where he took work as a shopkeeper and was appointed to be postmaster. By all accounts, Abe was well-liked and respected by the citizens of Salem. His popularity grew quickly, and he was admired throughout the area for his ability to tell entertaining stories. Abe was also widely respected for his strength, evidenced by his log-splitting ability and his celebrated wrestling skills.

Those were times before the advent of professional sports for entertainment. Foot races and horse races were popular forms of community entertainment and wrestling was a favorite form of amusement. Great wrestlers drew great respect and Abraham was a local champion. He grew up in a hard life, working throughout his youth at rough physical labors. He was tall, at six feet four inches, an unusual height at that time. He was gaunt and lanky, at less than 180 pounds and his lifetime of manual labor made him unusually strong.

Lincoln loved to wrestle. He was, in fact, so good that he was eventually inducted, posthumously of course, in the **Wrestling Hall of Fame**. Historians tell us that he was known to fight 300 times, over a period of twelve years and endured but a single loss.

Abraham, in 1830, at the age of 21, was the undisputed wrestling champion in his Illinois county. He was a clerk in a local store when a group known as the Clary's Grove Boys came to Salem. They were led by a well-known bully named Jack Armstrong. The gang boasted loudly that their man, Jack, could beat any contender in a wrestling match . . . and they singled out and publicly challenged Abe Lincoln. They were openly instigating a match between Jack Armstrong and Abe Lincoln. Abe gratified their challenge, enthusiastically accepting the challenge. All of New Salem showed up to watch the epic battle. The Clary's Grove Boys, Jack included, were not well-liked in the county. They were known for hateful and destructive "pranks", a favorite of theirs being to capture new arrivals to the area and forcing them into a barrel, nailing the barrel shut and rolling it down a long hill. Very unpleasant for the involuntary barrel rider. The locals were hoping for a Lincoln victory.

Lincoln the Wrestler

Their hopes were completely fulfilled. Jack Armstrong committed numerous "fouls" during the long fight, which ultimately caused Lincoln to lose his patience and his temper. Abe threw Armstrong fiercely to the hard ground and knocked him completely senseless. Consequently, added to Lincoln's many other wins, the Armstrong victory made Abe a local hero. Abe and Jack Armstrong would later become close friends and Abe even represented Armstrong in a court battle after Abe became a lawyer.

The Black Hawk Indian War took place in 1832 and Abe enlisted. He was elected captain of his military company. Of the war, he later wrote that he saw no "live, fighting Indians", but he had "a good many bloody struggles with the mosquitoes".

Living in Salem, Lincoln was a store clerk, but he toyed around with the idea of being a blacksmith and he learned to be a surveyor and he eventually decided the law would be his career. He began to pursue political ambitions and was defeated in his first attempt to be elected to the legislature. He kept trying and was eventually elected, in 1834, and then repeatedly re-elected to the Illinois State Assembly. His political beliefs led him to support the Whig Party. He had already taught himself reading, grammar and mathematics and he attacked the study of the law aggressively. He passed the bar exam in 1836.

Lincoln moved to the Illinois state capital, Springfield and worked for several years as a lawyer. He served all kinds of clients, from local residents to nationwide railroads. Over his years in Springfield, Lincoln had to keep busy in his law practice. At a time when the Governor of the state was being paid $1200 annually, Abe's diligence was earning him as much as $1500 per year. He couldn't do that by simply working out of his office in Springfield. He began to work the circuit court route, following the circuit court judge as he made his rounds through the small towns all across the countryside. Every spring and every fall, Abe would mount his horse or let the horse pull his buggy, riding hundreds of miles, traveling slowly from county seat to county seat. People would see him riding patiently along, letting the horse take the trail, as he read books for hours. The legal cases Abe encountered were generally petty issues which yielded small fees. The frontier roads were mostly just muddy trails and the weather could be brutal for both man and horse.

Lincoln was already well known for his dominance in the popular sport of wrestling. He was also, though, known as a man of great patience and tolerance. He was not easily angered, nor was he easily intimidated. In 1942, in Illinois, state politics were heated by a bank failure. **James Shields** was the State Auditor and was a Democrat. Lincoln, at the time, was a Whig. Lincoln chose to write a scathing critique of Shields.

Using a pen name, "Rebecca", Lincoln submitted his written attack to the editor of the local newspaper, who was a close friend. Lincoln's editorial didn't stick to politics. He also mocked Shields' personal life, writing "His very features, in the ecstatic agony of his soul, spoke audibly and distinctly – 'Dear girls, it is distressing, but I cannot marry you all. Too well I know how much you suffer; but do, do remember, it is not my fault that I am so handsome and so interesting.'

Shields did not take the lampooning well. He learned "Rebecca's" true identity. He demanded that Lincoln retract his statements. Lincoln refused. Shields then responded by challenging Abe to a duel. Abe accepted. As Shields issued the challenge, Abe had the right to choose the weapons. He selected military broadswords. He wanted the biggest swords available. Lincoln later explained that, when he chose the big, long, heavy swords, he was thinking "I didn't want the damned fellow to kill me". Lincoln was several inches taller than Shields and had much longer arms. He feared someone would die if pistols were the chosen weapons.

The two parties, Lincoln and Shields, and their "seconds" or back-ups, had to travel to Missouri. Dueling was illegal in Illinois. Once they arrived at the site selected for the engagement, they were placed on opposite sides of a plank which had been placed on the ground between them. The "rules" for the duel required that neither participant cross over the plank. As they prepared to battle, Abe casually, effortlessly, swung his broadsword high above him to slice off a branch of the tree under which they all stood. Seeing

Lincoln's reach and strength, Shields quickly realized he was almost certainly doomed. Supporters easily convinced both men that the event should be cancelled.

By 1850 the railroads had begun to spread across the frontier, making transportation easier, more efficient and much faster. Abe Lincoln was engaged to be a political lobbyist for the Illinois Central Railroad. After he helped the railroad obtain its essential state charter, the railroad hired him to represent them regularly in court. After successfully defending the railroad in an important case, Lincoln received the single largest fee, $5,000, of his legal career. He then had to sue the railroad himself, in order to gain payment of that fee. In his success, Lincoln was soon representing banks, insurance companies and other railroads. He was becoming well-known in Illinois.

One of Abe's most famous cases was the defense of a man named **Duff Armstrong**. Duff was the son of one of Abe's old friends, **Jack Armstrong**, Abe's old wrestling opponent. Duff was charged with the murder of James Preston Metzger, which happened back in Mason County, Illinois, not all that distant from Springfield. When Abe heard about the charges, he was shocked. He quickly posted a letter to Hannah Armstrong, who was Jack Armstrong's widow. This is the letter:

"I have just heard of your deep affliction and the arrest of your son for murder. I can hardly believe he can be capable of the crime alleged against him. It does not seem possible. I am anxious that he should be given a fair trial at any rate; and gratitude for your long-continued kindness to me in adverse circumstances prompts me to offer my humble services gratuitously in his behalf. It will afford me an opportunity to requite, in a small degree, the favors I received at your hand and that of your lamented husband, when your roof afforded me a grateful shelter, without money and without price."

(signed) Abraham Lincoln

The Duff Armstrong murder trial was moved to Beardstown, Illinois, along the Illinois River. As the trial proceeded, Charles Allen, who claimed to be a witness to the crime, testified that he saw Duff strike Metzker with what Allen called "a slungshot". Lincoln pressed Allen, questioning him about Allen's ability to see clearly, at nighttime, at his described distance, 150 feet away from the event. Allen claimed he could see the event "in the bright moonlight". Lincoln brought into evidence an almanac. The almanac proved there could have been no adequate moonlight on the night in question. Duff Armstrong was acquitted.

Over the course of his twenty-year career as a lawyer, Lincoln became well-known and highly respected for his brilliance and his honesty. He would soon become known to the nation as **"Honest Abe, the Railsplitter"**.

In his early political career, Lincoln was a supporter of the heroes of the **Whig Party**, **Henry Clay** and **Daniel Webster**. Along with them, he was against the spread of slavery to the new territories. He looked forward to the expansion of the United States westward and he believed that urban centers and commerce, rather than agriculture, would drive that expansion.

Abe Lincoln seemed not to be a romantic personality. He had a bond of affection, when he lived in New Salem, with a young lady named **Ann Rutledge**. Ann died very young, at the age of 22 and Lincoln grieved deeply, as did the rest of the small community. A year after Ann's death, Lincoln pursued a lackluster courtship of a woman named **Mary Owens**. Lincoln eventually proposed marriage. Mary rejected him, saying he was "deficient in those little links which make up the chain of a woman's happiness".

Lincoln met and was fascinated by **Mary Todd**, who was a well-known, affluent Kentucky belle. Mary had the reputation of being a quick-witted, clever socialite. She was pursued by numerous suitors, including a man, **Stephen A. Douglas**, who would become Lincoln's biggest political rival. At one point in their courtship, the couple broke up. Lincoln reacted to the break up seriously, falling into a deep and lengthy period of depression. Such episodes would pursue him throughout his life. Eventually, the couple reconciled.

Lincoln married Mary Todd in 1842 and the two would produce four children. Sadly, only one would survive to adulthood. The kids were Robert Todd, Edward Baker, William "Willie" Wallace and Thomas "Tad" Lincoln. Edward was still three years old when he passed away. "Willie" died, a victim of Typhoid, at the age of 11 years, when Lincoln was in the White House. Tad, who suffered a cleft palate and a pronounced lisp, lived longer than his father, but did not live to be an adult. Only Robert Todd, the oldest of the children, survived to adulthood.

The available evidence indicates that Abraham and Mary were very close and expressed their affection in letters, suggesting they missed each other dearly on Abe's long absences from the home. Both of them were subject to periods of deep depression, with Mary's becoming more severe after the deaths of three of their children and the assassination of Abraham. After the death of Willie, in 1862, Mary sought solace in the form of holding seances in the White House, desperately hoping to contact her dead son. She was eventually diagnosed, in the 1870's, with insanity. While in the White House, she was mocked for her proclivity to spending lots of money, often running up debts that embarrassed the President.

Abraham Lincoln's Pathway to the White House

Lincoln's political career continued to develop and he was elected to the U.S. House of Representatives in 1846. His opposition to the **Mexican-American War** made him unpopular with Illinois voters and Abe decided not to seek re-election. He returned to Springfield in 1849.

The inflammatory issue of slavery continued to increase in intensity. In 1854, the **Kansas-Nebraska Act** was passed. It provided that, as territories became states, each state would be able to vote to determine whether it would enter the Union as a free state or a slave state. Democrat **Stephen A. Douglas** was an enthusiastic supporter of the Act. Douglas was an Illinois Congressman and Lincoln would find himself running against Douglas for that office.

Stephen A. Douglas was an active and well-known politician in Illinois. He stood only 5' 4" and was known as **"The Little Giant"**. Coincidentally, Douglas had, at one time, courted Mary Todd, who would later become Lincoln's wife. Lincoln won the girl, but Douglas would defeat him in the 1858 Illinois Senate election.

The slavery issue was a final straw in the decline and ultimate end of the **Whig Party**, to which Lincoln had belonged. That same slavery issue would ignite the fire that resulted in creation of the new, anti-slavery, **Republican Party**. Lincoln was their first Presidential candidate.

Lincoln's journey to the White House most likely began in June of 1858 when Lincoln delivered the closing address at the end of the Republican State Convention. His speech was directed primarily at Stephen A. Douglas and at any Republicans who might be considering supporting Douglas. His speech of that day is now famously known as his **"House Divided"** speech. It included these comments:

"Mr. President and Gentlemen of the Convention.

If we could first know where we are and whither we are tending, we could better judge what to do and how to do it.

We are now far into the fifth year, since a policy was initiated, with the avowed object and confident promise, of putting an end to slavery agitation. Under the operation of that policy, that agitation has not only not ceased, but has constantly augmented.

In my opinion, it will not cease, until a crisis shall have been reached and passed...A house divided against itself cannot stand.

I believe this government cannot endure, permanently half slave and half free.

I do not expect the Union to be dissolved - I do not expect the house to fall - but I do expect it will cease to be divided.

It will become all one thing or all the other."

The "House Divided" speech enhanced Lincoln's reputation, explained his position which emphasized the protection of the Union and became a foundation for his eventual run for the Presidency.

The Lincoln-Douglas Debates, beginning in 1854, are now legendary. Each of the two men was a polished, shrewd, effective speaker. Lincoln was long, lanky and awkward and decidedly homely. Douglas was short and stocky in build and had a good speaking voice and graceful mannerisms. Lincoln's voice could be shrill and squeaky, but his words were beautifully eloquent and his arguments difficult to challenge. Lincoln had a gift for expressing powerful and persuasive arguments in efficient, concise terms.

The first of the **Lincoln-Douglas debates** took place on October 16, 1854, before a large and enthusiastic crowd in Peoria, Illinois. Neither of the two men were in favor of slavery. Neither, though, was an outright abolitionist. Douglas supported the Kansas-Nebraska Act, allowing each state to make their own laws pertaining to slavery. Lincoln, on the other hand, was adamant that Congress must act to stop the spread of slavery into new states. Lincoln believed that a complete ban of slavery throughout the Union, put in place at that time, would result in civil war. He knew slavery had to end, but he didn't want the process of ending it to destroy the Union. In Peoria, Lincoln openly denounced slavery, stated his opposition to seeing it spread to new territories and declared that the institution of slavery was a violation of the most fundamental tenets of our Declaration of Independence. Lincoln believed that the Union was of paramount importance, as it represented the grand experiment of allowing free citizens the liberty to govern themselves.

Lincoln may have been, in some ways, a winner of the Lincoln-Douglas debates, but Douglas defeated him in the Senate election. The debates served to illuminate Lincoln's national image. The Presidential election, two years later, would have a different outcome.

Lincoln's performance during the Lincoln-Douglas debates, followed by a popular speech made in 1860, made him a favored candidate among those in the new Republican party. He was focused on eliminating divisions among the Republicans and on preserving the integrity of the Union. Recognizing his speaking prowess and his popularity as "Honest Abe, the Rail-splitter", the Republicans passed over more well-established politicians, such as Senator William H. Seward and they nominated Lincoln to be their candidate for the 1860 presidential election. Lincoln had, at the time, served only one rather undistinguished Congressional term.

Stephen A. Douglas was Lincoln's opponent in the presidential race. He represented the Northern branch of Democrats. Unfortunately for Douglas, the Southern, pro-slavery Democrats nominated their own candidate, **John C. Breckenridge** of Kentucky. The brand new **"Constitutional Union Party"** also nominated a candidate, **John Bell**. The Southern vote was split between Breckenridge and Bell, taking votes away from Douglas and Lincoln won the battle, carrying the Electoral College by a sturdy margin.

The Lincoln administration was somewhat defined by his unusual decision to bring some of his most vocal opponents into his cabinet. He appointed William H. Seward, Salmon P. Chase, Edward Bates and Edwin M. Stanton, all political opponents to him, to his cabinet. Historians say Lincoln built an unusually strong cabinet. He wanted to hear all sides of each debate and he wanted to try to hold the Union together by enfranchising all the various political factions. His efforts, though laudable, would be unsuccessful and the nation would be split asunder.

Abraham Lincoln and The Civil War

Before Lincoln even took office and before his inauguration, the state of South Carolina, in response to Lincoln's election, declared its withdrawal from the Union. Hoping to prevent further secessions, Congress attempted some mollifying gestures. **The Crittenden Compromise**, which included amendments which would guarantee that slavery would continue to be legal wherever it was already in place, was proposed. It also provided that the territories would be permanently divided between slavery and freedom. Lincoln was opposed to the compromise. He feared that it would lead to permanent divisions between slave and free states and territories and he feared the process would put America "on the high road to a slave empire", a possibility he could not abide. Lincoln advised Republicans to oppose the compromise, which they did and the measure was defeated.

The failure of the Crittenden Compromise and other political trends, added to the election of Abraham Lincoln, which Southerners believed meant an inevitable attack on their culture, stimulated the rapid **secession** of six additional Southern states. Along with South Carolina, those states gathered to form **The Confederate States of America** (the CSA). No sooner was Lincoln elected than the Union he hoped to preserve was torn asunder. He hadn't yet even moved into the White House.

Many of Lincoln's actions during the Civil War will be shared later, when we cover the war in detail. We will, however, outline the essentials here.

Lincoln was not a president with a military background. His participation in the Black Hawk War offered no real experience. **Jefferson Davis**, President of the Confederate States of America, though, was a graduate of West Point, a former United States Secretary of War and a well-known hero of the Mexican War.

Lincoln was soon revealed to be a surprisingly sophisticated strategic and tactical wartime leader. He was handicapped by early choices for military leaders, **General McClellan** being the best example of the worst performers. McClellan seemed reluctant to pursue aggressive engagements with the enemy and Lincoln would have to replace him. Other Union Generals proved to be equally disappointing.

The CSA, on the other hand, benefited from the fact that almost all of America's best military leaders lived in the South. The Union was blessed with superiority in practically every essential military resource. The Union boasted far greater population from which troops could be drawn and a much greater railroad network for moving troops and supplies and more waterways for transportation and much greater manufacturing resources for making weapons, transports and ammunition. The more experienced, better educated Southern military leaders, though, were able to register many victories against the superior Union forces. The Southerners were fighting a passionately defensive war and they were able to drag the war out for four long, vastly destructive years.

Soon after a Union army victory at the **Battle of Antietam**, near Sharpsburg, Maryland, Lincoln chose to deliver his **Emancipation Proclamation**. It was January 1, 1863. He intended to do so during a moment of Union strength and Antietam granted him that opportunity. The Emancipation Proclamation proclaimed that all enslaved people living in CSA states were free. Slaves in Union states remained in bondage. Northern states were still governed by our Constitution, which meant that an actual **Constitutional Amendment** would have to be passed in order to free all slaves in the North. Lincoln would work hard to push passage of that Amendment.

Lincoln's Emancipation Proclamation was a **"war measure"**, meaning it could only apply to black people in the South. As a practical measure, it actually meant little to Southern black people because their owners did not recognize the Proclamation itself or the United States government. It did not apply to black people in Northern states, though many were still enslaved. Only a constitutional amendment could truly free all black Americans. Northern black people were emancipated by the **13th Amendment**, passed on December 6, 1865. The **14th Amendment** codified birthright citizenship and prohibited violation of basic American privileges and immunities or denying "due process" of any citizens, including Black citizens. The **15th Amendment** finally prohibited any kind of discrimination based on race.

Lincoln, by then, was becoming more and more influenced by his friend and consultant, black abolitionist **Frederick Douglass**. Douglass was initially unhappy with Lincoln's belief that the Union had to be preserved, above all and that freedom for American black people would have to wait until the nation was re-united. Douglass would eventually come to understand that, while Lincoln's beliefs were hard to accept, Lincoln was right in his opinion. Lincoln worked hard to advance the 13th Amendment, which would eventually free all Americans, black people included. It would be passed, but Lincoln would not live to celebrate the victory.

Equal rights for America's male Black citizens would be guaranteed, at least legally, by the 13th, 14th and 15th Amendments, the last of which was ratified in 1870. The rights of American women were still lagging far, far behind. Legal codification of the rights of Black men laid a foundation, but building beyond that point would prove very, very difficult. Many hard challenges would be faced by Black Americans over the next few decades. Southern Democrats would provide cover for a vast number of injustices, as **"Jim Crow"** would rise from the ashes of the Civil War.

Two important Union army victories, one at Vicksburg, Mississippi and a second at Gettysburg, Pennsylvania, promised an ultimate Union victory in the war. After **General**

George Meade disappointed Lincoln by failing to capitalize on a strategic opportunity to finish off Southern General Robert E. Lee's army at Gettysburg, Lincoln made **General Ulysses S. Grant** the Supreme Commander of all Union armies. Grant was a brilliant strategist and an aggressive fighter and he would lead the Union to a final, definitive victory.

Lincoln went to Gettysburg, November 19,1863, to view the tragic results of the great **Battle of Gettysburg**, where more than 22,000 men died on the field. On that sacred field, Lincoln delivered one of the most famous and most frequently quoted, speeches in American history. The eloquent oration delivered only 272 words, but they are epic in their importance.

Abraham Lincoln's Gettysburg Address

Four score and seven years ago our fathers brought forth on this continent, a new nation, conceived in Liberty and dedicated to the proposition that all men are created equal. Now we are engaged in a great civil war, testing whether that nation or any nation so conceived and so dedicated, can long endure. We are met on a great battlefield of that war. We have come to dedicate a portion of that field as a final resting place for those who here gave their lives that that nation might live. It is altogether fitting and proper that we should do this. But, in a larger sense, we cannot dedicate -- we cannot consecrate -- we cannot hallow this ground. The brave men, living and dead, who struggled here, have consecrated it, far above our poor power to add or detract. The world will little note, nor long remember what we say here, but it can never forget what they did here. It is for us the living, rather, to be dedicated here to the unfinished work which they who fought here have thus far so nobly advanced. It is rather for us to be here dedicated to the great task remaining before us - that from these honored dead we take increased devotion to that cause for which they gave the last full measure of devotion - that we here highly resolve that these dead shall not have died in vain - that this nation, under God, shall have a new birth of freedom - and that government of the people, by the people, for the people, shall not perish from the earth.

Abraham Lincoln

November 19, 1863

Lincoln's Administration Draws to a Close

Lincoln will always be remembered primarily for his management of the **Civil War**, for the **Emancipation Proclamation** and for the **13th Amendment**, which confirmed the right to freedom for All American citizens, white, black and brown.

Union General George McClellan had been a big disappointment for Lincoln during the war. McClellan became Lincoln's Democratic opponent for the 1864 Presidential election. During the election campaign, Union armies were registering definitive victories which assured an imminent end to the war. Lincoln was re-elected.

In his second inaugural address, Lincoln famously focused on re-uniting the Union. He had been working with Frederick Douglass and General Grant to design methods to create a successful transition of Southern Black Americans into their new state of freedom. They recognized the enormous challenges with which those freed slaves would be confronted. They anticipated the resistance that would persist among many Southerners, even after the end of the war.

Lincoln stressed the importance of re-uniting the North and the South and of assuring a successful transition for the former slaves. He said, in his address, that reunification must be achieved "With malice toward none; With charity for all".

Lincoln would speak again, on the brink of **Robert E. Lee's** surrender at **Appomattox** and would plead with Northerners to welcome the Southern states back into the fold. He had already shared parts of his wide-ranging plan for Southern reconstruction and for a successful transition of the formerly enslaved into a free lifestyle, with the assistance and support of abolitionist **Frederick Douglass**, among other trusted associates.

Sadly and tragically for the United States, Abraham Lincoln would not live to implement his plans.

Lincoln attended the play **"An American Cousin"** at the **Ford Theater** on the night of April 14, 1865. He was accompanied by his wife, **Mary** and by a young Union Army Major, **Henry R. Rathbone**. Henry was accompanied by his young fiancé, **Clara Harris**.

A well-known actor, Confederate sympathizer **John Wilkes Booth**, was well acquainted with the floor plan of Ford Theater and he was a person who would draw no attention for being in the area. Booth sneaked into the balcony level at the theater and slipped quietly into Lincoln's box. He drew a derringer pistol and quickly shot Abraham Lincoln, point blank range, directly in the back of Lincoln's head.

Major Rathbone attacked Booth, who drew a dagger and slashed Rathbone. Rathbone's intervention interrupted Booth's attempt to escape off the balcony, causing him to catch a foot in a flag hanging from the edge. Booth fell awkwardly onto the stage, breaking a leg, but still managed to run from the theater. As he ran away, Booth shouted in triumph "Sic semper tyrannis", Latin for "Ever Thus to Tyrants" and then "The South is Avenged!"

Booth's bullet entered behind Lincoln's left ear and lodged behind his right eye, paralyzing him and leaving him struggling to breathe. He was carried across the street to a familiar boardinghouse, where he was cared for through the night. He never regained consciousness. He passed away at 7:22 a.m. on the morning of April 15th, 1865.

Booth ran to the countryside and hid in a barn, where he was soon discovered. He was shot there and he died on that same day. He had four co-conspirators, who were assigned to other nefarious deeds and who were to carry out other assassinations. None succeeded, though a knife attack on **Secretary of State William Seward** was nearly fatal. Lewis Paine, also known as Lewis Powell, brutally beat one of Seward's sons and found Seward in his bed. Powell managed to slice twice at Seward's throat. Paine fought with two of Seward's sons as he made his way out of the Seward home, but was soon captured. Seward survived because he was protected by wearing a metal neck brace due to a previous injury. He would serve several more years in our government and would be best known for the purchase of Alaska.

Booth's four known co-conspirators were **Lewis Powell (or Paine), George Atzerodt, David Herold** and **Mary Surratt**. Mary ran a boardinghouse in which the conspirators developed their complex plans. All four, on July 7, 1865, were hanged by their necks on the gallows at the Old Penitentiary, where present-day **Fort McNair** rests.

The nation grievously mourned their lost President. His coffin was carried by train from Washington, D.C., to his home in Springfield, Illinois, where he would be buried on May 4, 1865. The funeral train was met by huge crowds as it passed through 180 towns and cities.

Abraham Lincoln Quotes

"How many legs does a dog have if you call his tail a leg? Four. Saying that a tail is a leg does not make it a leg."

"I am not bound to win, but I am bound to be true. I am not bound to succeed, but I am bound to live by the light that I have. I must stand with anyone who stands right and to stand with him while he is right and part with him when he is wrong."

"Most folks are as happy as they make up their minds to be."

"The philosophy of the school room in one generation will be the philosophy of government in the next."

"Always bear in mind that your own resolution to succeed is more important than any other."

"No man has a good enough memory to be a successful liar."

"You can fool all the people some of the time and some of the people all the time, but you cannot fool all the people all the time."

"Give me six hours to chop down a tree and I will spend the first four sharpening the axe."

"You cannot escape the responsibility of tomorrow by evading it today."

"Sir, my concern is not whether God is on our side; my greatest concern is to be on God's side, for God is always right."

"I don't like that man. I must get to know him better."

"The ballot is stronger than the bullet."

"Government of the people, by the people, for the people, shall not perish from the earth."

"When I do good, I feel good. When I do bad, I feel bad. And that's my religion."

"When you have got an elephant by the hind legs and he is trying to run away, it is best to let him run."

"As I would not be a slave, so I would not be a master. This expresses my idea of democracy."

"Do I not destroy my enemies when I make them my friends?"

"The shepherd drives the wolf from the sheep's throat, for which the sheep thanks the shepherd as his liberator, while the wolf denounces the shepherd for the same act as the destroyer of the wolf's liberty. Plainly, the sheep and the wolf are not agreed upon a definition of liberty."

Abraham Lincoln and Slavery

As a child in Kentucky, Abe Lincoln attended a Baptist church, where he absorbed moral standards which banned alcohol, dancing and slavery. The family was very poor and had little interaction with anyone wealthy enough to own slaves. The family moved to Indiana, a state in which slavery was forbidden. Lincoln later wrote that the move was partly caused by challenges to his father's title to their land and partly caused by discomfort with the allowance of slavery in Kentucky.

Lincoln, as a young adult, moved further to the West, into the free state of Illinois, where he would reside for the rest of his life. After being elected to the Illinois legislature, Lincoln became one of only six Representatives to vote against a resolution which expressed opposition to the growth of abolitionist movements and which declared that ownership of slaves was legal. He went on to file a formal protest against the resolution.

Lincoln was not, early in his career, an abolitionist. He did not believe in slavery, but he also did not want to antagonize Southern slave owners to the point that the Union was threatened. At one point in his career, he supported the **Liberia Project** or the **Colonization Society**, which was designed to offer American Black people the option of leaving America to go to a "Black" nation in Africa. Lincoln recognized the impossibility and foolishness of thinking all American Black people, numbering in the millions, would or could ever be transported out of the United States.

Lincoln wrote "I am naturally anti-slavery. If slavery is not wrong, then nothing is wrong. I cannot remember when I did not so think and feel". Lincoln, as he grew older, often expressed his concerns about the destiny of America's Black citizens, once freed. He understood that most would be living in the South, where white Southerners would not look kindly on working to create a safe and nurturing environment for the freed slaves. Lincoln understood the economic, educational and social challenges that would inevitably confront the freed slaves.

Lincoln delivered a speech to a large crowd in Peoria, Illinois, in October of 1854. He addressed his opposition to the **Kansas-Nebraska Act**, which allowed each state to decide for itself whether or not to permit slavery within its boundaries. Lincoln believed the "declared indifference" of the Act to the institution of slavery was actually a cover for an Act which performed, in reality, as a tool to permit the further spread of slavery. He said of the Kansas-Nebraska Act: "The Kansas-Nebraska Act's declared indifference, as I must think, coverts real zeal for the spread of slavery, I cannot but hate it. I hate it because of the monstrous injustice of slavery itself. I hate it because it deprives our republican example of its just influence in the world". Abe was saying that the very existence of slavery in America forced our country away from the moral high ground. He recognized the hypocrisy of a nation that declared itself the home of freedom and liberty for all having, within it, the awful, shameful institution of slavery.

The times in which Lincoln lived were far different from our world today. America was having massive growing pains. There was pressure from other "colonizing" nations, who were still hoping to occupy and take control of parts of North America, including, for example, Alaska. The issue of slavery had been inflammatory when the Declaration of Independence and the Constitution were written and had never been resolved. It was paramount that the Union of the existing states be protected or loss of all of America was still a possibility. The future existence of America as a free and independent nation was by no means guaranteed.

Compromises were constantly being made as the future of the institution of slavery was being determined. Lincoln, and many others, believed in less federal government intervention and believed that "states' rights" had to be respected. Still, he strongly believed that the spread of slavery into new states was not to be allowed. It put him in a "rock and a hard place" situation with slavery. This Lincoln quote, delivered long before he became President, best explains his quandary:

"I hold it to be a paramount duty of us in the free states, due to the Union of the states and perhaps to liberty itself (paradox though it may seem) to let the slavery of the other states alone; while, on the other hand, I hold it to be equally clear, that we should never knowingly lend ourselves directly or indirectly, to prevent that slavery from dying a natural death—to find new places for it to live in, when it can no longer exist in the old." As he grew older and more experienced and met people like abolitionist Frederick Douglass, his beliefs would change and he would come to believe that slavery had to be completely eradicated before the United States could move forward in accordance with our most fundamental values.

Lincoln met and became a friend and admirer of the great Black abolitionist, Frederick Douglass. Douglass initially resented Lincoln's policy, after becoming President, of focusing all of his attention on preserving the Union. Douglass wanted Black people universally freed and he wanted the issue to be the driving force behind Lincoln's administration's objectives. As time passed and the Civil War progressed, Douglass came to understand Lincoln's reasoning. He understood that should the Union not be reunited, the chances for Southern Black people ever to find freedom would likely be completely extinguished. Douglass began helping Lincoln find ways to engage the Black community in support of the Union. Douglass was, in large part, the reason Lincoln eventually had enough confidence in the Black population to move him to encourage the enlistment of Black men in the Union Army. Those Black troops soon gained the respect of Army leaders and built a reputation for being some of the best troops on the battlefields.

In 1863, **Frederick Douglass** delivered a speech to a huge gathering in Philadelphia. In that address, Douglass said: "Once let the black man get upon his person the brass letter, U.S.; let him get an eagle on his button and a musket on his shoulder and bullets in his pocket and there is no power on the earth or under the earth which can deny that he has earned the right of citizenship in the United States." Douglass was right.

Lincoln called for Black Americans to sign up with the Union Army. More than 180,000 Black men would answer his call. The first all-Black fighting force to be assembled and trained was the **54th Massachusetts Volunteer Infantry Regiment**. The 54th was quickly sent to South Carolina, where they first saw action in an attack on Confederate troops at **James Island**. The 54th lost 45 men. Then, after days without rest or sustenance, the 54th Regiment was assigned to attack **Fort Wagner** on Morris Island. The battle was led by **Colonel Shaw**, a white man, who perished in the fight. The 54th suffered the deaths of half of their troops, but showed incredible bravery and fought with great honor. Promised reinforcements did not arrive in time to be of assistance. The 54th Massachusetts did not win that battle, but they gained immense respect as a result of their courageous performance.

When Lincoln delivered his **Emancipation Proclamation**, he had to cope with constitutional complications. He was able to declare only the Black people living in the Southern Confederacy to be free and would have to get the **13th Amendment** passed before all American Black people could be finally, formally, set free. Lincoln worked hard to gain support for the 13th Amendment, but he would not live to see it passed. Lincoln, of course, was motivated to facilitate the movement to freedom for the Southern Black people, but he also hoped the Emancipation Proclamation would encourage those Southern Black people to rise up against their masters and slip away to join the Union Army forces. **General Grant** worked to get the information communicated throughout the South so that Black Southerners, slaves or freedmen, would be aware that Northern troops would welcome them. Many Black fugitives from slavery would find their way to General Grant's troops and he was happy to bring them into his service.

Lincoln, judged by current standards, was far from a perfect man in terms of opposing slavery. His experiences on early flatboat trips and in his first home in Kentucky, seeing the reality of slavery, ground into him a lifelong hatred of slavery. He has been attacked for his early support of the **Liberia Project**, but he consistently explained that he viewed it as a "possible option" for those who chose to participate. He never wanted America's Black people to be "deported". He believed deeply in liberty and individual freedoms. His belief in liberty extended to the "liberty" of each state to determine its own destiny. As he lived his life, growing older and being exposed to more points of view from people living in other circumstances, he became convinced that, states' rights or not, slavery had to go.

In 1842, Lincoln married **Mary Todd** in Springfield, Illinois. She was the daughter of a slaveholder in Kentucky.

Mary Todd was born in Lexington, Kentucky, in 1808. Almost 95% of the Black residents of Lexington were enslaved individuals at that time. Mary's family was well-to-do financially and owned slaves. Mary's personal attitude toward the institution of slavery was complicated and showed great change over the period of her lifetime. By the time she was living in the White House, most records indicate she had become deeply opposed to slavery.

The Todd family generally owned five or six slaves. This includes slaves owned by their own immediate family, close relatives and "rental slaves" obtained from other slave owners. They purchased one slave from a cruel "slave jail" near their home. The Todds lived in a vicinity in which one didn't have to go far, only three city blocks, to see slaves being whipped and sold on the courthouse square.

Slaves drove carriages for the Todds, cleaned houses, cooked meals and did other household chores. Slaves worked in Mr. Todd's cotton factory and on the family farm.

Todd's family records seem to indicate the family members had warm relationships with some of their slaves. They wrote about a slave nurse, **"Mammy Sally"**, whom they described as being religious and superstitious, but very loving. Of course, Mammy Sally, had she been able to, may have written a completely different perspective on the relationship she had with the family.

One Todd family slave, a woman named **Chaney Dickerson**, was ordered to accompany the Todd family's youngest son to establish a farm in another part of Kentucky. Chaney had primarily served the Todd family as a cook. When the son was killed fighting for the confederacy, Chaney was hired out to another family. After being freed at the end of the war, Chaney never returned to the Todd family. Census records indicate that Chaney had at least one child, **Pen**, but that child apparently did not live with the Todds. Records indicate Pen was "loaned out" to a Todd family relative, where he was frequently "whipped".

It was very common, sadly, for slave families to be forcibly separated and slave children were often sent off, sold or rented out, to serve other slave owners. At least one other female Todd slave, **Jane Wales Sanders**, was known to have a family with which she had little contact. It was common for slave families to somehow maintain contact, perhaps through an underground slave communications network, with other members of their families.

Being a slave in the deep South was known to be an especially dark and painful existence, with slaves working daylight to dark in the tobacco and cotton fields. The need for large numbers of slaves on the plantations, though, sometimes meant that slave families could be kept together, as there could never be too much free labor. Urban slaves, though, were more likely to work in small groups, as in the Todd family, where five slaves appear to have served all of their needs. Not needing additional slaves to run the household, urban slave families were more likely to be forcibly split apart.

Todd's family slave Jane Sanders was able to stay married to her slave husband for thirty-five years, during twenty-five of which years they were forcibly separated. The two were "married" at the Todd home in 1835, but slave marriages were not recognized as being legal.

A Todd family slave named **William** attempted to escape to freedom in 1849. When captured, he was most likely whipped and he was then caged in the slave jail in Lexington. Rather than taking him back, **Robert S. Todd** ordered him sold. It's likely William was destined for the ultimate misery of the Southern cotton fields.

Little hard evidence is available to judge Mary Todd's personal feelings about slavery. **Her family** contributed to the **Colonization Society**, supporting the **Liberia Project**. They donated money to a fund meant to provide support to fugitive slaves. She grew up in a household served by several slaves and so must have had some way of mentally rationalizing their ownership of slaves.

One historian wrote that "Mammy Sally" came to knock on Mary's door one night. Sally told Mary that she had made a "secret mark" on the Todd fence. The mark would tell fugitive slaves they could stop at the Todd house to receive food. Mary was, according to the story, "thrilled" that Sally trusted her in such a way and the episode may have marked the beginning of Mary's anti-slavery development.

After becoming First Lady and moving into the White House, Mary struck up a close friendship with **Elizabeth Keckley**. Elizabeth was black and a former slave and an accomplished dressmaker. Elizabeth was a big advocate of the **Underground Railroad** and was an active abolitionist. Her relationship with Elizabeth was undoubtedly another force moving Mary toward a more and more passionate opposition to slavery.

Once Mary had matured and married Lincoln, all indications are that she had adopted his views that slavery, as an institution, was morally reprehensible and unsustainable. She wrote glowingly of Lincoln's Emancipation Proclamation. Mary wrote of her sadness at viewing the plight of Black refugees who were flooding to the North and she wrote letters recommending employment for past slaves.

Mary Todd's family owned slaves. In the area where she grew up, almost all Black people were slaves. She had practically no exposure to Black people who were not slaves. Her early attitudes about slavery were certainly formed around the only experiences she had observed. As she grew, her attitude about slavery changed dramatically. Mary Todd, personally, never owned slaves and by the time she moved into the White House, she was basically an abolitionist.

America's Civil War

April 12, 1861 – April 26, 1865

Fort Sumter - The Civil War Begins

Abraham Lincoln was elected in 1860 and seven Southern states quickly seceded from the Union, the United States. Four additional states soon joined them. They were Virginia, Arkansas, North Carolina and Tennessee. Those eleven states formed the **Confederate States of America**, intending to become a nation separate from the United States. While other states did not secede, they were home to many Southern sympathizers. Among those were Maryland, Kentucky and Missouri.

The Confederate States of America, the CSA originally created a capital in Montgomery, Alabama, in 1861. Three months later, their capital was moved to Richmond, Virginia.

Confederate armed forces, as Lincoln took office, were already threatening facilities owned by the United States, but geographically located in the South.

The nation's attention was quickly focused on an American (Union) fort which was being constructed at Charleston Harbor, located on the Atlantic shoreline of South Carolina. The fort was the property of the United States but found itself within the boundaries of the new CSA, U.S. troops were stationed there, under the command of **Major Robert Anderson**. The Confederacy immediately laid claim to **Fort Sumter**, based on its location in a Southern state. They established fortified stations in locations around the harbor and they commenced threatening the fort.

Lincoln hoped to elude serious confrontations. He wanted to avoid any aggressive actions toward the South. He quietly directed **Winfield Scott**, who was the **General in Chief** of the **U.S. Army**, to be prepared to "either hold or to retake, Fort Sumter". Lincoln, in his inaugural address, attempted one more time to hold the Union together. He spoke of the indestructibility of the Union and he pleaded for harmony between the split factions. He tried to clearly define his policy regarding Fort Sumter, saying:

"The power confided to me, will be used to hold, occupy and possess the property (Fort Sumter) and places belonging to the government and to collect the duties and imposts; but beyond what may be necessary for these objects, there will be no invasion — no using of force against or among the people anywhere." Then, near the end, addressing the absent Southerners: "You can have no conflict, without being yourselves the aggressors." Lincoln was saying that, if war was to come, it would not be he who fired the first shots.

Lincoln ordered a messenger to go to the governor of South Carolina. The messenger was to say:

"I am directed by the President of the United States to notify you to expect an attempt will be made to supply Fort Sumter with provisions only; and that, if such attempt be not resisted, no effort to throw in men, arms or ammunition, will be made, without further notice or in case of an attack upon the Fort." Lincoln was saying that he would re-supply the troops at the Fort, but would not initiate any aggressive activities. He was still hoping to avoid a military confrontation and hoping to re-unite the Union.

Before Lincoln's message could be delivered, Confederate military leaders had already presented, to U.S. Army Major Anderson, their demand that all Union troops evacuate the Fort. Major Anderson refused their demand and, on the morning of **April 12, 1861**, CSA gun batteries opened fire on Fort Sumter. The fort was evacuated by U.S. Army troops. Later, after the war was well established, there would be another battle for control of Fort Sumter. The Union army, in 1863, attempted to regain control of the fort. They failed, but the fort was reduced to rubble.

The American Civil War was begun. Lincoln began his long fight to reunite the United States. It did not begin well. The outgoing President, **James Buchanan**, did nothing to limit the actions of the seceding states. In Texas, a very large garrison of Union troops, amounting to nearly one-fourth of the entire U.S. Army, was immediately "surrendered" to the Confederate States of America. The commanding officer of the Texas garrison was General **David E. Twiggs**. He subsequently joined the Confederacy.

Lincoln had hopes that the North, the Union Army, would be able to take advantage of the many advantages they had and would quickly end the conflict. His hopes were drowned by the outcome of the successful Southern attack on Fort Sumter and by the outcome of the first big battle between North and South.

President Lincoln's overall plan was to bring the South back into the Union. He wanted to establish a naval blockade along the Southern coastline and he wanted to push forces down the Mississippi River. If successful, he could control much commerce into the South and he could manage better transport of troops and supplies while denying Southerners the same advantages.

The President of the Confederate States of America, Jefferson Davis, knowing his side was disadvantaged in terms of numbers of troops and access to essential resources, chose to fight more of a defensive battle. His armies didn't have to defeat the North, they just had to survive the war without capitulating to the North. In many ways, a defensive battle is easier to fight. The army of the South rarely ventured into the North on offensive missions, though General Robert E. Lee became a persistent threat to Washington, D.C.

America's Civil War would last four long, devastating years. Historians report there were more than 10,000 military skirmishes or engagements and more than 100 battles significant enough to be given names. We will cover a couple of battles in some depth and discuss others in less detail.

The First Battle of Bull Run

The Battle of Manassas

It had been about two months since Confederate rebels fired on Fort Sumter in South Carolina. The citizens in the North and the Northern press, were anxious to press their government to respond. Union troops had scored some early victories over the South in small skirmishes that occurred in Western Virginia. Morale was high in the North and Northerners believed the war would be very short and their ultimate victory was assumed to be inevitable. Sentiment was strong to encourage Union troops to march on Richmond, where the South planned to hold the first gathering of their new Congress.

The first major battle of America's Civil War took place on July 21, 1861. The location was near Manassas Junction in Virginia. 35,000 Union troops had marched the twenty-five miles from Washington, D.C. Their objective was to attack a "rebel" Confederate States of America force of 20,000 troops who were encamped along the banks of the little river known as Bull Run.

Brigadier General Irvin McDowell was instructed, by President Lincoln, to coordinate an aggressive attack on Southern troops, hoping to hit the South quickly and decisively. The goal was to power through the Southern troops, opening a pathway for Northern troops to drive directly to Richmond. Lincoln hoped the war could be ended quickly by taking immediate control of a center of Southern military leadership.

General McDowell was soon revealed to be a very "cautious" general. He wanted Lincoln to give him more time to prepare and to train his troops. Lincoln's response was that the Southern troops were no better prepared or trained and that the speed of the response was more important. McDowell, it turns out, did not move so quickly. His troop movements were slow enough to give the Southern spy network, well-established in Washington, D.C., time to warn the rebels of the impending attack.

The Confederate troops were camped along Bull Run. They were under the command of **General P. G. T. Beauregard**. Beauregard took advantage of early warnings of McDowell's slow approach and had time to request support from fellow Southern **General Joseph E. Johnston**, who was in command of an additional 11,000 troops. Johnston, located in the Shenandoah Valley, successfully outmaneuvered a different Northern force and made his way to Manassas and Bull Run.

The battle was engaged when Union troops began firing artillery across Bull Run, aiming at the left flank of the Southern army. Union troops forced the rebels back. Northern citizens, Congressmen and reporters lined the hilltops in the surrounding countryside, observing the battle. They cheered what appeared to be an early Union victory.

As more troops from both Johnston and Beauregard's armies soon gathered to support the besieged Southerners, the Union advance was stopped. The two forces exchanged offensives for several hours. The Union army was hindered by poor communications and poor coordination of their forces. The possession, by the South, of proven, well-trained military leaders began to show its importance.

The North and the South both had just short of 20,000 soldiers on the battlefield by late afternoon. General Beauregard launched an aggressive counteract which drove directly into Northern forces all along the length of the front lines. Union soldiers, the Federals, for the first time, heard the notorious, fearsome **"rebel yell"** as thousands of Southerners came at them headlong, laying down a fierce barrage of musket and artillery fire. Union troops were overrun and began a chaotic flight from the field. As they ran back toward Washington, D.C., they ran into and were hindered by, hundreds of D.C. sightseers who had been picnicking and watching the battle from nearby fields.

The First Battle of Manassas/BullRun was a Confederate victory. Lincoln was disappointed in the performance of his military leaders. It wouldn't be the last time. The Southern population was elated and their confidence was boosted by the victory. Northerners were angered and began to be concerned that the war might not be so easily won as they had anticipated. They were right.

There were several future leaders on the battlefield at Bull Run. On the Northern side were **William T. Sherman** and **Ambrose E. Burnside**. On the Southern side were **Wade Hampton** and **Thomas J. Jackson**. Jackson's toughness was celebrated as he earned his enduring nickname, **"Stonewall" Jackson**, during the battle.

Jackson was leading a small force, a Virginia brigade, which arrived from the Shenandoah Valley at a critical time in the fight. His Confederate troops took control of high ground near **"Henry House Hill"**, from which they held off Union efforts to dislodge them. **General Barnard Bee** directed his own Southern troops to look up to see their General Jackson, where General Bee said Jackson was standing "like a stone wall". General Bee did not survive the battle. The nickname he gave General Jackson, though, would persist.

The young Confederate army was not yet well trained and disciplined enough to pursue the Northern army back toward Washington, D.C. The CSA leaders, **President Jefferson Davis** and the two Generals, Johnston and Beauregard, argued over who was most to blame for the failure to summarily wipe out the Northern army. The early opportunity the Southerners missed at the first Manassas may have been their best opportunity to win the war.

On the Union side, Lincoln quickly dismissed General McDowell. McDowell was replaced with **General George B. McClellan**. McClellan took on the task of re-organizing and training the Union army. He would turn it into a more skilled and disciplined fighting force. It would be known as the **Army of the Potomac**.

In the South, that first battle was known as **First Manassas**. The Confederate army lost 1,750 of their troops. In the North, the battle was known as the First **Battle of Bull Run**. The Union troops lost more than 3,000 men.

The outcome of **The First Manassas/Bull Run** was the first indication of the lethal seriousness of the impending war. The casualties exceeded all expectations. The early victory Northerners expected appeared to be in real jeopardy. Lincoln began to re-evaluate the condition of the Army of the Potomac and the availability of effective military leadership. His earliest call for volunteers was a request for 75,000 troops. He increased the call to 100,000 and, before long, to 400,000 troops.

Elderly General Winfield Scott, an American military leader with an extensive history and Brigadier General Irvin McDowell were Lincoln's early military leaders. Scott was relieved of command early in the war, partly due to physical limitations. McDowell was quickly re-assigned after the First Manassas, primarily due to his slow troop movements and lack of enthusiasm for aggressive initiatives.

The Virginia Peninsula Campaign

General George B. McClellan became Lincoln's top ranking military leader. He also soon gained Lincoln's distrust due to his apparent reluctance to take the troops forward into battle. McClellan eventually did move the Army of the Potomac up the **Virginia Peninsula** to confront the rebels. He began a **siege of Yorktown**, where the rebels were in occupation. On May 4, 1862, McClellan captured Yorktown.

After McClellan captured Yorktown, Southern Generals Stonewall Jackson and Robert E. Lee joined forces to engage McClellan's Army of the Potomac. The Confederate Generals, between June 25 and July 1, 1862, in actions to be known as "**The Seven Days Battle**", were able to push McClellan steadily back. McClellan's objective of moving on the Southern capitol at Richmond had to be discarded. McClellan was forced to retreat all the way back to Washington, D.C. McClellan was allowed to stay in command of the Army of the Potomac, but Lincoln replaced him with **General Henry W. Halleck**, who became the "General in Chief".

During the course of events along the peninsula, the Confederacy surprised the Northerners when their iron-clad ship, **the C.S.S. Virginia** showed up at the mouth of the James River. The Virginia was tasked with blocking movement of Union ships. On March 8, 1862, the C.S.S. Virginia attacked and destroyed two Union ships, the **U.S.S. Congress** and the **U.S.S. Cumberland**. Lincoln was deeply concerned, believing it was possible, with the two Union ships no longer able to offer protection, that the Southern iron-clad Virginia would then be able to attack Washington, D.C. Fortunately for the Northerners, **the U.S.S. Monitor**, also an iron-clad ship, arrived in time to meet the C.S.S. Virginia directly in a face-to-face naval battle. They blasted away at one another over a distance apart of only a few yards. Neither was able to destroy the other, but the Virginia's capability to attack more Union ships was eliminated.

USS Monitor vs. CSS Virginia

The Civil War in West Virginia

The state of Virginia, the home of vast stores of American history, was quick to secede after Lincoln was elected. Many Virginians, though, opposed the secession. Most of those were located in Northern Virginia, near Washington, D.C. Non-slave-owning Virginians, supporting Lincoln and the Union, hoped to organize to secede from the state of Virginia. They intended to establish a new state, which would be a Union state.

In the months of June and July of 1861, Lincoln's General McClellan ventured into Northern Virginia. He led around 20,000 troops. He managed to defeat smaller forces under the leadership of Southern General Robert E. Lee in three battles. McClellan won on June 3rd at **Philippi**. He won again on July 11th at **Rich Mountain** and then once more on July 13th at **Carrick's Ford**, along the Cheat River.

McClellan's Union forces pursued Confederate troops and after the three battles, had gained almost total control of Northern Virginia. Southern **General Robert S. Garnett** led the approximately 3500 CSA troops who were driven off by McClellan.

CSA General Garnett stood bravely alongside his men as they made a "last stand", following an exhausting retreat down the river. As Garnett sat his horse, openly directing his troops, he was struck by a musket ball and fell to the ground. Union troops would later discover his body, resting among wild flowers along the banks of the Cheat River. All of Garnett's troops had fled. General Garnett became the first General to die in the Civil War.

McClellan had cleared the area of Southern military influence. The path was cleared for the Northern Virginians to pursue secession from the confederacy and admission to the Union. **West Virginia** became a new Union state in June of 1863.

The Second Battle of Bull Run

Second Manassas

The **Shenandoah Valley Campaigns**, throughout the Civil War, including the two battles at Bull Run, near Manassas, were dominated by Southern generals. General Thomas "Stonewall" Jackson became famous due to his many successful confrontations with Union forces. The valley provided a geographical framework from which Southern forces could push northward to points near Washington, D.C. The Northern generals weren't able to drive the Southerners out of the valley until late in the war. The ability of the South to post troops near Washington made it necessary for Northern generals to draw their troops back to the North, fearing an attack on their own capital. Northern troops under General McClellan had to pull back, giving up their hopes of an early capture of Richmond, the Southern capitol.

Union General Pope hoped to establish a base at Gordonsville, Virginia, which was the location of the Virginia Central Railroad. The railroad provided essential access to resources for Southern troops. Pope wanted to take that away from the Confederacy, starving the South of resources. CSA General Jackson moved more quickly, occupied Gordonsville and began to push General Pope's forces back northward.

In August, 1862, Southern General Stonewall Jackson, under orders from General Lee, was leading one part of the Army of Virginia northward. Jackson drove his troops around Union General Pope's forces and was able to capture and destroy a huge Union supply depot at Manassas. The action was a surprise to Pope and he was forced to order his troops to retreat, evacuating their defensive line.

General Lee ordered **General James Longstreet** to take one arm of the Army of Virginia northward. Lee wanted Longstreet to intercept Union General Pope. Lee wanted to confront Pope before Pope could join forces with Union General McClellan. The Southerners, under Longstreet, were able to push north to a point from which they could actually observe the movements of Pope's troops.

General Lee sent Stonewall Jackson to advance around the other end of Union General Pope's line of troops. Lee brought his own troops to join with the Southern troops led by General James Longstreet. Lee had put Pope's Northern army between two Southern armies.

Union General Pope launched the **Second Battle of Bull Run**, known in the South as the **Battle of Second Manassas**, on August 29, 1862. He ordered a widescale attack on General Jackson's positions. Pope, seeing movements by the Southern forces, believed the rebels were retreating. They were not. The Southerners absorbed a lot of damage, but did not give up significant ground.

Next day, General Lee brought his own forces to bear on the Federal troops led by Pope. The South brought Lee, Jackson and Longstreet's forces against Pope's army and Pope was overwhelmed. The Northerners were driven back to Washington in defeat.

General Pope was disgraced by the embarrassing defeat at Second Manassas. The Northern troops lost all confidence, not just in Pope, but in their certainty that they would easily defeat the South. Lincoln quickly relieved Pope of his command. Pope's troops were to join those of McClellan's Army of the Republic.

General Pope's troops, from a total of 70,000, suffered 13,824 casualties at the Second Manassas. General Lee, from a force of 55,000, suffered 8,353 casualties. The South was the clear victor in the Second Battle of Bull Run. The Union Army, though it had superior numbers and resources, was driven out of Eastern Virginia. General Robert E. Lee's tactical genius was beginning to be revealed. General Lee began to plan a Confederate assault on the North.

The Battle of Antietam

Confederate Generals Lee, Jackson and Longstreet had dealt a crushing blow to Union forces at the Second Battle of Bull Run. General Lee hoped to follow up, while the Union armies were in retreat and re-organizing, by launching an offensive move Northward. Up to that point in the war, Southern forces were on Southern ground, fighting defensive battles. Lee wanted to impress Northerners with the real consequences of the war by putting it in the Northerner's back yards.

Robert E. Lee held out several main objectives for carrying out a successful drive into Northern territory. He hoped to encourage European support for the confederacy and he believed successful military offensives would be of benefit to that end. He believed a significant Southern victory, occurring in the North, would impact Northern Congressional elections. Lee wanted Northern Congressmen elected who would vote to end the war. Union losses on the battlefield would influence Congress. Lee also hoped to be able to bring slave state Maryland into the Southern confederacy and his northern trajectory might make that possible. Finally, Lee hoped to put himself in position to potentially be able to occupy the U.S. Capitol in Washington, D.C., which would re-define the balance of power in the war. Lee's planned offensive, if successful, would actually place the Army of Virginia north of the city of Washington. Outside of the political importance, Lee recognized the critical need to defeat and demoralize the Northern armies. He knew his armies need only survive until the North lost the motivation to fight.

President Lincoln's disappointment in his Eastern generals was growing. He quickly replaced General Pope after the disastrous defeat at the Second Manassas. Lincoln placed General George B. McClellan in charge of all the Union forces located in the vicinity of Washington, D.C. Lincoln knew the danger of allowing the rebels to capture and occupy the capitol city. He always felt the burden of maintaining enough troops in the area to protect the capitol. Doing so meant that troops that could have been used to serve vital needs in other areas were not available.

CSA General Robert E. Lee took advantage of the victory at Second Manassas to quickly move his troops across the Potomac River and drive to the North. He reached **Fredericksburg, Maryland**, on September 7, 1862, where his **Army of Virginia** would be based for the looming battle.

Union General McClellan, seemingly never eager to join battle, moved more slowly, having to re-organize his army after the Bull Run defeat. McClellan's troops approached the field of battle on the same day that Lee occupied Fredericksburg, on September 7th.

Historians believe McClellan made several errors that impacted the events of the battle. He wildly over-estimated the size of Lee's force, which led him to make bad tactical errors. Union troops, in an amazing stroke of good luck, stumbled across a copy of Lee's battle plans and orders, which were found lying on the ground wrapped around three of the general's cigars. McClellan was quoted, on learning of the find, saying "Here is a paper with which, if I cannot defeat Bobby Lee, I will be willing to go home".

McClellan, though, chose to delay any action based on the critical new-found tactical information. Instead of immediately taking advantage of the information, he waited for a day and a half before ordering any movement. General Lee's forces were not yet in position, were scattered in several positions and might well have been destroyed had McClellan moved quickly when he had the opportunity.

Meanwhile, General Lee had learned that his lines of communication and openings for troop movements were blocked by a garrison of Union troops who were protecting the Union armory at Harper's Ferry, Virginia. Lee ordered General Stonewall Jackson to lead three columns of troops to move on and capture Harper's Ferry. Lee sent the rest of his troops to occupy locations in the vicinity of Antietam. Unfortunately for the Southerners, the federal garrison at **Harper's Ferry** proved more difficult to dislodge than Lee had anticipated. While the Southerners did manage to drive off the Union troops, on September 9th, it took days longer than expected. Lee had planned to re-unite his forces quickly, pending resolution of the Harper's Ferry issue. Lee's plans were unraveling.

McClellan initiated fighting on September 14th when his troops defeated Southern forces at the **Battle of South Mountain**, near Sharpsburg. Lee's army was pushed back into a restricted position along **Antietam Creek** and had to assume a defensive attitude, something Lee had hoped to avoid. On the positive side, General Jackson arrived, on that same date, to reinforce Lee's troops. The morale of Jackson's troops had been boosted by their victory at Harper's Ferry, where they took 12,000 federal troops prisoner, while losing only 300 of their own men. It was a great achievement by General Jackson and a big encouragement to Southern troops.

Southern forces were defeated at South Mountain, but they bought enough time for General Lee to begin consolidating his forces. The rebels set up a defensive line all along Antietam Creek.

McClellan's forces followed the retreating Southerners through the passes of South Mountain, only to find themselves facing General Lee's army. Lee had arranged his 11,000 troops to offer the most intimidating visual array possible. McClellan erroneously estimated Lee's army at 120,000 men. McClellan could have over-run Lee had he moved aggressively and quickly. Instead, he spent many hours engaged in "reconnaissance". Lee's force was enhanced tremendously with the overnight arrival of General Jackson's forces, coming from their victory at Harper's Ferry. Jackson took position near Sharpsburg. Southerners named the ensuing battle the **Battle at Sharpsburg**, while Northerners named it the **Battle at Antietam**.

The arrival of Jackson's force was met, on the late afternoon of September 16th, by **Major General Joseph Hooker's** Union troops. A small skirmish was initiated after Hooker's troops crossed the Antietam just to the North of the Confederates' left flank. Nightfall quickly ended the minor engagement. The stage was set for a historic fight.

The Battle at Antietam, in Maryland, would become the bloodiest single day in American military history. It began on the morning of September 17, 1862. On the previous day, both Union and Confederate troops organized their resources. They were planted firmly on opposite sides of Antietam Creek.

Fog enveloped the battleground in the early morning hours of the 17th. The battle was joined. Fighting was savage, brutal, furious and bloody. One side and then the other would appear to have an advantage, depending on location along the length of the battlefield. McClellan had hoped to drive the Southerners into the nearby Potomac, where they could be destroyed. He had, in another tactical error, left a large portion of his force in a center location where they could not participate in the battle. The intense fighting continued all day long. Union forces were ultimately able to push the Confederates back, but the rebels were not defeated. Both armies managed to hold most of the ground on which they had begun the day. There was no clear victor.

On September 18th, a tragic day in our history, both sides tended to their wounded and buried their dead. Once those tasks were completed, Lee was forced to turn back to the South, his Northern invasion a failure. He had, however, in spite of the Northern advantages in numbers and resources, fought the Union army to a standstill. The South continued to bring superior leadership to the battlefields.

The Battle at Antietam brought the loss of 12,400 Union soldiers, including several thousand killed. It brought the loss of 10,316 Southern soldiers, also including thousands killed. McClellan put about 87,000 troops on the field, while Lee put about 45,000 troops on the field.

After viewing the tactical mistakes made by McClellan at Antietam and McClellan's sluggish movements, Lincoln immediately replaced him with General Ambrose E. Burnside.

Lincoln had been hoping for a victory on the battlefield. He wanted a moment of optimism and celebration in which he could deliver his **Emancipation Proclamation**. While Antietam was no major victory, he felt the Northern ability to push the rebels back into the South was good enough. He issued his seminal Proclamation on September 22, 1862, only four days after the Battle at Antietam. The Emancipation Proclamation would stimulate Black men to join the Union Army. 186,000 of them would do so and would fight fiercely and valiantly and 38,000 would die in the war.

The Battle of Fredericksburg

President Lincoln, disappointed in the performance of General McClellan at the Battle of Antietam, had replaced McClellan with General Ambrose E. Burnside. Lincoln had twice before asked Burnside to take the job, but Burnside was insistent that McClellan was the better choice. Lincoln must have thought otherwise and he went to Burnside a third time. This time, Burnside accepted.

Burnside was undoubtedly aware of Lincoln's belief that McClellan had moved too slowly and had not been sufficiently aggressive. Burnside quickly re-organized the Union **Army of the Potomac** and developed a plan focused on capturing the rebel capital at Richmond, Virginia. Burnside moved his Federals quickly away from their position in Northern Virginia toward Fredericksburg, which is located on the banks of the Rappahannock River. It was Burnside's objective to cross the Rappahannock and proceed south to capture Richmond.

General Burnside had placed two advance forces on the northern banks of the Rappahannock by the middle of November, 1862. Their location was directly across the wide river from Fredericksburg. General Robert E. Lee was well aware of Burnside's troop movements. Lee rapidly moved several CSA forces to hilly grounds on the south side of the river. Lee was able to place several defensive positions before the larger part of Burnside's forces could be brought into place.

At the outset, the Fredericksburg campaign looked good for Burnside. He had ordered construction of a pontoon bridge at Fredericksburg, to allow rapid troop movements to the South. The construction of the bridge was delayed for several days. The delay seriously impeded Burnsides plans. It gave General Lee time to move a substantial force of rebel troops into place on Marye's Heights, high bluffs looking over Fredericksburg. Confederate troops were able to plant themselves along a sunken road which was further protected by a stone wall. Below them they could see the wide open, sloping downgrade by which Union troops would have to approach them. One rebel officer declared "A chicken could not live on that field when we open up on it". He was soon to be proved correct.

The Army of the Potomac brought 120,000 soldiers to Fredericksburg. The CSA, led by General Lee, brought 80,000 soldiers. The tactical picture seemed dire for the Union, but General Burnside decided to go on the offensive. It was the fourteenth of December in 1862. Burnside ordered his artillery to begin shelling the rebels and his troops to attack. Burnside's forces attacked the Southerners from both the right and left flanks. Lee's forces held their favorable defensive positions.

Union soldiers were facing a six-hundred-yard open field across which they had to run toward the wall of confederate fire. Fourteen times Burnside repeated his orders to attack. The open field became a killing field for Union soldiers. Burnside persisted until his subordinates pleaded with him to give it up. No Union troops came close to reaching the rebel lines above them on Marye's Heights. General Lee, with General James Longstreet, was watching the devastating carnage from a high position behind the front line. Lee commented, sadly, "It is well that war is so horrible or else we should grow too fond of it". Many of the dead and wounded, lying on the ghastly battlefield, froze to death over the course of the long and bitterly cold night.

The dawn of December 14th brought a nightmarish spectacle on the battlefield. Burnside considered renewing the attack, but was talked out of it. The two armies called a truce to give both an opportunity to bury their dead and collect their wounded. General Burnside took advantage of rain and darkness to organize a retreat, fleeing back to the North.

Almost 200,000 troops fought at Fredericksburg, the most of any Civil War battle. Around 13,000 Union soldiers were lost, while the Southerners lost about 4,000. It was a decisive victory for the South and it was a devastating loss for the North. Lincoln had only recently appointed General Burnside and was once again disappointed. He was seriously depressed over the massive loss of life. President Lincoln quickly replaced General Burnside, in December, with **General Joseph "Fighting Joe" Hooker**. Lincoln continued to be frustrated by his dissatisfaction with Union Army leaders.

The Battle of Fredericksburg was a defeat for the North which came at a time when a bitter winter was approaching. The Northern population was losing confidence in their ability to win the war. Fredericksburg fed their doubts. On the other hand, Fredericksburg gave Southerners a big boost in confidence and in their morale. They knew that the North was losing interest in pursuit of the war. They knew they just had to hang on until the Northerners grew "war weary" enough to quit. General Robert E. Lee's reputation was growing. Once again he had defeated a Union force of better equipped troops while being outnumbered.

The Battle of Chancellorsville

Both Union and CSA forces settled along opposite sides of the **Rapahannock River** following the Union defeat at the Battle of Fredericksburg. They held their positions and suffered the hardships of winter. As spring approached, the armies began to organize for new activities.

Three Southern generals were meeting at an inn known as **"Chancellor Farm"**, only a few miles away from Fredericksburg, when a messenger arrived to tell them Union troops were crossing the river. The three, one of whom was **J.E.B. Stuart**, quickly departed their meeting to rejoin their respective military units. The women who ran the inn, knowing a battle was forthcoming, gathered their valuables and sewed them into pockets in their undergarments. They were Southerners and expected to be treated badly by Union soldiers. The slaves who had worked the inn and nearby farms had already fled across the river to the North, to the sanctuary of Union lines.

In the early spring, Union General "Fighting Joe" Hooker was about to launch an offensive, planning to move south toward Richmond. Several generals and other group leaders, working under Hooker's directions, had pushed southward, destroying Southern resources as they proceeded. Hooker had distributed his forces in a pattern he thought would encircle Lee's various forces. Hooker, on the evening of April 30, 1863, was celebrating what he anticipated would be a great victory over Robert E. Lee. In his exuberance, while surrounded by his officers, Hooker boasted "I have the rebellion in my breeches pocket and God Almighty himself cannot take it away from me". Some of his subordinates were worried that Hooker's words might be ill-advised. They were right.

The Union Army brought 80,000 soldiers to Chancellorsville. The CSA brought half as many, at around 40,000 troops. On the morning of May 1st, Union troops had been placed in a wide perimeter within which the bulk of Lee's army was trapped. Southern General "Stonewall' Jackson initiated an offensive against a larger force. The Union officers thought Jackson was bringing a much bigger force than he actually had and Northern troops pulled back. General Jackson pursued them aggressively, putting them in disarray. The same sort of confusion and mistakes marked the rest of the day for the North and Robert E. Lee, puzzled by the apparent retreat of the Northerners, quickly took advantage. Historians still don't understand how General Hooker mis-interpreted what was happening at the various locations of the battlegrounds. Evidence indicates communications between the several Northern leaders was very ineffective.

On May 2nd, both armies continued to thrust and parry their various forces, with the South seeming to dominate or control much of the action. In the late afternoon, General Stonewall Jackson led a wild surprise attack on Union forces. They came, screaming the terrifying "rebel yell", from the tree lines and they drove the Union soldiers back two miles. Southern troops were deeply saddened, though, when Stonewall Jackson was mortally wounded, shot accidentally by his own men. Jackson's arm had to be amputated and he died within days. Jackson was temporarily replaced by J.E.B. Stuart.

May 3rd yielded the fiercest and bloodiest battles of Chancellorsville. Both sides are in the thick woods and fighting is brutal. Losses and gains are difficult to evaluate. At one point, a cannonball bursts into a tree on which General Hooker is leaning. He is knocked unconscious. Some of his subordinates are reported to have hoped he might remain so, as they believed their forces were being very badly managed.

On May 4th, Southern forces, directed by General Lee, while still vastly outnumbered, manage to persistently drive the Union Army backward. The next day, May 5th, General Hooker holds a conference with his subordinates. To their dismay, he wants to give up the battle and move back northward, retreating. He overrules their objections and the Northern army begins to pack up. The morning of May 5th sees the Union army crossing back over the Rappahannock River.

Chancellorsville becomes another major victory for General Robert E. Lee and the Confederate States of America. **The Battle of Chancellorsville** saw almost 31,000 casualties. The South lost 13,460, with 1,724 killed. The North lost 17,304, with 1,694 killed. The Chancellorsville defeat dealt a crushing blow to the confidence of Northern citizens in the ability of the North to be victorious in the way. President Lincoln was in despair and still struggling to find the right military leadership to help him preserve the Union. Lincoln criticized General Hooker, but also said: "I do not know that I could have given any different orders had I been with them myself. I have not fully made up my mind how I should behave when minie-balls were whistling and those great oblong shells shrieking in my ear. I might run away".

Lincoln left Hooker in charge of the army, but would replace him soon after, on June 28th, 1863. By then, both armies were engaged in preparations for the campaign that would culminate in the next great battle. **Gettysburg**.

Southerners were jubilant over the perceived victory at Chancellorsville, but they were deeply depressed by the loss of their great General Andrew "Stonewall" Jackson. General Lee was not as convinced that Chancellorsville had been such a great victory. He was proud that his troops had performed with such courage and had gained great confidence in the belief that his army would do anything for him. Still, he wrote, after the battle, "Our loss was severe and again we gained not an inch of ground and the enemy could not be pursued".

The Battle of Gettysburg

Summer was approaching in 1863. CSA General Lee's **Army of Northern Virginia** had scored a major victory, fighting the Northerner's **Army of the Potomac** at Chancellorsville to a standstill. Lee's attempted first advance into Northern territory was blocked, but his forces held their own against a Union army of greater size. General Lee needed to find a way into the North, where he could find food for troops, sustenance for horses and mules and seek other resources. Lee knew that, if he could begin taking the reality of the ground war into Northern towns, he could wear away the North's motivation to continue the fight. Northerners known as **"Copperheads"** were pressuring Lincoln to end the war and Lee believed he could add strength to their movement by bringing the war to their back yards. Confederate troops were under siege at Vicksburg, Mississippi and Lee believed he might, by venturing northward again, draw Union troops away from Mississippi, offering some relief to confederate forces. Lee also hoped that, by showing strength for the Southern cause, European nations might be more likely to support the South.

President Lincoln was disappointed by the performance of "Fighting Joe" Hooker, as he had been disappointed by Generals Scott, McDowell and McClellan. In June, 1863, Lincoln appointed **Major General George Gordon Meade** to lead the Army of the Potomac. Meade quickly took firm control and organized an aggressive campaign to find and engage the rebels. Lee had already moved north across the Potomac River and passed through western Maryland. He was leading an army of 75,000 troops on a steady march into southern Pennsyvania. He was leading an army of 75,000 troops, many of whom were seasoned by previous battles, into northern territory.

Robert E. Lee learned that the Union Army was coming for him. He hoped to bring his several divisions together at Gettysburg, a busy town 35 miles Southwest of Harrisburg, Pennsylvania. On July 1, 1863, Lee's **General A. P. Hill** drew near Gettysburg, quickly observing that Union cavalry forces had occupied the town only a day earlier. It didn't take long for rebel troops led by Generals Hill and **Richard Ewell** to drive the much smaller Union force out of town. The Union troops gathered just south of Gettysburg at a location known as Cemetery Hill. General Lee ordered General Ewell to attack the Northerners and drive them back, taking advantage of their brief superiority in numbers. Ewell declined the order, which gave Northern General Meade time to bring significant reinforcements. Ewell probably cost the South an important early victory in the battle. By nightfall, the Union had established a lengthy and strong defensive line.

Battle of Gettysburg

The second day at Gettysburg, July 2nd, was marked by gory, blood-soaked engagements at positions known by their locations around the battlefield. **Culp's Hill**, **Little Round Top**, **Cemetery Ridge**, **the Orchard** and **Devil's Den** became killing fields for both the North and the South. General Lee had ordered his subordinates to launch attacks early in the day, but his **General Longstreet** didn't get his corps moving until late in the afternoon. The rebels attacked a Union regiment from Maine at Little Round Top. The Federals were able to hold Little Round top, but had to give up both the Orchard field and Devil's Den.

The battle raged, with both sides taking some ground and giving up some ground. On day two, each side endured nearly 10,000 casualties. In the first two days of the **Battle of Gettysburg**, the nation had suffered almost 35,000 casualties, with both sides contributing to the massacre.

Day 3 of the battle, July 3rd, found General Lee believing that his men had been close to victory the previous day. He intended to strike hard early on the third day, hoping to establish a dominant offense before the North could organize to respond effectively. Lee directed one group to attack Union troops at Culp's hill, which led to a day-long battle at that location. Lee ordered a barrage of artillery at Cemetery Ridge, wanting to "soften' the Union defenses there. He then ordered **Major General George Pickett** to attack the heavily defended Union force along the Ridge.

Pickett had arrived at Gettysburg late and his force of around 14,000 troops was not yet depleted. Pickett's corps was ordered to march directly across three-quarters of a mile of open fields to charge head-on into the Union lines. Lee's massive artillery bombardment, fired from 150 cannon, meant to soften the Union defense, had not been effective enough to drive off the Northern troops. The Federals were well established to defend their position, had the high ground and had a large numerical advantage.

Pickett's troops showed great courage, but had no chance of success. As they crossed the fields, they were cut down by Union infantry musket balls, fired from behind stone walls and other solid defenses. Union regiments from Ohio, New York and Vermont were divided to form up positions on each side of Pickett's advancing troops. Pickett's division was trapped and taking heavy fire from three sides. They were shredded by the avalanche of hot shells and musket balls. The onslaught of Union fire was horrifying and the killing fields were grisly nightmares.

Two-thirds of Pickett's men were casualties of the fight at Cemetery Ridge. Their brave efforts are remembered as **"Pickett's Charge",** though Pickett himself was leading from behind the lines. George Pickett lived for another fifty years, but he never forgave Robert E. Lee for the decision that caused his men such horrific losses. General Lee was forced, by the end of the day, to pull his forces back and to try to shore up a defensive line.

Day four at Gettysburg, July 4th, found Lee preparing to defend against what he expected to be a vicious attack from the North. General Meade, however, chose not to pursue the weakened rebels. Lee had lost nearly a third of his army and, had Meade been more aggressive, might have been completely defeated. Instead, by the end of the day, in a rainstorm, Lee's forces were in a forlorn retreat back to the South.

The Southern defeat at Gettysburg was definitive. It most likely marked a significant turning point in the war. Northerners celebrated while Southerners wept. General Lee realized that his hopes of enticing European support were dashed. No help would be coming.

The Union lost 23,000 troops at Gettysburg. The South lost 28,000, which was an irreparable loss for an army which was already badly outnumbered. Robert E. Lee, who took full responsibility for the crushing defeat, tendered his resignation to CSA President Jefferson Davis. Davis refused the offer, knowing he had no better officer with whom to replace Lee.

Four months later, in November, President Lincoln personally visited the battlefield. He was deeply grieved by the tens of thousands of young lives lost in the battle and in other battles and he delivered his **Gettysburg Address** on the site. It may be the most famous speech in history, though it went only 272 words. The entire text can be read in the Lincoln biography offered earlier in this book.

The Battle of Vicksburg

President Lincoln was still struggling to find a reliably effective General to lead his entire army. He was dismayed on learning that General Meade had failed to pursue Lee's defeated forces at Gettysburg. Meanwhile, out in the West, the city of Vicksburg, Mississippi, had become an essential target. It was occupied by the confederates. Vicksburg was resting on the eastern shore of the Mississippi River and was located between New Orleans, to the south and Memphis, to the north. Control of the river offered a convenient avenue for movement of troops and resources. While the South had control of Vicksburg, it was difficult for the North to move materials and troops to the South.

CSA President Jefferson Davis had seen, during 1862, the losses of **Fort Henry** and **Fort Donelson** to the North. The losses were engineered by Union **General Ulysses S. Grant**, who recognized very early on in the war that control of southern waterways would be a key factor in winning the ultimate conflict. Grant's victories at Fort Henry and Fort Donelson gave the North control of the Tennessee and Cumberland Rivers and also led to control of railways in the region. By forcing the Southerners out of the area, Grant offered the Union forces much easier routes into the homeland of the rebels. His victories gave the Union control of much of Kentucky and Tennessee and gave the North a location for a massive supply depot in Nashville.

Grant's victories forced the Southerners to retreat into Vicksburg, where they hoped to maintain control of the essential Mississippi River. General Grant realized that, if he could take Vicksburg, he not only would take control of the river but he would fatally divide the army of the confederacy. Dividing the army of the CSA would make it impossible for the South to gather a large force in any one area.

Ulysses S. Grant had moved his 70,000 troops almost 500 miles and fought and won five battles and captured thousands of rebel prisoners in less than a month. His confidence was strong as he planned the attack on Vicksburg. His forces had pushed Southern **General Pemberton** back into the town, where the rebels were building up a defensive perimeter. President Davis ordered Pemberton to stay in place and defend Vicksburg at all costs.

Vicksburg was placed in a very fortuitous defensive location. It sat high on bluffs above the river and on those bluffs the rebels had established batteries of artillery that would stop any river travel attempted by the North. A Union attempt, in 1862, to attack the gun batteries on the bluffs using ironclad vessels on the river had failed. Vicksburg was protected on the north side by a network of swampy areas. Union **General William Tecumseh Sherman** had attempted to bring a force down on Vicksburg from the north, through the swamps, but his effort also failed. General Grant even tried to cut a canal around the town, intending to divert the river, but quickly gave up on that unrealistic plan.

In spite of the defensive advantages of Vicksburg, Jefferson Davis's most successful General, **Joseph E. Johnston**, advised the evacuation of Southern troops. Johnston recognized the impact of the great advantage the North had in numbers of troops and could see the danger of being trapped in the town. President Davis ignored his advice.

Union General Winfield Scott had devised the **"Anaconda Plan"**. It was designed to shut down Southern access to riverways and to the gulf coast. General Grant's plan to take Vicksburg was an important component of the Anaconda Plan. In a preliminary round to the coming fight at Vicksburg, Grant defeated Southern General Pemberton on May 16, 1863, at a place called **Champion Hill**. Pemberton was then forced back into Vicksburg.

Grant planned an "end run" that would put his troops behind the lines of Southern forces. Union **Admiral David Porter** ran a flotilla of vessels down the Mississippi, through the gauntlet of Southern artillery batteries on the high bluffs. Grant took 40,000 Federal troops across the Mississippi, then traveled downward 30 miles on the west side of the river. He was then able to use Admiral Porter's flotilla to cross back to the east side of the river. Back in Mississippi, Grant's force easily defeated a Southern force near the state capitol, Jackson. He then pushed back toward Vicksburg. His path meant he had to leave his supply train behind, which meant his troops had to survive by foraging along the way.

Along the trail leading back to Vicksburg, Grant was able to defeat a Southern force at **Port Gibson**, along the river. He also encountered an attempt by Southern General Johnston to reach and reinforce Pemberton inside Vicksburg. Grant blocked Johnston's movement, increasing the certitude of Pemberton's ultimate defeat. Pemberton tried to lead a force to meet up with Johnston, but Grant was able to push him back into the city.

General Grant made some tentative efforts to launch attacks on Pemberton's forces in Vicksburg, but quickly realized the Southerners were too well entrenched. Grant knew that he could deprive the inhabitants of Vicksburg, military and civilian, of essential resources, including food, for as long as necessary. He saw no need to sacrifice thousands of lives in fighting to occupy the town. Grant's army began digging 15 miles of trenches around Vicksburg, preparing to fend off any efforts by Pemberton to escape the city. It was May 18th, 1863 and the **Siege of Vicksburg** had begun. Pemberton and his 29,000 troops were sealed in with no realistic path to freedom. The siege would last 47 days.

Conditions quickly deteriorated inside the perimeter around Vicksburg. Citizens, terrified by incoming artillery shells, fearing an imminent attack and hoping to evade the misery within the Union boundaries, began digging caves in the bluffs outside the city. More than 500 citizens of Vicksburg were eventually living in the caves and tunnels above the town. Union soldiers, observing their hardships, referred to the area as **"Prairie Dog Village"**.

The siege was accompanied by a daily barrage of Union artillery shells into Vicksburg. More citizens moved to the caves in the bluffs. CSA General Pemberton tried multiple efforts to break through Union lines and escape with his troops, but all failed. Confederate forces, coming from behind the Union perimeter, attempted to attack Union lines to break the siege, but also failed. Conditions within the perimeter continued to worsen.

General U.S. Grant continued to bring more troops and armaments into place. The Southerners were deprived of any possibility of escape. Rebel troops were running out of ammunition. People in the city of Vicksburg were nearing starvation. Southern General Pemberton had to surrender the city and all of his forces, nearly 30,000 men, on July 4th, 1863.

The Vicksburg victory was followed quickly by a Union victory at **Port Hudson**, at the low end of the Mississippi. The two successful events gave the Union complete control of the Mississippi, an enormous benefit. It proved the success of the Anaconda Plan, which effectively blocked Southern access to travel paths and to essential resources. It split Confederate forces in half and they would never completely re-assemble.

Combined with the Southern defeat at Gettysburg, literally on the previous day, the loss at Vicksburg marked a final turning point in the war. General Grant was recognized for his brilliant strategy and tactics. President Lincoln would soon put Grant in charge of ALL Union forces. As the news of the two battles spread, Northerners were greatly encouraged and Southerners were depressed, discouraged and grieving their losses.

The South, though, was not yet ready to quit. They produced a victory in September at **Chickamauga Creek** in Georgia. The event may have worried Lincoln. He made U.S. Grant commander of all forces in the region and Grant led Northern troops to a victory, in November, at the **Battle of Chattanooga**. Grant's good reputation and fame, continued to grow.

General Sherman's "March to the Sea"

After his great victory at Vicksburg, General U.S. Grant, now supreme commander of all Union forces, departed to travel back to Washington. He took command of the Army of the Potomac and began a series of confrontations with the South's General Robert E. Lee. The war was winding down and the two greatest generals would fight one another to the bitter end.

Meanwhile, Grant assigned Union **General William Tecumseh Sherman** to continue the progress of the Yankee troops across the South. Sherman led his 65,000 troops on their infamous "**March to the Sea**". Sherman's Yankees had occupied Atlanta, Georgia, by November of 1863.

Sherman, before the war, had many Southern friends. He planned a campaign that would be so definitively victorious that it would remove all hopes of winning the war by the Southerners. His goal wasn't cruelty, but clarity. He meant to take away the ability and the motivation of the South to fight back, hoping to end the war as quickly as possible. Sherman believed that, in the long run, a display of invincible power would make it very clear that further pursuit of the war, by the Southerners, would only cost more lives with no hope of victory.

In November, Atlanta was already decimated. Southern troops had already done much damage to the city as they dug out defensive entrenchments and used the city as a fortress throughout the fighting. It had absorbed devastating artillery bombardments. Sherman directed his own troops to destroy any facilities or assets that might be used to the advantage of rebel forces. The city was left in smoking ruins, with only about 400 buildings left standing. Then, Sherman directed his victorious army to the Southeast, toward Savannah.

Sherman's "March to the Sea" was characterized by a **"scorched earth"** policy, designed to eliminate any possibility of a Southern resurgence. The policy also cut his own supply lines and he knew his men would have to live off of the land, foraging for food and supplies as they moved. Sherman was fighting a psychological war. He wanted to convince Southern civilians that they had no hope of winning. He wanted to show them that, if they surrendered, they would be treated with kindness and respect. Before destroying military infrastructure in Atlanta, Sherman had the remaining civilians moved safely out of the smoking city.

Before embarking on what he knew would be a physically demanding and arduous march, Sherman directed his commanders to be certain the assigned troops were men who were fit and strong enough to withstand the hardships sure to come. Physicians assessed each man for fitness. Sherman also ordered two of his armies, commanded by his **General**

George H. Thomas, to march to Tennessee to block the moves of Southern **General John Bell Hood**. Thomas would ultimately be victorious over General Hood's rebel forces and the success would mean Sherman's armies could basically move on unmolested.

General Sherman's feelings on November 15ᵗʰ, as he led his armies away from the defeated city of Atlanta, are revealed in this note taken from his own memoirs:

"We rode out of Atlanta by the Decatur road, filled by the marching troops and wagons of the Fourteenth Corps; and reaching the hill, just outside of the old rebel works, we naturally paused to look back upon the scenes of our past battles. We stood upon the very ground whereon was fought the bloody battle of July 22d and could see the copse of wood where McPherson fell. Behind us lay Atlanta, smouldering and in ruins, the black smoke rising high in air and hanging like a pall over the ruined city.

Away off in the distance, on the McDonough road, was the rear of Howard's column, the gun-barrels glistening in the sun, the white-topped wagons stretching away to the South; and right before us the Fourteenth Corps, marching steadily and rapidly, with a cheery look and swinging pace, that made light of the thousand miles that lay between us and Richmond.

Some band, by accident, struck up the anthem of "John Brown's Body"; the men caught up the strain and never before or since have I heard the chorus of "Glory, glory, hallelujah!" done with more spirit or in better harmony of time and place."

[Copied from "William T. Sherman, Memoris (sic) of General W. T. Sherman".]

After leaving Atlanta, on November 15ᵗʰ, General Sherman still had a Confederate Army to contend with on his march toward Savannah. He split his army into two columns and left a small force to hinder Southern Lt. General John Bell Hood. As they marched across the countryside, Sherman's troops destroyed telegraph lines, tunnels and railroad tracks. They heated railroad rails so they could be twisted and left useless. Southerners called the damaged rails "Sherman's neckties". They burned food supplies they could not use, leaving nothing for Southern troops to forage.

Southern forces under **Lt. General William J. Hardee**, **Maj. General Gustavus W. Smith** and **General Joseph Wheeler** all attempted to harass or block the advances of Sherman's forces. The rebel forces were of small numbers and were often no longer "regular" troops. Sherman disseminated false intelligence that misled the Confederates, making the rebels believe he was headed for Augusta and Macon. Neither was true.

Sherman actually drove his army toward the Georgia state capital of Milledgeville. Southern **General Wheeler**, with 3,500 men, attempted to stop Sherman's advance into their capital city. **Brigadier General Judson Kilpatrick's** 5,000 Yankee horse soldiers or cavalry, overwhelmed Wheeler's much smaller, much less-experienced force. Yankee troops celebrated in Georgia's capitol building. They acted out a parody in which they voted Georgia back into the Union.

On November 22nd, 1863, Union troops in Sherman's army approached Griswoldville, Georgia. They occupied and burned factories in the industrial town. Union **General Howard** left a small force, less than 2,000 soldiers, to serve as a rear guard for his departing armies. Three Confederate forces, adding up to more than 4,000 troops, came across the destruction of Griswoldville. The rebels were under the command of the relatively inexperienced **Brigadier General Pleasant J. Phillips**. Soon after seeing the carnage at Griswoldsville, the Southerners encountered the "rear guard" Union troops.

General Phillips ordered his ragged force to attack the Union line. He was unaware of how well the Yankees were entrenched and of the fact that the Northerners had new repeating rifles. The rebels were shredded by the barrages of Union rifle shots and had no chance of victory. The Southerners suffered more than 1,000 casualties, while the Northerners lost only about 100 men. When the battle was over, Union troops were distressed and horrified at learning that many of their opponents on the battlefield had been young boys and old men. The Confederate army was clearly in desperate straits.

Meeting little significant resistance, Sherman's two major columns were nearing Savannah, Georgia, by mid-December. His troops easily captured Southern **Fort McCallister**, which rested on the city's south side. Sherman's forces had Savannah surrounded and Sherman was hoping to avoid the loss of time and resources that would be required of a siege. He sent this message into Savannah, on December 17th, to Southern General Hardee:

"I have already received guns that can cast heavy and destructive shots as far as the heart of your city; also, I have for some days held and controlled every avenue by which the people and garrison of Savannah can be supplied and I am therefore justified in demanding the surrender of the city of Savannah and its dependent forts and shall wait a reasonable time for your answer, before opening with heavy ordnance. Should you entertain the proposition, I am prepared to grant liberal terms to the inhabitants and garrison; but should I be forced to resort to assault or the slower and surer process of starvation, I shall then feel justified in resorting to the harshest measures and shall make little effort to restrain my army—burning to avenge the national wrong which they attach to Savannah and other large cities which have been so prominent in dragging our country into civil war."

Within the city, Confederate General Hardee soon realized the futility of his position. He quietly gathered his remaining troops out of their trenches and led them across the Savannah River into South Carolina. He chose to escape rather than surrender his garrison. The mayor of Savannah surrendered the city to the Federals and General Sherman sent President Lincoln this message on December 21st:

"I beg to present you as a Christmas gift the city of Savannah, with one hundred fifty heavy guns and also about twenty-five thousand bales of cotton."

General Sherman took time, while in the captured city of Savannah, to rest and recuperate his troops. They were ordered to behave well, with those practicing "unsoldierlike deeds" being rewarded with immediate execution. Confederate officers sent notes to Sherman, requesting gentle treatment for their relatives who were still in Savannah and Sherman did what he could to comply with their wishes. People in the city were starving and Sherman sold agricultural products stored in the area to the North, using the money gained to buy food for the Southerners.

After capturing Savannah, General Sherman continued his march, now heading back northward. His ultimate goal was to come up behind Southern General Lee's forces, trapping Lee between Sherman's vast armies and U.S. Grant's forces, now north of Richmond, Virginia.

Black Southerners often attempted to escape their owners to join the Union armies. In most cases, they were allowed to participate as laborers, assisting the Yankee troops, but, in other locations, they were allowed to take up arms. Ulysses S. Grant encouraged their contributions as soldiers and President Lincoln grew to have great admiration for the courage and commitment to the cause of freedom seen in Black volunteers. Sadly, on seeing Sherman's Federalist troops marching away from Savannah, hundreds of Black Americans drowned while trying to cross **Ebenezer Creek** to follow Sherman. A historical marker can now be seen at the location.

Sherman pursued his "scorched earth" policy aggressively through South Carolina, reminding the residents that their state had been first to secede, lighting the match that started the fire of war. Sherman's armies captured Columbia and Charleston in South Carolina. They continued northward and soon captured Fayetteville, Bentonville, Goldsboro and Raleigh in North Carolina.

Sherman's campaigns to Atlanta, then to Savannah and then north through the Carolinas devastated the Confederacy. Southern morale was taken to its lowest point. The armies of the Confederacy were split in half, never to assemble again. Southern troops in other regions began to desert, most hoping to return to their homes. Black people were fleeing their owners, hoping to make it to the North, where they anticipated far better lives. Historians estimate that as many as 25,000 enslaved black Southerners were freed as a consequence of Sherman's **March to the Sea**. Much of the agricultural and industrial capacity of the South was destroyed. It would take many decades to recover.

General Sherman's "scorched earth" policy would be imitated many times in other wars in the future. Americans would use what came to be known as a **'shock and awe'** strategy to demoralize both military and civilian inhabitants in war zones in World War Two and in places like Korea, Viet Nam and Iraq. Sherman's tactics and strategies have been studied carefully, as he broke some fundamental rules of battle. He divided his forces. He fought an aggressive, offensive campaign behind enemy lines. He chose to impose levels of destruction that would persuade the enemy that continued fighting was hopeless. His successes were the result of excellent planning, effective tactics, great organizational skills, great leadership abilities and, of course, a great advantage in manpower and Northern resources.

Grant and Lee's Epic Struggles

President Lincoln had struggled throughout the war to find the right man to lead his Union armies. When U.S. Grant ran up a string of victories in the western region, Lincoln decided to make him commander of the entire half of a million Federal troops in all of the Union armies. Lincoln appreciated Grant's aggressiveness. When Grant was defeated at the **Battle at Shiloh**, people demanded his dismissal. Lincoln replied, "I cannot spare this man. He fights".

Grant was promoted to **Lt. General**, a title not used in the American army since it was held by **George Washington**. Lincoln was able to make this move, bringing Grant back East, in part because General Sherman was being so effective, under Grant, in the West. Grant was brought back East to Washington, D.C., where he immediately began re-organizing the Federal armies and planning a massive offensive. Meanwhile, in the West, Sherman began his "March to the Sea".

Grant planned to move on to the Confederate capital at Richmond and to capture Lee's **Army of Virginia**, which would effectively end the war. Grant had a strong numerical advantage over the Army of Virginia. He planned his "**Overland Campaign**" with offensives on three fronts. He was aware that the campaign he planned would most certainly cost many lives on both sides of the line of battle. Still, he believed, as did General Sherman, that a short-term, high-casualty campaign would save many lives by significantly shortening the war. Grant also knew that, in a battle that cost thousands of lives on each side, the South had far fewer available troops to replenish their losses. He believed he could win by attrition.

Grant ordered his **General Meade** to lead the Union **Army of the Potomac** south toward Richmond, the Southern capital. "Wherever Lee goes, there will you go also" was Grant's order to Meade. General Grant intended to keep the entire Southern Army of Virginia, under Robert E. Lee, busily occupied. He wanted to prevent Lee from sending some of his troops south to help stop Sherman's march toward Atlanta. Grant then personally accompanied the force of 115,000 Union troops as they crossed the Rapidan River into Virginia. It was very early in the morning of May 4, 1864 and it marked the beginning of Lt. General Ulysses S. Grant's Overland Campaign.

The South's greatest general, Robert E. Lee, had been remarkably successful throughout the war. He was always outnumbered and out-resourced. He found victories by picking the right places to stand and fight or to fight from the woods, minimizing the impact of his lack of numerical superiority. He had been able to deceive and mislead Federal generals to his own advantage. He continued those tactics when he learned of Grant's advances in Virginia. Lee moved his forces rapidly to the tangled forest located near **Fredericksburg**, which would be known as "**The Wilderness**".

The **Battle of the Wilderness** began on the morning of May 5th, 1864, when Northern Yankees came in contact with rebel troops. The Southerners had arrived earlier and were entrenched in the woods. The brush and trees were so thick that soldiers were sometimes shooting their own people. The terrain defeated any effective use of the dominant Union cavalry. The forest seemed to be a curtain of constant gunfire. The dead blanketed the ground. Cannonballs from artillery set fire to the dry timber, which quickly became a deadly inferno in which the wounded were burned to death, being incapable of escape.

Reporters, following Grant's encampments, quoted Union **Colonel Horace Porter** saying "It was as though Christian men had turned to fiends and hell itself had usurped the place of earth". Grant lost nearly 20,000 soldiers at the Wilderness and reporters observed him sobbing grievously in his tent. The general told one reporter: "If you see the President, tell him from me that whatever happens there will be no turning back." Grant meant to see his campaign accomplish the finale to the Civil War, at whatever cost necessary.

Robert E. Lee was able to field only about half as many troops as General Meade brought to the Wilderness. His men fought valiantly, though and the terrain was Lee's friend in the battle. At the end of the first day, the battle was undecided. The Yankees had gained an advantage that put them in a good position to flank the rebels. Both sides were beneficiaries of the arrival of reinforcements overnight on May 5th.

The second day, May 6th, delivered an even more devastating series of conflicts. Both sides took everything they had to the front and the smoke from rifles and artillery was so heavy that troops, incapable of clearly viewing enemy targets, were reduced to shooting in the general direction of their opponents. Southern **General Longstreet**, one of the South's most effective leaders, was wounded around midday. Neither side, as the day progressed, was able to gain a meaningful advantage.

Late in the afternoon, Southern **General John B. Gordon**, known for his aggressiveness, was able to break through on the right flank of Union lines. The Yankees, seeing rebel troops rushing into their midst, fled back toward Grant's headquarters. The retreating troops, fearful and panicked, thought the Union forces had been defeated. General Grant calmed them, gained control of the chaos, stopped the flight of frightened troops and ultimately held his ground.

May 7th dawned with both armies holding essentially the same ground they occupied at the beginning of the battle. Grant's troops slept that night believing they had lost the offensive and would be retreating in the morning. They got up and got organized and began a slow, sad march toward the lower edge of the Wilderness. When they saw their revered leader, U. S. Grant, ride alongside them, heading to the front of the column, they realized they were still in pursuit of Lee and they were charged again with optimism and high morale. Grant was treated to enthusiastic, loud cheers.

The South won the "battle of numbers" at the Wilderness, losing about 10,000 rebel soldiers, while the Union lost nearly 18,000 troops. Grant accepted the loss and planned to continue his campaign toward Richmond. He knew he had enough men to exhaust Lee's resources, even while taking heavy losses on his own side. He was headed for **Spotsylvania Courthouse**, at the western end of the Wilderness.

The Battle of Spotsylvania Courthouse

General Lee, anticipating Grant's intentions, was able to move his forces to **Spotsylvania Courthouse** and to establish entrenchments and fortifications before Grant arrived. The two armies met on May 8th to continue their battle. Fighting in the vicinity of Spotsylvania Court House continued for 12 extremely costly days. Grant's forces repeatedly assaulted Confederate lines. He attacked on both flanks and in the center and experienced brief victories, but no significant breakthroughs. Lee's men held their ground against the furious assault.

The rebels had created a strong fortification that took the shape of a **Mule Shoe**, which projected northward toward Union lines. It seemed a place that would be vulnerable to attack, but Lee had placed imposing artillery emplacements on the perimeter and he believed it would hold. Near evening on May 10th, a young Union Colonel, **Emory Upton**, led 12 Federal regiments in a valiant open-field charge. They ran bravely and headlong into the Confederate ramparts. Upton's troops nearly broke through the Mule Shoe's barricades but were ultimately stopped and driven back. Upton survived and was promoted for his efforts.

The South's beloved **General J.E.B. (Jeb) Stuart**, leading his famous rebel cavalry regiment, attempted to block the advance of a Union cavalry advance to the north of Richmond. It was May 11th, the fourth day at Spotsylvania and Union **General Sheridan**, supported by a cavalry brigade led by **General George A. Custer**, was approaching **Yellow Tavern**. Northerners brought twice as many men to the fight as the Southerners did. Both sides suffered many losses. Sheridan and Custer were able to find victory over the rebels and the rebels lost their esteemed leader, J.E.B. Stuart, a casualty of the fighting. The overall battle remained at a standstill.

The entrenchments created by the Southerners, the Mule Shoe, had a section that formed an angle. On May 12th, in heavy, driving rains, Grant ordered **General Winfield Scott Hancock** to lead 20,000 troops in an attack on the **"Bloody Angle"**. Scott's assault would lead to twenty hours of intense, grisly fighting. Much of the combat became face-to-face, hand-to-hand, very personal engagements. **Lt. Col. Horace Porter** wrote of the battle: "Rank after rank was riddled with shot and shell and bayonet thrusts and finally sank, a mass of torn and mutilated corpses". Reports described the scene. The dead were piled on top of one another, four deep in places, some of the wounded, still alive, twitching beneath their fallen comrades.

General Robert E. Lee attempted to lead his forces personally into battle at the Bloody Angle. His troops intercepted him, as they had at the Wilderness and forced him to the rear of the battle. **General John B. Hood** took the field to lead the rebel troops. Hood was able to hold their lines and push the bluecoat's offensive back to where it began.

Two days of battle at the Bloody Angle cost Grant 18,000 soldiers. Lee lost 11,000 and they were 11,000 he could not replace. The battle, though, was indecisive. After Bloody Angle, Grant realized he would not be overcoming Lee in Spotsylvania. He moved his forces around the end of Lee's lines and left the area, putting his own army between the Southern capital, Richmond and General Lee. Lee was left with no realistic option other than to once again maneuver his forces to place them between Grant and Richmond.

The days of the battles of the Wilderness and at Spotsylvania Court House were tragic. The Army of the Potomac, led by Grant, from May 5th through May 12th, 1864, lost nearly 32,000 men, killed, wounded, missing in action or captured. It was the greatest loss ever experienced by the Union armies in any one week of the Civil War.

Grant grieved, but his offense was relentless. He led his army toward **Cold Harbor**.

Cold Harbor was only a few miles north of the Confederate capital in Richmond. As Grant approached Cold Harbor, Lee was forced once again to move his army to place himself between Grant and the capital. Yankees had control of the critical crossroads at Cold Harbor and Grant had hopes of finishing off Lee's army there. Union General Winfield Scott Hancock wasn't able to bring his corps in time for Grant to launch a fatal attack. The delay caused by Hancock's late arrival gave Lee time to establish an organized resistance. Grant's offensive was stopped. Grant brought 108,000 soldiers to Cold Harbor and lost 13,000 men. The Confederates brought 62,000 soldiers and lost 2,500 men. Lt. General Grant declared "I have always regretted that the last assault at Cold Harbor was ever made… no advantage whatever was gained to compensate for the heavy loss we sustained."

The battle at Cold Harbor was the final resting place for thousands of soldiers, both rebel and Yankee, but did not change Grant's strategy. He absorbed his losses and continued to edge his armies around Lee's forces, always moving toward Richmond. His next stop would be Petersburg.

The Siege of Petersburg

Petersburg, Virginia, lay just south of Richmond on the Appomattox River. Grant reached Petersburg in early June 1864. His men constructed a pontoon bridge almost half a mile in length and Grant's army crossed the river. Lee didn't realize the proximity of Grant's forces and Grant's people were able to begin establishing a front. Petersburg featured an intersection of several railroad lines and also lay near the James River, meaning the bustling town was an essential resource for the confederacy. Grant believed that, if he could occupy and hold Petersburg, he would most certainly be able to take Richmond. A seizure of the Confederate capital would be devastating for the South.

The **Battle of Petersburg** began on June 15th, 1864, when several thousand Federal bluecoats attacked a small force of rebels led by Southern **General P.G.T. Beauregard**. Beauregard's corps consisted of only a few thousand troops and many of his troops were boys or old men. Still, the rebels were able to hold off Yankee assaults until reinforcements arrived. Over the next few days, numbers were added to both sides as new reinforcements for both Grant and Lee joined the fray.

Grant realized, by June 18th, that it would be too costly in terms of lives and resources to continue repeating assaults on the rebel lines at Petersburg. He decided to settle in for a long siege of the Petersburg/Richmond area. His men built approximately forty miles of trenches and barricades. The siege of Petersburg would last for nine months. Several battles were fought along the lines. Throughout those many months and many conflicts, the North was able to field two to four times more troops than the South could bring to the fights. The Southern troops were in bad shape, poorly nourished, inadequately clothed and lacking the most modern rifles carried by Northerners. Still, they steadfastly held their lines, resisting the Federals for the better part of a year.

Battles were fought along the line being created by the Union armies as Grant patiently extended his forces toward Richmond. As each battle was fought, Grant's troops would continue to create longer lines and would continue to extend their supply railroad. Beginning in June and carrying through the end of 1864 battles were fought at Jerusalem Plank Road, the Crater, Weldon Railroad, Reams Station, Peebles Farm and Burgess Mill. Continuing into 1865, the lines grew longer, the supply railroad grew longer and battles were fought at Hatcher's Run, Fort Stedman, Lewis Farm, White Oak Road and Five Forks.

President Lincoln had made efforts, throughout the war, to travel to the battle fronts to meet with his generals. He boarded his steamship **River Queen** on March 24, 1865, to travel to City Point, Virginia. Along with him were his wife and their son, Tad and they were eager to see Lincoln's older son, **Robert Todd Lincoln**, who was on General Grant's staff. While the Lincoln's were in City Point, they witnessed General Lee's final offensive attack. Lee attempted, unsuccessfully, to breech Union lines in the conflict at **Fort Stedman**.

General Sherman, returning from his successful March to the Sea, joined U.S. Grant and Abraham Lincoln on the River Queen. The three planned out the final days of the Civil War.

The **Battle at Five Forks**, on April 1st, 1865, became an insurmountable defeat for the South. Grant was able to decimate Lee's position to the Southwest of Petersburg. The next day Union General Sheridan did the same thing on the right side of Lee's line. With both ends of Lee's line shredded, Grant ordered an all-out assault on all Southern Army locations. Lee had no alternative but to begin his retreat, preserving what lives he was able to save.

Lee's army departed Richmond on the evening of April 2nd and Grant's troops moved in to celebrate their ultimate victory. The Confederate capital was finally occupied by Union forces.

The Confederate Army of Northern Virginia, still led by General Lee, fled south from Richmond and Petersburg, pursued by Grant. Lee made a final, futile effort to resist Grant at Appomattox. He had hoped to rest and re-supply his remaining troops there. Grant had other plans. Union General Sheridan surprised Lee, coming from the South. General Grant's own army had approached, in darkness, from the West. Eight thousand soldiers of the **United States Colored Troops** were among Grant's forces. Meanwhile, Union **General George Custer** was attacking Confederate supply trains at Appomattox Station. Lee was surrounded and completely overwhelmed. He was finally resigned to being forced to surrender his army.

The loss left Robert E. Lee with no viable options for carrying on the fight. He said, "There is nothing left me to do but to go and see General Grant and I would rather die a thousand deaths".

Grant and Lee at Appomattox Courthouse

April 9, 1865

General Lee wrote a letter to Grant, offering to surrender. He sent copies of the letter in two directions, through two locations of the Union lines. On receipt of the letter, Grant returned a letter requesting that Lee select a location for their meeting. One of Lee's men entered the village at **Appomattox**, where the first person he encountered was **Wilmer McClean**, one of the few citizens who had not fled the village. McClean offered his home for the historical meeting between the two great generals.

Lee took his place in the **McClean House**. Grant arrived within the hour. Grant opened the meeting with a reminder to Lee of their previous meeting, when both represented the United States in the Mexican War. The agreement for Lee's surrender was formalized in two short letters. Grant's letter outlined the terms for surrender and Lee's letter confirmed his acceptance of the terms. Grant's letter was but five lines long and Lee's was even shorter, containing only three lines. **Charles Marshall**, General Lee's aide, wrote out the acceptance letter for the Confederates. **Lt. Col. Ely S. Parker**, long a friend of Grant's and a **Seneca Indian leader**, wrote the letter for Grant. Captain Robert Todd Lincoln was among those in the room.

Prior to leaving for the meeting with Grant, Lee had dressed in his finest uniform, telling his aides that he expected to be taken prisoner and "wanted to make his best appearance". Lee's troops must have been anxiously awaiting their own fates. Prisons in the North and the South, miserable places, were full of those previously captured.

Grant and Lee at Appomattox

Grant, knowing the war was near its end, intended to leave the Southerners with their dignity and with a way forward. General Grant was already considering the plans he, Lincoln and Douglass were making for the peaceful re-unification of the nation. Lee was relieved to learn that Grant's terms did not include taking prisoners. Lee himself would be released and allowed to return to his home, as would all of his men. Lee was not asked to surrender his dress sword, as was the custom. His officers were allowed to keep their horses. All of the rebel troops were to be paroled and so long as they did not again take up arms, would not be prosecuted. Lee asked if his men in the artillery and in the cavalry, who had brought their own horses and mules to the army, could keep them and take them home. Grant agreed to issue an order to that effect. It was April 9th, 1865 and Lee's **Army of Northern Virginia** had surrendered.

Horace Porter wrote that Grant, along with his staff, followed General Lee from the McClean House. They removed their hats in respect as Lee mounted his horse to ride away and Lee did the same in return.

General Ulysses S. Grant's message to his men was "The war is over. The Rebels are our countrymen again." He was already thinking about re-uniting the country, as was his President. Sadly, President Lincoln was assassinated on April 14th. He would not live to see the re-unification of his nation.

Jefferson Davis, President of the Confederate States of America, ran from the Yankees as the Union Army steadily approached the Southern capital of Richmond. He was captured by Union troops on May 10th, 1865, in Georgia. Davis was indicted for treason, but never went to trial. He spent two years in prison at **Fort Monroe** in Virginia. This book includes a brief biography of his life.

As the war wound down and more Southern forces were exhausted and defeated, the generous terms for surrender worked out by Grant and Lee would commonly be used. Communications being what they were, combatants on both sides, in locations around the Southern states, continued to fight. Confederate General Johnston's Army of Tennessee was being pursued by Union General Sherman. Johnston had to surrender, on April 26th, to Sherman. Other rebel forces continued the fight far to the south and in locations west of the Mississippi. The end of the Civil War was not a cut and dried stop to the action. The **last "named" battle** took place May 13th, 1865, at **Palmito Ranch** in Texas.

The official declaration to the end of the war and to the Union victory, did not come until August 20, 1866. **President Andrew Johnson** issued this proclamation: "I do further proclaim that the said insurrection is at an end and that peace, order, tranquility and civil authority now exists in and throughout the whole of the United States of America."

America's Civil War lasted from April of 1861 until May of 1865, though exact dates differ from one historian to another based on which events determined the actual "end of the war". Eleven states seceded from the Union to form the Confederate States of America. They elected Jefferson Davis their President. More than 10,000 military "engagements" were fought, ranging from skirmishes to huge battles. Again, numbers vary from historian to historian, but somewhere between 100 and 250 battles were considered "named, significant battles". The Battle of Gettysburg was one of the most deadly, resulting in more than 50,000 casualties and more than 7,000 deaths. By the end of the Civil War, somewhere between 750,000 and 875,000 Americans died.

The totals of all casualties during the Civil War are devastating. America lost a vast segment of a new generation of young men. Historians offer a range of estimates, and records are incomplete, but these numbers are close: The Confederate States of America lost some 485,000 men. 94,000 were killed outright in combat. Diseases killed 160,000 Southerners. Almost 200,000 rebels were wounded. On the Northern side, approximately 660,000 died. Approximately 111,000 Union troops were killed on the battlefields. The Yankees lost 225,000 to diseases. They suffered 276,000 wounded soldiers. It was common in early wars for disease and injury to be responsible for more deaths than was actual combat. In today's world, modern hygiene practices, medical care, and, especially, antibiotics would have saved a great many of the lives lost in the Civil War.

The most significant results of the war were, first, the re-unification of the United States of America and, second, the abolishment of slavery. Following President Lincoln's Emancipation Proclamation, the 13th, 14th and 15th Amendments to our Constitution were passed.

The end of the war was followed by the bitter, painful era known as **the Reconstruction**. Major socio-cultural problems, economic problems and political problems would surface as the nation tried to come back together. Among the worst of those problems would be the great difficulty of assimilating millions of America's Black citizens into the "free society". Most of the formerly enslaved new citizens were lacking in education, owned no property, were impoverished and had no useful training outside of common menial labor skills. Furthermore, in much of the South, the former slaves were not welcomed as free citizens and many obstacles were thrown in their paths. Many former slaves were destined to continue to work the farms and plantations, often laboring under their former "owners".

The Assassination of Abraham Lincoln

Robert E. Lee surrendered to U.S. Grant on April 9, 1865, an event that appeared to have sealed a victory for the North in the great American Civil War. Washingtonians were exuberantly celebrating in the streets. As the news traveled across the country, the nation itself began to either grieve, if a Southerner or to celebrate, if a Northerner. Spirits were very high on the side of the Union and very, very low in the hearts of pro-slavery Southerners.

Abraham Lincoln delivered a speech, on April 11th, in which he remarked that his administration would be seeking legislation to confirm voting rights for black men. The idea of allowing women to vote was still not considered realistic. A well-known and popular actor was in the audience. His name was **John Wilkes Booth** and he was fervently pro-slavery. Booth was planning a series of assassinations. His targets would be Lincoln himself as well as Lincoln's Vice President and Secretary of State.

John Wilkes Booth was the son of Junius Brutus Booth and Mary Ann Holmes. The Booth family immigrated from England, where they had a long history as popular and well-known actors. John Wilkes, born May 10th, 1838, was the ninth of ten children. When John was eight years old, the community was scandalized upon learning that Junius had eloped with Mary Ann while neglecting to first divorce his first wife. John, known to be passionately proud of his famous family's name, was most defensive of any implications of impropriety.

John Wilkes Booth followed the well-worn path of his parents and siblings into the acting arts. He was a physically attractive, athletic person and became a popular favorite among those who attended theater productions. Booth was known in many American cities, as he traveled through them with various plays. He was known to be especially appreciated by the ladies.

Booth was a special favorite as he traveled the South, performing in all the major cities. He was known to be an adamant supporter of slavery and to believe strongly that the white race was superior to other races. He spoke openly of his hatred for Abraham Lincoln. Booth had volunteered to serve in a Virginia militia group. As a participant of, that militia, he was present for the capture of and for the hanging of, abolitionist John Brown.

Booth gathered a small group of like-minded pro-Southerners. They wanted to do something spectacular. Something that would change the course of national events. Something that might still save the cause of the South. The group planned a series of abductions, intending to kidnap the President. All of the plans failed to materialize or were unsuccessful. Booth did not give up. When John Wilkes Booth stood in the crowd,

April 11th, 1865 and listened to Lincoln voice his plans to seek voting rights for negroes, John was outraged. He made this comment to one of his co-conspirators: "Now, by God, I will put him through. That is the last speech he will ever make". Only three short days later, Booth would act on his promise.

The Booth-led cabal conspired to assassinate Abraham Lincoln, his Vice President Andrew Johnson and his Secretary of State, William Seward. Booth took the assignment to personally assassinate Lincoln. The group of co-conspirators met frequently at the boarding house home of **Mary Surratt**, wherein they made their nefarious plans. Included were David Herold, Mary Surratt, Mary's son John Surratt, George Atzerodt and Booth himself.

Mary Todd Lincoln wanted to see the British comedy **"An American Cousin"**, which was playing at Washington's **Ford Theater**. **Laura Keene**, famous actress, was in the starring role. Lincoln had hoped to be accompanied to the theater by his greatest general, U.S. Grant, but Grant had left town to visit a son. The President and Mary were, instead, accompanied by young army **Major Henry Rathbone** and Rathbone's fiancée, **Clara Harris**.

His familiarity with the lay-out of Ford Theater and his well-known appearance, made it easy for Booth to gain entry and to access the seating areas. Booth, knowing the play well, waited for a point at which he knew the audience would be loud. He slipped into the back of Lincoln's box seats. He carried with him, in his left hand, a dagger. In his right hand Booth held a small Derringer pistol. He silently drew, from behind, very near the President. He fired the Derringer from a distance of only six inches.

Booth Assassinates Lincoln

As the President slumped forward, Henry Rathbone was stabbed multiple times as he attempted to detain Booth. Booth then dramatically vaulted from the railing of the President's box. His leg was caught up in a flag, which caused him to fall awkwardly to the stage, breaking his leg. He shouted to the astonished crowd as he waved his dagger above him. It would be his last stage performance. As he waved the dagger, some reports claimed he declared loudly "Sic semper tyrannis", Latin for "thus always to tyrants". Others reported that he shouted "The South is avenged!"

Booth ran, limping markedly, from the theater. He mounted his waiting horse and fled toward Virginia, back to the South. Booth would be captured by Union cavalry two weeks later.

President Lincoln suffered a single, mortal bullet wound to his head. The projectile entered his head just behind his left ear. It ripped through his brain and was lodged just behind his right eye. Physicians arrived and quickly realized that the President had been dealt a fatal blow. They enlisted the assistance of citizens to carry Lincoln's dying body across the street. He was taken to the **Petersen House**, which was, at the time, a boarding house.

Overnight the physicians did what they could in service of their dying President. They attempted to warm his deathly cold extremities. They removed large clots of blood that continuously formed over his wound. They drained excessive brain fluid and brain matter, hoping to reduce pressure on the injured brain. Hemorrhaging was constant.

Armed guards protected the Petersen House through the long, devastatingly sad night. A long list of Cabinet members, military leaders and prominent members of Congress passed through the room in which their President lay dying. Abraham Lincoln quietly passed away at 7:22 a.m. on the morning of April 15th, 1865. He was only 56 years old. In the room with him were Senator Charles Sumner, General Henry Wager Halleck, General Montgomery C. Meigs, General Richard James Oglesby, Secretary of War Edwin Stanton and Lincoln's son Robert.

Booth's co-conspirators failed to complete their assignments. **Secretary of State Seward's** home was breached by Booth accomplice **Lewis Powell**. Powell managed to assault Seward with a knife. Seward, due to prior injury, was wearing a neck brace which probably saved his life. Seward's son interrupted Powell's attack. Seward survived. Another Booth accomplice, **George Atzerodt**, lost his courage and chose to cancel his planned attack on **Vice President Andrew Johnson**.

John Wilkes Booth met up with co-conspirator **David Herold** and both escaped through Maryland. The state of Maryland had many Southern sympathizers and the two hoped to find assistance. Booth located **Dr. Samuel Mudd**, who treated his broken leg. Mudd would later be convicted of participating in the conspiracy, though it is unlikely he had any part in the incident prior to the arrival of Booth at his door.

Herold and Booth stayed together and hid out for a few days in thick woods near the Zekiah Swamp in Maryland. A reward of $100,000 had been offered for the capture of

Booth and there were many people hoping to catch up with him. The two conspirators made their way from Maryland to a tobacco barn in Virginia, where they were hiding when Union troops located them on April 26th. Herold quickly gave himself up to the soldiers, but John Wilkes Booth was determined to resist capture.

Army troops and other law enforcement agencies had been instructed to attempt to capture Booth alive, so he could stand trial. When Booth refused to give himself up, soldiers set fire to the barn, planning to burn him out. One report indicates that one of the troops, **Sergeant Boston Corbett**, sighted Booth and shot him. Other reports suggest that Booth, in a final act of defiance, shot himself. In either case, he was taken to the porch of the nearby farm home, on which spot he soon died. His body was identified by a physician who had previously operated on Booth.

All of the conspirators to the assassination were ultimately captured and imprisoned. David Herold, Lewis Powell, Mary Surratt and George Atzerodt were all tried by a military tribunal. They were sentenced to death and were executed at the Washington Arsenal.

President Lincoln's assassination brought the Union to its knees. The entire Northern population grieved. Lincoln's body was returned to his long-time home in Springfield, Illinois. He was carried home on a funeral train which took a "long way" route back to Illinois from Washington, making possible many stops along the way. Hundreds of thousands of grieving Americans paid homage to the passing train. Lincoln was the first American President to be assassinated. Sadly, there have since been three more Presidents added to that list.

Jefferson Davis

President of the Confederate States of America

Jefferson Davis and Varina Howell Davis

Jefferson Finis Davis was born in Kentucky on June 3, 1808. He was the last of ten children and was given the middle name "Finis", Latin for "final" or "end". He was named in honor of American patriot Thomas Jefferson. His father was **Samuel Emory Davis**, who was born in Georgia and had been a soldier in the **American Revolution**. Jefferson Davis's family moved to Mississippi when he was three-years-old, where they lived on a plantation named **Rosemont**. When he was seven, Jefferson was sent to be educated at a school in Kentucky which was operated by Dominican Catholics. In spite of his young age, Jefferson made the trip from Mississippi to Kentucky on horseback. On his arrival, he became the smallest pupil enrolled at the school.

Jefferson, who had left the Dominicans at the age of 13 to enter Transylvania College, departed that college in 1824. His father died that year and his older brother, Joseph, then became his role model and benefactor. Joseph was a very successful and affluent plantation manager and an attorney. Jefferson left the college when Joseph secured for him an appointment to the **U.S. Military Academy** at West Point. He was not a stellar student, but he did graduate after four years, finishing in the lower third of his class rankings. While at West Point, Jefferson was reprimanded and placed under "house arrest" for his part in what became known as the **"Eggnog Riot"** of 1826. The riot, and the punishment, were related to the illicit smuggling of whiskey into the barracks by the cadets.

Soon after graduating, Jefferson was assigned a post in an infantry regimented based in the state of Wisconsin. While in the infantry, he served very briefly as a lieutenant in the **Black Hawk War**. A man he would one day know all too well, Abraham Lincoln, also served briefly in the Black Hawk War. **Albert Sidney Johnston** was Jefferson's best friend both at the college and at West point. Johnston would later become a CSA general under Davis when the Civil War was fought. It is likely Davis was also very familiar with **Robert E. Lee** and **Joseph E. Johnston**, both of who followed in the class behind him at West Point. Both would become confederate generals in the Civil War.

During the Black Hawk War, Lt. Davis's superior officer was **Zachary Taylor**. Taylor would become an American President and also was the father of **Sarah Knox Taylor**. Acquaintances at the time described Jefferson as being an attractive, clever, athletic and popular young gentleman. He was also described, in not so glowing terms, as being impulsive and captive to a fiery anger. Jefferson soon fell deeply in love with **Sarah Taylor**. Sarah's father, Zachary Taylor, was not a big admirer of Davis and the two had a history of disagreements. At one point, Taylor became so angry with Davis that he challenged Davis to a duel, a challenge that the hot-tempered Davis accepted. Fortunately, before any actual conflict could occur, more responsible minds cooled the combatants down and the duel was not carried out.

Following the **Black Hawk War**, he was posted in Arkansas, where he resigned his commission and left the army. His brother Joseph set him up as a planter on land near Vicksburg, Mississippi. Jefferson and Sarah were married. Sarah's father did not attend the wedding. Sadly, both of the newly weds contracted malaria. Davis survived, but Sarah died only three months after their marriage.

Jefferson Davis was devastated by the death of his beloved new bride. He withdrew to his Mississippi plantation, **Briarfield** and became more or less of a recluse for several years. He built a cotton plantation out of a wilderness. He was an avid reader of world literature and of constitutional law books.

Davis eventually, after nearly eight years of solitude, re-entered the society of the South. He was interested by then in politics and was a fervent advocate of both states' rights and slavery. They were the primary issues that would fuel the coming Civil War. Davis was a delegate to the 1840 and 1842 Democratic state conventions. He was unsuccessful in his attempt to run for the state legislature in 1843. In 1845, though, he was victorious in his campaign to gain a seat in the U.S. House of Representatives.

Jefferson Davis, having somewhat recovered from his grief after losing Sarah, fell in love with **Varina Howell**. Varina was a Mississippi girl who was 18 years younger than Jefferson and her grandfather had been governor of New Jersey. Varina would deliver four sons, none of whom would survive to adulthood, and two daughters. She was notoriously unhappy in the role of a Southern politician's wife, but women in those times, especially in the South, followed the paths of their husbands. She often referred to herself as a "half-breed", with her heart being half in the North and half in the South. Her father was a prominent citizen of New Jersey and her grandfather had fought in the American Revolution. Sarah's "half-breed" reference may have also applied to her "olive complexion", which was viewed with disapproval from many Southerners.

As Jefferson's career progressed and he served in the U.S. House of Representatives, the couple spent much more time in Washington, D.C. and that was where Varina felt most at home. Varina's father, William, who lived in Mississippi, owned several "house slaves", so Varina knew that culture well. William went broke, bankrupt, as a consequence of the **"Panic of 1837"**. The family lost everything and relied on the support of affluent relatives. Varina had to learn household skills for cooking, cleaning, sewing and caring for her six siblings. Still, a wealthy relative financed her education at an elite girl's college. She was an avid reader and she acquired more academic knowledge than was generally characteristic of "Southern belles" of those times. Southern ladies were not expected to participate in "learned" discussions or to be active in political debates. After the Civil War, Varina became a writer. She finished Jefferson's autobiography.

Jefferson Davis, long before the Civil War, became one of the wealthiest of the plantation owners in the state of Mississippi and owned upwards of seventy slaves. By the end of the Civil War, Jefferson's properties would be home to almost 140 slaves. The wives of plantation owners were often involved in management of the slaves, as was Varina. She provided medical care, when necessary and she made clothing for the enslaved workers. Unlike her husband, Jefferson, Varina knew the names of all of the slaves. She once referred to the black workers as "human beings, with their frailties".

When the **Civil War** began, and her husband was chosen to be the **President of the CSA**, Varina had to move back to the South. She was opposed to the war and she did not believe her husband had the right character to be President. She served as the **"First Lady"** of the CSA, but she longed to be back in Washington. Her time in the South was made much more difficult because she was blessed with an "olive complection", which was too dark for many Southerners. She was often referred to, never to her face, as a "squaw" or a "mulatto". Varina was criticized for continuing to correspond with friends in the North. She occupied herself during the war by helping to care for the vast numbers of confederate wounded.

Varina was been criticized for her comments that "maybe women are not inferior" to men and that "perhaps it was not a good idea to deny women suffrage". Jefferson had a history of rumored inappropriate relationships with a series of women. The two were often separated for long periods of time and the separations were not always amicable.

Before the Civil War, in 1846, Jefferson Davis left his seat in Congress so that he could serve the U.S. in the **Mexican-American War**. He was commissioned as a colonel and he commanded the **First Mississippi Volunteers**. **General Zachary Taylor** led the Americans at the **Battle of Buena Vista**, a major battle of that war at **Angostura Pass** in Mexico. The Mexican army, led by **General Santa Anna**, far outnumbered the Americans. Santa Anna demanded that the Americans immediately surrender. General Taylor reportedly responded by sending a courier to Santa Anna to "Tell him to go to Hell!". Early the next day, Santa Anna launched at attack with 15,000 Mexican soldiers. Taylor had only 5,000 American troops, but was able to hold the line. Meanwhile, Jefferson Davis led his Mississippi riflemen in a tactically skilled defense of the critical Mexican flank. The Mexicans had to retreat. Jefferson Davis became an American hero based on his excellent performance at Angostura Pass. His name became known world-wide.

Davis was severely wounded in that war and returned home to recover. When he was well enough, he pursued and won a seat in the U.S. Senate, representing the state of Mississippi. He was made Chairman of the Military Affairs Committee and began acquiring the experience that would lead him to the Presidency of the Confederate States of America. **President Franklin Pierce** appointed Davis to be **Secretary of War**, which further prepared him for leading the CSA. In that position, he worked to strengthen the U.S. military. He increased the size of the American fighting forces, which he may have later regretted, as he would find himself fighting against them. He worked to increase the range and strength of American Coastal defenses. By 1857, Franklin Pierce was out of office and Davis had returned to the U.S. Senate. As tensions rose between the North and the South, Jefferson traveled widely to speak to supporters of both sides, encouraging continued unity for all. He did not want to see the Union split apart. Davis believed the Constitution gave "states' rights" authority to individual states to determine their own regulations regarding the institution of slavery.

When Abraham Lincoln was elected and South Carolina seceded, Jefferson Davis continued to argue against any further secessions. His own state, though, against his advice and his wishes, seceded from the United States on January 21, 1861, following the secession of Mississippi by only twelve days. Davis made a passionate and eloquent speech to the U.S. Senate, including an emotional farewell, as he knew he would have to leave Washington to return to his Brierfield plantation. His wife, Varina, argued to have them both stay in Washington, but she acquiesced to his directions and followed him back to the South.

Davis quickly returned to Brierfield, his Mississippi plantation. He was appointed, before he even arrived home, to lead the Mississippi military forces, such as they were, as a Major General. The **Confederate Convention** was being held in Montgomery,

Alabama, though and at that convention Jefferson Davis was chosen to serve as "provisional president" of the **Confederate States of America**. Davis was expecting to play a significant role in the imminent war with the North, but he expected to be a military leader in the field. He had, in fact, hoped to be the commander-in-chief of Southern forces. His expectation was realistic, as he offered considerable military experience and carried the label "hero" for his role at Angostura Pass in Mexico.

Davis was inaugurated as president of the Confederacy on February 18th, 1861. He delivered an eloquent speech. In that speech, he made it clear that his hope was that the North would allow the South to separate itself from the Union and to live according to its own moral codes. He said:

"I enter upon the duties of the office to which I have been chosen with the hope that the beginning of our career as a Confederacy may not be obstructed by hostile opposition to our enjoyment of the separate existence and independence we have asserted and which, with the blessing of Providence, we intend to maintain."

President Davis promptly took action to try and avoid open war with the North. He sent emissaries to Washington to try and negotiate peace with Lincoln. Lincoln would not see those emissaries, believing it would be a mistake to recognize, legitimize or validate the Southern government. Lincoln's ever-present first priority was to try to keep all of America's states in the Union. He questioned the constitutional right of the states to secede.

Lincoln sent U.S. Navy ships to deliver supplies to the Union garrison posted at **Fort Sumter**, near Charleston, South Carolina. Lincoln gave Davis prior notice of the arrival of the ships and supplies and informed Davis that U.S. ships and troops at the fort would not fire upon Southerners unless the Southerners fired the first shots. On April 12th, 1861, Jefferson Davis ordered that Fort Sumter be bombarded. Those were the shots that officially triggered the beginning of America's great Civil War.

Davis was faced with insurmountable challenges. He was burdened with numerous critical priorities, none of which could be ignored or delayed. He had to coordinate creation of a brand-new government. He had to plan to fight a war against an enemy that was far better prepared and equipped. Lincoln's North had more and better railways. More and better waterways. Much more manufacturing capacity. Lincoln had a navy. Lincoln had a fully-functioning government in place.

The Yankees had triple the number of white males in the population and the South would not be able to count on its black population to support their efforts. Southerners feared the consequences of the war on the morale of the enslaved black people. Would the Northern aggression tempt the slaves to escape, or worse yet, to revolt? All available white males would be expected to leave their farms and plantations to fight with the confederate army. Wives and children would be left home alone. Would they be able to manage the slaves and keep the agricultural economy of the South alive? Southern women, especially more affluent women, were traditionally expected to be "Southern belles". They were to try to be attractive and to manage house slaves. They were not expected to be well-educated or to participate in financial or other management-related tasks. It would all be left on their shoulders as their men left to fight the war. Would the slaves "behave"? No one knew, but everyone had fears of slave rebellions.

Davis had a single military advantage. The confederate army would be fighting a defensive war. They did not have to invade the North or to acquire any new lands from the North. They had only to defend what they now considered to be their "homeland". It is much easier, in most military opinions, to fight a defensive war. Davis would also be fortunate in that, as the war progressed, it became obvious that the South had better military leadership than did the North. Lincoln would struggle for years in his effort to discover effective generals to lead his forces. He would be disappointed time and time again by his choices.

In the aftermath of the Fort Sumter attack, Davis focused on building factories to produce military resources such as rifles, cannons, gunpowder and all kinds of ammunition. The South began to upgrade railroad lines and build railroad cars to move troops and military resources. They re-built old navy yards to begin building armored gunboats. Davis sent a revolving retinue of agents to Europe where they tried to buy military products and to secure financing for the war.

Probably the best decision made by President Davis was to appoint **General Robert E. Lee** to command the critically important **Army of Northern Virginia**. Lee was a brilliant tactician. His army was located right across the river from Washington, D.C. and Lee knew how to "thrust and parry" his forces. Lee's movements made it necessary for Lincoln to hold large numbers of troops in the immediate area to prevent any possible Southern occupation of the Union capital.

Davis was also fearful that the Union army might overtake forces protecting the confederate capital city of Richmond, Virginia. He pressured Lee to commit large numbers of troops to defend Richmond, which left the Western theater of war weakly defended. The result was the ultimate loss of Vicksburg, a critical intersection of railroad lines and a point of control of the Mississippi waterway. The loss of Vicksburg was a major turning point in the war and it was a fatal loss for the South.

Union victory in the Civil War was most likely inevitable. When Lee surrendered to Grant, it was against Davis's instructions. Davis gathered his remaining cabinet and fled to the South. His family, including his wife Varina, accompanied him. With Union army soldiers approaching, Varina covered Davis with her shawl and he attempted to slip away, hoping to be perceived as a woman. His height and build gave him away and he was captured. It was May 10th, 1865. The war was over for Jefferson Davis. He was taken near Irwinville, Georgia and removed to a prison camp where he was put in leg-irons and installed in a damp, cold cell. Public outrage over his condition pressured the Yankees to improve his living quarters, but he would be detained as a prisoner for two more years.

Jefferson Davis hoped to be tried for treason. Numerous lawyers offered to represent him. The U.S. government indicted Davis for treason, but the case never went to trial. The U.S. government introduced a series of delays and more delay was caused by the impeachment of President Johnson. The concern expressed by some Northerners was that a treason trial might actually end up confirming that, according to the original American Constitution, Southern states may actually have had the legal right to secede. It was a potential outcome that would have made the Northern war against the South illegal. Davis was eventually, in May of 1867, released without charges. He was bailed out of jail by Northerners, many of whom were staunch abolitionists, because they believed he deserved to either have a speedy trial or he should, in the interest of re-uniting the nation, be released. Released he was.

On his release, due to deteriorating health, Jefferson and Varina ventured to Canada, where he planned to regain his strength. They made several trips to Europe, also in an effort to regain his former healthy constitution. They moved to Memphis, Tennessee, where, for a few years, Davis served as president of an insurance company. He finally, in 1877, retired. He returned to his beloved Mississippi. Varina and Jefferson lived separately for an extended period. He was living on a small plantation estate named **Beauvoir** near Biloxi, Mississippi, on the Gulf of Mexico. The estate was offered to Jefferson by **Sarah Dorsey**, a widowed heiress. Varina very much disapproved of the relationship between Jefferson and Sarah, but eventually joined them at Beauvoir. Sarah and Varina became friends after Jefferson's death. Both were writers and had been classmates in school.

Throughout the remainder of his life, Davis was a defender of the confederacy. He never gave up his belief that states' rights gave the South a legal basis to secede. Supporters wanted him to run for the U.S. Senate again, but he would not apologize for his part in the war and his citizenship would not be restored until after his death.

Jefferson Davis died in New Orleans on December 6th, 1889. He was 81-years-old.

Jefferson Davis Quotes

- Never be haughty to the humble or humble to the haughty.

- I worked night and day for twelve years to prevent the war, but I could not. The North was mad and blind and would not let us govern ourselves and so the war came.

- It was one of the compromises of the Constitution that the slave property in the Southern States should be recognized as property throughout the United States.

- If the Confederacy fails, there should be written on its tombstone: Died of a Theory.

Jefferson Davis and Slavery

Jefferson Davis was a promoter of "states' rights" and of slavery throughout his adult life. As a politician he adamantly argued that each state was entitled, by the American constitution, to determine its own rules regarding slavery. He believed that, as the nation expanded and added more states, the institution of slavery should be permitted to expand as well. Davis defined slaves as "property" and he argued that our Constitution guaranteed citizens protection of their property. He said the Constitution promised that no one could legally take his "property" away from him. Davis also argued that the Constitution guaranteed the Southern states the right to secede from the Union, if they so desired. Davis may have been technically right about this last idea.

Davis was born in Kentucky, only about one hundred miles from the birthplace of Abraham Lincoln. He graduated from West Point in 1828, became a plantation owner by 1836 and owned more than 70 slaves by the 1840's. His performance during the Mexican-American War built his reputation and he entered politics. He represented Mississippi in office and he was opposed to secessionist plans being proposed by Southern states.

Jefferson Davis clearly believed that black people were intellectually inferior to white people. He said, as a Senator, that slavery was "a form of civil government for those who, by their nature (being black), are not fit to govern themselves". He believed the Bible identified black people as being best suited for slavery, saying "we recognize the negro (in "God's book") as being our inferior, fitted expressly for servitude".

He is known to have commended good treatment of slaves by their owners. Historians report that he was not known for cruel treatment of slaves. He seemed to have a good relationship with the overseers, themselves slaves, whom he "owned", who managed his agricultural properties. Records show that corporal punishment (physical discipline) was not permitted on Davis's properties. "Overworking" of slaves was forbidden and overseers were instructed to be certain that slaves were well-fed. His slaves were generally managed by other slaves and the outcome seems to have been quite productive. On Davis's plantations, slaves who misbehaved were tried by a jury made up of other slaves. Davis was known to have commuted harsh sentences.

Southern society of those times had developed into a system in which many slaves were "rented out" by their owners. The "renting season" began after the new year each year, as home and plantation owners tried to fill out their staffing needs for the oncoming year. The Davis family participated routinely in the practice and usually had rented slaves working in their residence. While serving as President of the Confederacy, Davis's wife Varina managed fifteen to twenty household slaves, some most probably "rented" from other owners. It would have been bad practice, in societal terms, to badly abuse the "property" of another owner.

Jeff Davis grew up with a slave named **James Pemberton**. James became a plantation overseer, supervising other working slaves under the authority of Davis. Pemberton managed Brierfield successfully until his death in 1852. Following the death of Pemberton, Davis relied heavily on the services of **Ben Montgomery**, another of his slaves. Davis made no provisions to free either James Pemberton or Ben Montgomery, though their service to him had been invaluable.

Davis is known to have advised good treatment of slaves by other owners. His belief that white people were innately superior led to his related belief that white people were responsible for good treatment of what he considered the inferior black race. On the other hand, he is known to have supported the lynching of slaves, if those slaves displayed "vile temper" or "low instincts" or "base purpose". He believed that black people, left on their own, would not be able to form a civilized society. Many would argue that life for black people on many Southern plantations did not reflect governance by a "civilized society".

In an address to Congress in 1861, Davis boasted that, due to "the increasing care and attention for the well-being and comfort of the 'laboring class' (slaves)", the African slaves grew in number from around 600,000 when the Constitution was written, to more than four million slaves. He said the "brutal savages" had been "elevated", by the good treatment of them by Southerners, to become "docile, intelligent and civilized agricultural laborers". He claimed the slaves were treated to "bodily comforts" and "careful religious instruction". It is very unlikely many slaves would have been in agreement with his descriptions of their conditions.

During the Civil War, Jefferson Davis's family rented out a number of slaves to be used to assist in digging entrenchments around Vicksburg. Plantation owners were paid $1.00 per day, by the Confederate government, for slave workers. Confederate soldiers at the time were being paid only about $15.00 per month, making the slaves, in the opinion of the soldiers, worth twice as much as a white infantryman. It did not go down easily with the troops.

When U.S. Grant laid siege to Vicksburg and let it be known that fugitive slaves would be welcomed at his lines, Jefferson Davis's plantation was clearly at risk. It wouldn't be long before Davis's Brierfield itself would be attacked by the Yankees. Slaves in the South had an "underground telegraph", a word-of-mouth communications system that passed information from field to field, plantation to plantation. Davis's slaves knew what was happening on the battlefields around Vicksburg. They knew that U.S. Grant would protect them, if they could make it to his lines.

Jeff Davis was already suffering as he had to accept the loss of Vicksburg and loss of control of the Mississippi and the loss of some 30,000 Southern troops. He was further devastated on learning that Yankees had occupied Brierfield. His 137 slaves had fled, with some stealing whatever they could carry. They were running headlong for the Union lines. Only half a dozen adult slaves stayed on the plantation.

Ben Montgomery, the slave who had been an overseer for Jeff's brother, Joseph and for Jeff, was soon hired by Union Rear Admiral David Porter. Porter paid Montgomery to work on Union military gunboats. He described Montgomery as "an ingenious mechanic". Admiral Porter also hired Ben Montgomery's son, Isaiah. Isaiah served the Admiral as a cabin boy aboard a Union gunboat. Montgomery's older son, William Thornton, was enlisted in the United States Navy.

Near the end of the war, as federal troops surrounded Richmond, Davis finally compromised his racist views of black people and authorized allowing slaves to sign up to serve the army of the confederacy. It was much too late to help his cause. He was, by then, desperate. He sold two of his fine horses for more than $7,000. He also sold two remaining slaves, receiving $1,612 for them.

Jefferson Davis's home state of Mississippi refused to ratify the 13th Amendment, abolishing slavery, until 1995. Then they neglected to complete the paperwork on the ratification until 2013.

Robert E. Lee

Confederate General

General Robert E. Lee with his famous horse Traveller

In the year 1639 a man named Richard Lee I, came to America from Shropshire, England. He settled in the colony of Virginia. 168 years later, or after the passing of about eight generations, on January 19, 1807, **Robert Edward Lee** was the fourth child born to **Henry Lee III** and **Anne Hill Carter Lee**. The Lee family lived on a plantation known as **Stratford Hall**, located in Westmoreland County, Virginia. At the time of his birth, the family was socially prominent and relatively well-to-do.

Some of Robert's ancestors were signers of the American **Declaration of Independence**. Some served in the Congress of the new United States of America. Robert's father, Henry, fought in the **American Revolution**, where he was respected by, befriended by and commanded by **General George Washington**. Henry Lee represented himself well in the revolution and earned the nickname **Colonel "Light-Horse Harry" Lee**. Unfortunately, he also is remembered for writing General Washington a bad check, perhaps presaging Henry's future financial failures.

Henry "Light-Horse Harry" Lee had a checkered reputation as a military leader during the revolution. He executed some tactically excellent maneuvers and contributed to victories in battle. He also, though, built a reputation for being brutal and impulsive. He was charged with insubordination, but the charge was dismissed. After his force was instrumental in assisting **General Anthony Wayne** in a victory at **Stony Point** fort in New York, in 1778, Lee captured three American deserters. He had one deserter hung until dead and then he ordered the man decapitated and the head sent to General Washington. In another incident, Henry Lee forced a glowing-hot shovel to a captive's feet, torturing the man for information.

Ann Hill Carter, Robert's mother, was a product of one of Virginia's wealthiest and most prominent families. Colonel Henry Lee, his father, in addition to his famous revolutionary war performance, had served as Governor of Virginia. Henry Lee was active in the new country's political arena until his reputation was stained by his financial shortcomings.

The Lee plantation was not profitable enough to survive Robert's father's bad investments and poor business management. The family went broke and Henry Lee went to debtor's prison. It was 1809 and Robert was only two years old. When Robert's father was released from prison, the family moved to Alexandria, which, at that time, was part of the District of Columbia. Alexandria would later become a part of the state of Virginia. Robert E. Lee grew up to consider himself a life-long devoted "Virginian".

The Lee family benefited from the support of Robert's mother Ann's affluent family. Shortly after the family moved to Alexandria, Henry Lee, still personally plagued by financial problems, moved by himself to the West Indies. Ann, though, gave birth to her sixth child, Mildred, before Henry fled. Robert, at the age of six, was left fatherless and the family became dependent on the generosity of relatives.

Henry Lee was, after the war, a tormented man. He was involved in failed land speculation schemes. He sold properties he did not actually own. He chained his doors so that those who sought payment from him could not enter. He was often away from home for long periods, avoiding those who pursued him. Henry Lee would return briefly to America, but would move permanently to the West Indies when Robert was still only six years old. Henry died in 1818 after coming back to America, where he stayed in the home of Revolutionary War hero **Nathaniel Greene**. Robert had little opportunity to establish a meaningful relationship with his distant father.

Robert was blessed with the advantage of having prominent, affluent relatives. Those relatives stepped in to aid the struggling family after Henry fled to the West Indies. **William Henry Fitzhugh** was an uncle to Robert and owned the house where Anne Lee and her children lived. Fitzhugh solicited an appointment to the **United States Military Academy** at West Point, Maryland, for Robert. Robert entered West Point in 1825 and performed very well during his tenure there. He graduated second in his class and was one of only five classmates who studied at the Academy for those four years while receiving not a single demerit. After graduating in June of 1829, Lee was commissioned as a second lieutenant and was assigned to the Corps of Engineers.

Lee returned to Virginia after graduating from West Point, where he became interested in a young lady named **Mary Anna Randolph Custis**. Mary came from a wealthy and prominent family. Mary's father, **George Washington Parke Custis**, was a grandson to Martha Washington. The family took great pride in their relationship to the nation's first president.

Lee was initially refused permission to court and wed Mary, apparently because her father did not like the idea of the son of the disgraced "Light-Horse Harry Lee" being brought into his family. Later, the two gained the approval of Mary's father and were married. Their union would produce four girls and three boys and would last for 39 years.

Lt. Lee was assigned to supervise engineering work at Fort Pulaski, Fort Monroe and Fort Wool. He also directed work in surveying the southern Michigan border. In 1834, Lee was posted at the office of the chief engineer in Washington, D.C., from which location he would work for the next three years. While in that position, he supervised engineering work all over the MidWest. He helped survey the border between Ohio and Michigan. He was involved in creation of the St. Louis harbor and worked on projects on the Mississippi and the Missouri rivers. His work was good and he was promoted to captain of engineers.

The United States, on May 13, 1846, declared war on Mexico. The U.S. government claimed that Mexicans had attacked Americans in Texas. Ownership of the part of Texas that was involved was in dispute, with Mexico refusing to acknowledge that it belonged to the United States. In fact, Mexico was also antagonized by the admission of Texas as an American state. **President Polk**, supported by a vote of the Senate, declared war.

Robert E. Lee went to Mexico under the command of American **General Winfield Scott**. Scott's forces pursued a campaign that ultimately led all the way from Veracruz to Mexico City itself. Lee served as a top aide to Scott and was considered a major factor in victories at the **Battles of Cerro Gordo**, **Contreras**, **Churubusco** and at **Chapultepec**, where he was wounded. He revealed tactical skills that would be recognized and rewarded as the Civil War began. He was able to move his command through routes over rough terrain which the Mexicans believed to be impassable. His ability to be successful in bad terrain would once again be a factor during the Civil War.

Lee was promoted, throughout the Mexican war, from captain to brevet major, then brevet lieutenant colonel and finally to brevet full colonel. The prefix "brevet" meant that Lee was promoted to battlefield authority and command, but was not given the salary increases associated with those promotions. In essence, the "brevet" promotions were temporary and, after the war, Lee was dropped back to his original status as captain. He would later be transferred to a cavalry group and would be promoted at that time. General Winfield Scott came to know Robert E. Lee well and would later state that Lee was "the very best soldier that I ever saw in the field". Scott would later find himself on the other side of the battle lines from Lee in the Civil War.

It was during the Mexican-American War that Robert E. Lee would meet, for the first time, **Ulysses S. Grant**. Both men performed well in Mexico. They would not meet again until Lee was left with no option but to surrender his **Army of Virginia** to Grant at **Appomattox**.

In the three years after the Mexican War, Lee was posted at Fort Carroll in Baltimore. His duties were varied and he was sent to Florida for part of that time, where he did surveying and mapping tasks. As the 1850's began and the tensions surrounding the issue of slavery steadily increased, Lee was assigned to be Superintendent of the **United States Military Academy**. Records suggest Lee enjoyed spending time with the West Point cadets. His son, **George Washington Custis Lee**, attended the Academy during Lee's tenure there. Young Lee graduated first in his class, one place higher than had his esteemed father. The older Lee was posted at West Point from 1852 to 1855. The curriculum at West Point is heavily colored by their Motto: "Duty, Honor, Country" and by their seven essential Army values: "Loyalty, duty, respect, selfless service, honor, integrity and personal courage". All indications are that Robert E. Lee took those values very seriously.

After completing his duties at West Point, Lee served as a lieutenant colonel in the 2nd Cavalry in the state of Texas. He was second in command and was very much gratified by being transferred out of the engineering corps over to a combat-ready command. In Texas, Lee served under **Colonel Albert Sydney Johnston**. They were kept busy protecting American settlers from raiding Apache and Comanche Indians.

Lee happened to be in Washington, D.C., in 1859, when the infamous abolitionist **John Brown** executed his attack on the U.S. Army Arsenal at **Harper's Ferry**. Lee was promptly ordered to proceed the short distance to Virginia with a detachment of U.S. Marines. He coordinated, the next morning, the termination of Brown's unsuccessful raid and captured the severely wounded Brown. Brown was soon charged with murder, treason and insurrection and was executed by hanging.

Robert E. Lee was serving in Texas when **Abraham Lincoln** was elected. Seven states almost immediately seceded from the Union. Lee was not a supporter of secession. Texas seceded in February, 1861. American **General David Twiggs** surrendered all American forces to the Texans, who were, at that point, no longer citizens of the United States. Twiggs accepted an appointment as a General in the Army of the new **Confederate States of America**.

Lee quickly returned to Washington, D.C. The new President, Abraham Lincoln, in March of 1861, appointed Lee to be Colonel of the First Regiment of U.S. Cavalry. Three weeks later, Lee was asked to take the role of Major General, a senior command position, in the frantically expanding United States Army. Lee was still very much opposed to secession, but one week after the first shots were fired at **Fort Sumter**, his beloved Virginia seceded from the Union. Lee was being asked to take command of Union military forces which would be attacking the new **Army of Virginia**. He could not do it. Senior presidential adviser Francis P. Blair offered Lee a command as a major general. The position would give Lee the responsibility of protecting and defending the capital of the United States. Hearing the offer, Lee replied: "Mr. Blair, I look upon secession as anarchy. If I owned the four millions of slaves in the South I would sacrifice them all to the Union; but how can I draw my sword upon Virginia, my native state?" Lee resigned his commission in the U.S. Army and he returned to Virginia.

Confederate leaders were meeting in Richmond, Virginia. Lee arrived in Richmond three days after turning in his resignation. The rebel convention immediately elected him to be commander of all Virginia state forces. Robert was given the Revolutionary sword carried by George Washington as a symbol of his leadership. The combined militia of Virginia would become the **Army of Northern Virginia** and it would play a major role in the Civil War. Almost half of the Virginia officers of the United States Army stayed faithful to the Union and fought for the North.

His personal family was torn asunder by the war, with many of his relatives staying true to the Union, while many others joined him in fighting for the South. Lee's three sons decided to join the confederacy, but only after their father had made his own decision.

General Robert E. Lee's activities during the Civil War were covered in previous chapters. He was officially designated Major General in the new army, but he insisted on wearing only the three stars of a Confederate colonel. He declared he would consider himself a legitimate general only after the South had won the war.

The first Civil War battle in which Lee engaged enemy troops was the **Battle of Cheat Mountain**. His detachment was defeated, and he would be, in the usual terms of measuring battle outcomes, defeated in many other encounters. In subsequent battles, Lee was almost always vastly outnumbered. He was fighting an army with more of everything essential to war. More men, more access to river and rail transport, more money, more manufacturing capacity and more of an established navy. Still, his thrust and parry, "guerrilla" tactics confounded Union generals. Lee was able to tie up and interfere with Union troop movements. He fought from the woods, rather than open fields. He was deceptive, often misleading Union generals as to his intentions. Lee's men were generally more highly motivated, as they believed themselves to be protecting their own homes, farms and families from an invading force. Southerners believed the war could end on any given day, if the Northerners would simply pack up, go home and leave the Southerners alone to live by their own rules.

Abraham Lincoln had no intention of ending the war until he could reunify the United States.

After the battle at Cheat Mountain, Lee was assigned the difficult chore of building up Southern coastal defensive fortifications. He built up and improved Fort Pulaski and Fort Jackson and built up shoreline defenses along the coasts of Georgia and the Carolinas. His plans created a strong defense for the river approach to Savannah, Georgia. Federal troops, would not occupy Savannah for nearly four years.

Jefferson Davis, once the United States Secretary of War, was now the President of the Confederate States of America. He appointed Robert E. Lee to be one of his senior military advisers. While posted in the rebel capital, Richmond, Lee invested time and troops in the digging of an expansive network of trenches around the city. The press mocked his efforts, calling him the **"King of Spades"**, as thousands of troops shoveled out the defensive ditches. The day would come when Southern troops and the residents of Richmond, would be very grateful for the protection of Lee's trenches.

Lincoln's **General McClellan** had begun his **"Peninsular Campaign"** in the spring of 1862. He steadily pushed the Southern army, under **General Joseph E. Johnston**, back toward the Southern capital. When Johnston was wounded at the **Battle of Seven Pines**, in June 1862, Jeff Davis put Lee in command. Lee renamed the **"Army of Virginia"** to call it the "Army of Northern Virginia", as he wanted to focus the Northerners on the threat he posed to Washington, D.C.

Lee was initially criticized for being too passive. He spent a few weeks strengthening defenses around Richmond. Then, on June 25th, he pressed the Northern **Army of the Potomac** with a series of intrepid surprise attacks, now known as the **Seven Days Battles**. Lee was able to push the forces of Northern General McClellan back to the North. His success was celebrated in the confederacy and he was able to significantly boost the confidence and morale of all Southerners.

Lee continued his push to the North. In August he defeated Union **General Pope** at the **Second Battle of Manassas/Bull Run**, taking out an entire Northern command force. Lee had, in a matter of weeks, forced McClellan off of the peninsula, protecting Richmond, and had defeated Pope at Bull Run. Lee was only twenty miles South of Washington, D.C.

Robert E. Lee continued his advance into Northern territory. He moved parts of his army into Maryland and Pennsylvania. He hoped that, by doing so, by taking the war into the North, he might kill off Northern motivation and enthusiasm for the war. Lee's army settled in at Antietam Creek, where they were attacked by McClellan's Army of the Potomac. The **Battle at Antietam** was fierce. Both sides suffered enormous numbers of casualties. Lee's rebels were ultimately forced to draw back, allowing McClellan to declare a very narrow victory.

Abraham Lincoln had been awaiting a victory. He wanted to present his **Emancipation Proclamation** from a position of power. Antietam gave him his opportunity. The Proclamation was delivered on January 1st, 1863. It declared all enslaved people living in the Confederate states to be free citizens. The South was outraged. Southerners feared the Emancipation Proclamation would encourage their slaves to attempt to escape or, worse yet, to revolt against their "masters". It motivated Southern troops to fight even more fiercely to defend their way of life. The Emancipation Proclamation changed the position of the "moral high ground". It focused the war on the issue of slavery, putting Southerners in the role of defending the distasteful, shameful institution. It deflected the focus from "states' rights", a more defensible position and re-focused attention on the Southern defense of slavery.

Over the next two years, Lee would lead Southerners into a series of crucial battles. He was victorious over Union **General Burnside** at **Fredericksburg**, where more than 5,000 rebels and almost 13,000 Yankees became casualties. It was a bloodbath, horrifying to see. After the win, Lee was quoted: "It is well that war is so terrible, else we should grow too fond of it."

Lincoln replaced the defeated Burnside with **General Joseph Hooker**. Hooker took the Army of the Potomac to Chancellorsville, Virginia. It would be the site of Lee's greatest military victory. In the **Battle of (Spotsylvania) Chancellorsville**, Lee would execute a daring tactical maneuver, one which military advisors would have predicted would end in disaster. He was faced with a Union force of twice as many men as Lee could field. He responded by doing the unthinkable. He split his army in two. As the battle progressed, over several days, Lee split his forces once more. His tactics resulted in a Southern victory. Sixty thousand rebels defeated 115,000 Northerners. Chancellorsville would go down as Robert E. Lee's greatest victory. Sadly, near the end of the battle, Southern **General Thomas J. "Stonewall" Jackson** was severely wounded. The bullet was delivered by a contingency of his own troops, mistaking Jackson's group for Yankees. He would die days later. While being treated, Jackson received a note from Lee. Lee's note said, "Could I have directed events, I would have chosen for the good of the country to be disabled in your stead."

While Lee was finding some level of success in the East, Northern General U.S. Grant was defeating Southern forces in the West. Southern base Vicksburg, a major railroad terminal and a defensive position for transport on the Mississippi River, was in danger. Lee made a mistake in convincing Jeff Davis that the next big move should be further invasion of the North, rather than building up forces to defend Vicksburg. Lee moved his army toward Gettysburg, Pennsylvania. Grant's Union forces in the West placed Vicksburg under siege and eventually occupied the city. It was an enormous loss for the South.

At the **Battle of Gettysburg**, the North and the South traded small victories, pushing one another back and forth across the lines. Fighting was fierce and the result was a grisly nightmare on the killing field. On the third day at Gettysburg, Lee planned a massive assault directly into the middle of Union lines. His subordinate, General Longstreet, tried to persuade him not to pursue the plan. Lee persisted.

Lee ordered his **General George Pickett**, coordinating with two other generals, to lead the frontal assault. Almost 13,000 Confederate troops were ordered to run across an open field three-quarters of a mile long, toward a stone wall, behind which stood the Union army. Pickett's men faithfully followed their orders, charging across the field into the barrage of Union musket balls and cannon fire. The assault, known infamously as **"Pickett's Charge"**, had no chance of success. The carnage was ghastly. More than half of the rebels were casualties of the battle.

Gettysburg was considered a turning point in the great Civil War. Losses there were massive, both for the North and for the South. Lee was defeated and the rebel troops had to retreat back to the South. He was almost cut off from behind, which may have ended the war. While he concentrated forces at Gettysburg, the South was losing Vicksburg. U.S. Grant was about to be given complete control over all Northern armies and the South was doomed.

Northern General **William Tecumseh Sherman** would be beginning his devastating **"March to the Sea"**. Black Southerners were escaping to join the Northern Army. The war continued for two more years after Gettysburg. The South was steadily depleted of resources, including soldiers. They were cut off from the Mississippi River, making the transport of resources and men much more difficult. They lost New Orleans.

Commands under Grant and Lee met several times during the years 1862 to 1864. Skirmishes or small battles were fought in what was known as the **"Overland Campaign"**. They took place at **The Wilderness**, at **Spotsylvania Courthouse** and at **Cold Harbor**. The Northern armies, under General Grant, patiently continued to pressure Lee, moving him steadily back to the southeast, toward Richmond. Grant pushed and pushed and Lee managed to resist large Northern advances. Still, each assault by Grant pushed the rebels farther back to the South.

After Grant had quietly moved his army across the James River, he attempted to capture Petersburg, Virginia, an important railroad crossing. The initial Northern attack was unsuccessful. General Lee had his men furiously digging entrenchments around the city. Grant closed off avenues of access to the city and laid siege to Petersburg. As things grew more and more desperate inside the city, citizens began to move into caves in the nearby hills, looking for safety. Confederate soldiers, hungry and hopeless, were deserting in large numbers. The siege would last for several months.

Robert E. Lee was appointed **General in Chief** of the **Armies of the Confederate States** in February of 1865. It put him in a position equal to that of U.S. Grant in the North. Southern armies were losing numbers, both to casualties in battle and to desertions. Lee began to order that slaves be armed and trained to shoot. Those first Southern "slave troops" were in training when the war came to an end. Lee planned to gradually "emancipate" the black troops. Things were getting really desperate.

Grant's **siege of Petersburg** was ultimately successful. Lee had to try to evacuate his troops. He had not given up. He wanted to move his troops to meet up with **General Johnston's Army of Tennessee**. Grant's Union troops caught up with Lee and surrounded him. Lee was finally forced to surrender his army. The formalities for the surrender were accomplished at **Appomattox Courthouse** on April 9, 1865. Smaller Confederate forces would fight on for months, but the result of the war was inevitable. The South was defeated.

Some Southerners demanded that the rebels fight on, using guerrilla tactics, fighting from the hills and forests. Lee adamantly insisted that the South accept the outcome, saying the war was over. He began a campaign to re-integrate the North and the South. Lee said: "So far from engaging in a war to perpetuate slavery, I am rejoiced that slavery is abolished. I believe it will be great for the interests of the South."

Robert E. Lee was never arrested or punished. He was indicted, but no indictment was pursued. He lost his voting rights and his family home, the **Custis-Lee Mansion**, was seized by the government. The location would become a national monument, the **Arlington National Cemetery**. The home can be visited today and the grounds for the cemetery are glorious.

General Lee resisted giving black men the right to vote. He explained that he believed they were not prepared educationally to vote intelligently. Lee campaigned for free public schools for black students. In 1869, shortly after U.S. Grant was inaugurated as President, Grant invited Lee to visit the White House. Lee graciously accepted the invitation. Their meeting lasted less than half an hour and very little is known about it.

General Lee was appointed President of Washington College, which is now Washington and Lee College. His presidency at the college lasted from October 1865, until his death in 1870. He is credited with making many improvements at the school and with making in a major Southern school. He drafted students from the North and insisted that they be treated well on his campus. The students idolized him. Lee created an honor system similar to that at West Point and said "We have but one rule here and that is that every student be a gentleman". One professor at the college wrote: "The students fairly worshipped him and deeply dreaded his displeasure; yet so kind, affable and gentle was he toward them that all loved to approach him. No student would have dared to violate General Lee's expressed wish or appeal." On several occasions, Lee expelled students from the college because they had abused black citizens.

Throughout the remainder of his life, General Lee encouraged the peaceful reintegration of the North and South. He counseled fellow Southerners, including Jeff Davis, to encourage citizens to forget the past and plan for the future. He advocated for good treatment of and support for, freed black Southerners.

Robert E. Lee had pneumonia in September of 1870, which led to a stroke. On October 12, 1870, the general passed away. At the time of his death, torrential rains had flooded rivers and roads. Coffins had been ordered but were washed away, floating down the Maury River. Local boys C. G. Chittum and Robert E. Hillis found one of the coffins in the mud along the river's shoreline. They rescued it. The undertaker was able to clean it up enough to make it a suitable vessel for the general's body. Lee was a bit too tall for the coffin and had to be buried without his boots. He was buried beneath University Chapel in the college where he served so successfully as President.

Benjamin Harvey Hill, speaking to the Southern Historical Society in 1874, said this of Robert E. Lee:

"He was a foe without hate; a friend without treachery; a soldier without cruelty; a victor without oppression and a victim without murmuring. He was a public officer without vices; a private citizen without wrong; a neighbor without reproach; a Christian without hypocrisy and a man without guile. He was a Caesar, without his ambition; Frederick, without his tyranny; Napoleon, without his selfishness and Washington, without his reward."

Robert E. Lee Quotes

- "Never do a wrong thing to make a friend--or to keep one."

- "I cannot trust a man to control others who cannot control himself."

- "It is well that war is so terrible or we should grow too fond of it."

- "The education of a man is never completed until he dies."

- Duty. Duty is the sublimest word in the language; you can never do more than your duty; you shall never wish to do less.

- A Union that can only be maintained by swords and bayonets has no charm for me. If the Union is dissolved and government disrupted, I shall return to my native state and share the miseries of my people and save in defense will draw my sword on none.

- In this enlightened age, there are few, I believe, but what will acknowledge that slavery, as an institution, is a moral and political evil in any Country. It is useless to expatiate on its disadvantages.

- If you have any fault to find with anyone, tell him, not others, of what you complain; there is no more dangerous experiment than that of undertaking to be one thing before a man's face and another behind his back.

- I have fought against the people of the North because I believed they were seeking to wrest from the South its dearest rights. But I have never cherished toward them bitter or vindictive feelings and I have never seen a day when I did not pray for them.

- We must expect reverses, even defeats. They are sent to teach us wisdom and prudence, to call forth greater energies and to prevent our falling into greater disasters.

Robert E. Lee and Slavery

Robert E. Lee grew up as a child of two of the most well-known families in Virginia. His mother was a descendant of **Robert "King" Carter**, who was a notorious slaver. He spent his childhood years on a small family plantation, **Stratford Hall**, on which lived and worked some thirty enslaved black people. The family struggled financially and had to sell off some property and move to Alexandria, but held onto possession of approximately six slaves. There is no record of Robert E. Lee, as an adult, personally owning any slaves. When his mother died, she bequeathed her remaining slaves to a daughter. Robert may or may not have obtained slaves in the "remaining estate" which was left to him, but there is no record to suggest that he did.

The situation changed dramatically in 1857 when his wife's father, **George Washington Park Custis**, passed away. Her father left **Mary Custis Lee** a single slave, but he left his entire estate to be executed by Robert. The **Arlington House** estate was a plantation on which an estimated 200 enslaved black people labored. Her father, in his will, insisted that all of his slaves be freed (granted manumission) within five years after his death.

The estate of Mary's father had many assets, but also many large debts. In his attempt to find an overseer to manage the plantation, Lee wrote: "I wish to get an energetic honest farmer, who, while he will be considerate and kind to the negroes, will be firm & make them do their duty." He could not find such a person and was left with no option but to personally manage the plantation and the execution of his father-in-law's will. Robert had to take a two-year leave of absence from his military position to cope with the disposition of the massive estate. Robert E. Lee didn't actually own the slaves, but he was left with the responsibility of managing the execution of his wife's father's estate and with responsibility for the many slaves attached to that estate.

Robert E. Lee suddenly found himself the manager of those many slaves and of plantations which were struggling financially. Lee felt he needed to retain the slaves until he could resolve outstanding debts left by his father-in-law. The slaves, however, had been under the impression that they were to be freed on the day of their master's death. The misunderstanding, if that is what it was, led to much hostility. Records indicate that Lee was relatively successful in managing disposition of the lands, but also suggest that he was not a gentle manager of the slaves. Some historical accounts described Lee's treatment of the slaves as being so harsh that it caused rebellious responses.

The most infamous examples of Lee's relationship with slave's laboring on the family plantations have been recorded with inconsistent, varying descriptions.

In one example, in the early summer of 1858, Lee wrote to Rooney, his son, that "I have had some trouble with some of the people (slaves). **'Reuben', 'Parks'** and **'Edward'** (slaves), in the beginning of the previous week, rebelled against my authority. They refused to obey my orders and said they were as free as I was, etc., etc. I succeeded in capturing them & lodging them in jail. They resisted till overpowered and called upon the other people (slaves) to rescue them".

The three slaves were held in jail in Alexandria for several weeks, after which Lee had the three men, along with three additional female "house slaves", chained up and delivered to William Overton Winston, in Richmond, Virginia. Winston was directed, by Lee, to keep the slaves in jail until "good and responsible" slaveholders could be found, who could be counted on to work the slaves productively until their five-year period of continued enslavement would end. Lee could not sell the slaves because, according to the will of his father-in-law, they were to be freed within a period "not to exceed" five years.

The other notorious example of the relationship between Robert E. Lee and the slaves he (temporarily) inherited is reflected in **"The Norris Case"**. As in the case of the slaves Reuben, Parks and Edward, records vary widely in several essential details. Much of the most reliable information comes directly from Norris, his being the voice of one of the slaves intimately involved in the tale. The story goes like this:

In 1859, slaves **Wesley Norris**, his sister **Mary** and an unnamed cousin, all attempted escape from Lee's **Arlington House**. They fled to the North, but they were unsuccessful in their desperate attempt and were captured before reaching the Pennsylvania border. Slaves recognized Pennsylvania, home of the Quakers, as an anti-slavery haven.

The **New York Daily Tribune**, famously unfriendly to slavery, posted a couple of anonymous letters. The letters made condemnatory claims about Lee's treatment of the three captured fugitive slaves. Lee, at the time in his life, was not the famous Southern general. He was just a Southern plantation manager. The two letters accused Lee of having had the slave Wesley Norris, his sister Mary and their cousin, mercilessly whipped or flogged. Lee wrote to Custis, one of his sons, saying ""The N. Y. Tribune has attacked me for my treatment of your grandfather's slaves, but I shall not reply. He has left me an unpleasant legacy."

One of the Tribune letters claimed that Lee's overseer refused to flog the woman, Mary, and that Lee responded by taking the whip from the overseer's hands, proceeding to brutally whip her himself. One article described Mary as having been "stripped to the waist" for the flogging. Most historians cast serious doubt on this claim, reporting that it is highly unlikely Lee ever personally whipped anyone or that he would have had the female stripped. His own writings show disgust for slave owners who were too harsh. In review, it seems likely Lee himself would not have lowered himself to participate personally in the abuse. On the other hand, there is little doubt about the truth of the fundamental story.

The leader of the run-away slaves, Wesley Norris, years later, was interviewed about the incident. Wesley declared that, after being caught and returned to Arlington House, Robert E. Lee promised them that "he would teach us a lesson we would not soon forget". Norris reported that Lee had all three of them bound firmly to whipping posts and assigned the overseer to deliver 50 lashes to the men and 20 lashes to Mary, the woman. When the overseer objected, especially refusing to whip Mary, Lee then called in the county's constable. The constable carried out Lee's orders. Wesley said "Lee frequently enjoined Constable Williams to 'lay it on well', an injunction which he did not fail to heed; not satisfied with simply lacerating our naked flesh, General Lee then ordered the overseer to thoroughly wash our backs with (salt) brine, which was done." Norris made no mention of Lee doing any of the actual flogging, though that fact does not absolve Lee of guilt in the incident.

Wesley Norris and his cousin were delivered to railroad construction projects in Virginia and Alabama, still working off their "five years". Wesley was working in Richmond in 1863, possibly helping to build confederate entrenchments. He says "I finally made my escape through the rebel lines to freedom". Union army records reported that Wesley Norris approached their lines on September 5th, 1863 and that he was holding "a pass from General Washington Custis Lee". If the Union records are correct, then it would appear that, rather than "escaping", Wesley had been released by Robert E. Lee's son, Custis.

All of the "Custis slaves" left to Robert E. Lee's custody when Mary's father died were left to work out the five-year period allowed in the will. Mary's father apparently wanted the slaves freed as quickly as possible after his death and to be held in enslavement no longer than a maximum of five years. In practice, though, Robert held them in bondage until the entire five years played out. His justification appears to have been that he was in need of the free labor in his efforts to pay off the father-in-law's debts. Lee finally freed the Custis slaves, including Wesley Norris, at the end of the five-year period. The deed of manumission was signed on December 29, in the winter of 1862. Records show that only a single family of slaves was still living on the Lee family plantation by 1860.

In his own writings and in reports of his personal declarations, it seems clear that Robert E. Lee recognized the fundamental evil and shame attached to the institution of slavery. In the manner of many slave owners of the times, his personal behavior was inconsistent with his own beliefs. He could not, in his estimation, give up the Custis slaves because they were necessary to work off their owner's debts. His own remaining slaves, most likely originally from his wife Mary's inheritance, were to be emancipated in the terms of his will. It turned out that Lincoln's **Emancipation Proclamation** came before Lee's death, and in that manner all of the Southern slaves were set free.

Lee is known to have assisted individual slaves in their desire to relocate to **Liberia**, where a nation of freed slaves was being established. Lee believed that the passage of time, directed by the hand of God, would eventually, gradually, release all people from the bonds of slavery. He did not believe that a sudden, universal emancipation could work, as the enslaved were, in his opinion, no where near being prepared to cope with freedom. After the war, he promoted a peaceful and practical assimilation of freed slaves into society.

Lee's philosophy, as it related to slavery, is abhorrent to our present-day culture but was customary in his times and in his region. Robert E. Lee wrote, in 1856, in a letter to Mary:

"In this enlightened age, there are few I believe, but what will acknowledge, that slavery as an institution, is a moral and political evil in any Country. It is useless to expatiate on its disadvantages. I think it however a greater evil to the white man than to the black race and while my feelings are strongly enlisted in behalf of the latter (black people), my sympathies are more strong for the former (white people). The blacks are immeasurably better off here than in Africa, morally, socially and physically. The painful discipline they are undergoing, is necessary for their instruction as a race and I hope will prepare and lead them to better things. How long their subjugation may be necessary is known and ordered by a wise Merciful Providence."

There is little doubt that Robert E. Lee was personally involved in ordering "discipline" of slaves and that the discipline sometimes including whipping. We know that he held onto the slaves he obtained from his wife's father for as long as he could, not freeing them until the five-year period completely played out. We know that he appealed to the courts to extend that five-year-period, as his father-in-law's estate was still in debt. The court refused his application.

Records also indicate that Lee divided up slave families, sending them to different locations to work. In polite Southern society, many affluent plantation owners looked down on cruel punishments and on splitting up slave families. Such activities were considered inappropriate in aristocratic Southern families. Lee seems to have crossed those lines on occasion. He would dispute those accusations. One of his personal friends reported that Lee told him "There is not a word of truth in it. No servant, soldier or citizen that was ever employed by me can charge me with bad treatment".

Lee's innate prejudices about black people were revealed, after the war, when he appeared before a Congressional committee. His comments included statements that black people were "not disposed to work" and that black people did not have the

443

intellectual ability to actively participate in American politics or to vote. He told the committee that he hoped that his state, Virginia, could "get rid of" black people.

Robert E. Lee held the prejudiced, certainly erroneous, opinions about black people that were "normal" opinions in his times and in his location. He did not want to see slavery spread and he knew it had to eventually end. He didn't want it ended precipitously, though, but rather he would like to have slowly weaned the South from its dependence on slave labor. He claimed that, in leading the Southern military, he was fighting against a Northern invasion and fighting to protect his beloved Virginia from Northern occupation. He would not have admitted to fighting to protect slavery.

Thomas Jonathan "Stonewall" Jackson

Confederate Civil War General

Confederate General Thomas "Stonewall" Jackson

John Jackson was Thomas's great-grandfather. John was an Irishman who was living in London, England, in the 1700's. He was caught stealing and sentenced to seven years of punishment called **"penal transportation"**. John was put on the **Litchfield**, an English merchant ship, along with 150 other convicts and sent to America, where several colonies were already established. While aboard the Litchfield, John met another thief, **Elizabeth Cummins**, a durable woman who measured nearly six feet tall. Elizabeth had also been sentenced to serve **"bonded service"** time in America, as a consequence of having stolen "19 pieces of silver, jewelry and fine lace". The two convicted thieves fell in love. They were discharged, on reaching America, to two different locations in Maryland. They overcame the distance between them, apparently served out their bondage and were married in July of 1755.

John and Elizabeth worked their way westward and settled in an area that is now West Virginia. They gradually acquired more and more parcels of virgin land. When the **American Revolution** began, John and his two teenage sons quickly joined the American rebels in the fight to seize independence from the English crown. They fought throughout the war and John continued to serve in the Virginia militia after the war. Elizabeth did not stand by passively during the revolution. She converted their home so as to provide refuge for returning western settlers who were attacked by Indians while the American military was busy with the English.

Thomas **Jonathan Jackson's** father was Jonathan Jackson. Jonathan was a lawyer who married **Julia Beckwith** and Thomas became their third child. He was born on January 21, 1824, while the family lived in Clarksburg, which is now located in West

Virginia. In 1826, Thomas, aged two years, watched as his six-year-old sister, Elizabeth, died. She was a victim of typhoid fever. Thomas's father nursed Elizabeth and then fell victim to typhoid himself, dying only days later. One day after Jonathan's death, Thomas's mother gave birth to a girl baby named Laura Ann.

Thomas's mother, Julia, found herself a widow at age 28. The family carried a burden of debt which became, along with three young children, Julia's responsibility. She was forced to sell off all of their belongings. She began taking in sewing jobs and she opened a private school. She moved the family to a small, one-room house and she steadily refused charity.

Several years later, ignoring the advice of friends, Julia remarried. Her new husband was Captain Blake Woodson, another lawyer and Blake did not relish the idea of taking on the burden of some other man's children. Julia's oldest son, Warren, Thomas's big brother, went to live with a distant uncle. Julia, in poor health and struggling, agreed to move Thomas and Laura Ann to live with their Grandmother Jackson. One of Grandmother Jackson's sons arrived to pick up the children, intending to transport them to live with the grandmother. The children, Thomas and Laura, were frightened by the prospect of leaving their mother behind to go and live with strangers.

Thomas, only six years old, fled to the forest. His uncle, after a couple of days of coaxing and attempted bribery, persuaded Thomas to join them. The two children found themselves in much improved conditions. The family surrounding their grandmother was kind, charitable and generous and treated the two children very well. Reports suggest they were "well-spoiled". When their grandmother died, in 1835, Thomas and Julia were moved once again. They were sent to live with a half-uncle, Cummins Jackson, who lived in Jackson's Mill, a town in present-day West Virginia. The little town was named for the mill that Cummins operated. Only a year later their mother lay dying and they were taken to be by her side. Julia's three children were left orphans. Julia's final resting place became a homemade coffin buried in an unmarked grave. Laura and Thomas returned to Jackson's Mill.

Laura Ann and Thomas spent four years at Jackson's Mill and then the two siblings were finally separated, each being sent to live with different relatives at different locations. Thomas went to live with his Uncle Isaac Brake and Aunt Polly. Uncle Isaac wasn't happy having to take on the burden of caring for Thomas and was harsh with the boy. Thomas endured the abuse for over a year, but then ran away. He trekked through the wilderness, covering almost twenty miles, to return to Jackson's Mill. His uncles welcomed him back and he lived there for several more years.

His uncle Cummins was a task-master. He expected Thomas to work for his food and his lodging. Cummins was a school teacher and Thomas respected him. Thomas had little and infrequent access to formal schooling himself, but was motivated to learn. Most of his education was self-taught. He is known to have convinced one of his uncle's slaves to bring him "pine knots", for which, in return, Thomas agreed to teach the slave to read. (Thomas used the pine knots to make fires so that he could read in the evenings). The law in Virginia, at that time, forbade teaching any black person to read or write, but Thomas had promised and he honored his promise. The young slave, after learning to read, found his way to the Underground Railroad and fled to Canada.

In Jackson's Mill, Thomas learned to care for and to herd, with assistance from a dog, sheep. He learned to drive teams of oxen and to participate in the growing and harvesting of grains. He was serving as a local school teacher by the time he was sixteen years old. His own education was "catch as catch can" and very sketchy.

Thomas Jonathan Jackson was accepted to **West Point**, The United States Military Academy, in 1842. His poor education led to chronic academic struggles and he began his tenure at West Point near the bottom of his class. He was doggedly determined, applied himself diligently, studied tenaciously and steadily advanced his standing. Jackson, in 1846, after four years of hard work, graduated 17th in his class of 59. Other students said that, if he had stayed one more year, he would have graduated first in the class.

The **Mexican-American War** was firing up just as Thomas Jackson left West Point. He was posted to the First U.S. Artillery brigade and was quickly sent to Mexico. Jackson soon earned great respect for his courage and his tactical intelligence. His commanding officer was future American President **General Zachary Taylor**. Lieutenant Jackson was dispatched to Veracruz, Mexico, where he participated in the **Siege of Veracruz** and then in the Battles at **Contreras**, **Chapultepec** and **Mexico City**. During the time he was in Mexico, Jackson, for the first time, encountered **Robert E. Lee**. The future would bring the two of them together in epic fashion.

In September of 1847, during the **Battle of Chapultepec**, Jackson was given an order that he considered very much ill-advised. He confronted his superior officer and presented an argument sufficient to convince his commander to retract the order. The result of the battle proved Jackson to have been correct in his assessments and Jackson's force was able to hold off Mexican advances and turn the battle in favor of the Americans.

Jackson, though, didn't always resist orders he considered to be in bad judgement. He reluctantly followed orders to assault a mob of civilians with artillery fire when Mexican officials refused to surrender Mexico City at an appointed time.

Thomas Jackson's overall performance in the Mexican-American War was judged to be very good. He received multiple brevet promotions, concluding the war as brevet major. (A "brevet" promotion gives you the title and the authority, but not the increased salary).

Following the end of the Mexican-American War, Jackson was assigned a series of short postings. At one point, he was sent to Florida, where he participated in the on-going effort to force the **Seminole Indians** to re-locate westward. Thomas Jackson continued his military career until 1851, when he accepted a position as a professor at the **Virginia Military Institute**, located in Lexington, Virginia. He taught natural philosophy (more similar to what we would call physics in today's world) and he taught artillery tactics. Cadets sometimes complained that Jackson was too gruff and lacking in sympathy and a bit eccentric. They ridiculed his rumored hypochondria and his odd inclination to hold one arm lightly elevated, to compensate for his perceived difference in the length of his extremities. Some cadets called Jackson **"Tom Fool"**. He was not a popular professor.

The governor of Virginia, in November of 1859 ordered a group of VMI cadets to Charles Town. He wanted them to add to the show of military force present at the execution, by hanging, of the famous abolitionist, **John Brown**. Brown was hung for leading an unsuccessful attack on the U.S. Army Arsenal at **Harper's Ferry**. Jackson, serving as a major, was in command of the artillery, which consisted of two army howitzers. The guns were manned by twenty-one VMI cadets. The guns were not fired. John Brown was hung without incident, other than a large gathering of enthusiastic witnesses.

Jackson had a lifelong run of bad luck in terms of the untimely deaths of his loved ones. He lost his mother and his father and his little sister Elizabeth. Thomas married the daughter of the president of Washington College, now Washington and Lee College, **Elinor Junkin**, in 1853. Elinor's father also served as a minister in the Presbyterian Church. Elinor, known as "Ellie", died only a short fourteen months later, in the throes of childbirth. The infant son did not survive.

Three years later, Thomas married **Mary Anna Morrison**, the daughter of another college president, this time being Davidson College. One year later, Mary Anna gave birth to a daughter, but the little girl survived for only a month. He would eventually have another daughter and she would survive, but Thomas would die, in the Civil War, less than a year after her birth.

His years living in Lexington gained Thomas a solid reputation. He was known to be a man of devout religious faith, honest, reliable and responsible. He refused tobacco and alcohol and was never known to gamble. His peaceful, successful civilian life in Lexington was rudely interrupted when Virginia elected to secede from the United States in 1861.

Thomas Jackson advised his home state of Virginia not to secede after the election of **Abraham Lincoln**, but secede Virginia did. Jackson, like **Robert E. Lee**, chose to support the new Confederacy, unwilling to fight against his neighbors and fellow Southerners.

He accepted appointment to the rank of colonel in the new **Confederate Army.** He departed Lexington to fight the war and would never return. He grumbled about his commission status and was quickly promoted, by CSA **General Joseph E. Johnston**, to the rank of Brigadier General. He developed a reputation for constantly drilling his troops and for expecting them to follow orders quickly and without question. The troops, like all troops, probably complained about the constant work, but the skills and discipline they learned under Jackson would serve them very well on the battlefields.

Thomas Jackson took with him, into the Southern army, a reputation as an "unconventional" horseman. Some would have said a poor horseman. William Andrews, a Southern army volunteer, wrote this about General Jackson: "He was a very ordinary looking man of medium size, his uniform badly soiled as though it had seen hard service. He wore a cap pulled down nearly to his nose and was riding a rawboned horse that did not look much like a charger, unless it would be on hay or clover. He certainly made a poor figure on horseback, with his stirrup leather six inches too short, putting his knees nearly level with his horse's back and his heels turned out with his toes sticking behind his horse's front shoulder. A sorry description of our most famous general, but a correct one."

General Jackson's horse was a small chestnut gelding which had been 'captured' off of a Union farm. The horse was named **"Little Sorrel"** or sometimes "Old Sorrel" and Jackson rode him throughout the war. Little Sorrel died at the age of 36, a long life for a horse and is buried near Jackson's statue on the parade grounds at Virginia Military Institute, where Jackson had been a professor.

Early in the Civil War, Jackson was in command of troops fighting at the **First Battle of Bull Run**, Manassas. It was July of 1861 and the Union Army was pushing hard to breach Confederate lines. General Jackson rushed his command toward the front lines, aggressively filling a weak spot in the rebel lines, stopping the Union advance. His troops held their ground against the Yankee onslaught. A fellow general, seeing the courageous stand of Jackson and his followers, is said to have remarked "Look, men, there is Jackson standing like a stone wall!" The comment gave birth to the nickname that would follow Thomas Jackson through his remaining time in the war and then into history. He became **General "Stonewall" Jackson**. He was, a couple of months later, promoted to Major General.

The war continued and Jackson was charged with leading the **"Shenandoah Valley Campaign"**. His main task was to defend Virginia from invasion by the Yankees and to protect the Confederate capital at Richmond. He was remarkably successful. Stonewall Jackson commanded a maximum of 18,000 rebel soldiers. He was fighting against Union armies that numbered upwards of 60,000 well-armed, well-resourced Yankees. Abraham Lincoln had ordered his **Army of the Potomac** divided into three separate assault forces. Stonewall Jackson was able to move his troops around so quickly that they became known as the **"foot cavalry"**, meaning they seemed to move around so quickly they might have been on horseback.

His Shenandoah Campaign lasted from March until June of 1862, during which time he was able to deceive and outmaneuver three Union armies. His army marched 646 miles in 48 days. He won several victories in battles while being vastly outnumbered. He was able to stop Union advances, preventing a planned combined Union assault on Richmond and was able to successfully protect the capital at Richmond. He became well-known and admired by Northern military leaders, including Abraham Lincoln.

When the Shenandoah Campaign was brought to a successful close, Stonewall Jackson "force marched" his troops overland to reinforce the command of Robert E. Lee. Together they would fight the Northerners at the **"Seven Days Battles"**. (A "forced march" is an unusually rapid march over an unusually long distance).

Stonewall Jackson and Robert E. Lee were able to join their commands in June of 1862. Robert E. Lee was very much aware of Jackson's courage and expertise in tactical planning. Lee meant to make maximum usage of Jackson's skills. Jackson and his "foot cavalry" served with distinction in the **Second Battle of Bull Run**, the **Battle of Antietam**, The **Battle of Fredericksburg** and the **Battle of Chancellorsville**.

When the fall of 1862 came around, Jackson had earned a national reputation. His troops idolized him. In personal relationships with his officers, though, his unpopularity with cadets back when he was a professor is recalled. His military subordinates described him as being too secretive and often too punitive. They felt he often punished his staff for infractions too minor to warrant discipline. They complained that he never shared or discussed his plans with them. Stonewall Jackson gave his orders and he expected them to be followed promptly and explicitly.

The Battle of Chancellorsville, in May of 1863, became the greatest victory of Robert E. Lee and Stonewall Jackson. The South brought nearly 60,000 men, but was heavily outnumbered by 130,000 Yankees, who were led by Union **General Joseph Hooker**. Stonewall 'force marched' 28,000 rebel soldiers over 15 miles of rough terrain to maneuver stealthily to the rear of Hooker's flank. Lee was simultaneously engaged in diversionary actions along the front lines. Jackson's surprise attack inflicted devastating casualties on Hooker's much larger force. Hooker, days later, had no realistic option except to retreat.

Jackson's assault on Hooker's flank was winding down as the sun was beginning to set. He led a few men into the forest, intending to scout the area where he planned to move his troops. A Southern regiment from North Carolina, not recognizing Jackson and his men, opened fire. Jackson was severely wounded, suffering a bullet wound to his left shoulder, a second bullet to his left arm and a bullet to his right hand. Several of his troops and some of their horses were also wounded or killed. In the chaos, as troops tried to evacuate Jackson, he was dropped from a stretcher. **Hunter McGuire**, physician and soldier, quickly amputated his arm. McGuire would later be the president of the American Medical Association. Numerous present-day medical facilities carry his name.

Stonewall was taken to a field hospital, where it was hoped he would recover. While in the hospital, he received a note from Robert E. Lee. The note said "Could I have directed events, I would have chosen, for the good of the country, to be disabled in your stead." Stonewall Jackson seemed to be recovering, but soon was infected with pneumonia. He died May 10th, 1863. He was only 39-years-old.

Dr. McGuire wrote later of his recollection of Stonewall Jackson's final moments. McGuire reported that a dying, delirious Jackson cried out "Order A.P. Hill to prepare for action! Pass the infantry to the front rapidly! Tell Major Hawks . . ." at which point the general paused, failing to complete his sentence. Soon thereafter, McGuire reported that "a smile of ineffable sweetness spread itself over his pale face and he said quietly and with an expression, as if of relief: "Let us cross over the river and rest under the shade of the trees." And, with that, he passed away.

In what must be one of the very first times the science of **forensic ballistics** identification was employed, an examination of the bullets retrieved from Jackson's body appeared to prove they were fired by Southerners. Rebel soldiers were using musket balls of 67 caliber, while federal troops were using balls of 58 caliber. The ones taken from Jackson were 67 caliber.

When Robert E. Lee learned that Jackson was dying, he sent a message to Jackson. It read: "Give General Jackson my affectionate regards and say to him: He has lost his left arm but I my right." After learning of Jackson's passing, Lee's cook said that Lee told him: "William, I have lost my right arm and I am bleeding at the heart".

Thomas "Stonewall" Jackson has been widely recognized as a brilliant military strategist. Military leaders as famous as **General George Patton, General "Chesty" Puller** and **General Douglas MacArthur** idolized him. Patton was said to consider Robert E. Lee and Stonewall Jackson to be "God and Jesus" in military terms. He said to his superior officer, **Dwight Eisenhower,** "I shall be your Jackson".

Thomas "Stonewall" Jackson Quotes

- "You may be whatever you resolve to be."

- "If the general government should persist in the measures now threatened, there must be war. It is painful enough to discover with what unconcern they speak of war and threaten it. They do not know its horrors. I have seen enough of it to make me look upon it as the sum of all evils."

- "The only true rule for cavalry is to follow the enemy as long as he retreats."

- "I yield to no man in sympathy for the gallant men under my command, but I am obliged to sweat them tonight, so that I may save their blood tomorrow."

- "Captain, my religious belief teaches me to feel as safe in battle as in bed. God has fixed the time for my death. I do not concern myself about that, but to be always ready, no matter when it may overtake me. Captain, that is the way all men should live and then all would be equally brave."

- "The business of a soldier is to fight. Armies are not called out to dig trenches, to throw up breastworks and live in camps, but to find the enemy and strike him; to invade his country and do him all possible damage in the shortest possible time. Such a war would, of necessity, be of brief continuance and so would be an economy of prosperity and life in the end. To move swiftly, strike vigorously and secure all the fruits of victory, is the secret of successful war."

- "Always mystify, mislead and surprise the enemy, if possible; and when you strike and overcome him, never let up the pursuit so long as your men have strength to follow; for an army routed, if hotly pursued, becomes panic-stricken and can then be destroyed by half their number. The other rule is, never fight against heavy odds, if by any possible maneuvering you can hurl your own force on only a part and that the weakest part of your enemy and crush it. Such tactics will win every time and a small army may thus destroy a large one in detail and repeated victory will make it invincible."

- His last words on his deathbed: "Let us cross over the river and rest under the shade of the trees."

Thomas "Stonewall" Jackson and Slavery

Thomas Jackson grew up in an area which is now West Virginia. Slavery was not as common in West Virginia as it was in Virginia, but Jackson certainly was exposed to slavery as he grew up. He was an extremely religious man and he rationalized ownership of slaves by reasoning that slavery had existed throughout the Bible. He reportedly recognized the evil of slavery, but believed it would gradually be eliminated, according to God's plans.

Jackson's uncle at Jackson's Mill owned slaves and Thomas must have worked alongside them. We know that Thomas, when he was a boy, secretly taught slaves to read and write. We know that he organized a clandestine, informal "school" for slaves. It was illegal to educate black people, but Jackson did so, anyway.

When he married Mary Anna, she brought with her six slaves. They included "Hetty", "Cyrus" and "George". Hetty was the mother of teen-agers Cyrus and George. A fourth slave, "Albert", was being rented out to serve as a waiter in a Lexington hotel. Albert asked Thomas Jackson to buy him, knowing Jackson would allow him to work to earn his freedom. Jackson purchased Albert and rented him out to work at the Virginia Military Institute. "Amy" was the family's fifth slave. Amy also asked Jackson to purchase her. He did so, "buying" her at a public slave auction. She became the Jackson family's cook and helped with housekeeping. Finally, the sixth slave, "Emma" was given to the Jackson's by an elderly widow. Emma was only four-years-old when she came to their home and she had learning disabilities. All reports indicate they were all treated as family.

Jackson was not prominent or well-known among the white population around Lexington at the time, but it seems his name was very familiar to the black population. His reputation for kind treatment of the family slaves must have been the basis for motivating other slaves to plead with him to buy them.

In 1855, Thomas and Mary Anna opened a Sunday School, within the Presbyterian Church, specifically for black children. Thomas said "I prefer that my labors should be given to the colored children, believing that it is more important and useful to put the strong hand of the Gospel under the ignorant African race, to lift them up". The pastor at the church said of Thomas: ""In their religious instruction he succeeded wonderfully. His discipline was systematic and firm, but very kind. His own servants reverenced and loved him, as they would have done a brother or father. He was emphatically the black man's friend." Thomas addressed his students by name and they referred to him as 'Marse Major'". When he went away to fight in the Civil War, General Stonewall Jackson often sent money home to continue to support the Sunday School for black children.

One of the slaves that came to Jackson when he married Mary Anna, George, was one who the Jackson's, contrary to the law, educated. Much later, after the Civil War, George would become a board member for a school for black children. He was very successful in his life. One historian shared George's obituary: "George Jackson, colored, died last week in his home in East Lincoln. He was one of the few remaining ex-slaves of this section. He was proud to tell he was the servant of Stonewall Jackson."

A slave was among the last contacts of Stonewall Jackson. As Jackson lay dying in Chancellorsville, a slave named Jim Lewis stayed by his side.

The Reverend L. L. Downing's parents had been slaves who benefited from Thomas Jackson's Sunday School for black children. The Reverend created a fund to raise money to memorialize Jackson. A memorial window has been installed at the Fifth Avenue Presbyterian Church in Roanoke, Virginia and dedicated to Jackson. It's a remarkable thing, finding an African-American church with a monument to a Confederate general.

In other locations, Jackson's history of kindness to black people is not enough to protect his reputation. The fact that he did, after all, own slaves is unforgiveable to many in today's cultural environment. Many statues and other monuments to Stonewall Jackson have been torn down and hidden away. This writer believes he should be remembered and his story should be remembered. He was not a man who would ever have claimed to be perfect. Still, he was a significant figure in American history. We can appreciate his brilliance and we can learn from his flaws and his mistakes. We must learn from the sins and defects of previous generations. As in all things, it is our failures that lead us to our successes.

Remembering all of history is not the same as glorifying all of its elements. We cannot learn from that about which we know nothing. Education is a bad thing only when it is inaccurate.

William Tecumseh Sherman

American Civil War General

William Tecumseh Sherman was born February 8th, 1820, near the Hocking River in Lancaster, Ohio. His father, **Charles Robert Sherman**, was a prominent citizen, an attorney and a judge who served on the Ohio Supreme Court. William's father, according to family records, was an admirer of the great **Shawnee** tribal chieftain **Tecumseh** and honored the chief by giving his son the middle name. William's mother was **Mary Hoyt** Sherman and she delivered eleven children.

The Sherman family is well-represented in American history. A younger brother was elected Senator and also served as Secretary of the Treasury and Secretary of State. An older brother was a federal judge.

Typhoid fever killed William's father in 1829, when William was nine-years-old. He left no inheritance and his mother was left a widow with eleven children and few assets. Many of the children were placed in the homes of other families. William, who had been nicknamed "Cump", was taken in by the family of a friend and neighbor to the Sherman's, **John Ewing**.

John Ewing was also a prominent citizen in Ohio. He was an Ohio Senator and he became the nation's first Secretary of the Interior. William was, for the most part, raised by John Ewing. As an adult, William married **Ellen Ewing**, a foster sister.

In 1836, at the age of 16, Sherman was appointed to the **United States Military Academy** at **West Point**. Senator Ewing secured the appointment for him and William became a good student in academics. Behaviorally, though, William was not so good. He did not conform well to rigid regulations and wasn't the neatest, best dressed cadet on campus. He received up to 150 demerits annually, but still managed to graduate sixth in his class. Other cadets described him as being "one of the brightest and most popular fellows". One wrote that Sherman was "a bright-eyed, red-headed fellow who was always up for a lark of any kind".

When he graduated from the Academy in 1840, William Tecumseh Sherman was commissioned a second lieutenant. His first assignment was to travel to Florida to assist in the forced relocation of the **Seminole Indians**. He had little enthusiasm for the task and said that "It was a great pity to move the Seminoles at all". He said Florida was "the Indian's Paradise".

While many of his contemporaries were sent to fight in the **Mexican-American War**, Sherman was sent to California, at the time considered "a captured territory", where he had administrative duties. His trip from New York City to California was a 198-day voyage around Cape Horn on the **USS Lexington**.

While in California, living in Monterey, Sherman was involved in surveying the infant city of Sacramento. It would eventually become the state's capital. He opened a General Store, which earned him $1500 in 1849. His army salary was $70 monthly. He used some of the money to buy real estate, which he then re-sold for profit. Sherman was given a brevet promotion to captain, but he was gaining no combat experience.

William married his foster sister, **Ellen Boyle Ewing**, in 1850. **President Zachary Taylor** and **Vice President Millard Fillmore** were in attendance at the wedding. The couple went on to have eight children. They moved to St. Louis, Missouri, where William served in the Commissary Department of the army. After three years, not feeling like his military career was showing sufficient advance, he resigned his commission. He became the manager of a San Francisco bank. On the way to San Francisco, he was able to survive two ship wrecks. He literally floated into the bay in San Francisco on the inverted hull of a sinking schooner.

Yerba Buena, the original settlement, had recently been renamed **San Francisco**. The area was becoming extremely busy, with the gold rush of 1849 adding to the usual chaos of the sea-going business around the bay. Speculation in real estate was frenzied. Sherman would later say "I can handle a hundred thousand men in battle and take the City of the Sun, but I am afraid to manage a lot in the swamp of San Francisco." Still, when **"Black Friday"**, the **Panic of 1855**, arrived, Sherman was able to keep his bank open, while many others failed and locked their doors. In the next year, during a period of lawlessness known as the **"Vigilante Period"**, Sherman served as **major general** of the California militia.

Sherman, moving back and forth from California to New York, continued working for the bank for three more years. After it failed in 1857, he proceeded to Leavenworth, Kansas, where his relatives Hugh Ewing and Thomas Ewing, Jr., ran a law firm. William was able to obtain a license to practice law, but found little success in that endeavor. He served as office manager for the firm.

William Tecumseh Sherman was appointed, in 1859, Superintendent of the Louisiana State Seminary of Learning & Military Academy in Pineville, Louisiana. The school, present day, is Louisiana State University. As the name implies, the school at that time was a military-based institution. **Colonel Joseph P. Taylor** wrote of Sherman's tenure there: "If you had hunted the whole Army, from one end of it to the other, you could not have found a man in it more admirably suited for the position in every respect than Sherman." Sherman enjoyed his time in the South and voiced no strong objection to the slavery he observed during his time there. He was, though, adamantly opposed to secession, believing the South had no realistic probability of defeating the much better prepared, much more industrialized North.

Sherman had a close friend, Professor David French Boyd, who was a Southerner with enthusiasm for secession. Boyd wrote that, when Sherman learned that South Carolina had seceded, "Sherman burst out crying and began, in his nervous way, pacing the floor and deprecating the step which he feared might bring destruction on the whole country." Sherman went on, as reported by Professor Boyd, to describe his fears:

"You people of the South don't know what you are doing. This country will be drenched in blood and God only knows how it will end. It is all folly, madness, a crime against civilization! You people speak so lightly of war; you don't know what you're talking about. War is a terrible thing! You mistake, too, the people of the North. They are a peaceable people but an earnest people and they will fight, too. They are not going to let this country be destroyed without a mighty effort to save it. Besides, where are your men and appliances of war to contend against them? The North can make a steam engine, locomotive or railway car; hardly a yard of cloth or pair of shoes can you make. You are rushing into war with one of the most powerful, ingeniously mechanical and determined people on Earth right at your doors. You are bound to fail. Only in your spirit and determination are you prepared for war. In all else you are totally unprepared, with a bad cause to start with. At first you will make headway, but as your limited resources begin to fail, shut out from the markets of Europe as you will be, your cause will begin to wane. If your people will but stop and think, they must see in the end that you will surely fail."

As we look back, with the advantage of history as a measure, Sherman's bleak forecast was, almost to the letter, an accurate prediction of the future development and inevitable end, of the Civil War.

When Louisiana did secede, in 1861, Sherman was directed to take possession of the U.S. Army weapons that had been assigned to the military school. Louisiana, now a Confederate state, wanted those weapons for the rebellion. Sherman refused, saying "on no earthly account will I do any act or think any thought hostile to or in defiance of the old Government of the United States." He chose, instead, to resign his position at the school.

Sherman then traveled to Washington, D.C., where he was able to meet briefly with President Lincoln. He expressed his fears to Lincoln, telling the President that he was gravely concerned that the North was insufficiently prepared for the coming fight. He found Lincoln less than receptive to his thoughts. Once again, future developments would prove the wisdom of Sherman's concerns.

Sherman went back to St. Louis, Missouri, where he served as president of a streetcar company. As the Civil War began, he continued to express concerns that the North was taking the threat of Southerners too lightly. He advised Lincoln to commit more troops, believing that the war could still be brought to a rapid termination. When Lincoln ordered up only 75,000 "three-month" volunteers, Sherman, privately, mocked the move, saying "Why, you might as well attempt to put out the flames of a burning house with a squirt-gun!"

Civil war seemed inevitable. In May, 1861, William's younger brother, **Senator John Sherman**, assisted him in obtaining a commission. William Tecumseh Sherman was back in the United States Army. A month later, Sherman wrote to a relative "I still think it is to be a long war—very long—much longer than any Politician thinks."

This book covered Sherman's Civil War activities in the earlier sections on the Civil War. We won't go into great detail in this short biography.

Sherman entered the Civil War as a colonel in the 13th Infantry Regiment, a new outfit. They participated in the Union defeat at the **First Battle of Bull Run**, where Sherman's command was the exception that performed well. He was promoted to "Brigadier General of volunteers". He was transferred to a command in the Union **Army of Cumberland** in Kentucky.

Sherman was still very much concerned that the North was seriously underestimating the South. He recommended that Lincoln call up an additional 200,000 troops. The press mocked him. Doubting himself and distressed by the attacks from the journalists, Sherman was relieved of his duties. He returned to his home in Ohio, where he suffered from depression and perhaps a type of "nervous breakdown". He later admitted that the weight of command had "broke me down" and he confessed that he had contemplated suicide. One newspaper labeled him "insane".

Only a few weeks later, regaining his strength, Sherman returned to duty. He was transferred to the Western theater of war and placed under the command of **Ulysses S. Grant**. The two became close. In April of 1862, Grant's **Army of Western Tennessee** was being pushed back by rebels at the **Battle of Shiloh**. Sherman suffered two minor bullet wounds and three horses were shot from under him, but he was able to stabilize the panicking Yankees and to coordinate a controlled retreat, preventing a bloody defeat. The Union Army was able to defeat the Southerners on the next day. Sherman was promoted to Major General of volunteers. One biographer wrote that "Shiloh marked the turning point in Sherman's life".

Sherman continued to serve under Grant through 1862 and 1863. He participated in battles at **Fort Henry**, **Fort Donelson**, **Shiloh**, **Vicksburg** and **Chattanooga**. After a successful **Jackson Expedition**, during which Sherman re-captured Jackson, Mississippi, he was promoted to Brigadier General in the regular U.S. Army, no longer a "volunteer". His family came to visit him at a camp near Vicksburg, once the siege was concluded and his nine-year-old son, known as Willie, the "Little Sergeant", contracted typhoid fever and died.

Union troops were under siege in October of 1863 and Sherman was ordered to go to Chattanooga to relieve them. He was aboard a train, carrying troops to Chattanooga, when it was attacked by 3,000 rebel troops. The Southerners had three pieces of artillery to support their attack. Sherman took command of a near-by garrison of Union troops and was able to fight off the Southerners. Not long after, President Lincoln re-organized his Western armies, putting Grant in command of the new **Military Division of the Mississippi**. William Tecumseh Sherman was put in command of the **Army of Tennessee**.

Sherman, in February of 1864, led his command to Meridian, Mississippi, which was a stronghold for Confederate communications and transportation resources. His forces captured the city on February 14th and proceeded to do all that they could to destroy Confederate infrastructure. Sherman destroyed 10 railroad locomotives, 28 train cars, 61 bridges and more than 100 miles of essential railroad tracks. Sherman's troops captured more than 4,000 prisoners. They took possession of large numbers of horses and transport wagons. Black and white Southern refugees rushed to join Sherman's long columns of troops and captives.

After taking Meridian, in Mississippi, Sherman headed into Georgia. He led three armies, which totaled almost 100,000 troops. Sherman loved the South, but he firmly believed that the best way to bring any war to an end was to do devastating damage and to convince the enemy to give up on the war. He believed more lives would be saved by shortening the duration of the war. He believed his "**scorched earth**" tactic would serve that purpose best.

Sherman's forces moved against Southern **General Joseph E. Johnston**, most often using indirect "flanking" maneuvers. Only at the **Battle at Kennesaw Mountain** did Sherman engage in a direct assault and it ended in a rare Confederate victory. The loss at Kennesaw Mountain barely slowed Sherman down, as he continued to advance his enormous force through Georgia. It was in July,1864, that Sherman was promoted to Major General. He was surprised by the promotion and said he had not desired it until after capturing the city of Atlanta.

In May of 1864, before his promotion, Sherman had already consolidated his armies and started the run to Atlanta. The campaign would take all of four months. Sherman would have to engage Southern Generals **Joseph E. Johnston** and **John B. Hood**, who fought him fiercely. Sherman's tactics and numbers could not be overcome, though and General Hood was forced to abandon Atlanta to Sherman on September 2nd, 1864.

Sherman was committed to making it clear that the South would suffer terribly if it did not totally capitulate to the North and do so quickly. He ordered all civilians to evacuate the city, for their own protection. He ordered that all military and government installations in the Atlanta area be burned to the ground. Many civilian properties were also destroyed. Troops were allowed to "forage" for food and other necessaries. Tremendous damage was done to Atlanta, but some of it was due to rebels, before fleeing, destroying any assets that might benefit the hated Yankees.

Sherman's decisive victory at Atlanta was a huge benefit to **Abraham Lincoln**, who had been anticipating a loss in the upcoming election of 1864. Northerners, who had been discouraged about the progress of the war, were motivated anew to complete the victory. Sherman's conquest of Atlanta also put an end, for all practical purposes, to the **"Copperhead"** movement in the Democrat party. "Copperheads" were Northern Democrats who did not foresee an imminent end to the war and were demanding an immediate termination of the war, leaving the nation divided and the South to govern itself. Sherman's victory at Atlanta may well have saved an electoral victory for Lincoln.

Following the victory at Atlanta, Sherman was more convinced than ever that the Southerners would never quit fighting, so long as they had any remote possibility of surviving as a separate nation. He wanted to show invincible dominance, intending to make the South understand that continuing the war was a hopeless and devastating choice. Sherman, as well as anyone could, understood the awful impact of war. He said "War is cruelty. There is no use trying to reform it. The crueler it is, the sooner it will be over."

He had experienced some success in earlier campaigns in which he counted on his men, during **"forced marches"**, to be able to survive by "foraging" along the trail. Now, having gained much confidence in the toughness and determination of his troops, Sherman did not worry about outrunning his supply lines. He wanted to move swiftly and do a lot of damage. He messaged Grant that, if he could pursue his strategy, he could "make Georgia howl". He received consent from Grant to separate from his supply and communications connections and to march south.

Union General Sherman's "March to the Sea"

Sherman and Southern General Hood were trading blows, back and forth, through the months of September and October, 1864. Hood began working his way to the North, hoping to isolate and cut Sherman off completely. Hood wanted to prevent any unification of the armies of Grant and Sherman. Sherman ordered his **Major Generals Thomas** and **Schofield** north to handle Hood. They crushed Hood's army in November and December, in the **Battles of Franklin** and **Nashville**. Sherman, meanwhile, was cutting a wide corridor across the South, heading relentlessly toward Savannah, Georgia. Sherman wrote to U.S. Grant "If you can whip Lee and I can march to the Atlantic, I think ol' Uncle Abe will give us twenty days leave to see the young folks".

Sherman proceeded, having divided his 62,000 men into two "corps", which were ripping up the countryside, destroying Southern assets along the way. His men created roads and built bridges along the way. They were "on their own" in very hostile territory, stealing food to survive. Southern railroad tracks were torn up wherever they were encountered, heated to a point at which they could be bent and twisted. The mangled tracks came to be known as **"Sherman's neckties"**. In his own writings, Sherman estimated he did more than 100 million dollars in damages during the "**march** to the **sea**". Sherman's plan was to destroy not only Southern military resources, but to devastate Southern morale and motivation to continue the fight. He was completely successful in destroying resources, but the fierceness of his attacks generated a burning hatred for Northerners among the Southern survivors.

Sherman took Savannah, Georgia, on December 21st, 1864. He was pleased to find a Union gunboat that was able to take him immediately to Washington, D.C., where he was able to deliver a message in person to President Lincoln. It read "I beg to present you, as

461

a Christmas gift, the city of Savannah, along with 150 heavy guns and plenty of ammunition and also about 25,000 bales of cotton." (The North, of course, was in need of cotton to make clothing and uniforms).

During his time at Savannah, General Sherman was informed that his infant son, Charles, whom Sherman had never seen, had died. He had lost a second son in the course of the war.

Sherman went back to rejoin his armies and began to march northward through the Carolinas. During that period, General Grant was struggling in his battles with Robert E. Lee. Sherman's successes were gathering public support and there was talk of replacing Grant with Sherman, leaving Sherman to lead all Northern armies. A piece of legislation was introduced which would give Sherman a promotion that would make it easier to put him in place of Grant. Sherman wanted nothing to do with the plan. He immediately, on hearing of it, wrote to General Grant and to Senator John Sherman (William's brother) to say: "General Grant is a great general. I know him well. He stood by me when I was crazy and I stood by him when he was drunk; and now, sir, we stand by each other always."

General Grant advised Sherman to utilize steam ships to transport his troops northward, where Grant hoped Sherman could reinforce the fight against Robert E. Lee. Sherman convinced Grant to allow him to drive his armies north through the Carolinas. Sherman could visualize his armies coming from the south to "squeeze" Robert E. Lee between Grant and himself. Sherman believed that his "scorched earth" strategy, so effective during his "March to the Sea", if carried on through the Carolinas, would further demoralize the South. He especially wanted to dominate South Carolina, as it was the first state to secede, triggering the sequence of secessions that led to the beginning of the war.

Sherman once more force-marched his army northward. In spite of the very rough terrain, his people were moving forward at a rate of up to 12 miles per day. When Southern **General Johnston** learned of the rapid progress, over washboard dirt roads, muddy fields and nearly impassable Salkehatchie Swamps, he declared he had "made up his mind that there had been no such army (as Sherman's) since the days of Julius Caesar".

Sherman's forces left little standing as they pushed through Columbia, South Carolina, on the 17th of February, 1865. Columbia, the capital of South Carolina, burned for days. Most blame Union troops, but Southerners set fire to thousands of bales of cotton before fleeing the city and it is possible much of the fire originated in those flaming bales.

As Sherman's army approached the Lumber River, in south-central North Carolina, torrential rains had created flooding conditions. The ground around the banks of the river included a network of swamps and creeks, making the movement of a large force incredibly difficult. Guides from the **Lumbee Indian** tribe, local indigenous people, led

Sherman's troops through the soggy morass. Sherman himself declared passage through the bogs and marshes was "the damnedest marching I ever saw". As the Union troops left South Carolina and proceeded into North Carolina, they curtailed much of their "scorched earth" activity. They did little damage in North Carolina, probably because Northerners believed that North Carolina had only joined the South very reluctantly. It was the "next to last" Southern state to secede and was perceived to have had little choice, being geographically "trapped" between Virginia, South Carolina and Tennessee.

The only "named" battle engaged during Sherman's drive north from Georgia was the **Battle of Bentonville**, March 19th through 21st, 1865. What little was left of the confederate army, led by General Joseph E. Johnston, took the battlefield near Bentonville, North Carolina, to resist Sherman's continued northward drive. Sherman's army dominated the battle and Johnston was soon left with no choice but to push open a narrow avenue of retreat. Johnston, under cover of darkness, quietly withdrew his remaining forces off the battlefield. He marched his people deeper into North Carolina but had to surrender his command in April. Many years later, Johnston would be a respectful pallbearer at Sherman's funeral.

The Battle of Bentonville would be the final significant, "named" battle of the Civil War. After Bentonville, Sherman traveled to City Point, Virginia, where he met with both Grant and President Lincoln. It was the only time, throughout the war, when the three great men came together personally. A famous painting by **G.P.A. Healy, "The Peacemakers"**, memorialized the intimate meeting.

Following the City Point meeting, Sherman returned to his army. He marched them to Raleigh, Virginia, where he planned to communicate with Southern General Johnston, hoping to offer terms for Johnston's surrender. Before that could be accomplished, though, Sherman received word of Lee's surrender at Appomattox. The great Confederate Army of Northern Virginia was history. Smaller Southern forces would continue to engage in skirmishes, in locations sprinkled around the South, but the great Civil War was over.

William Tecumseh Sherman remained in the army after the war. When Ulysses S. Grant was elected President, he put Sherman in charge of all U. S. forces. He resigned from his commission in 1884, after which he was asked repeatedly to run for public office. He equally repeatedly refused, saying "I will not accept if nominated and will not serve if elected."

Sherman was living in New York when he died on February 14th, 1891, at the age of 71. He was buried, though, in St. Louis, Missouri. His old enemy, General Joseph E. Johnston, in a gesture of respect, served as one of his pallbearers. The weather for the funeral was cold and Johnston performed his duties bare-headed. Days later, Johnston developed pneumonia and died soon after.

William Tecumseh Sherman Quotes

- Courage - a perfect sensibility of the measure of danger and a mental willingness to endure it.

- It's a disagreeable thing to be whipped.

- I make up my opinions from facts and reasoning and not to suit anybody but myself. If people don't like my opinions, it makes little difference as I don't solicit their opinions or votes.

- The scenes on this field would have cured anybody of war.

- If the people raise a great howl against my barbarity and cruelty, I will answer that war is war and not popularity seeking.

- In our Country... one class of men makes war and leaves another to fight it out. If I had my choice I would kill every reporter in the world, but I am sure we would be getting reports from Hell before breakfast.

- Grant stood by me when I was crazy and I stood by him when he was drunk and now we stand by each other.

- I am tired and sick of war. Its glory is all moonshine. It is only those who have neither fired a shot nor heard the shrieks and groans of the wounded who cry aloud for blood, for vengeance, for desolation. War is hell.

William Tecumseh Sherman and Slavery

Sherman was a Northerner who fought for the Union in the Civil War. His position regarding slavery, like that of Abraham Lincoln, evolved continuously as he lived his life. He was not, prior to the Civil War, an abolitionist and he did not believe that black people were the equals of white people. He expressed opposition, though, to the practice of separating slaves from their biological families and he was an advocate of education for the enslaved black population. His writings make it clear that his opinions about race changed steadily as he grew older and had more experiences.

During his tenure throughout the Civil War, Sherman resisted pressures to allow black freedmen or fugitive slaves to participate as armed combatants. He refused to encourage the slaves to revolt or to attempt escape. He explained, after the war, that "My aim then was to whip the rebels, to humble their pride, to follow them to their inmost recesses and make them fear and dread us. Fear of the Lord is the beginning of wisdom. I did not want them to cast in our teeth what General Hood had once done at Atlanta, that we had to call on their slaves to help us to subdue them."

When many thousands of escaped slaves, now refugees, joined Sherman's columns as he passed through Georgia and the Carolinas, some Northern abolitionists accused Sherman of not being supportive enough of the masses of black fugitives. **Secretary of War Edwin M. Stanton** was sent to Savannah to meet with Sherman, to investigate the complaints. Approximately twenty leaders of the black community, all invited by General Sherman, attended the meeting. After their meeting, black Baptist minister **Garrison Frazier** described the feelings in the black community about Sherman:

"We looked upon General Sherman prior to his arrival as a man in the providence of God specially set apart to accomplish this work and we unanimously felt inexpressible gratitude to him, looking upon him as a man that should be honored for the faithful performance of his duty. Some of us called upon him immediately upon his arrival and it is probable he would not meet Secretary Stanton with more courtesy than he met us. His conduct and deportment toward us characterized him as a friend and a gentleman."

Only days after that meeting, General Sherman published his famous **"Special Field Orders, No. 15"**. The orders proposed to take land from white property owners in the states of South Carolina, Georgia and Florida and re-distribute it to 40,000 former slaves and black refugees. The Sherman orders were consistent with the anticipated **"Reconstruction"** plans of Abraham Lincoln, Frederick Douglass and Ulysses S. Grant. The program was the basis for the widely shared claim that the U.S. government had promised freed slaves **"Forty Acres and a Mule"**. Unfortunately, when Andrew Johnson, a man many considered to be a racist, became President, he revoked Sherman's order, terminating the program. Johnson would be an obstacle to many of the re-unification plans made by Lincoln, Grant and Douglass.

Records indicate that William Tecumseh Sherman grew much more supportive of the black community as he aged. Records indicate he dealt with black people, in personal encounters, in a cordial and sincere manner. He was approaching his final days when he published an essay in which he advocated "full civil rights for black citizens". He implored Southerners to "let the negro vote and count his vote honestly, otherwise, so sure as there is a God in Heaven, you will have another war, crueler than the last when the torch and dagger will take the place of the muskets of well-ordered battalions".

Andrew Johnson

America's Seventeenth President

On December 29, 1808, **Mary "Polly" McDonough**, a washer-woman, gave birth to Andrew Johnson. She was married to **Jacob Johnson**, who was a man of little means. Jacob and Polly both were from the most humble of beginnings and worked mostly as servants in a tavern. They lived in a two-room home, little better than a shack. Jacob and Polly both were illiterate, but Jacob was able to become the town constable of Raleigh, North Carolina before the two were married.

Andrew was only three when Jacob, while ringing the town bell after rescuing three drowning men, suddenly died. He was probably the victim of a heart attack. Polly supported the family, in poverty, with her work as a laundress. In those days, washer-women went alone into the homes of other citizens, where they did their work. Women who were privately in the company of men to whom they were not married were often assumed to be of low character. Indeed, as young Andrew was considered to have no visible resemblance to his father, Jacob, rumors flew that Andrew may have been the son of some other citizen. Polly, after Jacob's early death, would eventually be remarried to **Turner Doughtry**, a man as bound by poverty as she was herself.

Polly "apprenticed" Andrew to **James Selby**, a tailor, when Andrew was but ten years old. The apprenticeship had the effect of "indenturing" Andrew to Selby until Andrew reached twenty-one years of age. His work and his family's poverty, kept Andrew out of formal education. In Raleigh, though, educated citizens gathered at Selby's tailor shop, where they would share readings with the busy tailors. Andrew Johnson was known to go often to the tailor shop, even before his apprenticeship, to listen to the readers. Fellow employees sometimes worked with Andrew to boost his fundamental reading and arithmetic skills. Andrew's drive to continue his education was probably initiated by his experiences in the tailor's shop. He would one day be known for his gifted public speaking abilities.

Both Andrew and his older brother, William, were apprenticed to James Selby. Neither boy was happy in their circumstances. Andrew had served for about five years, making him around 15 years old, when the two boys ran away from their "subscriber", James Selby. Selby quickly posted a reward for their return, offering "ten dollars reward to anyone who will deliver said apprentices to me in Raleigh or I will give the above reward for Andrew Johnson alone". It may be that the older brother, William, had already worked off most of his bondage and Selby was more concerned with getting Andrew back.

Both boys ran to Carthage, North Carolina, where Andrew obtained a job in another tailor shop. Still worried about being found and returned to Selby, Andrew moved on. He went to Laurens, South Carolina, where he once again easily found employment. Andrew soon fell in love, for the first time, with a young lady named **Mary Wood**. He used his tailoring skills to make her a beautiful quilt and, presenting it, he proposed marriage. She may have accepted the quilt, but she firmly rejected his proposal for marriage.

Broken-hearted and tired of running, Andrew returned to Raleigh, where he attempted to work out a mutually acceptable agreement with James Selby. Selby was not accommodating, which left Andrew at risk if he stayed nearby. Once again Andrew Johnson fled Raleigh. He moved westward. He worked in Tennessee, Alabama and back to Tennessee. In 1826, his mother and step-father, still living in poverty in Raleigh, convinced Andrew to return. They meant to gather all of the family, with the intention of moving west together. The group made their way through the Blue Ridge Mountains and rambled on until they reached Greeneville, Tennessee. The town was most agreeable to Andrew. The location they landed on when they arrived was so beautiful that he would one day purchase the property and plant on it a commemorative tree.

Andrew sat up his own tailor shop in Greeneville and was soon well-established. He met, and fell in love with, **Eliza McCardle**, the daughter of a shoemaker. The couple would produce five children. Eliza was somewhat educated and worked to improve Andrew's math and reading skills. Her affliction with tuberculosis undoubtedly made working, and later in Andrew's career, traveling, more difficult for her.

Andrew's tailor shop became prosperous and he began speculating in real estate. As the years passed, he became affluent enough to buy more properties, including several black slaves. The slaves worked in and around his residence or were "rented out". Some were with him throughout his entire life.

Johnson was elected to serve as an alderman in Greeneville. After the **Nat Turner Slave Rebellion**, which frightened many slave-owning Southerners, a new Tennessee constitution was proposed. Among other things, the new document would "**disenfranchise**" even free black Tennesseans. Andrew Johnson traveled the state, speaking in favor of it. He gained substantial public exposure and his public speaking skills were gaining recognition. He was elected Mayor of Greeneville in 1834. His political career had begun. His speeches communicated his dislike for the big planters and his opposition to a big central government. He avidly supported **"states' rights"** and **"populism"**, promoting more power for the people and less for the government. He was, from the beginning, pro-slavery or, at least, "pro" the right of each state to determine its own policies. While working in Greeneville, Johnson enlisted in the Tennessee militia, during which time he gained the rank of colonel and, thereafter, was often addressed by that title.

In 1836, Johnson was elected to serve in the legislature of the state of Tennessee. Johnson had not been solidly locked into either the Whig or the Democrat party but had generally practiced as a **Whig**. In 1837, though, he ran for election as a **Democrat** and would remain a Democrat throughout his remaining career. The Whig party, not long after, transitioned into the **Republican** party, which was founded on anti-slavery policies. Johnson would not be comfortable in that setting.

Andrew Johnson became a Tennessee Senator in 1841 and then, in 1843, was elected to serve in the United States House of Representatives. As a U.S. Congressman, Johnson proposed legislation that would be known as the **Homestead Act**. It would offer plots (160 acres) of undeveloped land to American settlers, but the bill would not pass until 1862. Meanwhile, his tailoring business, back in Greeneville, was doing well. He continued to speculate in real estate and he was able to invest in a larger personal residence and in a farm. His mother and his stepfather lived in his home and as many as nine slaves served their needs. He prospered financially.

As a Congressman, Johnson continued to lobby for less government, for states' rights, for the poor against the rich and, always, against the abolitionists. He firmly believed that the U.S. Constitution guaranteed citizens the right to own property, including slaves. Johnson himself, by that time, owned fourteen enslaved black people. As tensions built leading up to the Civil War, he opposed secession, supporting the preservation of the Union. He was elected governor of Tennessee in 1852 and left his Congressional seat. While serving as governor, Johnson had little support from a powerful opposition Whig party. Nonetheless, he was able to create the state's first **public library**, making books available to all citizens. He was also able to create their first common **public school system** and an agency to create uniformity in **weights and measures**. Johnson also created a **"State Fair"**, to be held each year to promote the affairs of craftsmen, businessmen and farmers. He was elected to the United States Senate and returned to Washington, D.C., in 1857. While making the trip, his train was derailed. Serious injury was incurred by his right arm and the residual damage would be an impairment for years to come.

Eliza, still burdened by tuberculosis, remained in Tennessee. Andrew eschewed social occasions and was known to spend much of his time studying in the **Library of Congress**. A fellow Tennessean, **James K. Polk**, was elected President in 1844, but the two never enjoyed a close relationship, often disagreeing on key issues. Johnson did support Polk's decision to engage in the **Mexican-American War**, but he adamantly opposed the administration's **"Wilmot Proposal"**, which would ban slavery in any territories gained from Mexico. While Johnson did oppose "big government", he compromised his philosophy in his support of a national program to expand railroads, knowing his own state of Tennessee needed the railroad. When Kentucky's "great compromiser", **Henry**

Clay, proposed the **Compromise of 1850**, Johnson supported all of its provisions except one: He would not vote to support the abolition of slavery in Washington, D.C.

In those times, U.S. Senators were elected by state legislatures and Presidents were elected by the Electoral College. Andrew Johnson pushed to have both senators and presidents elected by popular vote. He also pushed for a twelve-year limited tenure for all federal judges. None of his proposals were passed. He consistently pushed for the protection of slavery in the states where it was already an institution, but he also advocated strongly against secession and for the preservation of the Union.

Abraham Lincoln was elected President in 1860 and was inaugurated on March 4, 1861. Seven Southern states quickly announced they would secede. Johnson, still in the U.S. Senate, delivered a powerful speech, hoping to convince Southerners to resist secessionists. He said in that speech: "I will not give up this government. No, I intend to stand by it and I invite every man who is a patriot to rally around the altar of our common country and swear by our God and all that is sacred and holy, that the Constitution shall be saved and the Union preserved." Northerners applauded Johnson's oration, but Southerners were unmoved and Southern Senators resigned as their states departed the Union.

The Civil War began on April 12ᵗʰ with the rebel attack on **Fort Sumter**. Johnson's state, Tennessee, seceded from the Union in June. Andrew Johnson became the only Southern Senator to maintain his loyalty to the United States. Lincoln appointed him to be the military governor of Tennessee, for which duty Johnson resigned his seat in the Senate.

As military governor, Johnson attempted to re-unify the state with the Union. Tennessee was in the process of allowing a popular vote which would determine whether the state would or would not, secede. Johnson traveled widely, speaking against secession. Emotions were running hot. Secessionists were aggressive in their attacks against him. Threats were made and assaults were attempted. As he spoke, he kept a pistol on the podium, hoping to be able to defend himself against assassins. He was unsuccessful in his fight against secession and Tennessee became one of the **Confederate States of America**. Once Tennessee voters confirmed the state's secession, Johnson, now a "Northerner" in the eyes of the rebels, feared for his life. He fled Tennessee through the Cumberland Gap, during which passage his group was fired upon, though no injuries were incurred.

When Lincoln appointed Johnson military governor of Tennessee, the Senate confirmed his military rank to be that of Brigadier General. The Southerners reacted by immediately confiscating Johnson's home, his land and his slaves. Johnson's slaves apparently escaped the rebels and were able to return to the Johnson home.

The Confederates converted his residence into a military hospital. Meanwhile, in 1862, without the resistance of Southern legislators, Johnson's **Homestead Bill** was finally enacted by the United States Congress. In combination with the commitment to a **transcontinental railroad** and approval for **land-grant colleges**, the Homestead Act was the foundation for the massive westward expansion of the United States.

In his role as military governor of Tennessee, Johnson attempted to defend Nashville from frequent rebel raids. Southern **General Nathan Bedford Forrest** was a constant threat in Eastern Tennessee. Union **General William S. Rosecrans** finally arrived, early in 1863, to engineer a victory against Forrest at Murfreesboro. Eastern Tennessee was soon cleared of Confederates.

Lincoln issued his **Emancipation Proclamation** following the **Battle of Antietam**. Johnson persuaded him to exempt Tennessee from the provision in the proclamation which set all Southern slaves free. Lincoln cooperated. Northerners were debating about how the precipitous freedom of four million slaves could be managed. Immense problems were forecast as officials considered the obstacles that would be faced by the newly freed citizens, knowing most had no property, no assets, no education and no employment. Andrew Johnson finally came to understand that slavery had to end. He declared: "If the institution of slavery seeks to overthrow the Government, then the Government has a clear right to destroy it". He eventually came to support the enlistment of former slaves in the United States Army. He worked to recruit more than 20,000 black soldiers.

As the Civil War wound down and the election of 1864 was on the horizon, Abraham Lincoln selected Andrew Johnson to be his running mate. He believed that Johnson, as a "**War Democrat**" and a Union-supporter from the South, would balance out his campaign. ("War Democrats" were Southern Democrats who remained loyal to Lincoln when the war broke out). Lincoln won the 1864 election by a margin of 212 to 21 in the electoral college. Johnson became his Vice President. When the two were inaugurated into office in March of 1865, Johnson, who was in recovery from typhoid fever, drank heavily at celebrations the night before the big event. He then "medicated" himself with whiskey on the next morning, hoping it would improve his condition. It had the effect, instead, of impairing his speech, which became slurred and somewhat incoherent. The incident led to his being accused of being an alcoholic, which most historians agree he was not. Abraham Lincoln came to Johnson's defense, saying: "I have known Andy Johnson for many years; he made a bad slip the other day, but you need not be scared; Andy ain't a drunkard."

After Johnson became Vice President, but while he remained in Tennessee as military governor, the state had been made nearly free of confederate aggression. Tennessee's citizens voted to ratify a new constitution while Johnson was still in Nashville. His final act as military governor was to certify the new constitution . . . a constitution abolishing slavery in the state.

Andrew Johnson was Vice President only for a few weeks. Abraham Lincoln was assassinated on April 14th, 1865. Andrew Johnson was immediately sworn in as President. He was most fortunate on the night of the assassination, as the cabal that planned and carried out the President's death also planned to kill the Vice President, Johnson and the Secretary of State, **William Seward**. Seward was attacked but recovered. The man assigned to kill Johnson, **George Atzerodt**, spared the Vice President when he lost his courage, reportedly got drunk and abandoned the attack. He would hang, anyway.

Andrew Johnson became President without being elected, which probably diminished his power while in office. He was faced with the immense problems, on many fronts, which faced the nation as the Civil War was drawing to an end.

Johnson learned, soon after Lincoln's death, that union **General Sherman** had plans to offer a very lenient plan for the surrender of Southern **General Johnston's** forces in North Carolina. Sherman's offer would leave Confederate state governments in place and would not abolish slavery in the state. Johnson ordered Sherman not to offer such lenient terms of surrender and to make no political compromises, which direction Sherman soon followed.

Johnson then publicized his placement of a $100,000 bounty (almost two million dollars in present day) for the capture of Confederate President **Jefferson Davis**. It was an action that angered Southerners and stimulated resistance on some fronts.

As the time to execute the four members of the group that planned the Lincoln assassination approached, some citizens argued that **Mary Surratt** should not die with the other conspirators. Johnson ordered her to be hung with the rest. (Atzerodt, the man who got drunk instead of killing Johnson, was also hung).

These early actions suggested Johnson would be tough on Southerners as the re-unification of the nation began. Southerners were already making plans to protect their interests, especially in terms of keeping black people from gaining power.

Andrew Johnson argued that the Southern states never really left the union, because they didn't have the constitutional right to do so. This could be seen as inconsistent with his usual strong "states' rights" position. He wanted the Union restored quickly, though, and was willing to compromise his beliefs to make it happen. He was willing to let the Southern states elect new governments, knowing that many of the new officials would be former leaders of the rebel confederacy. He was hopeful that the common citizen would have an opportunity to occupy positions previously held by the wealthy plantation owners and their friends.

Johnson was not concerned about suffrage, the right to vote, for African-Americans. After all, women, even white women, were still nowhere near obtaining the right to vote in national elections. Johnson held, in this case, to his "states' rights" position, arguing that each state could work out its own decisions regarding voting rights.

"The Era of Reconstruction" was about to begin. It would define the manner in which Southern states were brought back into the Union and the way that millions of free black people would be assimilated into American society. As Southerners elected government officials, many of whom had been in power prior to the war, their new leaders began to create **"Black Codes"** which were designed to restrict the freedoms of black citizens.

Republicans wanted Johnson to use the financial desperation of the returning Southern states to be used as "leverage" to force the Southerners to accept guarantees of civil rights for freed black citizens. Andrew Johnson was not supportive, still believing each state should determine its own policies. His cabinet was split on the issue. On the 29th of May, 1865, President Johnson, with the full support of his cabinet, issued his first two "Reconstruction" proclamations. One proclamation was the first official recognition of a new state government in one of the rebel states and that state was Virginia. The second proclamation ordered amnesty for all former rebels, with the exception of those who owned properties worth more than twenty-thousand dollars. Johnson also authorized a temporary governor and new elections in North Carolina. He ordered constitutional conventions to be held in the other Southern states.

Northerners wanted the South to have to openly, publicly acknowledge their absolute defeat. They wanted apologies from the South. They wanted changes that would justify the devastation of the war, including civil rights for African-Americans. They wanted slavery abolished in all of America. The **"Black Codes"** that were already cropping up in the South were discouraging harbingers of things to come. Some of the new codes bound black laborers to farms based on annual contracts that could never be terminated. Many former slaves ended up having to keep working for the same people who were their former "owners" and "masters". Other new codes allowed law enforcement to arrest unemployed black people for "vagrancy" or "loitering" and then to rent the arrested victims out as laborers. Voting rights for black men were still only a dim light, far in the future. After all, black men were still not allowed to vote in most Northern states, either.

As the United States Congress began to come back together, many of the Southern representatives and senators were the same Southern Democrats who had previously held the offices. Republicans feared that allowing the Southerners back in too easily might mean Democrats would gain too much power in the government.

Andrew Johnson's lack of empathy for Southern blacks began to emerge in his early policy decisions. He vetoed the **Freedmen's Bureau Bill** and a **Civil Rights Bill**, both of which were meant to provide important protections for the newly freed black citizens. Congress went on to pass the **Fourteenth Amendment**, which granted full citizenship to black people, but Johnson also vetoed it. In spite of his veto, the Amendment passed in July of 1868. The Fourteenth Amendment, strangely, extended full citizenship to all Americans born in the United States . . . EXCEPT American Indians or Native Americans who lived on reservations.

Johnson's policies caused an impassable divide between him and his Republican colleagues. He tried to establish a new political party, the **National Union Party**, hoping that some Republicans and many Southern Democrats might come to his defense and support him. The "mid-term" elections of 1866, in which Southern states were still not allowed to vote, was a disaster for Johnson. Republicans won an overwhelming victory, taking a controlling 2/3 majority in the House. They began organizing their own plans for managing Reconstruction.

President Johnson had a vitriolic relationship with Secretary of War Stanton. The two often quarreled. Johnson eventually suspended Stanton, replacing him with General U.S. Grant. Grant was not a willing participant in the incident. Congress was unhappy with Johnson for many reasons and the suspension of Stanton may have given them a reason to attack him. Congress claimed Johnson had violated the **Tenure of Office Act** and began **impeachment proceedings**, making Johnson the first President to be impeached. The proceedings moved forward haltingly, starting and stopping, regaining momentum and then stopping again. Congress re-instated Stanton, over Johnson's objection and General Grant happily walked away from the situation. Johnson then dismissed Stanton from the office and replaced him. Stanton refused to leave. The House of Representatives then voted for Johnson's impeachment.

The impeachment trial began in March of 1868 and lasted for three months. In the end, the move to impeach fell short by a single vote and Johnson remained in office. There was speculation that some legislators voted in favor of Johnson because they could not accept the man who would succeed him, **Senator Wade**, president pro tempore of the Senate. Wade was a supporter of giving women the right to vote, which made him unacceptable to many of the legislators. There were unproven, but persistent, allegations that bribery may also have been involved in manipulating some of the impeachment votes.

One of the most significant achievements of the Johnson presidency, the Alaskan purchase, came with the help of Secretary of State Seward. Seward was an aggressive "expansionist", wanting to add territory to the United States, hoping to create a "sea to sea" nation. The Russian government owned what it called its **"North American Colony"**, which is now Alaska. The Russians feared the possible movement of Great

Britain from Canada into Alaska and considered the territory a financial liability. Seward tried to purchase all of Alaska from Russia for five million dollars. Russia negotiated to get the price increased to $7,200,000, which would be about $140,000,000 dollars in present day. America gained 600,000 square miles of property for approximately two-cents per acre.

Just before the 1868 election, Johnson pardoned all former confederate soldiers, with the exception of those in leadership roles. He hoped it would hasten re-unification and he certainly hoped it would help him gain favor with Southern Democrats. Johnson did not receive the Republican nomination for the 1868 election, which was easily won by U.S. Grant. Johnson played out his time in office by throwing a birthday party for his sixtieth birthday. He invited several hundred children to the affair. Grant, still angry with Johnson over the Stanton debacle, did not allow his children to attend the celebration.

Andrew Johnson issued a final and comprehensive amnesty to the Southern rebels on Christmas Day, 1868. This one covered all the rebels, including **Jefferson Davis** himself. Johnson, in his final weeks in office, also pardoned **Dr. Samuel Mudd**, who had treated the broken leg of **John Wilkes Booth**. Mudd's conviction had been controversial, with some believing he had nothing to do with the assassination conspiracy. On the day that U.S. Grant was to be inaugurated, Grant had announced he would refuse to ride to the event in a carriage with Johnson. Johnson, for his part, refused to attend the inauguration at all, under any conditions. He wrapped up some paperwork and quietly left the White House, riding to the house of a friend.

After failing to win re-election, Johnson returned home to Tennessee. He failed in an attempt to win a Senate seat in 1869 and failed to win a seat in the House in 1872. He was persistent, though, and was able to win a seat in the U.S. Senate in 1875. No other former President had done so. He was back in the Senate for only a very short time, as he suffered a stroke while back home visiting family in Tennessee and died shortly thereafter, on July 31st, 1875. He was 66-years-old.

Johnson's funeral drew immense crowds. His private secretary wrote "People came from the hills and valleys, everywhere near and far. The cortege was so dense the marshals were unable to control the masses or to make way for the passage of the hearse, carrying the coffined body to its sepulchral home, on the way to the apex of the knoll which was to be the final sleeping place of the deceased, pointed out by the negro Sam, a former slave, as having been so designated by his master".

Andrew Johnson Quotes

"Washington, DC is 12 square miles bordered by reality."

"When I die, I desire no better winding sheet than the Stars and Stripes and no softer pillow than the Constitution of my country." (When Johnson died, he was buried with an American flag and with a copy of the U. S. Constitution folded beneath his head.)

"The life of a republic lies certainly in the energy, virtue and intelligence of its citizens."

The following Johnson quote is shared with regrets and apologies for its content of crude racism:

"If blacks were given the right to vote, that would place every splay-footed, bandy-shanked, hump-backed, thick-lipped, flat-nosed, woolly-headed, ebon-colored in the country upon an equality with the poor white man."

Andrew Johnson and Slavery

Slavery was well-embedded in Southern society and not rare in Northern society, as Andrew Johnson was growing up. He accepted slavery as the way of things, as did many Southerners of those times. He was not a friend of the abolitionists, as he believed each state should have the right to determine its own policies regarding slavery. He was opposed to the fragmentation of the Union and argued adamantly against secession. When the Civil War broke out, he broke his ties with the government of Tennessee and went to work for the North. He did not believe that the black race was equal in all ways to the white race. It's not known whether his prejudices were based on his perception of the natural endowments of the races or were based on his understanding that African-Americans were generally deprived of any meaningful education.

In the year that Andrew Johnson purchased his first slave, 1843, he was a Tennessee State Senator. On November 29th of that year, he bought an African-American boy who was approximately 13-years-old and was named **Sam**. Sam cost Andrew $541.00. He would be with Andrew Johnson until Johnson's death. In January, only weeks later, Johnson purchased Sam's half-sister, **Dolly**, who was about 14-years-old. It seems likely Sam may have persuaded Andrew Johnson to obtain his sister, so the two could remain together.

In 1857, some fourteen years later, Johnson purchased another African-American youth, this one named **Henry**. Henry cost $1015.00 and was also about 13-years-old when purchased. The Bills of Sale for all three read the same, declaring that the slaves were "sound, healthy, sensible and a slave for life". Pretty much the same words would be found on the Bill of Sale for a horse or a pig. The phrase "slave for life" meant that there were no legal papers that would allow the slave to work off his term of slavery.

There happens to be a great deal of information about the slaves Johnson owned. He would eventually own ten and maybe as many as fourteen.

Records suggest they were, given the circumstances of the times, treated reasonably well.

The slave "Sam" took Johnson's last name, which was common practice. Sam married Margaret and the couple had nine children, three of whom were born into slavery. Their younger children were born after the Civil War and were born free. One of their daughters, "Dolly", had three children, all born into slavery and all with "questionable heritage", meaning the father, or fathers, were unknown. It wasn't unusual for slave owners to exploit female slaves and father children through their slaves. There is no indication anything like that happened in the Johnson family.

Andrew Johnson, or his family members, "rented out" Sam Johnson and other slaves to various other employers. Sam is known to have done work plastering houses, planting and harvesting crops and working as a janitor at the local courthouse. Andrew Johnson allowed his slaves to keep a share of their earnings, which other slave owners sometimes did as well. Many did not. Sam had been with the Johnsons for nearly twenty years when Andrew's son Charles wrote to his father, about Sam:

"A few days since Mother sent Sam word to cut wood at Pattersons. He came up in the house and said, he would 'be damed' if he wanted to cut wood there; and if you wanted to sell him you could do so just as soon as he pleased, he did not care a dam,' You will see he is quite an independent gentleman and just to show his notions of himself and his rights, at another time, he was asking Mother for his part of some money paid him for work. Mother remarked to him if he was as ready to pay others as he was to collect, he would do better; he replied that he did not get half enough no how and that he ought to have all that he could make". Indications are that the slave Sam had few restrictions on his own comments.

Andrew Johnson was President in 1867 and had already freed Sam. Sam had been appointed to the board of the new **"Freedmen's Bureau"**. (Andrew Johnson had been opposed to creation of the Freedmen's Bureau). Sam wrote a letter to the President, asking him if it might be possible for Sam to buy a plot of land from Andrew. On that property, he wanted to build a school for "the education of Coloured children". Sam hoped to be able to raise money to purchase an acre of land, which he clearly specified by carefully defining the location in his letter to the President. Johnson responded by directing Sam to lay out the boundaries of the property and to send him the necessary paperwork. Andrew Johnson gave the acre of land to Sam, but did not charge him for the purchase. In Sam's letter to Andrew, his former "owner", he closed by saying "I am getting along as well as usual and have not changed any in Politics, still being for you as much as ever. I would like to see you very much."

Sam Johnson and his wife, Margaret, were living, without charge, in Andrew's former tailor shop. Around 1870 a newspaper reporter went to the address to inquire about Sam. Margaret answered the door and told the reporter that "He (Andrew Johnson) lets me and my husband live in here now and don't charge us no rent". Later in life, Sam Johnson worked as a janitor in his church, where he became familiar in a silk top hat and a jacket with long tails. When Andrew Johnson was buried, it was Sam who led officials to the spot which Andrew had designated for his burial.

The slave Dolly (Johnson) was purchased at nearly the same time that Sam had been purchased. She grew to adulthood in the Johnson home and became a caretaker for the household and the children. Andrew Johnson's granddaughter wrote of Dolly: "My mind wanders back to the days when we children used to have a black mama (Dolly) as well as our own dear mama, but thank God the race is free. Slavery is a sin."

The Johnson slave Dolly had three children, Liz, Florence and William and the identity of the fathers are unknown. Her youngest son, Will, was born ten years after the first two children and his death certificate lists Andrew Johnson's son, Robert, as the boy's father. In a letter written to his son, Robert, in 1854, Andrew said "I have bought a basket and some other little notions for your little brother and a little chair for Liz and Florence". Dolly's son William wrote "When I was little, Mr. Andrew used to hold me on one knee and my sister on the other." William also wrote, much later, that: "One day Mrs. Johnson called us all in and said we were free now. She said we were free to go or we could stay if we wanted. We all stayed."

Dolly's daughter, Florence, joined Andrew in the White House. Others of her children may also have lived or visited there. After Andrew returned from the presidency, Dolly's son William wrote that "I was with him all the time. I slept in the same room with him". As an adult, William was invited to visit **Franklin Delano Roosevelt** in the White House. Roosevelt gifted William a cane with a silver tip. The famed reporter **Ernie Pyle** questioned Will, asking "Weren't you better off when Andrew Johnson owned you than since then?" Will responded "Yes, we were mighty well off then, but any man would rather be free than be a slave".

Andrew Johnson told about a time, during the Civil War, when Union troops "confiscated" his slaves, taking them away. The Union Army used confiscated slaves to assist in building entrenchments, repairing railroads and other tasks in service of the North. Johnson said his slaves soon escaped and returned to the Johnson home. A son-in-law to Johnson, Judge Patterson, supervised the transport of the escaped slaves back to the Johnson household.

After the war, Dolly Johnson continued to live in the little house beside the tailor shop. She described it in this way: "It is a small house, with two rooms and one fireplace and whitewashed like the shop. It stands on the street, there being no front yard." It is the house in which her mother, Margaret, had also lived. Sam was living in his own home, built by himself, on land that had been given to him by Andrew. Dolly, by 1880, had moved into the Johnson family Tailor Shop, which she converted into her own business. An advertisement was posted in the local Greeneville, Tennessee, newspaper on March 17th, 1881. It read: "Dolly Johnson, colored, has established a bakery in town."

Andrew Johnson grew up in a culture that was permeated with slavery. People of those times were never exposed to a society without slavery, they knew nothing else. Most people, even slave owners, understood the underlying sin and shame attached to the awful institution of slavery. The economic advantages of free slave labor, and the pleasure some took in having complete power over other humans, blocked all efforts to abolish the practice. Johnson was a racist and he carried all of the standard prejudices and misconceptions of the typical racist of his day. As he grew older, and as he experienced his own relationships with his own slaves, Johnson evolved. He grew to understand that slavery was a sin that had to be abolished.

Andrew set all of his own slaves free on August 8th, 1863, before the end of the war. They all chose to stay with him and his family and continued to work for wages. As military governor, before the war ended, he declared all of the slaves in Tennessee to be free. He wrote "If the institution of slavery seeks (through the Confederacy) to overthrow the Government, then the Government has a clear right to destroy it." Johnson came to support the encouragement of former slaves to enlist in the Union Army. He worked to recruit more than 20,000 black soldiers. The black people, former slaves, in Tennessee presented Andrew Johnson with a beautiful watch, on which was inscribed their gratitude to him "For his Untiring Energy in the Cause of Freedom". Sam Johnson, Andrew's first slave, attended Johnson's funeral and pointed out to officials the specific spot on which Johnson wanted to be interred.

It may be assumed, in reading these reports, that the experiences shared by Johnson family slaves could present a false impression of the typical experiences of enslaved African-Americans. In reality, it delivers an honest picture of one of many, many different true experiences of those in bondage.

Many "house slaves", especially in the northern United States, were treated more or less as family members. In those homes, the black people were often assumed to be of lower abilities than white people, not "equals", but were usually not horribly abused. In much of society, North and South, it was considered dishonorable, undignified and abusive to mistreat slaves. Racism was the norm in the sense that prejudices about capabilities and characteristics of black people were pervasive. Not everyone shared those prejudices, but many certainly did.

Slaves who did field work commonly were treated far worse than "house slaves". The farther south the slaves were taken, the worse their treatment generally became. Most farmers and plantation owners, if they were wealthy enough to own slaves, wanted them treated well enough to keep them strong for their labors. Some, though, took pleasure in having "power" over the slaves and went out of their way to demonstrate their control. Slaves were whipped mercilessly, beaten with chains, burned, bound, raped and, sometimes, murdered. Certainly, no records were kept that would document how common such activities were, but there can be no doubt that they happened far too frequently.

Treatment of slaves ranged from the apparent kindness and benevolence of the Johnson family to the horrors of some of the plantation overseers. In no case, though, could ownership of other human beings be justified. There is no acceptable defense of slavery.

Post-Civil War in America

The Era of Reconstruction

President Lincoln, General Grant and abolitionist **Frederick Douglass** shared a vision of **re-unification** which would bring the Union back together and would ease the transition of former slaves into their new lives as free souls. Lincoln had already labeled his plan "**Reconstruction**". Lincoln, in a speech in Louisiana, for the first time, suggested that some black people, including free black men and black men who had served in the Union Army, should have the right to vote. Only three days later Lincoln was assassinated. Reconstruction did not go as the three great leaders had hoped.

After the loss of Abraham Lincoln, **President Johnson** held onto his strong belief in states' rights, which was an impediment to any federal intervention in the policies of individual states. He supported the abolition of slavery, but he was reluctant to enforce penalties against states which were finding ways to keep their black citizens under control. Southerners began enacting "**Black Codes**" designed to limit opportunities for black people in employment, housing, social interactions and voting rights. Northerners were outraged by the restrictive and abusive practices of Southerners in their treatment of the former slaves. President Johnson claimed he opposed giving black men the right to vote because he feared that the dominant white population would control, through intimidation and sheer force, the black vote. Many free black people were still dependent on their former owners for work and sustenance.

The **Era of Reconstruction** began with the final throes of the Civil War and is considered to have ended with the **Compromise of 1877**. As the war wound down and a Confederate defeat was inevitable, Congress abolished slavery in all of the United States. The **13th, 14th and 15th Amendments**, known now as the "**Reconstruction Amendments**" were passed. On paper, at least, the United States had guaranteed black freedmen the same civil rights as white citizens. In practice, though, African-Americans would continue to suffer inequalities in almost every aspect of life, including education, voting opportunities, employment, housing and equal access to transportation.

Southerners reacted angrily to the new Amendments and attacks on black people became more frequent and more brutal. The threat of lynchings terrified black families. In response to the violence and to Southern resistance to the laws, Congress responded by federalizing national protection of civil rights for all citizens. States that had seceded were put under U.S. military control and legislation was passed which forced the Southern states, before being allowed re-admission to the Union, to guarantee the civil rights of their freed black people. Unfortunately, it is much easier to put laws on the books than it is to change the daily real-life behaviors instilled by decades of cultural practice.

Republicans formed organizations intended to force Southern states to fundamentally re-design their historical culture. President Johnson wanted power shifted from the wealthy plantation owners to the common citizens. The **Freedmen's Bureau** was created, with the goal of delivering assistance and resources to the former slaves. The U.S. Army was assigned to facilitate the transition of the black community by enforcing a free-labor economy, assisting in negotiation of fair labor contracts, coordinating establishment of wide-spread access to schools and churches and eliminating violence against black people. Sadly, when the military was withdrawn, with the Compromise of 1877, Southern Democrats quickly regained control, **"Jim Crow"** was brought to life and African-Americans continued to suffer.

The government allocated money to be spent in pursuing a litany of reconstruction projects. Money draws attention. Thousands of Northerners drifted southward, some with good intentions, hoping to help assimilate black Southerners successfully into society, while others were grifters and swindlers, hoping to make money on the miseries of others. The Northerners were known as "**Carpetbaggers**". Southerners who openly participated in, and supported, reconstruction policies were, in many places, in a minority position. They were known as "**Scalawags**" and they were generally disliked by other Southerners. Calling someone a Carpetbagger or Scalawag was not often meant as a compliment.

Most Southerners were, in political terms, "Southern Democrats". They were the party that forced the secession of Southern states in defense of "states' rights", including the right to own slaves. They were responsible for creation of the **Black Codes** and they worked to maintain control of the black population. The notorious **Ku Klux Klan** was born and nurtured in the heart of the society of Southern Democrats. The KKK would target, intimidate, terrorize and, sometimes, murder black men. The KKK also attacked white Republicans and Carpetbaggers. Arkansas Congressman **James M. Hines**, a supporter of rights for black people, was murdered by the Klan.

After the war, most Republican voters in the South were newly enfranchised black men. They were joined by the white Carpetbaggers and the Scalawags, but Democrats retained political control of the South. President Andrew Johnson maintained his "states' rights" position, putting him, for the most part, on the side of the Southern Democrats.

When President Grant took office in 1869, he attempted to pursue the re-unification and reconstruction plans visualized by Abraham Lincoln, Frederick Douglass and himself. He met many obstacles, both in the government and in the socio-culture structure of the American South.

The Northern passion in support of reconstruction began to wane as the years passed and memories of the horrors of the war faded. The presidential election in 1876 was contested and negotiations to resolve the conflict were pursued. The **Compromise of**

1877 was reached; an informal and unwritten "back room" type of deal. The compromise allowed **Rutherford B. Hayes**, a Republican, to become President, but only if he agreed to extract all federal troops from Louisiana, Florida and South Carolina, which he did. The action marked, for all practical purposes, the end of the Era of Reconstruction.

Abuse of black people and restrictions on the rights of black people, most especially in the South, would continue for decades into the future. Southern Democrats would also repeatedly block **women's suffrage,** or the extension of the right to vote, to women and also the passage of the **Civil Rights Act**, for many more years. Northern Democrats stood by their Southern colleagues in their demands that Southern states be re-admitted to the Union without conditions and in opposing the right of black people to vote.

Northerners were not without sin in their treatment of black citizens. Many Northern states persisted in refusing black Americans the right to vote. As late as 1865, as the war was ending, the states of Minnesota, Connecticut and Wisconsin all overwhelmingly voted against black voting rights.

As the period of reconstruction began, Northerners were outraged as they learned of the institution, in the South, of the new **Black Codes**, which Northerners considered little better than slavery. Northern Republicans were worried that being too lenient on the Southern states, allowing them re-admission too quickly, would result in the Southern Democrats regaining too much power in the government.

Black Codes enforced continued **segregation** of the races, restricting black people's access to many facilities. It became illegal for black people to attempt to utilize restaurants, rest rooms and other services designated for "Whites Only". Black laborers were forced into contracts that gave them no opportunity to improve their conditions or to quit their jobs. The Codes restricted the kinds of employment available to black people and the resources for education and access to medical care. Pressures were applied that forced black people to live in specifically defined residential areas, separate from white residents. Black men were lynched for perceived disrespect, insults or offenses against white people, especially white women.

Black people were technically allowed to vote, after passage of the 15th Amendment, but conditions were applied in the South that made voting nearly impossible. **"Literacy Tests"** were required for voters, but the tests given to white people were easily completed, while the tests given to the largely illiterate black voters were complex and difficult. Some states allowed black men to vote only if their pre-1867 ancestors had been legal voters, an impossible condition for former slaves. In many places, black men were simply not allowed to register. The Ku Klux Klan showed up at voting stations, clearly communicating their promise that black people who attempted to vote could expect a terrifying night-time visit from the hooded thugs. Lynchings were far too common. Over the years, in the face of continued intimidation and violence, the numbers of Southern black men who registered to vote steadily declined. In the enthusiasm that followed the Emancipation, 90% of black men registered to vote. By 1940, after decades of mistreatment, only 3% of black men were registered.

The 1866 Congressional elections, during which Reconstruction was the primary issue with voters, became an overwhelming victory for Republicans. The Republicans began to drive their own version of Reconstruction aggressively in 1867. Civilian governments in the South, mostly powered by Southern Democrats, were removed from power, with the U.S. Army taking control. New elections were conducted, but white people who had been in leadership roles in the former Confederacy were not allowed to vote or to take office. The Army protected voters who were former slaves. White Southerners who supported Reconstruction, mostly Republicans, white Northern 'carpetbaggers', Southern 'scalawags' and freed black people all came together in ten Southern states to form new governments. They promoted a series of Reconstruction-based new programs with objectives including raising taxes to fund public improvements, creating new jobs, establishing charities to support the black population, raising funding for public schools and resisting the Ku Klux Klan's activities.

Outrage over the wave of anti-black violence in the South, most perpetrated by the Ku Klux Klan, led President Grant, in 1871, to send in federal troops to gain control. The effort resulted in widespread suppression of the Klan, driving it underground, but certainly not eliminating it.

The Black Codes were mildly weakened when the **Reconstruction Act of 1867** was passed. It required all states to enforce "equal protection under the **14th Amendment**" and focused especially on the right of black men to vote. The **15th Amendment** soon followed, guaranteeing African-American men the right to vote. Southerners were able to find many avenues for avoidance of the intent of the law, though and voting as a black man continued to be a life-threatening experience in much of the South. The Klan was a constant threat and lynchings of black men who attempted to vote were far too common. Black men in the South soon gave up on their efforts to vote.

During the 1870's, white Southern Democrats began to regain control of government in the South. The **Panic of 1873** led to simultaneous gains for Democrats in the North, as well. Southern elections were rife with fraud and intimidation. Reformers were run out of office. Southern politicians began to enact discriminatory and restrictive legislation to once again strip black people of power and control. "**Jim Crow**" laws, effectively disenfranchising black people were put in place. "Jim Crow" was an insulting term for a black person. Jim Crow restrictions existed most openly in the South, but African-Americans all over America were impacted. Many areas in the North also practiced strict segregation, separating white and black people in schools, transportation and businesses.

Facilities serving white people were consistently of higher quality than those serving black people. Restricting black children to inferior schools may have been the most damaging of the segregationist conditions, although African-Americans also suffered poor access to quality housing and good jobs.

The Supreme Court, in 1896, long after Reconstruction, delivered a regrettable decision in the case of **Plessy vs. Ferguson**. The court decision ruled that segregation was constitutional, if "**Separate but Equal**" services, for instance in education and transportation, were offered to both races. "Separate but Equal" led to some very strange interpretations of what was considered "equal". Conditions for black people continued to be of far less quality than conditions for white people. Black schools were notoriously inferior and black people were forced to ride in separate parts of trains and buses.

All but one of the former Confederate states, following the example of Mississippi, initiated new laws pertaining to electoral regulations and voter registration requirements. The laws were meant to prevent the male black population from voting. (Even white females had not yet obtained the right to vote in America). From about 1890 to 1910 new state laws were built to intentionally disenfranchise the black vote. Poll taxes were instituted or increased, tests of academic literacy and reading comprehension were required and paperwork records of residency and other forms of identification were mandated. Black men, already discouraged after years of suffering under "Jim Crow", were further disheartened.

It would not be until eighty years after the Civil War that the Supreme Court, in the case of **Brown v. Board of Education** of Topeka, in 1954, would declare discrimination in education illegal in the United States. The law met with great resistance in the American South and it did not eliminate harsh treatment of black students who attempted to register at "white schools". It would be another decade before a more comprehensive civil rights bill could be passed.

Segregation, the separation of the races, was enforced throughout the South and in some other parts of the country, too, until the **Civil Rights Act of 1964** was finally passed. Democrats, engaging in the longest **filibuster** in American political history, were unsuccessful in their attempt to block it. The Civil Rights Act of 1964 made discrimination and segregation based on race illegal in the United States. Sadly, no laws effectively govern the behaviors of racist individuals and tensions between the races continue to present day.

Ulysses S. Grant

America's Eighteenth President and Civil War General

General Ulysses S. Grant on his famous horse Cincinnati

Grant's military performance was covered in the Civil War sections of this book, so we will only briefly review it in this biography.

Hiram Ulysses Grant was born on April 27th, 1822, in Point Pleasant, Ohio. His parents were **Jesse Root Grant** and **Hannah Simpson Grant**. His ancestry could be traced back to the arrival of **Matthew** and **Priscilla Grant** to the **Massachusetts Bay Colony** in 1630. Hiram's great-grandfather fought in the French and Indian War and his grandfather fought at **Bunker Hill** in the **American Revolution**. Hiram was named in honor of a grandfather, but was always addressed as "Ulysses".

Grant's father, Jesse, was a tanner by employment, a Whig politically and an avid abolitionist. The family relocated to Georgetown, Ohio, when Ulysses was one year old, where his parents would produce five more children. Ulysses began attending school at the age of five, around 1827, and would continue his education through 1838, when he was enrolled at an academy. Ulysses did not like working at the tannery, but he displayed an unusual talent for working with horses, so his father arranged for him to work driving wagons for transportation of goods and people.

His father engaged the assistance of a Democrat Congressman, **Thomas L. Hamer**, to obtain a nomination for acceptance at West Point for Ulysses. Ulysses had little interest in politics at that point in his life, but his father was a Whig and the Whig party, at the time, was transitioning into the anti-slavery Republican Party. In spite of their political differences, Hamer did recommend Ulysses for the appointment and Ulysses was accepted to the **United States Military Academy** at **West Point**. When Rep. Hamer submitted Grant's name, he erroneously wrote the name out as "Ulysses S. Grant", apparently misunderstanding and using Grant's mother's maiden name for the middle initial. Grant never made an effort to correct the mistake and went forward as "Ulysses S. Grant" for the remainder of his life. Fellow cadets at West Point began calling him "Sam", saying his initials stood for "Uncle Sam".

Grant's prowess as a horseman followed him through West Point, where he was judged "Most Proficient" among the cadets. He was remembered for guiding a large horse, "York", unmanageable to others, through a leap that set a high-jump record which stood for decades. He was not a sociable person and, while he made some very close friends, was known to spend much of his time in the library. He took classes in art and produced some paintings, at least nine of which still survive. Ulysses was most likely, in religious terms, an agnostic. He was required to attend church services while at the academy, but was known to find them an imposition. He grew close to **James Longstreet** and **Winfield Scott** while at the academy, both of whom he would encounter during the Civil War to come.

Ulysses graduated 21st out of his class of 39 in June of 1843. He was commissioned a brevet second lieutenant and, in spite of his well-known expertise with horses, was assigned to the infantry. He was sent to St. Louis where he was to serve at the nation's largest military base, Jefferson Barracks. He planned to serve out his four years enlistment and then resign his military commission. He hoped to pursue a career in teaching. While in Missouri, Ulysses visited with the family of Frederick Tracy Dent, a classmate from West Point. He met **Julia Dent** during that visit.

Ulysses was dispatched to Louisiana at the beginning of the **Mexican-American War**. America was in the process of annexing Texas and the relationship between Mexico and America was tense. Grant performed well during the conflict. His first experience with actual combat was at the **Battle of Palo Alto**, May 5th, 1846. He pressed for a larger role in leading combat forces and then participated in the **Battle of Resaca de la Palma**, in which he personally led a key advance. At the **Battle of Monterrey** Grant displayed his exceptional horsemanship, as he volunteered to run critical messages past enemy snipers, hanging low on the far side of his galloping horse, out of sight from the shooters.

Grant was sent, along with other forces, to form a new army. It would be led by **Major General Winfield Scott**. The new command was deployed by sea to land at Vera Cruz, Mexico and to march toward the Mexican capital at Mexico City. Scott's army encountered and fought Mexican forces at the **Battle of Molino del Rey** and the **Battle of Chapultepec.** Grant was promoted to brevet first lieutenant in recognition of his bravery at Molino del Rey. Soon after, at **San Cosme**, Grant discovered a howitzer, which he had his men dis-assemble and then drag up to a nearby church steeple, from which he was able to fire down upon Mexican soldiers. His creativity and initiative earned him another promotion, this time to Captain.

General Scott's army took Mexican City on September 14th, 1847. Vast amounts of new territory, from Texas to California, was ceded by Mexico to the United States. The Mexican-American War was over.

Ulysses S. Grant was a political opponent to the Mexican-American War. He believed it could lead to a wider distribution of the institution of slavery, which he had come to abhor. He wrote "I was bitterly opposed to the measure ... and to this day, regard the war which resulted as one of the most unjust ever waged by a stronger against a weaker nation." Grant came to believe that the coming Civil War was a punishment against the nation for what he saw as the immorality of the Mexican-American War.

The war, though, offered a perfect classroom for Grant, teaching him much about military tactics and strategies. He served as a **Quartermaster**, a job for which he initially showed little enthusiasm. In that position, though, Grant learned about the critical importance of "behind the front line" activities such as maintenance of sound supply lines, distribution of resources, management of transportation networks and communications systems. He learned how to manage the immense task of moving large military forces through lands occupied by enemy armies. He experienced a series of battles in combat. He learned from more seasoned commanders and he became proficient in the ability to sustain large armies. He was becoming a "complete soldier".

After the Mexican-American War ended, Grant returned to Missouri. He married Julia Dent in August of 1848. The couple would eventually have four children. Grant was assigned to a post in Detroit and then to a remote and bleak outpost in upstate New York, Madison Barracks, and then back to Detroit. When the gold rush of 1849 happened, Grant was assigned to move the 4th Infantry regiment to California, along with a contingency of a few hundred civilians, to reinforce a small garrison that was already there. The large group was sent by sea to Panama and then had to make the grueling overland march to the Pacific.

Before traversing Panama, while in Panama City, the group encountered an outbreak of cholera. Soldiers and civilians, women and children, were dying. Grant constructed a field hospital to treat the sick. He moved the most serious cases to a "hospital barge" away from other vulnerable people. He sent those civilians and soldiers who were not infected onward and he stayed behind with the sick. Orderlies resisted treating the infected victims and U.S. Grant stepped in and did much of the nursing himself. He risked being infected himself, but was fortunately spared. He was able to successfully deliver the civilians and the infantry to San Francisco by late summer.

Grant was then sent to serve in Oregon, at the Vancouver Barracks. In 1853 he was dispatched back to Northern California, where he served at Fort Humboldt. His position demanded little attention, he was far from home, he missed his family and he was drinking too much alcohol. His commander told him to "reform or resign". Grant decided to resign, with the War Department writing that there was "nothing against his name".

A friend, **Rufus Ingalls**, later wrote:

"Captain Grant, finding himself in dreary surroundings, without his family and with but little to occupy his attention, fell into dissipated habits and was found, one day, too much under the influence of liquor to properly perform his duties. For this offense Colonel Buchanan demanded that he should resign or stand trial. Grant's friends at the time urged him to stand trial and were confident of his acquittal; but, actuated by a noble spirit, he said he would not for all the world have his wife know that he had been tried on such a charge. He therefore resigned his commission and returned to civilian life."

Grant, himself, wrote: "The vice of intemperance (drunkenness) had not a little to do with my decision to resign".

While serving, before his resignation, Grant attempted a series of business ventures. One failed when a partner ran off with Grant's investment money, equivalent to $21,000 in present day. In California, during the gold rush, prices were ridiculously high for essentials such as food and lodging. He initiated a potato-growing project, expecting to make a great profit, but most of the potatoes rotted in the ground. He wrote to Julia, who was concerned about Indian attacks, that those Indians in his vicinity were harmless. He complained that white agents were exploiting and stealing from the natives. Grant wrote that the Indians were suffering tremendously with infection from diseases brought to them by the white man. He was shocked by the numbers of fatalities to measles and smallpox. Grant became a life-long advocate for better treatment of Native Americans.

Leaving the military, Grant returned to his family in St. Louis. He had no business on which he could rely. It was 1854 and Grant was 32-years-old. The family entered a period of several years in which they faced poverty and instability. His father offered Ulysses a position in a branch of the family business, tanning and leatherworks, in Galena, Illinois, on the Mississippi River. The condition, though, was that Ulysses go alone to Galena, leaving Julia and the kids with either her family, in St. Louis or the Grant family, then in Kentucky. Julia and Ulysses declined the offer.

Grant tried farming for the next few years. He worked on property owned by Julia's brother and he was helped by **Dan**, a slave owned by Julia and by other "rented" slaves or slaves owned by Julia's father. Julia came from a family of merchants and planters. The agricultural efforts of Ulysses, though, did not harvest a profit. He had to supplant the family's meager income by selling firewood on street corners in St. Louis. The family then relocated to a plot of land on Julia's father's farm. They built a simple cabin and named it **"Hardscrabble"**. The family lived in poverty, but was able to grow food, making them better off than others during the "**Panic of 1857**".

Grant exchanged his gold watch, in 1857, so he could buy Christmas presents for his kids. He had to rent Hardscrabble out in 1858 and he and his family had to move to Julia's father's large plantation. He soon contracted malaria. When he recovered, he gave up his effort to become a farmer.

Julia's father transferred a slave, **William Jones**, a thirty-five-year-old black man, to Ulysses in 1858. Ulysses was not a passionate abolitionist, though he was no advocate of slavery and he was not able to make himself force William to work. He set William free early in 1859. William would have been worth a minimum of $1000 if Ulysses had chosen to sell him. Ulysses badly needed money. He gave William his freedom anyway. (Some historians question whether Ulysses did or did not receive any form of compensation from William).

Ulysses went back to St. Louis and tried working for one of Julia's cousins in the real estate business. He made little money as a bill collector and soon gave up that position. His academy education and army quartermaster experience qualified him to be a County Engineer, but he was passed over based on political affiliation. The commissioners feared he would be a supporter of his father-in-law's Democrat Party policies.

Grant was able to move his family to Galena, Illinois, where he worked in the branch of his father's business which had been run by his brothers Simpson and Orville. He finally achieved some measure of financial success and was able to repay his debts. He voted against **Abraham Lincoln** in the 1860 election, fearing that efforts to end slavery would lead to secession of Southern states and to civil war. Grant was struggling more and more with the anti-slavery feelings that were growing in him. His wife was a loyal Democrat and her family had always owned slaves.

As noted earlier in this segment, Grant's record during the Civil War was covered in detail in the chapters about the war. We'll treat it lightly here.

Confederate forces attacked **Fort Sumter** on April 12, 1861 and the Civil War began. Three days later, President Lincoln called for 75,000 volunteers, thinking that would be sufficient to bring an expeditious close to the conflict. The day after Lincoln's call to arms, Grant attended a meeting at which he heard a passionate speech by **John Aaron Rawlins**. The patriotic oration motivated Grant so that he immediately began to assist in recruitment. He later wrote that "I never went into our leather store again". Grant was offered a commission as a captain in the militia which was being quickly organized. He refused the offer, believing his former military experience qualified him for a higher rank.

John Aaron Rawlins would become a "right-hand-man" aide to Grant when the war was underway. Rawlins would become a General in his own right and would later serve, under President Grant, as United States **Secretary of War**.

Grant was appointed to be a military aide to Illinois Governor Yates and he brought 10 regiments into the state militia. He was commissioned Colonel and soon brought the poorly organized and poorly disciplined 21st Illinois Volunteer Infantry up to military standards. His regiment, under his command, was dispatched to Missouri to drive out Confederates who were trying to take control of the "slave state". Grant was quickly promoted to Brigadier General of Volunteers. **Major General Fremont**, remembering Grant's exemplary performance during the Mexican war, passed over several other candidates to make Grant commander of all forces in Southeastern Missouri. He began to organize his plan to move down the Mississippi and then up the Tennessee and Cumberland Rivers. His first victory came when he took control of Paducah, Kentucky, with no fighting required.

Grant's early aggressiveness and willingness to go to the Confederate's positions and fight were noticed by Lincoln. As the war progressed, it became clear that Grant was perhaps the only Union general who truly understood Lincoln's objectives. Lincoln's overriding priority was to bring the Southern states back to the Union. He wanted to save the United States of America. As the war raged and aged, Lincoln began to understand that the institution of slavery had to be abolished or reunification of the U.S. would likely be impossible. After the **Emancipation Proclamation**, Grant, Lincoln and Lincoln's friend Frederick Douglass all began to focus on the best ways to assimilate the huge population of black slaves who would soon be free. Later in the war, Grant welcomed black refugees, slaves and freedmen alike, who fled their owners to come to the Union Army lines. He would advocate allowing black men to serve in the army.

In February of 1862, while Lincoln's armies back East were turning in a series of defeats, Grant led a coordinated attack on Fort Donelson, a critical rebel defensive location on the Cumberland River. The **Battle at Fort Donelson** was fought over several days. The Yankees made some gains and were forced to retreat and came back to try again. Union gunboats rained cannonballs on the Confederates and cannon fire from the fort drove the Union gunboats away. The rebels launched a furious attack on February 14th and Grant mounted his horse and rode hard over seven miles of frozen trails and trenches. He fiercely rallied his various group commanders, gathered information and organized a coordinated resistance to the rebel attack. The Confederate charge was blocked and their troops retreated to Fort Donelson. On February 16th, Grant ordered an artillery bombardment of the fort. Two Confederate generals fled with their troops. **General Simon Bolivar Buckner** was left to fight Grant. Grant demanded surrender. Buckner requested "surrender terms". Grant responded that the terms were

"Unconditional and immediate surrender". Buckner, having no choice, complied, becoming the first Confederate general to surrender an entire army. The Union army took 14,000 prisoners, including Buckner. Grant delivered the first Union Army victory to President Lincoln and Lincoln promoted him to Major General of Volunteers. The press began to call U. S. Grant **"Unconditional Surrender Grant"**.

Grant went on to lead his forces to the capture of **Vicksburg**, which took the Mississippi River away from the Southerners. He would proceed through a series of campaigns and battles and would become the commander of all of Lincoln's armies. He would defeat Robert E. Lee and accept Lee's surrender at **Appomattox**. Grant would be Lincoln's greatest general.

After the Civil War, Grant stayed in the army, still functioning as the commander of all forces. When Northerners wanted to put **Robert E. Lee** and Lee's generals on trial for treason, Grant stepped in to block the movement. He cited the terms he delivered to Lee at Appomattox as justification for granting amnesty to the Confederate officers.

Ulysses S. Grant became our 18th President on March 4th, 1869. His inaugural address, among other things, focused on encouraging the passage and ratification of the **15th Amendment**. As President of the United States, emerging from the great Civil War, Grant had a lot on his plate. He wanted **Reconstruction** to be successful. He wanted freed black Americans to find peace, security and success. He campaigned for "proper treatment" of the Indians and expressed his desire that they be civilized and would have the right to vote. He was concerned about French invaders in Mexico, not wanting a European nation being created right across the Rio Grande. He wanted the 15th Amendment ratified, guaranteeing black men the right to vote. He wanted all of the Southern states peacefully reunified with the Union.

Early in his administration, Grant appointed Confederate leaders to various positions in the government, a move not appreciated by many Northerners. He appointed more than 50 Jewish people to government positions, perhaps in an effort to remove the stain on his reputation left by his "**General Orders No. 11**". General Orders No. 11 was Grant's response to illegal trading practices going on while he was a General in the Union Army. It banned Jewish people from participating in certain activities and it actually caused a number of Jewish families to be driven from their homes. It brings to mind another "General Orders No. 11", which was issued by a different Union General. That one expelled all families with Southern sympathies from four counties in Missouri. Both "General Orders No. 11" were met with widespread resistance. President Lincoln was appalled by Grant's order and insisted that it be immediately rescinded.

Grant, as President, wanted the French to get out of Mexico. The French, under **Napoleon III**, had invaded Mexico. Mexican fighters, on May 5th, 1862, pushed the

French out at the **Battle of Puebla**, which event is the basis for the popular Mexican "**Cinco de Mayo**" celebration. The French, though, re-organized and came back, attempting another invasion. They successfully occupied Mexico City and they enthroned **Maximilian**, an Austrian prince, as **Emperor of Mexico**. It was 1864 and President Lincoln, while he refused to recognize the French government in Mexico, was occupied with the American Civil War. The Southern Confederacy actually supported the French, hoping to gain support for their own rebellion. As President, Ulysses S. Grant staunchly resisted the French invasion. He was incensed by the French support of the Confederates. He claimed that French soldiers had fired on Union troops from the south side of the Rio Grande and that the French protected Confederate troops who fled south.

Grant sent his trusted **General Sheridan** south to Texas, bringing along a force of 50,000 troops. His stated intent was to wipe out residual Confederate resistance, rebels who had not yet given up on the Civil War. Sheridan persisted in moving southward, though and the French could feel the pressure of the American advance. The French, at that time, had problems enough at home, as they were being threatened by Germany. The Mexicans, led by **Benito Juarez** organized a strong enough resistance to defeat the French. By 1867, the French were gone. General Sheridan ultimately had no need to launch an offensive against them. "Emperor" Maximilian was shot to death by Juarez's soldiers. U. S. Grant had achieved the result he hoped for and the Mexican people were left with the ability and the right to determine their own future.

The 15th Amendment was ratified and signed by President Grant in 1870. He also authorized legislation meant to curb the terrifying activities, in the South, of the **Ku Klux Klan**. He sometimes ordered troops to hotbeds of Klan activity, which resulted in accusations that Grant wasn't respecting "states' rights". Grant's primary focus was on making **Reconstruction** work, aiding and supporting the assimilation of freed black people. He lobbied to have schools and churches built to support the newly free black community.

President Grant established the **Department of Justice**. His administration created the **Weather Bureau** (now the National Weather Service). He also created **Yellowstone National Park**, our nation's very **first national park**. Grant worked to improve conditions for **Native Americans** but was met with little support. He negotiated the **Treaty of Washington** in 1871, which resolved conflicts founded in British activities during the Civil War. The treaty led to better relations between the United States and England. Grant was not so successful in his failed attempt to annex **Santo Domingo**, a Caribbean island nation known in present day as the **Dominican Republic**.

President Grant proposed a constitutional amendment in 1875 that was intended to limit "religious indoctrination" in federally funded public schools. In the proposal, he wrote that schools in the U.S. would serve all children "irrespective of sex, color, birthplace or religion". The proposed amendment was defeated in the Senate.

Grant aggressively prosecuted **Mormon polygamists**. He had their leader, **Brigham Young**, indicted for "lewd and lascivious cohabitation". He also vigorously prosecuted, under the terms of the **Comstock Act,** "indecent pornographers" and "abortionists".

Historians give Grant credit for doing all he could do to make Reconstruction work. He was successful in many ways and very much unsuccessful in others. Grant signed a law on March 18, 1869, which provided for equal rights for black people in America to serve on juries and to run for public office. He signed the **Naturalization Act** in 1870, which made foreign black people and black children born in the U.S. to foreign parents, all eligible for naturalization, the process of becoming a U.S. citizen. The Naturalization Act did not apply to Chinese people or people of other races, specifying only "free white people" and "black people".

Grant was able to bring all of the seceded Southern states back into the Union. It was Abraham Lincoln's greatest desire and Grant meant to fulfill it for him. Black Americans served, for the first time in history, in the U.S. Congress and each of them originated in a Southern state.

Motivated to find ways to curtail Klan activities, Grant established the **Justice Department**, including an **Attorney General** and a **Solicitor General**, meant to aggressively attack the Klan. During Grant's first administration, Republicans had control of the government. Southern Democrats had not yet been allowed to return to office. In that period, Reconstruction was supported strongly and Grant provided troops to protect the advancement of rights for Southern black citizens. 470 Klan members were arrested in South Carolina and wealthy Klan leaders had to flee the state. African-Americans voted in large numbers in the elections of 1872. When Grant entered his second term, though, **"Redeemer Democrats"** came back to power. Troops had to be removed from the South. The KKK regained power and a new Attorney General suspended prosecutions of Klan members. Grant signed the "**Civil Rights Act of 1874**", which guaranteed black people the right to use public facilities, but it was ruled unconstitutional in 1883. A meaningful civil rights act would not be passed in the United States for another 81 years.

U.S. Grant did not attempt to win a third term in the presidency. He was succeeded by **Rutherford B. Hayes**. Hayes had gained the support of Southern Democrats by promising to end federal government intervention in attempts to enforce racial equality for black people in the South. Hayes cooperated, signing the **Compromise of 1877**, removing all remaining federal troops from the South, indicating the termination of Reconstruction. The result would be decades of racist restrictions on the lives of black people in the American South. The end of Reconstruction marked the beginning of the era of **"Jim Crow" segregation** in the South. It would last for eight decades.

After leaving the White House, Grant remarked that he "had never been so happy in his life". He and his wife left for New York where they attended the birth of a granddaughter. They then traveled to visit several American cities. Ulysses, along with his family, then cruised the world for two years and was well-received by foreign crowds and dignitaries wherever they visited.

The bad luck in business ventures that plagued Ulysses as a young man followed him into his old age. He invested in a financial company, along with his son and another partner. His entire savings was tied up in the company. The other partner swindled the investors in 1884 and the company folded. Grant was bankrupt. He lost everything. He began writing his autobiography, with assistance from American author **Mark Twain**, in hopes of paying bills. Ulysses contracted throat cancer and died on July 23rd, 1885, at the age of 63. Mark Twain had the autobiography published and it became a popular and financially successful book.

Ulysses S. Grant Quotes

"The friend in my adversity I shall always cherish most. I can better trust those who helped to relieve the gloom of my dark hours than those who are so ready to enjoy with me the sunshine of my prosperity."

"I have never advocated war except as a means of peace."

"The art of war is simple enough. Find out where your enemy is. Get at him as soon as you can. Strike him as hard as you can and keep moving on."

"Leave the matter of religion to the family altar, the church and the private school, supported entirely by private contributions. Keep the church and state forever separate."

"Labor disgraces no man; unfortunately, you occasionally find men who disgrace labor."

"I know only two tunes: one of them is 'Yankee Doodle' and the other isn't."

Ulysses S. Grant and Slavery

Grant married **Julia Dent**, whose father owned, at times, up to thirty enslaved African-Americans. Grant made use of **"Dan"**, one of the Dent slaves, in his early attempts at farming. Grant purchased a slave, 35-year-old **William Jones**, via a transfer of ownership from Julia's father, in 1858. He also had assistance from several other of the Dent family slaves. A year later, in 1859, Grant issued a **deed of manumission**, freeing William. There is disagreement among historians as to whether Grant received any compensation in return for William's freedom. Family records claim William was freed based on Grant's discomfort about owning another man.

These are the terms of the **Document of Manumission** which made William Jones a free black man:

"I Ulysses S Grant of the City and County of St. Louis in the State of Missouri, for diverse good and valuable considerations me hereunto moving, do hereby emancipate and set free from Slavery my negro man William, sometimes called William Jones of Mullatto complexion, aged about thirty-five years and about five feet seven inches in height and is the same slave purchased by me of Frederick Dent. And I do hereby manumit, emancipate & set free said William from slavery forever."

The Grant's, while they lived on Julia's father's property and while they lived in St. Louis, continued to benefit from the labors of four of her father's slaves. Julia Grant considered four slaves to be her own, though it is possible her father retained legal ownership. They were named Eliza, Julia, John and Dan.

Grant's wife, Julia, a Democrat, was a staunch advocate of slavery and boasted of how "contented" were the family slaves. It is unlikely the slaves felt happy about their positions in bondage. Julia's association with slavery became a problem for Grant when Grant entered politics. As he grew older, Grant's feelings of opposition to slavery grew stronger.

As a General, Grant pushed to allow black volunteers to join the United States Army. He welcomed fugitive black slaves to his army camps. When Lincoln delivered the Emancipation Proclamation, Grant wrote to the President: "By arming the negro we have added a powerful ally. They will make good soldiers and taking them from the enemy weakens him in the same proportion they strengthen us."

As a President, Grant pushed for Amendments that promised to end discrimination based on color and that granted black men the right to vote. He supported the plans made by Abraham Lincoln to create ways for freed black people to be effectively and safely assimilated into American society. Grant supported the creation of public schools and churches for the black community.

Grant benefited, early in his working life, from slave labor. He owned a slave, whom he voluntarily set free before the Civil War began. His wife's family exploited thirty slaves on their plantation, White Haven. On the other hand, he promoted and supported many actions intended to benefit the black population. Grant will, though, forever be known as the "last slave-holding American President".

Beyond the American Civil War

America in the 1860's

The New York Draft Riots of 1863

As the Civil War approached, the business leaders of New York City were extremely apprehensive of losing their substantial trade relationship with the southern slave states. Cotton, especially, was an essential product for many of their businesses. New York even contemplated joining the southerners in seceding from the Union. New York politicians and businessmen warned their white, working-class neighbors, mostly of Irish and German heritage, that if the slaves were freed by Lincoln, the migrating black millions would come north and take their jobs.

When Lincoln did issue the **Emancipation Proclamation**, New York workers, along with New York military regiments, staged protests. The soldiers complained that they signed up to preserve the Union, but not to abolish slavery.

Early in 1862, with the Union Army facing dangerously low levels of new manpower, Lincoln's administration passed a stringent new **"conscription law"**. It made all American white males, aged 20 to 35, and all "unmarried" white males aged 35 to 45, eligible to be **"drafted",** involuntarily, to serve in the army. Problems arose when a lottery was established as a foundation for selecting which males would be selected for the draft. All males that fit the law's eligibility requirements were entered in the lottery. One section of the new conscription law, though, provided that a man could pay a "substitute" to serve in his name, or that a man could "buy his way out of the lottery" by paying the government, directly, three-hundred dollars. (Equal to $5800 in present-day money).

Three-hundred dollars was about the amount of an annual salary for working men in 1862. The "rent or buy-out" exemptions meant that only the most wealthy of men could avoid the draft. People began to speak out against conscription, especially as defined by the new law. The problems were exacerbated because the draft law also exempted all black males, aggravating existing racial tensions.

Anti-war newspapers ran headlines attacking the law. The first "lottery drawing" for conscription was on July 11th, 1863. Riots began firing up in several northern American cities, including Detroit and Boston, but the largest and most violent began on July 13th in New York City. Thousands of white working-class men, many of Irish heritage, began attacking government buildings and military installations. It wasn't long before the target list was expanded to include black businesses and black citizens.

Thousands of white people invaded a **"Colored Orphan Asylum"** which sheltered two hundred black children. The raiders stole the food, clothing and bedding from the home, but refrained from actually assaulting the children. Nothing can justify the shameful actions of the rioters who left these innocent children to the sad mercy of the city's **"alms houses"**.

The rioters also sought out for attacks the businesses, especially along the docks on the harbor, where black workers were employed. Families with "mixed race" marriages were attacked. Abolitionists were attacked. Several black men were lynched and many were brutally beaten to death. The protests against the draft law became riots against black citizens.

Accurate numbers are not available, but estimates of the number of people killed range from a couple of hundred to as many as a thousand.

New York City has not often been thought of as a "slave city", but the draft riots prove that there were far too many racists in the area and they were willing to be lethally violent in their hatred. Perhaps worse, it was the city's leadership, both politically and in the wealthy business class, that instigated the ruthless riots.

The Civil Rights Act of 1866

On March 13th, 1866, the **Civil Rights Act of 1866** was passed. It was intended to support and clarify the terms of the **Thirteenth Amendment**, which had recently been enacted. It was the first national legislation to address protection of rights assigned to African-Americans. Southern states had not yet been re-admitted to the Union, so northerners wanted to pass essential civil rights legislation while they had the power in congress to do so. The main argument used to oppose the Act was the "states' rights" position, which held that the federal government did not have the authority to create legislation regarding civil rights that would be binding for all of the individual states.

"The Civil Rights Act of 1866" was passed by both the House and the Senate. In the Senate, 33 Republicans voted for the Act, while not a single Democrat voted for it. Had the southern states been back in place, the Act would have had no chance of passing. 111 Republicans voted for the Civil Rights Act in the House, while, again, not a single Democrat voted to support it. President Johnson, arguing the "states' rights" issue, vetoed the bill. Both the House and the Senate voted to over-ride his veto.

The primary intention of the Civil Rights Act of 1866 was to support peaceful integration of freed black people into American society. It was focused on three issues. First, to clearly define the terms of American citizenship. Second, to more clearly define the rights attached to citizenship. Third, to make it unlawful in America to obstruct citizenship rights to any American based on "race, color or prior condition of slavery or involuntary servitude". Note that the Act provided no protection for American women, be they black or white.

In an attempt to "solidify" the intentions of the Civil Rights Act, when the **Fourteenth Amendment** was passed, in 1868, the very first sentence was a **"Citizenship Clause"**. It read: "All persons born or naturalized in the United States and subject to the jurisdiction thereof, are citizens of the United States and of the State wherein they reside". The amendment gave the conditions of the Civil Rights Act **"constitutional protection"**.

The Ku Klux Klan in America

The KKK was covered, to some extent, in the Civil War story in this book. We'll fill it out a bit here. The name "Ku Klux" was taken from the Greek word "Kyklos", meaning "circle", with the "Klan" being added, apparently, for the sake of alliteration.

Ku Klux Klan Meeting

The first "Klan" was organized on December 24th, 1865, by six former Confederate Army officers. They were J. Calvin Jones, John Kennedy, Frank McCord, John Lester, Richard Reed and, appropriately, James Crowe. (The name "James Crowe" was NOT the origin of the term "Jim Crow", which was applied to Klan activities). The six met in Pulaski, Tennessee. Early explanations for the purpose of the group did not mention racist intentions but suggested the organization was meant for "strange initiations, baffling the public and amusement for the members". No explanation is given for the origin of the Klan's strange costumes and high, pointed hats. It seems probable that the intention was to strike fear and intimidate.

The first incarnation of the **Ku Klux Klan**, existing primarily in the 1860's and early 1870's, utilized terrorism to gain control of political groups and voting conditions. Klan members, who claim to have originally had no purpose other than amusement, realized their "secret society" seemed to have powers beyond their anticipation. During 1867, they began to transform into a far more dangerous organization. Chapters began to form across the southern states. As their founders and many of their members were former Confederate soldiers, their attitudes toward African-Americans, the abolishment of slavery and the Reconstruction movement were predictably bitter, angry and resentful. The Klan began to interfere with local politics, especially with the opportunities for black Americans to vote. Their "interference" took the guise of terrifying threats and actual physical violence.

The Klan tried, sometimes successfully, to overthrow and toss out Republican governments in southern states. They targeted African-American leaders for intimidation and violence. Other groups with similar objectives began to spring up around the South. The **"Knights of the White Camelia"** were organized in Louisiana in 1867. The **"Invisible Empire of the South"** was a direct out-growth of the KKK, founded in a convention of representatives of former Confederate states which was held in Nashville, Tennessee, during the summer of 1867. The "Invisible Empire" was organized in a hierarchy of "officers" and was led by a **"Grand Wizard"**, who was **Nathan Bedford Forrest**. Below him was a network of **"Grand Dragons"**, **"Grand Titans"** and **"Grand Cyclopses"**.

The Klansmen of the KKK and the Invisible Empire adopted costumes intended to intimidate and to incite terror among black freedmen and any white people who supported the newly freed black population. The coverings and hoods worn by the Klan served not only to incite fear, but also to hide the identification of the cowardly terrorists. Their activities, most often carried out under cover of darkness, included raids on the homes of black freedmen and of white people who supported the people of color. Klansmen burned homes and destroyed crops. Their victims were beaten, whipped, tortured and lynched.

During the years from 1867 through 1870, the Klan reached levels of power that enabled them to dismantle Reconstruction efforts to bring the former slaves into American society peacefully. The Klan successfully replaced politicians in several southern states who supported Reconstruction with men who believed in their own racist causes. The powerful Klan operated with little resistance and the levels of violence increased in brutality and in frequency. Consequently, in 1869, Nathan Bedford Forrest, realizing the cruel direction taken by his organization, ordered the Klan chapters to be disbanded. The KKK, by then, had grown so big and powerful and so fearsome that it couldn't so easily be brought to an end. Black people and their white supporters were still living under the threat of local chapters of the Klan who chose not to give up their robes and pointy hats.

The American government was slow to respond to the violence perpetrated by the KKK. President Grant was a supporter of Lincoln's Reconstruction hopes and plans but felt he had little authority to interfere with the problems of individual states. A Grand Jury was convened in South Carolina to investigate KKK activities. This is part of their conclusion:

"During the whole session we have been engaged in investigations of the most grave and extraordinary character—investigations of the crimes committed by the organization known as the Ku Klux Klan. The evidence elicited has been voluminous, gathered from the victims themselves and their families, as well as those who belong to the Klan and participated in its crimes. The jury has been shocked beyond measure at the developments which have been made in their presence of the number and character of the atrocities committed, producing a state of terror and a sense of utter insecurity among a large portion of the people, especially the colored population."

The U.S. Congress was hearing from Americans who were outraged by reports of the horrors of Klan behaviors. The congressional reaction was enactment of three **"Force Acts"**. The first was **"The Enforcement Act of May 1870"**. It banned "going in disguise upon the public highways or upon the premises of another" and "banding together". It was clearly directed at Klan activity. **"The Second Force Act of February 1871"** put all federal elections under federal supervision. It was meant to prevent the Klan from obstructing the voting rights of black men and their white supporters. The final enforcement act was the **"Third Force Act of April 1871"**. It gave the President power to suspend **"Habeas Corpus"** and to utilize the American military to enforce all three of the enforcement acts. ("Habeas Corpus" is the legal requirement that anyone who is arrested and detained have the right to be brought before a judge and have the legitimacy of their detainment verified). The enforcement acts, especially the last two, are now known as the **"Ku Klux Klan Acts"**.

President Grant, having been blessed with congressional authority, sent American troops to several of the South Carolina counties where Klan violence was most prominent. He declared martial law in those areas. The **Seventh U.S. Cavalry** was sent to maintain peace, protect citizens and gather investigatory information about Klan members. Many Klan members fled the area, but hundreds were identified, arrested and prosecuted for "conspiracy and terroristic actions". Klan activity was soon largely suppressed, though isolated acts of violence would continue far into the future. The Klan prosecutions were among the first carried out by the new United States **"Department of Justice"**.

As Klan activity was being prosecuted, other groups were formed. They have been characterized as **"insurgent paramilitary organizations"** and they shared the nefarious objectives of the KKK. They were white southern Democrats and they intended to suppress voting by white Republicans and all black men. They wanted to drive the Republicans completely out of politics in the South. Among those groups were the **"White League"**, in Louisiana, the **"Red Shirts"**, in Mississippi and chapters of both in other southern states, including, of course, South Carolina. They are credited, along with the Klan, with putting southern Democrats back in control of state legislatures throughout the South. Their activity meant failure for many of the Reconstruction plans and hopes developed by Abraham Lincoln, Frederick Douglass and U.S. Grant.

Some aspects of the Ku Klux Klan "enforcement acts" were rescinded by the Supreme Court in 1882. (The United States v. Harris, 1882). American troops are not supposed to be used to control American citizens and the writ of Habeas Corpus is fundamental to our

504

judicial system. By the time the acts had been rescinded, though, the activities of the Klan had largely been terminated.

The ugly head of the KKK rose again in the late 1910's and carried into the 1920's. This time, the Klan added new activities to their agenda. They initiated their new version of the hooded robes and they began burning crosses to communicate their hatred. Millions of discontented Americans joined their organizations.

The 1920's incarnation of the Klan was not, sadly, the last. The Klan arose for a third time in the late 1900's, being a form of resistance to various civil rights movements. The Klan still meant to intimidate people of color, but it added other targets: Republicans who were trying to pass civil rights legislation, people of color, Jewish people, Catholics, homosexuals, unions and any others who opposed their agenda. Their agenda was focused on "purification of America", meaning they wanted racial segregation and restrictions on rights for black people and they wanted politics to be controlled by white Democrats. The final boost to Klan membership in the 1920's seems to have been their opposition to the Democrat nomination of **Alfred E. Smith** for President in 1928. Smith's sin, in their minds, was that he was a Catholic. A Catholic would not be elected President in the United States until **John F. Kennedy** came along.

The KKK found one more cycle of life beginning in the 1960's, lasting into the 1990's, a time when civil rights movements were very active and were making progress. Segregation was no longer enforced. Children of black families were attending integrated schools. The Klan was not adapting well to the objectives of the **"Civil Rights Act of 1964"**, which their southern Democrats had almost been able to suffocate in congress. Their opposition took the form of bombings, shootings, assassinations, beatings and whippings.

David Duke, a Grand Wizard of the Ku Klux Klan, won the primary election for governor of Louisiana in 1991. His selection drew national attention and international opposition to his candidacy was overwhelming. The news of his candidacy resulted in numerous boycotts of Louisiana and in the negative focus of many advocacy groups. Duke did not win the gubernatorial election, but more than half of Louisiana's white voters checked his box on the ballot. Hopefully, today's Louisianians would generate a completely different result.

In their core, groups like the KKK, the White League, the Red Shirts and others, were motivated primarily by fear. They feared the competition of people of color in the labor market. They feared loss of control of their southern society. They feared being deprived of their status as "dominant masters" of their culture. They feared having to compete on a level playing field.

We should all hope that we have seen the last of them.

Juneteenth

Southern states, during the Civil War, did not recognize the authority of the United States government over them. The **Emancipation Proclamation** was irrelevant to them. They were the **Confederate States of America** and they had their own government and they were keeping their slaves. In truth, slaves in the north were also still enslaved after the Proclamation. The northern states, still being part of the United States, could free slaves only by **Constitutional Amendment. The 13th, 14th and 15th Amendments** were quickly passed to finally truly abolish slavery and to guarantee certain civil rights to all Americans, including black Americans. Women were bitterly upset in learning that they were still forbidden the right to vote.

Two years and six months after President Abraham Lincoln delivered the Emancipation Proclamation, many thousands of black Americans were still bound in slavery. Once the war ended, as southern states began to be re-admitted to the union, each had to swear loyalty to the United States and each had to formally abolish slavery in their respective states. Texas was the last hold-out in which slavery was still fiercely defended. Technically, slavery in America was not ended until the last slave in Texas was set free. Communications of the day were rudimentary, especially in the deep south. The "underground word-of-mouth" transmission of information throughout the black community was the only way southern slaves could learn that they should no longer be slaves.

Many southern slaves, including some from Texas, had already managed to escape and flee to the North by June of 1865. On June 5th, an entire brigade of the 25th Army Corps, United States Army, arrived in Galveston, Texas. They drove what remained of the Confederate Army out of Texas, down into Mexico, where some would plot new attacks on the United States. The **25th U.S. Army Corps** was made up, in part, of one thousand black freedmen. They spread the word of freedom far and wide through Texas. Thousands of more enslaved black people heard the word and immediately fled their "owners" and headed north. **Major General Gordon Granger** arrived on **June 19, 1865,** to deliver **"General Orders, No. 3",** which officially put an end to slavery in Texas, meaning it had been abolished, finally, in all of America. Approximately 250,000 Texas slaves were set free. General Orders, No. 3 read:

"The people of Texas are informed that, in accordance with a proclamation from the Executive of the United States, that all slaves are free. This involves an absolute equality of rights and rights of property between former masters and slaves and the connection heretofore existing between them becomes that between employer and hired labor. The freedmen are advised to remain quietly at their present homes and work for wages. They are informed that they will not be allowed to collect at military posts and that they will not be supported in idleness either there or elsewhere."

The American government was already coping, very badly, with the large collections of Native Americans, who, being deprived of their historic ways of survival, were collecting around western forts, hoping to be fed. Northern workers were afraid that the millions of black freedmen would rush northward to take their jobs.

Black people in the South soon learned that the new federal laws could be bypassed or "worked around" and they were still in a world of trouble. As southern Democrats replaced the Republicans who had been put in place during the early Reconstruction period, the invidious "Black Codes" and "Jim Crow" laws began to take shape. The KKK was formed in Pulaski, Tennessee by six former Confederate soldiers. President Grant sent troops into the South to put down the KKK and to protect the black community. Free black Americans immediately began to have an impact on elections in the South. Challenges and obstacles were thrown constantly in their path, but steady progress has been made toward real freedom and real equality of opportunity.

Juneteenth is celebrated for memorializing the final act separating the United States from the shameful institution of slavery and for being the first national holiday created by and practiced continuously by and for the American black community. It reminds us that our Constitution works, driving us ever forward in our search for fairness and justice. The battle to establish equality in all things for America's minorities continues to be fought every day.

The Invention of the Typewriter

The first pragmatic typewriter was invented in 1866 by **S.W. Soule, Carlos Glidden**, a **mechanic** and **Christopher Sholes**, an inventor. Soule was quickly bought out of the business by **James Densmore**, who brought financing and personal energy to the project. Their first machine was a "numbering machine" and had no letters on the keyboard. The machine was patented by **E. Remington and Sons** in 1867 and then introduced, following some improvements, to the marketplace in 1874. It was called **"Remington No. 1"** or the **"Sholes and Glidden"** typewriter. (James Densmore would go on to develop and market similar machines which were called **"Densmore Machines"** or **"Densmore Typewriters"**.

It was Glidden who suggested adding letters to the numbers machine. As the development of the product continued, problems arose because the combinations of letters that most often occurred together were not allowing time for the machines' cylindrical "platen" to make the necessary up and down movements. The **"QWERTY"** arrangement of letters on the keyboard was created to physically separate the keys for those troublesome combinations. It is still, one hundred and fifty years later, the fundamental organization of keys on typewriters, phones and computers.

E. Remington and Sons had a very profitable firearms business, which had been established in 1816. They were interested in investing in other products and were fascinated by the machine Sholes, Glidden and Densmore were beginning to market. Remington negotiated deals with Densmore and Glidden and took control of the machine, patenting it in 1867. Densmore sold his part in the business for $12,000. Glidden preferred to take his share in permanent "royalties", meaning he would make a little money on each future sale. Glidden ended up making millions of dollars on the typewriter. Densmore must have deeply regretted his own decision, though he went on to market his own version of typewriter.

The earliest typewriters had no lower-case letters, so everything was typed in all capitals. The "Shift" key was first introduced in 1878. They had no number "1", as Sholes thought the letter "l" could be used. The main reason for the "QWERTY" arrangement of keys was that it separated letters that frequently were used together, making the cylindrical platen work better and it put all the letters needed to type the word "typewriter" together on the top line. It made it easier for salesmen to demonstrate usage of the machine. During those early years, all typists used the simple, but slow, "hunt and peck" method of typing. In 1888, during a typing competition, a law clerk named **Frank E. McGurrin** won the event by using the "touch typing" method. If you type, it's likely you use McGurrin's idea.

The first Remington typewriters sold for $125, a lot of money in those days, equal to about $4,000 in present-day money. The "Remington No. 2" provided both upper- and lower-case letters, among other improvements and was introduced in 1878. "Multiple language" typewriters soon followed.

As typewriters became more common and it became clear they could enhance speed, efficiency and legibility to business documents, "typewriter schools" began to pop up in the cities. Women, who had traditionally been excluded from American businesses, began to take the classes and develop a needed and marketable skill. Typewriters assisted women in their efforts to gain recognition and equality in the business environment, though they had a long, long way to go in those efforts. Keep in mind, they were not yet even allowed to vote. They were marginalized American citizens. The typewriter gave them a boost forward.

America Acquires Alaska

The **"Russo-American Treaty"** had been signed in 1824. It set the boundaries defining territories, including those belonging to Great Britain, Russia, Canada oregon, Washington and the United States. The treaty was an imperfect document and all parties continued to entertain disputes through the next few decades. The **Civil War** put a hold on all American efforts to resolve those disputes. **President Andrew Johnson** and his Secretary of State, **William H. Seward**, after the war ended, were eager to add this enormous tract of land to the United States of America. Some politicians and other American leaders were not so eager. The plan to acquire Alaska was called, in the press, **"Seward's Folly"** and **"Johnson's Polar Bear Garden"**. In spite of the derision, Johnson and Seward moved forward with their plans.

Russia was in possession of most of Alaska. The **Russian Tsar** had just lost the Crimean War against Great Britain and had taken huge financial losses. They feared military conflict with Great Britain or the United States over Alaska, believing it would be a fight they could not win. Gold had already been discovered in California and Russia was aware that Alaska might have great reserves of gold and other natural resources. At the same time, Russia knew they were lacking the money and military resources needed to fight America or Great Britain for the property. Russia approached Seward with an offer to sell.

Negotiating terms for the purchase of all of Alaska took only one month to complete. American added Alaska to its properties. The cost was only $7.2 million dollars, amounting to about two cents per acre. The **"Treaty of Cession of Russian America to the United States"** was signed on March 30th, 1867. America's area of territory was instantly increased by about twenty percent.

Tennessee - First State Re-Admitted

On June 1st, 1796, **Tennessee** was granted statehood and admitted to the United States. It has a long history of solid military participation on behalf of America, earning it the nickname **"Volunteer State"**. Tennessee depended on an agricultural economy and so was a **"slave state"** up until late in the Civil War. Slaves, in the 1860's, made up only twenty-five percent of the population in the state, which was the lowest percentage among all of the Confederate states.

When civil war began to look likely, Tennessee was one of the states wherein the populace was deeply divided in sentiment. Central and western Tennessee were dominated by supporters of the pro-slavery southerners. Eastern Tennessee citizens leaned more to the policy of protecting the Union above all else. Political infighting in the state delayed decision making to the extent that Tennessee became the last southern state to secede. Many disgruntled men from eastern Tennessee surreptitiously fought guerrilla type activities against the Confederates, burning bridges, destroying railroad tracks and doing what they could to hamper the progress of the rebels.

During the war, Tennessee lived up to its "Volunteer State" nickname, providing more troops to the Union than any other southern state and only Virginia delivered more troops to the Confederacy. Tennesseans showed up and fought, some for the Union, some for the Confederacy. Due to its geographical location, more battles were fought in Tennessee than in any other state, except for Virginia, which rested immediately on the border between the South and Washington, D.C., the nation's capital.

Union troops were occupying most of Tennessee by the time Lincoln delivered the **Emancipation Proclamation**, which meant the slaves in Tennessee could not be set free by the President. **President Johnson** came along, though, and in October of 1864 declared all Tennessee slaves to be free. The **Tennessee legislature**, in March of 1865, passed an **Amendment** to their state constitution which formally abolished slavery in the state. It was the only southern state to do so. Tennessee's politicians quickly ratified the **13th and 14th Amendments** to the U.S. Constitution. Having met all of the requirements, Tennessee became the first southern state to have its elected officials returned to their seats in the U.S. Congress, though they weren't immediately granted voting rights on federal issues. Tennessee, because they had quickly ratified the Amendments, was also spared being assigned a northern military governor at the end of the war.

Tennessee became the **first southern state** re-admitted to the Union after the war on **July 24th, 1866**.

The First Transcontinental Railroad

The United States still had a frontier beyond which land belonged to Territories rather than states. American businessmen and politicians had begun to understand the importance of being able to transport people and materials **"from sea to sea"**. Viable passages across the wide expanses of the west had been sought for decades. America's biggest businessmen and financiers were eager to participate in a venture which might yield massive investment returns.

Surveys were launched at northern, central and southern potential routes for a transcontinental railroad. Business interests with properties or enterprises in those various areas were aggressively trying to promote the routes that would take the railroad through their own areas of dominance. **Abraham Lincoln**, long before he became president, was engaged as an attorney by interests who favored a central route. Lincoln's assignment was to assist in choosing the best eastern terminus for the railroad. He selected the route that was most beneficial to his employer, **Thomas C. Durant**.

Once the basic information had been gathered, there were three potential routes for the proposed railroad. A **"northern route"** ran along the Missouri river westward through Montana and Oregon, which was, at that time, a Territory. Heavy winter snows and challenging terrain were obstacles for the northern route. A **"central route"** ran along the Platte River, passing from Nebraska through Wyoming to pick up the well-traveled **Oregon Trail**. Heavy snow in the mountainous regions was also a problem with this route. A potential **"southern route"** would run through Texas, New Mexico Territory and the Sonora desert. It would terminate in Los Angeles, California. The southern route had a problem in that much of it ran south of the American border with Mexico. The **"Gadsden Purchase"**, finalized in 1854, solved that problem when it added much of Mexico's property in Arizona and New Mexico to the United States.

The **central option** was ultimately selected. **Lincoln** was involved in choosing the **Omaha/Council Bluffs** location to be the eastern terminus. Council Bluffs put the railroad north of the fighting which was going on during the Civil War. It followed a river that would offer a fertile ground for establishment of towns and white settlers. It also led to the easiest passage through the Rockies. The central route also hooked the new railroad up with multiple railroads owned by Thomas C. Durant, the financier who had hired Abe Lincoln.

The government paid railroad companies $16,000 per mile of track laid across level ground, equal to about $525,000 in present-day money. They were paid $32,000 for track laid in the foothills and $48,000 per mile of track laid in the mountains. Throughout the process of selecting routes and building different sections of the transcontinental railroad there were rampant rumors of graft and corruption in assigning the contracts. Thomas C. Durant seemed to be the chief culprit in the nefarious dealings.

No owner of the Union Pacific segment of the track was permitted to own more than 10% of the railroad's stock. Thomas C. Durant purchased large amounts of stock through use of other people's names or businesses. He had the railroad built, in the early stages, by adding unnecessary digressions from the most advantageous route, meaning he made much more money by stretching the distance. Durant created and spread false rumors about the construction of the railroad, allowing him to manipulate stock prices to his advantage. Today's analysts have estimated that Durant probably added $5,000,000 to his profits by virtue of his fraudulent practices. Durant wasn't the first, and certainly wouldn't be the last, to use his wealth and power to dupe and swindle the government and American taxpayers.

The **transcontinental railroad**, known at the time as the **"Overland Route"**, began at **Council Bluffs**, in the east, where it attached to the existing U.S. rail network, proceeding westward to the **Oakland Long Wharf**, which rested on **San Francisco Bay**. The railroad was constructed during the years 1863 through 1869. It is remarkable that the nation was able to accomplish this tremendous feat while engaged in a furious civil war. Three railroad companies were involved in the construction. They were the **Western Pacific Railroad**, The **Central Pacific Railroad** and the **Union Pacific Railroad**. Western Pacific built 132 miles, beginning on the west coast. Central Pacific built 690 miles and Union Pacific built 1,085 miles. The finished railroad stretched **1,911 miles across America**, reaching from established rail lines all the way to San Francisco.

Union Pacific hired many recently discharged veterans of both the Union and Confederate sides of the Civil War. They especially valued the highly experienced engineers and surveyors who had built (and destroyed) railroads and bridges for military forces. Emigrant Irishmen numbered very highly among their laborers.

Central Pacific, due to their location, had more difficulty obtaining useful laborers. They brought in surveyors and engineers from Canada and Europe. They needed semi-skilled and unskilled laborers. White laborers in California were busy working in agriculture and in mining. **Chinese emigrants** were pouring into California, escaping wars and extreme poverty in their homeland. Central Pacific hired some to determine their effectiveness and learned that the Chinese, in spite of their smaller stature, were hard and reliable workers. The railroad set up a recruiting office in China and began hiring Chinese as preferred laborers. The Chinese were joined by a few black men, who were eager to leave the Civil War and their former status behind them. The Chinese did most of the hardest jobs, the heaviest manual labor, because, over much of the challenging terrain, the work could not be done by animals or explosives. Black and white laborers were paid $30 per month. One dollar per day for their very hard labors. They received food and lodging along with their wages. The Chinese were paid $31 per month, one dollar more than the white and black workers, because they preferred to concoct their own meals. The workers engaged in a strike in 1867. Their wages were increased to $35 per month. $35 at that time would equal about $730 in present-day money.

The railroad companies found ways to provide for basic human necessities along the construction routes. Union Pacific, for example, brought along several railroad cars customized to serve as bunkhouses for the workers. They also drove a herd of cows along with the construction workers to serve as a source of nutrition. One of the railroad cars was equipped to serve as a kitchen in which food for the workers could be prepared. Hunters were hired to search for and kill buffalo and other wild game for food. Scouts who were sent ahead of the ever-moving end of the constructed track were sometimes attacked and killed by Indians. The Native Americans often perceived the railroad to be a serious threat to their own safety. They were right to be concerned. The U.S. sent army detachments to reconnoiter the areas around the construction, searching for the Indians. As the Native Americans increased their resistance, the U.S. Army increased its own forces in the region.

Many **Native Americans** resisted the progress of the railroad. They knew the **"iron horses"** would bring an influx of white people and would increase exponentially the risk to their homelands. Some Native Americans, though, had decided to take advantage of whatever benefits the whites might bring. The transcontinental railroad provides a great example. **800 Pawnee scouts and warriors** were hired by the Union Pacific Railroad in 1864 to protect the workers and the laid tracks. The Pawnee were led by Major Frank North. The Indians wore uniforms and patrolled the crews and livestock. They also protected the railroad workers from raids by hostile **Sioux and Cheyenne** tribes. When, as the rails progressed westward, the railroad offered "excursions" on the trains, the

Pawnee were invited to participate. The Pawnee also staged, for entertainment of the riders on the excursions, mock Indian raids on the trains.

All along the way, as the tracks were extended farther and farther, temporary "towns" were constructed, generally consisting of little villages of canvas tents. They were sometimes called **"Hell on Wheels"** towns. The flimsy towns were similar to encampments that followed the Union army around during the war. They were populated by railroad men, gambling houses, prostitutes, saloons and dance halls. Many of the laborers lost their wages to the entertainments offered in the Hell on Wheels camps.

The Transcontinental Railroad or Overland Route, was finally completed when Central Pacific Railroad **President Leland Stanford**, on May 10th, 1869, ceremoniously tapped into place the "Last Spike", later called the **"Golden Spike"**. He used a silver hammer. The point where the railroad being built from the east was connected to the railroad being built from the west was located at **Promontory Summit**, near Promontory, Utah.

Creation of the transcontinental railroad changed the American landscape in several significant ways. It was the first real demonstration of the reality of **President Monroe's "Manifest Destiny"** declaration, which declared that all of the continental United States, "from sea to sea", would inevitably become part of the United States. The railroad bound the east to the west. The new railroad made it possible for Americans to travel from New York City to San Francisco. It revolutionized the economy of the American west. It made movement of goods and people more efficient, less costly, less dangerous, more comfortable and less expensive. It made the future for Native Americans much less optimistic, as it, to a large extent, locked in the relentless expansion of the white man.

Baseball in America

The origin of modern baseball can be tracked back to early folk games played in continental Europe, Ireland and Great Britain. The earliest versions required the hitter to pitch to himself, throwing the ball up and hitting it. The bases were run in the opposite direction of today's game and the hitter was put out by hitting him with the ball or "plugging" him, as he ran.

In the mid-1700's a game had been developed which involved pitching a ball, hitting it and running a circuit of bases. It was called **"Rounders"** and it was taken to the American colonies by traveling or emigrating Englanders. There were many variations in the rules of the game, but it became quite popular in the colonies. During the mid-1800's the game became more formal, with rules beginning to be established.

There was a **"base ball" club** in New York, in 1845, called the **Knickerbocker Club**. **Alexander Cartwright** was a member. He wrote up a Base Ball code of rules which are called the **Knickerbocker Rules**. The Knickerbocker Rules put an end to the practice of "plugging" the runner, which put a player out by hitting him with the thrown ball. Elimination of plugging allowed utilization of a new, smaller, harder ball. It changed the nature of both pitching and hitting. The Knickerbocker Rules still held, though, that catching a hit ball on the first bounce counted as an "out" and they still required all pitching to be "underhanded".

The first Base Ball game in the United States is generally accepted to be a game between the **New York Knickerbockers** and a team from Hoboken, New Jersey. It was June 19th, 1846 and the game was not played by professional, paid, players. The Hoboken team, named the **"New York Nine"** defeated the Knickerbockers soundly, 23 runs to one. The game lasted four innings.

The baseball association eliminated the "catch on first bounce is an out" rule in 1863. African-American players were officially banned from the game in 1867. Black players would not be re-admitted until 1947, when **Branch Rickey** brought **Jackie Robinson** on board with the **Brooklyn Dodgers**. Robinson, in his famous number 42 uniform, fought extensive racism within the players of the league to become a **"Hall of Famer"** and one of the game's greatest heroes. Jackie Robinson was the perfect man to run the gauntlet of angry racism that faced the first black man to play professional baseball. He was intelligent, courageous, highly skilled and willing to play the critical role assigned him. He opened doors for all African-Americans in fields far removed from the baseball field.

There was a National Association of Base Ball Players operating from 1867 to 1870. The teams were made up, mostly, of players who were not paid professionals. The Cincinnati Base Ball Club was formed in 1866. The **Cincinnati Red Stockings** were subsequently organized in 1866 and all of the players were paid to play. They were the first American professional baseball team. The Red Stockings traveled widely and were undoubtedly responsible for creating certain traditions. Other teams began to emulate their uniforms, including some using different colors for identification. The Red Stockings were not defeated until 1870. The Red Stockings, to this day, are the only baseball team to complete an undefeated season.

A widely accepted rumor circulated later in the 1800's claiming that Abner Doubleday had invented baseball in 1839. It was, obviously, not true and Doubleday never claimed any responsibility for creating the game.

A convention was held in 1857, in New York, which was attended by representatives of many "Base Ball" clubs. At that meeting rules were established which would largely define the game for decades to come. Previous to that date, games would be played to a set number of runs. Whichever team reached that number first, won the game. At the convention it was decided that the number of runs would be unlimited, but the number of innings, barring tie games, would be nine. It was determined that the distance between bases would be exactly 90 feet, that "force outs" could be made at any base and that each team would consist of nine players, no more, no fewer.

The first baseball game played in front of a paying crowd took place on July 20th, 1858. It featured a team made up of New York and Hoboken players in opposition to a team made up of players from Brooklyn. Four thousand spectators watched New York-Hoboken defeat Brooklyn by a score of 22 to 18. Each spectator paid ten cents for the privilege of watching the game.

Newspapers were already, by 1856, calling baseball our "national game" or our "national pastime". Some clubs, by the early 1860's, were able to play their games in enclosed fields created specifically for the game. As the Civil War proceeded, traveling Union and Confederate soldiers spread the game across the country.

Black players were not allowed to play in the white leagues until Jackie Robinson was introduced in 1947. Prior to that time and for some time after, African-American players engaged in league play made up of their own organizations. There were, over time, at least seven **"Negro Major Leagues"**. The **"National Colored Base Ball League"** was created in 1887, but survived for only weeks. In 1920, the **"Negro National League"** was organized. The **"Negro American League"** was the last recognized African-American league and it was created in 1951. The Negro Leagues faded away as more and more of their better players were accepted into the white baseball league.

The first game played by all-black players, according to historical records, featured the **"Henson Base Ball Club"**, of Jamaica, Queens, NYC, versus the **"Unknowns"** of

Weeksville, Brooklyn, NYC. The Unknowns may have remained unknowns, as they were defeated by the Henson Club 54 to 43.

More than 3,000 black men played in the Negro Leagues. Among them were such baseball greats as **Buck O'Neil** and **Jackie Robinson**, of the **Kansas City Monarchs**, and **Satchel Paige** and **Josh Gibson**, who began their astonishing careers with the **Pittsburgh Crawfords**.

John "Buck" O'Neil

Kansas City Monarchs

The Black Friday Gold Panic of 1869

The President was **Ulysses S. Grant**. The government was struggling to overcome the financial damage done to the nation's resources by the **Civil War**. Grant had a younger sister, Virginia, called **"Jennie"**. **Abel Corbin** was a somewhat sketchy financial speculator who married Jennie.

President Grant was selling Treasury gold at regular intervals. It was part of his plan to pay off the national debt. **James Fisk**, his partner **Jay Gould** and Abel Corbin, the President's son-in-law, formed a group called the **"Gold Ring"**. Their plan was to corner the gold market. Their tactic was to try to use the relationship between President Grant and Abel Corbin, Jennie's husband, to manipulate the marketplace.

Gould pushed Corbin to introduce him privately to Corbin's father-in-law, the President. Gould and Fisk hoped to gain **"insider information"** and influence over the President, that would help them drive the price of gold up. They were surprisingly effective. The "Gold Ring" partners successfully used the credibility they gained by their relationship with Grant to influence **Wall Street** investors. They convinced Grant that sales of gold were doing serious harm to America's farmers. Grant sent a letter to the Secretary of Treasury, **George S. Boutwell**, sharing his new-found concerns about the gold sales. Boutwell suspended all sales of the shiny metal. The price of gold immediately began to rise, making the gold already held by the Gold Ring far more valuable.

Gould and Corbin had encouraged the appointment of **Major General Daniel Butterfield** to be Assistant to the Secretary of Treasury. Butterfield was a Civil War hero who knew little about finance. As their scheme progressed, Gould gave Butterfield a $10,000 bribe, a huge amount to a man whose annual salary was only $8,000. In present-day money the bribe would be worth $225,000 dollars. Butterfield accepted the bribe and agreed to tip the Gold Ring off before the government released anymore gold. The insider tip would allow the Gold Ring to sell off their own gold at the highest prices. They "bought low" and expected to "sell high".

President Grant became aware of the Gold Ring scam. Grant apparently told his son-in-law, Corbin, to sell off his gold quickly, protecting his daughter. He then, on September 24th, 1869, directed Boutwell to sell $4 million worth of government gold. Gold prices dropped precipitously, destroying the Gold Ring's corner on the gold market.

As the episode unfolded, Wall Street investors fell into a panic. The national economy proceeded through several months of chaotic performance. The actions of the Grant administration prevented a devastating national depression. The best of defense lawyers protected Gould and Fisk from prosecution. Grant was exonerated of any knowledge of, or participation in, the Gold Ring scheme.

Celluloid – The Birth of Plastic

An inventor named **John Wesley Hyatt** was trying to find a way to replace ivory in the manufacture of billiard balls. In the 1860's Hyatt was most likely concerned with convenience more than with the ecological protection of ivory-producing creatures. He ignored the advice of a chemist, who told him he risked an explosion by the experiments he was pursuing. Hyatt mixed alcohol, nitrocellulose and camphor and then applied heat under pressure. The result was **celluloid**. Hyatt then developed the machinery and manufacturing process to produce celluloid in bulk.

Celluloid was, over the next couple of decades, used to replace all kinds of common products. It may have been created for billiard balls, but it was soon used for collar stays, buttons, toys, pens, knife handles, table tennis balls, inexpensive jewelry and much, much more. A process was developed, in the late 1880's, to use celluloid to create photograph film, which eventually replaced photographic plates.

The vast plastic industry grew from the seed planted by celluloid. In present day, plastics are seen both as a great asset and a great threat to our environment. Plastics are integral to the manufacture of agricultural products, electronics, furnishings, clothing, medical products, utensils, all kinds of packaging, sports and recreational products and much more. It would be incredibly difficult to stop using plastics. There are immense problems involved with disposal of used plastic materials. Plastics can be toxic and are largely resistant to biodegradation. The vast amounts of discarded plastic pose a serious threat to our health and our environment.

Celluloid itself, in today's world, is used primarily for making table tennis or Ping Pong, balls. Nothing else has served so well for that particular purpose.

Wyoming and Women's Suffrage

The **"Women's Suffrage Movement"** was a slow-moving fire that many believe was originally lit in the Wyoming Territory. One might expect that the centers of highest education, the homes of the most affluent and influential citizens, the inhabitants of New York City, Boston and Washington, D.C., might have led the fights for women's rights. In truth, the western frontier state of Wyoming might be more appropriately seen as the "home of suffrage" for America's women.

What does **"suffrage"** mean? It comes from the Latin word **"suffragium"**, which meant "vote" or "eligibility to vote". In America and Europe, the long battle to gain fundamental human rights for women was called the fight for **"women's suffrage"**.

Nebraska and Washington had voted down bills promoting suffrage for women. Legislators in Kansas, in 1867, had defeated a proposed bill meant to give women the right to vote. Similar bills had been repeatedly defeated in the U.S. congress. Wyoming was still part of a "Territory", not yet a state, so legislation could be passed by a majority vote. States were required to pass constitutional amendments to grant women the vote, a much more formidable task.

The Territorial legislature in Wyoming consisted entirely of men. Two women, **Anna Dickinson** and **Redelia Bates**, made independent speeches in Cheyenne, encouraging women's suffrage. **Ulysses S. Grant** was elected President in 1868 and he immediately appointed Republican supporters to govern Wyoming. (Political positions in the Territories were appointed, rather than elected, as they were in the states).

On December 10th, 1869, the all-male Wyoming territorial legislature voted to pass **"An Act to Grant Women of Wyoming Territory the Right of Suffrage and to Hold Office"**. We would like to believe that the men of Wyoming were deeply interested in human rights, but historians suggest that the rough new frontier territory desperately needed women. The men may have offered the right to vote as an incentive to draw more females to their state. Whatever the root cause for the vote, Wyoming women were given the right to vote and to hold political office. **Louisa Ann Swain**, of Laramie, on September 6th, 1870, became the first Wyoming woman or woman of any American state or territory, to exercise her right to vote.

Wyoming also passed, in 1869, resolutions which guaranteed women **property rights** separate from their husbands and that guaranteed that teachers, most of whom were women, would all receive the **same salaries**, regardless of sex. The changes taking place in Wyoming brought illumination of the problems faced by women across the nation. Wyoming was doing things no one had previously done. Wyoming gave hope to the suffragettes.

Wyoming women soon began to have a heavy influence on voting in Wyoming. They were putting too many Republicans in office. Democrats responded by trying to repeal the suffrage act, taking away the right of the ladies to vote. The territorial governor vetoed the effort and women continued to vote.

In 1890 Wyoming was being considered for statehood, which would bring many benefits, protections and supports to the territory. The federal government informed Wyoming it could not be entered in the Union because women were forbidden, in the United States, to vote. Wyoming was given the choice: Stop letting women vote or lose the opportunity to gain statehood. Wyoming stood by their women. The U.S. relented and Wyoming became a state on July 10th, 1890.

It should be noted here that women were permitted to vote, for a short time, in New Jersey. New Jersey was the first to grant women the constitutional right to vote, but they soon rescinded it. In their original constitution, written in 1776, people were allowed to vote based on owning a given minimum amount of property. The assumption was that people with property were more likely to be educated and capable of voting intelligently. It also limited voting to a certain class of people. Women with enough property and black people with enough property, were allowed to vote. Of course, black people and women didn't often meet the **"property ownership"** requirement. The constitution was changed in 1807. The changes were called "progressive" and they abolished the right to vote, in New Jersey, for women and black people. It would be 61 years before women once again gained the right to vote and it would be Wyoming territory that did so.

America in the 1870's

Hiram Rhodes Revels

The First African-American in Congress

Hiram Rhodes Revels was born on September 27th, 1827. His parents were free people of color and his ancestors were citizens who could be traced all the way back to before the **Revolutionary War**. He was born in North Carolina, but traveled widely during his life. He attended **Knox College** in Illinois.

Revels became a minister and served as a chaplain for the **Union Army** during the Civil War. He assisted in the successful recruitment, in the **"slave state"** of Maryland, of two regiments of black troops. He was active at the **Battle of Vicksburg**.

His ministerial work took Hiram to several states, both in the North and in the South. He lived in Indiana, Illinois, Ohio, Tennessee, Missouri, Kansas and Maryland. He was director of a high school for black students in Maryland. Hiram was briefly imprisoned, in 1854, for illegally preaching to a black congregation. Free black people, at that time, were forbidden to live in Missouri.

Revels had first served as a minister in Baltimore, Maryland. When the Civil War ended, Revels returned to his ministerial duties. He was a pastor for the Methodist Episcopal Church and he served congregations in Kansas and in Louisiana. Revels moved to Natchez, Mississippi, where he added a political element to his work.

Hiram became an **alderman**, and then a **state senator**, and then the Mississippi Senate voted to elect Revels to replace a Senator from pre-war times. Democrats, led by their southern members, attempted to block Revels' election. They claimed that Revels had not been a legal citizen until after the **14ᵗʰ Amendment** was passed, meaning he had not been a citizen long enough (nine years was required) to make him eligible for the job. A vote was taken. Every Republican voted to seat Revels, while every Democrat voted against him. He became a **U.S. Senator**.

Hiram became the **first black American** in the **United States Congress** on **February 25ᵗʰ, 1870**. He was a **Republican** representing the deep south state of Mississippi, making his achievement the more remarkable. While holding office in the **U.S. Senate**, Revels was an advocate for racial equality. He supported amnesty for former Confederates who would sign an oath of loyalty to the U.S. Hiram served on the Committee for Education and on the Committee for the District of Columbia.

After departing the Senate, Hiram Revels was appointed to be the first President of **Alcorn Agricultural and Mechanical College**. Alcorn is now known as **Alcorn State University** and is a "historically black college" **(HBCU)**. Hiram taught philosophy at the school. He also taught at Shaw College, which is now Rust College, another school that is now an HBCU. President Grant made offers to give him government **"patronage"** jobs, but he turned them down. He persisted in his busy pursuits, editing a Christian newspaper, teaching theology, preaching and advocating for civil rights.

Hiram Rhodes Revels passed away on January 16ᵗʰ, 1901, while attending a church meeting in Aberdeen, Mississippi. Hiram is buried in Holly Springs, Mississippi.

John D. Rockefeller and Standard Oil

William A. Rockefeller, Sr., was a lumberjack early in his career, but became a traveling salesman who used the names **"Devil Bill"** and **"Big Bill"**. He sold "elixirs" and claimed to be a "botanic physician". He was a rambling **"con man"**, according to historians and wasn't bound by the usual codes of ethics for sales people. He saw his family only infrequently. William lived a "gypsy-like" lifestyle and was known for his money-making schemes.

One day, late in 1836, a young man came to the door of the farmhouse of **Eliza Davison's** father. She opened the door to find a tall and handsome door-to-door salesman. On his shirt was pinned a card informing all whom he encountered that he was **"Deaf and Dumb"**. Eliza reportedly declared that, if that man was not deaf and dumb, she would marry him. When she discovered that Bill was neither deaf nor dumb, but only perpetrating a scam to encourage sales of his gimmicks, Eliza forgave his deception. Her father refused to bless the union, but the two married, anyway.

William married Eliza Davison in Niles, New York, on February 18th, 1837. Together they would produce six children, of whom John Davison was the second. **John D. Rockefeller** was born on July 8th, 1839. William, between encounters with Eliza, also had a lengthy relationship with a mistress, **Nancy Brown**, who worked for the family as a housekeeper. William and Nancy had two children, but only one survived.

William was known to pick berries and sell them as pills to his naïve customers by telling them that the "medicine" would cure a list of maladies. He would add to his sales story a warning that the "pills" should not be given to pregnant women because they would most surely cause abortions. Many desperate women purchased the pills, hoping to eliminate unwanted pregnancies. They were all very much disappointed.

Bill was charged with the rape of a family housekeeper in 1849. He seems to have avoided the charges by fleeing the area. He also, in 1855, secretly married **Margaret Allen**, who was only 17 years old when he met her. He went through with the marriage with no attempt to terminate his marriage to Eliza, making him a bigamist. Not long after, Bill took on the false identity of a physician. He pursued fraudulent medical activities for a few years. Bill always rode the edges of legality and morality, but he did make a fair amount of money.

Eliza was a religious and hard-working woman. She raised her large family while Bill traveled, which was most of the time. Their second son, John D., grew accustomed to working around the home to assist his mother. She was a frugal woman, though her family had some money and John remembered learning from her: "Willful waste makes woeful want". John raised extra money by raising turkeys and selling potatoes. He gained success enough to be able to occasionally lend money to his neighbors. John declared "From the beginning I was trained to work, to save and to give".

In 1851, probably to escape his father's pursuers, John's family moved to Moravia, New York and then to Owego, New York, where he attended the Owego Academy. His family moved again, in 1953, to Strongsville, Ohio, where John attended the very first high school in Ohio, which was also the high school furthest westward past the Allegheny Mountains. He continued to study bookkeeping at Folsom's Commercial College.

John was described by colleagues and instructors as a quiet, very studious, reflective, discreet and methodical student. He was a lover of music, at one time considering a full-time career as a musician.

John took a job as a bookkeeper at the tender age of 16 years. He began as an apprentice and was paid $16 monthly. After four years his salary had been increased to $58 per month. He wrote that he was thrilled to learn all of "the methods and systems of the office". His job involved the negotiation of transportation rates, a complicated system subject to manipulations. He worked directly with canal barge owners, ship captains and freight agents. The knowledge he gained would turn out to be an incredibly beneficial education for him. By the age of 20, he had engaged in a series of business ventures. He became knowledgeable of the oil refining business and began to focus on it.

John fell in love with a school teacher, **Laura Celestia Spelman**, called "Cettie" and they were married on September 8th, 1864. They produced five children, four daughters and one son. Their children went on, following the lives of John D. and Laura, to continue to serve many of the Rockefeller family's philanthropic ventures. Their children, grandchildren and great-grandchildren created a **"Rockefeller Dynasty"** in America. Among them were David Rockefeller, who became CEO of Chase Manhattan, now known as J.P. Morgan Chase; **Nelson Aldrich Rockefeller**, who became governor of New York and an American Vice President; **Winthrop Aldrich Rockefeller**, who was governor of Arkansas; and **Laurance Spelman Rockefeller**, who was an influential conservationist. Others among their descendants became arbiters of the trusts, charities and foundations which originated with John D. and Laura. Of Laura, John D. Rockefeller said "Her judgment was always better than mine. Without her keen advice, I would be a poor man".

John Davison Rockefeller, Sr., entered his first business partnership in 1858 with **William B. Clark**. The two sold $450,000 worth of produce, collecting commissions on each sale, in their first year together. They soon transitioned their attention from produce to oil production. The government was subsidizing the oil business and it became very profitable very quickly. Most of their revenue came from sales of kerosene, at that time more important than other oil products. The automobile's introduction, of course, made a huge impact on their business. Rockefeller, Clark and their partners built their first wholly-owned **oil refinery** in Cleveland, Ohio, in 1863.

Rockefeller voted for **Abraham Lincoln** before the **Civil War** started. He supported the new **Republican**, anti-slavery political party. He was an abolitionist. He was running a successful business when the war started, so he gave money to support the Union cause, but paid substitutes, which was legal at the time, to take his place in the army. He said that he wished to "do his part" in the war, but to go away to fight would mean closing his business, which would do harm to many workers. Rockefeller was devoutly religious and he was an outspoken **abolitionist**.

John D. Rockefeller was a gifted businessman. He introduced the **Standard Oil Company** to America in 1870. He built the company into a financial juggernaut in the United States. Kerosene, at that time, was used for many purposes and fueled much of the lighting in American homes. Rockefeller soon gained control of 90% of the American oil business. Then, electricity and electric lighting, began to eat into his kerosene business. John's good fortune was held as the gasoline-powered automobile drove onto the scene. Huge demand for gasoline swelled and John was the guy with the oil refineries needed to produce it. He also was soon to benefit from the symbiotic relationship between the railroads and the transportation of his fleet of tanker cars full of oil. Rockefeller became an essential customer for the railroads and gained great influence over the railroad business.

John was the boss at Standard Oil until 1897, but, when he gave up that front desk job, he held onto the majority interest in the company's stock. He became the richest of all Americans. He revolutionized big business practices in America, creating the first huge business trust in the country. His creativity and innovations impacted all large corporations. His changes resulted in easy access to low-cost fuels. He grew so large and powerful that other organizations considered him a risk, threatening the **"free market"** with his near **monopolization** of the oil business.

In 1911, the Supreme Court took notice. They ruled that Standard Oil was in violation of **federal anti-trust laws** and they fragmented the corporation into 34 separate business entities. Included were **Exxon-Mobil** and **Chevron** and those companies still generate some of the largest levels of revenue in the world. The transactions made John D. the first American **billionaire**. His wealth made up about 3% of the entire nation's gross domestic product or GDP.

John D. Rockefeller withdrew to his estate, **Kykuit**, in Sleepy Hollow, Westchester County, New York, when he retired. "Kykuit" is drawn from a Dutch word that means "look out". He was there for another four decades. He was a major innovator in the way American philanthropists invest their money to benefit the general society. He joined forces with other successful industrialists, men such as **Andrew Carnegie**. They created foundations that still impact modern America, including organizations to benefit the fields of science, medicine, education and the arts. **Rockefeller Foundations** were key players in the near-total elimination of several devastating medical conditions, including yellow fever and hookworm.

Rockefeller was profoundly religious and his money supported many church-based organizations. He was a "Northern Baptist" and never touched alcohol or tobacco. As mentioned before, he was an avid abolitionist. In his own local church, Rockefeller served on the board and as a clerk, a Sunday School teacher and a janitor. He was the founder of the Central Philippine University in the Philippines, Rockefeller University in New York City and the University of Chicago. In business, he believed in economic and social Darwinism, leading to one of his most-quoted declarations: "The growth of a large business is merely a survival of the fittest".

Rockefeller has critics who believe he was a ruthless bully in business affairs. Others say he was the least "ruthless" of all of the great corporate giants of early American industrialism.

Historian Robert Whaples wrote that what some saw as ruthlessness was actually Rockefeller's "Relentless cost-cutting and efficiency improvements, boldness in betting on long-term prospects while others were willing to take short-term profits and impressive abilities to spot and reward talent, delegate tasks and manage a growing empire".

John D. Rockefeller was resting at his Florida home, **"The Casements"**, on May 23rd, 1937, when he succumbed to arteriosclerosis at the age of 98. He is buried in Cleveland, Ohio.

The 1870's, continued

The **1870 national census** revealed an American population of 38,558,371. In the present day, the state of California, all by itself, has a population of over 40,000,000 citizens. It was the first census that did not have any slaves to count. The total increase of American citizens was lower than the rate of growth in earlier counts, largely due to the losses of life suffered during the **Civil War**. The **"geographic center"** of the United States, for the second consecutive time, was just west of Cincinnati, Ohio.

The **final Confederate state to be re-admitted** to the Union was **Georgia**. It was July 15th, 1870 and the **Confederated States of America** were finally and completely disintegrated.

The **great Chicago fire** occurred on October 8, 1871. In legend, the blaze began when **Mrs. O'Leary's cow** kicked over a lantern. Historians believe the fire was actually most probably started in the cowshed owned by **Daniel Sullivan**. Sullivan was the one who first reported the fire. The immense conflagration consumed more than a million acres of Chicago properties, burning nearly 18,000 buildings. It did nearly two million dollars in damages, left 90,000 citizens without homes and killed 250 citizens. In a strange coincidence, another huge fire started on the very same day. It began in **Peshtigo, Wisconsin** and it tore through six counties in a single day. The **Wisconsin fire** is reported to have killed between 1,200 and 2,500 people, which makes it, by far, the deadliest blaze in American history. The fires motivated city leaders across the nation to examine their firefighting resources.

President Ulysses S. Grant dedicated **America's first National Park, Yellowstone**, on March 1st, 1872. The dedication marked the first of a long and continuing series of actions intending to protect our nation's most precious resources. Yellowstone encompasses more than two million acres of diverse land. It includes geysers, waterfalls, great cliffs, "paint pots" or "mud pots", green forests and pure wilderness. The park protects a wide range of species of wildlife, including grizzly bears, wolves, foxes, coyotes, elk, moose and more than 3500 bison. The beautiful and variegated landscape is a consequence of a massive volcano eruption that took place 640,000 years ago.

The **Democrat Party**, in the 1870s, was dominated by a **"political machine"** known as **"Tammany Hall"**. Tammany was run by a political boss named **William Magear Tweed**, best known as **"Boss Tweed"**. Tweed and Tammany Hall, pretty much owned the Democrat Party in New York state. Tweed was a major stock shareholder or a Board member of a long list of prominent businesses, including utility companies, railroads, banks, mines, newspapers and more. He was one of the three largest real estate owners in New York City and that was some of the most expensive real estate in the world. Tweed was elected to the U.S. House of Representatives and then the New York County Board of Supervisors. By 1858 he was running Tammany Hall, which meant he could offer jobs and contracts in return for political loyalty. He had enormous power. "Boss Tweed" was arrested and found guilty of **theft by political corruption**. Estimates were that he had stolen between $25 and $45 million dollars from New York taxpayers. Later analysis suggested the amount could be as high as $200 million. In today's money that would be equal to over three billion dollars! Tweed escaped from jail, fleeing to Cuba and then Spain, but was captured and returned to custody. He died ignominiously in the **Ludlow Street Jail** in New York City. Most of the other inmates were serving time because they owed money and debtors could be jailed at that time. It seems ironic that the richest guy died among the poorest.

The **General Amnesty Act of 1872** was signed into law by **President U.S. Grant** on May 22nd, 1872. It was intended to support **Reconstruction** and to encourage the peaceful **reunification** of the North and the South. There had been previous amnesties and pardons for the citizens of the Confederacy, but most had harsh restrictions or exemptions attached. The Amnesty Act of 1872 **restored civil rights** to all citizens of the defeated Confederacy, including the right to hold federal office. The Act opened up political opportunities for more than 150,000 former rebels and it exempted only 500 former significant Confederate leaders.

Off the northwest coastline of Washington state lie the **San Juan Islands**. They carry beautiful landscapes, beaches, craggy cliffs and wildlife on land and in the waters and they were claimed by both the British and the Americans in the mid-1800s. One of the larger of the islands is **San Juan** itself. The British were encamped on one end of the island and the Americans on the other. **Washington Territory**, not yet part of the United States, claimed ownership of the islands, as did **America** and **Great Britain**. British Vancouver rested on the Canadian shore, with the San Juan Islands between them and land claimed by the Americans. **The Oregon Treaty** had assigned boundaries for lands between the British and the Americans, but the boundaries through the islands were left unclear. The British were herding sheep and raising other livestock on their end of the island. **Lyman Cutlar**, an American, shot a pig owned by the British **Hudson Bay Company**. The English threatened to imprison Cutlar. **The Pig War** was begun. **George E. Pickett**, who would later become a Confederate Army general, in command of the famously disgraced **"Pickett's Charge",** was sent to quell the disturbance. The British dispatched three warships with the objective of moving Pickett out. Both sides began to escalate their preparations to fight. The dead pig was causing a whole lot of trouble. **President Buchanan**, eager to prevent more military action, sent **General Winfield Scott** to the scene, where he negotiated a peaceful settlement. The British remained on the island, encamped at Garrison's Bay on San Juan Island over the ensuing twelve years. Previous to the "pig episode", Washington Territory attempted, in 1855, to levy a property tax against properties that were claimed by the British Hudson Bay Company. The company refused to pay, claiming it was them that owned the property on which they stood. The pig episode apparently escalated matters to approach military levels. The dispute was ultimately placed, for arbitration, in the hands of **Emperor Wilhelm I** of Germany. He declared the San Juan Islands to be the property of the Americans. The British departed the area in 1872.

President Ulysses S. Grant was re-elected in 1872, by an overwhelming margin, when his main opponent, **Horace Greeley**, died before the campaign ended. Women's suffragette **Susan B. Anthony** illegally cast a vote in the election, drawing attention to the ongoing battle to win the right to vote for America's women.

Epilogue

The author wildly underestimated the amount of time and space that would be required to write a "true American history". The book has grown too long, and the writer is too old, to continue through the more modern chapters of our nation's growth. We made it through the Civil War in this book. The next one hundred and fifty years would bring many more wars, some on devastating global scales and many more trials and tribulations for America. The Industrial Revolution would change our culture in many ways, some wonderful, some very bad. Civil Rights would continue to be a thread of infection that continues to this day to be addressed. Vast gains would be made in all aspects of life and much would still demand improvement.

This author believes, heart and soul, that our American government is the best to ever exist. Every nation has faults and challenges, but our government is designed to be continuously "self-correcting" and we have made enormous progress in our short national lifetime. The American "Grand Experiment", allowing the common people to control the government, rather than the other way around, has been a success. Going forward, it is paramount that we recognize and glorify our many amazing successes while identifying and remediating our inevitable shortcomings. God Bless America!

End of Manuscript